D1552457

TREATING RESISTANT DEPRESSION

TREATING RESISTANT DEPRESSION

Edited by
JOSEPH ZOHAR, M.D.
Jerusalem Mental Health Center and
Hebrew University
Hadassah Medical School
Jerusalem, Israel
and
ROBERT H. BELMAKER, M.D.
Beer Sheva Mental Health Center
Beer Sheva, Israel

PMA PUBLISHING CORP.
New York

NOTICE: The editors, contributors, and publisher of this work have made every effort to ensure that the drug dosage schedules and/or procedures are accurate and in accord with the standards accepted at the time of publication. Readers are cautioned, however, to check the product information sheet included in the package of each drug they plan to administer. This is particularly important in regard to new or infrequently used drugs. The publisher is not responsible for any errors of fact or omissions in this book.

Library of Congress Cataloging in Publication Data

Treating resistant depression

Includes bibliographies and index.
1. Depression, Mental – Treatment. 2. Depression, Mental – Chemotherapy. 3. Antidepressants.
I. Zohar, Joseph. II. Belmaker, Robert H. [DNLM:
1. Antidepressive Agents – therapeutic use.
2. Depressive Disorder – drug therapy. WM 171 S741]
RC537.S635 1987 616.85′27061 85-14424
ISBN 0-89335-225-X

Printed in the United States of America

Contributors

Hagop S. Akiskal, M.D.
Department of Psychiatry, University of Tennessee, Center for the Health Sciences, Memphis

Frank J. Ayd, Jr., M.D.
Baltimore

Robert H. Belmaker, M.D.
Beer Sheva Mental Health Center, Beer Sheva, Israel

Paul K. Bridges, M.D.
Department of Psychiatry, Guy's Hospital Medical School and Brook General Hospital, London, England

Robert M. Cohen, M.D.
Clinical Brain Imaging, National Institute of Mental Health, Bethesda

Gerard Cournoyer, M.D., F.R.C.P.
Fellow of the Medical Research Council of Canada, Department of Psychiatry, University of Montreal, Montreal, Canada

Hinderk M. Emrich, M.D.
Max Planck Institute for Psychiatry, Munich, F.R.G.

Claude de Montigny, M.D., Ph.D., F.R.C.P.
Faculty of Medicine, Department of Psychiatry, University of Montreal, Montreal, Canada

Max Fink, M.D.
Department of Psychiatry, Health Sciences Center, SUNY at Stony Brook, Stony Brook

Mark S. Gold, M.D.
Director of Research, Fair Oaks Hospital, Summit

David Greenberg, M.D.
Jerusalem Mental Health Center and Department of Psychiatry, Hebrew University, Hadassah Medical School, Jerusalem, Israel

P. Kielholz, M.D.
University Psychiatric Clinic, Basle, Switzerland

David J. Kupfer, M.D.
Department of Psychiatry, University of Pittsburgh, School of Medicine, Western Psychiatric Institute and Clinic, Pittsburgh

Bernard Lerer, M.D.
Department of Psychiatry, Hebrew University, Hadassah Medical School, Jerusalem, Israel

Alfred J. Lewy, M.D., Ph.D.
Departments of Psychiatry, Ophthalmology, and Pharmacology, School of Medicine, Oregon Health Sciences University, Portland

Paul S. Links, M.D.
Visiting Scientist, University of Tennessee, Memphis, and McMaster University, Hamilton, Canada

R. Bruce Lydiard, M.D., Ph.D.
Fair Oaks Hospital, Summit

David A. Martin
Psychiatric Diagnostic Laboratories of America, Summit

Roberto Mester, M.D.
Eitanim Hospital, and Department of Psychiatry, Hebrew University, Hadassah Medical School, Jerusalem, Israel

Stuart A. Montgomery, M.D.
Department of Psychiatry, St. Mary's Hospital Medical School, University of London, London, England

Daniel Moskovich, M.D.
Jerusalem Mental Health Center, Jerusalem, Israel

Edward Mueller, M.D.
Section on Clinical Neuropharmacology, National Institute of Mental Health, Bethesda

Dennis L. Murphy, M.D.
Laboratory of Clinical Science, National Mental Health Center Clinical Center, Bethesda

J. Craig Nelson, M.D.
Department of Psychiatry, Yale University School of Medicine, New Haven

Willem Nolen, M.D.
Department of Biological Psychiatry, Christlijk Psychiatrish Centrum Bioemendaal, The Hague, The Netherlands

Gerald Oppenheim, M.D.
Department of Psychiatry, Shaare Zedek Medical Center, Jerusalem, Israel

Robert Pohl, M.D.
Department of Psychiatry, Wayne State University, and Lafayette Clinic, Detroit

Robert M. Post, M.D.
Biological Psychiatry Branch, National Institute of Mental Health, Bethesda

A.L.C. Potash, M.D.
Fair Oaks Hospital, Summit

Arthur J. Prange, Jr., M.D.
Department of Psychiatry, University of North Carolina, School of Medicine, Chapel Hill

Robert L. Sack, M.D.
Department of Psychiatry, School of Medicine, Oregon Health Sciences University, Portland

Baruch Shapiro, M.D.
Jerusalem Mental Health Center, Ezrat Nashim, Jerusalem, Israel

Charles Shawcross, M.D.
Mapperley Hospital, Nottingham, England

Herzl R. Spiro, M.D., Ph.D.
Department of Psychiatry, Hebrew University, Hadassah Medical School, Jerusalem, Israel

Trey Sunderland, M.D.
Section on Clinical Neuropharmacology, National Institute of Mental Health, Bethesda

Michael E. Thase, M.D.
Department of Psychiatry, University of Pittsburgh School of Medicine, and Western Psychiatric Institute and Clinic, Pittsburgh

Peter Tyrer, M.D.
Mapperley Hospital, Nottingham, England

Thomas W. Uhde, M.D.
Biological Psychiatry Branch, National Institute of Mental Health, Bethesda

Herman M. van Praag, M.D., Ph.D.
Department of Psychiatry, Montefiore Hospital and Medical Center, and Albert Einstein College of Medicine, Bronx

Joseph Zohar, M.D.
Hebrew University, Hadassah Medical School, and Jerusalem Mental Health Center, Ezrat Nashim, Sarah Herzog Psychiatric Hospital, Jerusalem, Israel

Preface

Many books have appeared in recent years emphasizing the widespread problem of depression: the need to recognize depression, the good prognosis and satisfactory treatability of depression. However, there have been few attempts to deal with the problem of those patients who do not respond to standard antidepressant treatment; while only a small minority of depressed patients, these "resistant depressives" take up an increasingly large part of the clinical psychiatrist's time.

When the depressed patient does not get well, it does not mean that he must be rediagnosed or that the physician has necessarily prescribed the wrong drugs or doses. Instead, we propose to accept the concept of resistant depression since only by facing up to the existence of resistant depression can the clinician gauge the need for innovative treatments and treatment strategies now available to treat these depressed patients.

Innovative treatments in our view are treatments which, though not yet proven and standard, are no longer strictly experimental. It seems that in a resistant depressive, the ethical risk of such innovative but not proven treatment might be less than the risk of chronic illness.

In this volume, we have collected those treatments and treatment strategies that are promising and perhaps worth trying in resistant depressives. Treatments that are strictly experimental, without more than animal evidence, were not included. This volume is not aimed at the researcher with an eye to new compounds that might theoretically be antidepressants, but rather at the up-to-date clinician who is willing to expand his armamentarium while treating the resistant depressive.

J.Z. and R.H.B.

Contents

I

INTRODUCTION

1

Chronic and Intractable Depressions: Terminology, Classification, and Description of Subtypes

Paul S. Links and Hagop S. Akiskal

TERMINOLOGIC AND CONCEPTUAL ISSUES

Introduction

Chronic and intractable affective disorders are assuming greater prominence in psychiatric practice as are issues related to chronic care in other branches of medicine (Pless and Pinkerton, 1975). Classification is essential to any scientific endeavor, particularly in an area such as chronic affective disorders, where there is much confusion and ambiguity. These problems are compounded by nonrecognition and misdiagnosis. As noted by Weissman and Klerman (1977), most clinicians, including psychiatrists, are not accustomed to making the diagnosis of chronic depression because of a stereotype equating affective disorders with acuteness and episodic course. Many chronic depressives are diagnosed as having anxiety, somatoform or personality disorders. Indeed, Price (1978) has suggested that repeated treatment failures in chronic depressions may so frustrate the clinician that the diagnosis may be changed to personality disorder.

The terms "chronic," "intractable," "refractory," and "treatment-resistant" depression are often used synonymously. However, the word "chronic" is derived from the Greek *chronos*, or time, and refers to a prolonged, lingering condition. By contrast, both intractability and treatment resistance connote something which is difficult to treat or work with; refractoriness constitutes an extreme degree of treatment resistance or intractability. When applied to a medical condition, chronicity refers to an illness with a protracted history, while intractability and treatment-resistance relate to illness which is difficult to treat, regardless of duration. A depression lasting two years or more may be considered chronic (American Psychiatric Association, 1980). Although such an illness may also be intractable, or difficult to treat, not all chronic illness is intractable. Hypothyroidism usually runs a chronic course, but is amenable to appropriate treatment. Nor is all intractable illness chronic. Delirious mania, which runs its course very quickly, can be intractable.

Chronic Versus Refractory Depression

The distinction between chronic and refractory illness must be kept in mind in attempts to characterize the increasing number of patients referred to affective disorders clinics. Such patients are often considered to be "refractory" by referring clinicians who may not have exhausted treatment possibilities and who operate on the assumption that chronic depression implies treatment resistance. Ten years of experience at the University of Tennessee has led to the following schema in the approach to patients referred for such "treatment resistance" (Akiskal, 1984):

1. A depressive illness may appear refractory if the natural history of the disorder is insufficiently appreciated. For instance, many unipolar depressions making their first appearance in mid- or late-life pursue a 2-5 year course (Akiskal et al., 1981). By DSM-III criteria (1980), depression is chronic when it lasts for 2 or more years and symptomatic manifestations are present at least 80% of the time. Thus, chronicity would apply not only to those disorders with an unremitting course but also to protracted depressions with intermittent course. This category includes many intermittent depressions with bipolar familial background (Bipolar II/III disorders), which may or may not involve episodes of hypomania (Akiskal, 1983b).
2. Depression may persist because of inappropriate treatment. For example,

depressives encountered in primary care are often given large doses of anxiolytic and sedative-hypnotic medication because the affective nature of the illness is masked by somatic complaints (Weissman and Klerman, 1977; Akiskal et al., 1981).

3. Depression often persists because of inadequate treatment; i.e., the treatment (antidepressants or lithium) is correct, but is not given in proper dosage or duration. Alternatively, maintenance treatment may have been stopped too early, or the patient's compliance may have been suboptimal. Furthermore, some patients with chronic depression have considerable admixtures of personality disturbance; they may be demanding and manipulative, alienating their therapists (Akiskal, 1983a). Many of these patients are categorized under characterologic depression or borderline personality rubrics. Kielholz et al. (1979) defined treatment resistance in depression as failure to respond to two correctly selected tricyclic antidepressants given in adequate dosages. This threshold is too low. One should not consider a depression treatment-resistant before two standard tricylics, a monoamine oxidase inhibitor, lithium carbonate, one of the new heterocyclic antidepressants, and ECT have been tried.*

4. Finally, one must consider the possibility of missed diagnoses. For instance, intermittent depressions in the setting of a primary anxiety disorder, epilepsy, and hypothyroidism may not respond to standard antidepressants as long as the primary illness remains untreated.

To illustrate these concepts in the characterization of chronic and refractory affective disorders, we shall first review current clinical research on several chronic affective subtypes. Nosologic rubrics such as anxious, atypical, masked, hypothyroid, and borderline personality features often invoked in discussions of chronicity and treatment resistance will then be reviewed.

CHRONIC DEPRESSIONS

Early Studies

Perhaps most contradictory to the conventional concept of affective disorders as self-limiting illnesses are 15% of depressions which persist for several years

---

*Editor's note: See also Chapters 5 and 11.

(Robins and Guze, 1972). Many such patients are misdiagnosed (Akiskal et al., 1981) or improperly treated (Wissman and Klerman, 1977).

Weissman and Klerman (1977) did a 20-month follow-up of 150 female patients who had been treated for an acute depressive episode. All patients but one were located and assessed in terms of their persisting symptoms, level of social functioning, and interim help-seeking behavior. Twelve percent of these patients were judged to be chronically symptomatic on follow-up. Rather than exhibiting retardation, agitation, and depressed appearances, these chronic patients complained of such symptoms as anxiety, tension, fatigue, insomnia, and guilt; they made only sporadic contacts with their family physicians, outpatient clinics, or hospital emergency rooms. Minor tranquilizers were the most common forms of treatment they received. It was reported that these patients had elevated neuroticism scores on the Maudsley Personality Inventory (MPI). The authors concluded that premorbid neuroticism was important in the development of chronicity. However, because the MPI had been administered after patients had been in treatment for approximately four weeks, one cannot rule out the possibility that these neurotic features were the residual affective symptomatic phase of the depressive illness (Cassano et al., 1983).

The University of Tennessee Study

In a series of papers (Akiskal et al., 1980, 1981; Akiskal, 1982, 1983a), we reported on 137 outpatients with intermittent subsyndromal depressions lasting at least 2 years (meeting the DSM-III criteria for dysthymia) and systematically evaluated them to delineate factors involved in chronicity. The cohort was divided into three groups:

1. Patients who did not fully recover from episodes of primary major depression (N = 38) that occurred in the absence of preexisting validated psychiatric disorders; this group, which had late on set, was considered the residual phase of a major unipolar depression, henceforth referred to as *chronic residual depression*.
2. Early onset *characterologic depressives* (N = 50), who complained of dysphoria since their teens, failed to meet the criteria of a validated nonaffective disorder, but had character pathology so interwoven with depressive symptoms that separating between the two seemed impossible on clinical grounds.
3. Probands with *chronic secondary dysphoria* (N = 49) developing in the setting of preexisting nonaffective psychiatric or medical conditions.

Sleep electroencephalographic studies documenting abnormal shortening of REM latency were used as external validation. In a naturalistic follow-up approach, the groups were compared on phenomenologic, developmental, personality, and familial factors, as well as concurrent stressful situations.

Chronic Residual Depression

The chronic unipolar group permitted us to evaluate factors preventing full remission from episodes of major depression occurring in the absence of preexisting psychiatric illness. This group of patients was the oldest (mean = 50.8 years) at index evaluation, and sleep polygraphy revealed that their mean REM latency was in the low range characteristic of a control group of episodic primary depressives, thereby supporting the hypothesis that incomplete remission in an acute primary depression represents an ongoing affective process (Akiskal, 1982). Furthermore, chronic depressives did not show any more deviant personality attributes than the episodic primary depressive controls, suggesting that personality features were unlikely to explain the protracted course of their illness. Factors positively correlated with chronicity in this group included heredofamilial affective loading, multiple object losses through death, disabled spouses, superimposed incapacitating medical disease (including the use of depressant antihypertensives), secondary alcoholism, and sedative-hypnotic dependence. The appropriate diagnosis and treatment of these patients depend on the physician's recognition of the protracted natural history of affective disorders in late onset primary major depressives. Energetic chemotherapy with heterocyclic antidepressants provides significant symptomatic relief to most of these patients. The therapeutic gains made can often be potentiated by psychotherapeutic attention to these patients' marital and social lives, which are often disturbed because of the depression (Weissman and Akiskal, 1984).

Characterologic Depressions

Characterologic depressions represent a group of low-grade intermittent depressions with onset in late childhood or adolescence and pursuing a protracted, presumably lifelong course (Akiskal et al., 1980; Rosenthal et al., 1981).

Onset is usually insidious, with full manifestations apparent by the early 20's. If a major depressive episode supervenes, it tends to be short-lived, and return to the premorbid low-grade depressive baseline is the rule. This group of patients is most representative of the DSM-III dysthymic disorder category. Indeed, it has been elsewhere proposed that the nosologic territory of dysthymia be restricted to this early onset group (Akiskal, 1983a).

Keller and Shapiro (1982) have suggested the term "double depression" in reference to the coexistence of major and minor depressions. The rubric of "hysteroid dysphoria," denoting low self-esteem, an exquisite sensitivity to loss of romantic attachments, passive-dependent and histrionic personality traits, and a persistent tendency toward dysphoria and manipulative suicidal gestures, has also been invoked for some of these patients; the mood is typically geared toward and reactive to environmental praise (Liebowitz and Klein, 1979). In addition to such traits, our work has revealed introverted-obsessoid tendencies (Akiskal et al., 1980; Rosenthal et al., 1981). We have proposed that these different personality types may underlie two distinct subgroups described below.

Character-Spectrum Disorders

This pattern is primarily manifested in "unstable" characterologic pathology, including dependent, histrionic-sociopathic, and schizoid traits, reminiscent of the RDC categories of intermittent depression and labile personality. Two-thirds of the characterologic depressives in our studies were assigned to this category, based in part on failure to respond to systematic trials of tricyclics and lithium carbonate. Furthermore, REM latency values were within the normal range, and there were high rates of familial alcoholism but not of familial affective disorders. Broken homes and childhood parental losses formed the developmental background for these character disturbances. In our opinion, the chronic dysphoria of character-spectrum patients represents the adverse consequences of parental alcoholism, sociopathy, and related disorders.

Treatment results in this group are disappointing. This can be explained in part by poor compliance, in that patients seek help at times of crisis and demand symptom-relief. Also, these patients tend to have low thresholds for side effects of thymoleptic medications, and the treating physician may be inclined to change drugs before a trial of adequate dosage and duration has been given. Furthermore, trying to engage these patients in any formal psychotherapy is a difficult task. It is possible that the dysphoria of at least some of these patients—and their inability to form lasting transference—is secondary to residual attention deficit disorder. Therefore, drugs such as magnesium pemoline or methylphenidate, coupled with an educational approach (rather than formal psychotherapy), might prove beneficial in some of these cases.

Subaffective Dysthymia

In this subtype, reminiscent of RDC minor episodic depression, the personality disturbances are milder, although again of long duration, and appear to conform to admixtures of introversion, obsessionalism, and Schneiderian depressive traits. In 35%, family history is positive for bipolar affective disorder, which explains the high rate of pharmacologically occasioned hypomania seen in this subtype. REM latencies are shortened as in primary depressions. Furthermore, these patients are responsive to noradrenergic tricyclics, lithium, or both. These interventions seem to reverse the intermittent tendency towards psychomotor inertia, hypersomnia, and anhedonia. However, the gains made with pharmacotherapy are often short-lived, unless supplemented with psychotherapy, i.e., social skills and related behavioral approaches to provide these patients with appropriate social behaviors in which they are deficient. Taken together, these findings suggest that these predominantly subsyndromal depressions of early onset represent *formes frustes* of primary affective illness—hence the designation "subaffective dysthymia."

Chronic Secondary Dysphorias

Low self-confidence and self-esteem, varying degrees of social withdrawal, intermittent morose mood, and fleeting suicidal ideation are common findings in patients with disabling, disfiguring, and progressive medical or psychiatric illness. These dysphorias are usually understandable psychologic reactions to chronic neurologic, rheumatologic, somatization, obsessive-compulsive, phobic, and panic disorders. In our study (Akiskal et al., 1981), the joint presence of medical and psychiatric disorder was especially potent in producing refractory dysphorias. These dysphoric reactions tend to parallel the vicissitudes of the underlying disorder and therefore are best viewed as secondary demoralization responses, although cerebral dysrhythmia and endocrine factors can be implicated in some. Whether occurring in the setting of psychiatric or medical illness, onset is rarely with a major depressive episode, and family history is usually negative for affective disorders. Finally, DST and REM latency results are usually within the nonaffective range. As argued elsewhere (Akiskal, 1983a), low-grade dysphoric manifestations in the setting of disabling medical and neurotic disorders do not constitute a psychopathologic process distinct from the underlying disorder.

Although patients suffering from secondary dysphorias are commonly treated with soporific heterocyclic antidepressants, no controlled trials to document their efficacy have been undertaken. Group therapy, to address concerns common to dysphoric patients suffering from disabling medical disorders, represents a reasonable alternative but, again, its efficacy is not supported by controlled research. When an anxiety disorder forms the substrate for the dysphoric reaction, monoamine oxidase inhibitors are generally believed to be effective by some, but not all, investigators. Such patients, often labeled as "atypical depressives," will be discussed next.

ANXIOUS (ATYPICAL) DEPRESSIONS

Early British Experience

Although the concept of "atypical depression" has been around for more than two decades, no consensus exists on its definition. The origin of the concept is usually traced back to the work of West and Dally (1959) and Sargant (1960, 1961) in St. Thomas's Hospital, London. From these early reports it is not entirely clear why patients responding to the monoamine oxidase inhibitor (MAOI) iproniazid were considered to be "atypical." They constituted 57% of a consecutive cohort of 101 outpatients systematically followed in a special clinic. Compared to nonresponders, the responder or atypical group had less self-reproach, was worse in the evening, had less early morning awakening, more phobias, more hysterical conversion reactions, more tremor, and a worse prior response to ECT. Although these were the only characteristics significantly differentiating the responders, the authors discussed additional features such as fatigue, psychophysiologic symptoms, and "good" premorbid personality, which were also felt to be characteristic of the atypical group. Judging from this description, responders may have been considered atypical because: (1) in some respects their clinical manifestations were the reverse of more "typical" or endogenous depression, (2) admixtures of depression with anxiety and phobic symptoms occurred to such a degree that depression appeared as a nonconstant feature of a preexisting neurotic illness; and (3) hysterical and other personality inadequacies were present during the course of the illness, despite adequacy of the premorbid personality.

The main thrust of these early British studies was to identify an MAOI- responsive group of depressives as contrasted to the ECT-responsive endogenous group. This work was flawed because of retrospective bias and the failure to indicate what criteria were used to define MAOI-responsiveness. Furthermore, many cyclic recurrent and some endogenous depressions also responded to iproniazid (West and Dally, 1959).

Using less-toxic drugs like phenelzine and isocarboxazid, Sargant and Dally (1962) continued their efforts to refine the criteria for a group of depressions which seemed particularly responsive to MAOIs. The emerging profile of MAOI-responders included severe precipitating stress, initial insomnia, increased depth of sleep, evening worsening of mood, inordinate fatigue, variable depression on a day-to-day basis, irritability, tendency to blame others, and, in women, premenstrual tension. Premorbid personality, again, was felt to be "basically good" in those who responded to MAOIs, while the nonresponsive group had inadequate personality manifested by *chronic* tension and substantial marital and occupational difficulties. By contrast, panic attacks and phobias were so characteristic of the responders or atypical depressives that the authors concluded that no clear demarcation existed between atypical depressions and anxiety neurosis.

Recent Controlled Studies

In a carefully conceived investigation, Robinson et al. (1973) performed a double-blind placebo-controlled study to evaluate the efficacy of the MAOIs in depressive-anxiety states. The authors reported that these patients were more responsive to phenelzine than placebo, and that phenelzine was particularly effective in ameliorating anxiety, irritability, and agitation. The same group of investigators (Ravaris et al., 1976) extended these results using a multiple-dose controlled study comparing 60 mg. of phenelzine to 30 mg. of phenelzine and placebo in 62 outpatients with mixed anxiety-depressive states, and found out that only the higher dose was significantly more effective than placebo. In a third study, these investigators (Ravaris et al., 1980) compared phenelzine to amitriptyline in 105 patients with a broad spectrum of depressive and anxiety symptoms of moderate to severe intensity. Overall, the two drugs were found to be equally effective; however, anxiety measures improved significantly more with phenelzine treatment.

Paykel et al. (1971) attempted to characterize different depressive typologies using cluster analysis. Four typologies were identified: psychotic depressive, anxious depressive, hostile depressive, and young depressives with personality disorder. Paykel et al. (1979) also attempted to validate the concept of atypical depression by response to MAOIs. They followed a cohort of mixed depressed patients and then compared responders to nonresponders. The MAOI-responsive or atypical patients were best characterized by less severe illness and outpatient status. In a further attempt to clarify whether MAOIs has a differential effect from tricyclics, this group of investigators (Rowan et al., 1982) studied 131 outpatients with depression or mixed anxiety and depression. The drugs were compared by assessing effects on symptom ratings and by examining differential overall improvement in subgroups. Diagnostic assessments included the Research Diagnostic Criteria, ICD-8, criteria developed by Klein, the Nies-Robinson Diagnostic Index, the Newcastle Scale, cluster analytic typologies and a number of other judgments derived by the research group to characterize atypical depression. The patients were randomly assigned to amitriptyline, phenelzine or placebo after a 1-week washout. After 6 weeks of treatment, the results indicated that both drugs were equally effective in the diagnostic subgroups and of comparable overall efficacy. No differential response to phenelzine was seen either in terms of symptom ratings or on the basis of a diagnostic subgroup. There was only a weak tendency for phenelzine to be more beneficial for patients with anxiety and without evidence of chronic characterological depression.

Liebowitz and Klein (1979) have summarized their work with hysteroid dysphoria, a condition they feel is a subtype of atypical depression. The authors selected the study group on the basis of the following as characteristics of: loss of anticipatory pleasure, preservation of consummatory pleasure, hyperphagia, craving for sweets, hypersomnolence, reversed diurnal variation, lethargy or inertia, initial insomnia, rejection sensitivity, applause-hunger, history of liking amphetamines, and reactivity of depressed mood. Interestingly, these authors noted during a pilot study that brief hypomania appeared in several patients while taking MAOIs. Their more recent experience indicates that history of panic attacks is the most reliable predictor of phenelzine response (Leibowitz et al., 1984).

Heterogeneity of Atypical Depressions

In a scholarly review, Davidson et al. (1982) summarized the concept of atypical depression. They concluded that there were at least two types of atypical depression: Type A, depression accompanied by severe anxiety; and Type V, characterized by atypical vegetative symptoms. The V type was further subdivided into unipolar V and bipolar V subtypes. According to these authors, the atypical bipolar V subtype could take the form of a major bipolar depression or an attenuated form such as subaffective dysthymia as defined by Akiskal et al. (1980); this latter form of disorder, which does not manifest anxiety features, can be mobilized to hypomania by tricyclic antidepressant challenge. The common features in types A and V include: early age of onset, predominance in women, outpatient status, nonendogenicity, and minimal psychomotor change.

Zisook and Click (1983) reported that many of their patients who were characterized as "atypical" because of anxious, somatic, phobic and/or panic symptoms also met Research Diagnostic Criteria for "typical" major depression. They concluded that the validity of the atypical group as a distinct form of depression remains to be established.

Anxious Depressions

The definition of an atypical group of depressions is further complicated by the difficulties in conceptualizing the relationship between anxiety and depression.

Roth and Mountjoy (1982) proposed that anxiety and depression were distinct syndromes and reported success in separating the entities using factor analytic techniques. By contrast, Gersh and Fowles (1979) summarized the literature and concluded anxiety and depression were two symptomatic stages of affective disorders, with the ratio of symptoms varying over time.

In an attempt to clarify the relationship between panic and major depressive disorders, VanValkenburg et al. (1984) studied a cohort of 114 patients assessed at the University of Tennessee Center for the Health Sciences. Reliable diagnostic criteria were employed to define patients with panic disorders (DSM-III, 1980) and depression (Feighner et al., 1972). Four categories of patients were defined: primary panic disorder, primary depression, panic disorder with secondary depression, and primary depression with secondary panic attacks. These groups were compared across clinical, family history, and naturalistic outcome variables. It was found that patients with a combined picture of depression and panic (regardless of which came first) had a poorer response to treatment and poorer psychosocial outcome. Patients with primary panic disorder and secondary depression appeared to have a more severe variant of panic disorder, while those patients with primary depression and secondary panic attacks were felt to have a subtype of depression with a chronic course. However, the four groups were difficult to differentiate on clinical and familial grounds alone.

Recent family history studies indicate that panic disorders may be more closely related to depression than other anxiety disorders. Leckman et al. (1983) compared the families of depressed patients without anxiety symptoms to those with depression plus a specific anxiety disorder (agoraphobia, panic disorder and generalized anxiety disorder). The diagnostic assessments of family members were made blindly using direct interviews, medical records, and family history data systematically obtained from relatives. The relatives of patients with depression plus panic disorder were found to have markedly increased risk for major depression, panic disorder, phobia and/or alcoholism compared to relatives of probands with depression without anxiety. The authors felt these findings suggested that panic disorder and major depression may share a common underlying diathesis. Dealy et al. (1981) compared patients diagnosed as having generalized anxiety disorder or panic disorder with secondary depression to those without depression. The only major difference was the finding that the group with secondary depression reported a history of more frequent panic attacks. In another study, Raskin et al. (1982) attempted to differentiate patients with panic disorder from those with generalized anxiety disorder on the basis of developmental and psychiatric histories. They found that patients with panic disorder had suffered from significantly more major depressive episodes, again suggesting some kinship between the two disorders.

Recent research has compared anxious depressions to primary dysthymic disorders on the basis of sleep electroencephalography (Akiskal et al., 1984). The dysthymic group comprised 20 patients with early onset, longstanding, fluctuating subsyndromal depressive symptoms—falling short of the criteria of Feighner et al. (1972)—in the absence of an anxiety disorder. They were compared with 22 anxious-depressives who also had subsyndromal fluctuating depression occurring in the setting of anxiety neurosis by Feighner et al. criteria, and eleven nonpsychiatric controls. The dysthymic group showed a significantly higher percentage of REM sleep and shorter REM latency than both control groups. By contrast, the anxious depressives were characterized by sleep continuity difficulties in the form of multiple arousals and decreased sleep efficiency, particularly on the first night of study. Thus, although the two groups of depressives were similar clinically, psychophysiologic findings suggested that anxious depressives and primary dysthymics constituted distinct subtypes within the large universe of atypical depression (Table 1), thereby lending support to the distinction between anxiety and depressive states.

Conclusion

The findings reviewed in this section are not easily summarized. Under the rubric of "atypical depression" clinical investigators have studied an ill-defined group

TABLE 1. Comparison of Anxious Depression with Subaffective Dysthymia[a]

	Anxious depression	Subaffective dysthymia
Age of onset	Twenties	Teens
Sex ratio	F > M	F = M
Family history	Anxiety disorder; major depression	Bipolar disorder; major depression
REM latency	Insomnia > hypersomnia	Hypersomnia > insomnia
Psychomotor activity	Agitation	Psychomotor inertia
Substance abuse	Alcohol; sedative-hypnotic	Stimulant
Pharmacologic hypomania	No	Yes

[a]Summarized from Akiskal et al. (1984).

of fluctuating depressive conditions commonly encountered in the outpatient setting that do not meet the stereotype of "typical" inpatient endogenous depression. History of or concurrent panic attacks seem to be the most consistent characteristic of atypical depressions since their first description in the British literature. In this sense, atypical depressions may simply represent panic disorder complicated by chronic fluctuating depression. However, there also seems to exist a small subgroup who lack anxiety features but have distinct bipolar tendencies and varying degrees of personality disturbance, similar to the subaffective dysthymic group described by Akiskal and associates (1981).

MASKED DEPRESSION

Definition

There is considerable overlap between the somatic symptoms of anxiety and depression. The differentiation between anxiety and depressive disorders may be difficult if characteristic psychologic symptoms are not present. Many patients seen in medical settings suffer from subacute or chronic illnesses with medically unexplained symptoms. Such patients are often considered to have a "masked depression," wherein the somatic symptoms of depression occupy the foreground and the psychological symptoms recede into the background (Kielholz, 1973). The implications for clinical practice are obvious: These are patients who receive inappropriate treatment because the depression goes unrecognized. According to Kielholz et al. (1982), at least 10% of all patients consulting a doctor are depressed and in half of these, the depression will be masked. Lesse (1980) predicted that one-third to two-thirds of all patients over 40 years of age who are seen by general practitioners have masked depressions; sixty-five percent of the patients studied had a course of illness predating the first psychiatric consultation by 2 years, and thirty percent had had an unrecognized depression for 5 years before the initial psychiatric referrral.

In this section we shall describe the clinical features of these patients and discuss external validating guidelines that permit differentiation from anxiety disorders.

Clinical Presentation

Because patients presenting to family practitioners are different from those seen in secondary or tertiary care psychiatric settings (Links et al., 1982), the psychiatric consultant must have a good understanding of the context of the primary physicians' practice before proferring advice about the diagnosis and treatment of depressive patients presenting with somatic symptoms.

The clinical features of these patients have been described by Lesse (1977, 1980), who reported their frequent visits to their physicians with psychosomatic and hypochondriacal complaints. Kielholz et al. (1982) described sleep disturbances, chronic pain syndromes, cardiovascular complaints or anxiety symptoms. In nonliterate societies, depressed patients have also been known to manifest with such "masks" as simple confusion (Lesse, 1980). Although masked depressives do not complain of subjective depression, Lesse (1980) suggests that a "depressive core" is typically present and that careful, tactful questioning will usually elicit a history of restlessness, pacing, anorexia, persistent fatigue that is worse in the morning, decreased concentration and loss of interest in daily activities.

Masked depression is most commonly described in middle-aged females (Lesse, 1980). Often they give a detailed history of varied somatic ailments. These patients are typically aggressive, overbearing, and may obtain strong secondary gain from their symptoms.

There are two important dangers associated with a missed diagnosis of masked depression. First, up to forty percent of these patients have suicidal ideas and tendencies by the time they are assessed by a psychiatrist (Lesse, 1980) and the risk of suicide is not negligible (Kielholz et al., 1982). Second, many of these patients receive sedative-hypnotic drugs because of their initial presentations. These drugs can lead to iatrogenic substance abuse and perpetuation of the depressive condition (Akiskal, 1982).

External Validation

Recently, biological methods have been used in attempts to validate the affective basis of unexplained somatic complaints in primary care. "Unexplained" in this context refers to the absence of a medical disorder that could account for the somatic symptoms, as well as failure to meet the criteria for a definite psychiatric syndrome. In a study of 25 such patients with pain syndromes, gastrointestinal complaints, palpitations, fear of choking in sleep, insomnia, restless extremities, fatigue, difficulty getting out of bed in the morning and impotence, we found that REM latency was shortened on sleep polysomnography similar to that in primary depressive illness (Table 2). The similarity is striking, given the low level of symptomatology on psychometric measures in the masked depressive group. Such shortening of REM latency is not characteristic of Briquet's hysteria and anxiety states (Akiskal, 1983b).

TABLE 2. Comparisons of Masked and Chronic Residual Depressions on Selected Clinical and Sleep Variables[a]

Variables	Masked depression ($N=25$)	Chronic depression ($N=20$)	p
Age	45 ± 16	36 ± 12	ns
% female	36	65	ns
Beck depression score	7 ± 4	17 ± 8	$<.001$
MMPI D scores	60 ± 14	81 ± 16	$<.01$
MMPI scales >2 SD	2 ± 1	6 ± 2	$<.001$
REM latency (min)[b]	62 ± 23	53 ± 21	ns

[a]Summarized from Akiskal (1983c).
[b]Both groups significantly shorter than 11 nonpsychiatric controls ($\bar{X} = 89 \pm 25$, Scheffé, $p < .05$).

Blumer et al. (1982) have investigated chronic pain patients for biological indices of depression. In addition to shortened REM latency, they found that forty percent of their patients were nonsuppressors with the dexamethasone suppression test (DST). Nonsuppressors were found to be more responsive to antidepressants than those with normal DST responses. Atkinson et al. (1983) were able to replicate the finding of positive DST response in seven of twenty-four chronic pain patients.

Although much research remains to be done in this area, further work with biological indices may aid in unmasking many of these depressed patients so that they can receive appropriate treatment before their illness becomes chronically entrenched. At present, diagnosis must largely rely on skilled clinical history and interview, family history for affective illness, periodicity of somatic complaints, and prospective follow-up (Pichot and Hassan, 1973). A high degree of clinical suspicion would suggest a therapeutic trial with antidepressant medication.

"SUBCLINICAL" HYPOTHYROIDISM

Significance

Many physical conditions can present with depressive symptoms (Hall et al., 1980). If the underlying medical disorder is subacute or chronic, depressive symptoms may also persist. Lack of recognition of the physical basis of the depression and lack of adequate response to standard thymoleptic agents may create the false impression of intractability when the situation is really one of missed diagnosis and wrong treatment. Mild grades of thyroid failure without overt physical signs (Gold et al., 1981) and certain forms of epilepsy and cerebral dysrhythmias without a seizure component (Himmelhoch, 1984) may both manifest primarily with vague intermittent depressive complaints. This section focuses on subtle manifestations of thyroid disease as a paradigm for pseudointractable depression occurring in the setting of treatable medical disease.

Grades of Thyroid Failure

Gold and Pottash (1983) reviewed the use of the thyrotropin-releasing hormone (TRH) test in identifying three grades of hypothyroidism. In Grade 1 or overt hypothyroidism, the classical physical signs are present, and the standard laboratory findings of reduced L-triodothyronine (T3) resin uptake (RU) or serum thyroxine (T4) levels and increased thyroid stimulating hormone (TSH) are found; there will also be an exaggerated TSH response to TRH. In Grade 2 hypothyroidism, the patients have only a few of the physical signs and symptoms of hypothyroidism; T3,RU and T4 are normal while TSH levels and TSH response to TRH are increased. Patients with Grade 3 or subclinical hypothyroidism do not present with classical physical symptoms but may complain of depression or anergia; here T3,RU, T4 and TSH levels will be normal, and the diagnosis will be missed if TSH response to TRH is not measured. As a very small decrease in T4 and T3 can result in a marked augmentation of TSH response to TRH, this latter test will identify patients with so called "symptomless" hypothyroidism which presents with behavioral manifestations.

Clinical and Laboratory Studies

Gold et al. (1981) studied the complete thyroid function of two hundred fifty consecutive admissions to their neuropyschiatric evaluation unit. These patients had been referred for evaluation of depression or anergia. Twenty (8%) of the patients were found to have evidence of hypothyroidism; two had Grade 1 hypothyroidism; eight, Grade 2; and ten met criteria for Grade 3 hypothyroidism. All of the twenty patients had exaggerated TSH responses to the TRH test. The importance of these findings is highlighted by the fact that six of seven of patients who were subsequently given thyroid replacement showed a positive response.

The TRH test has received considerable attention in the psychiatric literature (Loosen and Prange, 1982). In primary depression, the major finding is the opposite of that found in hypothyroidism, i.e., *blunted* rather than exaggerated responses to the TRH infusion. The significance of this finding is still unclear as similar blunting has been found in alcoholics and lithium-free manic patients (Loosen and Prange, 1982). However, the blunted response has not been detected in schizophrenia, leading to the suggestion that the blunted TSH response to TRH may be a trait marker for affective illness. Although these explorations are clearly worthwhile, the discussion below is limited to the use of the TRH test as a state marker or diagnostic test for hypothyroidism.

Gold et al. (1982) have extended their findings by studying patients for symptomless autoimmune thyroiditis (SAT). Some patients who are clinically euthyroid are found to have augmented TSH responses to TRH and circulatory antithyroid antibodies (for example anti-M and anti-T antibodies) which are considered to be evidence of autoimmune disease. These patients may go on to develop Hashimoto's goiterous thyroiditis or, more often, atrophic thyroiditis. Based on such evidence, it has been hypothesized that many SAT patients present psychiatrically (with depression, loss of memory, and anergia) and that the underlying thyroid deficiency may go unrecognized. As a preliminary test of this hypothesis, the authors tested the thyroid functioning of one hundred consecutive admissions to their inpatient unit. All patients received the TRH test, and if this was abnormal, they were further examined for the presence of thyroid microsomal antibodies (anti-M antibodies). Fifteen patients were found to have mild or subclinical hypothyroidism, and ten of these patients were found to have autoantibodies (one patient was found to have thyroglobulin anti-T antibodies), thus meeting the criteria for SAT. A matched control group of fifteen patients with normal TRH tests were found to have no evidence of anti-M antibodies.

Clearly, then, the research by the New Jersey group is leading us to reconsider that group of patients who are now labelled as chronically and intractably depressed. As elaborated elsewhere, the evaluation of chronic and intractable depressives should include a selective medical work-up that considers occult malignancies, epilepsy, anemia, and subtle endocrine abnormalities (Akiskal, 1985).

A NOTE ON BORDERLINE PERSONALITY, CHRONIC DEPRESSION, AND INTRACTABILITY

Many patients with chronic affective conditions meet contemporary criteria for borderline personality. Conversely, patients selected on the basis of borderline features often exhibit clinical characteristics seen in chronic affective disorders (Stone, 1981; Akiskal, 1981).

As defined in DSM-III and other nosologic systems, borderline patients are impulsive, affectively labile, and drug-seeking; engage in polymorphous sexual behavior and bizarre attempts at self-harm; complain of boredom and anhedonia; lack a stable sense of self; and are prone to micropsychotic episodes (Links, 1982). They typically present to psychiatric facilities with complicated biographies and give histories of tempestuous interpersonal relationships, similar to patients with affective temperamental disorders (Akiskal, Khani and Strauss, 1979; Akiskal, 1983a).

Although the "borderline" label was originally used for dilute forms of schizophrenia, contemporary usage tends to emphasize, in Schmidberg's apt phrase, the "stable characterologic instability" (1959). There have been proposals that special subgroups may represent atypical forms of limbic epilepsy or adult forms of minimal brain dysfunction (Andrulonis et al., 1981). Finally, Stone (1979) has shown that a substantial proportion of Kernberg borderlines had familial-genetic loading for affective disorders. Indeed, in a University of Tennessee study (Akiskal, 1981) we found that many DSM-III borderlines had family histories replete with bipolar disorder, met criteria for cyclothymic, dysthymic, bipolar II, and panic (atypical depressive) disorders and developed major depressive, manic, and mixed states during prospective follow-up. Further, the REM latencies of borderline probands were shortened to levels seen in primary affective controls; this abnormality was not observed in non-borderline personality controls who were similar to noncase subjects. Bell et al. (1983) and McNamara et al. (1984) have replicated these REM sleep abnormalities. Consistent with these polysomnographic findings, abnormal DST results (Carroll et al., 1981) and blunted TSH response to TRH (Garbutt et al., 1983) have also been reported in borderlines.

It would appear that while borderline personality disorders are clearly heterogeneous, as many as two-thirds seem to suffer from chronic affective disorders. In these patients the characterologic instability appears secondary to chronic affective pathology.

The relationship of personality to affective disorders is a complex methodologic question reviewed elsewhere (Akiskal, Hirschfeld, and Yerevanian, 1983). Personality may predispose to affective episodes, pathoplastically modify the clinical expression of the episode, or result from the experience of recurrent affective episodes. In the latter perspective, episodes of illness prevent optimum ego maturation, giving rise to interpersonal friction, and postdepressive personality complications (Cassano, Maggini, and Akiskal, 1983). The available evidence supports the view that in many patients, borderline features may represent post-depressive complications. In other patients with chronic affective disorders, long-term personality disturbances may be independent of the affective disorder, having their roots in genetic and adverse developmental factors shaping personality formation. Whatever the origin and nature of these personality disturbances, the clinician treating chronic and intractable affective disorders cannot ignore them. Competent pharmacotherapy alone is often inadequate in ameliorating the suffering of patients with chronic affective disorders. One reason for this intractability may be the failure to attend to personality and social factors. Unfortunately the potential benefit of psychotherapeutic interventions in chronic depression has not been demonstrated in controlled studies, but their use can be clinically justified from indirect evidence for efficacy in other types of depression (Weissman and Akiskal, 1984).

SUMMARY

In this chapter we have argued that depressions can be chronic without necessarily being refractory. Such chronicity can be due to natural history (e.g., the residual phase of late onset unipolar depression), or nonrecognition of the medical basis of the depression, as is the case, for example, in the early phase of thyroid failure. Low-grade chronic, often fluctuating, depression can also occur as part of an "atypical" depressive syndrome, often secondary to an underlying anxiety condition such as panic disorder. Other depressions may progress to chronicity because somatic presentations mask the affective nature of the illness, leading to inappropriate treatment. Finally, in characterologic depressions the depressive and personality disturbances have been so closely interwoven since their insidious beginnings in late childhood and teens that it is often difficult to disentangle a true dysthymic component from personality malfunctioning. In addition to reviewing the literature, we have summarized recent findings from work conducted at the University of Tennessee as a framework for a descriptive and biologic classification of this group of affective disorders.

REFERENCES

Akiskal, H.S. Subaffective disorders: Dysthymic, cyclothymic, and bipolar II disorders in the borderline realm. *Psychiat. Clin. North Amer. 4*; 25-46 (1981).

Akiskal, H.S. Factors associated with incomplete recovery in primary depressive illness. *J. Clin. Psychiat. 43;* 266-271 (1982).

Akiskal, H.S. Dysthymic disorder: Psychopathology of proposed chronic depressive subtypes. *Amer. J. Psychiat. 140;* 11-20 (1983a).

Akiskal, H.S. Diagnosis and classification of affective disorders: New insights from clinical and laboratory approaches. *Psychiat. Developments* 1; 123-160 (1983b).

Akiskal, H.S. Overview of chronic depressions, in Ayd, F. et al (eds): *Affective Disorders Reassessed.* Baltimore, Ayd Medical Communications, pp 125-137 (1983c).

Akiskal, H.S. The challenge of chronic depressions: Diagnostic, etiologic and therapeutic aspects. In A. Dean, ed., *Depression in Multidisciplinary Perspective.* New York, Brunner and Mazel, pp 105-117 (1985).

Akiskal, H.S. Khani, M.K., and Scott-Strauss, A. Cyclothymic temperamental disorders. *Psychiat. Clin. North Amer.* 2; 527-554 (1979).

Akiskal, H.S. Rosenthal, T.L. Haykal, R.F. Lemmi, H., Rosenthal, R.H., and Scott-Strauss, A. Characterological depressions: Clinical and sleep EEG findings separating "subaffective dysthymias" from "character spectrum" disorders. *Arch. Gen. Psychiat. 37;* 777-783 (1980).

Akiskal, H.S., Hirschfeld, R.M.A., and Yerevanian, B.I. The relationship of personality to affective disorders: A critical review. *Arch. Gen. Psychiat. 40;* 801-810, (1983).

Akiskal, H.S., King, D., Rosenthal, R.H. Robinson, D., and Scott-Strauss, A. Chronic depressions: Part 1. Clinical and familial characteristics in 137 probands. *J. Affec. Disord. 3;* 297-315 (1981).

Akiskal, H.S., Lemmi, H., Dickson, H., King, D., Yerevanian, B.I., and VanValkenburg, C. Chronic depressions: Part 2. Sleep EEG differentiation of primary dysthymic disorders from anxious depressions. *J. Affec. Disord. 6*; 287-295 (1984).

American Psychiatric Association. *Diagnostic and Statistical Manual*, 3rd edition; Washington, D.C. (1980).

Andrulonis, P.A., Glueck, B.C., Strobel, C.F., Vogel, N.G., Shapiro, A.L., and Aldridge, D.M. Organic brain dysfunction and the borderline syndrome. *Psychiat. Clin. North Amer. 4,* 61-66 (1981).

Atkinson, J.H., Kremer, E.F., Risch, S.C., and Bloom, F.E. Neuroendocrine function and endogenous opioid peptide systems in chronic pain. *Psychosomatics 24;* 899-913 (1983).

Bell, J., Lycaki, H., Jones, D., Kelwala, S., and Sitaram, N. Effects of preexisting borderline personality disorder on clinical and EEG-sleep correlates of depression. *Psychiat. Res. 9,* 115-123 (1983).

Blumer D, Zorick F, and Heilbronn RT: Biological markers for depression in chronic pain. *J. Nerv. Ment. Dis. 170;* 425-428 (1982).

Carroll, B.J., Greden, J.F., Reinberg, M., Lohr, N., James, N. McI., Steiner, M., Haskett, R.F., Albala, A.A., DeVigne, J.P., and Taricka, J. Neuroendocrine evaluation of depression in borderline patients. *Psychiat. Clin. North Amer. 4;* 89-99 (1981).

Cassano, G.B., Maggini, C., and Akiskal, H.S. Short-term subchronic and chronic sequelae of affective disorders. *Psychiat. Clin. North Amer. 6;* 55-67 (1983).

Davidson, J.R.T., Miller, P.D., Turnbull, C.D., and Sullivan, J.L. Atypical depression. *Arch. Gen. Psychiat 39;* 527-534 (1982).

Dealy, R.S., Ishiki, DM., Avery, DH., Wilson, L.G., and Dunner, DL. Secondary depression in anxiety disorder, *Compr. Psychiatry 20*; 612-618 (1981).

Feighner, J.P., Robins, E., Guze, S.B., Woodruff, R. A., Winokur, G., and Munoz, R. Diagnostic criteria for use in psychiatric research. *Arch. Gen. Psychiat. 26;* 57-63 (1972).

Garbutt, H.C. Loosen, R.T., Tipermas, A., and Prange, A.J. The TRH test in patients with borderline personality disorder. *Psychiat. Res. 9;* 107-113 (1983).

Gersh, F.S., and Fowles, D.C. Neurotic depressions: The concept of anxious depression. In R.A. Depue, ed., *The Psychobiology of the Depressive Disorders.* New York, Academic Press (1979).

Gold, M.S., and Pottash, A.L.C. Thyroid function or depression? in F. Ayd, I.J. Taylor, and B.T.

Taylor, eds. *Affective Disorders Reassessed: 1983*. Baltimore, Ayd Medical Communcations, pp. 179-191 (1983).

Gold, M.S., Pottash, A.L.C., and Extein, I. Hypothyroidism and depression: Evidence from complete thyroid function evaluation. *J.A.M.A. 245*; 1919-1922 (1981).

Gold, M.S., Pottash, A.L.C., and Extein, I. "Symptomless" auto-immune thyroiditis in depression. *Psychiat. Res. 6*; 261-269 (1982).

Hall, R.C., Gardner, E.R., Stickney, S.K., LeCann, A.F., and Popkin, M.K. Physical illness manifesting as psychiatric disease. II. Analysis of a state hospital inpatient population. *Arch. Gen. Psychiat. 37*; 989-995 (1980).

Himmelhoch, J.M. Major mood disorders related to epileptic changes, in D. Blumer, ed., *Psychiatric Aspects of Epilepsy*. Washington, D.C., American Psychiatric Press, Inc, pp. 271-291 (1984).

Keller, M.B., and Shapiro, R.W. "Double depression": Superimposition of acute depressive episodes on chronic depressive disorders. *Amer. J. Psychiat. 139*; 438-442 (1982).

Kielholz, P., ed. *Masked Depression*. Berne Stuttgart/Vienna, Huber (1973).

Kielholz, P., Terzani, S., and Gastpar, M. Treatment for therapy resistant depressions. *Internat. Pharmacopsychiat. 14;* 94-100 (1979).

Kielholz, P., Poldinger, W., and Adams, C. Masked depression: A didactic concept for the diagnosis and treatment of somatized depressions. *Deutscher Arztc-Verlag* (1982).

Leckman, J.F., Weissman, M.W., Merikanges, K.R., Pauls, D.L., and Prusoff, B.A. Panic disorders and major depression: Increased risk of depression, alcoholism, panic and phobic disorders in families of depressed probands with panic disorder. *Arch. Gen. Psychiat. 40*; 1055-1060 (1983).

Lesse, S. Masked depression and depressive equivalents. *Psychopharmacol. Bull. 13*; 68-70 (1977).

Lesse, S. Masked depression: The ubiquitous but unappreciated syndrome. *Psychiat. J. Univ. Ottawa 5*; 268-273 (1980).

Liebowitz, M.R., and Klein, D.F. Hysteroid dysphoria. *Psychiat. Clin. North Amer. 2*;555-575 (1979).

Leibowitz, M.R., Quitkin, F.M., Stewart, J.W., McGrath, P.J., Harrison, W. Rabkin, J., Tricamo, E., and Klein, D.F. Atypical depression: Description and treatment. Paper presented at the American Psychiatric Association Annual Meeting, New York City, May 1983.

Links, P.S. The existence of the borderline diagnosis: Studies on diagnostic validity. *Can. J. Psychiat. 27*; 585-592 (1982).

Links, P.S., Kates, N., Gliva, G., and Clark, B. A Canadian community mental health program: A clerkship experience. *Gen. Hosp. Psychiat. 4*; 245-248 (1982).

Loosen, P.T., and Prange, Jr., A.J. Serum thyrotropin response to thyrotropin-releasing hormone in psychiatric patients: A review. *Amer. J. Psychiat. 139;* 405-416 (1982).

McNamara, E., Reynolds, C.F., Soloff, P.H., Mathias, R., Rossi, A., Spiker, D., Coble, P.A., and Kupfer, D.J. EEG sleep evaluation of depression in borderline patients. *Amer. J. Psychiat. 141;* 182-186 (1984).

Paykel, E.S. Classification of depressed patients: A cluster analysis derived grouping. *Brit. J. Psychiat. 118;* 275-288 (1971).

Paykel, E.S., Parker, R.R., Penrose, R.J., and Rassaby, E.R. Depressive classification and prediction of response of phenelzine. *Brit. J. Psychiat. 134;* 572-581 (1979).

Pichot, P., and Hassan, J. Masked depression and depressive equivalents—Problems of definition and diagnosis. In P. Kielholz, ed.; *Masked Depression*. Bern, Hans Huber Publisher, pp. 61-76 (1973).

Pless, I.B., and Pinkerton, P. *Chronic Childhood Disorders: Promoting Patterns of Adjustment*. Chicago, Year Book Medical Publishers (1975).

Price, J.S. Chronic depressive illness. *Brit. Med. J. 2;* 1200-1201 (1978).

Raskin, M., Pecke, H.V.S., Dickman, W., and Pinsker, H. Panic and generalized anxiety disorders. Developmental antecedents and precipitants. *Arch. Gen. Psychiat. 39;* 687-689 (1982).

Ravaris, C.L., Nies, A., Robinson, D.S., Ives, J.O., Lamborn, K.R. and Korson, L. A multiple-dose controlled study of phenelzine in the treatment of depressive anxiety states. *Arch. Gen. Psychiat. 33;* 347-350 (1976).

Ravaris, C.L., Robinson, D.S., Ives, J.O., Nies, A., and Bartlett, D. Phenelzine and amitriptyline in the treatment of depression: A comparison of present and past studies. *Arch. Gen. Psychiat. 37;* 1075-1080 (1980).

Robins, E., and Guze, S.B. Classification of affective disorders: The primary-secondary, the endogenous-reactive and the neurotic-psychotic concepts. In T. A. Williams, M. M. Katz, and J. A. Shields, eds., *Recent Advances in the Psychobiology of the Depressive Illness.* Washington, D.C., U.S. Government Printing Office (1972).

Robinson, D.S., Nies, A., Ravaris, C.L., Lamborn, K.R., and Burlington, V. The monoamine oxidase inhibitor, phenelzine in the treatment of depressive anxiety states. *Arch. Gen. Psychiat. 29;* 407-413 (1973).

Roth, M., and Mountjoy, C.Q. The distinction between anxiety states and depressive disorders. In E. S. Paykel, ed., *Handbook of Affective Disorders.* New York, The Guilford Press (1982).

Rosenthal TL, Akiskal HS, Scott-Strauss A, Rosenthal RH and David M. Familial and developmental factors in characterological depressions. *J. Affective Disord. 3;* 183-192 (1981).

Rowan RR, Paykel ES, and Parker RR: Phenelzine and amitriptyline: Effects on symptoms of neurotic depression. *Brit. J. Psychiat. 140;* 475-483 (1982).

Sargant, W: Some newer drugs in the treatment of depression and their relation to other somatic treatments. *Psychosomatics 1;* 14-17 (1960).

Sargant, W. Drugs in the treatment of depression. *Brit. Med. J. 1;* 225-227 (1961).

Sargant, W., and Dally, P. J. Treatment of anxiety states by antidepressant drugs. *Brit. Med. J. 1;* 6-9 (1962).

Schmidberg, M. The borderline patient. In S. Arieti, ed., *American Handbook of Psychiatry,* Vol. 1. New York, Basic Books, pp. 398-416 1959.

Stone, M.H. Contemporary shift of the borderline concept from a schizophrenic disorder to subaffective disorder. *Psychiat. Clin. North Amer. 3;* 517-594 (1979).

Stone, M.H. Borderline syndromes: A consideration of subtypes and an overview, directions for research. *Psychiat. Clin. North Amer. 4;* 3-24 (1981).

VanValkenburg, C., Akiskal, H.S., Puzantian, V.R., and Rosenthal, T.L. Anxious depressions: Clinical, family history, and naturalistic outcome comparisons with panic and major depressive disorders. *J. Affective Disord. 6;* 67-82 (1984).

Weissman, M.M., and Akiskal, H.S. The role of psychotherapy in chronic depressions: A proposal. *Compr. Psychiatry 25;* 23-31 (1984).

Weissman, M.M., and Klerman, G.L. The chronic depressive in the community: Unrecognized and poorly treated. *Compr. Psychiatry 18;* 523-532 (1977).

West, E.D., and Dally, P.J. Effect of iproniazid in depressive syndromes. *Brit. Med. J. 1;* 2491-2494 (1959).

Zisook, S., and Click, M.A. Atypical depression: Diagnostic and treatment considerations. Paper presented at the American Psychiatric Association Annual Meeting, New York, New York, May (1983).

2

Characteristics of Treatment-Resistant Depression

Michael E. Thase and David J. Kupfer

Approximately one-third to one-half of depressed patients do not respond satisfactorily to a given treatment regimen and it has been estimated that about 10-20 percent of depressives are refractory, given a variety of interventions (Ananth and Ruskin, 1974; Ayd, 1983). Since a substantial proportion of clinicians' time is spent caring for such treatment-resistant individuals, identification of characteristics which predict response or nonresponse would be of considerable practical and theoretical importance. Moreover, application of such findings for selection of appropriate alternative treatment modalities might lessen the suffering of individuals with chronic affective syndromes. In this chapter we discuss patient characteristics that might predict nonresponse to antidepressant treatment.

We begin with a brief review of methodological issues involved in studying treatment resistance. Next, evidence is summarized pertaining to sociodemographic, clinical, and psychobiological correlates of nonresponse to tricyclics, monoamine oxidase inhibitors, psychosocial treatments, and electroconvulsive therapy. Interrelationships between sociodemographic, clinical, and diagnostic subtype predictors of nonresponse are emphasized. Similarly, evidence for treatment-specific predictors of nonresponse will be discussed. Finally, we will integrate these diverse factors and provide recommendations for evaluation of treatment-resistant or chronically depressed patients in clinical practice.

METHODOLOGICAL ISSUES

Several investigators have proposed that the term "refractory depression" should be reserved for patients who have not responded to consecutively administered trials of several forms of antidepressant treatment (Ananth and Ruskin, 1974; Ayd, 1983; Gerner, 1983). In practical terms, this would include one or more trials with tricyclic antidepressants (TCAs) in dosages up to 300 mg per day of imipramine (or its equivalent), an aggressive trial with a monoamine oxidase inhibitor (MAOI; i.e., phenelzine in dosages up to 90 mg per day or its equivalent), and an "adequate" course of electroconvulsive therapy (ECT; up to 12-16 bilateral treatments) (Shaw, 1977). A definitive study of refractory depression would entail collection of a sizable sample of patients who failed to benefit from each of the modalities noted above. Unfortunately, to date such a series of patients has not been systematically collected. Therefore, we employ the concept of "relative" treatment resistance, the failure to respond to a trial of a given form of treatment.

Perhaps the single greatest hazard in identifying patients with resistant depression is determination if an adequate treatment trial has indeed been administered. As most pharmacotherapy trials employ a modest, fixed dosage of medication (i.e., 150-200 mg per day of imipramine or 45-60 mg per day of phenelzine), it is likely that a number of "resistant" patients actually would have responded to a higher dosage of antidepressant. Research on the relationship between drug dosage and tricyclic plasma level or level of platelet MAO inhibition has documented wide interpatient variability, with lower response rates generally observed in individuals with low TCA levels (Glassman and Perel, 1978; Nelson et al., 1982) or low percentage inhibition of platelet MAO (Davidson et al., 1978; Quitkin et al., 1979). Further, investigations employing low-dose versus high-dose strategies (Ravaris et al., 1976; Simpson et al., 1976; Watt et al., 1972), open trials of rather high dosages in "resistant" patients (Amsterdam et al., 1979; Schuckit and Feighner, 1972) or studies permitting upward titration of dosage guided by plasma levels (Nelson et al., 1982) document that the number of responders increases with more aggressive treatment.* This point also could apply

*See also Chapter 4, this volume.

to ECT, where switching from unilateral to bilateral electrode placement may result in fewer cases of resistant depression (Abrams et al., 1983). Thus, some degree of unwanted variance is present in grouped data on resistant depression derived from standard treatment protocols because of inclusion of potentially responsive, yet inadequately treated patients. Indeed, even patients considered so refractory as to be referred for psychosurgical interventions frequently are found to have received repeated trials of subtherapeutic doses of antidepressants (Bridges, 1983).

Another issue relates to differentiating resistant depressives from patients who were not able to tolerate an adequate trial of treatment because of the development of side effects. Results from one recent survey indicate that approximately one-third of a group of patients identified as tricyclic-resistant actually were not able to tolerate an adequate dosage of medication (Schatzberg et al., 1983a). Such patients often did well when prescribed an alternative medication with a different side-effect profile (Schatzberg et al., 1983a). Similarly, it is likely that outpatient samples with "resistant" depression include some individuals who did not respond because of noncompliance to the drug regimen. Again, inclusion of such patients in analyses to differentiate responders from resistant patients introduces unwelcomed "noise." Ideally, patients intolerant to conventional drug dosages and those suspected of noncompliance should be grouped separately from patients who did not respond to treatment.

Composition of the sample of depressed patients employed in treatment outcome research also is an important methodological factor. Patient samples employed in studies conducted prior to introduction of reliable, standardized criteria for primary or major depression frequenly were quite heterogeneous, including "depressed" patients with other pre-existing nonaffective disorders, covert medical or neurological conditions, or chronic subsyndromal affective states, in addition to patients now considered suitable for protocol participation. Even within the currently accepted primary major depression grouping, considerable heterogeneity still exists (Nelson and Charney, 1981). Clinical correlates of nonresponse might be obscured by combining the unipolar-bipolar, delusional-nondelusional, melancholic-nonmelancholic, typical-atypical dichotomies within the broad grouping of primary major depression (Kupfer and Thase, in press). One recent conservative solution to this problem is restriction of research samples to patients with nonbipolar, nondelusional primary endogenous depression (e.g., Kupfer et al., 1982; Nelson et al., 1982). Of course, such an approach limits the number of questions which can be addressed concerning predictors of nonresponse.

Another important source of methodological variance involves the definition of response and nonresponse categories. For example, a patient may be identified as a responder by one criterion (i.e., Hamilton Depression Rating Scale score reduction of >50 percent), yet be considered resistant using an alternative, more restrictive classification (i.e., final Hamilton score <10). Moreover, response rates differ as a function of number of weeks of treatment: some patients who are nonresponders after four weeks of treatment will "convert" to responders with two or four additional weeks of pharmacotherapy.

Finally, selected variables with possible significance for prediction of treatment outcome, such as length of episode or presence of marital disharmony, frequently are not assessed. If not controlled, such variables may obscure the value of other predictors.

We do not consider this summary of methodological issues to be exhaustive; certainly, other confounding factors might be considered pertinent. Nevertheless, this brief review should illustrate the complexity of the problem of defining nonresponse and identifying valid correlates of treatment outcome.

PREDICTION OF NONRESPONSE

Sociodemographic Factors

Nonresponse to TCAs has been associated with patient age, marital disharmony, and socioeconomic background (Deykin and Dimascio, 1972; Downing and Rickels, 1973; Raskin et al., 1970). Limited data from psychosocial treatment outcome studies suggest similar relationships exist between demographics and nonresponse (Steinmetz et al., 1983; Zeiss and Jones, 1983). Neither gender nor race appear to predict response, particularly when other variables are controlled.

Clinical experience and data from several controlled trials indicate a relative resistance to tricyclics exists in older depressed patients (i.e., >60 years old) when compared to younger samples (Brown et al., 1983; Hordern et al., 1965; Spar and LaRue, 1983; Wittenborn et al., 1973). Himmelhoch et al. (1982a) suggest that such a relationship reflects an interaction between declining neurobiological integrity and worsening social-psychological stressors. Of course, older patients also are often less tolerant to high dosages of antidepressant medication. Further, advancing age is correlated with a number of clinical factors which predict TCA nonresponse, such as increased global severity, presence of delusions, and melancholic features (Brown et al., 1983; Glassman and Roose, 1981; Himmelhoch et al., 1982a). These factors will be discussed in detail later in this chapter. Nevertheless, Brown et al. (1983) recently found relative resistance to TCAs in older patients even when factors such as severity and melancholic subtype were controlled. Older melancholic depressives resistant or intolerant to TCAs frequently benefit from ECT (Brown et al., 1983; Carney et al., 1965; Kiloh, 1982).

Nonresponse to tricyclics also has been noted in a subgroup consisting of relatively young female patients (Paykel et al., 1973; Raskin 1975; Raskin et al., 1973). Again, the relationship between a demographic factor and nonresponse may be associated with a cluster of clinical characteristics; irritability, anxiety, atypical neurovegetative symptoms, and characterological pathology are noted in these TCA resistant patients (Liebowitz and Klein 1979; Nies and Robinson, 1982). Such atypically depressed young females also are noted to respond poorly to ECT (Kiloh 1982; Nies and Robinson, 1982). This subgrouping may respond preferentially to treatment with MAOIs, particularly in the presence of hypersomnia and hyperphagia (Liebowitz and Klein, 1979; Nies and Robinson, 1982; Quitkin et al., 1982). Increasing experience with efficacious use of TCAs in depressed children and adolescents would suggest that the relationship between young age and TCA nonresponse may be specifically associated with a particular clinical subtype of depression. Young female patients seem to respond relatively well to psychosocial treatments (McLean and Hakstian, 1979; Steinmetz et al., 1983; Zeiss and Jones, 1983).

Results from several investigations indicate a significant association between marital discord and nonresponse to TCAs (Downing and Rickels, 1973) and ECT (Nyström, 1965). Naturalistic studies also reveal a relationship between marital discord and chronicity of depression (Akiskal, 1982; Rounsaville et al., 1979). At a broader level, a nonsupportive social environment has been associated with nonresponse to psychosocial treatment (Steinmetz et al., 1983) or open treatment with TCAs (Flaherty et al., 1983). Lower socioeconomic status also may predict poor outcome following treatment with TCAs (Downing and Rickels, 1972, 1973; Raskin et al., 1973; Rickels et al., 1964). However, it is possible that this latter relationship might actually reflect patient noncompliance, since each of these studies involved outpatient clinic samples. There is no evidence to implicate low socioeconomic status to nonresponse to ECT.

Sociodemographic correlates of nonresponse are summarized in Table 1.

Clinical Variables

Detailed reviews of clinical predictors of response/nonresponse to TCAs (Bielski and Friedel, 1976; Nelson and Charney, 1981), MAOIs (Nies and Robinson, 1982), and ECT (Kiloh, 1982) have been published elsewhere. In addition, our own group has published a study of clinical predictors of nonresponse to amitriptyline in a large (n = 76) inpatient series of depressives (Kupfer and Spiker, 1981).

A number of early studies found chronicity, whether defined in terms of a long index episode of depression or multiple previous episodes, to predict nonresponse to TCAs (see Bielski and Friedel, 1976) or ECT (Kiloh, 1982). However, neither index of chronicity was related to short-term outcome in our inpatient study (Kupfer and Spiker, 1981). A recent series of studies by Keller and associates (Keller and Shapiro, 1982; Keller et al., 1982a; 1982b; Keller et al., 1983) helps clarify the relationship between response and definition of chronicity. Patients with major depression superimposed upon a long-standing minor depressive syndrome (dysthymic disorder) were found to recover to their mildly symptomatic baseline more rapidly when compared to patients with acute, episodic disorders (Keller and Shapiro, 1982; Keller et al., 1982a). Further, presence of a long-standing minor depression antedating development of a full syndrome obscured other traditional predictors of treatment response (Keller et al., 1983). However, patients with these "double depressions" were less likely to achieve full remissions as rapidly and were significantly more likely to relapse than uncomplicated major depressives (Keller and Shapiro, 1982; Keller et al., 1982b; Keller et al., 1983). Among patients with no history of chronic minor depression, number of past episodes did not predict recovery, but was associated with risk of relapse during naturalistic follow-up (Keller et al., 1982b). Both severity and a short index episode were predictors of response in these acute depressives (Keller et al., 1982b).

Investigations examining the efficacy of psychosocial treatments for depression also generally have found that a long index episode of depression predicts poor response (McLean and Hakstian, 1979; Steinmetz et al., 1983; Zeiss and Jones, 1983). Such investigations did not differentiate between chronic minor and major

TABLE 1. Sociodemographic Correlates of Nonresponse

Variable	Relationship
Age	Curvilinear; relative resistance to tricyclics seen in younger (i.e., less than 30 years old) and older (i.e., more than 60 years old) age groups.
Sex	Relative resistance to tricyclics in young women; probably related to more "atypical" clinical presentation.
Marital status	Poorer response to antidepressants, ECT, and individual psychotherapy in patients with marital disharmony.
Social network	Preliminary data indicate that a nonsupportive social environment is related to nonresponse to psychosocial treatment or tricyclics.
Socioeconomic status	Poorer outcome in lower socioeconomic status groupings; possibly related to noncompliance.

depressive syndromes, however. While it is often assumed that chronic depressive disorders might preferentially respond to psychological treatments, little data have been collected to support this claim (Thase, 1983). Indeed, Akiskal (1982) has demonstrated that such chronic depressions are quite heterogeneous and include a number of patients who respond favorably to pharmacotherapy.

With respect to selected clinical signs and symptoms, the symptomatic criteria employed to diagnose an episode of major depression do not appear to uniformly predict TCA response (Nelson and Charney, 1981). However, major depressives respond preferentially to TCAs when compared to patients with milder, subsyndromal conditions (Stewart et al., 1983). Indeed, low levels of severity generally predict poor response or intolerance to TCA treatment (Bielski and Friedel, 1976; Stewart et al., 1983). In contrast, such mildly depressed patients may preferentially respond to psychosocial treatments (McLean and Hakstian, 1979; Steinmetz et al., 1983; Zeiss and Jones, 1983). In our own experience, the intermediate range of depressive severity (i.e., Hamilton scores in the range of 15-30) appears optimum for response to pharmacotherapy. This impression recently was confirmed by Abou-Saleh and Coppen (1983) in a study investigating clinical correlates of response to ECT or TCAs. Markedly severe depressions are associated with relative resistance to TCAs, MAOIs, and psychosocial approaches (Bielski and Friedel, 1976; McLean and Hakstian, 1979; Nies and Robinson, 1982). Such patients preferentially respond to ECT (Kiloh, 1982). It is of interest that this relationship parallels the pattern noted to exist between TCA response and aging.

Perhaps the best validated correlate of TCA response is psychomotor retardation (Bielski and Friedel, 1976; Nelson and Charney, 1981). Conversely, agitation and psychic anxiety generally are associated with a poor response to TCAs (Bielski and Friedel, 1976; Kupfer and Spiker, 1981; Nelson and Charney, 1981). Of note, phenelzine has been shown to be relatively effective in patients with anxiety (Nies and Robinson, 1982), while ECT may be favored over TCAs in patients with marked psychomotor agitation (Kiloh, 1982). It may be important to differentiate a history of panic attacks from that of generalized anxiety. There is increasing evidence that panic attacks are well-controlled by treatment with TCAs (Zitrin et al., 1983) or MAOIs (Sheehan et al., 1980; Robinson et al., 1983). Further research is needed to ascertain if patients with panic attacks and depression preferentially respond to MAOIs as opposed to TCAs (e.g., Robinson et al., 1983), or if depressed patients with generalized anxiety and no history of panic attacks gain greater benefits from MAOI treatment.

Other clinical variables traditionally grouped within the endogenomorphic symptom cluster, such as weight loss, middle insomnia, early morning awakening, and diurnal mood variation show modest positive correlations with TCA response (Bielski and Friedel, 1976; Nelson and Charney, 1981). Pervasive anhedonia also appears to be a powerful correlate of the need for treatment with a TCA or ECT (Nelson et al., 1980). As previously noted, "atypical" symptoms, such as hypersomnia, overeating, weight gain, mood lability, and reverse diurnal mood variation (i.e., mood worsening in evening) are predictive of response to treatment with an MAOI (Davidson, 1983; Nies and Robinson, 1982). Further, patients with a constellation of such features are often resistant to treatment with TCAs such as imipramine (Quitkin et al., 1982) and amitripytline (Paykel et al., 1973; Robinson et al., 1983). We would suggest that such patients should be preferentially treated with MAOIs, rather than with sedating and appetite-enhancing TCAs. In this case, nonresponse to TCAs reflects selection of the wrong class of antidepressant rather than an actual resistance.

The best studied clinical predictor of nonresponse to TCAs or MAOIs is the presence of delusions (Avery and Lubrano, 1979; Brown et al., 1982; Coryell et al., 1982; Glassman et al., 1975; Glassman and Roose, 1981; Kupfer and Spiker, 1981; Nelson and Bowers, 1978; Perry et al., 1982). Such patients frequently require either ECT (Avery and Lubrano, 1979; Perry et al., 1982) or a combination of TCA and neuroleptic (Brown et al., 1982). Psychotically depressed patients with mood incongruent delusions appear to show the greatest relative resistance to somatic treatments (Coryell et al., 1982; Brockington et al., 1982).

Among other clinical subtypes of major depression, results from one controlled trial (Kupfer and Spiker, 1981) indicate that bipolar II depressives exhibit relative resistance to amitriptyline. Preliminary data from an outpatient treatment trial currently in progress indicate that depressives with bipolar II disorder also respond less favorably to imipramine ($p < .05$) when compared to an otherwise matched group with recurrent unipolar depression (Thase and Kupfer, unpublished data). Anecdotal reports suggest that a relatively high proportion of bipolar I depressives also may be resistant to TCAs (Himmelhoch et al., 1972, 1982b). Further, bipolar depressives are at some risk for developing a pattern of rapid cycling during TCA treatment (Potter, 1983), although this observation is controversial (Lewis and Winokur, 1982). Some evidence suggests that lithium carbonate and/or MAOIs produce better results in such patients (Himmelhoch et al., 1972, 1982b; Potter, 1983). It is possible that these tentative conclusions are related to clinical observations of atypical neurovegetative symptoms, such as hypersomnia, hyperphagia, and weight gain, in a number of outpatient bipolar depressives (Kupfer et al., 1975).

One might expect that patients with endogenous (melancholic) subtype of depression would have a high probability of response to TCAs (e.g., Bielski and Friedel, 1976). Surprisingly little data have been collected to support this claim and at least several reports fail to document such a relationship (Kupfer and Spiker,

1981; Stewart et al., 1983). It should be kept in mind that several correlates of TCA nonresponse, including agitation and delusions, are more common in endogenous depressions. Similarly, many investigators consider bipolar depressions to be endogenous by definition. Thus, the endogenous grouping contains several subtypes which may show relative resistance to treatment with a TCA. However, it does appear likely that definite endogenous depression (as defined by Research Diagnostic Criteria) or melancholia (according to DSM-III) categorize depressions which are relatively resistant to psychosocial treatments (Prusoff et al., 1980; Thase, 1983).

Depressions complicated by antecedent nonaffective psychiatric disorders, alcoholism or sedativism, or intercurrent medical-neurological conditions tend to have more chronic or protracted courses (Akiskal, 1982; Clayton and Lewis, 1981; Weissman et al., 1978). It is unclear that such patients exhibit relative resistance to TCAs; conflicting results have been published (Andreason and Winokur, 1979; Kupfer and Spiker, 1981; Reveley and Reveley, 1981). Nevertheless, it is our clinical experience that such complicated cases definitely are more difficult to treat and are overrepresented in treatment-resistant samples. Indeed, review of patients admitted to our outpatient affective disorders clinic over a five-year period reveals that depressed patients with alcoholism, habitual sedative use or drug abuse, intercurrrent medical conditions, cerebral dysrhythmias or nonaffective primary psychiatric conditions exhibited significantly poorer response to openly administered, clinician's-choice treatment (Thase et al., 1984).

Particular attention needs to be given to rule out underlying medical-neurological conditions in treatment-resistant patients. Approximately 15 percent of depressed patients admitted to our Clinical Research Unit are found to have previously undiagnosed physical illnesses which are intimately related to their affective syndrome (Kupfer and Spiker, 1981). Further, such patients are most often diagnosed by referring clinicians as suffering from nonbipolar major depressins (Thase and Himmelhoch, 1983). While hypothyroidism and other endocrinopathies are most common, collagen vascular diseases, occult malignancies, myasthenia gravis, and multiple sclerosis also have been detected. Iatrogenic effects of a variety of medications also may be implicated, including antihypertensives, narcotic analgesics, contraceptives, and other steroids. Akiskal (1982) found similar intercurrent medical and iatrogenic factors to characterize his sample of chronic primary depressives. It is our experience that such depressions remain relatively refractory until that underlying medical problem is corrected or stabilized. Targum (1983a) has presented some pertinent preliminary data in this regard: patients with subclinical hypothyroidism were resistant to TCAs until thyroid supplementation was added to the regimen.

Finally, as previously noted, presence of selected "characterological" features is associated with nonresponse to TCAs or ECT relative to MAOIs (Liebowitz and Klein, 1979; Nies and Robinson, 1982). Other personality disturbances, such as hypochondriasis, extreme dependency, markedly low self-esteem, and neuroticism, may predict poor response across treatment modalities (Bielski and Friedel, 1979; Weissman et al., 1978; Zuckerman et al., 1980), particularly if the patient does not evidence either a typical or atypical neurovegetative symptom profile. However, Akiskal (1982) has noted that untreated or inadequately managed primary depressions may develop "characterological" overtones as a consequence of chronicity per se. Extremely early onset, lack of family history of affective disorder, and fluctuating or nonepisodic course represent clinical predictors of nonresponse to tricyclics in such chronically depressed patients (Akiskal, 1982).

Clinical correlates of response and relative resistance are summarized in Table 2.

TABLE 2. Clinical Correlates of Nonresponse

Variable	Relationship
Severity	Curvilinear; nonresponse to tricyclics most likely in mildest and most severe cases.
Delusions	Poor response to tricyclics alone; ECT or tricyclic plus neuroleptic preferred. Greatest treatment resistance when delusions are mood incongruent.
Agitation	Poor response to tricyclics alone; conversely, retardation is predictive of tricyclic response.
Anxiety	Generalized anxiety related to nonresponse to tricyclics or ECT, association with response to phenelzine. Panic attacks without chronic generalized anxiety predict response to phenelzine and possibly tricyclics.
"Atypical" features	Hypersomnia, weight gain, and hysteroid features associated with nonresponse to tricyclics relative to MAOIs, particularly seen in bipolar II subtype of depression
Medical illness and treatments	Intercurrent endocrinological illnesses, particularly thyroid disease, related to nonresponse. Chronic debilitating illnesses and antihypertensive medication associated with protracted course of depression
Alcohol and drug abuse, other primary psychiatry disorders	Alcohol abuse and sedativism related to nonresponse in an open treatment setting. Secondary depressions noted to run more chronic course longitudinally.

Psychobiological Correlates

In recent years, considerable attention has been devoted to identification and validation of objective biological correlates of endogenous depression. In this section, we will review application of four such biological "tests" for depression: the dexamethasone suppression test (DST; Carroll, 1982), the thyroid releasing hormone (TRH) stimulation test (Kirkegaard, 1981), electroencephalographic (EEG) sleep studies (Kupfer and Thase, 1983), and determination of 24-hour urinary excretion of 3-methoxy-4-hydroxyphenylglycol (MHPG) (Schildkraut, 1982; Kelwala et al., 1983). As each of these methods are felt to reflect evidence of core biological dysfunction in the brain, it has been hoped that their clinical application may enhance judgements with respect to selection of the most appropriate somatic antidepressant treatments (Carroll, 1982; Kupfer and Thase, 1983). In particular, such markers of "biological" depression might prove particularly useful in assessing and monitoring patients with resistant depressions.

Failure to suppress cortisol levels after administration of dexamethasone is a rather well-documented finding in depression, occurring in perhaps 30-60 percent of inpatient series, as well as a lesser percentage of outpatients (Carroll, 1982; Gwirtsman et al., 1982). Although originally specifically linked to the melancholic subtype of depression (Carroll et al., 1981), a number of recent investigations also have established clinical correlations between DST nonsuppression and aging, weight loss, recent alcohol withdrawal, anxiety, agitation, and the presence of delusions (Caroff et al., 1983; Edelstein et al., 1983; Mendlewicz et al., 1982; Newsom and Murray, 1983; Reus, 1982; Raskind et al., 1982; Schatzberg et al., 1983b; Spar and Gerner, 1982). Further, DST nonsuppression has proved to be less specific to endogenous depression than originally hoped (Graham et al., 1982; Meltzer et al., 1982; Newsom and Murray, 1983; Spar and Gerner, 1982). Thus, it should not be surprising that pretreatment DST nonsuppression has not been shown conclusively to predict response to TCAs. Several investigations have noted that pretreatment DST nonsuppression actually may predict relative resistance to TCA treatment (McLeod, 1972; Spar and LaRue, 1983; Amsterdam et al., 1983). Again, use of ECT may be indicated in TCA-resistant patients with DST nonsuppression (Coryell, 1982; Greden, 1982). Conversely, there is little evidence that a normal DST identifies a subgroup of major depressives who do not require somatic antidepressant treatment. Some very preliminary evidence indicates that patients with DST nonsuppression may benefit from somatic treatments relative to psychosocial interventions (Rush and Shaw, 1983).

The DST has shown promise in monitoring longitudinal treatment response. Abnormal test results generally normalize with clinical recovery; persistent nonsuppression often is associated with treatment resistance (Albala et al., 1981;

Greden et al., 1980; 1983; Papakostos et al., 1981; Yerevanian et al., 1983). One possible exception here may be noted during treatment with ECT: neurobiological effects of repeated seizures may induce a transient normalization which does not predict short-term response (Coryell and Zimmerman, 1983). Therefore, it may not be prudent to use DST normalization as a criterion for response during a course of ECT. A small precentage of clinically recovered patients will continue to evidence DST nonsuppression. Although more detailed study of such cases is needed, preliminary evidence would suggest that these patients are at high risk for relapse (Greden et al., 1983; Targum, 1983b; Yerevanian et al., 1983).

Experience with the TRH stimulation test has been similar to that with the DST: a minority (20-40 percent) of major depressives experience a blunted thyroid stimulating hormone (TSH) response to this challenge, but such blunting is not entirely specific to depression (Gold et al., 1981; Loosen and Prange, 1982; Kirkegaard, 1981). It is of some interest that there is little overlap between TRH and DST results (Gold et al., 1981; Rush et al., 1983). TRH test results often normalize with clinical recovery, such that treatment-resistant patients frequently manifest continued TSH blunting (Langer et al., 1983; Targum, 1983b). However, it would be premature to speculate that TRH blunting identifies a subgroup of depressives who require somatic treatment. As was the case with the DST, continued TSH blunting in apparently recovered patients may serve as a marker for increased risk of relapse (Kirkegaard, 1981; Langer et al., 1983; Targum, 1983b).

All-night EEG sleep studies have been increasingly used in affective disorders research. Four basic EEG sleep disturbances characteristically are seen in depression: (1) disturbances of sleep continuity and sleep maintenance, (2) diminished delta (slow-wave) sleep, (3) altered rapid-eye-movement (REM) sleep density and distribution, and (4) shortened REM latency (i.e., < 60 minutes) (Kupfer and Thase, 1983). Shortened REM latency is now widely considered to be a reliable marker of endogenomorphic depression and is present in bipolar, unipolar, delusional, most nonbipolar major (60–80 percent), and schizoaffective depressions (Kupfer and Thase, 1983).

Several lines of evidence indicate that EEG sleep studies may have some use in prediction of TCA response, at least with respect to amitriptyline (Kupfer, 1981). The work of Akiskal (Akiskal, 1982; Akiskal et al., 1980) also has demonstrated that modestly shortened REM latencies (i.e., 20-60 minutes) predict TCA response in patients with chronic, atypical, or characterological depressive syndromes. Conversely, such patients were found to seldom benefit from treatment with TCAs if REM latencies fell within the normal range (i.e., >70 minutes). Extremely shortened REM latencies, however, have been found to predict relative resistance to treatment with amitriptyline (Kupfer et al., 1982). We have found that patients with severe, delusional depression are most likely to evidence REM latencies of <20 minutes, particularly if they are older and have a history of several prior episodes of depression dating over a protracted period of time (Thase et al., 1986). Such patients generally require treatment with ECT to achieve a satisfactory response. Shortened REM latency (i.e., <60 minutes) also may identify outpatient major depressives who fail to respond to psychosocial treatments (Rush and Shaw, 1983: Thase, unpublished data). This curvilinear relationship between REM latency and TCA response shows considerable similarity to previously described curves for age and global severity. Indeed, previous work has documented significant inverse correlations between REM latency and both severity and age (see Kupfer and Thase, 1983).

Some evidence implicates other pretreatment EEG sleep disturbances with treatment response. For example, marked sleep continuity disturbances are present in a number of TCA nonresponders. Clinical correlates of this pattern include presence of delusions or intercurrent medical-neurological illnesses (Kupfer and Thase, 1983). Conversely, it has been our experience that hypersomnia, as documented by prolonged sleep time and minimal sleep maintenance problems, is predictive of response to MAOIs relative to sedating TCAs (Kupfer and Thase, 1983).

Beyond use of pretreatment REM latency for prediction of response/nonresponse, several investigations have studied correlations between drug effects during the first several nights of treatment with subsequent outcome (see Kupfer, 1981; Thase and Kupfer, in press). Briefly, patients who fail to respond to a standard course of treatment with amitriptyline (i.e., 150-300 mg per day for four weeks) evidence little change in sleep latency and less pronounced suppression of REM latency and REM percent during the first two nights of drug treatment when compared to responders (Kupfer, 1981; Thase and Kupfer, in press). Conversely, the degree of nonpharmacological REM deprivation produced by sleep deprivation procedures appears to predict subsequent response to TCAs (Duncan et al., 1980; Vogel, 1981; Wirz-Justice et al., 1979).

Accuracy of prediction of subsequent TCA response on the basis of the first two nights of sleep on 50 mg of amitriptyline is approximately 65 percent, compared to chance predictions of 33 percent (Thase and Kupfer, in press). Further, such predictive accuracy has been found to be superior to discriminant functions based on clinical data or pretreatment EEG sleep variables (Kupfer, 1981; Thase and Kupfer, in press).

In summary, several findings have emerged from EEG sleep studies which characterize patients who are resistant to treatment with amitriptyline: (1) either normal or extremely shortened REM latency during pretreatment studies, (2) failure to lengthen REM latency by at least 150 percent after a test dosage of 50 mg of amitriptyline, (3) relative nonsuppression of REM sleep by amitriptyline test dose (i.e., ≥ 50 percent suppression of REM time), and (4) lack of an initial sedative response to amitriptyline (see Table 3). Clinical correlates of such EEG sleep findings reveal links to advancing age, either marked severity or nonendogenous depressive syndromes, and presence of delusions. Not surprisingly, patients receiving amitripytline whose EEG sleep profiles are indicative of nonsuppression of REM sleep frequently require ECT (Thase and Kupfer, in press).

TABLE 3. EEG Sleep Correlates of Nonresponse

Variable	Relationship
REM latency at baseline	Curvilinear, nonresponse most common in patients with very short REM latency (i.e., less than 20 minutes) or normal REM latencies (i.e., greater than 70 minutes).
Sleep continuity changes following amitriptyline test dose	Poor response to amitriptyline associated with little initial sedative effect during the first two nights of treatment.
Inadequate REM suppression following amitriptyline test dose	Relative resistance to amitriptyline correlated with less than 50 percent suppression of REM time and failure to prolong REM latency by 150 percent during the first two nights of treatment.

Interest in hypothesized monoamine disturbances in major depression led to investigations of relationships between CNS amine metabolites and TCA response. Renal excretion of MHPG, a key metabolite of norepinephrine in the CNS, has received considerable attention as a possible predictor of TCA response (Kelwala et al., 1983; Schildkraut, 1982). In particular, it has been proposed that low levels of 24-hour excretion of urinary MHPG predict response to "noradrenergic" antidepressants, such as imipramine, desipramine, or maprotiline, relative to agents with more serotonergic effects (Schildkraut, 1982). Indeed, a considerable number of studies have found a significant association between urinary MHPG level and TCA response, with high values generally associated with relative resistance to agents like imipramine (see Kelwala et al., 1983; Maas et al., 1984; Schildkraut, 1982). Transient clinical improvement during several days' treatment with amphetamine or methylphenidate, noradrenergic agonists, may be similarly predictive of subsequent TCA response (e.g., Sabelli et al., 1983).

However, a number of investigators have not found a significant relationship between 24-hour urinary MHPG levels and either diagnosis or treatment response and several methodological problems may limit routine use of MHPG excretion for treatment prediction (Kelwala et al., 1983; Kupfer and Thase, in press). Clinical correlates of urinary MHPG levels include low levels in patients with motoric retardation and/or low anxiety levels (Kupfer and Thase, in press; Schildkraut, 1982). Conversely, high levels are observed in patients with prominent anxiety, marked agitation, or during panic attacks (Kupfer and Thase, in press; Ko et al., 1983). It is of interest that such clinical correlates respectively predict response or nonresponse to TCAs. Low urinary MHPG is most commonly seen in bipolar I depressions (Schildkraut, 1982). Indeed, much of the work by Schildkraut and associates relating urinary MHPG with imipramine response has been conducted with bipolar patients. Since we have previously noted that bipolar II depressives (and possibly bipolar I patients) may exhibit a relative resistance to TCAs (e.g., Himmelhoch et al., 1982b; Kupfer and Spiker, 1981), further research is needed to reconcile relationships between bipolarity, urinary MHPG, and TCA response.

SUMMARY AND RECOMMENDATIONS

In this section we integrate findings from the clinical and psychobiological studies described above. Review of characteristics of nonresponse to standard antidepressant treatment regimens reveals several general groupings of resistant depression. We describe these "types" of resistant depression, provide recommendations for assessment, and suggest alternative treatment regimens. Such treatment strategies are reviewed in more detail in subsequent chapters of this monograph.

Perhaps the most striking grouping of TCA-resistant depressives consists of patients with the most pervasive and severe, agitated affective syndromes. This grouping is of some conceptual interest because patients frequently evidence several or many clinical predictors of TCA responsiveness, i.e., endogenomorphic symptoms, shortened REM latency, and neuroendocrine test abnormalities. However, such patients are often delusional and over age 50. Given the marked agitation and psychic anxiety frequently seen in patients with these depressions, urinary and plasma MHPG levels actually may be elevated. Moreover, EEG sleep studies in these patients conducted following a test dose of 50 mg of amitriptyline reveal minimal changes in sleep efficiency and only modest or minimal suppression of REM sleep indices. Electroconvulsive therapy should be considered the first line of treatment for such severely depressed patients, although brief trials of neuroleptics or lithium carbonate (de Montigny et al., 1983; Heninger, et al., 1983) might be tried as an adjunctive to a large dose of TCA. Thorough medical evaluations also are important, as a variety of severe intercurrent illnesses may present in this fashion (e.g., Kronfol et al., 1982).

A second common form of TCA-resistant depression is characterized by an atypical neurovegetative profile, reactive or nonautonomous mood disturbance, and personality attributes such as rejection sensitivity or histrionic interpersonal style. This form of depression is most often seen in young women. Prominent anxiety may be a salient feature and panic attacks are common. Prevalence of bipolar II disorder is common in this grouping (Akiskal, 1981). Psychobiological profiles are often normal, although REM latency may be shortened (Akiskal, 1981; Quitkin et al., 1982). Evaluation of the integrity of the hypothalamic-pituitary-thyroid axis is of some use, as symptomless autoimmune thyroiditis is common in this age grouping and presents with "atypical" features such as anergia, irritability, hypersomnia, and weight gain (Gold and Pottash, 1983). If evidence of subclinical hypothyroidism is documented, then adjunctive use of T_3 (Cytomel) would appear indicated (Targum, 1983a). As previously noted, treatment with MAOI antidepressants should be used with these atypically-depressed individuals.

Third, another relatively common grouping of TCA-resistant patients includes patients with a chronic, nonepisodic, mild-moderate depressive syndrome which often has persisted since childhood or young adulthood. A variety of marital, family, and interpersonal disturbances may be identified which are intertwined closely with the depressive syndrome. Such individuals have relatively few neurovegetative signs (both typical and atypical), although they may have marked generalized anxiety and other, antecedent, nonaffective psychiatric disorders (Akiskal et al., 1978; Akiskal, 1982). Psychobiological studies generally are normal. Efforts to treat these patients with alternative somatic therapies often are unproductive. While psychosocial approaches probably are the cornerstone of treatment, available data would indicate that such interventions are hardly a panacea for these difficult patients (McLean and Hakstian, 1979; Rush and Shaw, 1983; Steinmetz et al., 1983; Zeiss and Jones, 1983).

Fourth, we would consider the subgroup of bipolar patients who develop a pattern of rapid cycling on TCAs. Withdrawal of TCAs often results in lengthening of cycles, at the expense of developing a prolonged, lithium-resistant depression (Potter, 1983). Again, integrity of thyroid function should be assessed and deficiencies corrected (Cowdry et al., 1983). If lithium alone is not effective, we would suggest preferential use of MAOI antidepressants, particularly if the patient has a profile of anergia, hypersomnia, and weight gain. Among available alternative, novel antidepressant agents, carbamazepine may hold particular promise (Post and Uhde, 1983).

Fifth, we would include a group of pseudoresistant patients who have received inadequate, low dosage trials of TCAs, who are rapid metabolizers of normally adequate dosages, or who are intolerant to usual clinical dosages of TCAs and/or MAOIs due to development of severe side effects. Outpatients who are noncompliant with medication also might fall into this grouping. This residual grouping would probably appear indistinguishable from TCA responders on the basis of clinical and psychobiological studies. Use of plasma TCA levels is helpful to identify rapid metabolizers and noncompliant patients, both of which would have low blood levels.

We recognize that this classification of TCA-resistant patients is rather stereotypic and some patients will not "cleanly" fit into these categories. However, thorough review of characteristics of patients who appear to have resistant depressions does provide a rational basis for selection of the next, most appropriate treatment or set of treatments for these long-suffering individuals.

ACKNOWLEDGMENTS

This work was supported in part by NIMH Grants MH 24652 and MH 30915 as well as a grant from the John D. and Catherine T. MacArthur Research Network on the Psychobiology of Depression.

REFERENCES

Abou-Saleh, MT., and Coppen, A. Classification of depression and response to antidepressive therapies. *Brit. J. Psychiat. 143,* 601-603 (1983).

Abrams, R., Taylor, M.A., Faber, T., Ts'o, T.O.T., Williams, R. A., and Almy, G. Bilateral versus unilateral electroconvulsive therapy. *Amer. J. Psychiat. 140,* 436-465 (1983).

Akiskal, H.S. Subaffective disorder: Dysthymic, cyclothymic and bipolar II disorders on the "borderline" realm. *Psychiat. Clin. N. Amer. 4,* 25-46 (1981).

Akiskal, H.S. Factors associated with incomplete recovery in primary depressive illness. *J. Clin. Psychiat. 43,* 255-271 (1982).

Akiskal, H.S., Bitar, A.H., Puzantian, V.R., Rosenthal, T.L., and Walker, P.M. The nosological status of neurotic depression. *Arch. Gen. Psychiat. 35,* 756-766 (1978).

Akiskal, H.S., Rosenthal, T.L., Haykal, R.F., Lemmi, H., Rosenthal, R.H., and Scott-Straus, A. Characterological depressions: Clinical and sleep EEG findings separating subaffective dysthymias from character spectrum disorders. *Arch. Gen. Psychiat. 37,* 777-783 (1980).

Albala, A.A., Greden, J.F., Tarika, J., and Carroll, B.J. Changes in serial dexamethasone suppression tests among unipolar depressives receiving electroconvulsive treatment. *Biol. Psychiat. 16,* 551-560 (1981).

Amsterdam, J., Brunswick, D.J., and Mendels, J. High dose desipramine, plasma drug levels and clinical response. *J. Clin. Psychiat. 40,* 141-143 (1979).

Amsterdam, J.D., Winokur, A., Bryant, S., Larkin, J., and Rickels, K. The dexamethasone suppression test as a predictor of antidepressant response. *Psychopharmacol. 80,* 43-45 (1983).

Ananth, J., and Ruskin, R. Treatment of intractable depression. *Int. Pharmacopsychiat. 9,* 218-229 (1974).

Andreason, N.C., and Winokur, G. Secondary depression: Familial, clinical, and research perspectives. *Amer. J. Psychiat. 136,* 62-66 (1979).

Avery, D., and Lubrano, A. Depression treated with imipramine and ECT: The DeCarolis study reconsidered. *Amer. J. Psychiat. 136,* 559-562 (1979).

Ayd, F.J. Treatment-resistant depression: Therapeutic strategies, in *Affective Disorders Reassessed: 1983.* F.J. Ayd, I.J. Taylor, and B.T. Taylor, eds., Ayd Medical Communications, Baltimore, pp. 115-125 (1983).

Bielski, R.J., and Friedel, R.O. Prediction of tricyclic antidepressant response. *Arch. Gen. Psychiat. 33,* 1479-1489 (1976).

Bridges, P.K. " . . . and a small dose of an antidepressant might help." *Brit. J. Psychiat. 142,* 626-628 (1983).

Brockington, I.F., Helzer, J.E., Hillier, V.F., and Francis, A.F. Definitions of depression: Concordance and prediction of outcome. *Amer. J. Psychiat. 139,* 1022-1027 (1982).

Brown, R.P., Frances, A., Kocsis, J.H., and Mann, J.J. Psychotic vs. nonpsychotic depression: Comparison of treatment response. *J. Nerv. Ment. Dis. 170,* 635-637 (1982).

Brown, R.P., Sweeney, J., Frances, A., Kocsis, J.H., and Loutsche, E. Age as a predictor of treatment response in endogenous depression. *J. Clin. Psychopharmacol. 3,* 176-178 (1983).

Carney, M.W.P., Roth, M., and Garside, R.F. The diagnosis of depressive syndromes and the prediction of ECT response. *Brit. J. Psychiat. 111,* 659-674 (1965).

Caroff, S., Winokur, A., Rieger, W., Schweizer, E., and Amsterdam, J. Response to dexamethasone in psychotic depression. *Psychiat. Res. 8,* 59-64 (1983).

Carroll, B.J. The dexamethasone suppression test for melancholia. *Brit. J. Psychiat. 140,* 292-304 (1982).

Carroll, B.J., Feinberg, M., Greden, J.F., Tarika, J., Albala, A.A., Haskett, R.F., James, N.M., Kronfol, Z., Lohr, N., Steiner, M., DeVigne, J.P., and Young, E. A specific laboratory test for the diagnosis of melancholia. *Arch. Gen. Psychiat. 38,* 15-22 (1981).

Clayton, P.J., and Lewis, C.E. The significance of secondary depression. *J. Affect. Disord. 3,* 25-35 (1981).

Coryell, W. Hypothalamic-pituitary-adrenal axis activity abnormality and ECT response. *Psychiat. Res. 6,* 283-291 (1982).

Coryell, W. Tsuang, M.T., and McDaniel, J. Psychotic features in major depression. Is mood congruence important? *J. Affect. Disord. 4,* 227-236 (1982).

Coryell, W., and Zimmerman, M. The dexamethasone suppression test and ECT outcome: A six-month follow-up. *Biol. Psychiat. 18,* 21-27 (1983).

Cowdrey, R.W., Wehr, T.A., Zis, A.P., and Goodwin, F.K. Thyroid abnormalities associated with rapid-cycling bipolar illness. *Arch. Gen. Psychiat. 40,* 414-420 (1983).

Davidson, J. MAO inhibitors: A clinical perspective, in *Affective Disorders Reassessed: 1983,* F.J. Ayd, I.J. Taylor, and B.T. Taylor, eds. Ayd Medical Communications, Baltimore, pp. 41-55 (1983).

Davidson, J.R.T., McLeod, M.N., and White, H.L. Inhibition of platelet monoamine oxidase in depressed subjects treated with phenelzine. *Amer. J. Psychiat. 135,* 470-472 (1978).

deMontigny, C., Cournoyer, G., Morissette, R., Langlois, R., and Caille, G. Lithium carbonate addition in tricyclic antidepressant-resistant unipolar depression. *Arch. Gen. Psychiat. 40,* 1327-1334 (1983).

Dewan, M.J., Pandurangi, A.K., Boucher, M.L., Levy, B., and Major, L.F. Abnormal dexamethasone suppression test results in chronic schizophrenic patients. *Amer. J. Psychiat. 139,* 1501-1503 (1982).

Deykin, E.Y., and DiMascio, A. Relationship of patient background characteristics to efficacy of pharmacotherapy in depression. *J. Nerv. Ment. Dis. 155,* 209-215 (1972).

Downing, R.W., and Rickels, K. Predictors of amitriptyline response in outpatient depressives. *J. Nerv. Ment. Dis. 154,* 248-263, (1972).

Downing, R.W., and Rickels, K. Predictors of response to amitriptyline and placebo in three outpatient treatment settings. *J. Nerv. Ment. Dis. 156,* 109-129 (1973).

Duncan, W.C., Gillin, J.C., Post, R.M., Gerner, R.H., and Wehr, T.A. The relationship between EEG sleep patterns and clinical improvement in depressed patients treated with sleep deprivation. *Biol. Psychiat. 15,* 879-889 (1980).

Edelstein, C.K., Roy-Byrne, P., Fawzy, F.I., and Dornfeld, L. Effects of weight loss on the dexamethasone suppression test. *Amer. J. Psychiat. 140,* 338-341 (1983).

Flaherty, J.A., Gaviria, F.M., Black, E.M., Altman, E., and Michell, T. The role of social support in the functioning of patients with unipolar depression. *Amer. J. Psychiat. 140,* 473-476 (1983).

Gerner, R.H. Systematic treatment approach to depression and treatment resistant depression. *Psychiatr. Ann. 13,* 40-49 (1983).

Glassman, A.H., Kantor, S.J., and Shostak, M. Depression, delusions, and drug response. *Amer. J. Psychiat. 132,* 715-719 (1975).

Glassman, A.H., and Perel, J.M. Tricyclic blood levels and clinical outcome: A review of the art, in *Psychopharmacology: A Generation of Progress.* M.A. Lipston, A. DiMascio, and K.F. Killam, eds., Raven Press, New York, pp. 917-922 (1978).

Glassman, A.H., and Roose, S.P. Delusional depression. *Arch. Gen. Psychiat. 38,* 424-427 (1981).

Gold, M.S., Pottash, A.L.C., Extein, I., and Sweeney, D.R. Diagnosis of depression in the 1980's *J.A.M.A. 245,* 1562-1564 (1981).

Gold, M.S. and Pottash, A.L.C. Thyroid dysfunction or depression?, in *Affective Disorders Reassessed: 1983.* F.J. Ayd, I.J. Taylor, and B.T. Taylor, eds., Ayd Medical Communications, Baltimore, MD, pp. 179-191 (1983).

Graham, P.M., Booth, J., Boranga, G., Galhenage, S., Myers, C.M., Teoh, C.L., and Cox, L.S. The dexamethasone suppression test in mania. *J. Affect. Disord. 4*, 201-211 (1982).

Greden, J.F. The dexamethasone suppression test: An established biological marker for melancholia, in *Biological Markers in Psychiatry and Neurology.* E. Usdin, and I. Hanin, eds., Pergamon Press, New York, pp. 229-240 (1982).

Greden J.F., Albala, A.A., Haskett, R.F., James, N.M., Goodman, L., Steiner, M., and Carroll, B.J. Normalization of dexamethasone suppression test: A laboratory index of recovery from endogenous depression. *Biol. Psychiat. 15*, 449-458 (1980).

Greden J.F., Gardner, R., King, D., Grunhaus, L., Carroll, B.J., and Kronfol, Z. Dexamethasone suppression tests in antidepressant treatment of melancholia. *Arch. Gen. Psychiat. 40*, 493-500 (1983).

Gwirtsman, J., Gerner, R.H., and Sternbach, H. The overnight dexamethasone suppression test: Clinical and theoretical review. *J. Clin. Psychiat. 43*, 321-326 (1982).

Heninger, G.R., Charney, D.S., and Sternberg, D.E. Lithium carbonate augmentation of antidepressant treatment. *Arch. Gen. Psychiat. 40,* 1335-1342 (1983).

Himmelhoch, J.M., Detre, T.P., Kupfer, D.J., Swartzburg, M., and Byck, R. Treatment of previously intractable depression with tranylcypromine and lithium. *J. Nerv. Ment. Dis. 155*, 216-220 (1972).

Himmelhoch, J.M., Auchenbach, R., and Fuchs, C.Z. The dilemma of depression in the elderly. *J.*

Clin. Psychiat. 43 (2), 25-32 (1982a).

Himmelhoch, J.M., Fuchs, C.Z., and Symons, B.J. A double-blind study of tranylcypromine treatment of major anergic depression. *J. Nerv. Ment. Dis. 170*, 628-634 (1982b).

Horden, A., Burt, C.G., and Holt, N.F. *Depressive States: A Pharmacotherapeutic Study*. Charles C. Thomas, Springfield, IL, pp. 70-97 (1965).

Keller, M.B., Lavori, P.W., Endicott, J., Coryell, W., and Klerman, G.L. "Double-depression": Two-year follow-up. *Amer. J. Psychiat. 140*, 689-694 (1983).

Keller, M.B., and Shapiro, R.W. "Double depression": Superimposition of acute depressive episodes on chronic depressive disorders. *Amer. J. Psychiat. 139*, 438-442 (1982).

Keller, M.B., Shapiro, R.W., Lavori, P.W., and Wolfe, N. Recovery in major depressive disorder. *Arch. Gen. Psychiat. 39*, 905-910 (1982a).

Keller, M.B., Shapiro, R.W., Lavori, P.W., and Wolfe, N. Relapse in major depressive disorder. *Arch. Gen. Psychiat. 39*, 911-915 (1982b).

Kelwala, S., Jones, D., and Sitaram, N. Monoamine metabolites as predictors of antidepressant response: A critique. *Prog. Neuro-Psychopharmacol. Biol. Psychiat. 7*, 229-240 (1983).

Kiloh, L.G. Electroconvulsive therapy, in *Handbook of Affective Disorders*. E.S. Paykel, ed., Guilford Press, New York, pp. 262-275 (1982).

Kirkegaard, C. The thyrotropin response to thyrotropin releasing hormone in endogenous depression. *Psychoneuroendocrinol. 6*, 189-212 (1981).

Ko, G.N., Elsworth, J.H., Roth, R.H., Rifkin, B.G., Leigh, H., and Redmond, D.E. Panic-induced elevation of plasma MHPG levels in phobic-anxious patients. *Arch. Gen. Psychiat. 40*, 425-430 (1983).

Kronfol, Z., Greden, J.F., Condon, M., Feinberg, M., and Carroll, B.J. Application of biological markers in depression secondary to thyrotoxicosis. *Amer. J. Psychiat. 139*, 1319-1322 (1982).

Kupfer, D.J., EEG sleep and tricyclic antidepressants in affective disorders, in *Clinical Pharmacology in Psychiatry*. E. Usdin, ed., Raven Press, New York, pp. 325-338 (1981).

Kupfer, D.J., Pickar, D., Himmelhoch, J.M., and Detre, T.P. Are there two types of unipolar depression? *Arch. Gen. Psychiat. 32*, 866-871 (1975).

Kupfer, D.J., Shaw, D.H., Ulrich, R., Coble, P.A., and Spiker, D.G. Application of automated REM analysis in depression. *Arch. Gen. Psychiat. 39*, 569-573 (1982).

Kupfer, D.J., and Spiker, D.G. Refractory depression: Prediction of non-response by clinical indicators. *J. Clin. Psychiat. 42*, 307-312 (1981).

Kupfer, D.J., and Thase, M.E. The use of the sleep laboratory in the diagnosis of affective disorders. *Psychiat. Clin. North. Amer. 6*, 3-25 (1983).

Kupfer, D.J., and Thase, M.E. Validity of major depression: A psychobiological perspective, in *DSM-III: An Interim Appraisal*. G. Tischler, and M.M. Weissman, eds., American Psychiatric Association, Washington, D.C. (in press).

Langer, G., Aschauer, H., Koing, G., Resch, F., and Schonbeck, G. The TSH response to TRH: A possible predictor of outcome to antidepressant and neuroleptic treatment. *Prog. Neuro-Psychopharmacol. Biol. Psychiat. 7*, 335-352 (1983).

Lewis, J.L., and Winokur, G. The induction of mania. A natural history study with controls. *Arch. Gen. Psychiat. 39*, 303-306 (1982).

Liebowitz, M.R., and Klein, D.F. Hysteroid dysphoria. *Psychiat. Clin. N. Amer. 2*, 555-575 (1979).

Loosen, P.T., and Prange, A.J. The serum thyrotropin response to thyrotropin-releasing hormone in psychiatric patients: A review. *Amer. J. Psychiat. 139*, 405-416 (1982).

Maas, J.W., Koslow, S.H., Katz, M.M., Gibbons, R.L., Bowden, C.L., Robins, E., and Davis, J.M. Pretreatment neurotransmitter metabolites and tricyclic antidepressant drug response. *Amer. J. Psychiat. 141*, 1159-1171 (1984).

McLean, P.D., and Hakstian, A.R. Clinical depression: Comparative efficacy of outpatient treatment. *J. Consult. Clin. Psychol. 47*, 818-836 (1979).

McLeod, W.R. Poor response to antidepressants and dexamethasone non-suppression, in *Depressive Illness: Some Research Studies*. B. Davies, B.J. Carroll, and R.M. Mowbray, eds., Charles C. Thomas, Springfield, IL, pp. 202-206 (1972).

Meltzer, H.Y., Fang, V.S., Tricou, B.J., Robertson, A., Piyaka, S.K. Effect of dexamethasone on plasma prolactin and cortisol levels in psychiatric patients. *Amer. J. Psychiat. 139*, 763-768 (1982).

Mendlewicz, J., Charles, G., and Franckson, J.M. The dexamethasone suppression test in affective disorder: Relationship to clinical and genetic subgroups. *Brit. J. Psychiat. 141* 454-470 (1982).

Nelson, J.C., and Bowers, M.B. Delusional unipolar depression. *Arch. Gen Psychiat. 35*, 1321-1328 (1978).

Nelson, J.C., and Charney, D.S. The symptoms of major depressive illness. *Amer. J. Psychiat. 138*, 1-13 (1981).

Nelson, J.C., Charney, D.S., and Quinlan, D.M. Characteristics of autonomous depression. *J. Nerv. Ment. Dis. 168*, 637-643 (1980).

Nelson, J.C., Jattow, P., Quinlan, D.M., and Bowers, M.B. Desipramine plasma concentration and antidepressant response. *Arch. Gen. Psychiat. 39*, 1419-1422 (1982).

Newsom, G., and Murray, N.: Reversal of dexamethasone suppression test nonsuppression in alcohol abusers. *Amer. J. Psychiat. 140*, 353-354 (1983).

Nies, A., and Robinson, D.S. Monoamine oxidase inhibitors, in *Handbook of Affective Disorders*. E.S. Paykel, ed., Guilford Press, New York, pp. 246-261 (1982).

Nyström, S. On relation between clinical factors and efficacy of ECT in depression. *Acta Psychiat. Scand. 40* (Suppl. 181), 121-134 (1965).

Papakostas, Y., Fink, M., Lee, J., Irwin, P., and Johnson, L. Neuroendocrine measures in psychiatric patients: Course and outcome with ECT. *Psychiat. Res. 4*, 55-64 (1981).

Paykel, E.S., Prusoff, B.A., Klerna, G.L., Haskell, D., and DiMascio, A. Clinical response to amitriptyline among depressed women. *J. Nerv. Ment. Dis. 156*, 149-165 (1973).

Perry, P.J., Morgan, D.E., Smith, R.E., and Tsuang, M.T. Treatment of unipolar depression accompanied by delusions. *J. Affect. Disord. 4*, 195-200 (1982).

Post, R., and Uhde, T.W. Alternatives to lithium: A focus on carbamazepine, in *Affective Disorders Reassessed: 1983*. F.J. Ayd, I.J. Taylor, and B.T. Taylor, eds., Ayd Medical Communications, Baltimore, MD, pp. 16-40, (1983).

Potter, W.Z. Rapid cycling bipolar disorder, in *Affective Disorders Reassessed: 1983*. F.J. Ayd, IJ. Taylor, and B.T. Taylor, eds. Ayd Medical Communications, Baltimore, MD, pp. 138-150 (1983).

Prusoff, B.A. Weissman, M.M., Klerman, G.L., and Rounsaville, B.J. Research diagnostic criteria subtypes of depression. *Arch. Gen. Psychiat. 37*, 796-801 (1980).

Quitkin, F., Rifkin, A., and Klein, D.F. Monoamine oxidase inhibitors: A review of antidepressant effectiveness. *Arch. Gen. Psychiat. 35*, 749-760 (1979)

Quitkin, F.M., Schwartz, D., Liebowitz, M.R., Stewart, J.R., McGrath, P.J., Halpern, F., Puig-Antich, J., Tricano, E., Sachar, E.J., and Klein, D.F. Atypical depressives: A preliminary report of antidepressant response and sleep patterns. *Psychopharmacol. Bull., 18*, 78-80 (1982).

Raskin, A. Age-sex differences in response to antidepressant drugs. *J. Nerv. Ment. Dis. 32*, 643-649 (1975).

Raskin A., Boothe, H., Schulterbrandt, J.G., Reatig, N., and Odle, D. A new model for drug use with depressed patients. *J. Nerv. Ment. Dis. 156*, 130-142 (1973).

Raskin, A., Schulterbrandt, J.G., Reatig, N., and McKeon, J. Differential response to chlorpromazine, imipramine, and placebo. *Arch. Gen. Psychiat. 23*, 164-173 (1970).

Raskind, M., Peskind, E., Rivard, M.F., Veith, R., and Barnes, R. Dexamethasone suppression test and cortisol circadian rhythm in primary degenerative dementia. *Amer. J. Psychiat. 139*, 1468-1471 (1982).

Ravaris, C.L., Nies, A., Robinson, D.S., Ives, J.O., Lamborn, K.R., and Korson, L. A multiple-dose controlled study of phenelzine in depression-anxiety states. *Arch. Gen. Psychiat. 33*, 347-350 (1976).

Reus, V.I. Pituitary-adrenal disinhibition as the independent variable in the assessment of behavioral symptoms. *Biol. Psychiat. 17*, 317-326 (1982).

Reveley, A. M., and Reveley, M.A. The distinction of primary and secondary affective disorders. *J. Affect. Disord. 3*, 273-279 (1981).

Rickels, K., Ward, C.H., and Schut, L. Different populations, different drug responses. *Amer. J. Med. Sci. 247*, 328-335 (1964).

Robinson D.S., Kayser, A., Corcella, J., Howard, D., and Ives, A. Hyperphagia, hypersomnia, panic attacks, hysterical traits and somatic anxiety predict phenelzine response in depressed outpatients. Poster presented at the Annual Meeting of the American College of Neuropsychopharmacology, San Juan, Puerto Rico, Dec. 13, 1983.

Rounsaville, B.J., Weissman, M.M., Prusoff, B.A., and Herceg-Brown, R.L. Marital disputes and treatment outcome in depressed women. *Comp. Psychiat. 20*, 483-490 (1979).

Rush, A.J., Schlesser, M.A., Roffwarg, H.P., Giles, D.E., Orsulak, P.J., and Fairchild, C. Relationships among the TRH, REM latency, and dexamethasone suppression tests: Preliminary findings. *J. Clin. Psychiat. 44*, 23-29 (1983).

Rush, A.J., and Shaw. B.J. Failures in treating depression by cognitive behavior therapy, in *Failures in Behavior Therapy*. E.B. Foa, and P.M.G. Emmelkamp, eds., Wiley-Interscience, New York, pp. 217-228 (1983).

Sabelli, H.C., Fawcett, J., Javid, J.L., and Bagri, S. The methylphenidate test for differentiating desipramine-responsive from nortriptyline responsive depression. *Amer. J. Psychiat. 140*, 212-214 (1983).

Schatzberg, A.F., Cole, J.O., Cohen, B.M., Altesman, R.I., and Sniffin, C.M. Survey of depressed patients who have failed to respond to treatment, in *The Affective Disorders*. J. M. Davis, and J.W. Maas, eds., American Psychiatric Press, Washington, DC, pp.73-85 (1983a).

Schatzberg, A.F., Rothschild, A.J., Stahl, J.B., Bond, T.C., Rosenbaum, A.H., Lofgren, S., MacLaughlin, R.A., Sullivan, M.A., and Cole, J.O. The dexamethasone suppression test: Identification of subtypes of depression. *Amer. J. Psychiat. 140*, 88-91 (1983b).

Schildkraut, J.J. The biochemical discrimination of subtypes of depressive disorders: An outline of our studies on norepinephrine metabolism and psychoactive drugs in the endogenous depressions since 1967. *Pharmakopsychiat. 15*, 121-127 (1982).

Schuckit, M.C., and Feighner, J.P. Safety of high-dose tricyclic antidepressant therapy. *Amer. J. Psychiat. 128*, 1456-1459 (1972).

Shaw, D.M. The practical management of affective disorders. *Brit. J. Psychiat. 130*, 432-451 (1977).

Sheehan, D.V., Ballenger, J., and Jacobsen, G. Treatment of endogenous anxiety with phobic, hysterical and hypochondriacal symptoms. *Arch. Gen. Psychiat. 37*, 51-59 (1980).

Simpson, G.M., Lee, J.H., Cuclic, A., and Kellner, R. Two dosages of imipramine in hospitalized endogenous and neurotic depressives. *Arch. Gen. Psychiat. 33*, 1093-1102 (1976).

Spar, J.E., and Gerner, R. Does the dexamethasone suppression test distinguish dementia from depression? *Amer. J. Psychiat. 139*, 238-240 (1982).

Spar, J.E., and LaRue, A. Major depression in the elderly: DSM-III criteria and the dexamethasone suppression test as predictors of treatment response. *Amer. J. Psychiat. 140*, 844-847 (1983).

Steinmetz, J.L., Lewinsohn, P.M., and Antonuccio, D.O. Prediction of individual outcome in a group intervention for depression.*J. Consult. Clin. Psychol. 51*, 331-337 (1983).

Stewart, J.W., Quitkin, F.M., Liebowitz, M.R., McGrath, P.J., Harrison, W.M., and Klein, D.F. Efficacy of desipramine in depressed outpatients. Arch. Gen. Psychiat. 40, 202-207 (1983).

Targum, S.D. Neuroendocrine challenge studies in clinical psychiatry. *Psychiatr. Ann. 13*, 385-395 (1983a).

Targum, S.D. The application of serial neuroendocrine challenge studies in the management of depressive disorder. *Biol. Psychiat. 18*, 3-19 (1983b).

Thase, M.E. Cognitive and behavioral treatments for depression: A review of recent developments, in *Affective Disorders Reassessed: 1983*. F.J. Ayd, I.J. Taylor, and B.T. Taylor, eds., Ayd Medical Communications, Baltimore, MD pp. 234-243, (1983).

Thase, M.E., and Himmelhoch, J.M. On the Amish study. *Amer. J. Psychiat. 140*, 1263-1264 (1983).

Thase, M.E., Himmelhoch, J.M., and Fuchs, C.Z. Epidemiology of an affective disorders clinic. Paper presented at the New Research section of the Annual Meeting of the American Psychiatric Association, Los Angeles, CA, May 7, 1984.

Thase, M.E., and Kupfer, D.J. Current status of EEG sleep in the assessment and treatment of depression, in *Advances in Human Psychopharmacology, Vol. IV*. G.D. Burrows, and J.S. Werry, eds., JAI Press, Greenwich, CT (in press).

Thase, M.E., Kupfer, D.J., and Ulrich, R. EEG sleep in psychotic depression. *Arch. Gen. Psychiat.* 43, 886-893, 1986.

Vogel, G.W. The relationship between endogenous depression and REM sleep. *Psychiatr. Ann. 11*, 423-428 (1981).

Watt, D.C., Crammer, J.L., and Elkes, A. Metabolism, anticholinergic effects and therapeutic effects and outcome of desmethylimipramine in depressive illness. *Psychol. Med. 2*, 397-405 (1972).

Weissman, M.M., Pottenger, M., Kleber, H., Ruben, H.L., Williams, D., and Thompson, W.D. Symptom patterns in primary and secondary depression. *Arch. Gen. Psychiat. 34*, 854-862 (1977).

Weissman, M.M., Prusoff, B.A., and Klerman, G.L. Personality and the prediction of long-term outcome of depression. *Amer. J. Psychiat. 135*, 797-800 (1978).

Wirz-Justice, A., Puhringer, W., and Hole, G. Response to sleep deprivation as a predictor of therapeutic results with antidepressant drugs. *Amer. J. Psychiat. 136*, 1222-1223 (1979).

Wittenborn, J.R., Kiremitci, N., and Weber, E. The choice of alternative antidepressants. *J. Nerv. Ment. Dis. 156*, 97-108 (1973).

Yerevanian, B.I., Olafsdottir, H., Milanese, E., Russotto, J., Mallon, P., Baciewicz, G., and Sagi, E. Normalization of the dexamethasone suppression test at discharge from hospital: Its prognostic value. *J. Affect. Disord. 5*, 191-197 (1983).

Zeiss, A.M., and Jones, S.L. Behavioral treatment of depression; Examining treatment failures, in *Failures in Behavior Therapy*. E.B. Foa, and P.M.G. Emmelkamp, eds., Wiley-Interscience, New York, pp. 197-216, (1983).

Zitrin, C.M., Klein, D.F., Woerner, M.G., and Ross, D.C. Treatment of phobias I. Comparison of imipramine hydrochloride and placebo. *Arch. Gen. Psychiat. 40*, 125-138 (1983).

Zuckerman, D.M., Prusoff, B.A., Weissman, M.M., and Padian, N.S. Personality as a predictor of psychotherapy and pharmacotherapy outcome for depressed outpatients. J. Consult. Clin. Psychol. 48, 730-735 (1980).

3

Psychological Management of Resistant Depression

David Greenberg and Herzl R. Spiro

Systematic psychosocial study of the treatment resistant depressions lags far behind the descriptive and somatic studies. Even the definition of the resistant depression generally is based on persistence of symptoms despite some specified course of *somatic* interventions. These somatic interventions vary from two well chosen tricyclics in adequate dose (Kielholz et al., 1979) to definitive treatment with trials of tricyclics (equivalent to 300 mg of imipramine), plus a monoamine oxidase inhibitor (equivalent to 90 mg per day of phenelzine), plus an adequate dose of ECT (12 to 16 bilateral treatments; Shaw, 1977). Nowhere can we find a clear definition of the resistant depression which calls for a course of psychotherapy of any kind, much less a course of family therapy or of environment-directed interventions appropriate to the patient's life circumstances, or a hospital stay in a psychiatric unit with a milieu program appropriate to the disorder. At minimum one would hope that somatic therapies be administered by a physician with psychosocial sophistication.

A major source of variance in clarifying the nature and outcomes of the resistant depressions may well stem from failures to take into sufficient account great variations in psychosocial treatment situations as well as the life circumstances of patients. Despite the efforts of leading writers to bridge the multiple models (Akiskal and McKinney, 1975; Arieti and Bemporad, 1978; Klerman and Weissman, 1984), there remains an unfortunate reductionism which has retarded the growth of psychiatry as a medical science. There are those few psychoanalysts who continue to debate whether medication can be used during analytic treatment and those few somaticists who might feel more comfortable were their patients not to trouble them with their disintegrating marriages, or their identification with hopelessly grandiose ego ideals. Even the wayward remarks of a confirmed somaticist may have profound impact on the susceptible dependent patient. It is close to impossible to avoid being psychologically important to the patient.

The premise of this chapter is that the resistant depressions constitute a nested set of complex psychosomatic and somatopsychic interactions; that whatever unknown biologic diathesis may predispose to resistant depressions, there are also cogent patterns of life experience and social events which predispose to, perpetuate, and mitigate resistant depressions.

Hard evidence is almost as scanty in the psychosocial realm as in somatic studies. The second section of the chapter reviews psychosocial treatment methods concerning which research findings are available.

Given the debilitating nature of these disorders, it would seem reasonable to develop "maximum push" strategies for intervention in which somatic, psychologic, and social interventions are combined for optimal effectiveness. We would suggest that certain core psychologic interventions should be utilized while the physician prescribes somatic interventions. The absence of a psychologic set *is* in itself a psychologic intervention of sorts. The doctor cloaked in Aesculapian authority who only writes prescriptions and inquires after side effects and symptoms fits quite nicely into a well demarcated nonhuman power role. While noncompliance to treatment regimes is excluded by definition from the treatment resistant syndrome, such unknown noncompliance can mimic the disorder. Moreover, the interaction effect between the medications and the significant other who renders the treatment remains largely unknown.

This chapter is intended to provide a core of information potentially useful to any physician utilizing any of the special treatment methods contained in this volume. The chapter is divided into three sections: (1) a review of specific psychosocial foundation material on depression which bears on doctor-patient interactions, (2) specific recommendations for the content of the doctor-patient relationship in the treatment of resistant depressions, and (3) therapies tailored for depressions whose efficacy has been systematically evaluated.

PSYCHOSOCIAL FOUNDATIONS FOR TREATMENT

Any treatment, be it prescription of a medication or elaborate psychological investigation, must take into account the nature and responsiveness of the subject. Severely depressed patients bear sufficient similarities to one another that the descriptions by Aeretaeus of Cappadocia (Lewis, 1934) show resemblances to clinical descriptions in a modern text (e.g., Arieti and Bemporad, 1978). It should also be recalled that 1700 years ago Aeretaeus struggled with the same mind-body problem which afflicts psychiatry today and chose (almost certainly incorrectly) to relegate to unimportant bile, phlegm, humours, and (by inference) the second century precursors of today's neurotransmittors, while declaring psychological factors to be paramount. What are the psychological variables which shape treatment response?

The existentialists, with their rejection of nonexperiential constructs, may provide the most direct description of the psychological world of the melancholic patient. Tellenbach (1974), in his study of 140 melancholics, describes a world of distorted time with excessive concern for a past which produces guilt and recrimination: a world of order, duty, and efforts to please others. The life space of the depressive is filled with efforts to find security and to escape uncertain situations which may produce further guilt.

The physician's role in this world is in large measure structured by the disease itself. Beck (1967) emphasizes the extreme pessimism which characterizes the depressive spectrum. The cognitive distortions through which the treating physician must work is characterized by a "cognitive triad" (Beck, 1970): negative expectations of the environment, a negative view of oneself, and negative expectations of the future. Seligman (1975) attributes the nature of this pessimism to a specific "learned helplessness" related to the expected ineffectiveness of one's own actions. Seligman's model, based on dog research, helps one understand the passivity and dependency of the depressed patient. The resistant depressive may reach for each external "cure," the new pill, the biofeedback treatment, the behavioral prescription as part of the compliant relationship to the doctor as significant other. It is the underlying sense of personal helplessness and hoplessness about self-effectiveness which remains the hub of the depression.

Bibring's work (1953) emphasizes this sense of personal helplessness and powerlessness before outside forces. The helplessness stands in contrast to the sense of unrealistic and unfulfilled aspirations.

The origins of these unrealistic expectations and predominant helpless hopelessness are best explicated in seminal work by Cohen et al. (1954) and a controlled follow up by Gibson (1958). The original Washington School of Psychiatry study uncovered evidence that the depressed patients often came from family backgrounds which called upon them to hold high a family banner, to enhance family reputation, to utilize human relations to promote desired ambitions. Gibson (1958) found that on questionnaires these pressures for achievement and prestige and the prevailing atmosphere of competitiveness and envy were striking, in contrast to the control group of schizophrenic patients. The Cohen group findings remain salient three decades later for the physician working with a patient even as a prescribing psychopharmacologist. They point out that the doctor is likely to be seen as stereotyped repetition of a parental figure: a moral authority who can and must be manipulated for sympathy, approval, and reassurance, but who basically is critical and rejecting.

Thus far we have emphasized approaches from cognitive, interpersonal, and ego psychology, theories which readily predict aspects of the doctor-patient interaction and whose findings are reasonably observable. Now we must shift to a body of material based on hypotheses less open to observation. Regrettably, psychoanalytic formulation is often presented in an either-or context in which the current orthodoxies are accepted in fairly complete form or rejected completely. For the somatically oriented psychiatrist working with patients with resistant depressions, that choice is not difficult. It is not that this body of theory is particularly difficult for the graduate of the modern psychiatric residency. It is the tendency to take sides in a prescientific debate about constructs which probably cannot be empirically tested in satisfactory control studies. Yet, these constructs serve as useful metaphors in listening to chronic, severely depressed patients. Moreover, the observations of great clinicians from the past should not be abandoned lightly. Given Freud's fascination with the somatic foundations of behavior one can imagine how closely he would have followed current research on biologic aspects of depression were he alive today.

The touchstone of Freudian theory as it applies to the physician-patient relationship is the concept of transference (Freud, 1912). The attitudes, beliefs, feelings, and thoughts of the depressed patient towards significant others from the past tend to be played out upon the person of the treating physician. The nature of these transactions may be heavily influenced by phenomena which Freud, Abraham, Rado, and Jacobson have described. We offer very abbreviated summaries here, together with references to more complete reviews. These are presented not in the expectation that physicians reading this book will refer their patients for psychoanalysis. The authors consider classic psychoanalytic techniques to be contraindicated in severe depressions. Rather, we are impressed that the fullness of psychoanalytic constructions can be helpful in understanding patient responses and that any psychiatrist can make use of such understanding in talking with his severely depressed resistant patients.

Several constructs were introduced by the psychoanalytic theorists. Abraham, in 1911, offered the first psychoanalytic formulation. He emphasized the ambivalent hostility poorly disguised by the depressive and the self-centered aspects of self-accusatory guilt. Subsequently (1916) Abraham noted the oral regression and dependent neediness which he related to severe injuries to infantile narcissism brought about by successive disappointments in love relations ("primal parathymia"). The importance of loss of significant objects, the tendency of patients to attach ambivalent attention to the physician, the difficulty ending sessions, the hostile edge to neediness—none of these are unfamiliar to the experienced clinician working with depressed patients.

Freud's formulations in Mourning and Melancholia (1917) follow Abraham's initial emphasis on ambivalence and self-reproach, but add the still controversial concept of anger turned in on an introjected lost object. The practical application of this concept is in the recommendation offered by many skilled clinicians that the patient must be helped to express this anger in socially acceptable ways. Some believe that such angry expression provokes antagonistic responses from significant others leading to a spiralling escalation of anger. The issue remains unresolved. The physician who treats resistant depressed patients can benefit from study of Freud's masterful clinical description and perhaps give thought to approaches one will take to the hostility problem in these patients.

Freud (1923) went on further to elaborate yet another series of issues which, to the authors, appear ubiquitous in resistant depressed patients. These concern internal structures which include conscience, standards of internalized others, values, morals, self-judgments, etc., clustered as "the superego." What physician can listen to depressed patients without being aware that these agencies are extraordinarily powerful, condemnatory, and even self-persecutory for them? The cruelty of the depressive superego becomes the main focus in Freud's later writings (Freud, 1933). The reader is referred to Meyer Mendelson's excellent, succinct book for a lucid exposition of these difficult topics (Mendelson, 1974).

Two other writers present clinical theory which may prove useful to the physician concerned with long-term resistant depressed patients.

Sandor Rado (1927) describes the hostility-guilt-contrition pattern which is the interaction often found between the patient and significant others in his life. We find this sequence a commonplace in supervising residents working with depressed patients even when the visits are limited to so-called medication checks. The pattern of passivity to be satisfied by an all-giving other along with outpourings of contrition will be recognized by those who have worked with these patients.

Edith Jacobson (1971) emphasizes both the pathologic superego bound concretely to persons from the past and defective ego ideal formation which renders it impossible for the depressive to measure up adequately. The treating physician may become one of the overvalued others used by the patient to maintain self esteem.

These constructs are synthesized in a useful way in two modern volumes. In both cases the treatment results are summarized below in the third section of this chapter. Arieti and Bemporad (1978) offer a psychodynamic approach based on their formulations concerning the depressed patient and the "dominant other": that person with whom the depressed patient is most involved. This volume contains both superior summaries of other writers' works and a major theoretical contribution in addition to a treatment approach. Klerman and Weissman (1984) have developed an interpersonal therapy which grew out of the NIMH cooperative study of depression. This remarkable work is not only important as a clinical approach but also offers the greatest future promise for rigorous research on resistant depressions with standardized psychotherapy methods.

RECOMMENDATIONS FOR PSYCHOSOCIAL INTERVENTIONS

The psychosocial world of the patient afflicted with a resistant depression is complex and the treating physician's role is not an easy one, whether it is limited to monitoring effects of somatic agents, or whether it involves more ambitious psychosocial interventions. We offer some clinical recommendations.

Initial Role

There are special problems in initiating treatment with these patients. They have usually experienced repeated treatment failures. The pervasive pessimism endemic to the disorder is reinforced by life experiences which further accentuate "learned helplessness." The initial problem is "getting the patient's attention" while avoiding nonachievable expectations or a role of dominance. Genuine warmth, accurate empathy, and relative forcefulness may help initiate a relationship. Early comments by the doctor should be realistic. The physician must avoid conveying to the patient unrealistic demands for self explanation (see Arieti and Bemporad, 1978). The patient does not know "why" the depression occurred, and must not feel any pressure to justify the illness. One must communicate concern and compassion without falling into the trap of pity which confirms helplessness.

Rational Hope, Positive Expectancy, and Treatment Planning

Having lived with timeless hopelessness for years, these patients need a physician who offers realistic optimism and hope, but not unfulfillable promises. The authors have found expectant patience vital to successful outcomes. We tell our chronic resistant patients:

> "While you have had many disappointments and you feel demoralized, there are, in fact many avenues of therapy yet available which truly have helped others with conditions similar to yours. Together we will explore each until we find what works for you, but you must allow us time."

After a thorough evaluation and appropriate tests, we outline the variety of psychological, social, and somatic treatments now available and make reference to some of the newer treatments in development stages. We reassure the new patient that in our personal experience most treated patients have in time recovered, but that the treatment period may be long, uncomfortable, and fraught with disappointments. We also discuss involvement of significant others in the treatment and arrange to meet with them. In most instances an adjunctive family therapy is recommended, sometimes with a second therapist. While most treatment begins on an outpatient basis, one of the authors (HRS) has found it helpful to take the new patient personally on a tour through the very modern, comfortable, milieu throughout therapy unit in the general hospital where his offices are. The patient is told that should the disorder become too painful we can offer a great measure of relief with a brief voluntary stay on the unit. We find it important to make clear recommendations, but to involve the patient *and* subsequently the family in developing a treatment plan.

Everything in these initial visits is directed towards powerful demand characteristics for a positive outcome, and "safety nets" to protect patients from suicidal impulses and devastating disappointments. We freely acknowledge that therapeutic interventions will, in part, be trial and error, and that we will be pressing medication dosages to levels that produce significant side effects. We emphasize that we will need an alliance to explore potential psychological explanations and to understand both the past and current social circumstances. We prepare the patient for disappointments and treatment changes by warning that we almost certainly will *not* hit the exact correct combination of interventions in the first several tries unless we are very lucky, but that we anticipate eventual success. This is what is meant by rational hope.

We invite the patient and family to become curious about the disorder and to report freely anything they think has "worked." Many patients keep both psychosocial event diaries and dream diaries, charting their depression on a global-rating scale against other variables. This strengthens both "the observing ego" and the therapeutic alliance. It also stabilizes identification with the future oriented, hopeful therapist.

The therapist who sets demand characteristics for long range failure generally achieves exactly what he expects. We have not found paradoxical statements of despair or reflection of patients hopelessness to be useful in treating depression. On the other hand, unrealistic promises come back to haunt the therapist. What should be conveyed is a sense of orderly process to find solutions, not false optimism about one given treatment.

Therapist Activity and Directiveness

It is not useful to leave the chronic resistant depression patient to suffer in painful silences. Therapist passivity rarely produces anything but pain and patient modeling of the role. The patient already feels useless and hopeless. Physician activity should be directed towards helping the patient find areas of competence and potential success. Questions should be brief, clear, and answerable. Patient growth will come from areas of health, not from demonstrations of pathology. We have found it necessary also to utilize limited directive comments. In the absence of any structure the patient feels lost and more hopeless. In situations where patients are incorrigibly passive or persist in leaving all to the therapist, we favor using a *non*regressive milieu oriented inpatient unit for a sufficiently long stay (3 to 6 weeks) to help "jar" the chronic resistant depression patient into a better, more active pattern.

The nature of the directiveness is a major issue. One can easily slip into the role of dominance and reinforce patient passivity. By directiveness, we mean focussing the session on the positive material that is forthcoming as well as offering quiet warm support for patient initiatives. The focus must always be on the alliance lest the therapist become "the dominating other."

Setting Achievable Goals

One must avoid joining the patient's grandiose ego ideal or punishing superego. In practical terms this means realistic goal setting. For some patients the goal may be as limited as keeping body and soul together while time is afforded for somatic interventions. Usually we join our patients in somewhat less modest goals. Unrealistic goal setting and subsequent experiences of failure are regular features of the depressive thought processes. We insist that this be brought into the psychiatric sessions and remind our patients that both the grandiosity of the goals and the sense of failure are products of the disorder. Teaching the depressive to make conscious and to disregard the "false goals" phenomena is akin to teaching the schizophrenic not to act on delusions while offering medication to mitigate their intensity.

Creating New Frames of Reference

During the periods of relative relief from depression afforded by somatic interventions, patients need help to develop new patterns of behavior and different sets of attitudes. The chronic, severe, resistant depression is seen as metaphorically like a car being stuck in the mud. If the patient uses new sources of energy to do the same things, he is told, it is akin to pressing the accelerator and spinning the wheels in deeper.

Beck's concept of pleasure schemata and concepts of mastery are invoked. The therapist seeks to help the patient develop a new set of references separate from his pessimism and chronic hopelessness. Techniques may be used to correct faulty thinking (see Beck, 1970), to foster constructive problem-solving, and to foster patient assertiveness. Physicians with a psychodynamic background may help the patient to understand life patterns as well as specific feelings and thoughts transferred from significant others to the person of the therapist. We generally recommend that the transference neurosis *not* be fostered and that transference distortions be interpreted early. One of us (HRS) does use dream material with selected patients but primarily to help the patient think "out of the box" through discussion of wishes and positive fantasy. The goal is more to get patients actively involved and intensely curious about themselves than to evolve some mutative interpretation.

The therapist thus introduces a new and distracting way of looking at the patient's problems, e.g., "What were you thinking about when you felt upset?" asks Beck (Beck et al., 1980); "How have you behaved towards others while you've been depressed?" asks Bellack (Bellack et al., 1981). The effort is to change the patient's frame of reference.

We have summarized some general recommendations for psychosocial intervention by the treating physician. The last section of this chapter is a review of three psychosocial approaches to therapy. The literature prior to the last decade emphasized the general superiority of antidepressant medication to treatments which excluded medication (Covi et al., 1974; Klerman et al., 1974; Friedman, 1975). We summarize studies of three treatment approaches which may be as effective as antidepressant medications. Multimethod treatments may prove superior. The therapies that are considered are those specifically tailored to depression whose efficacy in treating depression has been evaluated.

APPROACHES TO THERAPY

Interpersonal Psychotherapy

In this approach the patient's current depression is seen as having its roots in earlier relationships whose pathological forms have been maintained in the present, or where their loss has failed to be worked through. Arieti describes several categories of depression, one of which is outlined below. A review of the patient's life will show a narrowing of achievements and lack of fulfillment of earlier expectations. A life event is often the trigger for becoming overwhelmed by a sense of failure and lack of importance. Although the person feels sorrow at dreams unfulfilled and relationships lost, no sorrow work will have been done.

The therapist inquires into the development of the depression and the current circumstances, and discovers who the person is to whom the patient is most closely bound. Arieti calls this figure the "dominant other," the significant person in one's life for whom one may have denied one's own will and fulfillment. Arieti describes, for example, certain patients who blame themselves for everything, including their poor relationship with their spouse. "I am so careless," says the patient. "Perhaps," counters the therapist, "it is really your partner who is very obsessive," and carefully the patient's feelings towards the other are uncovered: In order to please the dominant other, the patient may have denied his own desires. Arieti suggests this attitude is particularly common in women and may account for the predisposition to depression found in women. In addition to pointing out the self-sacrificial relationships maintained until now, the positive wishes of the patient are uncovered, often by returning to childhood dreams and fantasies.

Arieti suggests a clear cognitive component in which the patient is made aware of his thoughts and discusses them, and also an assertive component, in which he identifies what is gratifying and meaningful to the patient, who is encouraged to go out and attain these ambitions.

Although no systematic work has been carried out using Arieti's method in severe depression, in the unit of one of the authors, several cases of resistant depression responsive to interpersonal psychotherapy have been described (Bechar et al., 1985), and Arieti claimed that nine out of seventeen cases of severe depression responded to psychotherapy (Arieti and Bemporad, 1978).

A similar method has been used in careful research by Klerman et al., (1982). They did not include the more cognitive and behavioral elements described by Arieti, but concentrated on a dynamic understanding of the current social context, including its parallels in earlier relationships. As in all of the major studies described below, the patients had nonbipolar, nonpsychotic acute primary major depressive disorder. Eighty-one patients were randomly allocated to one of four conditions—short-term interpersonal psychotherapy (IPT), tricyclic antidepressants (amitriptyline 100-200 mg for twelve weeks); IPT + tricyclic, or a nonscheduled control treatment. Patients were assessed using blind assessors throughout treatment and at one month follow up.

Eighty percent of the patients were classified as having endogenous or situational major depressive disorder. Across all measures the patients with endogenous depression responded well to the conditions that included a tricyclic and did not respond well to IPT. Situational depression, however, responded best to the combination of tricyclics and IPT, and did less well with the individual components alone. IPT alone is not the treatment of choice for either group.

Cognitive Therapy

Although there are several types of cognitive therapy for depressive disorder (Ellis, 1962, Meichenbaum and Genest, 1980), that of Aaron Beck in Pennsylvania is the most specifically tailored for depression and has been most carefully evaluated. Based on continuing research on the effects of cognitive processes on affect, the underlying principle is that the way that you think determines the way that you behave and feel. When a person is depressed, certain erroneous ways of thinking come to the fore and become automatic. The depressed person thinks of himself, events happening to him, and opportunities in the future in a negative way that accounts for the self-blaming, inactive, and despairing presentation of depression. The aim of therapy is to alter the patient's thoughts, thereby affecting his feelings and behavior. For the depressed inert patient, Beck recommends starting with behavioral techniques.

Unlike the behavior therapies discussed later, for whom increased activities are an end in themselves, the achievement of targets early on in therapy is in order to reveal the accompanying self-critical, pessimistic cognitions associated with the activities. In addition, the patient may be asked to plan the performance of activities that give a sense of pleasure; these should diminish the depression, but will again provide negative cognitions. The patient now starts to record the situations in which he feels low and the associated automatic "depressogenic" cognitions. These are reviewed with the therapist, who proceeds by form of Socratic dialogue to ask the patient if such thoughts are justified. The patient is encouraged to find alternative rational responses and note their effect on his affect.

The first well-designed study of a clinic population was carried out by the originator of the therapy in which 41 patients with nonpsychotic, nonbipolar major affective disorder were randomly allocated to twenty sessions of cognitive therapy over 12 weeks, or twelve weekly meetings in which they were given amitriptyline up to 250 mg although tapered off in the last two weeks. There were many more dropouts from the imipramine group. Improvement was significantly more at twelve weeks in the cognitive therapy group, of whom 15 out of 19 were markedly improved (BDI 0-9), while only 5 of 21 imipramine patients were markedly improved (Rush et al., 1977), although differences were no longer significant at one year follow up (Rush, 1982). It should be noted that the clientele was a highly motivated fee-paying group, and that the scores of the imipramine patients deteriorated after the drug was tailed off after ten weeks. It is also doubtful if the maximum benefit of imipramine was achieved in ten weeks.

These deficiencies were not present in the study of Blackburn et al. (1981). They randomly allocated 88 depressed outpatients who were attending a general health clinic or a psychiatric outpatient clinic to receive a tricyclic antidepressant (amitriptyline or clomipramine in a fixed dose), or a cognitive therapy, or a combination of the two therapies. Treatment was provided under the National Health Service in Scotland in a working-class area. The psychiatric outpatients responded best to the combination therapy, while the health clinic patients responded best to the combination or the cognitive therapy alone. It has been observed, however (Goldberg, 1982), that the response of the drug group in the health clinic was even lower than the usual placebo response. Treatment was discontinued after twenty weeks and patients were followed up for one year. These two studies indicate the clear value of cognitive therapy.

Two important studies have been published recently. Murphy et al. (1984) allocated 95 patients with unipolar primary affective disorder to one of four conditions: cognitive therapy, or tricyclic antidepressant (nortriptyline), or a combination of the two, or cognitive therapy plus placebo. Drug and cognitive therapies ended at twelve weeks and there was one month follow up. At no stage in the trial were there significant differences between the depression measures of any of the conditions. Both therapies were effective and there did not appear to be an additive effect. Nevertheless, the depression scores measured at follow up were lowest in the combination group, although this was not statistically significant; larger studies are awaited to investigate the importance of a combination of tricyclic and cognitive therapy.

Teasdale et al. (1984) randomly allocated depressed patients in health clinics in Oxfordshire, England, to a treatment as usual regime (medication) with or without cognitive therapy. Both groups showed improvement by the end of therapy after twelve weeks, although the patients who received cognitive therapy were much less depressed on all measures. Three months after the end of cognitive therapy, however, the remaining patients had continued to improve until there was no difference between the outcome of the two groups. The deficiencies of the earlier studies having been corrected, the addition of cognitive therapy to tricyclic medication appeared to speed up recovery and was associated with fewer overdoses and fewer referrals to psychiatrists.

Social Skills Training

In a series of studies, Lewinsohn has demonstrated that depressed patients have poor social competence (Libet and Lewinsohn, 1973; Lewinsohn et al, 1980), consequently receive little social reinforcement, may even evoke rejection from others, and are less assertive. They have difficulties relating to their families, friends, work associates, and strangers, and Lewinsohn has suggested these behavioral deficits may cause and maintain depression.

The focus in behavior therapy is the modification of the performance itself. A particular area of social functioning is selected, e.g., work associates, and a hierarchy of difficult situations is constructed. Starting with the least difficult situation, a format is used of instructions of how to handle the situation, followed by a modeling of the patient's role by the therapist, after which the patient role-plays the situation. He is then given constructive feedback on his performance and, after replaying the scene, is asked to carry it out "in vivo" as homework.

There has been only one large study of a clinic population by one of the pioneering units (Bellack et al., 1981; 1983) in which 125 depressed patients were randomly allocated to tricyclic medication (amitriptyline 200-300 mg), or twelve weekly sessions of social skills training plus placebo, or a time-limited dynamic psychotherapy plus placebo. The drug-only group had the highest dropout rate (53%), while the social skills training plus placebo group had the lowest dropout rate and the highest number of significantly improved patients. Overall, however, all conditions were associated with improvement with no therapy emerging as significantly better. Of interest, all the conditions were equally beneficial for vegetative depressive features and measures of social effectiveness outside of sessions.

THE IMPLICATIONS FOR RESISTANT DEPRESSION

It is clear from all of the above studies that there are specific psychotherapies that are at least as effective as tricyclics in treating nonpsychotic, nonbipolar major affective disorder. Some studies have found an advantage in a combination of the two therapies, Klerman et al. (1982) finding the combination most effective for situational depressives, and Teasdale et al (1984) finding the combination led to a more rapid recovery. Kupfer and Thase have noted in Chapter 2 that tricyclic nonresponse is more common in mild depression, and their definition is similar to Klerman's situational depression, so that this may well be the population for whom the psychotherapies outlined above are the treatment of choice.

Although the studies reviewed were nonpsychotic, nonbipolar populations and included severe depressions, they were not treatment-resistant cases. Is there evidence that patients with resistant depression will respond to the psychotherapies we have discussed? Many of the cases in the recent manual of Beck et al. (1979) were medication nonresponders, although no details of drugs, doses, or duration of treatment are provided. Similarly, of the three cases of chronic depression responsive to cognitive therapy described by Rush et al. (1975), two had received ECT and all of them medication with only a partial response.

The only study of treatment resistant depressives was by Harpin et al. (1982) who allocated six patients to a waiting list and six patients to receive twenty sessions of a cognitive-behavior therapy, including a variety of components. Although there was some change in depression in the treated group, the differences between the two conditions were neither clinically nor statistically significant. Although these patients were described as chronic depressives who had been treated with drugs and ECT, a limitation is that no details are given of the past therapies. Furthermore, throughout the study patients received 25 mg daily of a tricyclic antidepressant, a clinically inadequate dose. In a resistant population, it remains to be shown if an adequate dose of an antidepressant improves the benefits of psychotherapies; our own experience suggests that this is so.

Psychotic depressions were conspicuous by their absence from these studies, and our own experience has not found these relatively brief therapies to be suitable. The use of cognitive/behavioral techniques in psychotic states in general has not been notably successful. Although a recent trial of thought stopping in chronic paranoid schizophrenics demonstrated a reduction in frequency of delusion and hallucinations (Lamontagne et al, 1983), the modest results require replication and have yet to be applied to a more acute population or to psychotic affective states. In addition to the use of neuroleptics, tricyclics, and ECT in psychotic depression, the role of psychotherapy is more supportive, combining the rational hope and muted compassion mentioned earlier with cautious use of target-setting, which may be resisted by a psychotic patient, and then regarded as a furtherr failure.

SUMMARY AND CONCLUSION

Psychosocial management of resistant depression is not confined to specific psychotherapies. The treating physician is a psychologically important figure who needs to be aware of the effects of his comments and mannerisms. This chapter summarizes the depressed patient's past orientation, guilt, pessimism, helplessness, grandiose ego ideal, dependent neediness, ambivalence, self-directed anger, punishing conscience, and relationship to "dominant others." Taking these features into account, we recommend some general features of effective intervention with these patients. These include a stance of warmth, empathy, rational hope, and positive expectancy. We suggest that the therapist should be active in hepling patients problem solve, correct faulty thinking, set achievable goals, and create new frames of reference. Treatment should proceed from positive areas of mastery and "grow outward," creating expanding circles of success.

During the past eight years there have been several clinical studies which suggest the effectiveness of interpersonal dynamic, cognitive, and behavioral methods of psychotherapy developed for depressed patients. Methodologic issues have been addressed which will make possible future outcome studies of psychotherapy and family therapy for resistant depressions. Even in the absence of clear cut evidence, we recommend "total push" combinations of psychosocial and somatic interventions.

REFERENCES

Abraham, K. Notes on the psychoanalytic treatment of manic-depressive insanity and allied conditions, in *Selected Papers on Psychoanalysis,* Basic Books, New York, pp. 137-156 (1960, orig. 1911).

Abraham, K. The first pregenital stage of the libido, in *Selected Papers on Psychoanalysis.* Basic Books, New York, pp. 248-249 (1960, orig. 1916).

Akiskal, H.S. Factors associated with imcomplete recovery in primary depressive illness. *J. Clin. Psychiat. 43,* 266-271 (1982).

Akiskal, H.S. Dysthymic disorder: psychopathology of proposed chronic depressive subtypes. *Amer. J. Psychiat. 140,* 11-20 (1983).

Akiskal, H.S., and McKinney, W.T. Overview of recent research in depression. Integration of ten conceptual models into a comprehensive clinical frame.*Arch. Gen. Psychiat. 32,* 285-305 (1975).

Ananth, J., and Ruskin, R. Treatment of intractable depression, *Internat. Pharmacopsychiat. 9,* 218-229 (1974).

Arieti, S. The psychotherapeutic approach to depression. *Amer. J. Psychother. 16,* 397-406 (1962).

Arieti, S. Psychotherapy of severe depression. *Amer. J. Psychiat. 134,* 864-868 (1977).

Arieti, S., and Bemporad, J. *Severe and Mild Depression: The Psychotherapeutic Approach.* Basic Books, New York, (1978).

Bechar, A., Dasberg, H., Shefler, G., and Zohar J. Psychotherapy for resistant depression. In: *Terapis Bereves,* J.A. Itzigsohn and H. Dasberg, eds. Universidad Pontificia de-Salamanca, p. 113-123 (1985).

Beck, A. *Depression: Clinical, Experimental, and Theoretical Aspects.* Paul B. Hoeber, New York (1967).

Beck, A. The core problem in depression: the cognitive triad, in *Science and Psychoanalysis 17,* J. Masserman, ed. Grune and Stratton, New York (1970).

Beck, A. *Cognitive Therapy and the Emotional Disorders*. International Universities Press, New York (1976).

Beck, A. Rush, A.J., Shaw, G.F., and Emery, G. *Cognitive Therapy of Depression*. Wiley, Chichester (1980).

Bellack, A.S., Hersen, M., and Himmelhoch, J. Social skills training compared with pharmacotherapy and psychotherapy in the treatment of unipolar depression. *Amer. J. Psychiat. 138,* 1562-1567 (1981).

Bellack, A.S., Hersen, M., and Himmelhoch, J. A comparison of social skill training, pharmacotherapy and psychotherapy for depression. ***Behaviour Research and Therapy 21***, 101-107 (1983).

Bemporad, J. Psychotherapy of the depressive character. *J. Amer. Acad. Psychoanal. 4,* 347-372 (1976).

Bibring, E. The mechanism of depression, in *Affective Disorders,* P. Greenacre, ed. International Universities Press, New York (1953).

Blackburn, I.M., Bishop, S., Glen, A.I.M., Whalley, L.J., and Christie, J.E. The efficacy of cognitive therapy in depression: A treatment trial using cognitive therapy and pharmacotherapy, each alone and in combination. *Brit. J. Psychiat. 139,* 181-189 (1981).

Bonime, W. Dynamics and psychotherapy of depression, in *Current Psychatric Therapies,* J. Masserman, ed. Grune and Stratton, New York (1962).

Bonime, W., and Bonime, E. Depressive personality and affect reflected in dreams: a basis for psychotherapy, in *The Dream in Clinical Practice,* J. M. Natterson, ed. Aronson, New York (1980).

Chodoff, P. The core problem in depression, in *Science and Psychoanalysis, 17,* J. Masserman, ed. Grune and Stratton, New York (1970).

Chodoff, P. The depressive personality. *Arch. Gen. Psychiat. 27,* 666-673 (1972).

Cohen, M.B., Baker, G., Cohen, R.A., Fromm-Reichman, F., and Weigert, E.V. An intensive study of twelve cases of manic-depressive psychosis. *Psychiatry 17,* 103-138 (1954).

Covi, L., Lipman, R.D., Derogatis, L.R. Smith, J.E., L Pattison, J.H. Drugs and group Psychotherapy in neurotic depression. *Amer. J. Psychiat. 131,* 191-198 (1974).

Ellis, A. *Reason and Emotion in Psychotherapy*. Lyle Stuart, New York (1962).

Flaherty, J.A., Gaviria, F.M., Black, E.M., Altman, E., and Mitchell, T. The role of social support in the functioning of patients with unipolar depression. *Amer. J. Psychiat. 140,* 473-476 (1983).

Forrest, T. The combined use of marital and individual therapy in depression. *Contemporary Psychoanalysis 6,* 76-83 (1969).

Freud, S. Papers on technique: The dynamics of transference. *Standard Edition, 12,* 97-108. Hogarth Press, London (1957, orig. 1912).

Freud, S. Papers on metapsychology: Mourning and melancholia. *Standard Edition, 14,* 243-258. Hogarth Press, London (1957, orig. 1917).

Freud, S. The ego and thc id. *Standard Edition, 19,* 12-67. Hogarth Press, London (1957, orig. 1923).

Freud, S. New intoductory lectures on psychoanalysis. Lecture XXXIII. *Standard Edition, 22,* 81-111. Hogarth Press, London (1969, orig. 1933).

Friedman, A. Interaction of drug therapy with marital therapy in depressed patients. *Arch. Gen. Psychiat. 32,* 619-637 (1975).

Gibson, R.W. The family background and early life experience of the manic depressive patient: A comparison with the schizophrenic patient. *Psychiatry 21,* 71-90 (1958).

Goldberg, D. Cognitive therapy for depression. *Brit. Med. J. 284,* 143-144 (1982).

Harpin, R.E., Liberman, R.P., Marks, I., Stern, R., and Bohannon, W.E. Cognitive-behavior therapy for chronically depressed patients. *J. Nerv. Ment. Disease 170,* 295-301 (1982).

Himmelhoch, J.M., Auchenbach, R., and Fuchs, C.Z. The dilemma of depression in the elderly. *J. Clin. Psychiat. 43,* 25-32 (1982).

Jacobson, E. The effect of disappointment on ego and superego formation in normal and depressive development. *Psychoanalytic Review 33,* 129-147 (1946).

Jacobson, E. *Depression.* International Universities Press, New York (1971).

Jacobson, E. The psychoanalytic treatment of depressive patients, in *Depression and Human Existence,* E.J. Anthony and T. Benadek, eds. Little, Brown, Boston (1975).

Kielholz, P., Terzani, S., and Gaspar, M. Treatment for therapy resistant depressions. *Int. Pharmacopsychiatry 14,* 94-100 (1979).

Klerman, G.L., Dimascio, A., Weissman, M., Prusoff, B., and Paykel, E.S. Treatment of depression by drugs and psychotherapy. *Amer. J. Psychiat. 131,* 186-191 (1974).

Klerman, G.L., Weissman, M.M., and Prusoff, B.A. RDC endogenous depression as a predictor of response to antidepressant drugs and psychotherapy. *Advances in Biochemical Pharmacology 32*, 165-174 (1982).

Klerman, G.L., and Weissman, M.M. *Interpersonal Psychotherapy of Depressive Disorders.* Basic Books, New York (1984).

Kupfer, D.J. and Spiker, D.G. Refractory depression: prediction of nonresponse by clinical indicators. *J. Clin. Psychiat. 42*, 307-312 (1981).

Lamontagne, Y., Audet, N., and Elie, R. Thought stopping for delusions and hallucinations: a pilot study. *Behavioural Psychotherapy 11*, 177-184 (1983).

Lesse, S. Psychotherapy in combination with antidepressant drugs in patients with severe masked depression. *Amer. J. Psychother 31*, 185-203 (1974).

Lewinsohn, P.M., Mischel, W., Chaplin, W., and Barton, R. Social competence and depression: The role of illusory self-perceptions. *J. Abnormal Psychol. 89*, 203-212 (1980).

Lewis, A. Melancholia: A historical review. *J. Mental Sci. 80*, 1-42 (1934).

Libet, J., and Lewinsohn, P.M. The concept of social skill with special reference to the behavior of depressed persons. *J. Consulting Clin. Psychol. 40*, 304-312 (1973).

Meichenbaum, D., and Genest, M. Cognitive behavior modification: An integration of cognitive and behavioral methods, in *Helping People Change*, 2nd ed, F.H. Kanfer and A.P. Goldstein, eds. Pergamon Press, New York (1980).

Mendelson, M. *Psychoanalytic Concepts of Depression.* Spectrum Publications, New York (1974).

Murphy, G.E., Simons, A.D., Wetzel, R.D., and Lustman, P.J. Cognitive therapy and pharmacotherapy. *Arch. Gen. Psychiat. 41*, 33-41 (1984).

Prusoff, B.A., Weissman, M.M., Klerman, G.L., and Rounsaville, B.J. Research diagnostic criteria subtypes of depression. *Arch. Gen. Psychiat. 37*, 796-801 (1980).

Rado, S. The problem of melancholia, in *Collected Papers, Vol. I*, S. Rado. Grune and Stratton, New York (1956, orig. 1927).

Rado, S. Psychodynamics of depression from the etiologic point of view. *Psychosomatic Medicine, 13*, 51-55 (1951).

Rounsaville, B.J., Weissman, M.M., Prusoff, B.A., and Herceg-Brown, R.L. Marital disputes and treatment outcome in depressed women. *Comp. Psychiat. 20*, 483-490 (1979).

Rush, A.J., Beck, A.T., Kovacs, M., and Hollon, S. Comparative efficacy of cognitive therapy and pharmacotherapy in the treatment of depressed outpatients. *Cognitive Therapy and Research 1*, 17-37 (1977).

Rush, A.J., Beck, A.T., Kovacs, M., Weissenburger, J., and Hollon, S. Comparison of the effects of cognitive therapy and pharmacotherapy on hopelessness and self-concept. *Amer. J. Psychiat. 139*, 862-866 (1982).

Rush, A.J., Khatami, M., and Beck, A.T. Cognitive and behavior therapy in chronic depression.

Behavior Therapy 6, 398-404 (1975).

Seligman, M.E.P. *Helplessness*. W.H. Freeman, San Francisco (1975).

Shaw, D.M. The practical management of affective disorders. *Brit. J. Psychiat. 130*, 432-451 (1977).

Teasdale, J.D., Fennell, M.J.V., Hibbert, G.A., and Amies, P.L. Cognitive therapy for major depressive disorder in primary care. *Brit. J. Psychiat. 144*, 400-406 (1984).

Tellenbach, H. *Melancholic problemgeschichte-endogenitat-typologie-pathogeneseklinik*. Springer-Verlag, Berlin (1974).

Weissman, M.M., Potenger, M., Kleber, H., Ruben, H.L., William, D., and Thompson, W.D. Symptom patterns in primary and secondary depression. *Arch. Gen. Psychiat. 34*, 854-862 (1977).

Weissman, M.M., Prusoff, B.A., and Klerman, G.L. Personality and the prediction of long term outcome of depression. *Amer. J. Psychiat. 135*, 797-800 (1978).

Zuckerman, D.M., Prusoff, B.A., Weissman, M.M., and Padian, N.S. Personality as a predictor of psychotherapy outcome for depressed outpatients. *J. Consult. Clin. Psychol. 48*, 730-735 (1980).

II

MAJOR STEPS

4

The Contribution of Blood Levels to the Treatment of Resistant Depression

Mark S. Gold, R. Bruce Lydiard, A.L.C. Pottash, and David M. Martin

INTRODUCTION

Since the discovery of the antidepressant properties of imipramine by Kuhn (1958), there have been considerable advances of the pharmacotherapy of depression. The efficacy of tricyclic antidepressants (TCA) in treating depressive illness has been established beyond doubt (Klerman and Cole, 1965; Klein and Davis, 1969; Morris and Beck, 1974). The spectrum of conditions to which the term "depression" is applied ranges from a dysphoric response to adverse environmental events to a medical syndrome which occurs spontaneously and is characterized by fixed, depressed mood and physiological symptoms such as disturbed sleep and appetite patterns (Goodwin, 1977). The former end of this spectrum is often referred to as "reactive" or "neurotic" depression; the latter end of the spectrum is termed "endogenous" depression and is approximately equivalent to the Diagnostic and Statistical Manual of Mental Disorders (DSM-III) category of major depressive disorder with melancholia (American Psychiatric Association, 1980). While there is some controversy as to whether all types of depressive illness respond to pharmacologic treatment (Paykel, 1972; Reisby et al., 1977; Bielski and Friedel, 1979), it is generally accepted that patients meeting descriptive criteria for endogenous depression or having neurobiological evidence for an active major depression are most likely to respond to somatic treatments (Klein, 1974; Bielski and Friedel, 1976; Baldessarini, 1981; Gold et al., 1983).

However, within the descriptively homogenous endogenous subgroup of depressives, at least 35% of patients fail to respond to treatment with standard dosages of TCA (Klein and Davis, 1969). Among many of the "responders" the quality of response is quite variable. Furthermore, many "responders" in a research study relapse within six months and some are even included in another study. Others are treated and studied by other physicians. Undoubtedly, some patients are treatment resistant because they have been misdiagnosed and suffer from medical illness (Koranyi, 1979; Gold et al., 1981; Hall et al., 1981; Estroff and Gold, 1983).

There are several reasons why "nonmedical" endogenously depressed patients may fail to respond to standard treatment. First, the subgroup of endogenous depression is a heterogenous group of illnesses. Patients may meet criteria for a major depression but have an undiagnosed medical, neurobiological, endocrinological, drug or substance abuse illness (Gold et al., 1983). Patients may have an endogenous depression but since neither pathophysiology nor prediction of treatment response are considered in the diagnosis, the clinical diagnosis fails to predict who will respond to which treatment, for what duration, at what dose, etc. Demonstrable biochemical differences as indicated by variable patterns of 24 hour urinary 3-methoxy-4-hydroxyphenylglycol (MHPG) (Schildkraut, 1973; Maas, 1975; Hollister et al., 1980; Schatzberg et al., 1982) excretion and CSF 5-hydroxyindoleacetic acid (HIAA) levels suggest many differences exist between "similar" patients (Maas et al., 1982; Asberg et al., 1973; Appelbaum et al., 1979). Given the probable biochemical heterogeneity of endogenous depression, it is no more reasonable to expect that every individual will respond to a given antidepressant than it is to assume that all sore throats with fever will respond to the same pharmacological treatment. However, another reason why many patients fail to respond to treatment is that they have not received an adequate therapeutic trial of antidepressant drug therapy. Most physicians do not even know the definition of an antidepressant trial. The use of standard dose regimens unrelated to plasma levels has been identified as a major source of antidepressant nonresponse. The reasons for this fact are numerous but include pharmacokinetic, pharmacodynamic, and other factors. This confusion contributes to nonresponse and undertreatment (Keller et al., 1982). Other, less obvious factors may contribute to inadequate drug treatment and include interpatient pharmacokinetic variability resulting in nontherapeutic blood levels, drug-drug interactions, generic substitution, noncompliance, and inadequate duration of drug treatment. Of these factors, since the majority of depressed patients do not seek treatment, and those who do seek treatment feel a stigma upon filling a prescription (they may even go to a pharmacy outside their area), compliance must be lower than that reported for hypertension. This chapter examines these variables and suggests ways in which therapeutic drug monitoring can help the clinician to reduce the failure rate in pharmacological treatment of depressed patients by assuring the adequacy of the therapeutic trial. Additionally, a review of the relationship between blood levels and clinical response is presented, along with some methodologic considerations for obtaining antidepressant (AD) blood levels.

PHARMACOKINETICS

The basis of all pharmacologic treatment, including the treatment of depression with AD, is the assumption of a relationship between drug concentration at the site of action (i.e., the receptor) and drug response. A number of factors affect active drug concentration and therefore response (see Table 1). The concentration of active drug circulating free in the plasma is, in turn, related to the tissue (and presumably receptor) concentration of drug and should be correlated with clinical response. Plasma drug concentration is affected, not only by the dosage of drug

TABLE 1. Factors Affecting Blood Concentrations during Therapeutic Monitoring

Dosage	Storage
Route of administration	Induction of inhibition of microsomal enzymes
Gastrointestinal absorption	Sex
Weight	Menstrual cycle
Dosage form	Disease state
Tissue binding at active and inactive sites	Synergistic or antagonistic action of other drugs
Body water	Tolerance
Rate of detoxification	Time of sampling
Rate of elimination	Method of analysis (including metabolites)

Adapted from Koch-Wesser, 1972, and Winek, 1975.

administered, but also by the amount of drug absorbed, distribution, and the rate of metabolism and excretion of the drug. Since all of these factors ultimately affect the amount of drug available at the site of action, each is an important variable to consider in drug treatment. As an illustration of just how important the sum of these variables can be, steady-state plasma concentration can vary as much as 36-fold between patients receiving standard dosages of antidepressants (Gram and Fredericson-Overo, 1975; Alexanderson et al., 1973; Molnar and Gupta, 1980). Five to ten-fold interpatient variations in TCA steady-state levels are commonly encountered (Matuzas et al., 1982). The following sections examine more closely some reasons for this pharmacokinetic variability.

Absorption

After all ingestion, TCAs are absorbed rapidly, with peak blood levels being achieved within two-four hours. The amount of drug actually reaching the bloodstream, however, is highly variable as a result of rapid hepatic metabolism immediately after absorption. This is known as the "first-pass" effect. The amount of a given dosage of drug reaching the bloodstream varies widely from individual to individual and from drug to drug; bioavailability may thus range from as little as 13% to 90% (Alexanderson et al., 1973; Gram and Fredericson-Overo, 1975; Friedel, 1982) of the administered dose. As a result of this first-pass effect, the dosage of a particular drug required to achieve a therapeutic steady-state blood level may vary dramatically from patient to patient.

Metabolism

TCAs are metabolized in the liver by N-demethylation, hydroxylation, and glucuronide formation with hydroxylated metabolites. Both the rate and pathway of metabolism have been shown to vary according to genetic and environmental (see below) variables. Tertiary amines such as amitriptyline (AT), imipramine, and doxepin are demethylated to form the secondary amines nortriptyline (NT), desipramine, and desmethyl doxepin, respectively. The secondary amines are active antidepressant compounds as are some hydroxy metabolites of both the tertiary and secondary amines (Potter et al., 1980). Thus, when a patient is given a tertiary amine tricyclic, the secondary amine metabolites form in vivo and also must be taken into account when determining TCA blood levels. In patients receiving tertiary amines, there is a significant variation in a ratio of tertiary to secondary amines. These ratios can vary from 0.25 to more than 3 for amitriptyline/

nortriptyline and from 0.1 to 3 for imipramine (Amsterdam et al., 1980). Jungkunz and Kuss (1978) have suggested that the ratio of nortriptyline to amitriptyline correlated better with response to treatment than did the plasma level of amitriptyline plus nortriptyline. However, there is currently little information available to support or dispute these data and further work is needed to evaluate the clinical importance of the ratio of tertiary to secondary amines. Similarly, the contribution of the active hydroxy metabolites to clinical effect requires further study before it can be meaningfully applied to clinical practice.

At steady-state levels, the elimination of drug equals the amount ingested daily. The steady-state levels reflect the amount of drug available at the site of action. The time required for a drug to achieve the steady-state concentration is approximately equal to five elimination half-lives. Since the half-lives of the various TCAs range from 8 to over 100 hours (Van Brunt, 1983), the length of time to reach a steady-state varies considerably (see Table 2). The importance of this point is that for patients who have reduced metabolic rates or are receiving drugs with long half-lives, the time at which blood levels are obtained after beginning therapy must be considered. One could underestimate the steady-state plasma TCA level unless the appropriate amount of time to reach steady state is allowed.

TABLE 2. Half-Lives of Various Tricyclic Antidepressants

Tricyclic antidepressant	Half-life (hr) Mean	Range
Nortriptyline[a]	27	13-47
Imipramine	8	4-18
Amitriptyline	15	10-26
Desipramine[a]	17	13-26
Doxepin	17	8-25
Desmethyldoxepin	51	33-81
Protriptyline	78	55-125

[a]Half-life may be longer when derived from a tertiary amine compound.

Free Versus Bound Drug

Once absorbed into the bloodstream TCAs are largely bound to plasma proteins, with only a relatively small percentage of unbound or "free" drug being available for equilibration with tissue as pharmacologically active agent. The interindividual difference in the percent "free" drug for imipramine, for example, has been estimated to be as high as nine-fold (DeVane, 1980). The proteins to which TCA bind include albumin, alpha-acid-glycoprotein, and lipoproteins. Alpha-l-acid-glycoprotein (AGP) is felt to be "an acute phase reactant" and may be elevated in acute inflammatory illness, malignancy, hepatic and renal disease, and also may be elevated in elderly patients. Piafsky and Borga (1977) found that the amount of imipramine available as unbound was inversely related to the concentration of AGP in some clinical situations. In addition, the elderly often have a reduced serum albumin concentration, and as a result, may have more pharmacologically active drug as a percentage of total plasma levels (Thompson et al, 1983). Hyperlipoproteinemia may cause a decrease in the fraction of free drug. Patients with high levels of very low and low density lipoprotein may have less free drug available. Danon and Chen (1979) have reported that up to a third of the total circulating imipramine may be bound in hyperlipoproteinemic patients. It is in general assumed that the degree of protein binding is similar across patients, and is not usually an important variable (Friedel, 1982; Amsterdam et al., 1980). However in certain cases, particularly in treatment-resistant patients, it may be wise to consider some of the more unusual pharmacokinetic possibilities for nonresponse.

Drug Interactions

A number of pharmacologic agents are commonly coadministered with TCA and may alter steady-state levels. Agents which stimulate the hepatic microsomal enzyme system, which is responsible for the metabolism of TCA, may lower drug levels (see Table 3). Sedative-hypnotics (barbiturates, alcohol, glutethimide, chloral hydrate) and anticonvulsants may cause a lowering of TCA levels by inducing hepatic microsomal metabolism. Other agents reported to accelerate metabolism include cigarettes and oral contraceptives. Conversely, agents which

TABLE 3. Important TCA-Drug Interactions

Decrease TCA levels	Increase TCA levels
Alcohol[a]	Phenothiazines
Anticonvulsants	Butyrophenones
Barbiturates	Methylphenidate
Cigarette smoking	
Chloral hydrate	
Glutethimide	
Oral contraceptives	

[a]Chronic use; acute administration may increase TCA levels acutely.

inhibit hepatic metabolism may cause increases in TCA levels. Neuroleptics are often coadministered with TCA and have been shown to cause significant increases in TCA blood levels (Gram and Fredricson-Overo, 1972; Gram, 1975; Nelson and Jatlow, 1980). Methylphenidate, and agent occasionally used to potentiate TCA-treated nonresponders, has also been shown to inhibit microsomal metabolism and cause a rise in TCA levels (Wharton et al., 1971). Benzodiazepines reportedly have little effect on TCA levels (Gram et al., 1974) and are probably the best choice for a combination with TCA if sedation or anxiolytic action is desired.

Age, Race, and Sex

Age may be an important factor in determining steady-state blood levels. Elderly patients have a reduced capacity to metabolize TCA, and aging has been associated with higher TCA levels in this patient subgroup (Thompson et al., 1983). Similarly, very young patients may have less metabolic capacity and require lower dosages to achieve therapeutic levels. Race may be a significant factor in determining TCA steady-state levels. Black patients have been reported to have higher TCA levels than white patients (Ziegler and Biggs, 1977). Sex does not seem to be a critical variable (Cooper et al., 1975).

COMPLIANCE

It is well known that the majority of patients do not take medications prescribed. This is a fact in outpatient *and* inpatient psychopharmacology. Noncompliance or partial compliance causes wide fluctuations in plasma levels and reduced response to treatment. Frequent monitoring of antidepressant levels is the best way to insure compliance and guarantee the integrity of the medications trial. Prevention of compliance problems is recommended to avoid wasted hospital time and risk of untreated severe depressions. It is this "pharmacokinetic" aspect of treatment resistance that is rarely considered. It is remarkably common for patients to fail to take their medications regularly (Stewart and Cluff, 1972; Kessler, 1978). Over 70% of patients in one study failed to take between 25 and 50% of their prescribed dose of medication on a q.i.d. schedule. In one study 7% of patients failed to take 100% of their dose when a once-daily medication regimen was substituted (Ayd, 1972). More recently Loo et al. (1980) reported 10 of 17 outpatients were noncompliant with outpatient antidepressant regimens as assessed by plasma levels. Since TCA can be given on a once-daily basis, it seems prudent to recommend this simple schedule. However, noncompliance must be considered a major cause of treatment failure and therapeutic drug monitoring is very helpful in preventing noncompliance, or at least identifying noncompliant patients. Rather than the occasional use of "surprise" blood level determinations during routine visits to encourage compliance we prefer involving the patient, the treatment staff, and the patient's loved ones in an externally validated trial. The trial is clearly defined by blood levels to enhance compliance and therapeutic response to drug treatment. When the patient is given a nortriptyline (NT) prescription, the patient and family are instructed that a minimum trial is 21 consecutive days at therapeutic levels. A dose prediction test is administered using a 50 mg test dose of NT and blood levels rather than office visits. Telephone contact or short and occasional visits are necessary to monitor for target symptom relief and side effects. In this way the patient and physician have in mind a common goal—symptom relief—and a common plan—use of physiologically active doses. This simple protocol will convert the majority of so called treatment resistant patients to responders within the first month of treatment.

DURATION OF TREATMENT

Impatience on both the part of the patient and the treating physician can result in premature termination of treatment. Dose adjustments, adding additional medications, and so on are made all together and for no apparent reason. If a trial or dose is not defined by blood levels it is frequently difficult to decide when to raise or lower dose or switch medications. The usual lag time between the initiation of treatment and the onset of therapeutic effect is usually two to three weeks. There does not seem to be any significant evidence that this lag time can be shortened by choice of drug (Lydiard, 1983), route of administration, or adjunctive medication treatment (Kessler, 1978). A therapeutic drug trial, then, should consist of a minimum of 21 (post steady-state) consecutive days at a therapeutic blood level of the TCA being used, with documented blood level determinations to assure compliance.

It is best to do single medication trials at a time in order to be sure which intervention is having a therapeutic effect. As emphasized below, it is important that medication trials be well defined so that they are adequate in dosage and duration in order to assess the efficacy of a medication for a given patient. Equally important, a medication which has not been helpful after an adequate trial should be discontinued. Though there are some patients who do better on combinations, such as tricyclics plus neuroleptics, or antidepressants plus lithium, it is best to add the second medication in a step-wise fashion. There is little place for medications combining a fixed ratio of two medications (e.g., Trilafon and Elavil are more effectively prescribed individually than as Triavil). If two medications are needed, the dosages are best adjusted independently.

PLASMA TCA LEVELS AND TCA RESPONSE

There have been many studies of the relationship between steady-state plasma levels of antidepressants (especially tricyclics) and antidepressant effects (Amsterdam et al., 1980). As is the case for psychiatry and psychiatric research, not all of the studies in the literature are in agreement. However, the literature suggests that there are clinically important relationships, and therapeutic thresholds or windows have been defined for many of the antidepressants.

The concept of a "therapeutic window" means that there is a plasma level range within which a patient receives maximum antidepressant benefit, but above which or below which the antidepressant efficacy falls off. This is not simply the same as the observation that efficacy falls off at high levels as toxic effects are seen. The therapeutic window has been best defined for nortriptyline (Asberg et al., 1971), approximately 50-140 ng/ml at steady-state (see Figure 1). Steady-state is measured 8-12 hours after the last dose of antidepressant in a patient who has been on the same dosage for 5-7 days. This is usually most practically done in the morning when the patient has had his or her most recent dosage of medication at bedtime the night before.

For other tricyclics, other antidepressants, and most anticonvulsants, therapeutic levels are best described as thresholds required for therapeutic efficacy (Amsterdam et al., 1980; Risch et al., 1979). For antidepressants that are metabolized to substances that are themselves antidepressant, these "active metabolites" must be taken into account also. Thus, amitriptyline is metabolized to nortriptyline, and imipramine is metabolized to desipramine. For patients taking either of the parent medications, plasma levels of both parent and active metabolite must be measured. Therapeutic steady-state plasma levels for patients on amitriptyline are amitriptyline plus nortriptyline, greater than 120 ng/ml; for patients on imipramine are imipramine plus desipramine, greater than 180 ng/ml; for desipramine a therapeutic window may exist, but this remains unclear at present. There are preliminary data on therapeutic levels of other antidepressants as well. Table 4 summarizes the usual dosage ranges and therapeutic concentrations which we currently suggest as guidelines for treatment. Measurement of platelet MAO activity can guide proper dosage of MAOI. There are a number of reports that optimal phenelzine response requires at least 80% inhibition of platelet MAO from pretreatment baselines (Robinson et al., 1978a).

Many clinicians have delayed use of the plasma levels because of suggestions in the past that all nonresponders merely require a higher dose of the antidepressant. To say that no antidepressant trial (in the face of nonresponse) is complete without a period on high or very high doses is incorrrect and dangerous, since some patients end up with extremely toxic levels. Some physicians feel that antidepressant levels are too expensive for routine use. However, given the much greater expense of a single hospital day or an office visit, if the tests decrease hospital length of stay by even one day, or reduce outpatient visits, it is extremely cost effective. In addition there are serious risks of being on an antidepressant with substandard levels—the risks of not getting better, suicide, and suffering, as well as the medical risks being exposed to the risks of a medication without chance of benefit. Finally, psychiatrists have been similar to neurologists in their response to the introduction of medication levels. Neurologists once felt that clinical judgment was adequate in determining patient medication dosages and felt that anticonvulsant levels were an unnecessary expense. Now, while levels haven't eliminated judgment, very few neurologists fail to utilize these levels.

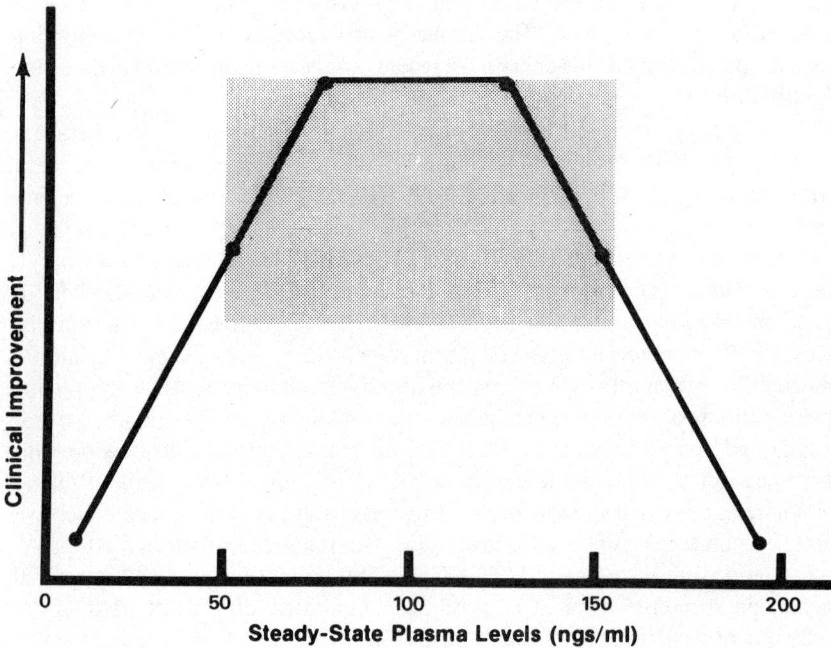

Figure 1. Schematic representation of the therapeutic window for nortriptyline in depression.

TABLE 4. Comparison of Tricyclic Antidepressants for Clinical Use[a]

Drug	Initial dose (mg)	Therapeutic plasma level (ng/ml)	Average daily maintenance dose (mg)
Imipramine (Tofranil, Janimine, SK-Pramine)	100-300	With desipramine[b] 180	75-150
Amitriptyline (Elavil, Endep)	150-300	With nortriptyline[b] 120	75-150
Desipramine (Norpramine, Pertofrane)	100-300	>125	75-100
Nortriptyline (Pamelor)	50-150	50-140	50-100
Doxepin (Adapin, Sinequan)	200-400	With desmethyldoxepin[b] 110	150-250
Protriptyline (Vivactil)	30-60	90-170	20-40
Maprotiline (Ludiomil)	75-150	180-300	75-125
Amoxapine (Asendin)	200-1400	30-120 (150-450)[c]	200-300
Trazodone (Desyrel)	50-600	>750	100-300

[a] In average adults, (middle-aged, 150-200 lbs., taking no other medication).
[b] Major active metabolite must be measured along with original tricyclic.
[c] 8-hydroxyamoxapine.

Nortriptyline

The best correlation between plasma TCA levels and clinical response has been demonstrated for nortriptyline (NT). The majority of studies have been conducted in patients with endogenous depression (major depressive disorder with melancholia, DSM-III). Asberg and associates (1971) reported that a minimum level of 50 ng/ml and an upper level of 150 ng/ml were associated with the maximum probability of therapeutic response in patients treated with nortriptyline. With few exceptions (Burrows et al., 1972; Burrows et al., 1977) the results of the majority of well-controlled studies have been remarkably consistent in substantiating this curvilinear plasma-clinical response relationship (see Table 5). The use of the "therapeutic window" has been prospectively shown to be an effective way of monitoring drug response (Kragh-Sorensen et al., 1976). These investigators used

TABLE 5. Nortriptyline Plasma Levels and Clinical Response

Investigator	Therapeutic range (ng/ml)
Asberg et al. (1971)	50-140
Burrows et al. (1972, 1974)	None apparent
Kragh-Sorensen et al. (1973, 1974, 1976)	50-150
Montgomery et al. (1978)	<200
Montgomery et al. (1977)	50-140
Ziegler et al. (1976, 1977)	50-140

a dosage of nortriptyline which resulted in plasma levels under 150 ng/ml in one group of patients, and in a second group used dosages which resulted in plasma levels over 180 ng/ml. The patients with plasma levels over 180 ng/ml did significantly less well than did the group with levels under 150 ng/ml after four weeks of treatment. The nonresponders in the high plasma level group were then randomly assigned to treatments which either maintained them at their previously high level or to dosages which allowed the plasma levels to fall below 150 ng/ml. Those patients whose dosages were reduced recovered after an additional two weeks, while the patients whose nortriptyline plasma levels remained high did not improve. The results of Lehmann et al. (1982) indicate that a strategy of promptly determining tricyclic plasma concentrations and requiring that the psychiatrist systematically adjust dosage can achieve the goal of bringing plasma concentration into a targeted range, resulting in improved clinical response. Additionally, a greater percentage of NT-treated discharged patients had improved at 3 weeks, suggesting that the dosage adjustment speeded clinical response. This was in contrast to amitriptyline (AT).

Sorensen et al. (1978) did require one dosage adjustment after 2 weeks in an open trial with NT if the drug level was outside the 50-150 ng/ml range. Of 34 patients, 14 had their dosage increased from 25-50 mg at the discretion of the clinician, but 9 of 14 had plasma levels above 50 ng/ml at the time of the change (51-78 ng/ml at 2 weeks). The response rate at the end of 4 weeks was approximately 80%. The authors suggested that the strategy was effective in achieving results near the best reported for any antidepressant (Morris and Beck, 1974).

Our experience (Gold and Martin, 1982) and the data reported by others (Lehmann et al., 1982; Dawling et al., 1981) suggest that use of the NT window with regular monitoring may increase both response time and response rate.

The tricyclic "dose prediction test" has been employed to try to ascertain in advance whether a patient is a rapid or slow metabolizer, and hence the approximate dosage that will be needed to achieve therapeutic levels (Cooper and Simpson, 1978). This test consists of measurement of plasma level 24 hours after administration orally of a test dose of 50 or 100 mg of a tricyclic. Nanograms have been worked out relating level at 24 hours to anticipated daily dosages needed.

Imipramine

Imipramine (IMI) appears to be the only other TCA for which a robust relationship between plasma levels and clinical response has been demonstrated. Table 6 shows the summary of the important studies demonstrating this relationship. Glassman and co-workers (1977) found that 90% of unipolar nondelusional depressed patients with plasma levels of IMI plus its metabolite desipramine (DMI) above 225 ng/ml responded to treatment with IMI, while only 30% of the patients with total plasma levels below 150 ng/ml, responded satisfactorily. Similar results were reported by Reisby and co-workers (1977). Nonresponders had plasma levels of IMI and DMI below 240 ng/ml, while 10 of 12 responders had total tricyclic levels above 240 ng/ml. It thus appears that a combined tricyclic plasma level above 225 to 240 ng/ml is necessary for optimal therapeutic effect in patients taking IMI.

It has been demonstrated that from data obtained from a single blood drawing after a loading dose of IMI or DMI, steady-state plasma levels of IMI and its active metabolite DMI is predictable (Brunswick et al., 1979).

In contrast to the "therapeutic window" for nortriptyline, there appears to be a sigmoidal-shaped plasma level-clinical response curve for imipramine. The data

TABLE 6. Imipramine Plus Desipramine Plasma Levels and Clinical Response

Investigator	Therapeutic levels (ng/ml)
Olivier-Martin et al. (1975)	>200
Gram et al. (1976)	>45 imipramine and >75 desipramine
Glassman et al. (1977)	>225
Reisby et al. (1977)	>240
Muscettola et al. (1978)	>240
Matuzas et al. (1982)	>180
Simpson et al. (1982)	Weak correlation

indicate that the maximal therapeutic response is obtained at levels of imipramine plus its demethylated metabolite desmethylimipramine of greater than 200 ng/ml. As an example of the potential value of rigorous attention to TCA levels as a guide to treatment, Glassman et al. (1977) treated 42 nondelusional, depressed patients with imipramine. Of the subgroup of patients achieving imipramine plus desmethylimipramine plasma levels of greater than 225 ng/ml, 93% responded. Thirteen of sixteen patients who did not respond at plasma levels of less than 180 ng/ml were treated with levels over 200 ng/ml; of these, 7 were promptly converted to drug responder status.

Amitriptyline

Amitriptyline (AT), like imipramine, is a tertiary amine which is demethylated to form nortriptyline, a secondary amine which is also an active antidepressant. Studies assessing the relationship between total amitriptyline and nortriptyline levels have yielded conflicting results to date (see Table 7). Some investigators suggest that a sigmoidal plasma level-response is obtained (Braithwaite et al., 1972; Kupfer et al., 1977; Ziegler et al., 1976). Others suggest a curvilinear or "therapeutic window"-type relationship (Gruvstad, 1973; Vandel et al., 1978; Montgomery et al., 1979; Moyes and Moyes, 1980). Still others have reported no relationship (Coppen et al., 1978; Robinson et al., 1979; Mendlewicz et al., 1980; Jungkunz and Kuss, 1978). Until further studies are completed and adequately address critical issues (Friedel, 1982), such as the possible inhibitory effects of high concentrations of nortriptyline and the possible contribution of active hydroxy metabolites, it is difficult to establish definitive guidelines for therapeutic

TABLE 7. Amitriptyline Plus Nortriptyline Plasma Levels and Clinical Response

Investigator	Therapeutic levels (ng/ml)
Grustad (1973)	70-180
Vandel et al. (1978)	60-220
Montgomery et al. (1979)	80-200
Moyes et al. (1980)	75-150
Braithwaite et al. (1972)	>120
Ziegler et al. (1976)	>160
Kupfer et al. (1977)	>200
Coppen et al. (1978)	None apparent
Robinson et al. (1979)	None apparent
Mendlewicz et al. (1980)	None apparent

blood levels of amitriptyline. However, it seems prudent to use greater than 100 ng/ml of amitriptyline plus nortriptyline and to avoid excessively high levels (i.e., greater than 300 ng/ml). For these reasons amitriptyline should be relegated to a secondary or tertiary treatment. AT should not be prescribed because it is NT with a sedative component. If a sedative is needed it should be prescribed (e.g., diphenhydramine).

Desipramine

There are few data on the relationship between clinical response and plasma levels of desmethylimipramine (see Table 8). Friedel et al. (1979) reported a "therapeutic window" effect for desipramine for plasma levels between 40 and 160 ng/ml. Two other poorly controlled studies (Amin et al., 1978; Khalid et al., 1978) found no relationship. Recently, Nelson et al., (1982) reported that levels of greater than 125 ng/ml were most effective in a sample of 31 depressed inpatients. In this study, 84% of patients who were treated with greater than 125 ng/ml responded well to treatment; no upper therapeutic limit was found in this study. Thus, a minimum level of 125 ng/ml seems a reasonable guideline until further studies establish the possibility of an upper therapeutic limit for desipramine plasma concentrations.

TABLE 8. Desipramine Plasma Levels and Clinical Response

Investigator	Therapeutic range (ng/ml)
Friedel et al. (1979)	40-160
Amin et al. (1978)	None apparent
Khalid (1978)	None apparent
Nelson et al. (1982)	>125

Other Antidepressants

The relationship between doxepin (plus desmethyldoxepin) levels and clinical response has been reported by only a few investigators. Friedel and Raskind (1975) reported a minimum concentration of doxepin plus desmethyldoxepin of 125 ng/ml. Ward et al (1982) replicated this finding and suggested an upper limit of 250 ng/ml. Two studies have reported the relationship between protriptyline and clinical response. Biggs and Ziegler (1977) reported that plasma levels of greater than 70 ng/ml are necessary for a clinical response. In this small group of patients, it was not possible to ascertain a therapeutic ceiling level. Whyte et al., (1976) reported a curvilinear relationship for protriptyline (165-240 ng/ml). For the newer antidepressants, trazodone (Greenblatt, 1983), maprotiline (Woggon et al., 1976), bupropion (Angst and Rothweiler, 1973; Gaertner et al., 1982), and amoxapine (Boutelle, 1980; Click and Zisook, 1982), there are insufficient data on the relationship between blood levels and clinical response to guide therapeutic drug level monitoring. At the present time, blood levels of these newer antidepressants can be useful in determining whether patients are complying with treatment or whether extremely low or excessively high blood levels are resulting from the regimen being prescribed.

STANDARD DOSE

To avoid pitfalls of PDR prescribing, medications should be used which have well understood plasma level-response relationships. In our opinion, there are no alternatives to starting most patients on NT or at least IMI or DMI. In order to prescribe antidepressants properly, it is important to define target symptoms for the treatment (Klein et al., 1980; Goodwin, 1977; Baldessarini, 1975). In many clear-cut cases of major depressive episodes with good premorbid functioning one can aim for virtually an absolute and complete remission of the depressive syndrome. In cases that are less clean cut, especially where there have been characterological and other long-standing problems that may be difficult to sort out from the depression in question, one may aim for improvement and symptom reduction without expecting remission from all the depressive symptomatology. The physician as a general rule can expect antidepressants at best to return the patient to his or her baseline level of functioning before the depression, but seldom affect baseline character structure or functioning. Well-designed studies of female outpatients with major depression have shown that antidepressant medications and psychotherapy have additive benefits, but on different target symptoms (Klerman, 1974). The antidepressants were necessary to alleviate depression symptoms, whereas psychotherapy was necessary to improve social functioning.

TARGET SYMPTOMS MAINTENANCE

Even some patients in clinical remission on maintenance antidepressants may benefit from plasma antidepressant concentration determinations. As noted above, a variety of exogenous factors may alter steady-state concentrations of antidepressant medications. For example, neuroleptics, methylphenidate, corticosteroids, disulfiram, dipropylacetamide, vitamins, and weight loss may all markedly increase plasma levels of antidepressant agents with "therapeutic windows." Conversely, barbiturates and tobacco smoking may markedly lower plasma tricyclic concentrations and allow relapse in patients treated with certain classes of antidepressants. There are likely to be numerous other drug-drug interactions affecting tricyclic plasma concentrations in the outpatient and, when adding or deleting a concurrent medication to a patient's pharmacological regimen, a plasma level determination may be appropriate.

Finally, differences in bioequivalence among pharmaceutical preparations of the same tricyclic agent have resulted in changes in plasma tricyclic concentrations and caused clinical relapses or precipitated toxicity, and the clinician must be alert to this if an outpatient changes pharmacies or is taking a generic product.

METHODOLOGIC CONSIDERATIONS

While there is considerable variation in TCA half-life among individuals, and some difference among the various TCAs as well as their monomethylated metabolites, in general their elimination half-lives are in the range of 18 to 48 hours, although longer for protriptyline. The implications of this for therapeutic monitoring is that seven to ten days should be allowed to achieve a steady-state plasma concentration with any given dosage. Using electron impact mass fragmentography, Ziegler et al. (1978) have reported intraindividual variations in steady-state levels of the various TCAs, ranging from 13% for nortriptyline to 26% for desipramine. With careful control of compliance and sampling time, the consistency of steady state concentrations is an excellent indicator of the reliability of the laboratory analysis. As with most drugs, it is usually desirable to monitor through levels, e.g., sampling just prior to the next dose.

In order to provide meaningful information to the practitioner, therapeutic drug monitoring must be timely and accurate. As was mentioned above, the collection of samples for plasma levels should be measured once steady-state concentrations have been achieved. This is usually after at least one week or longer for slow metabolizers or patients receiving protriptyline, a drug with a long elimination half-life. The timing of blood level determinations should be done in a consistent fashion. Ziegler et al. (1977) have suggested that TCA levels should be measured 12 to 16 hours after the last dose on a once-daily dosage schedule or 3 to 7 hours after the last dose on a TID schedule; there seems to be general agreement on this point (Baldessarini, 1979; Risch et al., 1981; Amsterdam et al., 1980). The method used to obtain samples can also be critical. Vacutainer tubes® should be avoided since a component contained in the stoppers of these tubes is believed to interfere with plasma protein tricyclic binding, driving the TCAs into the erythrocytes and causing spuriously low TCA levels to result (Brunswick and Mendels, 1977; Cochran et al., 1978, Risch et al., 1981). Although this component has reportedly been removed by the manufacturer of the stoppers, inventories of tubes may still be available in the field and used in the collection of plasma samples for TCA analysis. Therefore, it is advisable that Venoject® heparinized tubes or glass syringes should be employed for sample collection. Once the sample is drawn, it should be centrifuged as soon as is feasible to avoid hemolysis and the plasma separated from the cells. Blood level testing results should be available to the clinician within 24 hours if it is to save prolonged suffering, patient days, or outpatient visits. The assay technique used is also important, as is the reliability of the laboratory being used. There is little doubt that much of the controversy surrounding the measurement of ADs is a consequence of the difficulty encountered in performing the analysis.

ANALYTIC PROCEDURES

The determination of therapeutic concentrations of the ADs in plasma is technically demanding and requires sophisticated analytical instrumentation. A variety of analytical approaches has been utilized for this purpose as discussed below.

Isotope Dilution

Much of the early work on the significance of plasma tricyclic concentrations, nortriptyline in particular, was performed with this procedure (Hammer and Brodie, 1967). This procedure has largely been supplanted by various chromatography techniques.

Gas Chromatography

All of the chromatography methods involve separation of the drug from its biological matrix, generally by liquid-solvent extraction techniques. For gas chromatography, double extraction cleanup procedures are required, in view of the relatively low concentrations of the ADs and interferences encountered in the chromatographic areas of interest. The ADs are among the most difficult drugs to analyze, and unpredictable losses can occur if scrupulous care is not taken in cleaning and siliconizing of glassware, injector port septums, and careful deactivation of columns. An appropriate internal standard is also critical; a tricyclic drug other than that being measured is generally used. While early gas chromatography studies employed flame ionization detectors, most would agree that this approach is not adequately sensitive for optimal measurement of therapeutic concentrations of the TCAs. Much more widely applied is the nitrogen-phosphorus detector which has an enhanced sensitivity for nitrogenous compounds such as TCAs.

(GC/MS) Mass Fragmentography

Mass fragmentography represents the state of the art for the sensitive and specific measurement of TCAs as well as most other drugs. Unfortunately, the very high cost (generally $100,000 or more) and technical complexity of gas liquid chromatography-mass spectrometer systems make this approach unsuitable for cost-effective therapeutic monitoring.

High-Pressure Liquid Chromatography (HPLC)

HPLC is one of the most versatile tools available for drug analysis. A variety of HPLC procedures have been reported (Proelss et al, 1978; Kraak and Bijster, 1977; Vandemark et al., 1978; Martin et al., 1983) for the measurement of therapeutic concentrations of the TCAs employing normal-phase or reversed-phase chromatographic systems. The sensitivities of HPLC systems approach those achievable with gas-liquid chromatography nitrogen detection or mass fragmentography, and the less involved sample preparation and ease of automation make HPLC the most suitable approach for routine monitoring of plasma TCA levels.

Radioimmunoassay

Following conjugation to albumin, the various TCAs have been used for the generation of antibodies that are suitable for radioimmunoassay (Robinson et al, 1978b). Radioimmunoassay is potentially an attractive alternative to the more time consuming chromatographic assays in that the samples could be batch processed, yielding a high rate of analysis. Unfortunately, most of the assays reported to date demonstrate varying sensitivities for the tertiary amines and their secondary amine metabolites, as well as cross-reactivity with non-TCA psychoactive compounds which may be prescribed concurrently.

In summary, since the actual concentration of TCA in blood is very low (usually 50-200 ng), a reliable and sensitive assay technique is important. Undoubtedly the most specific method is gas chromatography-mass spectrometry (Jenkins and Friedal, 1978; Biggs et al., 1976), but is limited by expense and availability. Other clinically applicable methods include gas chromatography with nitrogen phosphorous detection, high performance liquid chromatography with ultraviolet detection, or radioimmunoassay with sample preparation prior to analysis (Jatlow, 1980; Martin et al., 1983; Perel et al., 1978). As with all specialized laboratory procedures the buyer (in this case the physician) beware. Almost all commercial laboratories claim that they can accurately measure ADs. This has yet to be demonstrated. In fact, Gelenberg (1983) recently reviewed reports of variation in TCA blood levels reported by various commercial laboratories. One study of six patients receiving amitriptyline revealed an interlaboratory *difference* of 362 ng/ml of amitriptyline plus nortriptyline plasma levels in one patient, with an *average* interlaboratory difference of 96 ng/ml (Bank and Bridenbaugh, 1982). The reviewer appropriately suggested that the reliability of the facilities could be tested by sending split samples either to different laboratories or to the same laboratory to test internal consistency.

WHAT TO DO

The physician may begin treatment of the supposed nonresponder with any AD since no clinical differences in response to various ADs have been demonstrated conclusively. This of course assumes a careful and comprehensive neuropsychiatric evaluation allowing the physician to make a diagnosis of exclusions like major depressive disorder. In general, in the absence of a positive personal or family history of clear response we prefer to begin therapy with nortriptyline or imipramine and to monitor the plasma level closely to insure trial at a therapeutic level for 21 days or longer. It is usually advisable to begin therapy with the nortriptyline dose prediction test. Medication given in an amount sufficient to maintain therapeutic plasma levels should, if effective, produce within ten days some improvement in sleep, appetite, and even mood. However, the full effect does not appear until the end of the third week, or occasionally even later. If response to 21 days (after steady-state) at a consistent therapeutic plasma AD level is negligible or minimal, a change to another antidepressant is recommended. Only after two well-controlled trials, each with a different antidepressant, should using a monamine oxidase inhibitor be considered.

Normally, once a clinical response is documented, antidepressant medication is continued for at least six months. During this time, the dosage may be altered as necessary to keep the plasma level in the therapeutic range. Plasma levels are usually monitored on an at least monthly basis or at any time that depressive signs and symptoms reemerge. The tricyclic may be given prophylactically thereafter if episodes of depression recur.

INTERPRET BLOOD LEVELS IN CONTEXT

Like all other chemical determinations, drug concentrations are most useful when they are interpreted in the broad context of the patient's problem. Taken out of this context, such measurements may prove misleading.

The availability of drug level measurements constitutes a major advance in the prevention of therapeutic accidents with an important group of potent, commonly used drugs which have low therapeutic indices. However, this approach carries significant drawbacks even for a small group of carefully selected drugs. An occasional patient may experience toxic reactions at therapeutic drug blood levels, nonresponse at therapeutic levels, and even clinical response at subtherapeutic levels.

One possible explanation for these so-called anomalies is that receptor sites on which drugs act may be aberrant in several disease states.

CONCLUSION

This chapter has focused on factors which can result in an inadequate therapeutic drug trial. These factors include inadequate dosage, interpatient pharmacokinetic variability, drug interactions, noncompliance, and insufficient duration of drug treatment. The use of accurate therapeutic blood level monitoring in documenting the adequacy of drug treatment has been presented. No patient should be considered a nonresponder unless an adequate drug trial with documented therapeutic blood level monitoring has been completed. In fact, a case can be made for avoiding the inadequate drug trial from the outset of treatment. Initiation of treatment with a TCA such as nortriptyline or imipramine, which have fairly robust plasma concentration-clinical response relationships established, is recommended. As seen in the two studies utilizing specific groups of depressed patients, nortriptyline with nortriptyline levels monitoring of antidepressants levels can improve efficacy (Gold and Martin, 1982). For carefully selected major depressives, response rates to antidepressants have been reported as low as 50-60% without monitoring of plasma levels, and as high as 70-90% of adolescents and adults with monitoring of levels (Klein et al., 1980; Goodwin, 1977; Baldessarini, 1975; Gold et al., 1980). Many clinicians, including ourselves, find the monitoring of plasma levels at approximately weekly intervals quite useful, especially in the early weeks of dosage adjustment. It is especially useful in patients at the extremes of normal—those who require extremely low or extremely high dosage to achieve therapeutic effects. Early documentation of therapeutic drug levels could save the unnecessary expense of prolonged hospitalization, additional outpatient visits, medication costs, and undue patient suffering. Additionally, occasional surprise blood level checks can maximize compliance and reduce the treatment failure rate significantly.

Some patients are truly nonresponsive to treatment, and other chapters in this volume address the treatments which follow nonresponse, such as use of hospitalization, monoamine oxidase inhibitors, lithium salts, neuroleptics, thyroid hormone, tryptophan, and electroconvulsive therapy (ECT). It is the hope of the authors that the optimization of standard treatments by using therapeutic blood level monitoring will reduce the need for innovative or adjunctive treatment in the majority of depressed patients. It is the severity of symptoms such as poor nutritional status, psychosis, suicidality, and presence of family supports and cooperativeness of the patient that go into the decision whether to treat the patient as an outpatient or inpatient. In view of the generally favorable response to treatment of depression, it is best in uncertain cases to err on the side of hospitalization.

REFERENCES

Alexanderson, B., Borga, O., and Alvan, G. The availability of orally administered nortriptyline. *Eur. J. Clin. Pharmacol. 5*, 181-185 (1973).

Amin, M.M., Cooper, R., and Khalid, R. A comparison of desipramine and amitriptyline plasma levels and therapeutic response. *Psychopharmacol. Bull. 14*, 45 (1978).

Amsterdam, J., Brunswick, D., and Mendels, J. The clinical application of tricyclic antidepressant pharmacokinetics and plasma levels. *Amer. J. Psychiat. 137*, 653-662 (1980).

Angst, J., and Rothweiler, R. Blood levels and clinical effects of maprotiline (Ludiomil)—A preliminary study, in *Classification and Prediction of Outcome of Depression*, Symposium Medica Hoechst 8, Schattauer, Stuttgart, p. 237 (1973).

Appelbaum, P.S., Vasile, R.G., Orsulak, P.J., and Schildkraut, J.J. Clinical utility of tricyclic antidepressant blood levels: a case report. *Amer. J. Psychiat. 40*, 58-69 (1979).

Asberg, M., Bertilsson, L., Tuck, R., Cronholm, B., and Sjoqvist, F. Indoleamine metabolites in the cerebrospinal fluid of depressed patients before and during treatment with nortriptyline. *Clin. Pharmacol. Ther. 14*, 277-286 (1973).

Asberg, M., Cronholm, B., Sjoqvist, F., and Tuck, D. Relationship between plasma level and therapeutic effect of nortriptyline. *Brit. Med. J. 3*, 331-334 (1971).

Ayd, F.J. Patient compliance. *Internat. Drug Ther. Newsletter 7*, 33-40 (1972).

Baldessarini, R.J. *Chemotherapy in Psychiatry*, Harvard University Press, Massachusetts and London p. 201 (1975).

Baldessarini, R.J. Status of psychotropic blood level assay and other biochemical measurements in clinical practice. *Amer. J. Psychiat. 136*, 1177-1180 (1979).

Baldessarini, R.J. A summary of the biomedical aspects of mood disorders. *McLean Hosp. J. 6*, 1-21 (1981).

Bank, R.L., and Bridenbaugh, R.H. Clinical reliability of tricyclic antidepressant levels. *Psychiat. Forum (Summer-Fall,)* 30-31 (1982).

Bielski, R.J., and Friedel, R.O. Prediction of tricyclic antidepressant response: a critical review. *Arch. Gen. Psychiat. 33*, 1479-1484 (1976).

Bielski, R.J., and Friedel, R.O. Depressive subtypes defined by response to pharmacotherapy. *Psychiat. Clin. North Amer. 2*, 483-497 (1979).

Biggs, J.T., and Ziegler, V.E. Protriptyline plasma levels and antidepressant response. *Clin. Pharmacol. Ther. 22*, 269-273 (1977).

Biggs, J.T., Holland, W.H., and Chang, S.S. The electron beam ionization mass fragmentographic analysis of tricyclic antidepressants in human plasma. *J. Pharm. Sci. 65*, 261-268 (1976).

Boutelle, W.E. Clinical response and blood levels in the treatment of depression with a new antidepressant, amoxapine. *Neuropharmacology 19*, 1229-1231 (1980).

Braithwaite, R.A., Goulding, R., and Theano, G. Plasma concentration of amitriptyline and clinical response. *Lancet 2*, 1297-1300 (1972).

Brunswick, D.J., Amsterdam, J.D., Mendels, J., and Stern, S.L. Prediction of steady-state imipramine and desmethylimipramine plasma concentrations from single-dose data. *Clin. Pharmacol. Ther. 25*, 605-610, (1979).

Brunswick, D.J., and Mendels, J. Reduced levels of tricyclic antidepressants in plasma from vacutainers. *Commun. Psychopharmacol. 1*, 131-134 (1977).

Burrows, G.D., Davies, B., and Scoggins, B.A. Plasma concentration of nortriptyline and clinical response in depressive illness. *Lancet 1*, 619-623 (1972).

Burrows, G.D., Turecek, L.R., and Davies, B. Plasma nortriptyline and clinical response—a study using changing plasma levels. *Psychol. Med. 7*, 87-91 (1977).

Click, M.A., and Zisook, S. Amoxapine and amitriptyline: serum levels and clinical response in patients with primary unipolar depression. *J. Clin. Psychiat. 43*, 369-371 (1982).

Cochran, E., Carl, J., Hanin, I., Koslow, S., and Robins, E. Effect of vacutainer stoppers on plasma tricyclic levels: a re-evaluation. *Commun. Psychopharmacol. 2*, 495-504 (1978).

Coppen, A., Montgomery, S., and Ghose, K. Amitriptyline plasma concentration and clinical effect. A World Health Organization collaborative study. *Lancet 1*, 63-66 (1978).

Cooper, T.B., Allen, D., and Simpson, G.M. A sensitive GLC method for the determination of imipramine and desmethylimipramine using a nitrogen detector. *Commun. Psychopharmacol. 1*, 445-454 (1975).

Cooper, T.B., and Simpson, G.M. Prediction of individual dosage of nortriptyline. *Amer. J. Psychiat. 135*, 333-335 (1978).

Danon, A., and Chen, Z. Binding of imipramine to plasma proteins: effect of hyperlipoproteinemia. *Clin. Pharmacol. Ther. 25*, 316-321 (1979).

Dawling, S., Crome, P., Heyer, E.J., and Lewis, R.R. Nortriptyline therapy in elderly patients: Dosage prediction from plasma concentration at 24 hours after a single 50 mg dose. *Brit. J. Psychiat. 139*, 413-416 (1981).

DeVane, C.L. Tricyclic antidepressants, in *Applied Pharmacokinetics: Principles of Therapeutic Drug Monitoring*. W. Evans, J. Schentag, and W. Jusko, eds. Applied Therapeutics, Inc., San Francisco, pp. 549-585 (1980).

Diagnostic and Statistical Manual of Mental Disorders, 3d ed. Washington, American Psychiatric Association (1980).

Estroff, T.E., and Gold, M.S. Psychiatric misdiagnosis, in *Advances in Psychopharmacology: Pre-*

dicting and Improving Treatment Response. M.S. Gold, R.B. Lydiard, and J. Carman, eds. CRC Press, Inc., Boca Raton, (1983) pp. 1-31.

Friedel, R.O. The relationship of therapeutic response to antidepressant plasma levels: an update. *J. Clin. Psychiat. 43*, 37-42 (1982).

Friedel, R.O., and Raskind, M.A. Relationship of blood levels of Sinequan to clinical effects in the treatment of depression in aged parents, in *Sinequan (Doxepin): A Monograph of Recent Clinical Studies*. J. Mendels, ed. Excerpta Medica, Lawrenceville (1975).

Friedel, R.O., Veith, R.C. Bloom, R.C., and Bielski, R.J. Desipramine plasma levels and clinical response in depressed outpatients. *Commun. Psychpharmacol. 3*, h1-87 (1979).

Gaertner, H.J., Golfinopoulos, G., and Breyer-Pfaff, U. Response to maprotiline treatment in depressive patients. Relationship to urinary MHPG excretion and plasma drug level. *Pharmacopsychiatry 15*, 170-174 (1982).

Gelenberg, A.J. Commercial laboratories and antidepressant blood levels: caveat emptor. *Biological Therapies in Psychiatry 6*, 17-19 (1983).

Glassman, A.H., Perel, J.M., Shostak, M., Kantor, S.J., and Fleiss, J.L. Clinical implications of imipramine plasma levels for depressive illness. *Arch. Gen. Psychiat. 34*, 197-204 (1977).

Gold, M.S. and Martin, D. Diagnosis and Treatment with Tricyclic Antidepressants. Presented at the 34th Institute on Hospital and Community Psychiatry, Louisville, October 11-14, 1982.

Gold, M.S., Pottash, A.L.C., and Extein, I., Hypothyroidism and depression. *J.A.M.A. 245*, 1919-1922 (1981).

Gold, M.S., Lydiard, R.B. and Carman, J.S. *Psychopharmacology in the 1980's: Improvement of Treatment Response*. CRC Press, Inc., Boca Raton (1983).

Gold, M.S., Pottash, A.L.C., Stoll, A., Martin, D.M. Extein, I., Mueller, E.A., and Finn, L.B. Nortriptyline plasma levels and clinical response in familial pure unipolar depression and blunted TRH test patients. *Int. J. Psychiat. Med.* 13(3) 215-220 (1983).

Goodwin, F.K. Drug treatment of affective disorders: general principles. In Jarvik, M.E., ed., *Pschopharmacology in the Practice of Medicine*. Appleton-Century-Crofts, New York, pp. 241-253 (1977).

Gram, L.F. Effects of perphenazine on imipramine metabolism in man. *Commun. Psychopharmacol. 1*, 165-175 (1975).

Gram, L.F., and Fredricson-Overo, K. Drug interaction-inhibitory effect of neuroleptics on metabolism of tricyclic antidepressants in man. *Brit. Med. J. 1*, 463-465 (1972).

Gram, L.F., and Fredricson-Overo, K. First-pass metabolism of nortriptyline in man. *Clin. Pharmacol. Ther. 18*, 305-314 (1975).

Gram, L.F., Fredricson-Overo, K., and Kirk, L. Influence of neuroleptics and benzodiazepines on metabolism of tricyclic antidepressants in man. *Amer J. Psychiat. 131*, 863-866 (1974).

Gram, L.F., Reisby, N., and Isben, I. Plasma levels and antidepressive effect of imipramine. *Clin. Pharmacol. Ther. 19*, 318-324 (1976).

Greenblatt, D.J. Editorial reply "Can plasma levels of trazodone be measured? If so, what is the therapeutic range?" *J. Clin. Psychopharmacol. 3*, 61-62 (1983).

Gruvstad, M. Plasma levels of antidepressants and clinical response. *Lancet 1*, 95-96 (1973).

Hall, R.C.W., Gardner, E.R., Popkin, M.K., LeCann, A.F., and Stickner, S.K. Unrecognized physical illness/prompting psychiatric admission: A prospective study. *Amer. J. Psychiat. 138*, 629-635 (1981).

Hammer, W., and Brodie, B.B. Application of isotope derivative technique to assay of secondary amines: Estimation of desipramine by acetylation with ^{3}H-acetic anhydride. *J. Pharmacol. Exp. Ther. 157*, 503-507 (1967).

Hollister, L.E., Davis, K.L., and Berger, P.A. Subtypes of depression based on excretion of MHPG and response to nortriptyline. *Arch. Gen. Psychiat. 37*, 1107-1110 (1980).

Jatlow, P. Therapeutic monitoring of plasma concentrations of tricyclic antidepressants. *Arch. Pathol Lab. Med. 104*, 341-344 (1980).

Jenkins, R.G., and Friedel, R.O. Analysis of tricyclic antidepressants in human plasma by GLC-chemical-ionization mass spectrometry with selected ion monitoring. *J. Pharm. Sci. 67*, 17-23 (1978).

Jungkunz, G., and Kuss, H.J. Amitriptyline and its demethylation rate. *Lancet 2*, 1263-1264 (1978).

Keller, M.B., Klerman, G.L., Lavori, P.W., Fawcett, J.A., Coryell, W., and Endicott, J. Treatment received by depressed patients. *J.A.M.A. 248*, 1848-1852 (1982).

Kessler, K.A. Tricyclic antidepressants: mode of action and clinical use, in *Psychopharmacology: A Generation of Progress*. M.A. Lipton, A. DiMascio, and K.F. Killam, eds., Raven Press, New York (1978).

Khalid, R., Amin, M.M., and Ban, T.A. Desipramine plasma levels and therapeutic response. *Psychopharmacol. Bull. 14*, 43-44 (1978).

Klein, D.F. Endogenomorphic depression: A conceptual terminological revision. *Arch. Gen Psychiat. 31*, 447-454 (1974).

Klein, D.F. and Davis, J.M., eds. *Diagnosis and Drug Treatment of Psychiatric Disorders*, Williams and Wilkins, Baltimore, pp. 187-298 (1969).

Klein, D.F., Gittelman, R., Quitkin, F., and Rifkin, A. *Diagnosis and Drug Treatment of Psychiatric Disorders*. Williams and Wilkins, Baltimore, p. 849 (1980).

Klerman, G.L., and Cole, J.O. Clinical pharmacology of imipramine and related antidepressant compounds. *Pharmacol. Rev. 17*, 101-141 (1965).

Klerman, G.L., DiMascio, A., Weissman, M., Prusoff, B., and Polytel, E.S. Treatment of depression by drugs and psychotherapy. *Amer. J. Psychiat. 131*, 186-191 (1974).

Koch-Wesser, J. Drug therapy. Serum drug concentrations as therapeutic guides. *New Engl. J. Med. 287*, 227-231 (1972).

Koranyi, E.K. Morbidity and rate of undiagnosed physical illness in a psychiatric clinic population. *Arch. Gen. Psych. 36*, 414-417 (1979).

Kraak, J.C., and Bijster, P. Determination of amitriptyline and some of its metabolites in blood by high pressure liquid chromatography. *J. Chromatogr. 143*, 499-512 (1977).

Kragh-Sorensen, P., Eggert-Hansen, C.E., and Asberg, M. Plasma levels of nortriptyline in the treatment of endogenous depression. *Acta Psychiat. Scand. 49*, 444-456 (1973).

Kragh-Sorensen, P., Eggert-Hansen, C.E., and Larsen, N.E. Long-term treatment of endogenous depression with nortriptyline with control of plasma levels. *Psychol. Med. 4*, 174-180 (1974).

Kragh-Sorensen, P., Eggert-Hansen, C., and Baastrup, P.C. Self-inhibiting action of nortriptyline antidepressive effect at high-plasma levels. *Psychopharmacologia 45*, 305-312 (1976).

Kuhn, R. The treatment of depressive states with G 22355 (imipramine hydrochloride). *Amer. J. Psychiat. 115*, 459-464 (1958).

Kupfer, D.J., Hanin, I., and Spiker, E.G. Amitriptyline plasma levels and clinical response in primary depression. *Clin. Pharmacol. Ther. 22*, 904-911 (1977).

Lehmann, L.S., Bowden, C.L. Redmond, F.C., and Stanton, B.C. Amitriptyline and nortriptyline response profiles in unipolar depressed patients. *Psychopharmacology 77*, 193-197 (1982).

Lydiard, R.B. Speed of onset of the newer antidepressants. Presented at the National Institute of Mental Health Workshop. "Antidepressant Drug Therapy: The Role of the Newer Antidepressants." Washington, DC April 7 & 8, 1983.

Loo, H., Benyacoub, A.K., Rovei, V., Altamura, C.A., Vadrot, M., and Morselli, P.L. Long-term monitoring of tricyclic antidepressant plasma concentrations. *Brit. J. Psychiat. 137*, 444-451 (1980).

Maas, J.W. Biogenic amines and depression: Biochemical and pharmacological separation of two types of depression. *Arch. Gen. Psychiat. 32*, 1357-1361 (1975).

Maas, J.W., Kocsis, J.H., Bowden, C.L., Davis, J.M., Redmond, D.E., Hanin, L., and Robins, E. Pre-treatment neurotransmitter metabolites and response to imipramine or amitriptyline. *Psychol. Med. 12*, 37-43 (1982).

Martin, D.M., Petroski, R.E., Alrazi, J., Hahn, R., Pottash, A.L.C., and Gold, M.S. High performance liquid chromatographic electrochemical detection and gas liquid chromatographic analysis of 3-methoxy 4-hydroxyphenylglycol in human urine. *Society for Neuroscience*, Abstract 9:431 (1983).

Matuzas, W., Javaid, J.I., Glass, R., Davis, J.M., Ross, J.A., and Uhleuhuth, E.H. Plasma concentrations of imipramine and clinical response among depressed outpatients. *J. Clin. Psychopharm. 2*, 140-142 (1982).

Mendlewicz, J., Linkowski, P., and Rees, J.A. A double blind comparison of doxepin and amitriptyline in patients with primary affective disorder: Serum levels and clinical response. *Brit. J. Psychiat. 136*, 154-160 (1980).

Molnar, G., and Gupta, R.N. Plasma levels and tricyclic antidepressant therapy: part 2. Pharmacokinetic, clinical and toxicological aspects. *Biopharm. Drug Dispos. 1*, 283-305 (1980).

Montgomery, S.A., Braithwaite, R.A., and Crammer, J.L. Routine nortriptyline levels in the treatment of depression. *Brit. Med. J. 2*, 166-167 (1977).

Montgomery, S., Braithwaite, R.A., and Dawling, S. High plasma nortriptyline levels in the treatment of depression. *J. Clin. Pharmacol. Ther. 23*, 309-314 (1978).

Montgomery, S.A., McAuley, R., and Rani, S.J. Amitriptyline plasma concentration and clinical response. *Brit. Med. J. 1*, 230-231 (1979).

Morris, J.B., and Beck. A.T.: The efficacy of antidepressant drugs. A review of research (1958-1972). *Arch. Gen. Psychiat. 30*, 667-674 (1974).

Moyes, I.C., and Moyes, R.B. Some factors affecting the plasma levels of tricyclic antidepressants. *Postgrad. Med. J. 56*, 103-106 (1980).

Muscettola, G., Goodwin, F.K., Potter, W.Z., Claeys, M.M., and Marken, S.P. Imipramine and desipramine in plasma and spinal fluid. *Arch. Gen. Psychiat. 35*, 621-625 (1978).

Nelson, J.L., and Jatlow, P.I. Neuroleptic effect on desipramine steady-state plasma concentrations. *Amer. J. Psychiat. 137*, 1232-1234 (1980).

Nelson, J.L., Jatlow, P., Quinlan, D.M., and Bowers, M.B. Desipramine plasma concentration and antidepressant response. *Arch. Gen. Psychiat. 39*, 1419-1422 (1982).

Olivier-Martin, R., and Marzins, D. Concentration plasmatique di'imipramine et du desmethylimipramine et effet antidepresseur au cours d'un traitement control. *Psychopharmacologie 41*, 187-195 (1975).

Paykel, E.S. Depressive typologies and response to amitriptyline. *Brit. J. Psychiatry 120*, 147-156 (1972).

Perel, J.M., Stiller, R.L., and Glassman, A.H. Studies on plasma level effects relationships in imipramine therapy. *Commun. Psychopharmacol. 2*, 429-439 (1978).

Piafsky, K.M., and Borga, O.: Plasma protein binding of basic drugs. II. Importance of alpha 1-acid glycoprotein for interindividual variation. *Clin. Pharmacol. Ther. 22*, 545-549 (1977).

Potter, W.Z., Calil, H.M., and Zavadil, A.P. Steady-state concentrations of hydroxylated metabolites of tricyclic antidepressants in patients: relationship to clinical effect. *Psychopharmacol. Bull.* 32-34 (1980).

Proelss, H.F., Logman, H.J., and Miles, D.G. High performance liquid chromatographic simultaneous determination of commonly used antidepressants. *Clin. Chem. 24*, 1948-1953 (1978).

Reisby, N., Gram, L.F., Bech, P., Nagy, A., Petersen, G.O., Ortmann, J., Isben, I., Dencker, S.J., Jacobsen, O., Drautwald, O., Sondergaard, I., and Christiansen, J. Imipramine: clinical effects and pharmacokinetic variability. *Psychopharmacology 54*, 263-272 (1977).

Risch, S.C., Huey, L.Y., and Janowsky, D.S. Plasma levels of tricyclic antidepressants and clinical efficacy: a review of the literature, Parts I and II. *J. Clin. Psych. 40*, 6, 58 (1979).

Risch, S.C., Kalin, N.H., Janowsky, D.S., and Huey, L.: Indications and guidelines for plasma tricyclic antidepressant concentration monitoring. *J. Clin. Psych. 1*, 59-63 (1981).

Robinson, D., Neis, A., Ravaris, C., Ives, I., and Bartlett, D. Clinical pharmacology of phenelzine. *Arch. Gen. Psychiat. 35*, 629-635 (1978a).

Robinson, D.J., Braithwaite, R.A., and Dawling, S. Measurement of plasma nortriptyline concentrations: Radioimmunoassay and gas-chromatography compared. *Clin. Chem. 24*, 2023-2025 (1978b).

Robinson, D.J., Cooper, T.B., and Ravaris, C.L. Plasma tricyclic drug levels in amitriptyline-treated depressed patients. *Psychopharmacol. 63*, 223-231 (1979).

Schatzberg, A.F., Orsulak, P.J., Rosenbaum, A.H., Maruta, T., Kruger, E.R., Cole, J.O., and Schildkraut, J.J. Toward a biochemical classification of depressive disorders, V: Heterogeneity of unipolar depressions. *Amer. J. Psychiat. 139*, 471-475 (1982).

Schildkraut, J.J. Norepinephrine metabolites or biochemical criteria for classifying depressive disorders and predicting response to treatment: Preliminary findings. *Amer. J. Psychiat. 130*, 695-699 (1973).

Sorenson, B., Kragh-Sorenson, P., Larsen, N.E., Hvidberg, E.F. The practical significance of nortriptyline plasma control. *Psychopharmacology 59*, 556-563 (1978).

Stewart, R.B., and Cluff, L.E. A review of medication errors and compliance in ambulant patients. *Clin. Pharmacol. Ther. 13*, 463-468 (1972).

Thompson, T.L., Moran, M.G., and Neis, A.S. Psychotropic drug use in the elderly. *New Engl. J. Med. 308*, 134-138, 194-199 (1983).

Van Brunt, N. The clinical utility of tricyclic antidepressant blood levels: a review of the literature. *Ther. Drug Monitoring 5*, 1-10 (1983).

Vandel, S., Vandel, B., and Sandoz, M. Clinical response and plasma concentration of amitriptyline and its metabolite nortriptyline. *Eur. J. Clin. Pharmacol. 14*, 185-190 (1978).

Ward, N.G., Bloom. V.L., Wilson, L., Raskind, M.N., and Raisys, V.A. Doxepin plasma levels and therapeutic response in depression: Preliminary findings. *J. Clin. Psychopharmacol. 2*, 126-128 (1982).

Wharton, R.N., Perel, J.M., and Dayton, P.G. A potential clinical use for the interaction of methylphenidate (ritalin) with tricyclic antidepressants. *Amer. J. Psychiat. 127*, 1619-1625 (1971).

Whyte, S.F., Macdonald, S., and Ghose, K. Plasma concentration of protriptyline and clinical effects in depressed women. *Brit. J. Psychiat. 128*, 384-390 (1976).

Winek, C.L. *Toxicology Annual—1974*. Marcel Dekker, New York, (1975) p. 206.

Woggon, B., Angst, J., Gmuer, M., Hess, K., Hurwitz, E., Martens, H., Rothweiler, R., and Steiner, A. Clinical double-blind study with two different dosages of maprotiline (150 to 225 mg per day). *Archiv fur Psychiatrie und Nervenkrankheiten 222*, 13 (1976).

Ziegler, V.E., and Biggs, J.T. Tricyclic plasma levels—effect of age, race, sex and smoking. *J.A.M.A. 238*, 2167-2169 (1977).

Ziegler, V.E. Clayton, P.J., and Taylor, J.R. Nortriptyline levels and therapeutic response. *Clin. Pharmacol. Ther. 20*, 458-463 (1976a).

Ziegler, V.E., Co. B.T., and Taylor, J.R. Amitriptyline plasma levels and therapeutic response. *Clin. Pharmacol. Ther. 19*, 795-801 (1976b).

Ziegler, V.E., Knesevich, J.W., Wylie, L.T., and Biggs, J.T. Sampling time, dosage schedule, and nortriptyline plasma levels. *Arch. Gen. Psychiat. 34*, 613-615 (1977).

Ziegler, V.E., Wylie, L.T., and Biggs, J.T. Intrapatient variability of serial steady-state plasma tricyclic antidepressant concentrations. *J. Pharm. Sci. 67*:554-555 (1978a).

Ziegler, V.E., Biggs, J.T., and Rosen, S.H. Imipramine and desipramine plasma levels: relationship to dosage schedule and sampling time. *J. Clin. Psycchiat. 39*, 660-663 (1978b).

5

Does It Make Sense to Change Tricyclic Antidepressants in Resistant Depression?

Stuart A. Montgomery

This chapter addresses the question of whether there is a rational basis for the selection of a tricyclic antidepressant to treat a depressed patient who has not responded to medication. An affirmative answer to this question would presuppose that there was a clear basis for the selection of particular treatments for the patient in the first instance. Regrettably, this is not the case. The clinician has a range of possible interventions in treating depressive illness but little rationale for the precise selection of an appropriate treatment for a particular patient.

The lack of a scientific basis for the selection of an antidepressant for individual patients would matter less if the overall response rate to treatment were higher than it is. If a treatment has a near 100% success rate the mechanism mediating the antidepressant effect would be primarily of academic rather than practical interest. The introduction of the tricyclic antidepressants (TCA) undoubtedly marked considerable progress in relieving the suffering of depressed patients. Nevertheless, a substantial proportion of patients do not respond at all, or respond only poorly.

Estimates of response in depressive illness vary among investigators, but even the most optimistic reports suggest that some 20% of patients do not respond to pharmacotherapy. In the United Kingdom in hospital practice it is the general experience that one-third of patients respond well, one-third have a fair response, and one-third respond quite poorly.

Response to treatment covers short-term response during an episode or long-term outcome in terms of relapse rates, and the reasons and management for each may be different. The subject of this chapter concerns more specifically the management of a particular episode by changing drug therapy.

If the TCAs are effective in some patients and not in others who were considered equally appropriate for treatment it seems possible that some patients do not respond because of an unknown biological determinant. There appear to be a certain number of refractory patients who do not respond at all, and who become chronically and severely depressed. This kind of nonresponse occurs in a relatively small group, although it is one which is worrying for the clinician attempting to treat them. The much larger group consists of patients who may not respond to one TCA but in whom response is seen with another, or who may respond during one episode to a TCA but not during another. It therefore seems quite possible that there are different kinds of depression in which the TCAs are not uniformly effective, and therefore produce a variable response. The positive identification of subtypes in depressive illness would have practical as well as theoretical implications for the treating clinician.

CLINICAL FEATURES ASSOCIATED WITH RESPONSE

Diagnosis

The search for distinct diagnostic categories fits with the medical model of disease entities, an approach which can be useful if there are corresponding differential treatments. Attempts to establish a valid and widely accepted classification of the affective disorders have, however, produced as much controversy as agreement, and many issues remain unresolved. Much of the early disagreement concerned the nature of the distribution of the affective disorders—whether they lie on a continuum, or whether qualitatively distinct categories of depression exist. The early work on classification was focused on this problem. A considerable literature on this area of enquiry was reviewed by Kiloh and Garside (1963), who concluded that the balance of the evidence supported the concept of a dichotomy separating depressed patients into groups suffering from endogenous or neurotic depression.

Some of the most exhaustive and elegant work has been carried out by the Newcastle group who took careful clinical observation of phenomenology as the starting point for describing different types of depression. Multivariate statistical analyses were performed in a series of studies to detect whether phenomenology was associated with syndromes, and response to treatment was used as an independent evaluation of the diagnostic hypotheses. From these analyses indices of weighted items to differentiate endogenous and neurotic depressions, and for the prediction of response to ECT, were proposed. (Carney et al., 1965). The two indices are closely related, but not identical, in their weightings of different items. Response to treatment was not sufficient to establish diagnosis, nor was diagnosis sufficient to predict response. Outcome studies confirmed previous clinical observation that a better response is seen in endogenous depression associated with weight loss, depressive psychomotor activity, early morning waking, feelings of guilt, adequate premorbid personality. A poorer response is seen in neurotic depression associated with anxiety, hysterical features, aggravation of symptoms in the evening.

Later studies have concentrated on the differentiation of anxiety states from depressive illness rather than on the endogenous neurotic dichotomy (Gurney et al., 1972; Roth et al., 1972; Mountjoy and Roth, 1982). The separation of these conditions has an important bearing also on response to treatment. The close association between anxiety and depression is clearly recognized, but there is much uncertainty about the separation of the two conditions. The labels used for the patients falling in the uncertain ground reflect this uncertainty. The terms "atypical depression," "masked depression," "anxiety-depression," may be misleading. They engender an expectation of response to antidepressants which is not fulfilled, probably because a substantial number of anxiety states are subsumed under these headings. If the anxiety states could be reliably differentiated from depressive illness, response rates to antidepressants might be much improved.

The Newcastle group showed that with the help of multiple regression analysis it was possible to separate patients with anxiety states and depression into two distinct groups with relatively little overlap (Gurney et al., 1972; Roth et al., 1972). Moreover, extensive follow-up studies showed the outcome of the patients with anxiety states to be poorer than the patients with depression, whether of the endogenous or neurotic variety. The prognostic implications of a separation between anxiety states and depression are confirmed also by other investigators (Derogatis et al., 1972). The diagnosis of anxiety or depression was found to be stable over time, so the differentiation is clearly an important one (Kerr et al., 1974). Some of the newer research diagnostic systems, including the DSM III, are held by many investigators to be too loose in the categorization of depression, so that it may be possible for what are actually anxiety states to fulfill the criteria for depression. It is therefore very important that these findings of a differential outcome should not be overlooked.

Although endogenous depression is more likely to respond to treatment, these are only probabilities and there are reports of antidepressants being effective in both endogenous and nonendogenous depression. The diagnosis is insufficient for the prediction of response, and more information is needed on the specific features which are consistently associated with good response.

There have been several careful reviews of antidepressant studies which have attempted to identify the common features in the depressed patients who responded to treatment during a particular episode. Such reviews are hampered by the problems associated with comparing studies which were not consistently rigorous in their methodologies, have used different methods of measurement from each other, and also different criteria for patient selection. Some caution is needed also when drawing conclusions from a review of papers which have appeared from widely different sources and over long periods of time when psychiatric diagnostic and treatment habits may have undergone considerable change. Nevertheless, the consensus is that the endogenous/nonendogenous dichotomy is a useful one with prognostic implications. Bielski and Friedel (1976) in their review conclude that where there is substantial evidence of an endogenous picture with several biological signs a good response is more likely. The predictive features include insidious onset, poor appetite, weight loss, middle and late insomnia, and psychomotor retardation. From this type of review, however, it is not possible to say how many of these signs or which particular ones, are needed. A more recent review (Nelson and Charney, 1981) has confirmed the importance of psychomotor retardation as a strong predictor of response to treatment. In the Newcastle studies of outcome variables the symptoms which correlated positively with good outcome were also those which are characteristic of endogenous depression, although not all of the conventional vegetative signs were found to be predictive. The authors also concluded that groups of symptoms were themselves insufficient as predictors, but predictive power was considerably improved if they were taken in conjunction with clinical diagnosis.

The delineation of a syndrome based on painstaking clinical observation can be of practical value in identifying those patients who are most susceptible to presently available treatments. It may also be productive as a first step in investigating the etiology of depression. However, response to pharmacological intervention does not necessarily inform us about pathogenesis of depression. As biochemical knowledge of the substrates of depressive illness is widened it could well turn out that these syndromes derived from observation and supported by response to treatment do not exactly match the biological data. This is very possible in depressive illness where there appear to be considerable areas of uncertainty as to which patients will respond, and where there is much overlap between categories thought likely to be responders or nonresponders. Even where the clinical picture accords most closely to the suggested predictors of response and prognosis would appear most favorable, there is frequent failure to respond (Schatzberg et al., 1983).

Severity of Depression and Response

In deciding the management of a patient who has not responded to treatment the clinician must consider whether the failure is attributable to patient or drug centered variables. The patient's response to pharmacotherapy will depend on accurate diagnosis in the first place, and the presence of certain predictive features. However, diagnosis is not sufficient, and the severity of the illness must also be taken into account. It is mistaken to equate endogenous depression with the more severe manifestations as some diagnostic systems, including the DSM-III, appear to do since there can be mild degrees of severity of endogenous as well as other depressions. It appears from the assessment of antidepressant efficacy of the TCAs that marked response is seen only in patients with moderate to severe degrees of depression. Where patients suffer from only a mild degree of depression, significant differences between active medication and placebo are unlikely to be apparent. It is of course possible that differences do exist but current measures of severity of depression are not sufficiently sensitive to register extremely small differences. However, it is inappropriate to expose patients to the potential risks of antidepressant medication if significant improvement is unlikely to be seen.

Poor Response as Failure of Treatment

A clearly diagnosed patient with moderate or worse depression still may not respond, and this may be due to inappropriate therapy. The dose given may have been inadequate, or it may have been too high; it may have been causing side effects, and the patient may not have been complying with tablet-taking. Before seeking an alternative antidepressant these are issues which should be examined. Many patients are referred to the psychiatrist because of nonresponse to antidepressants in the primary care setting. On investigation it is often found that the dosage of antidepressant was so far below the recommended therapeutic dose as to be at best a substitute for placebo. The problem for the psychiatrist is that the patient may have lost faith in the treatment, necessitating a change, although there is no rationale for such a change from the pharmacological point of view.

Nonresponse may also be caused by too high a dosage of an antidepressant.

With certain TCAs high levels of drug in the plasma are associated with poorer response. With nortriptyline, for example, the first TCA to be widely investigated in this respect, the majority of studies showed that high levels of nortriptyline are associated with a poorer response. Only three studies did not demonstrate a relationship between plasma levels and response and some of these may have been biased by the patient selection. There appears to be a consensus that in treating endogenous depression with nortriptyline the best clinical response is associated with steady state plasma concentrations approximately between 50-175 or 200 μg/*l* and that a poorer response is seen in patients with plasma concentrations outside this range (Montgomery, 1980). The results indicate that high levels of nortriptyline have a self-inhibiting effect. In the study of Montgomery et al. (1978), there was no further response after two weeks in the group who developed high concentrations, whereas the group with concentrations within the range 80-200 μg/*l* continued to improve. Since improvement due either to random variables or to spontaneous remission would have been expected, the result is interesting. Kragh-Sorensen et al., (1976) demonstrated the significant clinical advantage of adjusting the dosage of patients to bring their plasma nortriptyline concentrations from above to within the optimum range between the fourth and sixth week of treatment.

Amitriptyline is probably the most widely used TCA and there has been considerable interest in whether a similar relationship exists between levels and response as with nortriptyline. The position is less clear with amitriptyline, and while the majority of studies have reported a relationship between plasma level and response, not all studies are in agreement about the type of relationship. There are reports of linear and curvilinear relationships. However, there is a more consistent finding that high levels of the active metabolite nortriptyline are associated with poorer outcome (Cf. Montgomery, 1980).

The findings from investigations of imipramine show much less agreement than has been reached concerning the association of high levels of nortriptyline and poor response. There are three reports of an association between higher levels and better response (Glassman et al., 1977; Gram et al., 1976; Reisby et al., 1977). Later studies have, however, not confirmed these findings, and it seems that the association is very much open to question. The early studies used flexible dosages, confusing the relationship between level and response, and the exclusion of severely depressed psychotic patients from some of these studies would also have the unavoidable effect of biasing the sample. The later more rigorous studies which used a standard constant dose have not confirmed the finding of a relationship between a good response and high levels (Simpson et al., 1982; Montgomery et al., 1983). There is no rational basis for the practice of raising the dosage in the face of nonresponse, and it certainly cannot be justified without plasma level monitoring. There are in any case good reasons for avoiding high concentrations of TCAs since toxic effects, including cardiotoxicity of the TCAs, are related to plasma concentrations.

It does not appear possible to identify clinically the patients who are likely to achieve very high TCA levels. It might be thought that the appearance of side effects would be a guide to plasma levels but this is not reliable since patients vary considerably in their tolerance of unwanted effects. Correlations between plasma levels and side effects are therefore not consistently reported. The rational approach to the management of nonresponse to treatment with a standard dose of a TCA would include the monitoring of plasma levels to check if the patient has levels outside an optimum therapeutic range. Before considering changing the medication it would be appropriate to change the dose and bring the plasma levels within the recommended therapeutic range.

Side Effects and Noncompliance

TCAs have marked anticholinergic effects and these can be a real challenge to the patient's willingness to comply with tablet-taking. The side effects often prove unacceptable to patients, and closer investigation may lead to noncompliance as the source of nonresponse. It is estimated that as few as 30% of patients in outpatient practice may take the medication as prescribed. Where side effects are a major problem there is good reason for changing antidepressants. Selection of another TCA would be easier in such cases if they were not all associated with the well known anticholinergic side effects. Unfortunately there is not a great deal to choose from among the TCAs in this respect, although claims are made that the relative newcomer lofepramine has fewer side effects than the older compounds (Pugh et al., 1982). Treatment with one of the newer generation antidepressants, which are associated with fewer side effects than the TCAs, provides an alternative to the TCAs that is often more acceptable to patients.

Length of Treatment

Before changing medication in the face of nonresponse, consideration should be given to whether there has been an adequate trial of medication. Antidepressant effect is usually not seen before three weeks, and significant differences from placebo are not consistently found before four weeks. Patients may have suffered from their depressive symptoms for a considerable period before reaching a psychiatrist and, being unwilling to accept this delay, may prematurely reject medication as ineffective. An adequate dosage of an appropriate antidepressant for a sufficient period of time is required before accepting that a patient is a nonresponder.

CHOICE OF ALTERNATIVE ANTIDEPRESSANT

Given that all these prescriptions have been rigorously applied and patients do not respond, what then? Is there anything better than trial and error on which to base a choice of an alternative antidepressant? The clinical indicators for response to antidepressants can help in selecting patients appropriately for pharmacotherapy. The response of the individual patient, however, remains a matter of relative probabilities. There is little pharamacological basis for the selection of an antidepressant for a particular patient.

We do not know what causes depression, nor do we understand how the available antidepressants work. The TCAs were not developed as a result of theoretical expectation; their antidepressant efficacy was discovered by chance. The pharmacological actions of the TCAs on central neurotransmitters and their behavioral effects in depressed patients led to the hypothesis that monoamines play a role in the pathophysiology of depression. It was proposed that disturbances in the availability of noradrenaline (NA) (Schildkraut, 1965; Kety, 1962) or 5-hydroxytryptamine (5-HT) (Pare & Sandler, 1959) at the functionally relevant synapse are involved in the etiology of the affective disorders, and the therapeutic effect of the TCAs is mediated by their action in inhibiting reuptake of the amines, thereby increasing the amount of neurotransmitter in the synaptic cleft. This attractive and simple notion could supply the basis for rational treatment since compounds with appropriate pharmacological action could be prescribed for patients with specific amine deficits.

Two decades of research have not been able to establish a causal link between supposed central disturbance of monoamine metabolism and depressive illness, but there seems little doubt that the monoamines are involved in the therapeutic effects. If, as the therapeutic hypothesis suggests, the change in the depressed patient's mood is brought about by a stabilization of central monoamine levels, it follows that pretreatment monoamine profile should correlate with response to drug.

AMINE HYPOTHESES OF DEPRESSION AND RESPONSE

The original amine hypotheses were undoubtedly at best an oversimplification of a very complex biological process. They cannot account for many of the phenomena observed clinically in depression. The rapid time course of the pharmacological effects of antidepressants does not match the delay in clinical response. Not all compounds that have amine uptake inhibiting properties are antidepressants (Sugrue, 1983), nor do all the currently available antidepressants have uptake inhibiting effects.

The possibilities for testing the amine deficit hypotheses of depression in depressed patients include: (a) the measurement of monoamine transmitter function in relation to mood state; (b) the measurement of neurotransmission in relation to treatment; (c) testing for differential drug response; and (d) manipulation of amine turnover by the use of precursors or blockers of amine synthesis.

The major constraint on investigation is that there can be no direct measures of neurotransmission in man. Attempts have been made to estimate brain activity by measurement of amine metabolites at peripheral sites, for example the measurement in urine of 3-methoxy-4-hydroxy-phenyl glycol (MHPG), a major metabolite of noradrenaline originating in the brain. This is of course not a pure indicator of brain noradrenergic activity, as the levels in urine are affected also by peripheral noradrenaline metabolism. There is evidence that an interaction exists between central catecholamine system and the peripheral systems, but while they may function together, the power of a peripheral measure to indicate central activity is uncertain (Jimerson et al., 1981; Ziegler et al., 1980; Maas et al., 1982). The levels of 5-hydroxy indoleacetic acid (5HIAA), the main metabolite of serotonin, in the CSF have been taken as a measure of brain serotonin metabolism. While closer in registering brain activity than urinary measurements, these levels will still be affected by serotonin metabolism outside the brain. Postmortem brain examination might seem to offer direct measures of neurotransmission, and relative changes have been reported in the brains of suicides, (Shaw et al., 1967; Bourne et al., 1968). However, the results of such studies are very difficult to interpret because of the likelihood of postmortem changes in levels.

BIOCHEMICAL SUBGROUPS OF DEPRESSION

Noradrenaline

In general, clinical studies have not produced very strong evidence to explain the role that deficiency in amines might play in depression. If low noradrenergic activity plays a role in the etiology of depression, reduced amounts of the amine metabolites measured peripherally might be expected. Many of the early studies which examined these relationships were based on very small numbers of patients, and the results were often variable and inconsistent. Shaw et al. (1973) found that levels of MHPG in the CSF of depressed patients dropped with recovery; this is not consistent with the hypothesis that a deficiency is associated with depression.

One of the more consistent findings has been that urinary MHPG is lowered in depressed patients (review Schatzberg et al., 1982). Several studies have suggested that this phenomenon is more consistently and more noticeably observed in bipolar patients than in unipolar patients. The implication could be that this is a biochemical discrimination of a biologically distinct illness for which there is evidence from independent sources. Based on this measure, unipolar depressives would appear to be a biochemically heterogeneous group. The suggestion has been made (Schildkraut, 1978) that multivariate discriminant function analysis on urinary catecholamine metabolites could be used to identify patients who, in the absence of a history of manic episodes, are mistakenly classified as unipolar.

Many depressed patients do not produce lower levels of urinary MHPG, and groups of patients with low, normal, and high levels are seen. Schildkraut has suggested that three types of depression might be identified by low, intermediate, or high urinary MHPG levels, relating to a disturbance of noradrenaline synthesis, disturbance of a different monamine, or to alterations in noradrenergic receptors (Schildkraut et al., 1983). If such subgroups can be identified, the possibility of a differential response to different pharmacological intervention could be systematically investigated. As already suggested, a differential response does not necessarily further our knowledge of the pathogenesis of depressive illness, but it certainly carries the possibility of providing the means to improve response by appropriate selection of treatment.

Serotonin

The early TCAs were found to have effects on both NA and 5-HT, the tricyclic tertiary amines having a greater effect on 5-HT uptake and the secondary amines a greater action on NA. Following the clinical observation of a difference in profile of effect, it was thought possible that serotonin might be more specifically related to mood regulation than noradrenaline (Carlsson et al., 1969).

The results of studies of levels of 5HIAA in the CSF of depressed patients compared with controls have been inconsistent. Some investigators have reported lower levels, but differences from controls were often not statistically significant. Interindividual variation was frequently greater than the difference between derpessives and controls. However, it has been suggested that there may be a group of patients suffering from a serotonin depression characterized by a disturbance in serotonin metabolism rather than of noradrenaline metabolism. Early data from Asberg et al. (1976a) suggested a possible bimodal distribution of 5HIAA levels in CSF. This type of distribution was also present in the findings of van Praag (1977), who used the probenecid-induced accumulation of 5HIAA rather than baseline levels. It seemed possible that there might be a biochemical subgroup within the depressive spectrum characterized by a disturbance in serotonin metabolism. Later studies in larger numbers of patients have not confirmed the bimodality of the distribution of levels. However, this does not rule out the possibility that subgroups of depression might be identified by levels of 5HIAA in the CSF. There is in fact clinical evidence that the group of depressives in whom low levels of 5HIAA are seen may differ from other depressives in their clinical picture. There is a consistent finding from investigators in different countries that low levels of 5HIAA in CSF are associated with an increase in suicidal behavior. (Asberg et al., 1976b; Brown et al., 1979; Montgomery et al., 1981; Banki and Arato, 1983; van Praag, 1983). This behavioral characteristic appears to be associated with low levels of CSF 5HIAA irrespective of the presence of depression and may represent a vulnerability factor.

PRACTICAL CLINICAL RELEVANCE OF AMINE METABOLITE MEASURES

The existence of subgroups of depression characterized by deficits of different amines is only suggestive of a role for central amine disturbance in the etiology of depression. Possible subgroups are, however, very relevant for testing the therapeutic hypothesis that antidepressants achieve their effect by enhancing neurotransmitter function.

There are obvious methodological difficulties associated with the assessment of amine metabolite status. Peripheral levels of amine metabolites as an estimate of central monamine metabolism obtained by noninvasive techniques are difficult to interpret. They are subject also to wide interindividual variation, and also variation within individuals, according to time of day. The reported differences in levels between categories of patients are small, so much overlap is seen. CSF measures are impractical as a routine clinical procedure and are in any case also subject to variability, being affected by sex, height, age, exercise, site of spinal tap, etc. Nevertheless, if it could be shown that amine status was relevant for prediction of response, the methodological problems would doubtless be overcome.

The test of practical clinical relevance of lowered levels of amine metabolites is whether there is a differential response to antidepressants, which selectively affect particular amine pathways. Investigation of this possibility has been restricted by the inadequacy of existing antidepressants as pharmacological tools. The older TCAs have many different actions, making it difficult to relate therapeutic effect with particular pharmacological properties. The picture is further complicated by the presence in many cases of active metabolites, which often have different actions than the parent compound.

Nevertheless, there have been attempts to predict response to the older TCAs on the basis of initial status of MHPG in urine. The proposition was that patients with low levels of MHPG might be expected to respond better to an antidepressant which acted by blocking the reuptake of noradrenaline thereby increasing amounts of available neurotransmitter at the synapse. Most of the studies which report correlations between levels of urinary MHPG before treatment and response to a TCA have been carried out on rather small numbers of patients and in some studies no conclusions could be drawn because of the high variance in MHPG levels. A further methodological problem has been that the TCAs used were not selective in their action and had pharmacological effects on both NA and 5 HT. It is not surprising that the results of the earlier studies have not been consistent. Some studies have found that lower levels of urinary MHPG are associated with a better response to imipramine, but others have produced equivocal or contradictory results. Nevertheless, a number of studies have now reported that patients with low levels of urinary MHPG respond more favorably to nortriptyline (Hollister et al., 1980), imipramine (Maas et al., 1972; Beckman and Goodwin, 1975), and to maprotiline (Rosenbaum et al., 1980; Schatzberg et al., 1981). The finding that patients with high levels of MHPG respond better to another antidepressant such as amitriptyline are, however, much more equivocal (Coppen et al., 1979a; Spiker et al., 1980).

SELECTIVE AMINE UPTAKE INHIBITORS AND RESPONSE

The current trend in the development of antidepressants has been to identify pharmacologically active molecules which are selective in their action and which are specific for a single amine pathway. This has led to the development of a series of antidepressants with selective 5 HT-uptake-inhibiting activity. The possibility that as a class such compounds would be more effective does not appear to be fulfilled. Only one, zimelidine, has reached general use and this was subsequently withdrawn, so their place in clinical usage is not yet established. However, the results of the clinical studies do not promise that these compounds will have greater overall antidepressant efficacy than those already available. They appear to be of the same order of antidepressant efficacy as the TCAs with which they have been compared (Montgomery et al., 1981; Coppen et al., 1979b).

The development of relatively more specific antidepressants has, however, made it possible to test directly whether biochemically identified subgroups of depressed patients respond differentially to antidepressants with different pharmacological actions.

The advent of zimelidine, the first available 5 HT uptake inhibitor, made such comparisons possible, and it has been compared with the noradrenaline uptake inhibitors maprotiline and desipramine. As might be expected from the different pharmacological activity of the drugs, there is some evidence of clinical differences in profiles of actions (Montgomery et al., 1981). The relative disadvantage of the 5 HT uptake inhibitors with regard to reduced sleep and reduced appetite have, for example, been quite consistently reported (Montgomery et al., 1981; d'Elia et al., 1981). A less expected finding was the apparent advantage in affecting the anxiety component of depression reported for zimelidine (Montgomery et al., 1981; Montgomery, 1983; d'Elia et al., 1981). It appears fairly consistently to have a more rapid effect on anxiety than the comparator antidepressants.

In spite of these differences in profile of action, the evidence for a differential clinical effect in biochemically different subgroups of depression is weak. The approach adopted to test the proposition has been to measure amine metabolites in the CSF of depressed patients prior to antidepressant treatment. Patients have then been randomly allocated double-blind to treatment with different selectively acting amine reuptake inhibitors and their subsequent responses investigated in relation to the amine metabolite profile.

In the large study reported by Montgomery (1981), levels of MHPG, 5HIAA, and HVA were measured in the CSF of depressed patients. This study could detect no correlation between levels of 5HIAA in the CSF and response to a 5 HT uptake inhibitor. Neither was there any correlation between pretreatment levels of MHPG in the CSF and response to treatment with maprotiline, the noradrenaline uptake inhibitor.

A claim for differential response was made by Aberg-Wistedt (1982), who compared zimelidine with desipramine. This study reported that patients who had very low levels of 5HIAA in CSF before treatment responded significantly better to the 5 HT uptake inhibitor than the patients with higher levels. This finding is, however, based on only 3 patients who had very low 5HIAA levels. Conclusions drawn from such a small number of patients must be treated with more than a modicum of caution.

It is of course possible that the compounds studied in these investigations were not sufficiently specific to be able to demonstrate a differential effect. Desipramine, for example, affected 5 HT uptake as well as noradrenaline, and norzimelidine, an active metabolite of zimelidine, has some noradrenaline uptake inhibiting properties. It is, however, considered to be more likely that the pharmacological specificity does not have clinical relevance for response. Any specificity of action appears to be overwhelmed by a general antidepressant effect (Montgomery, 1981).

It is known that there are functional connections between the noradrenaline and serotonin systems, and it is very unlikely that an adjustment in one pathway can be made without consequent effects on the other. Support for this concept is provided by recent pharmacological research findings. The focus of investigation has tended to move away from the simple notion that increasing the available neurotransmitter at the synapse is directly related to antidepressant effect. More attention has been paid to the role of alterations in pre and postsynaptic receptor function. Reduction in the density of beta adrenoceptors, which is seen with imipramine-like antidepressants, is thought to be the mechanism mediating their antidepressant effect. Recent findings have shown that both noradrenergic and serotonergic neuronal input are required to bring about this reduction in density of beta adrenoceptors (Sulser, 1984) This is in accord with the early clinical observation of Friedman et al. (1974), who found that patients who had responded to imipramine deteriorated when synthesis of 5 HT was blocked. It appears that the 5 HT system must be intact for response, and that both the NA and 5 HT systems contribute to mediating the antidepressant effect.

PROFILES OF ACTION AND IMPROVING RESPONSE

The inability to produce a clear differential response is disappointing for clinicians who had hoped the selective compounds might provide the means to tailor treatment more closely for particular patients. However, the different profiles of action of specific NA and 5 HT uptake inhibitors may mark some progress in treatment. If it is possible to affect one amine pathway by pharmacological intervention on another, the likely profile of clinical effect can influence the choice of treatment for a particular patient rather than any postulated mode of action of antidepressant effect. If, for example, the finding of earlier effect on the anxiety element of depression is sustained with other 5 HT uptake inhibitors, this class of compound might be used more appropriately for patients where anxiety is more prominent. Similarly, the choice might be made by the need to avoid particular side effects. The side effects of the TCAs are a frequent cause of noncompliance with treatment and consequent nonresponse. Patients are often unable to tolerate the drowsiness which amitriptyline, for example, can cause during the day. Where a patient is not complying with treatment with a TCA for this reason, and is consequently not responding, the medication might be changed with advantage to a 5 HT uptake inhibitor, which is less likely to be sedating. The importance of a particular side effect will depend on the patient, but there are other possibilities such as avoiding the weight gain associated with some TCAs by using a selective 5 HT uptake inhibitor.

CONCLUSIONS

In spite of the introduction of new antidepressants with selective amine uptake inhibiting properties, the overall antidepressant response has not been improved. Nor do we have a very much clearer idea of how antidepressants achieve their effect. Major encouragement for a rational basis for the selection of an antidepressant would be provided if subgroups of depression characterized by biochemical measures had a differential response to specific antidepressants. There is very little evidence that patients with low amine metabolite levels may respond better to some antidepressants than patients with high levels. The studies to date which have compared pharmacologically specific antidepressants indicate that any differñpial effect of selectively acting compounds is overwhelmed in a general antidepressant effect.

Improving response to antidepressants must therefore still be based primarily on selecting the patients who best fit the general clinical picture associated with response. The development of new antidepressants has broadened the range of choice of pharmacotherapy, and differences in pharmacological action provide the basis for some tailoring of treatment to avoid particular side effects. They are a clear advance on the TCAs, which differ little from each other in being associated with marked anticholinergic side effects.

Where a patient fails to respond, adequate consideration of the current medication must be given before any change of antidepressant is justified. An antidepressant must have been given a long enough trial at an adequate dose and with confidence in the patient's compliance before judgment of its efficacy is made. With some TCAs there is a relationship between drug plasma levels and response, and there may therefore be a sound pharmacokinetic basis for changing the dose of a particular TCA rather than changing the TCA itself. Monitoring plasma levels and adjusting dosage to bring plasma levels within therapeutic range may improve response.

Where an antidepressant has been given an adequate trial for sufficient length of time, and where pharmacokinetic factors are not responsible for nonresponse, a change of antidepressant is appropriate. There is, however, no sound pharmacological basis for making the change from one to another. The selective pharmacological action of the new antidepressants does not appear to have clinical relevance in changing overall antidepressant response, and a change from one to another in the face of nonresponse is based on the clinical imperative rather than scientific knowledge. There is even less pharmacological reason for changing from one TCA to another, since they generally have mixed effects on both NA and 5 HT. Since we do not understand the mechanism by which antidepressants achieve their antidepressant effect, and there is no sound pharmacological basis for changing medication, the choice of an alternative antidepressant is made clinically and on the basis of trial and error.

It has, however, to be accepted that depression is a periodic illness with a certain spontaneous remission rate. It is therefore quite easy to attribute the eventual response of a refractory depressed patient mistakenly to the pharmacotherapy that happens to have been used at the time when response was observed.

REFERENCES

Aberg-Wistedt, A. A double-blind study of zimelidine, a serotonin uptake inhibitor, and desipramine, a noradrenaline uptake inhibitor, in endogenous depression. I. Clinical findings. *Acta Psychiat. Scand. 66;* 50-65 (1982).

Asberg, M., Traskman, L., Thoren, P., Bertilsson, L., and Ringberger, V.A. Serotonin depression: A biochemical subgroup within the affective disorders? *Science 191;* 478-480 (1976) (a).

Asberg M., Traskman L., and Thoren P. 5HIAA in the cerebrospinal fluid—A biochemical suicide predictor? *Arch. Gen. Psychiat. 33*; 1193-1197 (1976) (b).

Banki, C.M. and Arato, M. Relationships between cerobrospinal fluid amine metabolites, neuroendocrine findings and personality dimensions (Marke Nyman scale factors) in psychiatric patients. *Acta Psychiat. Scan. 67;* 272-280 (1983).

Beckmann, H., and Goodwin, F.K. Antidepressant response to tricyclics and urinary MHPG in unipolar patients. Clinical response to imipramine or amitriptyline. *Arch. Gen. Psychiat. 32;* 17-21 (1975).

Bielski, R.J., and Friedel, R.O. Prediction of tricyclic antidepressant response. *Arch. Gen. Psychiat. 33;* 1479-1489 (1976).

Bourne, H.R., Bunney, W.E., Colburn, R.W. Davis, J.M., Shaw, D.M., and Coppen, A.J. Noradrenaline, 5 hydroxytriptamine and 5 hydroxyindoleacetic acid in hindbrains of suicide patients. *Lancet 2.;* 805-808 (1968).

Brown, L.G., Goodwin, F.K., Ballenger, J.C., Goyer, P.F. and Major, L.F. Aggression in humans, correlates with cerebrospinal fluid amine metabolites. *Psychiat. Res. 1;* 131-139 (1979).

Carlsson, A., Fuxe, K., and Hokfelt, T. Effect of antidepressant drugs on the depletion of intraneuronal brain 5 hydroxytryptamine stores caused by 4 methyl-a-ethyl-meta-tyramine. *Eur. J. Pharmacol.* 5; 357-366 (1969).

Carney, M.W.P., Roth, M., and Garside, R.F. The diagnosis of depressive syndromes and the prediction of ECT response. *Brit. J. Psychiat. 111;* 659-674 (1965).

Cobbin, D.M., Requin-Blow, B., Williams, L.R., and Williams, W.O. Urinary MHPG levels and tricyclic antidepressant drug selection. A preliminary communication on improved drug selection in clinical practice. *Arch. Gen. Psychiat. 36;* 1111-1115 (1979).

Coppen, A., Rama Rao, V.A., Ruthven, C.R., Goodwin, B.L., and Sandler, M. Urinary 4-hydroxy-3-methoxyphenylglycol is not a predictor for clinical response to amitriptyline in depressive illness. *Psychopharmacology (Berlin) 64;* 95-97 (1979) (a).

Coppen, A. Rama Rao, V.A., Swade, C., and Wood, K. Zimelidine: a therapeutic and pharmacokinetic study in depression. *Psychopharmacology 63;* 199-202 (1979) (b).

Derogatis, L.R., Lipman, R.S., Covi, and L. Rickels, K. Factorial invariance of symptom dimensions in anxious and depressive neuroses. *Arch. Gen. Psychiat. 27;* 659-665 (1972).

d'Elia, G., Hallstrom, T., Nystrom, C., and Ottosson, J.–O. Zimelisine vs maprotiline in depressed outpatients. A preliminary report. *Acta Psychiat. Scan. 63;* (Suppl. 290).

Friedman, E., Shopsin, B., and Goldstein, H. Interactions of imipramine and synthesis inhibitors on biogenic amines. *J. Pharm. Pharmacol. 26;* 995-997 (1974).

Glassman, S.H., Perel, J.M., Shostak, M., Kantor, S.J., and Fleiss, J.L. Clinical implication of imipramine plasma levels for depressive illness. *Arch. Gen. Psychiat. 34;* 197-204 (1977).

Gram, L.F., Reisby, N., Ibsen, I., Nagy, A., Dencker, S.J., Bech, P., Petersen, G.O., and Christiansen, J.C. Plasma levels and antidepressant effect of imipramine. *Clin. Pharmacol. Therapeut. 19;* 318-324 (1976).

Gurney, C., Roth, M., Garside, R.F., Kerr, T.A., and Schapira, K. Studies in the classification of affective disorders: The relationship between anxiety states and depressive illnesses II *Brit. J. Psychiat. 121;* 162-166 (1972).

Hollister, L.E., Davis, K.L., and Berger, P.A. Subtypes of depression based on excretion of MHPG and response to nortriptyline. *Arch. Gen. Psychiat. 37;* 1107-1110 (1980).

Jimerson, D.C., Ballenger, J.C., Lake, C.R., Post, R.M., Goodwin, F.K., and Kopin, I.J. Plasma and CSF MHPG in normals *Psychopharmacology Bull. 17;* 86-87 (1981).

Kerr, T.A., Roth, M., and Schapira, K. Prediction of outcome in anxiety states and depressive illnesses. *Brit. J. Psychiat. 124;* 125-133 (1974).

Kety, S.S. Amino acids, amines and behavior. In *Ultrastructure and Metabolism of the Nervous System*. S.R. Korey. A. Pope, and E. Rodins, eds. Williams & Wilkins Co., Baltimore, pp. 311-324 (1962).

Kiloh, L.G., and Garside, R.F. The independence of neurotic depression and endogenous depression. *Brit. J. Psychiat. 109;* 451-463 (1963).

Kragh-Sorensen, P., Eggert-Hansen, C., Baastrup, P.C., and Hvidberg, E.V. Self inhibiting action of nortriptyline's antidepressant effect at high plasma levels. *Psychopharmacologia 45;* 305-316 (1976).

Maas, J.W., Fawcett, J.A., and Dekirmenjian, H. Catecholamine metabolism, depressive illness, and drug response. *Arch. of Gen. Psychiat. 26;* 252-262 (1972).

Maas, J.W., Davis, J. Hanin, I., Kocsis, J.H., Redmond, D.E., Bowden, C., and Robins, E. Pretreatment neurotransmitter metabolites in response to imipramine and amitriptyline treatment. *Psychol. Med. 12;* 37-43 (1982).

Montgomery S.A. Measurement of serum drug levels in the assessment of antidepressants. *Brit. J. Clin. Pharmacol. 10;* 411-416 (1980).

Montgomery, S.A. The nonselective effect of selective antidepressants. In *Typical and Atypical Antidepressants*. E. Costa and G. Racagni, eds. Raven Press, NY, pp. 49-56 (1981).

Montgomery, S.A. Anxiety as part of depression. *Acta Psychiat. Scand. 687*; Suppl. 308, 171-174 (1983).

Montgomery, S.A., and Asberg, M. A new depression scale designed to be sensitive to change. *Brit. J. Psychiat. 134*; 382-389 (1979).

Montgomery, S.A., and Montgomery, D.B. Pharmacological prevention of suicidal behaviour. *J. Affect. Disord. 4*; 291-298 (1982).

Montgomery, S.A., Braithwaite, R. Dawling, S., and McAuley R. High plasma nortriptyline levels in the treatment of depression. *Clin. Pharmacol. Therapeut. 32*; 309-314 (1978).

Montgomery, S.A., McAuley, R., Rani, S.J., Roy, D., and Montgomery, D.B. A double blind comparison of zimelidine and amitriptyline in endogenous depression. *Acta Psychiat. Scand. 63*; Suppl. 290, 314-327 (1981).

Montgomery, S.A., Roy, D., Wynne-Willson, S., Robinson, C., and Montgomery, D.B. Plasma levels and clinical response with imipramine in a study comparing efficacy with mianserin and nomifensine. *Brit. J. Clin. Pharmacol. 15*; 205S-211S (1983).

Mountjoy, C.Q., and Roth, M. Studies in the relationship between depressive disorders and anxiety states. *J. Affect. Disord. 4*; 149-161 (1982).

Nelson, J.C., and Charney, D.S. The symptoms of major depressive. *Amer. J. Psychiat. 138*; 1-12 (1981).

Pare, C.M.B., and Sandler, M. A clinical and biochemical study of a trial of iproniazid in the treatment of depression. *J. Neurol. Neurosurg. Psychiat. 22*; 247-251 (1959).

Pugh, R., Bell, J., Cooper, A.J., Dunstan, S., Greedharry, D., Pomeroy, J., Raptopoulos, P., Rowsell, C., Steinert, J., and Priest, R.G. Does lofepramine have fewer side effects than amitriptyline? *J. Affect. Disord. 4*; 355-363 (1982).

Reisby, N., Gram, L.F., Beck, P., Nagy, A., Petersen, G.O. Ottman, J., Obsen, I., Dencker, S.J., Jacobsen, O., Krautwald, O., Sondergaards, I., and Christiansen I. Imipramine: Clinical effects and pharmacokinetic variables. *Psychopharmacology 54*; 263-272 (1977).

Rosenbaum, A.H., Schatzberg, A.F., Maruta, T., Orsulak, P.J., Cole, J.O., Grab, E.L., and Schildkraut, J.J. MHPG as a predictor of antidepressant response to imipramine and maprotiline. *Amer. J. Psychiat. 137*; 1090-1092 (1980).

Roth, M., Gurney, C., Garside, R.F., and Kerr, T.A. Studies in the classification of affective disorders: The relationship between anxiety states and depressive illnesses. II. *Brit. J. Psychiat. 127*; 147-161 (1972).

Schatzberg, A.F., Rosenbaum, A.H., and Orsulak, P.J. Toward a biochemical classification of depressive disorders. III. Pretreatment urinary MHPG levels as predictors of response to treatment with maprotiline. *Psychopharmacology 75*; 34-38 (1981).

Schatzberg, A.F., Rosenbaum, A.H., and Orsulak, P.J. Towards a biochemical classification of depressive disorders. Heterogeneity of unipolar depression. *Amer. J. Psychiat. 139*; 471-475 (1982).

Schatzberg, A.F., Cole, J.O., Cohen, B.M., and Altesman, R.I. Survey of depressed patients who have failed to respond to treatment. In *The Affective Disorders*. J.M. Davis and J.W. Maas, eds. American Psychiatric Press, pp. 73-86 (1983).

Schildkraut, J.J. (1965) The catecholamine hypothesis of affective disorders: a review supporting the evidence. *Amer. J. Psychiat. 122*; 509-522 (1965).

Schildkraut, J.J. Toward a biochemical classification of depressive disorders. II. Application of multivariate discriminant function analysis to data on urinary catecholamines and metabolites. *Arch. Gen. Psychiat. 35*; 1436-1439 (1978).

Schildkraut, J.J., Schatzberg, A.F., Orsulak, P., Mooney, J. Rosenbaum, A.H., and Gudeman J.E. Biological discrimination of subtypes of depression. In *The Affective Disorders*. J.M. Davis and J.W. Maas, eds. American Psychiatric Press (1983).

Shaw, D.M., Camps, E.E., and Eccleston, E.G. 5 hydroxy triptamine in the hindbrains of suicide patients. *Lancet ii*: 801-808 (1967).

Shaw, D.M., O'Keefe, R.O., MacSweeney, D.A., Brooksbank, W.L., Noguera, R. and Coppen, A. 3 methoxy-4-hydroxy phenolglycol in depression. *Psychol. Med. 3*; 333-336 (1973).

Simpson, G.M., White, K.I., Boyd, J.L., Cooper, T.B., Halaris, G., Wilson, I.C., Raman, E.J., and Ruther, E. Relationship between plasma antidepressant levels and clinical outcome for inpatients receiving imipramine. *Amer. J. Psychiat. 139*; 358-360 (1982).

Spiker, D.G., Edwards, D., Hanin, I., Neil, J.F., and Kupfer, D.J. Urinary MHPG and clinical response to amitriptyline in depressed patients. *Amer. J. Psychiat. 137*; 1183-1187 (1980).

Sugrue, M.F. Chronic antidepressant therapy and associated changes in central monoaminergic functioning. *Pharmacol. Ther. 21*; 1-33 (1983).

Sulser, F. Antidepressant treatments and regulations of norepinephrine receptor coupled adenylate cyclase systems in brain. In *Frontiers in Biochemical and Pharmacological Research in Depression*. E. Usdin, ed. Raven Press, NY, pp. 249-262 (1984).

van Praag, H.M. New evidence of serotonin deficient depressions. *Neuropsychobiology 3*; 56-63 (1977).

van Praag, H.M. Depression, suicide and serotonin metabolism. In *Neurobiology of Manic Depressive Illness*. R.M. Post and J.C. Ballenger, eds. Williams & Wilkens, Baltimore (1983).

Ziegler, M. Lake, C. Wood, J. and Brooks, B. Relationships between cerebrospinal fluid and norepinephrine and blood pressure in neurological patients. *Clin. Exper. Hypertension* 2; 995-1008 (1980).

6

The Place of Monoamine Oxidase Inhibitors in the Treatment of Resistant Depression

Charles Shawcross and Peter Tyrer

Monoamine oxidase inhibitors "should only be used in cases of resistant depressions after failure to respond to other antidepressants" (Hollister, 1973); "are drugs of narrow therapeutic utility, have not emerged as drugs of choice in the treatment of any type of depressive illness" (Simpson, 1974); "are used only under special circumstances: the history of responsiveness to MAOIs, when unresponsive to tricyclics, and exceptionally in combination with tricyclics" (Kingstone, 1980).

These quotations, taken at random from authoritative publications, suggest that this chapter should be devoted entirely to an extensive literature on monoamine oxidase inhibitors (MAOIs) and resistant depression. Indeed, they give the impression that MAOIs should only be regarded as therapy for this relatively small group of disorders. In our view these notions misrepresent completely the place of MAOIs in clinical psychiatry, and in discussing the reasons for rejecting them it is necessary to look beyond the therapeutic spectrum of depression to anxiety, phobic and other common symptoms and syndromes that often coexist with depression.

MAOIs are classed as antidepressants and so it is not surprising that many clinicians consider them only in this light. Unfortunately from the point of view of drug classification, MAOIs had the misfortune to be the first group of drugs to be specifically tested as antidepressants. This happened in the late 1950s, when the diagnosis of depression was still impressionistic and the methodology of drug trials of psychotropic drugs was still in its infancy. It was the age of enthusiasm, in which every positive finding was heralded as a major breakthrough and interpretation of data was often fanciful and speculative.

It was in this setting that many of the fixed ideas about the proper use of MAOIs developed, even though the results of clinical studies gave contradictory results that could in no way be regarded as conclusive. With hindsight it is now possible to see why errors of interpretation developed, but in order to understand these it is necessary to retrace the history of clinical studies with MAOIs.

The psychotropic effect of iproniazid was observed initially as an unwanted side effect during the search for a more effective antituberculous agent (Bosworth, 1959). In early clinical trials of iproniazid in pulmonary tuberculosis, using doses of 300 mg daily, increased appetite associated with large gains in weight were noticed, accompanied in a proportion of patients by mood changes that sometimes developed into frank psychosis. The changes were reversible on stopping the drug (Bloch et al., 1954; Dally, 1958). The closely related hydrazine drug, isoniazid, subsequently became established as a highly effective antituberculous drug and iproniazid was no longer used to treat the condition.

In 1957, following investigations in the United States (Crane, 1957; Loomer, Saunders and Kline, 1957; Kline, 1958), iproniazid was introduced into psychiatry for the treatment of depressed patients. During a symposium held in New York later that year, it was concluded that iproniazid was of value in the treatment of depressive illness and claims were made that as many as 75% of patients improved as much as or better than on E.C.T. for this disorder (Kline, 1958). At this time many psychiatrists viewed iproniazid as an alternative to E.C.T., but it must be remembered that no other antidepressant drug was then available. Loomer and his colleagues (1957) concluded after their study that the drug acted by improving energy and initiative and so they used the descriptive term "psychic energizer." They also suggested that the therapeutic benefit of iproniazid was due to inhibition of monoamine oxidase. It has previously been shown (Zeller et al., 1952) that iproniazid, but not isoniazid, was capable of inhibiting this enzyme.

Following the 1957 symposium, Dally carried out two studies (Dally, 1958; West and Dally, 1959) in the United Kingdom, on the value of iproniazid in depression. Although these studies were by today's standards methodologically poor, they were carefully conducted and came to conclusions that were subsequently shown to be accurate. Unfortunately, these were eclipsed during the next 15 years and have only been accepted recently. Both found that iproniazid was of particular value in treating a group of "atypical" depressive illnesses. Analysis of symptoms of patients who responded, compared with those who did not respond, showed significant differences for the following clinical characteristics: less self-reproach, depressed mood which is better in the morning and worse in the evening, absence of early morning waking, presence of phobias, presence of hysterical conversion symptoms, presence of tremor, and personality disorder. The authors stated that these patients were often dismissed as being "inadequate" and that their symptoms may have been present for many years. On closer analysis, however, they felt that most had good premorbid personalities before their illness started. Patients with lifelong "inadequate" personalities, who often presented with similar symptoms of depression, did not respond well. It was also found that iproniazid was less effective in typical "endogenous depressive illnesses."

By 1959, the efficacy of iproniazid as an antidepressant was more or less accepted and there were useful indications of the kind of patients and symptom profile that responded better to this form of treatment. Soon afterwards, however, there followed a period of increasing disillusionment with MAOIs. Following some reports of fatal hepatitis caused by administration of iproniazid, Dally and Rohde (1961) compared iproniazid with newer monoamine oxidase inhibitors and imipramine. Similar therapeutic potential of the MAOIs was found as in their earlier studies, but the newer antidepressants were less effective than iproniazid, and nialamide was the least effective. The study also suggested that imipramine was more effective in patients with "endogenous" depression. Shortly after this paper, Dally appeared to change his mind over the meaning of the anxiety symptoms; whereas in 1961 he wrote "in some patients the phobic and anxiety symptoms predominated and sometimes obscured the underlying depression," in a later paper written with William Sargant (Sargant and Dally, 1962) more stress was made on the efficacy of monoamine oxidase inhibitors on anxiety even in the absence of underlying depression. Sargant was perhaps instrumental in making this important change of emphasis, which derived almost entirely from his clinical experience (Sargant and Slater, 1962).

The early studies that showed MAOIs to be effective in treating depression were methodologically poor in that few used double-blind procedure, the diagnosis of depression was unclear, and assessments were often crude. They were followed in the 1960s by other studies that were superior in design but that gave largely negative results. Harris and Robin (1960) investigated the efficacy of phenelzine in the treatment of depression. They found no benefit, but their patients were severely depressed inpatients, and the drugs were only given for two weeks. Hare et al. (1962) compared the antidepressant effects of lactose, dexamphetamine, and phenelzine. Again no difference in antidepressant effect was found, but it was noted that phenelzine was marginally better in treating anxiety and agitation. Again it should be noted that inpatients were used and that phenelzine, although prescribed as an appropriate dose, was only given for two weeks. A large study carried out by Greenblatt and his colleagues (1964) compared imipramine, phenelzine, isocarboxazid, placebo, and E.C.T. in hospitalized depressed inpatients. E.C.T. was the best treatment, followed by imipramine, and phenelzine was not significantly different from placebo. In 1965 the results of a multi center trial carried out by the Medical Research Council in the United Kingdom almost administered the coup de grace to MAOIs in clinical psychiatry. Phenelzine, placebo, E.C.T., and imipramine were compared in depressed inpatients. Treatment was given for four weeks and phenelzine was no better than placebo. Again it should be noted that in this study the treatment was given almost exclusively to patients with severe endogenous depression, and possibly some patients had other psychotic disorders with depressive symptomatology. Although the dosage of phenelzine given was probably adequate (60 mg a day), this was only given for four weeks. Subsequent studies have shown that many of these early trials were using an inadequate dose of drug or too short a period of treatment, and so in retrospect these negative results were predictable (Tyrer, 1976).

Thus, early encouraging studies were followed by a series of largely negative findings because of differences in dosage, selection of patients, and duration of treatment.

A further issue that dominated clinical thinking at this time was that of safety. In 1963 Blackwell first demonstrated that MAOIs could interact with certain foods with potentially fatal results. The importance of tyramine in this interaction was subsequently elucidated (Blackwell et al., 1967). As there were continuing reports of liver toxicity (Pare, 1964) and other drug interactions (Sjöqvist, 1965), it was not surprising that MAOIs fell into disfavor. Most clinicians seemed never to be aware that the negative studies had looked at subpopulations of depressed patients for whom MAOIs had never been recommended.

Sporadic reports continued to be published by the champions of MAOIs, particularly Kline in the United States and Sargant in England, attesting to the efficacy of these drugs in patients clinically more similar to the population originally described as being helped by MAOIs. Kline (1967) published three case reports of a favorable response to a combination of MAOIs and neuroleptic drugs given for 4-6 months in the treatment of phobic disorders. In 1969 Roth amd Myers stated that MAOIs may be of use in the treatment of depression accompanying an anxiety state or even in an anxiety state in the absence of depression, although no evidence was given to support this view. But in 1970, Kelly and his colleagues published a retrospective study on the treatment of phobic states with antidepressants. This suggested that MAOIs, alone or in combination with chlordiazepoxide or a tricyclic antidepressant, led to a significant clinical improvement in patients who had phobias as their main symptoms. MAOIs were also of use in treating panic attacks. Pollitt and Young (1971) attempted to resolve the conflict between clinical response in anxiety states and depression. They found that depressive symptoms change with increasing age and that anxiety symptoms are more prominent in younger patients. They speculated that anxiety states responsive to MAOIs are a form of depression. By this time it was becoming clear that MAOIs were effective agents in the treatment of phobic disorders whether or not depression was present as an accompanying symptom (Tyrer, Candy and Kelly, 1973). An important series of studies by Robinson, Ravaris and their colleagues in the United States was carried out between 1973 and 1980 in a population of depressed patients with significant anxiety. These patients were somewhat similar to the original group described by West and Dally (1959) and showed some characteristics of "anxious depressions" identified in a cluster analysis of depressed patients (Paykel, 1971). In their first study (Robinson et al., 1973), patients received either a placebo or phenelzine after withdrawal of previous medication. They took phenelzine in a dosage to 45-75 mg daily for six weeks. Phenelzine was found to be superior to placebo for the symptoms of depression (total), anxiety (total), somatic anxiety, hypochondriasis, agitation, and psychomotor change. In their later study (Ravaris et al., 1976), two dosages of phenelzine were compared, 30 mg and 60 mg daily. Those given 60 mg a day showed a superior response, while those on 30 mg daily fared no better than those on placebo. A later study by Tyrer et al. (1980), showed a similar superiority of a high dosage of phenelzine (90 mg daily) over lower dosages (45 mg) in a mixed group of patients with anxiety, depressive, and phobic neuroses. No significant differences in improvement were found between any of the diagnostic groups.

These studies showed convincingly that phenelzine was significantly superior to placebo in treating mixed anxiety and depressive disorders if it was given in adequate dosage. It was now time to look again at the efficacy of MAOIs compared with tricyclic antidepressants in this type of depressed patient. One study (Kay et al., 1973) had shown amitriptyline to be marginally superior to phenelzine in depressed outpatients, but again the period of treatment was too short and the dosage on the low side. In a study by Ravaris and his colleagues (1980), the patients chosen had an admixture of anxiety and depression. Altogether 160 patients took part and were treated with phenelzine (60 mg daily) or amitriptyline (150 mg daily) for six weeks. There were no significant differences between amitriptyline and phenelzine for the major symptoms of depression, anxiety, hypochondriasis, and psychomotor change. However, although in general the two drugs showed similar improvement, there were certain therapeutic differences of possible clinical importance. Phenelzine was superior to amitriptyline on some measures of anxiety, and the authors concluded that phenelzine had a strong antianxiety as well as antidepressant action. Ravaris and his colleagues went further and suggested that the antianxiety effects of phenelzine may well be central to antiphobic action. It is important to stress that the antianxiety effect of phenelzine was being shown in patients suffering from mixed anxiety-depressive disorders. The only controlled study of a MAOI and placebo in pure anxiety states (Mountjoy et al., 1977) showed very little difference between phenelzine and placebo, but the only significant difference actually favored placebo. Paykel and his colleagues (1982), in a large-scale study using fairly strict criteria, compared the efficacy of amitriptyline and phenelzine in patients defined as having neurotic depression. They were treated for six weeks with phenelzine up to 75 mg daily, amitriptyline up to 187 mg daily, or placebo in a double-blind controlled trial. Severe depression was excluded and phobic and anxious patients with secondary depression were also excluded. After four weeks, amitriptyline showed the greater superiority, but by six weeks both amitriptyline and phenelzine were significantly superior to placebo. There was little difference in efficacy between phenelzine and amitriptyline, but there was a tendency for patients with additional anxiety to improve more on phenelzine.

These studies were all primarily concerned with clinical syndromes; other factors influencing clinical response were not evaluated. One important factor, mentioned originally by Sargant and later by West and Dally, was to study the personality of patients suffering from depression and to see if this affected response to MAOIs. Sargant and Slater (1962) stated that patients who responded well to MAOIs had a good premorbid personality in that they tended to be "conscientious, rather sensitive, highly strung people with a lot of energy and drive." Kay et al. (1973) found that a high neurotic (N) score on the Eysenck Personality Inventory (EPI) was unfavorable only in patients treated with phenelzine. Tyrer et al. (1983) found that in a clinical trial of the efficacy of two dosage regimes of phenelzine in 60 patients, the presence of personality disorder significantly impaired clinical outcome. Similarly, in comparing response to phenelzine and amitriptyline (Paykel et al., 1982) there was some evidence that patients with "characterological depression" responded better to amitriptyline. These studies all suggest patients with abnormal personalities who become depressed are more likely to respond to a tricyclic antidepressant than to a MAOI.

DIFFERENCES AMONG MONOAMINE OXIDASE INHIBITORS

Although one early study suggested that there were some differences in the efficacy of different MAOIs (Bates and Douglas, 1961), a tendency developed to regard the class of drugs as though they were a single agent. Retrospective assessment of published studies, however, shows that iproniazid is probably the most effective MAOI, followed by tranylcypromine, phenelzine, and isocarboxazid. This is only based on indirect evidence, as no satisfactory study comparing all these compounds has yet been published. It is unfortunate, and a common occurrence in psychopharmacology, that the most effective drugs are also the most toxic. This is true of the MAOIs, with isocarboxazid the safest compound and iproniazid the most dangerous (Tyrer, 1982). It is perhaps therefore predictable that the compound in the middle of the therapeutic and toxic range, phenelzine, is preferred in many quarters. Most recent clinical trials have been carried out with phenelzine, and there is a tendency to generalize from these results to other MAOIs. This may not be appropriate, particularly with tranylcypromine.

Tranylcypromine is the only monoamine oxidase inhibitor in clinical use that is not a hydrazine. It is therefore not metabolized by acetylation and, unlike all other MAOIs in clinical use, is not a suicide inhibitor (Singer and Salach, 1981). Although there are no definite clinical correlates of these pharmacological properites, there are some indications that tranylcypromine differs in several ways from hydrazine MAOIs. Its speed of action is more rapid, clinical response occurring within three weeks of starting treatment and often long before. Hydrazine MAOIs take up to six weeks before full clinical response is shown. There are also some indications that tranylcypromine possesses greater energizing properties. Its clinical configuration is like that of the amphetamines and there has long been concern that it might carry some of the disadvantages of these compounds. Cases of true pharmacological dependence on tranylcypromine have been described (Ben-Arie and George, 1979), but there is no published comparison of dependence risk with tranylcypromine and hydrazine MAOIs. Phenelzine is associated with a greater risk of relapse after withdrawal than tricyclic antidepressants (Tyrer, 1984), suggesting that pharmacological dependence may be a risk of regular treatment with hydrazine MAOIs.

Possibly because of its alleged amphetaminelike actions, tranylcypromine has been used more frequently in the treatment of severe depression than other MAOIs. It is important to realize that almost all the studies showing MAOIs to be inferior to other antidepressants were carried out with phenelzine and the results may not apply to tranylcypromine. In a suggested program of treatment for resistant depression by a recognized authority (Shaw, 1977) tranylcypromine is given an important place. However, there is no real evidence that the drug has greater antidepressant effects; a recent study (White et al., 1982) showed tranylcypromine to be similar to phenelzine in that it has equivalent efficacy to amitriptyline in the treatment of depression, but with some superiority for anxiety symptoms.

MONOAMINE OXIDASE INHIBITORS COMBINED WITH ANTIDEPRESSANTS

Although combinations of MAOIs with other proven antidepressant compounds has been part of clinical practice for more than 20 years, there is remarkably little research that answers satisfactorily the questions of safety and efficacy. In view of the absence of definitive data it is not surprising that the practice of combining antidepressant drugs has therefore aroused much controversy.

COMBINATION WITH TRICYCLIC ANTIDEPRESSANTS

In the early 1960s MAOIs were commonly prescribed with tricyclic antidepressants. According to Marks (1965) as many as 5% of all antidepressant prescriptions involved the usage of combined antidepressants. Current usage is considerably less than this, well under 1% of all prescriptions (Crammer, personal communication). A major concern has been that of toxicity. According to White and Simpson (1981) there are over 40 reports in the literature of adverse reactions to combined antidepressants. As scientific evidence many of these leave much to be desired. There are several reports referring to serious toxicity of the combination in overdose. Most of these reports describe nothing more than a simple summation of the adverse effects of the individual drugs in the combination, and in many cases their value is limited because of the concurrent use of other drugs. However, there are some exceptions. For example, Davies (1960) described a patient who had taken phenelzine 45 mg daily for three weeks and then took an overdose of 200 mg of imipramine. She developed profuse sweating and extreme restlessness before collapsing with hyperpyrexia. She died soon afterwards. A similar case was reported soon afterwards (Brachfield et al., 1963) in which a 41-year-old woman was given tranylcypromine 20 mg daily for three weeks. The drug was stopped and three days later she was treated with a single dose of imipramine. She became restless, complained of headache, lost consciousness, had an epileptic seizure, and developed hyperpyrexia. There are several other reports reviewed by White and Simpson (1981) of adverse reaction of varying severity following the addition of a tricyclic antidepressant to a patient who was taking or had recently taken monoamine oxidase inhibitors. The reports of adverse reactions are most frequent with imipramine, fewer with amitriptyline, and none with the other closely related antidepressants such as trimipramine and dothiepin. There have been no reports of adverse reactions between MAOIs and the newer antidepressants such as maprotiline, mianserin, trazodone, and nomifensine. This, of course, may only represent a change in prescribing habits in that such combinations are now seldom used.

Although there are several reports of severe toxic reactions following the administration of a tricyclic antidepressant *after* an MAOI, there are no reports of serious adverse reactions when the MAOI is added to the drug regime of a patient already taking a tricyclic antidepressant. In one report (Kane and Freeman, 1963) a patient taking imipramine 25 mg daily became flushed and had to "fight to breathe" after taking a single tablet of etryptamine, a monoamine oxidase inhibitor. As the patient was discharged later the same day, this reaction sounds more like an acute episode of panic than a true drug reaction.

There is also debate about which combinations of MAOIs and tricyclic antidepressants are the most dangerous. White and Simpson (1981) have reviewed 26 relatively uncomplicated cases that probably represent adverse central nervous system reactions to combined antidepressant. They found that tranylcypromine was involved in 6 cases (1 fatal), phenelzine in 5 (1 fatal), isocarboxazid in 6 (1 fatal), iproniazid in 4 (none fatal), nialamide in 3 (2 fatal), mebanazine in 1 (fatal), and etryptamine in 1 (not fatal). It is obviously difficult to interpret these figures, but they do not appear to support the view that tranylcypromine is more dangerous than other MAOIs. The pattern of symptoms described in these cases is similar to those mentioned earlier in that similar adverse effects are found when a tricyclic antidepressant is added to a patient established on MAOIs. The symptoms include confusion, delirium, coma, seizure, and hyperpyrexia.

Once combined therapy is established, an overdose is only marginally more dangerous than would be predicted from the summation of the individual toxic effects of the two drugs. Although the addition of a tricyclic antidepressant to someone established on MAOIs is generally to be avoided, some authors (e.g., Davidson, 1982) feel that this regimen is possible if the new drug is introduced gradually.

Imipramine and its congeners (e.g., desimpramine, clomipramine) appear to be particularly at risk of producing adverse reactions when combined with MAOIs, but the reason for this is not quite clear. When using combined antidepressants, it is wiser to begin with the combined treatment simultaneously, but as many patients are only considered for treatment after other drug therapy has failed, this may not always be possible. If a patient is already established on a tricyclic antidepressant, it is reasonable to add an MAOI, but to start this in lower dosage and build up gradually. There is some evidence (Pare et al., 1982) that patients on combined MAOIs and amitriptyline show reduced pressor response to intravenous tyramine. If so, such patients may be partly protected from an adverse reaction to eating tyramine-containing foods. If this work is replicated, it suggests that this particular combination is safer than taking an MAOI alone.

The issue of safety becomes relevant only if it can be established that combined antidepressants are therapeutically more powerful than either drug given alone.

Research in this area is remarkably sparse. In an earlier report Dally (1965) reported that 8 patients receiving either a combination of amitriptyline and iproniazid or amitriptyline and isocarboxazid had responded after previously being depressed for between 2 and 7 years and failing to respond to antidepressant drugs when given singly. It was noted that attempts to withdraw the drugs had led to a recurrence of symptoms. Although these data are uncontrolled, they are supported by those of other studies (e.g., Winston, 1971) and suggest that combined antidepressants have a role in the treatment of resistant depression. However, the potential adverse effects of the combination had a greater effect on prescribing practice, and combined antidepressants fell into disfavor. Schuckit and his colleagues (1971) commented on the virtual demise of combined antidepressant therapy following warnings from the FDA and drug industry about the dangers of combining antidepressants. They regarded this as an overreaction and pointed out that when the drugs were combined correctly they were safe and predictable in their effects, as Dally (1965) and Gander (1965) had previously described.

A careful study of the use of combined antidepressants in the treatment of depressive illness was reported by Sethna in 1974. These patients had failed to respond to, or consistently relapsed after, treatment with tricyclic antidepressants and monoamine oxidase inhibitors separately, and E.C.T. Ten patients received a combination of phenelzine (45 mg/day) and amitriptyline (50-75 mg nocte). Ratings of depression and anxiety using the Hamilton scales showed that all patients had a considerable admixture of anxiety and depressive symptoms, and had chronic illness (mean duration 11.3 years). Most of the patients responded well and remained improved after 16 months. Although the study was uncontrolled, at least it was concerned with the patients who are normally treated with combined antidepressants in clinical practice.

The first properly controlled study of combined antidepressants was carried out by Davidson and his colleagues in 1978. Patients with unipolar depressive illness or depression secondary to anxiety or character disorder were treated if they had failed to respond to conventional antidepressants singly. One group of patients received bilateral E.C.T. and the other was treated with combined amitriptyline (mean 71 mg daily) and phenelzine (mean 34 mg daily). Seventeen patients completed the study; E.C.T. was more effective in depressive psychosis but combined antidepressant therapy was almost as effective in neurotic depressive illness. Patients with character disorder were not helped by drug therapy. A well designed and well conducted trial was carried out by Young and his colleagues (1979). The patients differed from those in earlier studies in that they presented with mild or moderate depression and did not require E.C.T. or inpatient treatment. One hundred and thirty-five patients were randomly allocated to one of five treatment groups: trimipramine and placebo, phenelzine and placebo, isocarboxazid and placebo, phenelzine and trimipramine, and isocarboxazid and imipramine. The drugs were given in adequate dosage and the study used a double-blind procedure. The results showed a clear superiority for the tricyclic antidepressant, trimipramine, over MAOIs and combined antidepressants, and there were some indications that combined antidepressants were the least effective. Again the findings give no special support for the efficacy of combined antidepressants, but the patients treated were not those who would normally receive this combination

A further controlled trial was carried out three years later (White et al., 1982). Seventy-one inpatients and outpatients satisfying the diagnostic criteria for major depressive illness (DSM-III) were randomly assigned to four weeks of treatment with either tranylcypromine, amitriptyline, or the combination of both drugs. In the case of the combined treatment, the drugs were introduced together to a maximum of half the dosage used when the drugs were given separately. The average maximum doses were tranylcypromine (40 mg daily), amitriptyline (239 mg daily) and, in the combined treatment group, tranylcypromine (24 mg daily) and amitriptyline (128 mg daily). Sixty patients completed the study; the dropout rate was highest in the group treated with amitriptyline alone and lowest in the combined antidepressant group. The groups were well matched on clinical and demographic characteristics and side effects were similar. The only small differences found were that patients on amitriptyline complained more frequently of dry mouth and tremor, and patients on tranylcypromine had a greater number of anticholinergic effects. Patients on each of the three treatments improved to a similar degree and at the same rate. Hypochondriasis responded significantly better to tranylcypromine or combined antidepressant therapy, insomnia to amitriptyline or combined antidepressant therapy, and anxiety to tranylcypromine alone.

These results indicate quite similar therapeutic and adverse effects for the three treatments. There was certainly no evidence of increased toxicity when combined antidepressants were used, but the results failed to show any advantage for combined therapy over treatment with single drugs.

COMBINED MAOI AND TRYPTOPHAN THERAPY

On pharmacological grounds it would be predicted that tryptophan, a precursor of 5-hydroxytryptamine, would be of value in combination with monoamine oxidase inhibitors. Although there have been few published reports about the results of the combination, there is evidence that tryptophan does potentiate the therapeutic effects of monoamine oxidase inhibitors (Pare, 1963) and has no adverse effects. It is not known whether the same clinical effects might otherwise be achieved by simply raising the dosage of the MAOI. As tryptophan is now becoming established as an antidepressant in its own right it is reasonable to consider the combination in cases of resistant depression. In practice we have tended to use the combination when a patient has made only a partial response on a monoamine oxidase inhibitor alone. Tryptophan is gradually added to the drug regime, beginning in a dose of 1 gm daily and rising up to 6 gms.

COMBINED THERAPY WITH MAOIs AND NEWER ANTIDEPRESSANTS

Although there are no published reports on the efficacy of MAOIs combined with newer antidepressants such as trazodone, mianserin, nomifensine and viloxazine, many clinicians use such combinations. The use of these combinations appears to be rational as the newer antidepressants tend to have fewer adverse effects than their tricyclic counterparts. The combination with an MAOI is also likely to have fewer adverse effects. Nevertheless, because most of the new antidepressants are monoamine reuptake inhibitors, it is preferable to avoid adding the new antidepressant to a patient already taking an MAOI.

COMBINED THERAPY WITH MAOIs AND LITHIUM

Because lithium has an established place in the treatment and prophylaxis of manic-depressive disorders, it is quite common for patients in clinical practice to receive lithium together with other antidepressants and MAOIs. The combination of MAOIs and lithium appears to be safe but to carry no special advantages. However, a recent report describes several patients who had not responded to a combined therapy with MAOIs and other antidepressants who dramatically improved after lithium was added to this combination (Joyce et al., 1983). There is no other pharmacological or clinical evidence that supports a synergistic therapeutic effect of this three-way combination, but as all these drugs act in different ways it is reasonable to consider the combination if all other treatments have failed.

SUMMARY AND CONCLUSIONS

Twenty-five years of clinical experience with MAOIs have shown that they do have a place in the treatment of depressive illness and in some cases of resistant depression. The patients for whom MAOIs are most likely to be of value are likely to have the following characteristics:

(1) to have a depression of moderate severity, more likely to be encountered as an outpatient than as an inpatient;
(2) to show an absence of self-reproach, to feel better in the morning and worse in the evening, with an absence of early morning waking;
(3) to have additional agoraphobic and anxious symptoms in association with their depressive ones, and also to have other associated symptoms, particularly lack of energy, hypochondriasis, and obsessional features;
(4) to have stable premorbid personalities without prominent traits of anxiousness or hypochondriasis. However, as many patients with resistant depression have chronic illnesses, the main characteristics of the premorbid personality may not have been shown for many years. The personality that has developed since the onset of depression must not be taken as the premorbid one.

Patients with resistant depression chosen according to these criteria can be expected to do well on MAOIs. If treatment is chosen purely because other measures have failed, a poor response is more likely. Treatment must be continued for an adequate period and in suitable dosage before being abandoned (See Table 1).

Although in general the MAOIs can be regarded as a single group of drugs, there are some important differences among individual members. At present there are no selected monoamine oxidase inhibitors recommended for clinical use in psychiatry, but these may have a place in the future. The main differences between hydrazine and nonhydrazine MAOIs are illustrated (in Table 1); for most clinical purposes phenelzine, isocarboxazid, or tranylcypromine should be used.

Evidence for the clinical value of combined antidepressants is still unsatisfactory. There is no indication that combined antidepressants have a place in the first line treatment of depressive illness, but many of the published studies are concerned with this group of patients. Combined antidepressant therapy should be considered only when patients have failed to respond to adequate doses of a MAOI and tricyclic antidepressant (or new antidepressant alone). If after these treatments have failed, and E.C.T. may also have been tried, it is important to reassess the diagnosis to avoid the crime of Procrustes in forcing the diagnosis to fit the treatment. If after this reevaluation the disorder is still felt to be that of resistant depression, combined antidepressant therapy may be tried. This may be a combination of MAOIs with tryptophan, tricyclic antidepressants, newer antidepressants or lithium, or similar combinations of three or more of these drugs. The combination of amitriptyline and phenelzine is probably the safest. Treatment should be continued for at least six weeks before an assessment of efficacy can be made. There is still a great need for suitably designed studies to test the efficacy of combined antidepressants in resistant depressive disorders, and until this has been carried out, combined therapy cannot be recommended with confidence.

TABLE 1. Comparison of Hydrazine and Nonhydrazine MAOI's and Combined Antidepressants in the Treatment of Resistant Depressive Disorders

	Hydrazine MAOI's	Non-hydrazine MAOI's	Combined Antidepressants
Clinical indications	See text	See text	See text
Adverse effects	Anticholinergic side effects Anti-adrenergic side effects Weight gain Food and drug interactions Relapse on withdrawal	As for hydrazines Probable higher rate of relapse on withdrawal	Summation of adverse effects of individual drugs
Toxicity	Low if drugs taken as directed	Low if drugs taken as directed	Low except with certain combinations
Onset of therapeutic action	2-6 weeks	1-3 weeks	2-6 weeks but evidence less good
Duration of treatment months. May be	At least 3 months. May be used long-term but clear evidence lacking	At least 2 months. May be used long-term but clear evidence lacking	May need to be long-term in view of nature of patient treated
Published evidence of efficacy in adequately designed studies	Yes	Equivocal	Yes (1 study only)
Efficacy compared to tricyclic antidepressants	Equivalent efficacy in some forms of depression; possibly superior if phobic and anxious symptoms prominent	Equivalent efficacy in some forms of depression	Conflicting evidence: no conclusion possible.

REFERENCES

Bates, T.J.N., and Douglas, A.D.M. A comparative trial of four monoamine oxidase inhibitors on chronic depressives. *J. Ment. Sci. 107*, 538-543 (1961).

Ben-Arie, O., and George, G.C.W. A case of tranylcypromine (Parnate) addiction. *Brit. J. Psychiatry 135*, 273-274 (1979).

Blackwell, B. Hypertensive crisis due to monoamine oxidase inhibitors. *Lancet ii*, 849-851 (1963).

Blackwell, B., Marley, E., Price, J., and Taylor, D. Hypotensive interactions between monoamine oxidase inhibitors and foodstuffs. *Brit. J. Psychiatry 113*, 349-365 (1967).

Bloch, R.G., Doonief, A.S., Buchberg, A.S., and Spellman, S. The clinical effect of isoniazid and iproniazid in the treatment of pulmonary tuberculosis. *Ann. Intern. Med. 40*, 881-900 (1954).

Bosworth, D.M. Iproniazid: A brief review of its introduction and clinical use. *Ann. N.Y. Acad. Sci. 80*, 809-819 (1959).

Brachfield, J., Wirtshafter, A., and Wolfe, S. Imipramine-tranylcypromine incompatibility. *J.A.M.A. 186*, 1172-1173 (1963).

Crane, G.E. Iproniazid (Marsilid) phosphate, a therapeutic agent for mental disorders and debilitating diseases. *Psychiat. Res. 8*, 142-152 (1957).

Dally, P.J. Indications for use of iproniazid in psychiatric practice. *Brit. Med. J. 1*, 1338-1339 (1958).

Dally, P.J. In: *The Scientific Basis of Drug Therapy in Psychiatry*. eds. J. Marks, and C.B.B. Pare, Oxford, Pergamon Press, p.149 (1965).

Dally, P.J., and Rohde, P. Comparison of antidepressant drugs in depressive illness. *Lancet i*, 18-20 (1961).

Davidson, J. Adding a tricyclic antidepressant to a monoamine oxidase inhibitor. *J. Clin. Psychopharmacol. 3*, 216 (1982).

Davidson, J., McLeod, M., Law-Yone, B., and Linnoila, M. A companion of electroconvulsive therapy and combined phenelzine-amitriptyline in refractory depression. *Arch. Gen. Psychiat., 35*, 639-642 (1978).

Davies, G. Side effects of phenelzine. *Brit. Med. J. 2*, 1019 (1960).

Gander, D.R. Treatment of depressive illnesses with combined antidepressants. *Lancet, ii*, 107-109 (1965).

Greenblatt, M., Grosser, G.H., and Wechsler, H. Differential response of hospitalized depressed patients to somatic therapy. *Amer. J. Psychiat. 120*, 935-943 (1964).

Hare, E.H., Dominian, J., and Sharpe, L. Phenelzine and dexamphetamine in depressive illness; a comparative trial. *Brit. Med. J. 1*, 9-12 (1962).

Harris, J.A., and Robin, A.A. A controlled trial of phenelzine in depressive reactions. *J. Ment. Sci. 106*, 1432-1437 (1960).

Hollister, L.E. *Clinical Use of Psychotherapeutic Drugs*. Springfield, Illinois, Charles C. Thomas, 1973.

Joyce, P.R., Hewland, H.R., and Jones, A.V. Rapid response to lithium in treatment-resistant depression. *Brit. J. Psychiat., 142*, 204-205 (1983).

Kane, F.L., and Freeman, D. Nonfatal reaction to imipramine-MAO inhibitor combination. *Amer. J. Psychiat.* 120, 79-80 (1963).

Kay, D.W.K., Gasside, R.F., and Fahy, T.J. A double-blind trial of phenelzine and amitriptyline in depressed out-patients. A possible differential effect of the drugs on symptoms. *Brit. J. Psychiat. 123*, 63-67 (1973).

Kelly, D., Guirguis, W., Frommer, E., Mitchell-Hoggs, N., and Sargant, W. Treatment of phobic states with antidepressants. *Brit. J. Psychiat. 116*, 387-398 (1970).

Kingstone, E. In S.E. Greber, et al., eds. *A Method of Psychiatry*. Philadelphia, Lea & Febiger, p. 314 (1980).

Kline, N.S. Clinical experience with iproniazid (Marsilid). *J. Clin. Exp. Psychopathol. 19* (Suppl 1), 72-78 (1958).

Kline, N.S. Drug treatment of phobic disorders. *Am. J. Psychiatry. 123*, 1447-50 (1967).

Loomer, H.P., Saunders, J.C., and Kline, N.S. A clinical and pharmacodynamic evaluation of iproniazid as a psychic energizer. *Psychiat. Res. Rep. 8*, 129-141 (1957).

Marks, J. Interactions involving drugs used in psychiatry. In: J. Marks and C.B.B. Pare, eds. *The Scientific Basis of Drug Therapy in Psychiatry*. Oxford, Pergamon Press, pp 191-201 (1965).

Medical Research Council. Clinical Trials Subcommittee. Clinical trial of the treatment of depressive illness. *Brit. Med. J. 1*, 881-886 (1965).

Mountjoy, C.Q., Roth, M., Garside, R.F., and Leitch, I.M. A Clinical trial of phenelzine in anxiety, depressive and phobic neuroses. *Brit. J. Psychiat. 131*, 486-492 (1977).

Pare, C.M.B. Potentiation of monoamine oxidase inhibitors by tryptophan. *Lancet ii*, 527-528 (1963).

Pare, C.M.B. Toxicity of psychotropic drugs: side effects and toxic effects of antidepressants. *Proc. Roy. Soc. Med. 57*, 757-778 (1964).

Pare, C.M.B., Kline, N., Hallstrom, C., and Cooper, T.B. Will amitriptyline prevent the "cheese" reaction of monoamine-oxidase inhibitors? *Lancet ii*, 183-186 (1982).

Paykel, E.S. Classification of depressed patients: a cluster analysis derived grouping. *Brit. J. Psychiat. 118*, 275-288 (1971).

Paykel, E.S., Rowan, P.R., Parker, R.R., and Bhat, A.V. Responses to phenelzine and amitriptyline in subtypes of out-patient depression. *Arch. Gen. Psychiat. 39*, 1041-1049 (1982).

Pollitt, J. and Young, J. Anxiety state or masked depression? A study based on the action of monoamine oxidase inhibitors. *Brit. J. Psychiat. 119*, 243-249 (1971).

Ravaris, C.L., Nies, A., Robinson, D.S., Ives, J.O., Lamborn, K.R., and Korson, L. A multiple-dose, controlled study of phenelzine in depressive-anxiety states. *Arch. Gen. Psychiat., 33*, 347-350 (1976).

Ravaris, C.L., Robinson, D.S., Ives, J.O., Nies, A., and Bartlett, D. A comparison of phenelzine and amitriptyline in the treatment of depression. *Arch. Gen. Psychiat. 37*, 1075-1080 (1980).

Robinson, D.S., Nies, A., and Ravaris, C.L. The monoamine oxidase inhibitor phenelzine in the treatment of depressive-anxiety states. *Arch. Gen. Psychiat. 29*, 407-413 (1973).

Roth, M., and Myers, D.H. Anxiety neuroses and phobic states—II diagnosis and management. *Brit. Med. J. 1*, 559-562 (1969).

Sargant, W., and Dally, P. Treatment of anxiety states by antidepressant drugs. *Brit. Med. J. 1*, 6-9 (1962).

Sargant, W., and Slater, E. *An Introduction to Physical Methods of Treatment in Psychiatry*. 5th ed. Churchill Livingstone, Edinburgh (1962).

Schuckit, M., Robins, E. and Feighner, J. Tricyclic antidepressants and monoamine oxidase inhibitors. *Arch. Gen. Psychiat. 24*, 509-514 (1971).

Sethna, E.R. A study of refractory cases of depressive illnesses and their response to combined antidepressant treatment. *Brit. J. Psychiat. 124*, 265-271 (1974).

Shaw, D.M. The practical management of affective disorders. *Brit. J. Psychiat. 130*, 432-451 (1977).

Simpson, L., and Cabot, B. Monoamine oxidase inhibitors. In *Drug Treatment of Mental Disorders*, ed. L. Simpson. New York, Raven Press, p. 155 (1974).

Singer, T.P., and Salach, J.I. Interaction of suicide inhibitors with the active site of monoamine oxidase, in *Monoamine Oxidase Inhibitors—The State of the Art*. M.B.H. Youdim and E.S. Paykel, eds. John Wiley, New York, pp 17-29 (1981).

Sjöqvist, F. Psychotropic drugs (2): Interaction between monoamine oxidase (MAO) inhibitors and other substances. *Proc. Roy. Soc. Med. 58*, 967-968 (1965).

Tyrer, P. Towards rational treatment with monoamine oxidase inhibitors. *Brit J. Psychiat. 128*, 354-360 (1976).

Tyrer, P.J. Monoamine oxidase inhibitors and amine precursors, in *Drugs in Psychiatric Practice*, P.J. Tyrer, ed. Butterworths, London, pp. 249-279 (1982).

Tyrer, P. Effects of sudden withdrawal of monoamine oxidase inhibitors and tricyclic antidepressants after long-term therapy. *J. Affect. Dis. 6*, pp. 1-7 (1984).

Tyrer, P., Candy, J., and Kelly, D. Phenelzine in phobic anxiety: a controlled trial. *Psychol. Med. 3*, 120-124 (1973).

Tyrer, P., Lambourn, J., and Whitford, M. Clinical and pharmacokinetic factors affecting response to phenelzine. *Brit. J. Psychiatry, 136*, 359-365 (1980).

Tyrer, P., Casey, P., and Gall, J. Relationship between neurosis and personality disorder. *Brit. J. Psychiatry, 142*, 404-408 (1983).

West, E.D., and Dally, P.J. Effects of iproniazid in depressive syndromes. *Brit. Med. J. 1*, 1491-1494 (1959).

White, K., and Simpson, G. Combined MAOI-tricyclic antidepressant treatment. A re-evaluation. *J. Clin. Psychopharmacol. 1*, 264-282 (1981).

White, K., Razari, J. Simpson, G., Rebal, R., Bruce Sloane, R., O'Leary, J., and Palmer, R. Combined MAOI-tricyclic antidepressant treatment: a controlled trial. *Psychopharmacol. Bull. 18*, 180-181 (1982).

Winston, F. Combined antidepressant therapy. *Brit. J. Psychiat. 118*, 301-304 (1971).

Young, J.P.R., Lader, M.H., and Hughes, W.C. Controlled trial of trimipramine, monoamine oxidase inhibitors and combined treatment in depressed outpatients. *Brit. Med. J. 4*, 1315-1317 (1979).

Zeller, E.A., Barsky, J., Berman, E.R., and Fouts, J.R. Action of isonicotinic acid hydrazide and related compounds on enzymes involved in the autonomic nervous system. *J. Pharmacol. 106*, 427-428 (1953).

7

The Use of Antipsychotic Drugs in the Treatment of Depression

J. Craig Nelson

The use of neuroleptic drugs in the treatment of depression raises three basic questions: (1) Do neuroleptic drugs have antidepressant properties? (2) Are there specific depressive disorders for which use of neuroleptics constitutes a primary treatment modality? (3) Are there symptoms for which adjunctive neuroleptic treatment is beneficial? I discuss in this chapter information pertaining to these questions in order to identify specific indications for the use of neuroleptics in depression, and to facilitate consideration of the use of neuroleptics in depressed patients who are resistant to conventional tricyclic antidepressant treatment.

Neuroleptic or "antipsychotic" drugs are not generally regarded as antidepressants. The conventional drugs of choice for treatment of serious depression are the tricyclic compounds such as imipramine or amitriptyline. The pharmacologic distinction between these two drug classes appears well established. It has been clear since their initial description (Kuhn, 1958) that tricyclic antidepressants are not effective for treatment of psychotic symptoms, yet it is not confirmed that neuroleptic drugs are without antidepressant properties. Several studies addressing this question suggest the opposite.

Early reports (Cohen, 1958; Brougher, 1960) suggested thioridazine was beneficial in the treatment of certain depressed patients. In 1965, Hollister and Overall reported that neuroleptic drugs were effective for the treatment of depression in patients having an "anxious profile." They questioned the "specificity" of the two drug classes and noted that the effects of neuroleptics were not limited to the treatment of anxiety, but that these drugs were effective for all symptoms associated with anxious depression, including depressed mood. A 1982 review of neuroleptic efficacy in depression concluded that there is considerable evidence to support the use of these drugs in depression (Robertson and Trimble, 1982). This review is timely and comprehensive. Nevertheless, the question of whether neuroleptics have a "true" or specific antidepressant effect remains, and is pursued further here.

Aside from the question of the antidepressant properties of neuroleptics, specific uses of neuroleptic drugs in depression have been suggested. In 1978, the successful treatment of delusional depression with antipsychotic-antidepressant drug combinations was described (Nelson and Bowers). Subsequent studies confirmed the efficacy of combined treatment in this disorder and indicated that psychotic depression is a specific disorder for which antipsychotic drugs can play a primary role.

In this chapter the possible antidepressant effects of the neuroleptic drugs are reconsidered. The use of neuroleptic drugs in the treatment of delusional depression is discussed and other possible indications for antipsychotic drugs in depression are explored. The risk of tardive dyskinesia in depressed patients is discussed, since that bears directly on the decision to use neuroleptics in the treatment of depressive disorders.

ARE NEUROLEPTICS ANTIDEPRESSANTS?

Robertson and Trimble (1982) recently reviewed the double-blind studies comparing the antidepressant effects of neuroleptic drugs with placebo, antianxiety agents, and tricyclic antidepressant drugs. They concluded that "drugs of the major tranquilliser class possess some antidepressant effects." However, the implications of these studies vary with the type of depression being examined and are limited by several methodologic considerations.

Studies in Nonendogenous Depression

Most studies of neuroleptic drugs in depression have involved patients having depressions variously described as anxious, neurotic, mild-to-moderate, or reactive. While terminology has varied, these descriptions usually indicated nonendogenous depression. In studies of this syndrome, antipsychotic drugs were prescribed in doses below an antipsychotic range, e.g., doses of thioridazine less than 200 mg per day.

In eight studies of anxious or neurotic depression, neuroleptics were compared with placebo. They were superior to placebo in six (Karn et al., 1961; Felger, 1965; Predescu et al., 1973; Fann et al., 1974; Frolund, 1974; Ovhed, 1976), comparable in one study (De Jonge et al., 1976), and less effective than placebo in one (Raskin et al., 1970). When compared with benzodiazepines, neuroleptic drugs have been found to be comparable in six studies (De Jonge et al., 1976; Hollister et al., 1971; General Practitioner Trials, 1971; Rosenthal and Bowden, 1973; Kurland, 1976; Johnson, 1979) and superior in one (Schuster et al., 1972). Neuroleptic agents were comparable to tricyclic drugs in nine studies of anxious or neurotic depression (Lodge Patch et al., 1967; Paykel et al., 1968; Rickels et al., 1968; General Practioner Trials, 1971; General Practioner Trials, 1972; Glick, 1973; Wittenborn and Kiremitci, 1975; Young et al, 1976; Johnson 1979) and superior to tricyclics in three other studies (Overall et al., 1966; Hollister et al., 1967; Raskin et al., 1970). In those studies which included both nonendogenous and endogenous patients, only the results for the former patients are included here.

Several authors noted that anxious, neurotic, or nonendogenous depressed patients showed significant improvement with all active drug treatment and that the differences between drugs, if present, were slight in comparison to overall improvement. That these three drug classes are comparable for the treatment of nonendogenous depression suggests that either all three drug classes are antidepressants or that the improvement noted was not a "true" or specific antidepressant effect.

The definition of specific antidepressant effect is not well established. Such an effect might be demonstrated in relation to a core symptom or process, but this symptom is not established. Klein has suggested that an inability to experience pleasure is the central feature of endogenous depression (1974), but this clinical observation requires validation. For now, treatment of the standard or "classic" disorder appears to be the best method of establishing specific antidepressant action. This disorder has most commonly been described as endogenous depression or in DSM III as "melancholia." Specific antidepressant activity would also be supported by evidence that the drug results in remission of the depressive syndrome rather than partial improvement or moderate symptomatic benefit.

Studies in Endogenous Depression

With these thoughts in mind, I reviewed the studies of neuroleptic drugs in the treatment of endogenous depression. Three of these studies found neuroleptic drugs superior to placebo (Fink et al., 1964; Klein, 1966; Raskin et al., 1970). Of nine studies comparing neuroleptic drugs and tricyclics, six found the two drugs similar in effectiveness (Fink et al., 1964; Klein, 1966; Paykel et al., 1968; Kiev, 1972; Simpson et al., 1972; Wittenborn and Kiremitci, 1975). One of these (Simpson et al., 1972), noted that the differences, while not significant, favored the tricyclic. Three other studies found the tricyclic drugs superior to neuroleptic drugs for endogenous patients (Overall et al., 1966; Hollister et al., 1967; Raskin et al., 1970). In the Overall and Hollister studies, the group which they described as similar to endogenous depression was their "retarded" profile. This sample was selected using a "profile" analysis and thus differed from that of the other studies.

Several of these studies noted the symptomatic benefits of neuroleptics, particularly for the treatment of agitation. However, only three of the nine studies described outcome so that frequency of remission can be compared. These three studies (Klein, 1966; Kiev, 1972; Simpson et al., 1972) indicated that the percentage of patients who were much improved or remitted was similar for the neuroleptics and tricyclics, and that neuroleptic drugs do treat some patients to the point of remission.

Methodologic Issues

The methodologies of the studies reviewed were quite variable—the studies span a 25 year period. While it is easy to criticize prior studies, it is more difficult to determine what methodologic changes would have had significant effects. The most important factor in these studies appeared to be patient selection. In the studies of endogenous depression, it is not clear the samples were comparable to each other or similar to the DSM III concept of melancholia. The Overall and Hollister "retarded" profiles were clearly selected in a different manner and appeared to be a subgroup of endogenous patients.

Several studies included bipolar as well as unipolar patients. One of these (Klein, 1966) demonstrated the problem of assessing outcome in bipolar patients. In that study, three patients treated with tricyclics developed manic symptoms and two of these were judged as having an unfavorable outcome. These patients accounted for half of the tricyclic failures.

None of these studies differentiated between delusional and nondelusional depressed patients. Since delusional patients respond less well to tricyclics or antipsychotics administered independently, their inclusion would lower response rates and decrease the chances of finding significant drug differences.

None of these studies measured plasma drug levels. It has been reported that 40% of those patients receiving a conventional tricyclic dose, e.g., nortriptyline 150 mg per day or imipramine 225 mg per day, will not achieve a therapeutic drug concentration (Kragh-Sorenson et al., 1973; Glassman and Perel, 1978). Failure to achieve adequate treatment levels would lower response rates and diminish the chances of finding a difference between treatments.

Conclusions

In evaluating these studies, the following conclusions seem warranted. As Robertson and Trimble noted, there is considerable evidence that neuroleptics are useful in the treatment of depression. While specific neuroleptics have been promoted as having antidepressant action, these studies indicate that all the neuroleptics examined appear similar with regard to their effectiveness. There is no evidence that one antipsychotic is more useful in treating depressed patients than any other.

In nonendogenous depression, the neuroleptic drugs are more effective than placebo but comparable to the tricyclics and antianxiety agents. None of these agents appears superior to another drug or class or drugs. The most important finding is that acute nonmelancholic patients do well with all forms of active treatment and may be best managed with the most benign drug. Hollister et al. (1971), in a comparison study of acetophenazine and diazepam, specifically noted that while the two drugs were comparable, in acute uncomplicated anxious depressives diazepam had the edge. The similar efficacy of the three drug classes suggests their effect may not be a true antidepressant effect in this patient group but that these drugs have some other effect in common, such as mild sedation.

The findings in patients with endogenous depression are more difficult to interpret. As a group the studies suggest that the antipsychotics and tricyclics are comparable, with a minority favoring the tricyclics. There is almost universal agreement that neuroleptic drugs are useful for the treatment of certain symptoms, especially agitation, but also delusions, guilt, and insomnia. There is also agreement that neuroleptic drugs can result in considerable global improvement in melancholic patients. The critical question is whether neuroleptics have a true antidepressant effect. Do they treat melancholic patients to remission, and how does the response rate compare with that of the tricyclics?

The above studies do not resolve these questions, and the methodologic problems cited limit the conclusions which can be drawn. While it is difficult to estimate the magnitude of the effects of these methodologic problems, there are some clues. Recent studies of tricyclic effectiveness in nondelusional unipolar melancholic patients have reported response rates of 85% in patients who achieved an adequate tricyclic plasma level (Glassman et al., 1977; Nelson et al., 1982a). In these studies the criterion for response required that patients remitted or were minimally symptomatic. The three neuroleptic-tricyclic comparison studies which provided response rate data were reexamined using a similar criterion for response. In these three studies the actual tricyclic response rates for patients who were much improved or remitted ranged from 28% to 44% (Klein, 1966; Kiev, 1972; Simpson et al., 1972). It seems reasonable to conclude that inclusion of bipolar and delusional patients and treatment without assurance of adequate plasma drug concentrations resulted in response rates which are not representative of tricyclic efficacy.

Another body of data bears on the question of the antidepressant effects of the neuroleptic drugs. Several studies examining the value of antipsychotics used alone in delusional depression report a low rate of response (Minter and Mandell, 1979a; 1979b; Kaskey et al., 1980; Charney and Nelson, 1981; Spiker, et al., 1985). As two studies note (Nelson and Bowers, 1978; Minter and Mandell, 1979a), antipsychotic drugs were useful for treatment of agitation and delusional thinking and resulted in considerable improvement; however, depressive symptoms such as anhedonia, lack of energy, and motor retardation frequently persisted until a tricyclic was added. These observations are similar to those of Raskin et al. (1970) who noted that lack of interest and retardation were responsive to imipramine but not chlorpromazine.

It is my opinion that the studies comparing tricyclic and neuroleptic efficacy in endogenous depression have not established the comparability of the two drug classes since these studies did not achieve representative response rates for the tricyclic antidepressants. While a "true" antidepressant effect has been demonstrated for the tricyclic antidepressants, similar effects appear doubtful for the antipsychotic drugs. Neuroleptics are not effective for treatment of anhedonia, a symptom suggested as central to melancholia, and neuroleptics are not usually effective for the treatment of delusional depression when given alone. It is acknowledged, however, that demonstration of the superiority of the tricyclics is limited to just a few studies and not well confirmed. In addition, the observation that some endogenous patients can be treated to remission with neuroleptics indicates that these drugs can be useful in individual cases. Presumably these are agitated depressives, but there is little descriptive data to indicate which individual patients can be successfully treated with neuroleptics alone.

NEUROLEPTICS IN THE TREATMENT OF DELUSIONAL DEPRESSION

One specific use of neuroleptic drugs is in the treatment of delusional depression. Early psychopharmacology texts (Klein and Davis, 1969; Detre and Jarecki, 1971; Hollister, 1975) commented on the possible value of antipsychotic drugs in depressed patients who were agitated or psychotic, but initially there were few data to support these observations. The issue took on added importance in 1975 when Glassman et al. noted that the rate of response to imipramine was much lower in delusional patients than in nondelusional patients, even when plasma drug concentrations were obtained to insure that the patients had received adequate treatment. Subsequent reports noted similar findings (Simpson et al., 1976; Glassman et al., 1977; Davidson et al., 1977; Charney and Nelson, 1981), and one study (Nelson et al., 1979) noted that tricyclics were not only less effective but that they might precipitate or exacerbate psychotic symptoms in vulnerable patients.

In 1978 Nelson and Bowers described successful treatment of delusional depression with combined antipsychotic-tricyclic drug regimens. This report, as well as subsequent studies (Minter and Mandell, 1979a; Kaskey et al., 1980; Charney and Nelson, 1981; Brown et al., 1982; Clower, 1983), provided retrospective evidence for the value of this drug combination in delusional depression. Recently Spiker and associates (1985) have described a prospective study of delusional depression in which combined antipsychotic-antidepressant treatment proved superior to either drug alone. In this study 78% of the patients receiving amitriptyline and perphenazine responded, while 41% of those receiving amitriptyline and only 19% of those receiving perphenazine responded. The superiority of the combination was not explained by higher plasma drug concentrations resulting from drug interactions.

DESCRIPTIVE FEATURES

Identification of delusional patients is clearly important for planning treatment since delusional patients are at increased risk for successful suicide (Roose et al., 1983). Several studies have described the characteristics of delusional patients (Nelson and Bowers, 1978; Charney and Nelson, 1981; Glassman and Roose, 1981; Frances et al., 1981; Frangos et al., 1983). Delusional depression is invariably endogenous; it is not responsive to placebo treatment or drug-free hospitalization and thus appears to be a subcategory of melancholia. Delusional patients are similar to melancholic patients in other respects. The average age of onset is 45 years of age. Women outnumber men 2 or 3 to 1. Delusional depression is a recurrent illness. Over 70% of delusional patients have had prior episodes (an average of two), and presumably some of the remaining 30% will go on to have future episodes. Ninety-five percent of those with prior episodes were psychotic during a prior episode. In fact the actual delusional thought is quite similar from episode to episode.

DSM-III designates this syndrome "psychotic" major depression and indicates that the patient is considered psychotic in the presence of delusions, hallucinations, or depressive stupor. Delusions are most common. Frangos et al. (1983) recently described 145 psychotic depressives of whom 136 were delusional. Of the nine patients without delusions, five had hallucinations and four patients were stuporous.

Delusions are defined by most authors as beliefs which are clearly false and are not common in other members of the patient's subculture. Depressive worries which are merely exaggerated or distorted are not necessarily delusional. The patient who thinks she is an utter failure is not delusional. The patient who thinks he has failed and as result is about to be put to death is delusional. The most common delusional themes are of guilt and paranoia. Somatic delusions are common and nihilistic delusions may occur. DSM-III also recognizes mood-incongruent delusions, but at present it is unclear what the diagnostic or treatment implicvations of mood-incongruent delusions are.

Other symptoms which are prominent in psychotic depression are psychomotor disturbance and guilt. Three studies (Charney and Nelson, 1981; Frances et al., 1981; Frangos et al., 1983) found agitation to be more common in delusional than nondelusional patients. Glassman and Roose (1981) found motor retardation more prevalent. Pathological guilt, the sense that one is bad or evil, is also more frequent in delusional patients and often reaches delusional proportions.

TREATMENT

Two treatments have been demonstrated to be effective in psychotic depression: electroconvulsive therapy (ECT) and combined antipsychotic-antidepressant drug therapy, as described above. Electroconvulsive therapy is effective for treatment of psychotic depressives (Avery and Winokur, 1977; Avery and Lubano, 1979) and one report found ECT superior to drug treatment (Perry et al., 1982). While both treatments appear to be effective, it seems likely that in most clinical situations drug therapy will be preferred by patients and clinicians. In addition, drug therapy will be a consideration even if ECT is administered since maintenance treatment following ECT has been shown to reduce relapse rates (Quitkin et al., 1976).

When combined treatment is administered, I usually begin treatment with the antipsychotic drug first since: (1) agitation responds rapidly to the antipsychotic, (2) the presence of the antipsychotic blocks exacerbation of the psychosis by the tricyclic, and (3) side effects can be more easily evaluated if one drug is given at a time. It has been generally recognized that side effects are more common when two or more psychotropic drugs are administered (Hollister, 1978) and specifically it has been demonstrated that major adverse reactions are four times more common during combined antipsychotic-antidepressant treatment than when the tricyclic is administered alone (Nelson et al., 1982b). This increase does not appear to be the result of increased tricyclic plasma levels.

Authors describing combined drug treatment have administered the antipsychotic at usual antipsychotic doses. Dosage recommendations for the tricyclic are of limited value because of the wide interpatient variability of tricyclic plasma levels; however, it is usually not necessary to give high doses of the tricyclic since neuroleptic drugs increase the plasma concentration of the tricyclic as much as twofold through inhibition of tricyclic metabolism (Gram and Overo, 1972; Nelson and Jatlow, 1980). The actual tricyclic plasma level required for effective treatment is not well established, but our experience suggests that levels similar to those in nondelusional patients are required.

Lithium augmentation of combined drug therapy has also been reported to be effective in some cases of psychotic depression (Price et al., 1983) and would appear to be useful in patients who fail to respond to combined drug treatment. Our experience suggests that patients with a history of hypomania or a family history of bipolar illness are overrepresented in the group of psychotic depressives refractory to combined therapy. The addition of lithium was usually effective for these probable bipolar patients but less effective in refractory unipolar patients (Mazure and Nelson, 1985). Some of these patients responded to lithium within the first 48 hours, consistent with the "augmentation" hypothesis (DeMontigny et al., 1981). Other probable bipolar depressives responded to lithium over a two-to three-week period, suggesting that lithium may be having a primary antidepressant effect as described for bipolar patients (Noyes and Dempsey, 1974; Mendels, 1976). It is possible that bipolar psychotic depression deserves to be studied independently and that lithium may play a fundamental role in the antidepressant treatment of these patients.

Preliminary reports suggest loxapine and amoxapine are also effective in the treatment of psychotic depression (Goldschmidt and Burch, 1982; Anton and Sexauer, 1983). The rational for this treatment is that loxapine has antipsychotic properties while its metabolite, amoxapine, may have both antidepressant and anitpsychotic effects. The use of either drug thus results in both antidepressant and antipsychotic effects. The advantage of administering one drug, however, is offset by the disadvantage of being unable to adjust the dose of the antipsychotic and antidepressant independently.

Effective maintenance treatment for psychotic depression has not been determined. While it has been established that relapse rates in patients with recurrent depression are diminished with maintenance tricyclic therapy (Davis, 1976), it is not known if delusional patients require maintenance treatment with both the antipsychotic and the antidepressant. In my experience, attempts to discontinue the antipsychotic sometimes have been unsuccessful and continuation of both drugs was necessary. This problem is particularly pressing, since prolonged treatment with an antipsychotic carries the risk of tardive dyskinesia, as discussed below.

OTHER USES OF NEUROLEPTICS IN DEPRESSION

While it seems questionable that the antipsychotic drugs possess true antidepressant properties, neuroleptics are of value for combined treatment of delusional depression and can be of adjunctive value in other clinical conditions. In the following situations, neuroleptics might be employed first or could be considered in patients resistant to conventional antidepressant treatment. At the outset it should be emphasized that any use of neuroleptic drugs requires serious consideration of the risks of tardive dyskinesia. If less hazardous treatment alternatives exist, they should be employed.

Probable Psychotic Depression

In clinical practice, patients are encountered who appear very similar to patients with psychotic depression but in whom psychotic symptoms cannot be verified. Their thinking may be clearly distorted and ruminative, their behavior may be guarded and suggestive of delusional thinking, but psychotic content or experiences may not be explicitly stated. Such patients, especially outpatients, may be best managed if initially treated as though they were delusional. Tricyclics alone may exacerbate psychotic symptoms (Nelson et al., 1979), and once the patient is frankly psychotic the patient's awareness of the nature of the illness decreases, the ability to understand and comply with treatment diminishes, and the need for hospitalization will increase. Neuroleptics may prove useful during the acute stage of treatment of such patients; however, if it is questionable that the patient was delusional, discontinuation of the neuroleptic should be attempted once the patient's condition is stable.

Agitated Melancholic Patients

Neuroleptics are clearly of value for the treatment of agitation in melancholic patients. They are useful also for treatment of disturbed sleep, and are of considerable value in reducing distress associated with painful thoughts of guilt or hopelessness. When the agitation subsides, the patient's lack of interest or anhedonia may be more prominent and tricyclic antidepressants may then be employed. As the patient's condition improves the neuroleptic dose can be tapered off and then discontinued.

Neuroleptics can be very useful in the negativistic melancholic patient who is actively refusing to eat and whose physical status is deteriorating. Frequently this behavior is associated with delusional or near delusional thoughts of hopelessness, guilt, or of being harmed. Neuroleptics can reduce their distress and distorted thinking so that the active resistance to eating is no longer a problem. While this clinical situation has sometimes been cited as an indication for ECT, in my experience neuroleptics have all but eliminated this use of ECT.

Organic Affective Syndrome

Older patients with organic syndromes may present with symptoms suggestive of melancholia. These patients are frequently agitated, distraught, sleeping poorly, somatically preoccuppied, may be delusional and are at an age when melancholia is more common. In addition, as the concept of pseudodementia has become more familiar, the overdiagnosis of depression in patients with a primary dementia has increased, leading one author to describe "pseudodepression" (Morstyn et al., 1982). Diagnosis of such patients can be very difficult and may be possible only after a trial of an antidepressant. If an organic affective syndrome is suspected, transient use of a neuroleptic at a low dose can be employed, either initially, or if an antidepressant is unsuccessful. Antipsychotic drugs are frequently quite effective in organic affective syndromes, especially if agitation or paranoid symptoms are prominent.

Nonmelancholic Depression

In nonmelancholic patients, the literature suggests that neuroleptics, tricyclics, and benzodiazepines are comparable in terms of effectiveness. Acute nonmelancholic major depressives are likely to respond well to all treatments. Thus, selection of the safest agent is dictated, and for this reason the benzodiazepines are the drugs of choice, if any drug is to be given. If the patient is unresponsive and depressive symptoms continue, then a trial of an antidepressant or monoamine-oxidase inhibitor might be considered. The availability of safer alternative treatments, including nonpharmacologic therapies, should discourage the use of neuroleptics in this syndrome.

THE RISK OF TARDIVE DYSKINESIA

The use of neuroleptics in the treatment of depression poses a serious dilemma for the clinician. In the conditions described above, the seriousness of the clinical state and the potential value of antipsychotic drugs must be weighed against the risk of tardive dyskinesia. This clinical dilemma is further complicated by a growing literature suggesting that the risk of tardive dyskinesia may be higher in affective disorder (Davis et al., 1976; Yassa et al, 1983; Casey, 1983; Kane et al., 1983; Alpert et al., 1983). This issue becomes especially important during maintenance treatment when exposure to pharmacologic agents is prolonged. The use of antipsychotic drugs for maintenance treatment of depressive disorders is not established, and the APA Task Force (1980) advises that if neuroleptics are used in the acute treatment of depression,they be withdrawn when symptoms subside. Neuroleptics may be required for maintenance treatment of delusional depression, but this clinical issue requires study. Until further information is forthcoming, clinicians would be well advised to attempt the discontinuation of the neuroleptic in any depressed patient who has received this drug during the acute phase of treatment. In individuals for whom there is a demonstrated need for continuing treatment, the patient must be advised of the risks.

REFERENCES

Alpert, M., Rush, M., and Diamond, F. Affective signs and treatment response in patients with tardive dyskinesia. In *Tardive Dyskinesia and Affective Disorders*, G. Gardos and D. Casey, eds. American Psychiatric Association, Washington, D.C., 1983.

Anton, R.F., and Sexauer, J.D. Efficacy of amoxapine in psychotic depression. *Amer. J. Psychiatry 140,* 1344-1347 (1983).

Avery, D., and Lubrano, A. Depression treated with imipramine and ECT: the DeCarolis study reconsidered. *Amer. J. Psychiatry 136,* 559-562 (1979).

Avery, D., and Winokur, G. The efficacy of electroconvulsive therapy and antidepressants in depression. *Biol. Psychiat. 12,* 507-523 (1977).

Brougher, J.C. The treatment of emotional disorders in obstetrics and gynaecology with thioridazine. *Quart. Rev. Surg. Obstet. Gynec. 17,* 44-47 (1960).

Brown, R.P., Frances, A., Kocsis, J.H., and Mann, J.J. Psychotic vs. nonpsychotic depression: comparison of treatment response. *J. Nerv. Ment. Dis. 170,* 635-637 (1982).

Casey, D.E. Tardive dyskinesia and affective disorders. In *Tardive Dyskinesia and Affective Disorders,* G. Gardos and D. Casey, eds. American Psychiatric Association, Washington D.C., 1983.

Charney, D.S., and Nelson, J.C. Delusional and nondelusional depression: further evidence for distinct subtypes. *Amer. J. Psychiat. 138,* 328-333 (1981).

Clower, C.G. Recurrent psychotic unipolar depression. *J. Clin. Psychiat. 44,* 216-218 (1983).

Cohen, S. TP-21, A new phenothiazine. *Amer. J. Psychiat. 115,* 358 (1958).

Davidson, J.R.T., McLeod, M.N., Kurland, A.A., and White, H.L. Antidepressant drug therapy in psychotic depression. *Brit. J. Psychiat. 131,* 493-496 (1977).

Davis, J.M. Overview: maintenance therapy in psychiatry: II. Affective disorders. *Amer. J. Psychiat. 133,* 1-13 (1976).

Davis, K.L., Berger, P.A., and Hollister, L.E. Tardive dyskinesia and depressive illness. *Psychopharmacol. Commun. 2,* 125-130 (1976).

De Jonghe, F.E.R.E.R., Schalken, H.F.A., and van der Helm, H.J. Thioridazine in the treatment of depressive patients. *Acta Psychiat. Scan. 53,* 271-276 (1976).

De Montigny, C., Grunberg, F., Mayer, A., and Deschenes, J.-P. Lithium induces rapid relief of depression in tricyclic antidepressant drug nonresponders. *Brit. J. Psychiatry 38,* 252-256 (1981).

Detre, T., and Jarecki, H.G. *Modern Psychiatric Treatment.* J. B. Lippincott Co., Philadelphia, pp. 172-174 (1971).

Fann, W.E., Lake, C.R., and Majors, L.F. Thioridazine in neurotic, anxious, and depressed patients. *Psychosomatics 15,* 117-121 (1974).

Felger, H.L. Depressed hospitalized patients treated with chlorprothixene concentrate. *J. New Drugs 5,* 240-248 (1965).

Fink, M., Pollack, M., Klein, D.F., Blumberg, A.G., Belmont, I., Karp, E., Kramer, J.C., and Willner, A. Comparative studies of chlorpromazine and imipramine. In *Neuro–Psychopharmacology,* Vol. 3. P.B. Bradley, F. Flugel, and P.H. Hoch, eds. Elsevier, Amsterdam, pp.370-372 (1964).

Frances, A., Brown, R.P., Kocsis, J.H., and Mann, J.J. Psychotic depression: a separate entity? *Amer. J. Psychiat. 136,* 831-833 (1981).

Frangos, E., Athanassenas, G., Tsitourides, S., Psilolignos, P., and Katsanou, N. Psychotic depressive disorder, a separate entity? *J. Aff. Dis. 5,* 259-265 (1983).

Frolund, F. Treatment of depression in general practice; a controlled trial of flupenthixol (Fluanxol). *Curr. Med. Res. Opin. 2,* 78-79 (1974).

General Practitioner Clinical Trials. Antidepressant effects of tranquillizers. *Practitioner 206,* 146-148 (1971).

General Practitioner Clinical Trials. Thioridazine as an antidepressant. *Practitioner 209,* 95-98 (1972).

Glassman, A.H., and Perel, J.M. Tricyclic blood levels and clinical outcome: A review of the art. In *Psychopharmacology: A Generation of Progress.* M.A. Lipton, A. DiMascio, and K.F. Killam, eds. Raven Press, New York, pp. 917-922 (1978).

Glassman, A.H., and Roose, S.P. Delusional depression: a distinct clinical entity. *Arch. Gen. Psychiat. 38,* 424-427 (1981).

Glassman, A.H., Kantor, S.J., and Shostak, M. Depression, delusions, and drug response. *Amer. J.*

Psychiat. 132, 716-719 (1975).

Glassman, A.H., Perel, J.M., Shostak, M., Kantor, S.J., and Fleiss, J.L. Clinical implications of imipramine plasma levels for depressive illness. *Arch. Gen. Psychiat. 34,* 197-204 (1977).

Glick, B.S. Comparison of doxepin and thioridazine in outpatients. *Dis. Nerv. System 34,* 37-39 (1973).

Goldschmidt, T.J., and Burch, E.A. Use of loxapine to treat a patient with psychotic depression. *Amer. J. Psychiat. 139,* 946-947 (1982).

Gram, L.F., and Overo, K.F. Drug interaction: inhibitory effect of neuroleptics on metabolism of tricyclic antidepressants in man. *Brit. Med. J. 1,* 463-465 (1972).

Hollister, L.E. *Clinical Use of Psychotherapeutic Drugs.* Charles C. Thomas, Springfield, Ill. pp. 92-93 (1975).

Hollister, L.E. Tricyclic antidepressants (second of two parts). *New Engl. J. Med. 299,* 1168-1172 (1978).

Hollister, L.E., and Overall, J.E. Reflections on the specificity of action of antidepressants. *Psychosomatics 6,* 361-365 (1965).

Hollister, L.E., Overall, J.E., Shelton, J., Pennington, V., Kimbell, I., and Johnson, M. Drug therapy of depression. *Arch. Gen. Psychiat. 17,* 486-493 (1967).

Hollister, L.E., Overall, J.E., Pokorny, A.D., and Shelton, J. Acetophenazine and diazepam in anxious depressions. *Arch. Gen. Psychiat. 24,* 273-278 (1971).

Johnson, D.A.W. A double-blind comparison of flupenthixol, nortriptyline, and diazepam in neurotic depression. *Acta Psychiat. Scand. 59,* 1-8 (1979).

Kane, J.M., Woerner, M., Weinhold, P., Kinon, B., Lieberman, J., and Borenstein, M. Incidence and severity of tardive dyskinesia in affective illness. *In Tardive Dyskinesia and Affective Disorders,* G. Gardos and D. Casey, eds. American Psychiatric Association. Washington, D.C., 1983.

Karn,W.N., Mead, B.T., and Fishman, J.J. Double-blind study of chlorprothixene (Taractan), a panpsychotropic agent. *J. New Drugs 1,* 72-79 (1961).

Kaskey, G.B., Nasr, S., and Meltzer, H.Y. Drug treatment in delusional depression. *Psychiat. Res. 1,* 267-277 (1980).

Kiev, A. Double-blind comparison of thiothixene and protriptyline in psychotic depression. *Dis. Nerv. System 33,* 811-816 (1972).

Klein, D.F. Chlorpromazine-procyclidine combination, imipramine and placebo in depressive disorders. *Canad. Psychiat. Assn. J. 11* (suppl), 146-149 (1966).

Klein, D.F. Endogenomorphic depression. *Arch. Gen. Psychiat. 31,* 447-454 (1974).

Klein, D.F., and Davis, J.M. *Diagnosis and Drug Treatment of Psychiatric Disorders.* Williams and Wilkins, Co., Baltimore, pp. 213-214, 304-305 (1969).

Kragh-Sorenson, P., Hansen, C., and Asberg, M. *Acta Psychiat. Scand. 49,* 444-456 (1973).

Kuhn, R. The treatment of depressive states with G22355 (imipramine hydrochoride). *Amer. J. Psychiat. 115,* 459-464 (1958).

Kurland, M.L. Neurotic depression; an empirical guide to two specific treatments. *Dis. Nerv. Sys. 37,* 424-430 (1976).

Lodge Patch, I.C., Pitt, B.M., and Yeo, Y.M. The direct comparison of antidepressants; imipramine and chlorprothixene. *J. Psychiat. Res. 5,* 273-280 (1967).

Mazure, C., Nelson, J.C. Lithium in psychotic refractory depression. *Sci. Proc. Am. Psych. Assoc.* Washington, D.C. (1985).

Mendels, J. Lithium in the treatment of depression. *Amer. J. Psychiat. 133,* 373-378 (1976).

Minter, R.E., and Mandell, M.R. The treatment of psychotic major depression with drugs and electroconvulsive therapy. *J. Nerv. Ment. Dis. 167,* 726-733 (1979a).

Minter, R.E., and Mandell, M.R. A prospective study of the treatment of psychotic depression. *Amer. J. Psychiat. 136,* 1470-1472 (1979b).

Morstyn, R., Hochanadel, G., Kaplan, E., and Gutheil, T.G. Depression vs. pseudodepression in dementia. *J. Clin. Psychiat. 43,* 197-199 (1982).

Nelson, J.C., and Bowers, M.B. Delusional unipolar depression: description and drug treatment. *Arch. Gen. Psychiat. 35,* 1321-1328 (1978).

Nelson, J.C., and Jatlow, P.I. Neuroleptic effect on desipramine steady-state plasma concentrations. *Amer. J. Psychiat. 137,* 1232-1234 (1980).

Nelson, J.C., Bowers, M.B., and Sweeney, D.R. Exacerbation of psychosis by tricyclic antidepressants in delusional depression. *Amer. J. Psychiat. 136,* 574-576 (1979).

Nelson, J.C., Jatlow, P.I., Quinlan, D.M., and Bowers, M.B. Desipramine plasma concentration and antidepressant response. *Arch. Gen. Psychiat. 39,* 1419-1422 (1982a).

Nelson, J.C., Jatlow, P.I., Bock, J., Quinlan, D.M., and Bowers, M.B. Major adverse reactions during desipramine treatment. *Arch. Gen. Psychiat. 39,* 1055-1061 (1982b).

Noyes, R., and Dempsey, G.M. Lithium treatment of depression. *Dis. Nerv. System 35,* 573-576 (1974).

Overall, J.E., Hollister, L.E., Johnson, M., and Pennington, V. Nosology of depression and differential response to drugs. *J.A.M.A. 195,* 946-948 (1966).

Ovhed, I. A double-blind study of flupenthixol (Fluanxol) in general practice. *Curr. Med. Res. Opin. 4,* 144 (1976).

Paykel, E.S., Price, J.S., Gillan, R.U., Palmai, G., and Chesser, E.S. A comparative trial of imipramine and chlorpromazine in depressed patients. *Brit. J. Psychiat. 114,* 1281-1287 (1968).

Perry, P.J., Morgan, D.E., Smith, R.E., and Tsuang, M.T. Treatment of unipolar depression accompanied by delusions. *J. Aff. Dis. 4,* 195-200 (1982).

Predescu, V., Ciurezu, T., Timofte, G., and Roman, I. Symptomatic relief with flupentixol (Fluanxol) of the anxious-algetic-depressive syndrome complex in neurotic states. *Acta Psychiat. Scand. 49,* 15-27 (1973).

Price, L.H., Conwell, Y., and Nelson, J.C. Lithium augmentation of combined neuroleptic-tricyclic treatment in delusional depression. *Amer. J. Psychiat. 140,* 318-322 (1983).

Quitkin, F., Rifkin, A., and Klein, D.F. Prophylaxis of affective disorders. *Arch. Gen. Psychiat. 33,* 337-341 (1976).

Raskin, A., Schulterbrandt, J.G., Reatig, N., and McKeon, J.J. Differential response to chlorpromazine, imipramine, and placebo. *Arch. Gen. Psychiat. 23,* 164-173 (1970).

Rickels, K., Jenkins, B.W., Zamostien, B.Z., Raab, E., and Kanther, M. Pharmacotherapy in neurotic depression. *J. Nerv. Ment. Dis. 145,* 475-485 (1968).

Robertson M.M., and Trimble, M.R. Major tranquilizers used as antidepressants: a review. *J. Aff. Dis. 4,* 173-193 (1982).

Roose, S.P., Glassman, A.H., Walsh, B.T., Woodring, S., and Vital-Herne, J. Depression, delusions, and suicide. *Amer. J. Psychiat. 140,* 1159-1162 (1983).

Rosenthal, S.H., and Bowden, C.L. A double-blind comparison of thioridazine (Mellaril) versus diazepam (Valium) in patients with chronic mixed anxiety and depressive symptoms. *Curr. Ther. Res. 15,* 261-267 (1973).

Schuster, T.S., Winslow, W.W., and Kellner, R. A comparison of thioridazine and diazepam in non-psychotic anxiety-depression: a pilot study. *Curr. Ther. Res. 14,* 131-135 (1972).

Simpson, G.M., Amin, M., Angus, J.W.S., Edwards, J.G., Go, S.H., and Lee, J.H. Role of antidepressants and neuroleptics in the treatment of depression. *Arch. Gen. Psychiat. 27,* 337-345 (1972).

Simpson, G.M., Lee, J.H., Cuculic, Z., and Kellner, R. Two dosages of imipramine in hospitalized endogenous and neurotic depressives. *Arch. Gen. Psychiat. 33,* 1093-1102 (1976).

Spiker, D.G., Weiss, J.C., Dealy, R.S., Griffin, S.J., Hanin, I., Neil, J.F., Perel, J.M., Rossi, A.J., and Soloff, P.H. The pharmacologic treatment of delusional depression. *Amer. J. Psychiat. 142*, 430-436 (1985).

Task Force on Late Neurological Effects of Antipsychotic Drugs. Tardive Dyskinesia: Summary of a task force report of the American Psychiatric Association. *Amer. J. Psychiat. 137,* 1163-1172 (1980).

Wittenborn, J.R., and Kiremitci, N. A comparison of antidepressant medications in neurotic and psychotic patients. *Arch. Gen. Psychiat. 32,* 1172-1176 (1975).

Yassa, R., Ghadirian, A.M., and Schwartz, G. Prevalence of tardive dyskinesia in affective disorder patients. *J. Clin. Psychiat. 44,* 410-412 (1983).

Young, J.P.R., Hughes, W.C., and Lader, M.H. A controlled comparison of flupenthixol and amitriptyline in depressed outpatients. *Brit. Med. J. 1,* 1116-1118 (1976).

8

Lithium Addition in Treatment-Resistant Major Depression

Claude de Montigny and Gérard Cournoyer

The introduction of lithium in psychiatry can probably be compared to that of antibiotics in microbiology. Its remarkable mood-stabilizing effect in most bipolar affective disorders has been a major pillar in the edification of biological psychiatry. As has been the case for most medical advances, the discovery of the therapeutic effect of lithium by Cade (1949) was serendipitous. The clinical phenomenon has prompted a tremendous fundamental research endeavor in search of its neurobiological substratum. Lithium thus rapidly became one of the most documented psychotherapeutic agents in neuropharmacology. However, in spite of the impressive amount of knowledge accumulated, the mechanism of its therapeutic effect in bipolar affective disorders remains elusive.

However, far from being useless, the data generated by this search permitted the formulation of a new therapeutic hypothesis: that lithium addition should bring about a rapid amelioration of depression in patients treated with, but not responding to, a tricyclic antidepressant drug. (The basis for this hypothesis is reviewed in the second section of this chapter.) Thus, from the perspective of the history of science, it is most interesting that the sequence of events has been as follows: the discovery of the mood-stabilizing effect of lithium prompted a vigorous neurobiological search; this search provided data which, instead of explaining the first clinical finding, led to the formulation and the discovery of a new therapeutic application for lithium. This crucial passage from deductive thinking to inductive logic is the hallmark of the contemporary revolution of medicine: serendipitous discoveries of therapeutic agents soon belong to the history of medicine, while advancement of the medical armamentarium proceeds from progress in fundamental knowledge.

The first goal of this chapter is to review clinical data on the antidepressant effect of lithium addition in major depression resistant to different types of antidepressant treatments. To begin with, it must be emphasized that this approach is newborn. At the time of writing this chapter, only seven studies have been published (de Montigny et al., 1981b; Nelson and Byck, 1982; Price et al., 1983; Louie and Mellzer, 1984; de Montigny et al., 1983; de Montigny et al., 1985; Heninger et al., 1983) and two brief reports have been printed (Birkhimer et al., 1983; Joyce et al., 1983). Only a few questions can as yet receive a definite answer, whereas many more remain unanswered or can at best be tentatively answered from pilot observations. Thus, special effort is made in this chapter to distinguish as clearly as possible the few facts that can be considered as established from the others which will require further investigation.

OVERVIEW OF THE SYSTEMATIC STUDIES

The first report of the rapid antidepressant effect of lithium addition in major depression resistant to tricyclic antidepressant (TCA) drugs was published in 1981 (de Montigny et al., 1981b). This was a prospective study conducted in eight unipolar depressed patients who had failed to respond satisfactorily to one of the following TCA drugs: amitriptyline (3 patients), imipramine (1 patient), doxepin (2 patients), or iprindole (2 patients). These drugs had been administered at a therapeutic dosage for at least three weeks (30 ± 7.5 days; mean ± s.e.m.). Two criteria had been used to define these patients as treatment resistant: first, the decrease of the total score on the Hamilton Rating Scale for Depression (HRS-D) had to be less than 40% from the pretreatment value; second, the two examining psychiatrists, the nursing staff, and the patients themselves had to agree that there had been no substantial improvement of depression, and that there was still a clinically significant functional impairment. Lithium carbonate was added at a daily dose of 900 mg (300 mg t.i.d.). Patients were reevaluated 48 hours later. All patients showed some improvement which ranged from 47% to 88% (67% ± 13%; mean ± s.e.m.) on the HRS-D.

In 1982, Nelson and Byck reported the response to lithium addition in three patients who had failed to respond to phenelzine, a monoamine oxidase inhibitor (MAOI), administered at a therapeutic dosage for at least one month. Lithium was administered at a dose of 900 mg/day. The three patients experienced a rapid and marked improvement of their depressive state. The authors emphasized the presence of a clinically significant improvement within the first 24 hours in two of the patients.

Heninger et al. (1983) were the first investigators to conduct a controlled study of the therapeutic effect of lithium addition in 15 patients who had failed to respond to a treatment of at least three weeks with high doses of amitriptyline (6 patients), desipramine (5 patients), or mianserine (4 patients). In the first phase of the study, lithium carbonate, 900-1,200 mg/day (8 patients), or placebo (7 patients) were added in a double-blind manner to the antidepressant drug which was maintained at the same dose. All patients receiving lithium showed some improvement whereas none improved significantly with placebo addition. In most patients, the improvement became clinically significant only several days after lithium addition. In the second phase, lithium was added in a single-blind manner to patients who had received placebo during the first phase. Their response to lithium was superimposable on that of the lithium group of the first phase.

We have recently reported the results of three studies carried out in a total of 34 unipolar TCA-resistant patients (de Montigny et al., 1983). In the first study, the 34 patients were given lithium carbonate (300 mg. t.i.d.) and reevaluated 48 hours later. Eight of these patients underwent a second lithium trial after having been treated unsuccessfully for three further weeks with another TCA drug. Thus, a total of 42 observations were made. The TCA drugs administered were amitriptyline (16 observations), imipramine (12 observations), trimipramine (6 observations), desipramine (4 observations), and doxepin (4 observations), at a mean dosage of 216 ± 6 mg per day (range: 150-300 mg per day) for an average duration of 45 ± 5 days. After 48 hours, lithium had brought about a mean 62% improvement on the HRS-D scale. Seventy-four percent of the patients showed a greater than 50% improvement on the HRS-D scale.

In the second study, ten female unipolar patients not improved after a three-week treatment with either amitriptyline (225 mg per day; 5 patients) or placebo (5 patients) administered on a double-blind basis were given lithium carbonate, 900 mg/day. All five amitriptyline-treated patients showed a greater than 50% improvement 48 hours after lithium addition whereas only one of the patients receiving placebo improved by more than 50% on lithium.

The third study consisted of the withdrawal of lithium 48 hours after its addition in nine patients of the first study who had improved by more than 50% when lithium had been added to their therapeutic regimen. Unexpectedly, only five had relapsed five days after lithium withdrawal whereas the four others showed a sustained remission.

Since most TCA drugs interfere with monoamine reuptake, we recently undertook a study with iprindole, an atypical TCA drug which does not affect monoaminergic reuptake (de Montigny, 1982), in order to ascertain that the prim ng of lithium action by TCA drugs could not be attributed to their presynaptic actions (see second section of this chapter). Lithium carbonate (900 mg/day) was administered to seven patients unimproved by a three-week treatment with iprindole (90 mg/day). In six of the seven patients, lithium addition brought about in 48 hours a greater than 50% improvement of depression as measured from the HRS-D scale (de Montigny et al., 1985).

Price et al. (1983) have recently reported their prospective study of lithium carbonate addition in six patients with psychotic depression unresponsive to a combined neuroleptic-tricyclic treatment. In four patients lithium addition produced a good to dramatic improvement. It is noteworthy that the one patient who showed only a moderate response was also suffering from Parkinson's disease and that the sixth patient who failed to respond to lithium addition had a mild hypothyroidism and subsequently proved unresponsive to a 6-week trial with maprotiline and a series of 10 ECT sessions.

We have recently completed a double-blind cross-over study comparing the effects of placebo and lithium addition in 12 patients not satisfactorily improved by trimipramine (9 patients) or amitriptyline (3 patients), both administered at a dosage of 200 mg/day for 3 or 4 weeks. These 12 patients were selected from an initial group of 34 patients, half of which were given amitriptyline and half trimipramine on a double-blind basis. Six of the TCA-resistant patients received lithium carbonate (900 mg/day) for 48 hours during the fourth week of the trial and placebo for 48 hours during the fifth week. The other six patients received placebo first and lithium second. In all cases, the TCA drug dosage was maintained constant. The detailed results of this study will be reported shortly. In brief, lithium addition induced a statistically significant mean improvement of 40% on the HRS-D within 48 hours, whereas placebo failed to modify significantly the depressive syndrome (mean improvement of 14%). As observed in our previous study, a high proportion of the patients who showed a marked improvement with lithium addition maintained this improvement after lithium discontinuation. It is possible that the smaller proportion of patients improved in this study with lithium addition as compared to that in our three previous studies and in the studies by other groups might be due in part to the fact that the majority of these patients (9 out of 12 patients) were receiving trimipramine (see below).

In conclusion, the results of these seven systematic studies converge unanimously on the conclusion that lithium addition can bring about a profound alleviation of major depression unresponsive to a tricyclic or tetracyclic antidepressant drug or to a MAOI. We now examine in more detail some specific issues of this therapeutic approach.

SPECIFIC CLINICAL ISSUES

Which Type of Depressive Disorders Resistant to a TCA Drug Will Respond to Lithium Addition?

The vast majority of the TCA-resistant patients reported thus far, in whom the effect of lithium addition was assessed, were presenting a unipolar affective disorder. However, rapid relief from depression with lithium addition has been reported by Joyce et al. (1983) in three antidepressant-unresponsive bipolar patients and by Price et al. (1983) in one other bipolar patient and in two unipolar patients with "bipolar-like" features. In the controlled study of Heninger et al., (1983), one bipolar patient unresponsive to mianserin improved markedly with lithium addition. Thus, it would appear that bipolar treatment-resistant depression is at least as responsive to lithium addition as is unipolar treatment-resistant depression.

As far as depressive disorders other than those meeting RDC or DSM-III criteria for major affective disorders are concerned, there is no data available.

It is noteworthy that major depression with psychotic features appears to respond particularly well to lithium addition. This is all the more interesting as it is well documented that the rate of response of delusional depression is much lower than that of major depressions without psychotic symptoms (Charney and Nelson, 1981). In the report of Price et al. (1983), the patients studied were receiving both a TCA and a neuroleptic (to which combination they were resistant) at the time of lithium addition. However, it is likely that lithium potentiated the action of the TCA rather than that of the neuroleptic, since, in our studies, five treatment-resistant patients presenting a delusional depression and receiving a TCA only markedly improved when lithium was added. It is possible that the greater severity of the depressive syndrome in these patients accounted for the apparently greater responsiveness of these patients simply by rendering the response more dramatic. At any rate, the number of delusional patients treated thus far with this novel approach is too small to allow a valid comparison with non-psychotic major depression.

Responding Symptoms

In contrast to the usual "patchy" time course of the improvement usually seen with TCA drugs, lithium addition produces a remarkably uniform improvement in all spheres affected by the illness, with the exception of sleep (Cournoyer et al., 1984). It is possible that the different temporal patterns of the responses to TCA drugs and to lithium addition might be explained on the basis of a successive sensitization to serotonin (5-HT) by TCA drugs in different forebrain regions (Wang and Aghajanian, 1980), whereas, at the time of lithium addition (i.e., after at least three weeks of treatment with a TCA drug), all forebrain regions receiving a serotonergic input can be presumed to be sensitized to 5-HT. Hence, lithium, acting presynaptically on the 5-HT neuron, unveils the sensitization of these forebrain regions to 5-HT in a simultaneous manner. As for sleep, most patients do not report a lengthening of sleep time. However, one striking and frequent observation is that insomnia is no longer perceived by the patient as a disturbing symptom: whereas before lithium addition intense depressive rumination and anxiety often supervene during periods of insomnia, following lithium addition insomnia is no longer accompanied by painful feelings.

Response Predictors

With the possible exception of psychotic symptoms (see above), we have been unable to identify any predictor of the response to lithium addition. The rate of response is similar in men and in women and in all age groups. Neither duration nor severity of the depressive episode appear to be determinant factors (de Montigny et al., 1983). It will be certainly most interesting to look at the predictive value of neuroendocrinological or other neurobiological markers.

Successful Lithium Addition

In the eight studies reviewed above, six TCA drugs had been administered before lithium was added: amitriptyline, imipramine, trimipramine, doxepin, desipramine, and iprindole. The response of lithium addition appeared quite comparable among the drug groups, with the possible exception of trimipramine. In our second open study (de Montigny et al., 1983), the mean improvement (51%) obtained with the addition of lithium to the trimipramine treatment was of a somewhat smaller magnitude from that (64%) obtained with lithium addition in the four other TCA drug groups, and from that seen in iprindole-pretreated patients (de Montigny et al., 1985). Consistent with these results, in our recent controlled study (de Montigny et al., unpublished observations), the response to lithium addition in the amitriptyline-resistant group (56%; 3 patients) was greater than that of the trimipramine-resistant group (33%; 9 patients). However, since these figures are derived from relatively small numbers of observations, any definite conclusion must be withheld until further investigations are carried out. It would seem that lithium addition in clomipramine-resistant patients produces an improvement of at least the same magnitude as that reported with other TCA drugs (personal communications from R. Duguay, from F. Grunberg, and from L. Traskman).

We have briefly reviewed the report of Nelson and Byck (1982) on the dramatic effect of lithium addition in three phenelzine-resistant depressions. Although a similar response was observed in some further phenelzine-resistant patients by Nelson (personal communication) and by Louie and Meltzer (1984) and in one tranylcypromine-resistant patient by Joyce et al. (1983), the small number of patients studied thus far precludes any valid comparison of the priming effect of MAOI drugs with that of TCA drugs. Nonetheless, the remarkable results obtained by these investigators certainly warrant further investigation.

As far as non-TCA non-MAOI drugs are concerned, the only drug which has been conclusively shown to prime the effect of lithium addition is mianserin (Heninger et al., 1983). However, several other antidepressant drugs have been observed in small numbers of patients to prime the effect of lithium, namely maprotiline (J. Bellwald, personal communication), trazodone (Birkhimer et al., 1983), zimelidine (Joyce, 1985; Pecknold, personal communication; de Montigny, unpublished observation) and amoxapine (Louie and Meltzer, 1984). Given the increasing use of these new antidepressant drugs, further investigations of the possible benefit of lithium addition in resistant patients is certainly warranted.

Length of Treatment

There is no precise data as to the "minimal" length of pretreatment with an antidepressant drug necessary to obtain a clinically significant potentiation by lithium. This information is of considerable theoretical interest. However, it would probably be of little practical value since the clinician must have a sufficient degree of certainty concerning the "resistance" to the antidepressant drug before adding lithium, and it is generally accepted that a three-week period is the minimal one to assess responsiveness to an antidepressant drug (Klein et al., 1980).

In the same line of thought, we cannot see any valid rationale for initiating the treatment with the combination of an antidepressant drug and lithium. First, on theoretical grounds, lithium would not be expected to potentiate the antidepressant drug until the postsynaptic sensitization (occurring only after at least two weeks of treatment) is induced by the antidepressant drug (see page 158). Second, from a practical point of view, lithium would be administered without any benefit to approximately 70% of the patients since this is generally the rate of response to the antidepressant drug alone. It is most probably these factors which precluded the demonstration of a clear superiority of the combination of a TCA drug with lithium over a TCA drug alone in two studies where the drug combination was administered from the onset of treatment (Lingjaerde et al., 1974; Nick et al., 1976).

In conclusion, at this state of knowledge, it would seem advisable to administer the antidepressant drug for at least three weeks and only then add lithium if no substantial improvement has occurred.

Plasma Lithium Level

In our study in iprindole-resistant patients a significant negative correlation with lithium plasma level emerged (de Montigny et al., 1984). However, in our three other studies comprising a much greater number of patients, there was no statistically significant correlation between the degree of improvement and the plasma lithium level (ranging from 0.4 to 1.2 mEq/L) (de Montigny et al., 1981b; de Montigny et al., 1983; Cournoyer et al., 1984). This absence of correlation is not surprising in the light of a serotonergic hypothesis (see page 157) since levels as low as 0.1 mEq/L of lithium already increase 5-HT synthesis in the rat brain (Broderick and Lynch, 1982). In practice, it would be logical to aim at "low" levels (0.4 to 0.6 mEq/L) since higher levels might not be more efficacious but might produce more side effects.

Main Side Effects

Surprisingly, very few side effects were observed in our trials. Obviously, the dramatic relief of depression produced in many patients might have shadowed the side effects since these patients were obviously more interested by the sudden relief of their depression than preoccupied by side effects. However, systematic collection of data by the research nurse revealed an extremely low incidence of side effects. These consisted mainly of abdominal discomfort, nausea, skin rash, and tremor. The relatively low plasma levels of lithium attained in our patients certainly account in good part for the low incidence of side effects. However, it is plausible that, as proposed by O'Flanagan (1973), the TCA drug pretreatment might reduce the incidence of lithium side effects.

Length of Lithium Trial

In our studies, the effect of lithium addition was assessed after 48 hours. The rationale for measuring the effect of lithium addition after such a brief exposure was based on the short time constant of the effect of lithium on 5-HT neurons (see page 157). As reviewed above, the majority of the patients showed a clinically significant response to lithium addition within this time lapse. Due to the design of our studies, we cannot know whether some "nonresponders" to lithium addition administered for 48h only would have shown a "late" response to a longer administration of lithium. Nelson and Byck (1982) have also observed a very rapid onset of the antidepressant effect of lithium addition in MAOI-resistant patients. However, for reasons that remain unclear, Heninger et al. (1983) found that a longer than 48 hour treatment with lithium was required in most of their antidepressant-resistant patients before a significant alleviation of depression could be detected. Thus, in practice, it would seem that lithium should be added to the antidepressant drug for at least five to seven days before a definite judgment is made on the effectiveness of the combination for a given patient.

Maintenance of Combined Treatment

This is obviously the most crucial question and, at the same time, that to which, unfortunately, it is at present almost impossible to give a satisfactory answer. Initially, we pursued the combined treatment for 2-3 months and then discontinued lithium. Although the absence of formal evaluation and of systematic data collection precludes any precise estimation, it appeared that most patients remained well after lithium discontinuation. Later, however, we made the unexpected observation reported above that a large proportion of patients improved by a 48-hour exposure to lithium remained in remission following lithium withdrawal. Hence, this raises the question of the extent to which the continuation of the lithium in our first patients was responsible for the sustained improvement. We would like to underscore here the striking parallel between this phenomenon and the sustained improvement of TCA-resistant depression induced by a single or two consecutive injections of reserpine (Poldinger, 1963; Haskovec and Rysänek, 1967; Hopkinson and Kenny, 1975).* Since both lithium and reserpine result in an enhanced release of 5-HT in the synaptic cleft, we have proposed that a maximal transient augmentation of 5-HT neurotransmission might induce a long-lasting neurobiological modification, the nature of which remains totally unknown (de Montigny et al., 1983).

Given the present uncertainty on the issue, it is impossible to derive any therapeutic rule. Physicians who use this approach, keeping in mind that the remission might persist without lithium in some patients, should consider the possibility of attempting to withdraw lithium for patients showing a sustained remission on the combined treatment, if need be reinstating it for a longer period of time in patients in whom depressive symptoms recur.

---

*Editor's note: For a detailed discussion of this issue, see Chapter 19.

ON THE NEUROBIOLOGICAL SUBSTRATUM OF THE THERAPEUTIC EFFECT OF LITHIUM ADDITION IN ANTIDEPRESSANT-RESISTANT PATIENTS

Is the Effect of Lithium Addition a True Pharmacological Potentiation?

The first possibility to envisage is a pharmacokinetic interaction. This can be ruled out on the basis of the unchanged plasma levels of TCA drugs and their demethylated metabolites following lithium addition (de Montigny et al., 1981; de Montigny et al., 1983; de Montigny et al., 1985).

Second, the possibility that lithium alone might have produced the improvement has to be considered. In their recent thorough review of the controversy on the antidepressant efficacy of lithium alone in major depression, Ramsey and Mendels (1981) conclude that it seems to exert a definite antidepressant effect in some major depressions, particularly in patients with bipolar depression, but that, in most responsive patients, several weeks of lithium administration are required before it is clinically significant. Thus, the fact that lithium addition in many patients not responding to a long-term antidepressant treatment produces a marked effect within 48 hours makes it very unlikely that lithium alone might produce this improvement. As improbable such a possibility might be, it would nevertheless be important to rule out the possibility that the pretreatment with an antidepressant would somehow sort out "lithium-responsive" patients (resistant to the antidepressant drug) from "lithium-unresponsive" patients (responding to the antidepressant drug alone). We are presently conducting a clinical study in which patients receive lithium for 48 hours before the antidepressant drug is started. This should provide a definite test for this hypothesis. In this regard, it is highly interesting that Neubauer and Bermingham (1976) have attempted to define from their observation of 20 patients a depressive syndrome which would rapidly respond to lithium alone. It is striking that all 20 patients had received a TCA drug before lithium was administered. Thus, although the exact treatment schedules were not given, it might have well been that the response to lithium they observed was a potentiation of the TCA drug pretreatment.

Effects of Antidepressant Drugs and of Lithium on 5-HT Neurotransmission

Novel electrophysiological evidence has been provided in the last few years for the long-standing hypothesis that antidepressant treatments produce their therapeutic effect via an "intensification of the central serotoninergic processes" (Lapin and Oxenkrug, 1969). In brief, long-term TCA-drug administration induces a sensitization of rat CNS neurons to microiontophoretically-applied 5-HT (de Montigny and Aghajanian, 1978; de Montigny et al., 1981a; Gallager and Bunney, 1979; Menkes and Aghajanian, 1981; Menkes et al., 1980; Wang and Aghajanian, 1981). Mianserine also sensitizes forebrain neurons to 5-HT (Blier et al. 1984) and repeated electroconvulsive shock treatments produce a similar sensitization to 5-HT (de Montigny, 1984). Long-term zimelidine treatment in the rat does not modify postsynaptic neuron sensitivity to 5-HT but enhances the response of the target neurons to the electrical activation of the ascending 5-HT pathway (Blier and de Montigny, 1983b), presumably via 5-HT reuptake blockade (Ross and Renyi, 1977). Concerning trazodone, Scuvée-Moreau and Dresse (1982) have shown its potent effect on the firing activity of 5-HT neurons.

The 5-HT potentiating effect of lithium has been well documented in various paradigms. Grahame-Smith and Green (1974) have elegantly demonstrated, using the hyperactivity syndrome, that lithium enhances 5-HT neurotransmission via its action on the 5-HT neurons itself. This is consistent with the increased synthesis (Broderick and Lynch, 1982) and release (Treiser et al., 1981) of 5-HT produced by lithium. We have confirmed recently, using an electrophysiological approach, the enhancement of 5-HT neurotransmission after two days of lithium administration in the rat (Blier and de Montigny, 1985).

It is from these two series of fundamental neuropharmacological data that we have formulated the hypothesis that lithium addition in patients treated with, but not responding to, an antidepressant drug should produce a rapid and marked antidepressant effect. It was postulated that enhancing the activity of 5-HT neurons by adding lithium should potentiate the serotoninergic effect of the antidepressant drug.

Are Clinical Data Consistent with the Postulated 5-HT-Mediated Potentiation of Antidepressant Drugs by Lithium?

We would like here to make conspicuous the remarkable congruence between available neuropharmacological data and the clinical phenomenology of the therapeutic response in support of the notion that the 5-HT system might mediate the therapeutic effect of lithium addition in treatment-resistant depression.

1. Time constants

The 5-HT neurotransmission enhancement by antidepressant drugs and that by lithium have different time constants: a long-term treatment with a TCA drug is required before the postsynaptic neuron sensitization to 5-HT is detectable, whereas the enhancing effect of lithium on 5-HT neurons is already present after 24 to 36 hours. Thus, the clinical phenomenon conforms to these time constants: lithium addition exerts a rapid antidepressant effect in most patients pretreated on a long-term basis with an antidepressant drug.

2. Types of antidepressant treatments potentiated by lithium

Lithium addition produces a similar effect in patients pretreated with various TCA drugs which have different presynaptic effects on monoaminergic reuptake, but a common property of producing sensitization to 5-HT. Furthermore, lithium exerted the same effect when added in patients pretreated with iprindole (de Montigny et al., 1985), an atypical TCA drug devoid of presynaptic effect on monoaminergic reuptake (Ross et al., 1971) but sharing with other TCA drugs the ability to induce a sensitization to 5-HT (de Montigny and Aghajanian, 1978; Menkes et al., 1980; Wang and Aghajanian, 1981). We have recently reported that long-term mianserin administration in rats also induces a sensitization of forebrain neurons to 5-HT (Blier et al. 1984). This provides a neurobiological basis for the potentiation of mianserin by lithium found by Heninger et al. (1983). Similarly, the lithium potentiates the action of MAOI drugs, trazodone, and zimelidine which all have the ability to enhance 5-HT neurotransmission (Blier and de Montigny, 1983; Dowdall and de Montigny, 1984). Hence, the 5-HT system appears to be the Ariadne's thread which can account for the potentiation by lithium of such different drugs as TCAs, iprindole, mianserin, MAOIs, zimelidine, and trazodone.

3. Lithium plasma levels

Lithium plasma level as low as 0.4 mEq/L appears sufficient to potentiate markedly antidepressant drugs. This clinical observation provides a powerful characterization of the phenomenon, permitting us to focus on a limited number of neurobiological actions of lithium. For instance, it rules out a possible involvement of the noradrenergic system since much higher levels are required to decrease cAMP response to NE (Katz et al., 1968). On the contrary, it constitutes another degree of congruence with the neurobiological data supporting the implication of the 5-HT system since low plasma levels prove sufficient to affect the 5-HT neurotransmission in biochemical (Broderick and Lynch, 1982), behavioral (Grahame-Smith and Green, 1974), and electrophysiological (Blier and de Montigny, 1985) paradigms.

4. Would other "5-HT agents" mimic lithium?

If one assumes that lithium produces its potentiation of antidepressant drugs through enhancing 5-HT neuron action [presumably via an enhanced release (Treiser et al., 1981)], other agents capable of increasing the availability of 5-HT in the synaptic cleft should also be expected to potentiate the therapeutic effect of antidepressant drugs. There have been three reports that reserpine, which releases 5-HT (Garattini et al., 1959), can improve depressions treated with but not responding to a TCA drug (Poldinger, 1963; Haskovec and Rysänek, 1967; Hopkinson and Kenny, 1975). An anecdotal report by Cole (1980) mentions that the addition of fenfluramine, a 5-HT releaser, can induce an improvement in patients not responding satisfactorily to a long-term treatment with amitriptyline. Hence, these two series of observations would support the validity of the basic assumption, i.e., that pharmacological agents capable of increasing synaptic availability of 5-HT do share with lithium the ability to potentiate the therapeutic effect of antidepressant treatments.

Note: Two recent reports (Louie and Meltzer, 1984; Price et al., 1984) have called attention to the apparent induction of hypomania or mania by lithium addition in treatment-resistant depressed patients. These authors have reported four such events and we have also observed a switch into hypomania in two patients shortly after lithium addition. As unexpected as this observation might be, the close temporal relationship would suggest that the switch into hypomania or mania was induced by lithium. The incidence of this phenomenon cannot be precisely evaluated at the present time, but it would appear to be very low. It is noteworthy that the occurrence of such a switch upon lithium addition was not limited to bipolar patients, as four of the six patients were definitely unipolar.

ACKNOWLEDGMENTS

Clinical research was conducted at the Psychiatric Research Center of the L. H. Lafontaine Hospital, Montreal, and preclinical research at the Neuroscience Research Center of the University of Montreal supported by Research Grants from the Medical Research Council of Canada and the Fonds de la Recherche en Santé du Québec.

REFERENCES

Birkhimer, L.J., Alderman, A.A., Schmitt, C.E., and Ednie, K.J. Combined trazodone-lithium therapy for refractory depression. *Am. J. Psychiat. 140*, 1382-1383 (1983).

Blier, P., and de Montigny, C. Electrophysiological studies on the effect of repeated zimelidine administration on serotoninergic neurotransmission in the rat. *J. Neurosci. 3*, 1270-1278 (1983a).

Blier, P., and de Montigny, C. Short-term lithium administration enhances serotonergic neurotransmission: electrophysiological evidence in the rat CNS. *Eur. J. Pharmacol. 113*, 69–77 (1985).

Blier, P., de Montigny, C. and Tardif, D. Effects of two antidepressant drugs, mianserine and indalpine, on the serotonergic system: single-cell studies in the rat. *Psychopharmacology 84*, 242-249 (1984).

Broderick, P., and Lynch, V. Behavioral and biochemical changes induced by lithium and L-tryptophan in muricidal rats. *Neuropharmacology 21*, 671-679 (1982).

Cade, J.F. Lithium salts in the treatment of psychotic excitement. *Med. J. Australia 36*, 349-352 (1949).

Charney, D.S., and Nelson, J.C. Delusional and nondelusional unipolar depression: further evidence for distinct subtypes. *Am. J. Psychiat. 138*, 328-333 (1981).

Cole, J.O. Fenfluramine. In *Psychopharmacology Update*, J.O. Cole, ed. Collamore Press, Lexington (1980), pp. 81-91.

Cournoyer, G., de Montigny, C., Ouellette, J., Leblanc, G., Langlois, R. and Elie, R. Lithium addition in tricyclic-resistant unipolar depression: a placebo-controlled study. *Coll Int. Neuropsychopharmacol. 14*, F-177 (1984).

de Montigny, C. Iprindole: a corner stone in the neurobiological investigation of antidepressant treatments. *Mod. Probl. Pharmacopsychiat. 18*, 102-116 (1982).

de Montigny, C. Electroconvulsive shock treatments increase responsiveness of forebrain neurons to serotonin. *J. Pharmacol. Exp. Ther. 228*, 230–234 (1984).

de Montigny, C., and Aghajanian, G.K. Tricyclic antidepressants: long-term treatment increases responsivity of rat forebrain neurons to serotonin. *Science 202*, 1303-1306 (1978).

de Montigny, C., Blier, P., Caillé, G., and Kouassi, E. Pre- and postsynaptic effect of zimelidine and norzimelidine on the serotoninergic system: single cells study in the rat. *Acta Psychiat. Scand. 63* (Supp. 290), 79-90 (1981a).

de Montigny, C., Grunberg, F., Mayer, A., and Deschenes, J.-P. Lithium induces rapid relief of depression in tricyclic antidepressant drug nonresponders. *Br. J. Psychiat. 138*, 252-256 (1981b).

de Montigny, C., Cournoyer, G., Morissette, R., Langlois, R., and Caillé, G. Lithium carbonate addition in tricyclic antidepressant-resistant unipolar depression. *Arch. Gen. Psychiat. 40*, 1327-1334 (1983).

de Montigny, C., Elie, R., and Caillé, G. Rapid response to lithium addition in iprindole-resistant unipolar depression. *Am. J. Psychiat. 142*, 220-223 (1985).

Dowdall, M., and de Montigny, C. Pre- and postsynaptic effects of trazodone on serotonin neurotransmission: single cell studies in the rat. *Neurosci. Abst. 10*: 9.5 (1984).

Gallager, D.W., and Bunney Jr., W.E. Failure of chronic lithium treatment to block tricyclic antidepressant-induced 5-HT supersensitivity. *Naunyn-Schmiedeberg's Arch. Pharmacol. 307*, 129-133 (1979).

Garattini, S., Mortavi, A., Valsecchi, A., Valzelli, J. Reserpine derivatives with specific hypotensive or sedative activity. *Nature 183*, 1273-1274 (1959).

Grahame-Smith, D.G., and Green, A.R. The role of brain 5-hydroxytryptamine in the hyperactivity produced by lithium and monoamine oxidase inhibition. *Br. J. Pharmacol. 52*, 19-26 (1974).

Haskovec, L., and Rysänek, K. The action of reserpine in imipramine-resistant patients. *Psychopharmacology 11*, 18-30 (1967).

Heninger, G.R., Charney, D.S., and Sternberg, D.E. Lithium carbonate augmentation of antidepressant treatment. *Arch. Gen. Psychiat. 40*, 1335-1342 (1983).

Hopkinson, G., and Kenny, F. Treatment with reserpine of patients resistant to tricyclic antidepressants. *Psychiat. Clin. 8*, 109-114 (1975).

Joyce, P.R. Mood response to methylphenidate and the dexamethasone suppression test as predictors of treatment response to zimelidine and lithium in major depression. *Biol. Psychiat. 20*, 598-604 (1985).

Joyce, P.R., Hewland, H.R., and Jones, A.V. Rapid response to lithium in treatment-resistant depression. *Br. J. Psychiat. 142*, 204-206 (1983).

Katz, R.I., Chase, T.N., and Kopin, I.J. Evoked release of norepinephrine and serotonin from brain slices: inhibition by lithium. *Science 162*, 466-467 (1968).

Klein, D.E., Gittelman, R., Quitkin, F., and Rifkin, A. *Diagnosis and Drug Treatment of Psychiatric Disorders: Adults and Children*, 2nd edition. Baltimore, Williams and Wilkins Co. (1980).

Lapin, J.P., and Oxenkrug, G.F. Intensification of the central serotoninergic processes as a possible determinant of the thymoleptic effect. *Lancet i*, 132-136 (1969).

Lingjaerde, O., Edbend, A.H., Gormsen, C.A., Gottcries, C.G., Haugstadt, A., Hermann, I.L., Hollnagel, P., Mäkimattila, A., Rasmussen, K.E., Remvig, J., and Robak, O.H. The effect of lithium carbonate in combination with tricyclic antidepressants in endogenous depression. *Acta Psychiat. Scand. 50*, 233-2422 (1974).

Louie, A.K., and Meltzer, H.Y. Lithium potentiation of antidepressant treatment. *J. Clin. Psychopharmacol. 4*, 316-321 (1984).

Menkes, D.B., and Aghajanian, G.K.α_1-Adrenoreceptor-mediated responses in the lateral geniculate nucleus are enhanced by chronic antidepressant treatment. *Eur. J. Pharmacol. 74*, 27-35 (1981).

Menkes, D.B., Aghajanian, G.K., and McCall, R.B. Chronic antidepressant treatment enhances α-adrenergic and serotonergic responses in the facial nucleus. *Life Sci. 27*, 45-55 (1980).

Nelson, J.C., and Byck, R. Rapid response to lithium in phenelzine nonresponders. *Br. J. Psychiat. 141*, 85-86 (1982).

Neubauer, H., and Bermingham, P. A depressive syndrome responsive to lithium: An analysis of 20 cases. *J. Nerv. Ment. Dis. 163*, 276-281 (1976).

Nick, J., Luante, J.P., Des Lauriers, A., Moinet, A., and Monfort, J. L'association clomipramine-lithium: essai contrôlé. *Encéphale 2*, 5-6 (1976).

O'Flanagan, P.M. Chlorimipramine infusion and lithium carbonate: a synergistic effect. *Lancet ii*, 974 (1973).

Poldinger, W. Combined administration of desipramine and reserpine or tetrabenazine in depressive patients. *Psychopharmacology 4*, 308-310 (1963).

Price, L.H., Charney, D.S., and Heninger, G.R. Manic symptoms following addition of lithium to antidepressant treatment. *J. Clin Psychopharmacol. 4*, 361-362 (1984).

Price, L.H., Conwell, Y., and Nelson, J.C. Lithium augmentation of combined neuroleptic-tricyclic treatment in delusional depression. *Am. J. Psychiat. 140*, 318-322 (1983).

Ramsey, T.A., and Mendels, J. Lithium ion as an antidepressant. In *Antidepressants: Neurochemical, Behavioral and Clinical Perspectives*, S.J. Enna, J.B. Malick, and E. Richelson, eds. Raven Press, New York (1981), pp. 175-182.

Ross, S.B., Renyi, A.L., and Ogren, S.-O. A comparison of the inhibitory activities of iprindole and imipramine on the uptake of 5-hydroxytryptamine and noradrenaline in brain slices. *Life Sci. 10*, 1267-1277 (1971).

Ross, S.B., and Renyi, A.L. Inhibition of the neuronal uptake of 5-hydroxytryptamine and noradrenaline in rat brain by (Z)-and (E)-3-(4-bromophenyl)-N, N-dimethyl-3-(3-pyridyl) allylamines and their secondary analogues. *Neuropharmacology 16*, 57-63 (1977).

Scuvée-Moreau, J., and Dresse, A. Effect of trazodone on the firing rate of central monoaminergic neurons. *Arch. Int. Pharmacodyn. 260*, 299-301 (1982).

Treiser, S.L., Cascio, C.S., O'Dohohue, T.L., Thoa, N.B., Jacobowitz, D.M., and Kellar, K.J. Lithium increases serotonin release and decreases serotonin receptors in the hippocampus. *Science 213*, 1529-1531 (1981).

Wang, R.Y., and Aghajanian, G.K. Enhanced sensitivity of amygdaloid neurons to serotonin and norepinephrine after chronic antidepressant treatment. *Commun. Psychopharmacol. 4*, 83-90 (1980).

9

ECT: A Last Resort Treatment for Resistant Depression?

Max Fink

INTRODUCTION

Despite a wide range of interventions, depressed patients may fail to respond to treatment, and are then viewed as "therapy-resistant." While some authors speak of therapy resistance among ambulatory patients, we reserve the term for those patients who have not improved after adequate courses of different therapies and are so ill as to need hospitalization. This is not to dispute the occurrence of treatment resistance in ambulatory depressed patients, but such patients are inherently less ill, and the variety of their disabilities so broad, as to make their classification using modern diagnostic criteria (as DSM-III or RDC) difficult. Further, there are many interventions which are reserved for hospitalized patients, and it seems practical to reserve the term "therapy-resistance" for the patients who have been given maximum opportunities for relief.

Among the many probable reasons depressed patients fail to improve with treatment are improper treatment and misdiagnosis; inadequate dosing, due to physician error or poor patient compliance; and the inherent inefficiency of the recommended treatments. The philosophical rejection of convulsive therapy (ECT), a useful treatment for patients with major depressive disorders, also encourages therapy resistance.

With the introduction of tricyclic antidepressant drugs, a hierarchy of treatment administrations developed; a hierarchy which obliges patients first to be treated with a tricyclic antidepressant; then an alternate tricyclic antidepressant, probably at higher dosages; followed by a monoamine oxidase inhibitor. For some therapists, more dramatic treatments follow, such as newer antidepressants ("second-" and "third-generation" drugs); or lithium therapy; or lithium combined with a tricyclic; or lithium combined with a newer antidepressant; or a tricyclic combined with an antipsychotic drug; or intravenous infusions of tricyclic substances. In this hierarchy, ECT is usually seen as a treatment of last resort, with therapists insisting on numerous "adequate" courses of therapy to which a patient has failed to respond before referral for ECT is made.

Such a philosophy and practice consign patients to prolonged illness and suffering. Our review of the clinical data finds the indications for convulsive therapy in patients with severe depressive disorders to be well defined. The practice of ECT is inherently safe, but it is arduous, expensive, frightening, and inelegant in its administration. Despite these caveats, the efficacy of ECT is so high as to encourage the belief that earlier use of ECT will significantly reduce the population of therapy-resistant depressed patients and the duration and severity of their disability.

EVIDENCE OF EFFICACY

When the efficacy of tricyclic antidepressant drugs was discerned in the early 1960s, it was generally assumed that these substances would replace the use of ECT, much as the introduction of antipsychotic drugs affected the use of insulin coma and leucotomy. In the ensuing decades, this expectation was not fulfilled; antidepressant substances were inherently less specific and less effective, leading to our present interest in "therapy-resistant depression." Many in the profession and some among the laity, puzzling at the continued use of ECT, wondered whether such use reflected a medical abuse of a potentially intrusive treatment. In the early 1970s, these concerns led to demands for political and legislative proscription of ECT. To the surprise of many and the chagrin of some critics, reviews of comparative clinical studies found compelling evidence that ECT was singularly effective in patients with major depressive disorders, particularly those with symptoms of melancholia, delusions, severe inanition, and suicidal preoccupation (Avery and Winokur, 1977; APA, 1978; Fink, 1978, 1979; Scovern and Kilmann, 1980; Kendell, 1981; d'Elia et al., 1983; Pippard and Ellam, 1981). If one restricts the analyses to those studies which meet the criteria of random assignment, independent ratings, and defined outcome criteria, six studies compare ECT and tricyclic antidepressants in patients with depressive disorders (Fink, 1981). ECT is the superior treatment ($\chi^2 \pm 25.5, p \pm 4 \times 10^{-7}$). It is also superior in outcome to MAOI, drug placebo, and sham ECT.

When one considers subtypes of depressions, special consideration should be given to patients with delusions, particularly delusions of guilt, worthlessness, or somatic concern; to those with catatonic symptoms; and to those with suicidal preoccupations.

Delusional Depression

A compelling case for the superior efficacy of ECT to tricyclic drugs is made in a study reported in 1964 by deCarolis and his associates. This report was recently translated and republished by Avery and Lubrano (1979). All patients hospitalized for depression were first treated with high doses of imipramine—at least 200 mg/day to a maximum of 350 mg/day for 25 days. Patients whose trial of imipramine was unsuccessful after 30 days were started on a course of ECT, with a minimum of eight and a maximum of ten treatments. Of the 437 patients treated with imipramine, 244 improved (56%). Of the 190 imipramine failures referred for ECT, 137 improved (72%). When the population is divided into subsamples by diagnosis, the success rate with imipramine is significantly poorer (40%) in the 181 patients with delusional depression. When the 109 delusional depressed patients who failed to improve with imipramine received ECT, however, 91 (83%) were considered improved.

The deCarolis study is a large study, and the efficacy rate with imipramine is comparable to later therapeutic trials, suggesting that the dosage and duration of imipramine treatment was adequate. The study is also unique in administering ECT to all imipramine treatment failures—patients who may be considered "therapy-resistant"—and it demonstrates the efficacy of ECT in such patients.

Delusional depression compels special consideration. In the treatment of depressive disorders, the presence of delusions has assumed prognostic significance, demarcating a subtype of depressive disorder with a particular prognosis and for whom a particular course of therapy may be recommended (Coryell et al., 1980; Coryell and Tsuang, 1982). This awareness has developed gradually, and was given a special impetus in comparative drug studies. In the deCarolis study, these patients responded poorly to imipramine but much better to ECT. Avery and Lubrano cite three additional studies (Simpson et al., 1976; Hordern et al., 1963; Glassman et al., 1975) in which the success rate for antidepressants in delusional depressed patients varied from 15% to 53%, while the success rate with nondelusional patients varied from 67% to 86%.

The finding that delusional depressives respond poorly to antidepressants alone has been repeatedly confirmed, even when plasma levels of tricyclics are monitored (Kantor and Glassman, 1977; Davidson et al., 1977; Avery and Winokur, 1977; Nelson and Bowers, 1978; Brockington et al., 1978; Rao and Coppen, 1979; Homan et al., 1982). Whether patients with delusions are a more severe variety of depression, as suggested by Guze et al., (1975), or a separate disorder remains controversial. Some authors suggest that these patients are adequately treated by the combination of a tricyclic antidepressant and a major antipsychotic drug, with the combination of amitriptyline and perphenazine recommended (Minter and Mandell, 1979 b6; Kaskey et al., 1980; Charney and Nelson, 1981; Spiker et al., 1985). These findings are disputed also by authors who suggest that the poor response to antidepressants alone in the earlier studies resulted from inadequate dosages, and that increasing the dosage (and the plasma levels) of tricyclics alone to higher than usual levels will be effective (Quitkin et al., 1978).*

We lack a prospective study comparing the efficacy of ECT with that of the drug combination in patients with psychotic major depressive disorders. But in a chart review, Perry et al. (1982) reported favorable treatment responses in 86% of ECT treated patients compared to a 42% rate in those treated with antidepressant-antipsychotic drug combinations. A similar greater efficacy for ECT (82%) compared to TCA alone (34%), antipsychotic drugs alone (51%), and the combination of TCA and antipsychotic drugs (77%) was reported by Kroessler (1985).

Antipsychotic drugs alone exhibit antidepressant activity (Robertson and Trimble, 1982). These authors identify 34 double-blind studies evaluating major tranquillizers for antidepressant activity, and conclude that some neuroleptics do, indeed, have antidepressant properties. These observations raise the question whether, in combined drug therapy of delusional depression, the contribution of the antipsychotic drug is as an "antipsychotic" agent, or whether the greater efficacy may result from the synergism of two "antidepressant" substances, effectively supporting the contention by Quitkin et al., that delusional depressed patients will respond to antidepressants alone, if they are given high enough dosages.

In some studies of the efficacy of ECT, the presence of psychotic features or delusions has been seen as a good prognostic sign (Hamilton and White, 1960; Nyström, 1964; Mendels, 1965; Carney et al., 1965; and Weckowicz et al., 1971).

Thus, from different perspectives, the treatment of delusional depression by antidepressant drugs is complex, often unsuccessful, while treatment with ECT is more often successful. Depressed patients with delusions who have responded

*See also Chapter 7, this volume.

poorly to treatment should not be considered therapy-resistant until a trial of ECT has been accomplished.

Catatonic Symptoms

Although catatonia is described as a form of schizophrenia, it is a syndrome which has a high prevalence among patients with bipolar affective disease (Abrams and Taylor, 1976, 1977; Taylor and Abrams, 1977). Like delusional symptoms in depression, catatonic symptoms are poorly responsive to antidepressant drugs alone, often requiring treatment with antipsychotic drugs. But the symptoms of catatonia are particularly responsive to ECT (Fink, 1979). To the extent that a sample of depressed patients concurrently exhibit the syndrome of catatonia, they should not be considered therapy-resistant until they have had a course of ECT.

Suicide

As the principal complication and risk in treating patients with depressive disorders, suicide is an important consideration in therapy-resistant patients. The age-corrected death rate among depressed patients is nearly three times that of the general population (Taylor, 1982). Suicide accounts for 15% of all deaths in patients with mood disorders and 60% of all deaths in the year post-depression. Among depressed patients, the non-suicide death rate, due to cardiovascular disease and infection, is also significantly higher than that of an age-corrected population. When comparisons are made of the efficacy of antidepressant drugs and ECT in preventing death by suicide, ECT is clearly superior (Avery and Winokur, 1976, 1977, 1978; Taylor, 1982). Avery and Winokur reviewed the records of more than 600 hospitalized depressed patients and found ECT superior to drug therapies in global antidepressant effect, but not in relapse rates. At 6-month follow-up, the drug groups had four to seven times more suicide attempts than the ECT group, and there was a lower overall mortality in the ECT treated group. They reviewed similar studies reporting on more than 4500 patients and concluded that ECT improves the survival rate in the natural course of depressive disorders.

In the treatment of severely depressed patients, there is a subgroup of patients who refuse to eat and who develop severe emaciation and inanition. In such instances, ECT may be life-saving, and such patients should not be considered therapy-resistant without a trial of ECT.

Other Considerations

While greater use of ECT would surely reduce the population of patients classified as having "therapy-resistant depressions," the indiscriminate use of ECT among all types of depressed patients would be a disservice. Convulsive therapy is effective for defined populations, but not for all who exhibit depressive symptoms. It is not effective for those with dysthymia; nor for those patients in whom the depressive symptoms are part of a more complex syndrome of anxiety, hypochondriasis, or neurosis; nor where the depression is complicated by alcoholism and drug dependence (Fink, 1978, 1979, 1982). There are many useful clues in identifying ECT responders in many of the efficacy reviews and in studies of predictors of outcome (Fink, 1979; Kendell, 1981; Kiloh, 1982). The predictors of good outcome are age (over 40), severity of the depression and associated vegetative symptoms, presence of delusions, and absence of neurotic symptoms. Much interest has recently been shown in measures of neuroendocrine dysregulation as a feature of major depressive disorders. The elevation and loss of rhythmicity of plasma cortisol, and its failure to be suppressed by exogenous dexamethasone is a reliable index of the severity of major depressive disorders. Normalization of an abnormal DST is associated with a good clinical prognosis after a course of ECT (Papakostas et al., 1980).

PRACTICAL CONSIDERATIONS IN ECT THERAPY

Much hesitation in the use of convulsive therapy results from difficulties in its administration. In the first decades of its use, seizures were unmodified by anesthesia, and the risks of fracture, pain, missed and tardive seizures, panic, and even death were high. In the 1950s, the acceptance of anesthesia as routine made ECT a distinctly different therapy. Oxygenation, unilateral electrode placements, and threshold brief stimulus induction currents each contributed to an increased efficacy, decreased risk, and greater acceptance of treatments. If the incidence of therapy-resistant depressions are to be reduced by ECT, our optimized present practice must be more widely adopted. Recent guidelines for treatment should be consulted for details of treatment (APA, 1978; Fink, 1979; Fraser, 1982), but some aspects warrant consideration here.

Concern was recently expressed that the induction of a seizure may not be necessary for a therapeutic result (Crow, 1979). At the time these doubts were raised, it was a puzzlement to many of us, since earlier studies had shown that sham-ECT or subconvulsive inductions were significantly less effective than grand-mal ECT (Fink, 1979). A recent survey of ECT usage suggests an explanation for these concerns. Pippard and Ellam (1981) examined the use of ECT in Great Britain in 1980. They visited 100 clinical centers to observe the practice of ECT. Using the guidelines of the Royal College of Psychiatrists (1977), they estimated that 59 clinics met the standards "with no more than minor deficiencies" and "(they had) few reservations about accepting treatment (as a patient)." But 27 had serious deficiencies, such as poor and indifferent care and obsolete apparatus, and could not easily be brought to a satisfactory standard. They rated 31% of the psychiatrists as unsatisfactory in their handling of ECT treatments.

There was a high incidence of missed seizures. "On several occasions during the visits, . . . we often saw 'missed fits,' even in those units which denied them. In some hospitals fewer than 50% of the patients in a session received fits, usually because of incorrect criteria for a fit or because the staff did not look at the patient to see . . . . In some clinics staff did not look to see whether a bilateral clonic convulsion had occurred. Sometimes we saw the operator press the button, remove the electrodes and, while turning his head to complete the notes, say that a fit had occurred when it had not."

If in one-third of the centers the therapists were unable to distinguish an adequate from an inadequate fit, it is probable that the doubts expressed by Crow resulted from similar experience. Nevertherless, the doubts were translated into five published studies in which ECT was compared to sham-ECT. Two studies were inconclusive (Lambourn and Gill, 1978; Freeman et al., 1978). Johnstone et al. (1980) found ECT to be more effective at the end of three and four weeks of treatment, but that, after a few months, the clinical results in the ECT and sham-ECT treated groups were not distinguishable. There was, however, no control for subsequent treatment during the aftercare period. West (1981) reported a clear advantage for ECT. The most recent study, that of Brandon et al. (1984), was a collaborative effort in which 138 patients were randomly assigned to real or simulated ECT given twice weekly, with a maximum of eight treatments. The clinical improvement in the group given real treatments was significantly greater than in the group given simulated treatment both at two and at four weeks of treatment. These studies confirm the belief that the repeated induction of cerebral grand-mal seizures is central to the antidepressant efficacy of ECT.

To maximize the efficacy of ECT, we need to improve its administration by monitoring the duration of seizures, and by modifying electrode placement and the induction currents. It is difficult to determine whether a satisfactory seizure has indeed occurred when a patient is fully anesthetized by barbiturate and succinylcholine. But it is possible to define the onset and duration of a grand-mal seizure if an EEG recording is made during the actual fit, or if a limb is allowed to have a full motor seizure. This latter may be observed by inflating a blood pressure cuff above the systolic pressure in a limb before succinylcholine is administered, allowing the full seizure to be timed in the "isolated" extremity. In our own practice, we use both monitoring methods and have recommended that an observed motor fit of at least 25 seconds in duration be accepted as an "effective" fit (Fink and Johnson, 1982).

Memory impairment is a principal objection to the use of ECT. This complaint may be reduced by administering seizure-inducing currents through electrodes which are so placed as to minimize the direct effects of currents on brain centers which subserve verbal memory functions. This is feasible since there is no specificity to electrode location (and current path) for the induction of a seizure. Since we believe that the essential part of the treatment is the induction of grand-mal seizures, the mode of induction has assumed less significance. Beginning more than two decades ago, numerous authors have described that the induction of seizures when electrodes are applied to one side of the head over the nondominant cerebral hemisphere is associated with a significant reduction in memory dysfunction. But this advantage may be associated with a decrease in clinical efficacy. While some authors find bilateral ECT to be more effective than unilateral ECT, many others find the two treatments equivalent in efficacy. At the worst, the advantage of bilateral ECT can be translated into a need for some additional treatments if patients are treated with unilateral ECT. We regularly treat all patients with unilateral ECT and change the induction to bilateral ECT for those patients in whom we fail to observe a therapeutic effect by 10 inductions.

A similar relationship exists between cognitive deficits and the energy used in induction currents. In general, instruments which induce seizures using alternating currents are accompanied by greater degrees of cognitive defect than those which use brief pulse stimuli. Again, we now use brief pulse stimuli for all treatments, and change to an alternating current instrument if there is a limited clinical response or we have increasing difficulty in inducing an effective seizure.

CONCLUSION

ECT is an effective therapy for severely delusional, catatonic, and suicidal depressed patients. Those patients who do not respond to pharmacotherapy should not be considered "therapy-resistant" until they have failed an adequate course of ECT. This is particularly true for patients over the age of 40, with delusions, melancholia, or catatonia.

ACKNOWLEDGMENTS

This study was aided in part by the International Association for Psychiatric Research, Inc., St. James, New York 11780

REFERENCES

Abrams, R., and Taylor, M.A. Catatonia: A prospective clinical study. *Arch. Gen. Psychiat. 33:*

579-581, 1976.

Abrams, R., and Taylor, M.A. Catatonia: Prediction of response to somatic treatments. *Amer. J. Psychiat. 134:* 70-80, 1977.

American Psychiatric Association. *Electroconvulsive Therapy*. Task Force Report #14. Washington, D.C., 200 pp., 1978.

Avery, D., and Lubrano, A. Depression treated with imipramine and ECT: The deCarolis study reconsidered. *Amer. J. Psychiat. 136:* 559-562, 1979.

Avery, D., and Winokur, G. Mortality in depressed patients treated with electroconvulsive therapy and antidepressants. *Arch. Gen. Psychiat. 33:* 1029-1037, 1976.

Avery, D., and Winokur, G. The efficacy of electroconvulsive therapy and antidepressants in depression. *Biol. Psychiat. 12:* 507-524, 1977.

Avery, D., and Winokur, G. Suicide, attempted suicide, and relapse rates in depression: Occurrence after ECT and antidepressant therapy. *Arch. Gen. Psychiat. 35:* 749-753, 1978.

Brandon, S., Cowley, P., McDonald, C., Neville, P., Palmer, R., and Wellstood-Eason, S. Electroconvulsive therapy: results in depressive illness from the Leicestershire trial. *Brit. Med. J. 288:* 22-25, 1984.

Brockington, I.F., Kendell, R.E., Kellett, J.M., Curry, S.H., and Wainright, S. Trials of lithium, chlorpromazine and amitriptyline in schizoaffective patients. *Brit. J. Psychiat. 133:* 162-168, 1978.

Carney, M.W.P., Roth, M., and Garside, R.F. The diagnosis of depressive syndromes and the prediction of ECT response. *Brit. J. Psychiat. 111:* 659-674, 1965.

Charney, D.S., and Nelson, J.C. Delusional and nondelusional unipolar depression: Further evidence for distinct subtypes. *Amer. J. Psychiat. 138:* 328-333, 1981.

Coryell, W., and Tsuang, M.T. Primary unipolar depression and the prognostic importance of delusions. *Arch. Gen. Psychiat. 39:* 1181-1184, 1982.

Coryell, W., Ziegler, V.E., and Biggs, J.T. Symptoms as predictors of response to amitriptyline and nortriptyline. *J. Affective Disorders 2:* 27-35, 1980.

Crow, T. The scientific status of electro-convulsive therapy. *Psychol. Med. 9:* 401-408, 1979.

Davidson, J.R.T., McLeod, M., Kurland, A.A., and White, H.L. Antidepressant drug therapy in psychotic depression. *Brit. J. Psychiat. 131:* 493-496, 1977.

d'Elia, G., Ottosson, J.-O., and Strömgren, L.S. Present practice of electroconvulsive therapy in Scandinavia. *Arch. Gen. Psychiat. 40:* 577-584, 1983.

Fink, M. Efficacy and safety of induced seizures (EST) in man. *Comprehens. Psychiat. 19:* 1-18, 1978.

Fink, M. *Convulsive Therapy: Theory and Practice*. Raven Press, New York, 308 pp., 1979.

Fink, M. Convulsive and drug therapies of depression. *Ann. Rev. Med. 32:* 405-412, 1981.

Fink, M. ECT in anxiety: An appraisal. *Amer. J. Psychother.36:* 371-378, 1982.

Fink, M., and Johnson, L. Monitoring duration of ECT seizures: 'Cuff' and EEG methods compared. *Arch. Gen. Psychiat. 39:* 1189-1191, 1982.

Fraser, M. *ECT A Clinical Guide*. John Wiley & Sons, New York, 134 pp., 1982.

Freeman, C.P.L., Basson, J.V., and Crighton, A. Double-blind controlled trial of electroconvulsive therapy (E.C.T.) and simulated ECT in depressive illness. *Lancet 1:* 738-740, 1978.

Glassman, A.H.,Kantor, S.J., and Shostak, M. Depression, delusions and drug response. *Amer. J. Psychiat. 132:* 716-719, 1975.

Guze, S. B., Woodruff, R.A., and Clayton, P.J. The significance of psychotic affective disorders. *Arch Gen. Psychiat. 32:* 1147-1150, 1975.

Hamilton, M., and White, J.M. Factors related to the outcome of depression treated with ECT. *J. Ment. Sci. 106:* 1031-1041, 1960.

Homan, S., Lachenbruch, P.A., Winokur, G., and Clayton, P. An efficacy study of electroconvulsive therapy and antidepressants in the treatment of primary depression. *Psychol. Med. 12:* 615-624, 1982.

Hordern, A., Holt, H.F., Burt, C.G., and Gordon, W.F. Amitriptyline in depressive cases. *Brit. J. Psychiat. 109:* 815-825, 1963.

Johnstone, E., Lawler, P., Stevens, S., Deakin, J.F.W., Frith, C.D., McPherson, K., and Crow, T.J. The Northwick Park electroconvulsive therapy trial. *Lancet 2:* 1317-1320, 1980.

Kantor, S.J., and Glassman, A.H. Delusional depressions: Natural history and response to treatment. *Brit. J. Psychiat. 131:* 351-360, 1977.

Kaskey, G.B., Nasr, S., and Meltzer, H.Y. Drug treatment in delusional depression. *Psychiat. Res. 1:* 267-277, 1980.

Kendell, R.E. The present status of electroconvulsive therapy. *Brit. J. Psychiat. 139:* 265-283, 1981.

Kiloh, L.G. Electroconvulsive therapy. In: E.S. Paykel (ed.): *Handbook of Affective Disorders*. Guilford Press, New York, 262-275, 1982.

Kroessler, D. Relative efficacy rates for therapies of delusional depression. *Convulsive Therapy 1*: 173-182, 1985.

Lambourn, J., and Gill, D. A controlled comparison of simulated and real ECT. *Br. J. Psychiat. 133:* 514-519, 1978.

Mendels, J. Electroconvulsive therapy and depression. *Br. J. Psychiat. 111:* 675-690, 1965.

Minter, R.E., and Mandel, M.R. The treatment of psychotic major depressive disorder with drugs and electroconvulsive therapy. *J. Nerv. Ment. Dis. 167:* 726-733, 1979a.

Minter, R.E., and Mandel, M.R. A prospective study of the treatment of psychotic depression. *Amer. J. Psychiat. 136:* 1470-1472, 1979b.

Nelson, J.C., and Bowers, M.B. Delusional unipolar depression—Description and drug response. *Arch. Gen. Psychiat. 35:* 1321-1328, 1978.

Nyström, S. On relation between clinical factors and efficacy of E.C.T. in depression. *Acta Psychiat. Scand. (Suppl.) 181:* 115-118, 1964.

Papakostas, Y., Fink, M., Lee, J., Irwin, P., and Johnson, L. Neuroendocrine measures in psychiatric patients: Course and outcome with ECT. *Psychiat. Res. 4:* 55-64, 1980.

Perry, P.J., Morgan, D.E., Smith, R.E., and Tsuang, M.T. Treatment of unipolar depression accompanied by delusions. *J. Affective Dis. 4:* 195-200, 1982.

Pippard, J., and Ellam, L. *Electroconvulsive Therapy in Great Britain, 1980*. Gaskell, London, 162 pp., 1981.

Quitkin, F., Rifkin, A., and Klein, D.F. Imipramine response in deluded depressive patients. *Amer. J. Psychiat. 135:* 806-811, 1978.

Rao, V.A.R., and Coppen, A. Classification of depression and response to amitriptyline therapy. *Psycholog. Med. 9:* 321-325, 1979.

Robertson, M.M., and Trimble, M.R. Major tranquillizers used as antidepressants. A review. *J. Affective Disorders 4:* 173-193, 1982.

Royal College of Psychiatrists. Memorandum on the use of electroconvulsive therapy. *Brit. J. Psychiat. 131:* 261-272, 1977.

Scovern, A.W., and Kilmann, P.R. Status of electroconvulsive therapy: Review of the outcome literature. *Psychol. Bull. 87:* 260-303, 1980.

Simpson, G.M., Lee, H.L., and Cuculic, A. Two doses of imipramine in hospitalized endogenous and neurotic depressions. *Arch. Gen. Psychiat. 33:* 1093-1102, 1976.

Spiker, D.G., Weiss, J.C., Dealy, R.S., Griffin, S.J., Hanin, I., Neil, J.P., Perel, J.P., Rossi, A.J., and Soloff, P.H. The pharmacological treatment of delusional depression. *Am. J. Psychiatry 142*: 430-436, 1985.

Taylor, M.A. Indications for electroconvulsive treatment. In: R. Abrams and W.B. Essman (eds.): *Electroconvulsive Therapy*. Spectrum Publications, New York, 7-40, 1982.

Taylor, R.A. and Abrams, R. The prevalence and importance of catatonia in the manic phase of manic-depressive illness. *Arch. Gen. Psychiat. 34:* 1223-1225, 1977.

Weckowicz, T.E., Yonge, K.A., Cropley, A.J., and Muir, W. Objective therapy predictors in depression: A multivariate approach. *J. Clin Psychol. (suppl.) 27:* 3-29, 1971.

West, E.D. Electric convulsion therapy in depression: a double blind controlled trial. *Brit. Med. J. 1:* 155-157, 1981.

10

Carbamazepine as a Treatment for Refractory Depressive Illness and Rapidly Cycling Manic-Depressive Illness

Robert M. Post and Thomas W. Uhde

Carbamazepine is increasingly recognized as an alternative treatment for patients with lithium resistant, rapid cycling, manic-depressive illness. In addition, preliminary evidence suggests that carbamazepine may have a spectrum of clinical efficacy in a variety of typical and atypical depressive syndromes of the unipolar type. We review the evidence for the efficacy of carbamazepine in the treatment of primary and secondary affective disorders and discuss important clinical management issues for the clinician. Use of carbamazepine as a supplemental treatment, and the use of other treatments in conjunction with carbamazepine, are outlined. The potential side effects and the importance of clinical monitoring are discussed. The relationship of clinical response to blood levels of carbamazepine and its metabolite are also addressed.

While we acknowledge the preliminary nature of the clinical evidence and research in the use of carbamazepine in the depressive disorders, we nonetheless attempt to outline the current state of the evidence, the possible clinical and biological predictors of carbamazepine response, and recommendations for its clinical use. The possible physiological and biochemical mechanisms of action of carbamazepine are reviewed elsewhere (Post et al., 1982b; 1983b; 1984a; Post and Uhde, 1983) and are only addressed in here insofar as they may shed light on issues of clinical import. For example, because carbamazepine does not appear to directly block dopamine receptors, in contrast to classical neuroleptic treatments, it is not associated with the development of acute parkinsonian or longer term tardive dyskinesia side effects. Similarly, because it appears to have vasopressin agonist-like effects, it does not produce diabetes insipidus, a relatively common side effect during the use of lithium carbonate.

ACUTE ANTIDEPRESSANT RESPONSE IN PRIMARY AND SECONDARY AFFECTIVE ILLNESS

Figure 1 illustrates the time course of improvement observed during acute treatment with carbamazepine in a double-blind, placebo-controlled clinical trial. Several points are noteworthy.

First, apparent clinical response was observed in slightly less than one-half of our patients. However, it is important to note that this relatively low rate of antidepressant response may be more impressive when it is considered in the context of our NIMH clinical research ward, which is a secondary and tertiary referral source. The majority of our patients are referred because of treatment-resistant unipolar and bipolar affective disorders. The majority of them have had unsuccessful clinical trials with traditional tricyclic, monoamine oxidase inhibitor antidepressants, or lithium carbonate. The demographic characteristic of our patient population are enumerated in Table 1. This illustrates the high incidence of rapid cycling disorders with large numbers of episodes and hospitalizations in the years prior to NIH hospitalization. Responders and nonresponders in this table are classified according to both their acute and prophylactic responsivity with a large group of equivocal responders being omitted. These data are suggestive that patients with more rapid cycling illness, particularly in the year prior to NIH hospitalization, may be among those who respond acutely or prophylactically to carbamazepine. While the statistical significance of these observations is only at or below the trend level in the relatively small sample gathered so far, these data are consistent with our clinical impressions that many patients with lithium-resistant, rapid-cycling affective disorders are among those who respond acutely or prophylactically to carbamazepine.

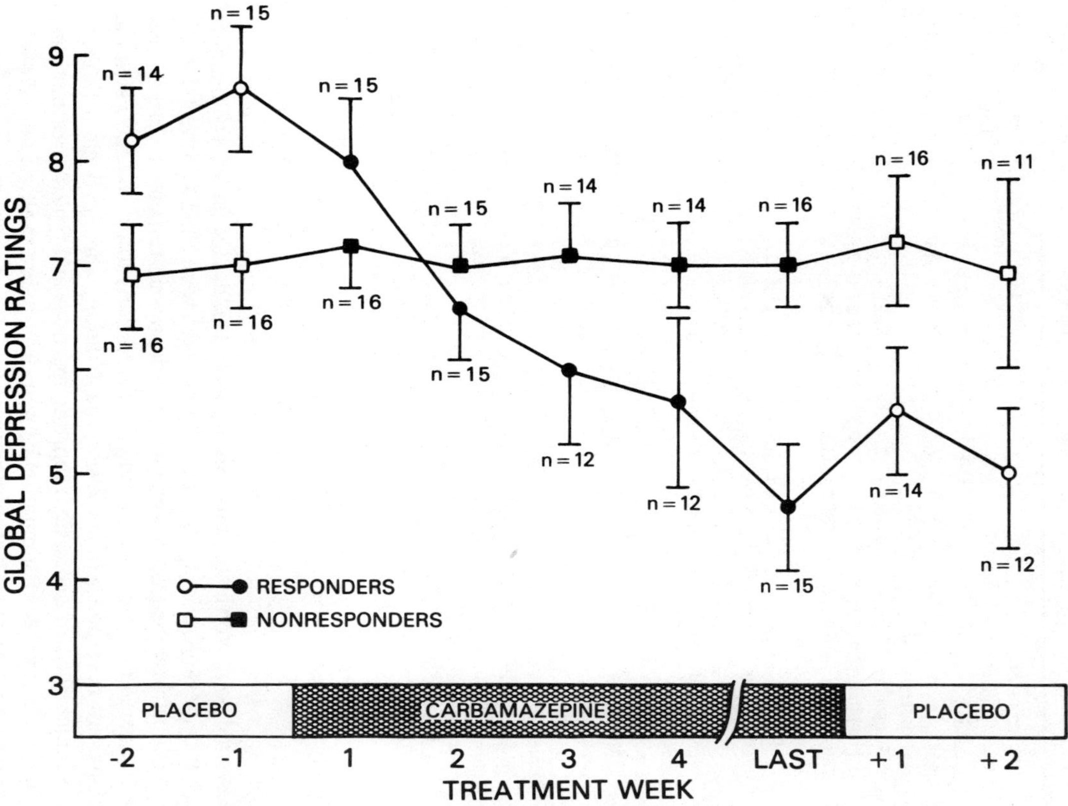

Figure 1. Time course of antidepressant response to carbamazepine.

TABLE 1. Demographic and Course of Illness Variables in Manic-Depressive Illness and Carbamazepine Response[a]

Variable	Nonresponders	Equivocal	Responders
Subject number	14	14	12
Male/female	5/9	7/7	3/9
UP/BP	5/9	1/13	3/9
Age	39.0 ± 3.5	35.29 ± 3.0	45.1 ± 3.8
Age onset:			
Symptoms	20.6 ± 2.3	20.21 ± 1.7	24.6 ± 3.0
Hospitalization	24.6 ± 2.0	27.29 ± 2.6	32.3 ± 4.6
Duration of illness	18.4 ± 3.2	15.25 ± 2.8	20.3 ± 2.3
Hospitalizations:			
Mania	1.1 ± 0.7	3.17 ± 1.1	2.0 ± 0.9
Depression	4.8 ± 1.1	2.58 ± 0.7	3.5 ± 1.6
Total	5.9 ± 1.1	6.29 ± 1.2	5.5 ± 1.7
Weeks hospitalized	31.8 ± 5.5	33.92 ± 10.2	154.1 ± 86.5
Weeks ill	277.4 ± 41.6	221.92 ± 65.6	278.0 ± 74.2
Episodes:			
Mania	5.3 ± 2.1	16.39 ± 8.0	17.7 ± 8.5
Depression	8.2 ± 1.9	22.54 ± 11.8	16.6 ± 5.6
Total	13.5 ± 3.8	38.92 ± 19.7	34.2 ± 13.9
Episodes/yrs ill	1.1 ± 0.3	2.54 ± 0.8	2.1 ± 0.9
Wks ill/yrs ill	26.0 ± 6.7	20.32 ± 4.6	15.4 ± 3.6
Hosps/yrs ill	0.7 ± 0.2	1.10 ± 0.2	0.4 ± 0.1
Year prior to NIMH:			
Episodes	3.0 ± 1.1	4.79 ± 1.3	5.8 ± 1.5
Weeks ill	42.6 ± 3.4	38.86 ± 3.7	33.7 ± 5.2

[a]Carbamazepine response was based on combined clinical assessment of acute and prophylactic response whenever both data were available on the first 40 patients studied up to 1983.

A second point worthy of emphasis in Figure 1 is that the patients with higher levels of depression ratings, assessed by nurses who were blind to patients' medication status, were associated with better antidepressant response to carbamazepine compared to those with lower initial depression ratings. We have seen the same pattern in response to acute sleep deprivation, where patients with more severe initial levels of depression, more endogenous and typical presentations, respond better to that manipulation as well (Roy-Byrne et al., 1984a; 1984b).

Third, the nonresponsive group shows no evidence of a withdrawal syndrome during the period of double-blind discontinuation of active treatment with placebo substitution. However, in the group of responders, mild and usually transient exacerbation of depressive symptoms may occur. This does appear to interact with clinical state and degree of carbamazepine responses as only 1 of 16 (6.3%) patients who did not respond showed evidence of clinical exacerbation during the withdrawal period while 7 of 15 (46.7%) showed exacerbation in the responsive group.

A fourth point of interest is the relative lag in onset of clinical response during carbamazepine treatment. In contrast to the rapid onset of antimanic efficacy, where improvement is often noted in the first several days of treatment, acute antidepressant response is less likely to develop until after the first or second week of treatment with carbamazepine. This conforms to the usual lag in onset of antidepressant efficacy observed with more routine agents such as tricyclic and monoamine oxidase inhibitor antidepressants.

Fifth, responders illustrated in Figure 1 included both unipolar (n ± 3) and bipolar (n ± 11) depressed patients. Further clinical trials will be required to assess whether there is a differential antidepressant response in these two subgroups. We have seen substantial, essentially complete, clinical response in both unipolar and bipolar patients, however. These results are illustrated in Figures 2 and 3. Six patients showed essentially complete clinical remission while nine showed slight to moderate improvement during carbamazepine administration. The potential for potentiating the incomplete responses to carbamazepine with adjunctive medication is discussed below.

Patient #243 was a 40-year-old bipolar I depressed female with a 1.3 year history of continuous illness (predominately depressive with episodic mild hypomania) following the birth of a child. The illness did not respond to desmethyl-imipramine (300 mg) alone or in combination with lithium or neuroleptics prior to NIMH admission.

She presented with a classical retarded depression with sleep and appetite disturbance and suicidal hopelessness about her condition and unremitting illness. Her EEG was normal but her CAT scan, while read as clinically normal, showed a large ventricular-brain ratio (VBR ± 11). She had marked cognitive disturbance subjectively and on the Luria-Nebraska battery. Cortisols and dexamethasone suppression tests were also abnormal.

She remained severely depressed (ratings › 9) for an additional 13 weeks, but as illustrated (Figure 2), by the second week following blind institution of carbamazepine (initially 200 mg/day raised to 600 mg/day by week 2), she showed dramatic improvement, and by week 3 of treatment showed a complete remission of symptoms. (Luria-Nebraska impairments normalized during her improved state.) Carbamazepine was discontinued because of mild elevations of SGOT and SGPT (bilirubin, alkaline, phosphatase, and LDH were normal) and she remained well off active medications.

Patient #252 was a 49-year-old unipolar depressed patient with a history of

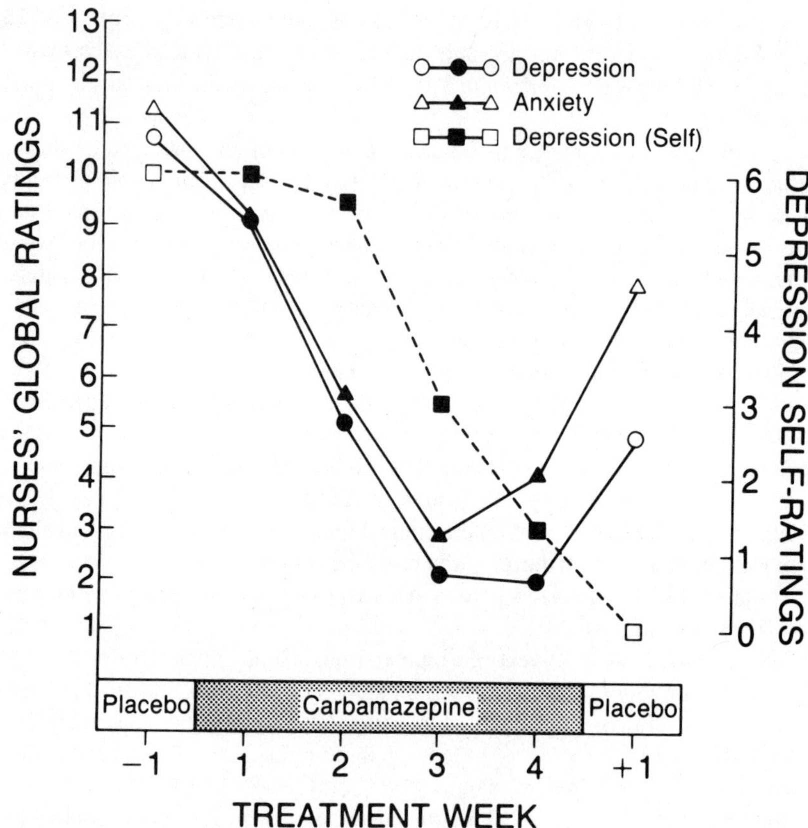

Figure 2. time course of antidepressant response to carbamazepine in a treatment-resistant bipolar depressed female.

four prior depressions and a chronic depression of 15 months' duration unresponsive to amitriptyline and trazadone. At NIMH she was markedly anxious and agitated, but by the second and third weeks of carbamazepine treatment was substantially improved (Figure 3). Only mild increases in dysphoria occurred following carbamazepine discontinuation.

These two cases are thus illustrative of patients with severe recurrent and/or prolonged depressive illness requiring previous hospitalization which did not respond to traditional agents, including tricyclic antidepressants or lithium carbonate. Both patients were moderately to severely agitated and expressing feelings of hopelessness and helplessness. Within several weeks of the onset of active treat-

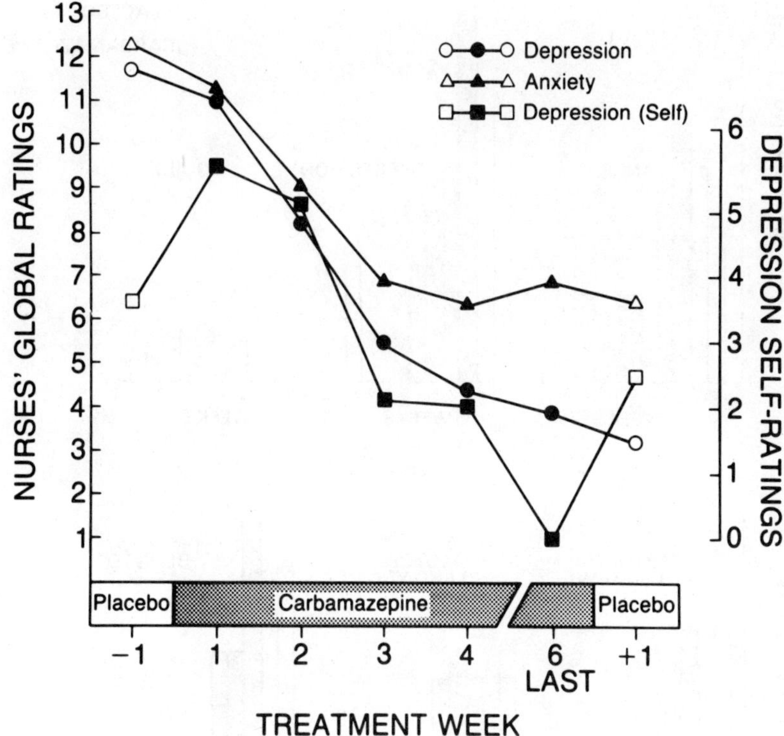

Figure 3. Time course of antidepressant response to carbamazepine in a unipolar depressed female.

ment with carbamazepine on a blind basis, improvement was observed rapidly and within 4 weeks an essentially complete clinical remission was achieved. Again, it is noteworthy that clinical relapses were not observed following placebo substitution as is often the case during the acute treatment of manic episodes.

A more detailed pattern of the different areas of symptom improvement observed during carbamazepine treatment is illustrated in Figure 4 in another bipolar depressed woman showing a notable antidepressant response to carbamazepine. Essentially all aspects of her depressive symptoms improved during treatment and at a roughly parallel rate. Both her mood and motor components improved as rated on the Brief Psychiatric Rating Scale by nurses who were blind to her treatment status. In addition, anxiety, restlessness, and guilt also showed parallel improvement. These observations conform with our clinical impression that the depressive syndrome, when it does respond to treatment with carbamazepine, tends to im-

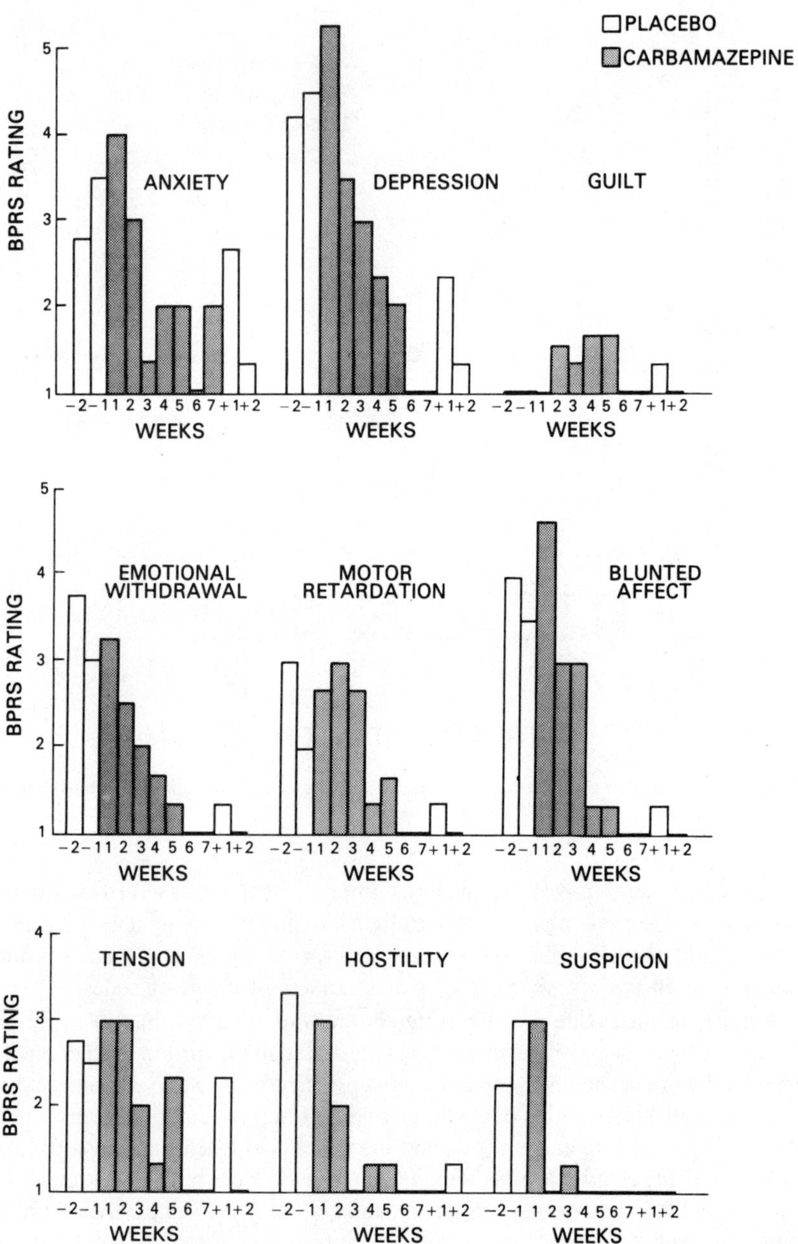

Figure 4. Profile of symptomatic improvement on carbamazepine in a bipolar depressed female.

prove in a relatively uniform fashion and it is not isolated components such as motor or agitated behavior which are specifically targeted. As illustrated below, sleep does improve during treatment with carbamazepine and often does so prior to the onset of other measures of clinical antidepressant response, however.

These observations in a single patient also conform to our observations in a wider clinical sample. In the same patients illustrated in Figure 1, anxiety ratings are plotted in Figure 5 illustrating a relatively parallel, although slightly less great amplitude of improvement in anxiety, compared to depression during carbamazepine treatment. It is also of interest that a single bipolar depressed patient who had prominent anxiety symptoms and periodic panic attacks, showed substantial improvement in his generalized anxiety and an absence of panic attacks during treatment with carbamazepine, even though his clinical antidepressant response was not complete. The findings are suggestive in several other patient populations that carbamazepine may be useful in targeting anxiety symptoms (Puente, 1976; Groh, 1976). A double-blind clinical trial is now ongoing of patients with anxiety and panic anxiety disorders in Dr. Uhde's outpatient program. Tricyclic antidepressant and monoamine oxidase inhibitor antidepressant agents have been reported effective in patients with panic anxiety disorder; it remains an area for further study to

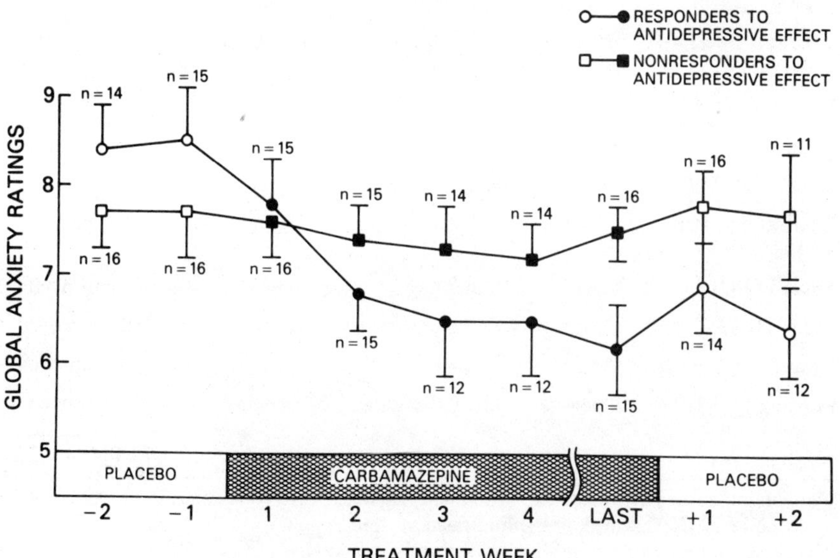

Figure 5. Time course of anti-anxiety response to carbamazepine.

determine whether carbamazepine will have an overlapping spectrum of antianxiety effects in this patient population, and whether a differential subgroup of patients may be responsive to this agent in comparison to more traditional pharmacological approaches.

LONG-TERM OR PROPHYLACTIC ANTIDEPRESSANT RESPONSE IN RECURRENT UNIPOLAR AND RECURRENT BIPOLAR AFFECTIVE DISORDER

As summarized in Table 2, two double-blind, controlled studies and a number of open studies and clinical case reports suggest that carbamazepine may have useful longer-term prophylactic efficacy in the management of recurrent affective

TABLE 2. Carbamazepine Prophylaxis in Affective Illness

Investigator	Design	Dose range	Duration	Results[a]
Takazaki & Hanaoki (1971)	Open[c]	200-600 mg/day	1-11 months	6/10 improved
Okuma et al. (1973, 1975)	Open[c]	400-600 mg/day (1200 mg)	Approx. 25 weeks	4/51 improved
Ballenger and Post (1978)	*Blind*[b,e]	800–2000 mg/day	6-51 months	6/7 improved
Post et al. (1982b)				
Okuma et al. (1981)	*Blind*	400-600 mg/day	12 months	6/12 improved
Inoue et al. (1981)	Open[d]	400-600 mg/day	18-32 months	2/3 improved
Lipinski and Pope (1982)	Open[d]	Not listed	3-8 months	3/3 improved
Yassa (1982)	Open[e]	600 mg/day	8 months	1/1 improved
Nolen (1983)	Open[e]	400 mg/day	2-6 months	6/12 improved
Kwamie et al. (1982)	Open[e]	—	—	5/12 improved
Keisling (1983)	Open[c,d]	600-1400 mg/day	2-8 months	3/3 improved
				72/144 = 63%

[a]Patients noted to have moderate to marked response were considered improved.
[b]Four patients studied in double-blind fashion; three open.
[c]Carbamazepine used in combination with other agents.
[d]Carbamazepine used in combination with lithium.
[e]Most patients lithium-nonresponsive.

disorders. In our initial group of rapidly cycling patients followed for an average of 1.7 years on carbamazepine, marked improvement in rapid cycling course was observed in both the manic and depressive phases of the illness. While patients had an average of 16.4 ° 5.7 episodes in the year prior to carbamazepine administration, this was reduced to an average of 5.6 ° 2.4 episodes per year of carbamazepine treatment ($p < .02$). As illustrated in Figure 6, this improvement occurred equally in decreasing the frequency of recurrent depressive as well as recurrent manic episodes. In six of the seven patients, evidence of relapse was observed during periods of carbamazepine dose reduction or discontinuation, suggesting that the improvement in rapid cycling was, in fact, attributable to treatment with carbamazepine rather than spontaneous improvement in the natural course of the illness. Moreover, when episodes did occur during carbamazepine administration they also tended to be less intense than those observed prior to carbamazepine treatment.

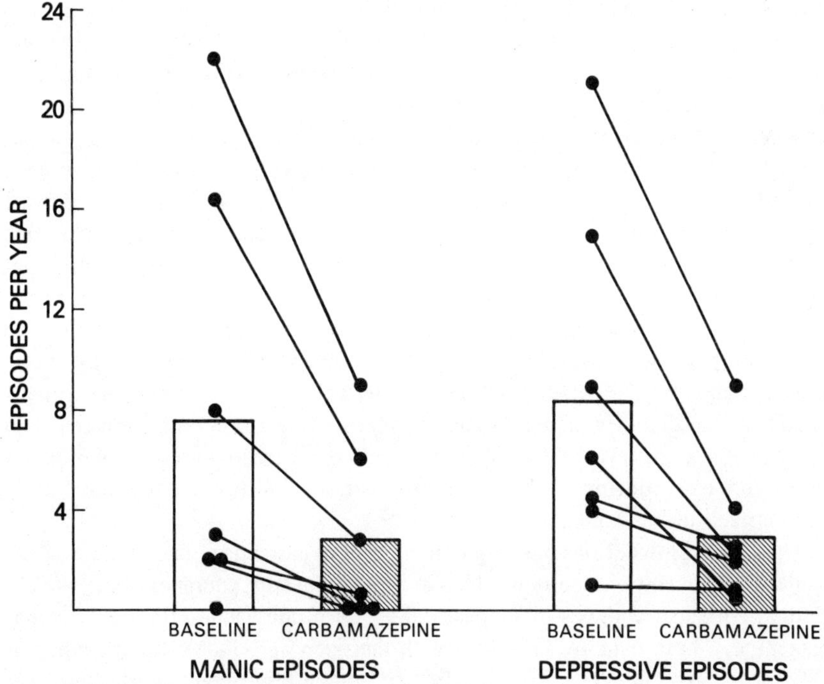

Figure 6. Significant reduction in number of manic and depressive episodes during carbamazepine prophylaxis.

This reduction of the severity of depressive episodes is illustrated during a prolonged double-blind clinical trial in a rapidly-cycling treatment resistant inpatient. Figure 7a summarizes the malignant, rapidly-cycling course in this 53 year old bipolar patient who required essentially continuous hospitalization since 1955. Severe manic episodes often requiring seclusion are plotted above the line and severe depressive periods characterized by marked psychomotor retardation are plotted below the line, based on doctors' and nurses' observations during her prolonged state hospitalization prior to NIMH admission. It is noteworthy that medication trials with lithium carbonate, neuroleptics, and tricyclic antidepressants were all ineffective in decreasing the frequency or magnitude of her rapid cycling illness. Daily ratings of mania and depression performed by nurses unaware of her medication status at the NIMH are illustrated in Figure 7b. A prolonged period of placebo observation was felt to be justified in light of her prior course of treatment-resistant affective illness which had been managed with high doses of neuroleptics and resulted in the appearance of tardive dyskinesia.

While on placebo the pattern of severe rapid-cycling illness was again documented, as illustrated on the left-hand portion of Figure 7b. In contrast, during periods on carbamazepine treatment at doses above 800 mg/day, illustrated on the right portion of the figure, the severity of mania and depression ratings was markedly attenuated. Moreover, during each period of placebo substitution, relapses were observed and increases in manic, psychotic, or depressive ratings were again observed. Manic ratings above 5 and depressive ratings greater than 7 have been shaded in Figure 7b to indicate periods of more severe illness. As is observed in the figure, these periods of severe illness were notably reduced during carbamazepine treatment, except for one period immediately following placebo substitution, when severe mania was again observed and did not respond as rapidly to carbamazepine treatment alone. Therefore, haloperidol on a blind basis was added to carbamazepine, which resulted in notable improvement in manic and psychotic symptomatology; the patient continued to do well on this combination of treatments for the duration of her NIMH hospitalization. The 85% improvement in number of days of severe depression, as well as the increase in relative number of improved days during carbamazepine treatment compared to placebo, is summarized in this patient in Figure 8.

Thus, the results of our ongoing clinical trial of carbamazepine in the prophylactic management of recurrent affective illness in a small number of intensively studied patients continues to suggest the useful prophylactic efficacy of carbamazepine. These data are in accord with the open and double-blind studies of Okuma and associates (1973; 1981). In their double-blind evaluation, where they followed patients for one year on carbamazepine, they observed improvement in 6 of 10 patients, compared to only 2 of 9 patients during the placebo period ($p < .10$).

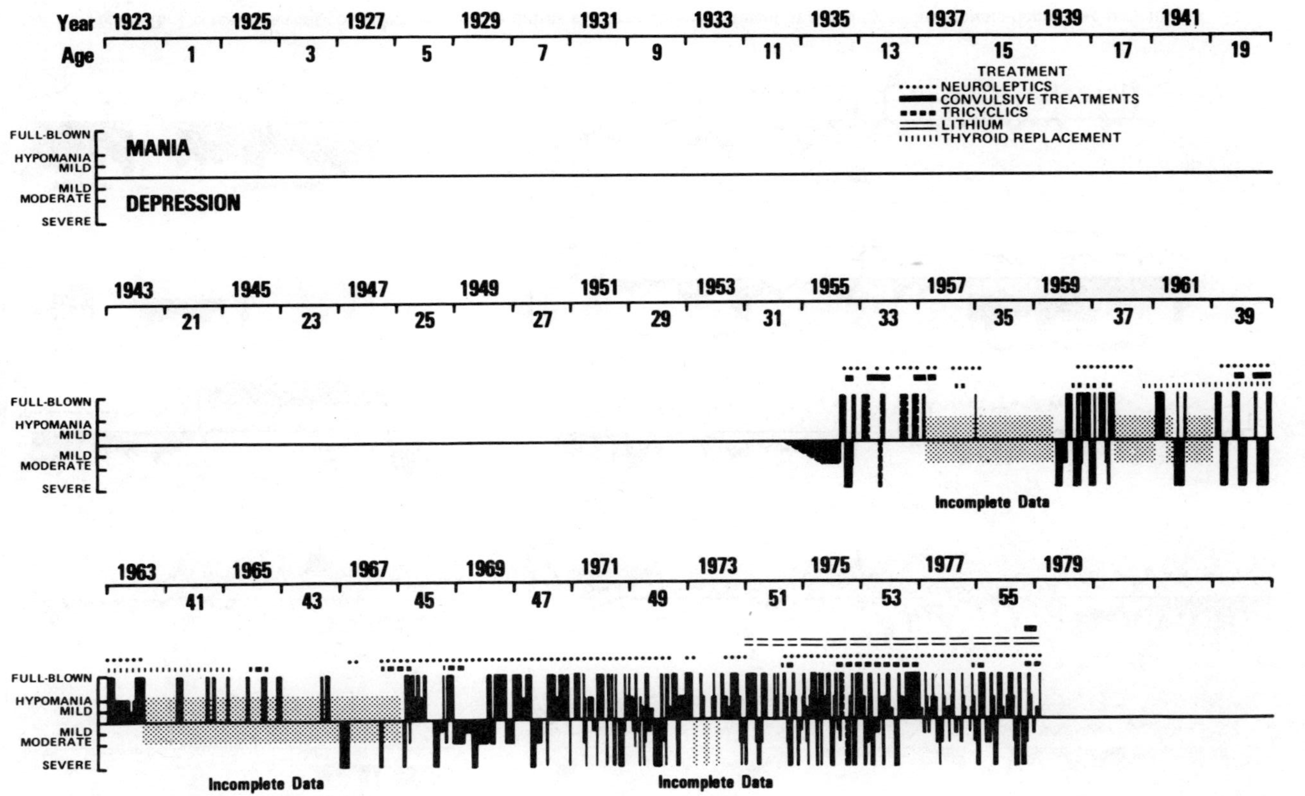

Figure 7a. Life chart of a medication-resistant rapidly cycling manic-depressive patient.

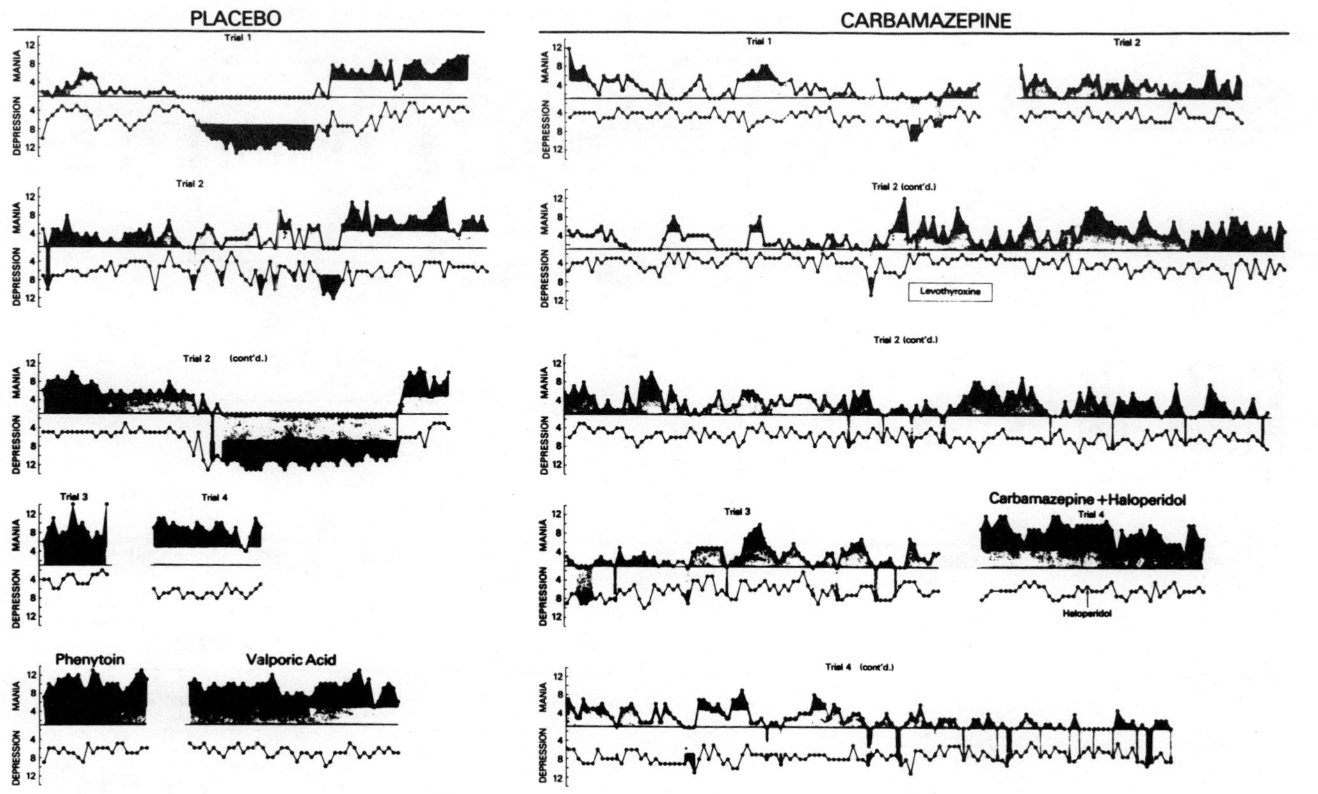

Figure 7b. Decreased severity of affective episodes during carbamazepine treatment in a rapidly cycling manic-depressive patient.

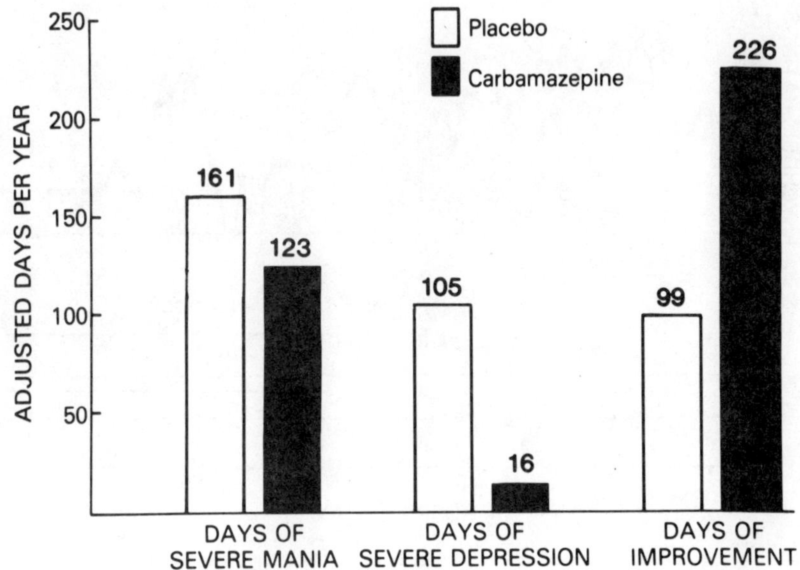

Figure 8. Improvement in manic and depressive phases during carbamazepine prophylaxis.

In their open study they reported that while 17% of patients had an acute antidepressant response, 14 of 27 patients (51.9%) showed a prophylactic antidepressant response to carbamazepine.

SCHIZOAFFECTIVE AND ATYPICAL DEPRESSIVE PSYCHOSES

We have also observed patients with less than classical presentations of recurrent affective illness who also respond to carbamazepine, either alone or in combination with other psychotropic agents. Figure 9 illustrates the clinical response in a 45-year-old patient with a history of approximately yearly severe depressive paranoid psychosis, each requiring acute hospitalization. During periods of lithium administration, the frequency of these episodes was, if anything, increased. Interestingly, the episodes were often precipitated by acute separations or loss of a family member or heralded by the onset of a minor viral illness (Silberman and Post, 1980). Once the depressive episode was initiated it proceeded with a fulminant and incapacitating course of increasing agitation, clinging, and helplessness, with a crescendo of paranoid anxiety and nihilistic delusions. As described in de-

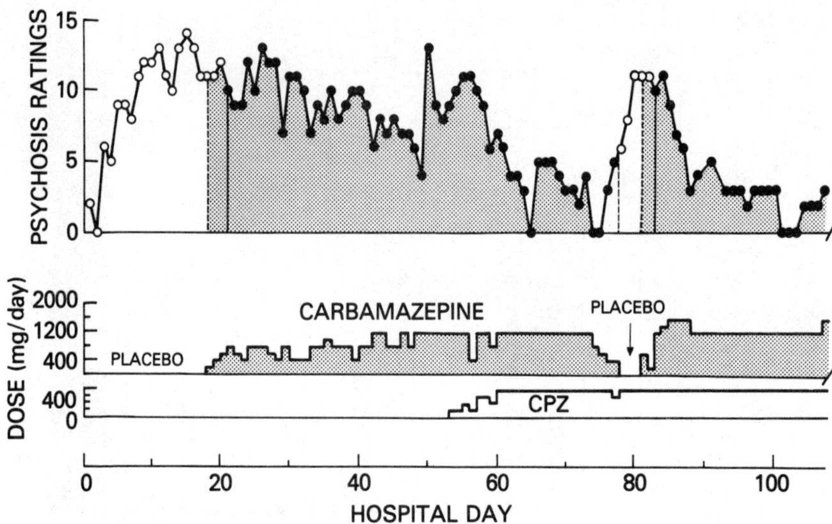

Figure 9. Effects of carbamazepine in an atypical depressive psychosis.

tail elsewhere (Silberman and Post, 1980), with the blind institution of carbamazepine treatment there was mild to moderate improvement in the degree of her depressive agitation, but continued improvement was not observed during carbamazepine treatment alone, so that neuroleptic supplementation with chlorpromazine at 400 mg/day was initiated. This combined treatment resulted in dramatic improvement in her depressive psychosis, as illustrated in Figure 9. At this point it was unclear to what extent carbamazepine was responsible for the improvement and it was discontinued on a double-blind basis. Following carbamazepine dose reduction and placebo substitution, the whole psychotic depressive syndrome rapidly reemerged, indicating that carbamazepine had been important to her initial improvement. When active treatment with carbamazepine was again instituted, improvement was again noted. This patient has been maintained on carbamazepine in combination with a neuroleptic for more than four years now without further recurrence of these episodes, except for one transient episode occurring with carbamazepine dose reduction. This case study suggest that some patients with recurrent atypical or schizoaffective depressive psychoses may respond to carbamazepine, either alone or in conjunction with a neuroleptic, as has been reported for more classical tricyclics when used in combination with neuroleptic treatment (Nelson and Bowers, 1978; see also Chapter 7, this volume). It is noteworthy that this patient was not responsive to lithium carbonate prophylaxis.

We have also observed response to carbamazepine in patients with other atypical or organic presentations. In one patient with approximately monthly occurrences of confusional depressive episodes that had in the past responded only to electroconvulsive shock, carbamazepine alone was partially effective in the treatment of these episodes, while carbamazepine in conjunction with lithium was markedly effective.

Depressive episodes occurring in conjunction with patients with psychomotor seizures or complex partial seizures have also been successfully treated with carbamazepine. These data are highlighted by Dalby (1975) in his review of the psychotropic effects of carbamazepine and in his own study, in 1971, where he documented that 11 of 18 epileptic patients with periodic depressions improved during carbamazepine therapy. The data in his epileptic series are also notable because, in some instances, he observed improvement in depressive episodes even though the seizure disorder was not adequately controlled. Data of Robertson (1983) are also consistent with these observations. She observed that epileptic patients who had been treated with carbamazepine had lower depression ratings than those who had been treated with other anticonvulsants.

Improvement in depressive symptoms occurring in conjunction with schizoaffective and schizophrenic syndromes has not so far been well documented in the literature (see Figure 9), although preliminary evidence from several clinical trials of carbamazepine used in conjunction with neuroleptics in schizophrenic syndromes are suggestive of positive results. In particular, the study of Klein et al. (1984) reports that carbamazepine compared to placebo (when added to previously inadequate neuroleptic treatment) was effective in treating schizophrenic patients. Other clinical trials in schizophrenic patients have reported parallel results (Neppe, 1982; de Vogelaer, 1981; Hakola and Laulumaa, 1982). In addition, there is preliminary evidence that carbamazepine may be useful in some aggressive psychotic states, as suggested by the data of Hakola and Laulumaa (1982), as well as Luchins (1983), and Bracha (unpublished observations, 1979).

While the spectrum of clinical efficacy of carbamazepine in depressive syndromes has not been entirely delineated, the emerging preliminary data do suggest that it may be useful in a subgroup of unipolar and bipolar affectively ill patients with either primary or secondary affective illness, with responses occurring in some patients who were previously resistant to treatment with lithium carbonate and other, more traditional agents. The antimanic efficacy of carbamazepine is summarized elsewhere (Post et al., 1982b; 1984a), but it is worthy of note that the profile of carbamazepine's efficacy in mania compared to depression appears somewhat in parallel with that of lithium carbonate. That is, there is good evidence of carbamazepine's antimanic efficacy, while its antidepressant efficacy is less well established, particularly because relapses upon placebo substitution are not consistently observed as they often are in manic trials. Similarly, the acute antimanic efficacy of lithium is not debated, while its acute antidepressant efficacy is still controversial even after more than a decade of research.

DOSE AND BLOOD LEVEL RELATIONSHIPS TO CLINICAL RESPONSE AND SIDE EFFECTS

In the treatment of trigeminal neuralgia, doses over 400 mg/day are generally associated with improvement. In patients treated for epilepsy, doses usually range from 600-1600 mg/day. In our clinical series the average dose has been just under 1000mg/day. Consistent with the neurological literature, we have observed wide individual variation in the ability of a given patient to tolerate doses of carbamazepine without side effects and also wide individual variability in the dose necessary to achieve clinical response. However, within an individual patient, we have observed clear dose-response relationships as illustrated in Figure 10. Marked antimanic and antipsychotic responses to carbamazepine were observed in this individual, particularly at doses higher than 800 mg/day.

Also consistent with the neurological literature, we have not observed impressive relationships between blood levels of carbamazepine and degree of clinical response. In seizure patients, blood levels between 6 and 12 μg/ml have generally been considered to be within the therapeutic range. Blood levels above this range have often been reported to induce a higher incidence of side effects. However, there is still considerable controversy regarding the exact therapeutic window for carbamamezpine in the treatment of seizure disorders. As illustrated in Figure 11, there is little evidence of a relationship of carbamazepine levels to degree of psychotropic response in our patient population.

In contrast, an active metabolite of carbamazepine, carbamazepine-10,11-epoxide, appears to show some trend for higher levels being associated with greater degree of clinical response. The same relationship is also observed in employing the CSF levels of carbamazepine and the epoxide (Figure 12) where CSF levels are thought to reflect more of the free fraction or unbound carbamazepine and its metabolite. Again we observed little evidence of a relationship between carbamazepine levels in CSF and degree of clinical response, while greater degrees of antidepressant response were associated with higher levels of carbamazepine 10,11-epoxide ($r \pm .71$, $p < .01$) (Post et al., 1983a).

Carbamazepine is metabolized by the liver microsomal enzyme system that can be induced with alcohol, barbiturates, and a variety of sedative and anticonvulsant drugs. These data are of import in several respects. Carbamazepine induces its own metabolism, particularly after two to three weeks of treatment (Bertilsson,

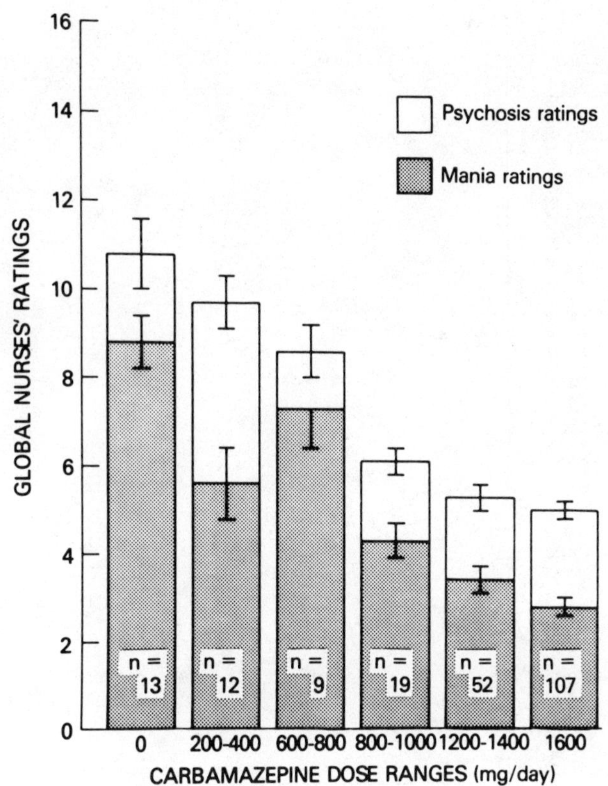

Figure 10. Dose-dependent therapeutic effects of carbamazepine during a prolonged manic episode.

1978). The half-life is 25 to 37 hours following acute administration, but decreases substantially to 18-24 hours following more chronic administration. This may be associated with a fall in plasma carbamazepine levels and may be associated with transient exacerbation of depression with chronic treatment. If this should occur, it may be an indication for a dose increase, although further study of this issue is required.

Because of this catabolic dependence on liver microsomal enzymes, carbamazepine appears to have important interactions with several different agents. A variety of anticonvulsants and sedative drugs, when used in combination with carbamazepine, will reduce levels, as summarized in Table 3. In addition, the monoamine oxidase inhibitors have been consistently reported to increase plasma

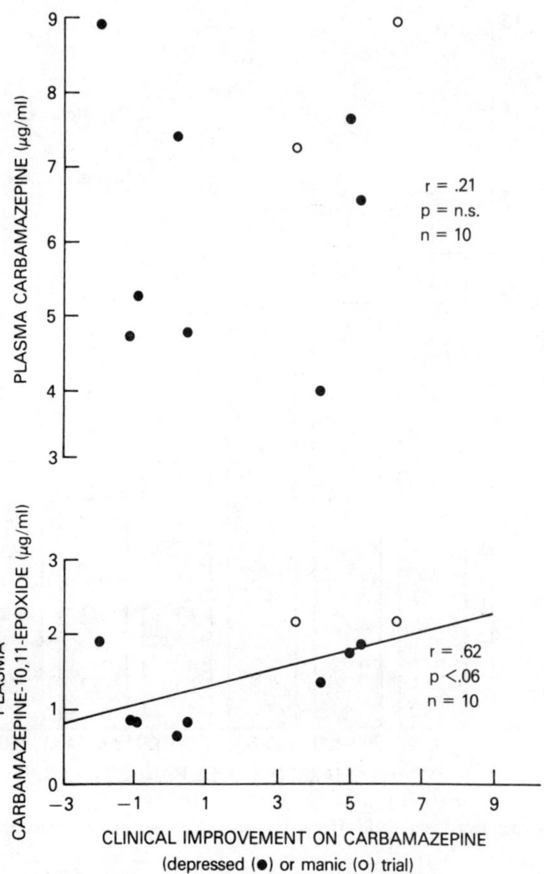

Figure 11. Plasma carbamazepine-10, 11-epoxide correlates better with clinical response than does carbamazepine itself.

carbamazepine levels, in some instances resulting in clinical toxicity (Wright et al., 1981, 1982; Valsalan and Cooper, 1982; Block, 1982). Erythromycin can also have the same effect.

Treatment with carbamazepine may be initiated with starting doses of 200-400 mg/day and increased slowly thereafter, titrating against clinical response and side effects. A slow increase in dose appears to be particularly important in avoiding initial side effects such as sedation or other typical "anticonvulsant" side effects

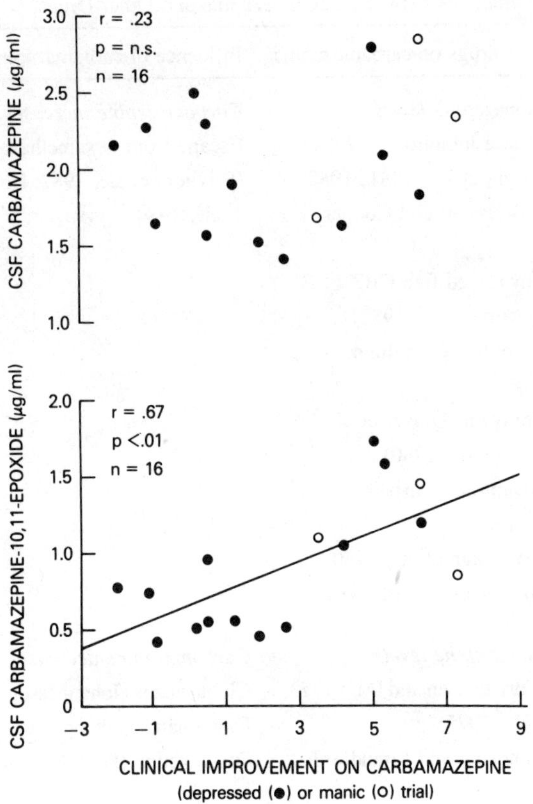

Figure 12. Degree of clinical improvement is correlated with CSF carbamazepine-10, 11-epoxide but not with carbamazepine itself.

such as ataxia, dizziness, clumsiness, etc. We would suggest continued increases in dose until an adequate clinical response is achieved, or until side effects supervene, or until a maximum of 1600-2000 mg/day is administered. It would appear indicated to continue the antidepressant trial of carbamazepine for 2-3 weeks, as there is often a lag in onset of acute antidepressant response, as indicated in Figures 1-3. However, in our clinical experience, clinical response in the manic phase of the illness is often quite rapid and if no response is evident within the first week or two of treatment at moderate doses of 600-1200 mg/day, we have seen a few manic patients then respond to higher doses.

TABLE 3. Interactions between Carbamazepine and Other Drugs[a]

Influence of other drugs on carbamazepine	Influence of carbamazepine on other drugs
Increased carbamazepine levels	*Carbamazepine increases:*
Monoamine oxidase inhibitors; Isoniazid (Wright et al., 1981, 1982; Block, 1982; Valsalan and Cooper, 1982)	Escape from dexamethasone suppression (Privitera et al., 1982; Rubinow et al., 1984)
Valproic acid (increased free CBZ in vitro— Mattson et al., 1982) (CBZ epoxide only—Cereghino, 1982)	
Triacetyloleandomycin (Dravet et al., 1977; Mesdjian et al., 1980)	
Propoxyphene (Dam and Christiansen, 1977)	
Erythromycin (Mesdjian et al., 1980)	
Nicotinamide (Bourgeois et al., 1982)	
Decreased carbamazepine levels	*Carbamazepine decreases the effects of:*
Phenobarbital (Christiansen and Dam 1973; Cereghino et al., 1975)	Clonazepam (Johannessen, 1981)
Phenytoin (Johannessen and Strandjord, 1975)	Dicoumarol (Johannessen, 1981)
	Doxycycline (Penttilä et al., 1974)
Primidone (Callahan et al., 1980)	Phenytoin (Hansen et al., 1971)
	Sodium valproate (Johannessen, 1981)
	Theophylline (Rosenberry et al., 1983)
	Ethosuximide (Warren et al., 1980)
	Warfarin (Hansen et al., 1971)
	Pregnancy tests (Lindhout and Meinardi, 1982)

[a]Adapted and expanded from S.I. Johannessen (1981) and Levy and Pitlick (1982).

The dose-response relationships for adequate antidepressant response are not entirely delineated and at this time one should use the blood levels between 4 and 12 μg/ml accepted in neurological patients only as rough guidelines. In an affectively ill patient who has levels on the high end of this range, but in whom clinical responses are not adequate and no side effects are evident, an increase in dose may be indicated.

SIDE EFFECTS AND CLINICAL MONITORING

As illustrated in Figure 13, carbamazepine is reported by our patients to be generally well tolerated. In fact, in comparison to ratings of "drug-related side effects" during placebo, ratings on carbamazepine show few differences. These data are interesting in suggesting that many presumed "drug-related" side effects are occurring in conjunction with the symptoms of depressive illness and are not drug related. We saw no increase in the subjective side effects during the acute phases of treatment with carbamazepine in the first several weeks or at week 4, as illustrated.

These data conform with our general clinical impression in a larger series of more than 50 patients that side effects of carbamazepine are generally not problematic. In instances where sedation or dizziness is prominent, it usually responds to transient dose reduction or may be attenuated merely with time and holding the dose constant before proceeding with further dose increases.

The majority of our patients appear to have improvement in sleep, as illustrated in Figure 14. It is of interest that improvement in sleep often occurs within the first week of treatment with carbamazepine, in some instances anticipating the antidepressant response to the drug.

Okuma et al. (1979) compared the side effects of carbamazepine (300-900 mg/day) to those of chlorpromazine (150-450 mg/day). In that study they reported generally fewer side effects on carbamazepine compared to chlorpromazine and, in particular, lesser degrees of sedation (see Table 4). Reynolds (1975) reported parallel incidence of these types of side effects in his neurological patients (see Table 4).

In the neurological literature (Reynolds, 1975) and in our series, we have not observed acute parkinsonian side effects or the emergence of tardive dyskinesia. Thus the use of carbamazepine instead of neuroleptic treatment in affectively ill patients may help avoid these problematic side effects. Moreover, if carbamazepine is used in conjunction with a neuroleptic, lower doses of the neuroleptic may be required and fewer neuroleptic-related side effects may be manifest. Dystonias and choreoathetoid movements have very rarely been reported during carbamazepine treatment, and usually only in conjunction with acute overdoses (Bimpong-Buta and Froescher, 1982; Jacome, 1979; Chadwick et al., 1976; Martinon et al., 1980). Moreover, carbamazepine has been used in the treatment of some dystonias

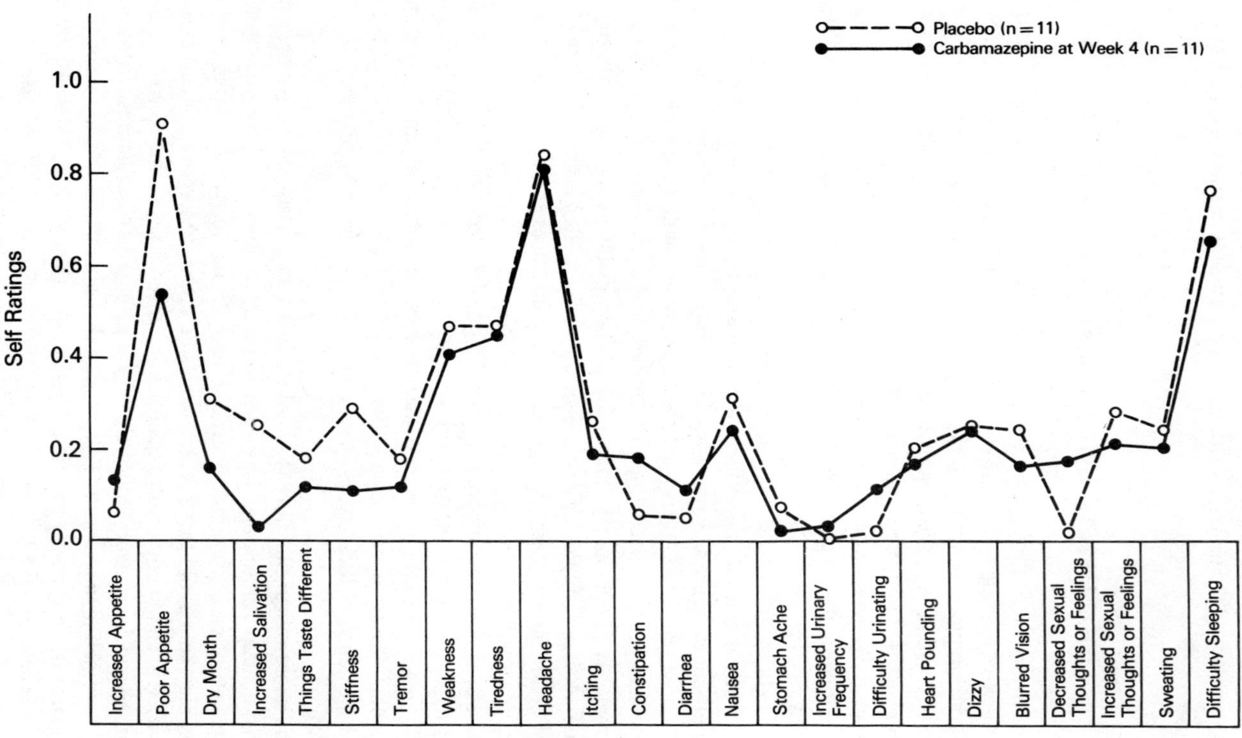

Figure 13. Lack of subjective side effects during carbamazepine treatment in depressed patients.

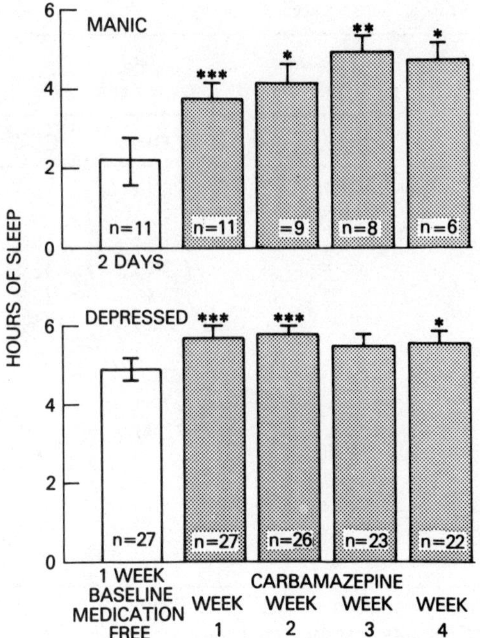

Figure 14. Effect of carbamazepine on sleep in manic and depressed patients.

(Garg, 1982; Geller, et al., 1974). In this regard carbamazepine appears to be a relatively safe drug with rare reports of fatalities even after relatively massive overdoses (see Table 5, data of Masland, 1982).

Hematological Toxicity

One of the major concerns of acute and long-term carbamazepine therapy is the development of major hematological toxicity, including thrombocytopenia, pancytopenia, and aplastic anemia. In 1975, Pisciotta reviewed 13 cases of aplastic anemia, 10 of which ended lethally, thought to be related to carbamazepine at that time. However, in many of the cases patients were medically ill (often they were older women with pain syndromes) and were concurrently on a number of other medications. Therefore, the conclusion that carbamazepine itself was directly related to the development of aplastic anemia in each of these cases could not be reached. However, it does appear that carbamazepine treatment may be associated

TABLE 4. Adverse Reactions to Carbamazepine[a]

	Ballenger and Post (1980)[b]	Okuma et al., 1979		Reynolds, 1975[f]
Symptom	CBZ	CHLORPZ[c]	CBZ[d]	CBZ
Overall incidence		(86%)[e]	59%	60.0%
Drowsiness	13%	(59%)[e]	29%	11.8%
Headache	—	(31%)	26%	.8%
Dizzyness	29%	(28%)	12%	11.4%
Dry mouth		(24%)	15%	
Lassitude		(21%)	15%	
Orthostatic hypotension		(17%)		
Feeling of weakness	4%	(17%)		
Hypersalivation		(17%)		
Nasal stuffiness		(17%)[e]		
Exanthema	16%		16%	
Ataxia	21%			9.0%
Diplopia	13%			0.2%
Confusion	4%			0.6%
Parasthesia	4%			0.4%

[a]None of these data were placebo corrected (see Figure 13).
[b]Data from first 24 patients, except exanthema, which were observed in 8 of first 56 patients.
[c]Twenty-eight manic-depressive patients.
[d]Thirty-two manic-depressive patients.
[e]$p < .05$.
[f]510 patients with trigeminal neuralgia.

with the development of agranulocytosis or aplastic anemia in a small number of patients. Recently, Hart and Easton (1982) and Pisciotta (1982) reviewed the world literature on hematological toxicity to carbamazepine. They suggested that the drug was generally safe with long periods of usage, both in children and in adults, for the prophylactic management of seizure disorders as well as trigeminal neuralgia. Based on their latest information, not only from the literature but also from CIBA-Geigy, they estimated that the risk for major hematological toxicity was on the order of magnitude of 1 in 10,000-40,000. With increasing use of the drug from 1972 to 1979, there was an increase in the number of blood dyscrasias, but the ratio of toxicity to patients at risk remained relatively constant at about 1 patient in 15,000-25,000. This small incidence of hematological toxicity is perhaps not different from that reported with other major psychotropic drugs, as the phenothiazines. Pisciotta (1982), for example, monitored a total of six white

TABLE 5. Case Reports of Massive Overdosage with Carbamazepine

Investigator	Age (yr)	Dose (g)	Respiration	Pupillary reaction	Labyrinth response	Tendon reflexes	Babinski reflex	Convulsion	Coma (days)	Recovery (days)
de Zeeuw et al. (14)	23	16	Respiratory support	NA	NA	NA	NA	NA	3	5
Gruska et al. (26)	41	20	Respiratory support	Slow	NA	Active	Normal	"Spasms"	6	17
Güntelberg (27)	14	17	—	Slow	NA	Absent	Abnormal	—	3	NA
Hager (28)	2	1.4	Cyanotic	Absent	NA	Weak	Abnormal	Convulsion	½	1
Hajnsek and Sartorius (29)	31	20	—	Slow	NA	Active	Normal	—	2	14
Lang-Petersen (45)	19	10-14	Respiratory support	Normal	NA	Absent	Abnormal	Status	4	?
Livingston et al. (48)	18	10-12	—	(Papilledema)	NA	Weak	?	Convulsion	2	4
Livingston et al. (48)	14	5+	—	NA	NA	NA	NA	—	2	7
Saleman and Pippenger (64)	NA	5.8	—	Normal	Absent	Active	Normal	—	1	4
Smoot and Wood (71)	15	10	—	Slow	NA	Weak	Abnormal	—	1½	2
Taghevy and Naumann (79)	16	1.2-2	—	NA	NA	NA	NA	—	0	5
Taghevy and Naumann (79)	38	10	—	NA	NA	NA	NA	—	?	4
Volmat et al (86)	15	3	—	NA	NA	Normal	Normal	—	0	2
Volmat et al. (86)	30	10	—	NA	NA	NA	NA	—	3	9
Warot et al. (88)	28	10	—	Slow	Depressed	Normal	Normal	—	1	3

NA-not available.
From: Masland, 1982

counts between weeks 2 and 10 of phenothiazine treatment. In 40,000 leukocyte counts (presumably in 6,666 patients), he found 5 cases of agranulocytosis and 500 cases of transient leukopenia). Nevertheless, because of the initial reports on the development of aplastic anemia, the *Physicians' Desk Reference* (1982) continues to flag this as a major problem with a special warning that the drug should not even be used as a first-line anticonvulsant. Yet, neurologists are increasingly using carbamazepine, in many cases in preference to phenytoin, and in this instance, current neurological practice appears to be somewhat different from that indicated in the *Physicians' Desk Reference*. Similar conclusions are reached by Hart and Easton (1982) and Pisciotta (1982) in their more recent reviews indicating that carbamazepine still appears to be one of the drugs of choice for the treatment of not only trigeminal neuralgia and related pain syndromes but also major motor seizures and, in particular, complex partial seizures. We have plotted the data from Pisciotta (1982) in Fig. 15a, which illustrates the greater risk for major blood dyscrasias in the first 4 to 6 months of treatment with carbamazepine. Thirteen of the 22 patients with aplastic anemia died while 1 of the 16 patients with agranulocytosis died. Thus, only 4 additional deaths have been reported since the initial survey in 1975. There did not appear to be a relationship to age (2-90 years), dose (200-1,400 mg/day; all but 5 patients were treated with 800 mg/day or less), or sex (22 females and 14 males). Pisciotta suggests that the drug should be discontinued when indices fall below certain guidelines:

lymphocytes < 4000/cu mm
erythrocytes < 4.0 x 10^6/cu mm
hematocrit < 32%
platelets < 100,000/cu mm
hemoglobin < 11 grams/100 ml
reticulocytes < 0.3% (20,000/cu mm)
serum iron < 150 µg/100 ml

Hart and Easton (1982) had generally similar guidelines for discontinuing carbamazepine, but a WBC limit of 3,000/cu mm or <1,500 neutrophils/cu mm.

The suggestions in the neurological literature are that the blood indices should be followed at weekly or bi-weekly intervals during the first 2 to 3 months of carbamazepine administration and then followed at quarterly intervals thereafter. These recommendations are made in the face of knowledge that the development of aplastic anemia appears to be a highly idiosyncratic process and probably not related to the more typical, possibly dose-response-related mild to moderate decreases in white count that occur routinely in association with carbamazepine administration. Thus, Hart and Easton suggest that after initial dose monitoring

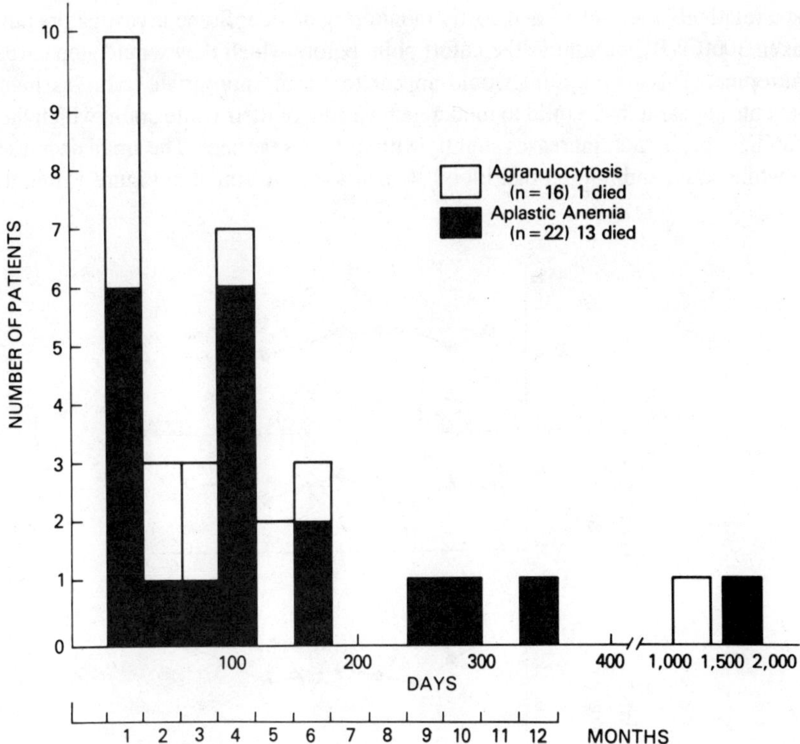

Figure 15a. Distribution of cases of aplastic anemia and agranulocytosis as a function of duration of carbamazepine treatment* (data from Pisciotta, 1982).

*3 additional cases of agranulocytosis and 2 of aplastic anemia were reported without onset data.

(twice a month complete white counts), patients should be cautioned to immediately notify their doctors if an infection or severe intercurrent illness or rash develops and only quarterly blood count monitoring is recommended. This latter recommendation appears more consistent with much of the use of carbamazepine in neurological patients, where the conservative degrees of monthly blood monitoring do not appear to be routinely utilized and patients are asked to notify their physician should side effects emerge.

Given the fact that carbamazepine has not yet been approved as a psychotropic agent (and is not likely to be so for some period of time), it might be wise to adopt the more conservative posture of monitoring blood levels weekly during the first several months and then approximately monthly thereafter, even though this may be a relatively ineffective and costly monitoring device. Some investigators have taken 3000 WBC/cu mm as the cutoff point before which they would stop carbamazepine. This lower limit would appear to be an appropriate value as many patients appear to have mild to moderate lowering of their white count which then stabilizes or, in fact, increases slightly with further treatment. The small decreases in white count and not in other blood elements are illustrated in Figure 15b in the

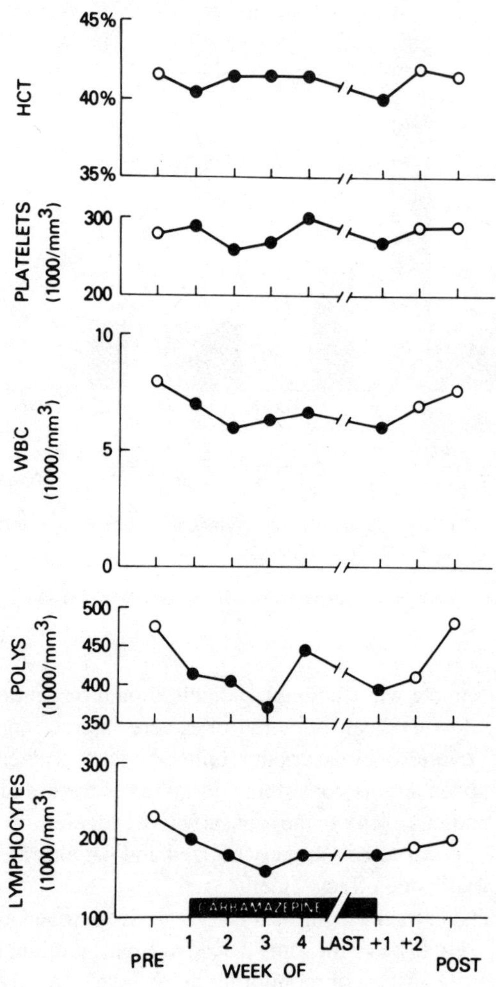

Figure 15b. Hematologic indices during carbamazepine treatment.

first series of our psychiatric patients treated with carbamazepine as the only drug. While the decreases in white count are statistically significant and quite consistent across individual patients, they are clinically insubstantial and in the majority of patients, the white count remains within the therapeutic range. We have not had to discontinue carbamazepine in any of the first 70 patients in our series because of a low WBC.

DOSE AND BLOOD LEVEL RELATIONSHIPS TO CLINICAL RESPONSE AND SIDE EFFECTS

Recently, Gerson et al. (1983) have described a patient who developed aplastic anemia following use of both the anticonvulsants phenytoin and carbamazepine. They thought that this was related to the formation of toxic arene oxide metabolites. Using a sample of a patient's lymphocytes and incubating them with phenytoin and carbamazepine in the presence of a microsomal drug metabolizing system (which presumably facilitated the formation of toxic metabolites), they found that this individual patient's white cell elements were markedly more sensitive to cytotoxicity than normal controls. They also studied the lymphocytes of the patient's mother and found that she too was more sensitive in this particular test. These results, if replicated, may lead to an important screening device for patients with some increased vulnerability to developing major hematological reactions to anticonvulsants such as carbamazepine.

These data do again emphasize the differential nature of the rare idiosyncratic development of aplastic anemia, potentially in response to this toxic metabolite, in contrast to the more routine and expected minor decreases in white counts achieved with routine carbamazepine administration, possibly occurring in a dose-related fashion. In fact, it is of some interest that the decreases in white count of carbamazepine contrast with the consistent increases in white count observed during lithium carbonate administration, although the factors for each of these white count changes are so far not known. When these factors are identified, it may be of some interest to consider whether this differential effect on white count is related to other physiological effects of these agents.

Effects on Thyroid Indices

Carbamazepine does appear to produce mild and clinically insubstantial effects on thyroid function. A number of studies as summarized in Table 6 document that it decreases either total levels of free circulating T_3 or T_4. However, in contrast to

TABLE 6. Effects of Carbamazepine on Thyroid Indices in Neurological and Psychiatric Patients

Indices						
T_4	T_3	Free T_3	Free T_4	TSH	TRH→TSH	Reference
—	—	↓	↓			Luhdorf et al., 1977
↓	↓,—					Rootwelt et al., 1978
	↓					Liewendahl et al., 1978
	↓	↓			—	Fischel and Knopfle, 1978 (children)
				—	↓	Joffe et al., 1984
↓	↓	—	↓	—		Strandjord et al., 1981[a]
↓	—	↓		—		Bentsen et al., 1983
↓	↓		↓	↑		Roy-Byrne et al., 1984

Key: ↓ = decreased; — = no significant change; blank indicates variable not reported or studied.

[a]Patients remained clinically euthyroid in this study and in most instances thyroid replacement is not required. One case of hypothyroidism with elevated TSH has been reported.

lithium carbonate, there is no associated increase in levels of TSH, suggesting that the mechanism of mild suppression of thyroid by carbamazepine is different from that achieved by lithium carbonate. Also in marked contrast to the small but substantial number of patients who develop clinical hypothyroidism and require thyroid replacement during lithium carbonate treatment, this appears to be an extremely rare occurrence during carbamazepine administration (Bentson et al., 1983) and to our knowledge only one patient has required thyroid replacement (Aanderud and Strandjord, 1980). Thus, monitoring of initial levels of thyroid function may be advisable prior to the initiation of carbamazepine therapy, but routine assessment of these indices would not appear to be necessary thereafter.

Antidiuretic Effect, Vasopressin, Hyponatremia

In contrast to lithium carbonate which induces the diabetes insipidus syndrome in a small, but substantial number of patients so treated, carbamazepine has not been associated with this problematic side effect. In fact, carbamazepine has been used in the treatment of non-lithium-induced diabetes insipidus with some success, particularly prior to the development from more potent arginine vasopressin analogs (Wales, 1975).

The effects of carbamazepine on vasopressin function therefore appear to be of both clinical and theoretical interest. Because it does not induce diabetes insipidus, carbamazepine may be a useful treatment alternative to those who have intolerable lithium-induced diabetes insipidus and associated renal side effects. It is also possible that if carbamazepine is used conjointly with lithium that lower lithium levels might be sufficient, producing less induction of diabetes insipidus. Lithium is thought to induce the diabetes insipidus syndrome at the level of inhibiting adenylate cyclase activity, while preliminary evidence from our laboratory (Gold et al., 1983; 1984; Berrettini et al., 1982) suggest that carbamazepine may be acting as a direct vasopressin receptor agonist. Gold et al. observed that during treatment with carbamazepine there was decreased secretion of plasma arginine vasopressin in response to a hypertonic saline load. This contrasts with the observations during lithium treatment where an increased amount of plasma vasopressin was secreted in response to a hypertonic saline load.

These findings would thus be consistent with what might be expected if carbamazepine was acting directly as a vasopressin agonist or facilitating available arginine vasopressin function. In this case less arginine vasopressin "needed" to be secreted into the plasma following the hypertonic saline challenge. The data of Berrettini et al. indicating that carbamazepine, albeit weakly, displaces I^{125} arginine vasopressin from a putative platelet vasopressin binding site do suggest that carbamazepine may be acting directly at the vasopressin receptor. If this were the case, it would be consistent with the clinical observations that co-treatment with carbamazepine of lithium-treated patients is not sufficient to reverse lithium-induced diabetes insipidus (Ghose, 1978; Post et al., unpublished observations). Since lithium carbonate is inhibiting vasopressin function at the level of adenylate cyclase, i.e., below the vasopressin receptor, even if carbamazepine were acting as an agonist directly at the receptor it would not be expected to reverse the lithium-induced defect. However, we are aware of several patients in whom persistent lithium-induced diabetes insipidus was adequately treated with carbamazepine once lithium carbonate administration had been discontinued (Brooks and Lessin, 1983).

Because of the effects of carbamazepine in potentiating antidiuretic effects, there is some risk for developing hyponatremia and/or water intoxication. Hyponatremia appears to be mild, dose related (Uhde and Post, 1983; Perruca and Richens, 1980), and clinically not problematic in the majority of patients. This is illustrated in Figure 16 showing that most patients have small decreases in serum sodium which are almost always within the therapeutic range. However, in several patients who had initially low levels of serum sodium, carbamazepine induced more major hyponatremia. These data might suggest more cautious monitoring of serum sodium in patients with low initial baseline levels. Dr. Uhde reviewed all

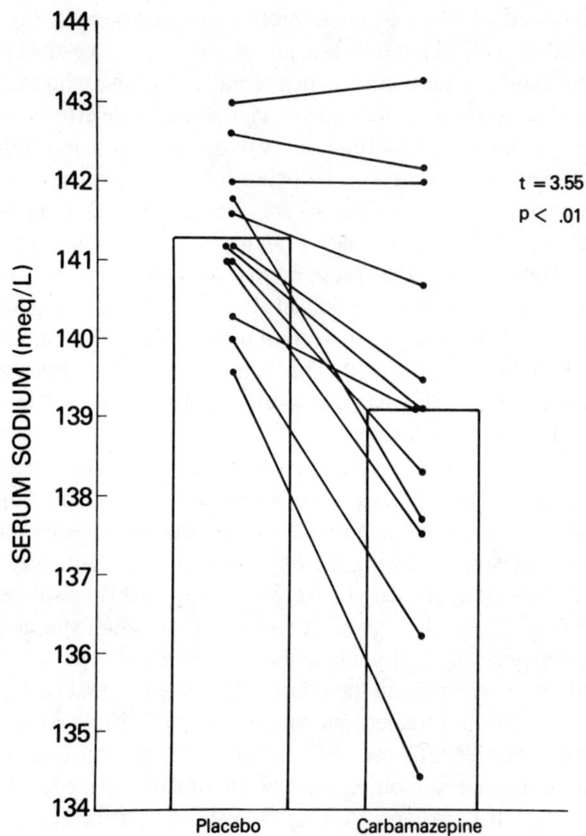

Figure 16. Reduction in mean serum sodium following carbamazepine treatment.

individual values of serum sodium before and after treatment with carbamazepine in our initial group of patients. As illustrated in Figures 17a and 17b, all of the abnormal single values were observed when the patients were on carbamazepine treatment. These data suggest that, if a patient develops confusion or other signs of impending hyponatremia or water intoxication, that serum sodium and associated biochemical measurements be rapidly obtained, and that the differential diagnosis of hyponatremia and potential water intoxication should be added to the clinician's awareness when he is considering whether side effects are merely dose-related

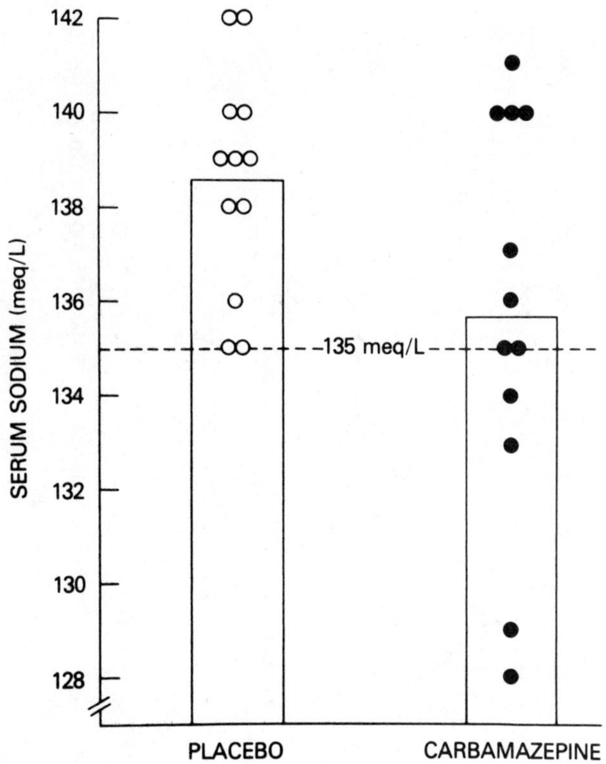

Figure 17a. Comparison of lowest sodium levels during placebo and carbamazepine treatment.

responses to carbamazepine or whether they may be because of alterations in fluid and electrolyte balance.

Because of the inability to excrete a full water load during carbamazepine treatment, clinicians should be aware of the potential danger of water intoxication, particularly in patients with psychogenic polydypsia or other instances of large water intake. Since carbamazepine does not affect the threshold of arginine vasopressin secretion following a hypertonic saline load, the incidence of water intoxication would be expected to be extremely low (Gold et al., 1984). In fact, this appears to be the case as there are few reports in the literature of water intoxication (Ashton et al., 1977; Perucca et al., 1978; Stephens et al., 1977).

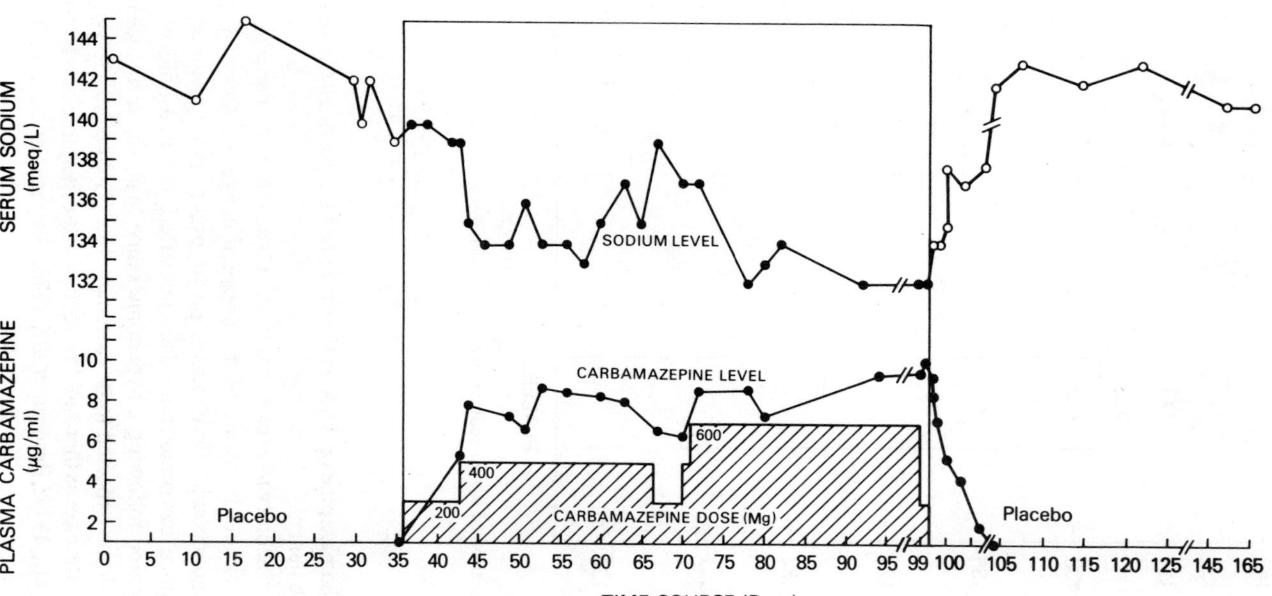

Figure 17b. Effect of carbamazepine on serum sodium in a patient with affective illness.

In addition to the renal and fluid and electrolyte aspects of carbamazepine's vasopressin agonist-like effects, these properties are also of potential interest in relationship to the drug's effects on mood and cognition. Gold et al. (1984) postulated that alterations in arginine vasopressin may play a role in some aspects of the symptomatology of manic-depressive illness. De Wied (1976), in animals, and Weingartner (1981), in man, have reviewed the substantial literature indicating that arginine vasopressin may play a role in various paradigms of learning and memory. To the extent that carbamazepine has direct or indirect agonist-like effects at the vasopressin receptor, it is possible that these could account for some aspects of carbamazepine's relatively positive effects on cognition. Thompson et al. (1980), for instance, reported that phenytoin, but not carbamazepine, led to dose-related deterioration in intellectual performance in normal volunteers. Subjective mood changes were also more favorable on carbamazepine. Trimble et al. (personal communication, 1983) has also indicated that in epileptic subjects, those with higher levels of carbamazepine showed more positive effects on mood than patients on other anticonvulsant regimens. Maitre et al. (1983) reviewed work of Mondadori and Classen (1984) indicating that carbamazepine differs from other anticonvulsants (phenytoin, clonazepam, ethosuximide, sodium valproate, and phenobarbitone), which worsen electroshock (ECS)-induced amnesia, in that it diminished ECS-induced amnesia in mice. It does so at doses about 30 times lower (0.1 mg/kg p.o.) than those reported to produce initial anticonvulsant effects.

Thus, it remains a possibility for further testing whether carbamazepine's effects on vasopressin may account for aspects of its effects on cognition or side effects. It is also of interest that patients on lithium frequently complain about slowness in intellectual performance and/or loss of creativity. In specifically designed scales to measure aspects of this cognitive defect, it is demonstrated that lithium does, in fact, impair some aspects of cognitive functioning (Reus et al., 1979). While it is not clear whether lithium's interference with arginine vasopressin function accounts for this altered subjective and objective sense of cognitive performance, it remains an interesting issue for further observation and testing because of carbamazepine's opposite effects on this system, whether the drug will not share this problematic side effect. If this turns out to be the case, use of carbamazepine might lead not only to less cognitive impairment during maintenance treatment, but also may improve patient compliance.

Dermatological Side Effects

In various studies of the neurological literature, carbamazepine has been reported to produce rashes in percentages of patients ranging from several to more than 10%. In our own experience, eight of the first 56 patients (14%) studied developed rashes while taking carbamazepine, which led us to discontinue the clinical trial. These rashes rapidly resolved upon drug discontinuation. There are several reports in the pediatric literature of restarting patients on the anticonvulsant once a rash has been experienced, although conservative procedure would suggest that this not be routinely employed in adult patients in light of possible risk of increasing the presumed hypersensitivity reaction. Moreover, there are several cases of severe skin reactions, including exfoliative dermatitis (Ford and Bieder, 1968; Harman, 1967), and the possible relationship of this syndrome to repeated exposure to carbamazepine has not been adequately delineated.

Other Side Effects

Hepatitis appears to be an extremely rare side effect of carbamazepine treatment (Zucker et al., 1977; Levy et al., 1981; Sheridan, 1982). There are relatively few reports of liver abnormalities in spite of close monitoring of these values in large numbers of epileptic and affectively ill patients. There are several reports in the literature of hepatitis associated with carbamazepine that led to a fatal outcome. However, one of these patients was a chronic alcoholic and the precise relationship of carbamazepine to her hepatic problems remains to be delineated. The rare, mild, and usually transient elevations of liver enzymes that do occasionally occur on carbamazepine appear to be quite distinct from the more major problem associated with liver enzyme abnormalities and hepatitis in patients taking sodium valproate (Jeavons, 1982). An initial liver battery might be desirable prior to starting carbamazepine treatment, and occasional monitoring of liver function would be conservative, but does not appear to be part of the routine medical practice in the treatment of neurological patients. Rare types of other hypersensitivity reaction to carbamazepine include pneumonitis (Stephan et al., 1978) and glandular fever-like syndrome (Lewis and Rosenbloom, 1982).

Carbamazepine is a potential antiarrhythmic agent for digitalis-induced ventricular arrhythmias and those induced by experimental coronary artery ligation and adrenaline in the dog (Steiner et al., 1970; Corday et al., 1971; Perez-Olea et al., 1979). It has been reported to moderately decrease A-V conduction, thus potentially predisposing to increased A-V block or slowing idioventricular rhythm in those already having complete block (Beermann and Edhag, 1978). Thus, carbamazepine should be used with caution in those with varying degrees of block (Meyrignac et al., 1983). Clinically useful antiarrhythmic effects have been reported in seven of nine patients (78%) with digitalis intoxication and in a smaller percentage (58%) in other types of arrhythmias (Perez-Olea et al., 1979).

SPECTRUM OF CLINICAL EFFICACY AND PREDICTORS OF CLINICAL RESPONSE

Carbamazepine appears to have a well-documented role in the treatment of trigeminal neuralgia and related paroxysmal pain syndromes (Table 7) as well as in epilepsy, particularly the psychomotor type thought to arise from temporal lobe and limbic system structures (Penry and Daly, 1975). As reviewed above, there is emerging evidence that carbamazepine may also be useful in a variety of psychiatric syndromes including primary and secondary affective illness. Further work needs to be carried out in order to assess the possible utility of this drug in schizoaffective and schizophrenic syndromes, although several preliminary clinical trials (reviewed above) suggest that it may be a useful adjunct to neuroleptic treatment of these patients. In addition, it may have some utility in the treatment of the aggressive patient (Roy-Byrne and Post, 1984). These preliminary clinical data on the use of carbamazepine in violent patients parallel initial studies indicating in different animal paradigms that carbamazepine is effective in some, but not all, animal behavioral pharmacological tests thought to predict anti-aggressive properties (Koella et al., 1976).

At this point, one can prepare a preliminary list of indications and possible predictors for carbamazepine's use; as further clinical trials are performed and more data are collected, this list will no doubt undergo substantial revision (see Table 8). One of the major clinical and theoretical issues to be resolved is the degree of overlap in lithium and carbamazepine responsivity. Are the two drugs useful in different subgroups of patients? The data from our own clinical series does not reveal the answer, as the majority of our patients had been previously not responsive to lithium carbonate and the relatively high percentage of carbamazepine responders in this group could either parallel those of the general population or be related to this preselected, lithium-nonresponsive group. There is some suggestion from the data of Okuma et al. (1973) that there may not be great overlap in response to the two agents and that positive response to one will relatively infrequently predict positive response to the other. Paul Grof (personal communication, 1983) has discontinued lithium in a small number of responsive patients with manic-depressive illness because of problematic side effects. None of these patients responded when they were switched to carbamazepine. Clearly, more systematic clinical trials are required to sort out this issue, including randomized assignment to carbamazepine and lithium as well as crossover trials. The data may emerge in some similarity to those in trigeminal neuralgia where patients appear to be responsive either to carbamazepine or phenytoin, a small percentage being responsive to both agents, and a very small group being responsive to neither.

If the data in affective illness eventually do suggest two relatively distinct sub-

TABLE 7. Carbamazepine in Paroxysmal and Dysrhythmic Syndromes

Seizures	
Temporal lobe epilepsy (TLE) (Complex partial seizures)	(Penry and Daly, 1975)
Grand mal seizures	(Penry and Daly, 1975)
Alcohol withdrawal seizures	(Chu, 1979)
Amygdala kindled seizures	(Wada, and Osawa, 1976; Babington, 1977; Ashton and Wauqier, 1979; Albright & Burnham, 1980)
Seizure management (Acute intermittent porphyria)	(Peters, 1981)
Paroxysmal pain syndromes	
Trigeminal neuralgia	(Blom, 1962; Bonduelle, 1976; Killian and Fromm, 1968; Davis, 1969)
Tabes (Lightning pain)	(Ekbom, 1972; Killian and Fromm, 1968)
Phantom limb pain	(Elliott et al., 1976)
Post-herpetic neuralgia[a]	(Davis, 1969)
Glossopharyngeal neuralgia	(Yang and Nagaswami, 1978)
Recurrent episodes of headache	(Kurata, 1982)
Cardiac arrhythmia	
Digitalis-induced ventricular arrhythmias	(Steiner et al., 1970; Corday et al., 1971; Perez-Olea et al., 1979)
Motor and verbal tics	
Gilles de la Tourette's syndrome	(Zawadzki, 1972; Lutz, 1977; Neglia et al., 1984; Gualtieri & Evans, 1984)
Hemifacial spasm	(Alexander and Moses, 1982)
Paroxysmal dysarthria	(Harrison and McGill, 1969)
Muscle irritability	
Myokymia	(Katrak et al., 1980; Hughes and Matthews, 1969)
Muscle hypertonicity	(Hershkowitz et al., 1982)
Myoclonic tinnitus[b]	(Shea and Harell, 1978; Rahko and Hakkinan, 1979; Melding and Goodey, 1979; Hess et al., 1980)
Autonomic dysregulation	
Autonomic epilepsy (with flushing and hypertension)	(Metz et al., 1978)
Autonomic epilepsy (with headaches and abdominal pain)	(Kurata 1982)
Affective dysregulation	
Manic-depressive illness	(Post et al., 1984a)
Affective dysregulation of TLE	(Dalby, 1975)

[a]Effective only on lancinating component of pain.

[b]In three studies of tinnitus, acute response to lidocaine was predictive of longer-term response to carbamazepine.

TABLE 8. Preliminary Indications for Individual Trials of Carbamazepine in Affective Illness.[a]

I. Primary affective illness	
A. Acute and prophylactic treatment of mania	++
B. Acute and prophylactic treatment of depression	+
C. Indicated in bipolar patients:	
1. Not responsive to lithium carbonate	++
2. Unable to tolerate lithium side effects including diabetes insipdus, allergy, or tremor	++
3. As supplement for lithium partial responder	++
D. Consider in schizoaffective illness, especially if cyclic; use in combination with a neuroleptic appears effective and should be further explored	+
E. Consider in recurrent atypical psychotic syndromes with depressive or confusional features	+
II. Secondary affective illness	
Mood and behavioral disturbance of:	
Complex partial seizures	++
Alcohol withdrawal symptoms	+

[a]Further studies are warranted in each area. ++, evidence from controlled studies or several laboratories; +, based on few studies or small numbers of patients.

groups of lithium and carbamazepine responders, however, this would not only be of clinical import in delineating predictors of clinical response, but would also suggest the possibility of different pathophysiological mechanisms underlying the two types of affective illness. Elsewhere, we have outlined some of the possible mechanisms of action of carbamazepine on classical and neuropeptide transmitter systems, which may account for its actions either in epilepsy or affective illness (Post et al., 1982b, 1983b, 1984a; Post and Uhde, 1983). In many instances these biochemical and physiological effects appear to differ considerably from those of lithium carbonate, neuroleptics, tricyclic antidepressants and more traditional psychotropic agents. As such, if a carbamazepine-responsive subgroup of patients were to emerge, it might suggest that one of these differential biochemical effects of carbamazepine may be related to its therapeutic efficacy in this subgroup.

At the present time we suggest carbamazepine as an alternative agent for patients who do not respond to lithium carbonate. It is also of interest that patients who show extremely rapidly cycling manic-depressive illness often do not respond as well to lithium carbonate as those with less rapid cycles (Dunner et al., 1977; Schou, 1982; Kukopulos et al., 1980). In addition, Kukopulos also identified the pattern of continuous cycling with short cycles (in 20% of his patients) and "depression-mania-free interval" (in 25% of his patients) as particularly lithium-resistant, especially if tricyclic antidepressants were administered concomitantly. We have observed carbamazepine responses in these types of patients and these patterns of rapidly cycling illness may thus be another indicator for a clinical trial of carbamazepine. Since Kraepelin's initial observation, multiple investigators have observed that affective illness tends to accelerate with repeated occurrences, both as a function of age and of number of prior episodes (Grof et al., 1974; Cutler and Post, 1982; Squillace et al., 1984; Roy-Byrne et al., 1985).

Therefore, it remains a possibility that carbamazepine may be differentially useful at different stages of the illness within an individual patient rather than within subgroups of patients. Thus just as in parkinsonian syndromes where, initially, levodopa may be adequate to control symptomatology, but with further deterioration a direct dopamine receptor agonist such as bromocryptine is required in order to continue successful treatment, it may be also that an agent like carbamazepine may be required later in the course of resistant affective illness when previously effective treatments become overwhelmed by the illness process. As illustrated in Table 1, the life course of illness variables do not differ significantly for carbamazepine responders compared to nonresponders with a group of equivocal patients omitted from the analysis. However, there is a trend for patients in the responder group to have more previous episodes of manic and/or depressive illness and more episodes in the year prior to NIH admission. This conforms to our clinical impression that rapidly cycling patients are among those who do respond to the drug, even if this is not a selective criterion.*

It is our clinical impression that many patients with extremely rapid onset of

* Parenthetically, one might emphasize the importance of following the life course of illness in some detail with an affectively ill patient as an important clinical and treatment response assessment tool. We have learned that estimates of numbers of affective episodes based on an insensitive measure such as number of hospitalizations bear no resemblance to estimates of episodes of illness based on more refined criteria (Squillace et al., 1984; Roy-Byrne et al., 1985). The data would suggest the utility of visually graphing the patient's daily mood ratings or the physician's weekly or monthly mood ratings over the patient's entire life course of illness (see Fig. 7a) in order to better understand the individual's patterns of illness and evolution of episodes to date. From this baseline one would then be able to make a more precise estimate of expected episode frequency and, ultimately, an evaluation of the nature and adequacy of prophylactic pharmacological response. A very simple rating instrument, such as the patient indicating on a 100 mm line from 0, the worst they have ever felt, to 50, their usual self, to 100 mm, the best they ever felt, can be a highly effective monitoring and evaluation device. The use of this type of system and the recognition of key signs and symptoms that herald the early onset of the patient's manic or depressive episodes may lead to better patient management by more careful and more rapid titration of the dose of primary or adjunctive medications at the first sign of an exacerbation of either phase of the illness.

illness in a given episode also are among those who respond to carbamazepine (for example, see Figs. 7a and 7b). These findings need to be more specifically explored and formally tested, but if substantiated might be consistent with the clinical profile of carbamazepine in other syndromes where the paroxysmal aspect of the illness appears to be particularly benefitted. For example, in the pain syndromes, carbamazepine is not especially effective for the chronic types of pain, but the lancinating or paroxysmal pain associated with trigeminal neuralgia and related syndromes appears to be markedly benefitted by the drug.

Paul Grof (personal communication, 1982) suggested that patients who responded to carbamazepine had a lower incidence of family history of affective illness than lithium responders. As illustrated in Table 9, this is not the case in our series, and is not the case in the Japanese series (Okuma, 1983). These investigators also indicated that carbamazepine response was associated with earlier onset of illness, presence of atypical features, and continuous rather than intermittent course of illness.

In our series, the severity of initial depression appears associated with degree of clinical response to carbamazepine (Fig. 1); the more severe the initial depression, the more likely the patient is to be a responder to carbamazepine. These findings parallel those we have observed with sleep deprivation, where the transient deprivation of one night's sleep sometimes results in dramatic mood improvement, particularly in those who are most severely depressed in the baseline period (Post et al., 1976; Roy-Byrne et al., 1984a). The type of presentation of depression (i.e., retarded or agitated) does not appear at this time to be a useful predictor of carbamazepine responses, although it is our clinical impression that the more agitated unipolar and bipolar patients respond best. For the acute antimanic effects of carbamazepine we have also observed a clinical profile of more severe mania and dysphoria and more rapid cycling in the manic patient who will respond to carbamazepine. In the studies of Okuma and associates they found a weak, but not

TABLE 9. Lack of Association of Carbamazepine Response to Family History of Affective Illness

Carbamazepine response[b]	Family history of affective illness[a]	
	Positive	Negative
Good	8/24	1/10
Equivocal	6/24	4/10
Poor	10/24	5/10

[a] First degree relatives

[b] Combined evaluation of acute and/or prophylactic response.

consistent, parallelism between acute responders and prophylactic responders. In fact, they had a higher incidence of prophylactic antimanic response (74%) than they did acute antimanic response (42%). Fifty-two percent of patients showed a prophylactic antidepressant response (i.e., those rated "markedly effective" and "effective"). Therefore, taken together, our data (Fig. 6) and those in the literature might suggest the utility of a prophylactic trial of carbamazepine in patients with sufficiently rapid cycling illness who require pharmacological intervention, even in some patients who were not acutely responsive to the drug during a given episode.

Although we have examined several possible biological markers for subsequent clinical response, only a few suggestive and preliminary patterns have emerged and considerable work is required in order to delineate possible biological markers of response (Table 10) (Post et al., 1984a). For example, we have observed that those patients with higher CSF opiate binding activity showed a better clinical response to carbamazepine (Post et al., 1981a). These findings are of interest from several perspectives. We have observed that patients with initially higher ratings

TABLE 10. Factors Affecting Response to Carbamazepine in Affectively Ill Patients

Clinical Correlates of Positive Response to Carbamazepine in Affectively Ill Patients

Typical manic-depressive symptoms (some atypical patients may also respond)
Carbamazepine responders may include:
- Lithium nonresponders
- Rapid cyclers

More severe depression responds better than less severe
History of positive response to sleep deprivation predicts antidepressant response
Patients with normal neurological exams and normal EEGs respond
History of psychosensory phenomena (usually associated with temporal lobe epilepsy) is *not* predictive
Family history of affective illness is controversial[a]

Biochemical Correlates of Positive Response

High CSF opioid binding in depressed patients
Low CSF cyclic-GMP and HVA in depressed patients
CSF GABA and somatostatin levels do *not* predict response

[a]P. Grof has observed negative family history of affective illness is predictive while we and Okuma have observed the opposite.

of anxiety had significantly higher opiate levels and anxiety appears to be one of the symptom clusters improved during the antidepressant response to carbamazepine. It is also of interest that carbamazepine has been shown to enhance the opiate-induced running behavior in laboratory animals, but it does not appear to directly interact with opiate receptors. It is possible that patients with higher CSF opiate binding levels would respond well to any acute antidepressant treatment and that there is nothing specific about the carbamazepine relationship.

We have not yet systematically explored other neuropeptide or endocrine predictors of clinical response. It will be particularly interesting to assess whether those with cortisol hypersecretion (based on either urinary free cortisol or escape from dexamethasone suppression) are differentially responsive to the drug. Preliminary data do not suggest that baseline levels of either urinary or CSF MHPG or CSF norepinephrine themselves are predictive of the degree of acute antidepressant response to carbamazepine. However, in several of our manic patients with extremely elevated levels of CSF norepinephrine, improvement was noted. As detailed elsewhere (Post et al., 1982a), we observed that carbamazepine significantly decreased probenecid-induced accumulations of cyclic GMP in cerebrospinal fluid. There were no changes in baseline levels. However, those patients who had the lowest initial levels of cyclic GMP in CSF showed the best acute antidepressant response to carbamazepine. These preliminary findings on biological predictors need to be more systematically explored before their possible clinical relevance is ascertained.

As noted above, blood levels of carbamazepine itself do not appear to be well correlated with degree of clinical response. There is wide individual variability in the blood level at which a patient might show either a therapeutic effect or side effects. While the active metabolite of carbamazepine, its 10,11-epoxide, did show a better correlation with a degree of clinical response, measurements of this substance are not widely available and further replications of these observations are required before the clinical utility of this measure is determined. Blood levels of carbamazepine in the 4-12 μ g/ml range that are generally accepted as the therapeutic range in the treatment of epileptic patients should be used only as a very rough guideline, and titration of a patient's clinical trial with dose increases against side effects and clinical response appears to be warranted at this time.

Carbamazepine would appear to be the drug of choice for patients with psychomotor seizure disorders and secondary affective illness. Based on Dalby's study in 1971 and his more extensive review of more than 2,500 patients in 1975, the evidence, albeit largely based on uncontrolled studies, appears to be quite substantial that carbamazepine is beneficial in controlling mood swings similar to those observed in primary affective illness. However, it has been argued that the psychotropic efficacy of carbamazepine in epilepsy is related to either substitution of this agent for other, more behaviorally toxic, drugs, low drug doses, or the achievement of better seizure control (Parnas et al., 1979). Several of the studies reviewed by Dalby and five of the eight controlled studies reviewed by Parnas (Tables 11a,b) suggest that this is not the case and our own series of patients with primary affective illness without any evidence of the seizure disorder provide indirect evidence that carbamazepine may indeed possess independent psychotropic properties separate from its anticonvulsant efficacy. Robertson and Trimble (1983) found that in epileptic patients meeting criteria for depression, patients treated with phenobarbital were more depressed, and those treated with carbamazepine were less depressed. Moreover, doses and blood levels of carbamazepine were inversely correlated with severity of trait anxiety measured on the Spielberger inventory (Robertson, 1983).

Successful use of carbamazepine, either alone or in combination with neuroleptics, has also been reported in patients with more atypical affective illness including schizoaffective disorder (Silberman and Post, 1980; Folks et al., 1982; Klein et al., 1982). In addition, as mentioned above, there is preliminary evidence that carbamazepine may also be a useful adjunct to neuroleptic treatment in some schizophrenic patients. Similarly, preliminary evidence seems to be emerging that carbamazepine may ultimately achieve a useful role in the treatment of some aggressive patients (Hakola and Laulumaa, 1982; S. Bracha, personal communication, 1980; Luchins, 1983; Trimble and Richens, 1981; Monroe, 1982).

CLINICAL USE OF CARBAMAZEPINE IN COMBINATION WITH OTHER AGENTS

All of the data in our series, unless otherwise indicated, referred to clinical trials of carbamazepine as the only treatment agent. In some instances, after this initial evaluation we have also found it useful to add a secondary psychotropic agent. During the trials of carbamazepine alone we have sometimes seen complete remission of manic and depressive episodes and we would recommend that treatment be initiated, if the patient is medication-free, with carbamazepine as the single agent. However, in a number of circumstances, carbamazepine does not seem to be completely effective in targeting all of the associated symptoms of a manic or depressive episode and supplementary medication might be considered. While no systematic clinical trials have been conducted to examine possible pharmacokinetic interactions between carbamazepine and other agents, we have not observed substantial alterations in blood levels of carbamazepine or lithium carbon-

TABLE 11A. Controlled Studies on Psychotropic Action of Carbamazepine (CBZ)

Author	Subjects	Design	Doses mg/day	Concomitant treatment	Blood levels reported	Psychotropic effect
Raotte et al. (1967)	24 epileptics from a mental hospital	CBZ vs PHT crossover 2 x 6 months	CBZ 600 PHT 300	Reduced	No	Positive
Marjerrison et al. (1968)	21 epileptic inpatients with personality disorders	CBZ vs Pb crossover 2 and 4 months	CBZ 400–120 PB?	Dosage halved	No	Positive
Pryse-Phillips & Jeavons (1970)	22 epileptics from a mental hospital	CBZ vs placebo group comparative 15 weeks	CBZ 600	Add-on	No	None
Groh et al. (1971)	20 non-epileptic children with behavior disorders	CBZ vs placebo cross-over 2 x 6 weeks	CBZ?	None	No	Positive
Cereghino et al. (1974)	45 mentally subnormal epileptic inpatients	CBZ vs PHT & Pb crossover 3 x 3 weeks	CBZ 1200 PHT 300 Pb 300	Withdrawn	Yes	None
Rodin et al. (1974)	37 epileptic inpatients	CBZ vs placebo cross-over 2 x 3 weeks	CBZ 600-1200	Slightly reduced	Yes	Negative
Puente (1975)	27 brain-damaged subnormal children	CBZ vs placebo cross-over 2 x 4 weeks	CBZ 200-300	No information	No	Positive
Dodrill & Troupin (1977)	40 epileptic outpatients	CBZ vs PHT cross-over 2 x 4 months	CBZ 18 mg/kg PHT 6mg/kg	None	Yes	Positive

Phenytoin (PHT).
Phenobarbital (Pb).
Adapted from Parnas et al., 1979.

TABLE 11B. Controlled Studies on Psychotropic Action of Phenytoin (PHT)

Author	Subjects	Design	Doses mg/day	Concomitant treatment	Blood levels reported	Psychotropic effect
Lefkowitz (1969)	50 delinquent boys with behavior disorders	PHT vs placebo group comparative 76 days	PHT 200	No information	No	Negative
Stephens & Shaffer (1970)	30 neurotic outpatients	PHT vs PHT cross-over 2 x 3 weeks	PHT 300 PHT 15	None	No	Positive
Malitz & Kanzler (1971)	312 depressed outpatients	PHT vs 6 antidepressants and placebo group comparative 4 weeks	PHT 400	Add-on	No	Negative
Uhlenhuth et al. (1972)	80 psychoneurotic outpatients	PHT vs Pb group comparative 8 weeks	PHT 300 Pb 90	No information	No	None
Stephens et al. (1974)	107 normal volunteers	PHT vs PHT cross-over 2 x 2 weeks	PHT 300 PHT 15	None	No	None

Phenobarbital (Pb).
Adapted from Parnas et al., 1979.

ate when these agents have been used together or neuroleptics have been added. The one notable exception to this, as indicated previously and in Table 3, is the use of carbamazepine with monoamine oxidase inhibitors where there was a clearcut and marked pharmacokinetic interaction resulting in substantially higher levels of carbamazepine and, in some cases, toxicity when it is combined with monoamine oxidase inhibitors.

If a patient with bipolar manic-depressive illness were showing some apparent response to lithium carbonate in one or the other phase of the illness, but not adequate control, we would recommend adding carbamazepine. The combination has produced better results than either drug alone in several of our patients as well as those of Lipinski and Pope (1982) and Okuma et al. (1973) without problematic side effects. However, we have recently become aware of several cases where carbamazepine has been added to previously existing lithium treatment and side effects, including nausea and vomiting, have been produced (Maria Del Zompo, personal communication, 1983; Post, personal observations, 1983). In several patients observed by Dr. Del Zompo, she found that addition of neuroleptic medication was sufficient to alleviate the nausea associated with the addition of carbamazepine to lithium therapy. The reports of Lipinski and Pope (1982) and others do suggest that patients may be inadequately responsive to either lithium carbonate or carbamazepine alone but show a more complete response to the combination of these two agents.

If a patient had been maintained on lithium carbonate with inadequate results and one were unsure to what extent lithium was continuing to be helpful to the rapid cycling patient, one might consider adding carbamazepine to the existing lithium treatment regimen and then withdrawing lithium after the patient had been suitably stabilized on the combination. If the patient showed some evidence of relapse during this lithium discontinuation phase, it would indicate that the combination had been useful. However, if the patient continued to remain stable on carbamazepine alone, monotherapy might be considered.

For the patient experiencing breakthrough depressions or inadequate control of depressive phases of the illness on carbamazepine, one might again consider the addition of lithium carbonate. Lithium carbonate appears to potentiate the antidepressant response to other tricyclic antidepressant compounds (de Montigny, Chapter 8, this volume) and, although convincing evidence is lacking to date, might also achieve the same effect with carbamazepine and may also ultimately lead to a better prophylactic response as well. Thyroid potentiation of carbamazepine treatment has not been systematically studied, although this might be indicated in patients with low thyroid indices. The use of more traditional tricyclic antidepressants in conjunction with carbamazepine has also not been systematically explored. As noted above, the use of carbamazepine in conjunction with monoamine oxidase inhibitors could lead to markedly higher levels of carbamazepine and potential toxicity. Neuroleptic supplementation of carbamazepine for the psychotically depressed patient has been documented as useful in at least one case report (Silberman and Post, 1980) and would also appear consistent with emerging data that neuroleptic use in combination with more routine tricyclic antidepressants is useful in the psychotic or delusional depressed patient (Nelson and Bowers, 1978; Chapter 7, this volume).

To our knowledge, carbamazepine has not been used in conjunction with electroconvulsive therapy and on theoretical grounds would not appear to be an uncomplicated procedure since carbamazepine is potent in inhibiting maximal electroconvulsive seizures and elevating the threshold for seizures in experimental animals (Albright and Burnham, 1980; Albright, 1983). We have observed that electroconvulsive seizures themselves, like carbamazepine, exert potent anticonvulsant effects on amygdala-kindled seizures in animals (Post et al., 1984b), so that it is possible that both seizures and anticonvulsants might be exerting their therapeutic effects in affective illness through similar common pathways. Nonetheless, it would appear prudent to discontinue carbamazepine treatment if electroconvulsive therapy were being considered and to reinstitute carbamazepine, lithium or some other suitable prophylactic agent following the course of electroconvulsive therapy if the patient appears to be at high risk for relapse based on previous life course of illness (Squillace et al., 1984; Coppen and Abou-Saleh, 1983).

Lambert et al. (1975) and Emrich et al. (1980) have reported the use of valproic acid in the management of acute manic episodes and, in combination with lithium carbonate, in the prophylactic management of the bipolar patient. Thus, another anticonvulsant agent, valproic acid, would appear to represent an alternative treatment strategy for the lithium-resistant bipolar patient. Chouinard et al. (1983) have also recently reported that another anticonvulsant agent, clonazepam, has acute antimanic effects, although this agent has not so far been studied in a prophylactic trial and appears to have fairly marked sedating side effects.

Thus carbamazepine would appear to be a first-line alternative to lithium carbonate in the bipolar patient. Its sequence of use in the unipolar depressed patient is less well established. We have seen several patients show complete clinical remission during treatment with carbamazepine when they have previously been resistant to other tricyclic antidepressants and, in some cases, lithium carbonate. Given the current state of relative ignorance regarding the acute antidepressant effects of carbamazepine (Post et al., 1984a), one might suggest the use of carbamazepine after a series of more routine tricyclic antidepressant or monoamine oxidase inhibitor treatments have been utilized.

INFORMED CONSENT AND THE FDA

If a bipolar depressed patient is not responsive to lithium carbonate or is unable to tolerate it because of side effects, then carbamazepine would appear to be a drug of choice, even though it is not yet FDA approved for this indication. The FDA makes it quite clear that one might be able to prescribe a drug that is available for other indications on a physician option or discretion basis. In their 1982 guidelines they state:

> The appropriateness or the legality of prescribing approved drugs for uses not included in their official labeling is sometimes a cause of concern and confusion among practitioners . . . .
>
> The FD&C Act does not, however, limit the manner in which a physician may use an approved drug. Once a product has been approved for marketing, a physician may prescribe it for uses or in treatment regimens or patient populations that are not included in approved labeling. Such "unapproved" or, more precisely, "unlabelled" uses may be appropriate and rational in certain circumstances, and may, in fact, reflect approaches to drug therapy that have been extensively reported in medical literature.
>
> The term "unapproved uses" is, to some extent, misleading. It includes a variety of situations ranging from unstudied to thoroughly investigated drug uses. Valid new uses for drugs already on the market are often first discovered through serendipitous observations and therapeutic innovations, subsequently confirmed by well-planned and executed clinical investigations. Before such advances can be added to the approved labeling, however, data substantiating the effectiveness of a new use or regimen must be submitted by the manufacturer to FDA for evaluation. This may take time and, without the initiative of the drug manufacturer whose product is involved, may never occur. For that reason, accepted medical practice often includes drug use that is not reflected in approved drug labeling. (*FDA Drug Bulletin*, 12;1:4-5, April 1982).

We have found it useful to explain the current status of this drug to our patients in some detail, indicating that it is, in fact, FDA approved for use in trigeminal neuralgia and in seizure disorders, but it is not likely to be approved for use in affective disorders in the near future. The risk:benefit ratio can then be discussed with the patient in the context that it has been given to many tens of thousands of patients for other indications with relative safety and that the emerging evidence seems to indicate that it may also be useful in the treatment of affective illness as well.

Carbamazepine is emerging as an effective alternative treatment agent in the primary and secondary affective disorders. While we do not know whether its proclivity to inhibit limbic system excitability is related to its psychotropic effect, several techniques are being employed to assess this possibility: EEG and averaged evoked response topographic mapping, regional glucose utilization (PET scan), paraepileptic and psychosensory symptom profiling, and intravenous procaine. Intravenous local anaesthetics such as procaine are thought to affect limbic system substrates, particularly altering EEG and glucose utilization in structures such as amygdala and hippocampus (Post, 1981). We are administering a series of graded intravenous doses of procaine to patients in order to study whether their electrophysiological or behavioral response to this agent will predict subsequent response to carbamazepine.

We have also systematically explored the degree to which patients with affective illness report signs and symptoms usually associated with psychomotor epilepsy. In collaboration with Ed Silberman we have developed a psychosensory questionnaire based on the reports of common subjective experiences during psychomotor seizures (Silberman et al., 1985). In this study, we found that patients with primary affective illness had as many psychosensory symptoms as patients with temporal lobe epilepsy, and both groups had significantly more symptoms than a medical hypertensive control population. Contrary to our expectations, we found that those affectively ill patients who reported greater numbers of psychosensory symptoms were the ones who responded best to lithium carbonate and showed a similar trend toward better response to tricyclic antidepressants. Preliminary inspection of the data suggested that this was not the case for carbamazepine, and that this potential clinical marker of signs and symptoms thought to emanate from limbic system structures was not a good correlate of carbamazepine response. These data also appear to parallel the EEG data where even mild abnormalities on the clinical EEG (which have been read as normal in our patient series) do not correlate with clinical response to carbamazepine.

Given the nonapproved status of carbamazepine, at the present time it would appear optimal to use it as a second-line drug in patients who are lithium carbonate failures or who respond inadequately to this and related agents. In the typical affective disorders, it would appear warranted to try several more routinely accepted agents prior to a clinical trial with carbamazepine. In patients with schizoaffective illness and excited schizophreniform psychosis, a cautious clinical investigatory trial may at times be indicated, particularly if not only further clinical benefit could be derived from the drug but also a lessening of the chance for long-term side effects such as tardive dyskinesia that are associated with long-term high dose maintenance of neuroleptic treatment.

Carbamazepine would appear to be an effective treatment alternative for the rapid cycling bipolar patient and in some unipolar depressed patients. We are seeking to elucidate further clinical and biological markers of response to carbamazepine as well as its mechanism of action. These data may further our understanding of the neural substrates underlying the affective disorders.

REFERENCES

Aanderud, S., and Standjord, R.E. Hypothyroidism induced by antiepileptic therapy. *Acta Neurol. Scand. 61,* 330-332 (1980).

Albright, P.S. Effects of carbamazepine, clonazepam, and phenytoin on seizure threshold in amygdala and cortex. *Exp. Neurol. 79,* 11-17 (1983).

Albright, P.S., and Burnham, W.M. Development of a new pharmacological seizure model: effects of anticonvulsants on cortical- and amygdala-kindled seizures in the rat. *Epilepsia 21,* 681-689 (1980).

Alexander, G.E., and Moses, H., III. Carbamazepine for hemifacial spasm. *Neurology 13,* 286-287 (1982).

Ashton, D., and Wauquier, A. Behavioral analysis of the effects of 15 anticonvulsants in the amygdaloid kindled rat. *Psychopharmacology 65,* 7-13 (1979).

Ashton, M.G., Ball, S.G., Thomas, T.H., and Lee, M.R. Water intoxication associated with carbamazepine treatment. *Brit. Med. J. 1,* 1134-1135 (1977).

Babington, R.G.: The pharmacology of kindling, in *Animal Models of Psychiatry and Neurology,* I. Hanin and E. Usdin, eds. Pergamon Press, Oxford/New York, pp. 141-149 (1977).

Ballenger, J.C. and Post, R.M. Therapeutic effects of carbamazepine in affective illness: a preliminary report. *Commun. Psychopharmacol. 2,* 159-178 (1978).

Beermann, B., and Edhag, O. Depressive effects of carbamazepine on idioventricular rhythm in man. *Brit. Med. J. 2,* 171-172 (1978).

Bentsen, K.D., Gram, L., and Veje, A. Serum thyroid hormones and blood folic acid during monotherapy with carbamazepine or valproate. *Acta Neurol. Scand. 67,* 235-241 (1983).

Berrettini, W.H., Post, R.M., Worthington, E.K., and Casper, J.B. Human platelet vasopressin receptors. *Life Sci. 30,* 425-432 (1982).

Bertilsson, L. Clinical pharmacokinetics of carbamazepine. *Clin. Pharmacokinet. 3,* 128-143 (1978).

Bimpong-Buta, K., and Froescher, W. Carbamazepine-induced choreoathetoid dyskinesias. *J. Neurol. Neurosurg. Psychiat. 45,* 560 (1982).

Block, S.H. Carbamazepine-isoniazid interaction. *Pediatrics 69,* 494-495 (1982).

Blom, S. Trigeminal neuralgia: its treatment with a new anticonvulsant drug G32883. *Lancet i.* 839-840 (1962).

Bonduelle, M. Current approaches to the treatment of trigeminal neuralgia, in *Epileptic Seizures-Behavior-Pain,* W. Birkmayer, ed. Hans Huber Publishers, Bern/Stuttgart/Vienna, pp. 321-326 (1976).

Bourgeois, B.F.D., Dodson, W.E., and Ferrendelli, J.A. Interactions between primidone, carbamazepine, and nicotinamide. *Neurology 32,* 1122-1126 (1982).

Brooks, S.C., and Lessin, B.E. Treatment of resistant lithium-induced nephrogenic diabetes insipidus and schizoaffective psychosis with carbamazepine. *Amer. J. Psychiat. 140,* 1077-1078 (1983).

Callaghan, N., Duggan, B., O'Hare, J., and O'Driscoll, D. Serum levels of phenobarbitone and phenylethylmalonamide with primidone used as a single drug and in combination with carbamazepine or phenytoin, in *Antiepileptic Therapy: Advances in Drug Monitoring,* S.I. Johannessen, P.L. Morselli, C.E. Pippenger, A. Richens, D. Schmidt, and H. Meinardi, eds. Raven Press, New York, pp. 307-313 (1980).

Cereghino, J.J. Relation of plasma concentration to seizure control, in *Antiepileptic Drugs,* D.M. Woodbury, J.K. Penry, and C.E. Pippenger, eds. Raven Press, New York, pp. 507-519 (1982).

Cereghino, J.J., Brock, J.T., van Meter, J.C., Penry, J.K., Smith, L.D., and White, B.G. Carbamazepine for epilepsy. A controlled prospective evaluation. *Neurology 24,* 401-410 (1974).

Cereghino, J.J., Brock, J.T., van Meter, J.W., Penry, J.K., Smith, L.D., and White, B.G. The efficacy of carbamazepine combinations in epilepsy. *Clin. Pharmacol. Ther. 18,* 733-741 (1975).

Chadwick, D., Reynolds, E.H., and Marsden, C.D. Anticonvulsant-induced dyskinesias: a comparison with dyskinesias induced by neuroleptics. *J. Neurol. Neurosurg. Psychiat. 39,* 1210-1218 (1976).

Chouinard, G., Young, S., and Annable, L. Antimanic effect of clonazepam. *Biol. Psychiat. 18,* 451-466 (1983).

Christiansen, J., and Dam, M. Influence of phenobarbital and diphenylhydantoin on plasma carbamazepine levels in patients with epilepsy. *Acta Neurol. Scand. 49,* 543-546 (1973).

Chu, N-S. Carbamazepine: prevention of alcohol withdrawal seizures. *Neurology 29,* 1397-1401 (1979).

Coppen, A., and Abou-Saleh, M.T. Lithium in the prophylaxis of unipolar depression: a review. *J. Royal Soc. Med. 76,* 297-301 (1983).

Corday, E., Enescu, V., Vyden, J.K., Lang, T.W., Carvalho, M.T., and Serruya, A. Antiarrhythimic properties of carbamazepine. *Geriatrics 26,* 78-82 (1971).

Cutler, N.R., and Post, R.M. Life course of illness in untreated manic-depressive patients. *Compr. Psychiat. 23,* 101-115 (1982).

Dalby, M.A. Antiepileptic and psychotropic effect of carbamazepine (Tegretol) in the treatment of psychomotor epilepsy. *Epilepsia 12,* 325-334, (1971).

Dalby, M.A. Behavioral effects of carbamazepine, in *Complex Partial Seizures and Their Treatment: Advances in Neurology, Vol. 11,* J.K. Penry and D.D. Daly, eds. Raven Press, New York (1975).

Dam, M., and Christiansen, J. Interaction of propoxyphene with carbamazepine. *Lancet ii.* 509 (1977).

Davis, E.H. Clinical trials of Tegretol© in trigeminal neuralgia. *Headache 9,* 77-82 (1969).

de Vogelaer, J. Carbamazepine in the treatment of psychotic and behavioral disorders. *Acta Psychiat. Belg. 81,* 532-541 (1981).

de Wied, D. Behavioral effects of intraventricularly administered vasopressin and vasopressin fragments. *Life Sci. 19,* 685-690 (1976).

Dodrill, C.B., and Troupin, A.S. Psychotropic effects of carbamazepine in epilepsy: a double-blind comparison with phenytoin. *Neurology 27,* 1023-1028 (1977).

Dravet, C., Mesdjian, E., Canraud, B., and Roger, J. Interaction between carbamazepine and triacelyloleandomycin. *Lancet i.* 810-811 (1977).

Dunner, D.L., Patrick, V., and Fieve, R.R. Rapid cycling manic-depressive patients. *Compr. Psychiat. 18,* 561-566 (1977).

Ekbom, K. Carbamazepine in the treatment of tabetic lightning pains. *Arch. Neurol. 26* 374-378 (1972).

Elliott, F., Little, A., and Millrandt, W. Carbamazepine for phantom-limb phenomena. *New Engl. J. Med. 295,* 678 (1976).

Emrich, H.M., von Zerssen, D., Kissling, W., Möller, H.-J., and Windorfer, A. Effect of sodium valproate in mania. The GABA-hypothesis of affective disorders. *Arch. Psychiat. Nervenkr. 229,* 1-16 (1980).

Fischel, H., and Knopfle, G. Effects of anticonvulsant drugs on thyroid hormones in epileptic children. *Epilepsia 19,* 323-336 (1978).

Folks, D.G., King, L.D., Dowdy, S.B., Petrie, W.M., Jack, R.A., Koomen, J.C., Swenson, B.R., and Edwards, P. Carbamazepine treatment of selected affectively disordered inpatients. *Amer. J. Psychiat. 139,* 115-117 (1982).

Ford, G., and Bieder, L. Exfoliative dermatitis due to carbamazepine (Tegretol). *New Zeal. Med. J. 68,* 386-387 (1968).

Garg, B.P. Dystonia musculorum deformans—implications of therapeutic response to levodopa and carbamazepine. *Arch. Neurol. 39,* 376-377 (1982).

Geller, M., Kaplan, B., and Christoff, N. Dystonia symptoms in children: treatment with carbamazepine. *J.A.M.A. 229,* 1755-1757 (1974).

Gerson, W.T., Fine, D.G., Spielberg, S.P., and Sensenbrenner, L.L. Anticonvulsant-induced aplastic anemia: increased susceptibility to toxic drug metabolites in vitro. *Blood 61,* 889-893 (1983).

Ghose, K. Effect of carbamazepine in polyuria associated with lithium therapy. *Pharmakopsychiatry 11,* 241-245 (1978).

Gold, P.W., Ballenger, J.C., Weingartner, H., Rubinow, D.R., Hoban, M.C., Goodwin, F.K., and Post, R.M. Vasopressin in affective illness: direct measurement, clinical trials and response to hypertonic saline, in *Neurobiology of Mood Disorders,* R.M. Post and J.C. Ballenger, eds. Williams & Wilkins, Baltimore, pp. 323-339 (1984).

Gold, P.W., Robertson, G.L., Ballenger, J.C., Kay, W., Chen, J., Rubinow, D.R., Goodwin, F.K., and Post, R.M. Carbamazepine diminishes the sensitivity of the plasma arginine vasopressin response to osmotic stimulation. *J. Clin. Endocrinol. Metab.,* 1983, 952-957.

Grof, P., Angst, J., and Haines, T. The clinical course of depression: practical issues, in *Symposia Medica, HKoest, Vol. 8: Classification and Prediction of Outcome of Depression,* F.K. Schattauer, ed. Schattauer-Verlag, New York, pp. 141-148 (1974).

Groh, C. The psychotropic effect of Tegretol in non-epileptic children, with particular reference to the drug's indications, in *Epileptic Seizures—Behavior—Pain,* E.W. Birkmeyer, ed. Hans Huber Publishers, Bern/Stuttgart/Vienna, pp. 259-263 (1976).

Groh, C., Rosenmayr, F., and Birbaumer, N. Psychotrope wirkung von carbamazepin bei nicht-epileptischen kindern. *Med. Mschr. 25,* 329-333 (1971).

Gualtieri, C.T., Evans, R.W. Carbamazepine-induced tics. *Dev. Med. Child Neurol. 26,* 546-548 (1984).

Hakola, H.P.A., and Laulumaa, V.A.O. Carbamazepine in treatment of violent schizophrenics. *Lancet,* 1358 (1982).

Hansen, J.M., Siersbock-Nielsen, K., and Shovsted, L. Carbamazepine induced acceleration of diphenylhydantoin and warfarin metabolism in man. *Clin. Pharmacol. Ther. 12,* 539-543 (1971).

Harman, R.R.M. Carbamazepine (Tegretol) drug eruptions. *Brit. J. Dermatol. 79,* 500-501 (1967).

Harrison, M., and McGill, J.I. Transient neurological disturbances in disseminated sclerosis: a case report. *J. Neurol. Neurosurg. Psychiat. 32,* 230-232 (1969).

Hart, R.G., and Easton, J.D. Carbamazepine and hematological monitoring. *Ann. Neurol. 11,* 309-312 (1982).

Hershkowitz, N., Mahany, T.M., and Raines, A. Effects of carbamazepine on muscle tone in the decerebrate cat. *J. Pharmacol. Exp. Ther. 224,* 473-481 (1982).

Hess, J.C., Viada, J., and May, A. Evaluacion de la prueba de la lidocaina y del tratamiento con carbamazepine en pacientes con tinnitus. *Rev. Laryngol. Otol. Rhinol. 40,* 5-10 (1980).

Hughes, R.C., and Matthews, W.B. Pseudo-myotonia and myokymia. *J. Neurol. Neurosurg. Psychiat. 32,* 11-14 (1969).

Inoue, K., Arima, J., Tanaka, K., Fukui, Y., and Kato, N. A lithium and carbamazepine combination in the treatment of bipolar disorder—a preliminary report. *Fol. Psychiatr. Neurol. Jpn. 35,* 465-475 *(1981).*

Jacome, D. Carbamazepine-induced dystonia. *J.A.M.A. 241,* 2263 (1979).

Jeavons, P.M. Valproate: toxicity, in *Antiepileptic Drugs,* D.M. Woodbury, J.K. Penry, and C.E. Pippenger, eds. Raven Press, New York, pp. 601-610 (1982).

Joffe, R.T., Gold, P.W., Uhde, T.W., and Post, R.M. The effects of carbamazepine on the thyrotropin response to thyrotropin-releasing hormone. *Psychiat. Res. 12,* 161-166 (1984).

Johannessen, S.I. Antiepileptic drugs: pharmacokinetics and clinical aspects. *Ther. Drug. Monit. 3,* 17-37 (1981).

Johannessen, S.I., and Strandjord, R.E. The influence of phenobarbitone and phenytoin on carbamazepine serum levels, in *Clinical Pharmacology of Anti-Epileptic Drugs,* H. Schneider, D. Janz, C. Gardner-Thorpe, H. Munardi, and A.L. Sherwin, eds. Springer-Verlag, Berlin/Heidelberg/New York, pp. 201-205 (1975).

Katrak, S.M., Pollack, M., O'Brien, C.P., Nukada, H., Allpress, S., Calder, C., Palmer, D.G., Grennan, D.M., McCormack, P.L., and Laurent, M.R. Clinical and morphological features of gold neuropathy. *Brain 103,* 671-693 (1980).

Keisling, R. Carbamazepine and lithium carbonate in the treatment of refractory affective disorders. *Arch. Gen. Psychiat. 40,* 223 (1983).

Killian, J.M., and Fromm, G.H. Carbamazepine (Tegretol) in the treatment of neuralgia: use and side effects. *Arch. Neurol. 19,* 129-136 (1968).

Klein, E., Bental, E., Lerer, B., and Belmaker, R.H. Carbamazepine and haloperidol versus placebo and haloperidol in excited psychoses. *Arch. Gen. Psychiat. 41,* 165-170 (1984).

Koella, W.P., Levin, P., and Baltzer, V. The pharmacology of carbamazepine and some other anti-epileptic drugs, in *Epileptic Seizures—Behavior—Pain,* W. Birkmayer, ed. Hans Huber Publisher, Bern/Stuttgart/Vienna, pp. 32-50 (1976).

Kukopulos, A., Reginaldi, D., Laddomada, P., Floris, G., Serra, G., and Tondo, L. Course of the manic-depressive cycle and changes caused by treatments. *Pharmakopsychiatria 13,* 156-167 (1980).

Kurata, S. Clinical trials of carbamazepine for autonomic seizures with and without generalized epileptic seizures. *Brain and Development 4,* 81-86 (1982).

Kwamie, Y., Persad, E., and Stancer, H.C. The use of carbamazepine in the management of affective disorders. Presented at U. of Toronto, Department of Psychiatry, Research Day, (1982).

Lambert, P.A., Carraz, G., Borselli, S., and Bouchardy, M. Le dipropylacetamide dans le traitement de la psychose maniaco-depressive. *Encephale 1,* 25-31 (1975).

Lefkowitz, M.M. Effects of diphenylhydantoin on disruptive behaviour. Study of male delinquents. *Arch. Gen. Psychiat. 20,* 643-651 (1969).

Levy, R.H., and Pitlick, W.H. Carbamazepine: interactions with other drugs, in *Antiepileptic Drugs,* D.M. Woodbury, J.K. Penry, and C.E. Pippenger, eds. Raven Press, New York, pp. 497-505 (1982).

Levy, M., Goodman, M.W., Van Dyne, B.J., and Sumner, H.W. Granulomatous hepatitis secondary to carbamazepine. *Ann. Int. Med. 95,* 64-65 (1981).

Lewis, I.J., and Rosenbloom, L. Glandular fever-like syndrome, pulmonary eosinophilia and asthma associated with carbamazepine. *Postgrad. Med. J. 58,* 100-101 (1982).

Liewendahl, K., Majuri, H., and Helenius, T. Thyroid function tests in patients on long-term treatment with various anticonvulsant drugs. *Clin. Endocrinol. 8,* 185-191 (1978).

Lindhout, D., and Meinardi, M. False-negative pregnancy test in women taking carbamazepine. *Lancet ii.* 505 (1982).

Lipinski, J.F., and Pope, H.G., Jr. Possible synergistic action between carbamazepine and lithium carbonate in the treatment of three acutely manic patients. *Amer. J. Psychiat. 139,* 948-949 (1982).

Luchins, D.J. Carbamazepine for the violent psychiatric patient. *Lancet i.* 766 (1983).

Lühdorf, K., Christiansen, P., Hansen, J.M., and Lund, M. The influence of phenytoin and carbamazepine on endocrine function: preliminary results, in *Epilepsy. The Eighth International Symposium,* J.K. Penry (ed.). Raven Press, New York, pp. 209-213 (1977).

Lutz, E.G. Alternative drug treatments in Gilles de la Tourette's syndrome—Letter to the Editor. *Amer. J. Psychiat. 134,* 95-96 (1977).

Maitre, L., Baltzer, V., Mondadori, C., Olpe, H.R., Baumann, P.A., and Waldmeier, P.C. Psychopharmacological and behavioral effects of antiepileptic drugs in animals. *Abstracts, VII World Congress of Psychiatry,* Vienna, July (1983), Excerpta Medica.

Malitz, S., and Kanzler, M. Are antidepressants better than placebo? *Amer. J. Psychiat. 127,* 1605-1611 (1971).

Marjerrison, G., Jedlicki, S.M., Keogh, R.P., Hrychuk, W., and Poulakakis, G.S. Carbamazepine: behavioral, anticonvulsant and EEG effects in chronically-hospitalized epileptics. *Dis. Nerv. Syst. 29,* 133-136 (1968).

Martinon, J.M., Docampo, G., Martinon, F., Viso, J.A., and Pena, J. Dostonia por carbamacepina: a proposito de cuatro observaciones en el niño. *Ann. Esp. Pediatr. 13,* 789-792 (1980).

Masland, R.L. Carbamazepine: neurotoxicity, in *Antiepileptic Drugs,* D.M. Woodbury, J.K. Penry, and C.E. Pippenger, eds. Raven Press, New York, pp. 521-531 (1982).

Mattson, G.F., Mattson, R.H., and Cramer, J.A. Interaction between valproic acid and carbamazepine: an *in vitro* study of protein binding. *Ther. Drug Monit. 4,* 181-184 (1982).

Melding, P.S., and Goodey, R.J. The treatment of tinnitus with oral anticonvulsants. *J. Laryngol. Otol. 93,* 111-122 (1979).

Mesdjian, E., Dravet, C., Cenraud, B., and Roger, J. Carbamazepine intoxication due to triacelyloleandomycin administration in epileptic patients. *Epilepsia 21,* 489-496 (1980).

Metz, S.A., Halter, J.B., Porte, D., Jr., and Robertson, R.P. Autonomic epilepsy: clonidine blockade of paroxysmal catecholamine release and flushing. *Ann. Intern. Med. 88,* 189-193 (1978).

Meyrignac, C., Berges, C., Benhothman, A., Toulette, K., Tillement, J.P., Albengres, E., and Blatrix, C.H. Bradycardie sinusale et bloc sino-auriculaire induits par la carbamazepine. *La Presse Medicale 12,* 577 (1983).

Mondadori, C., and Classen, W. The effects of various antiepileptic drugs on E-shock-induced amnesia in mice: dissociability of effects on convulsions and effects of memory. *Acta Neurol. Scand. 99,* 125-129 (1984).

Monroe, R.R. Limbic ictus and atypical psychosis. *J. Nerv. Ment. Dis. 170,* 711-716 (1982).

Neglia, J.P., Glaze, D. G., and Zion, T.E. Tics and vocalizations in children treated with carbamazepine. *Pediatrics 73,* 841–844 (1984).

Nelson, J.C., and Bowers, M.B. Delusional unipolar depression. *Arch. Gen. Psychiat. 35,* 1321-1328 (1978).

Neppe, V.M. Carbamazepine in the psychiatric patient. *Lancet ii,* 334 (1982).

Nolen, W.A. Carbamazepine, a possible adjunct to or alternative for lithium in bipolar disorder. *Acta Psychiat. Scand. 67,* 218-225 (1983).

Okuma, T. Therapeutic and prophylactic efficacies of carbamazepine in affective disorders. Proc. VII

World Congress of Psychiatry, Vienna, Austria, July 11-16, (1983).

Okuma, T., Inanaga, K., Otsuki, S., Sarai, K., Takahashi, R., Hazama, H., Mori, A., and Watanabe, M. Comparison of the antimanic efficacy of carbamazepine and chlorpromazine: a double-blind controlled study. *Psychopharmacology 66*, 211-217 (1979).

Okuma, T., Inanaga, K., Otsuki, S., Sarai, K., Takahashi, R., Hazama, H., Mori, A., and Watanabe, M. A preliminary double-blind study of the efficacy of carbamazepine in prophylaxis of manic-depressive illness. *Psychopharmacology 73*, 95-96 (1981).

Okuma, T., Kishimoto, A., Inoue, K., Matsumoto, H., Ogura, A., Matsushita, T., Naklao, T., and Ogura, C. Anti-manic and prophylactic effects of carbamazepine on manic-depressive psychosis. *Folia Psychiatr. Neurol. Jpn. 27*, 283-297 (1973).

Okuma, T., Kishimoto, A., and Inoue, K. Anti-manic and prophylactic effects of carbamazepine (Tegretol) on manic-depressive psychosis. (in Japanese) *Seishin Igaku 17*, 617-630 (1975).

Perucca, E., and Richens, A. Reversal by phenytoin of carbamazepine-induced water intoxication: a pharmacokinetic interaction. *J. Neurol. Neurosurg. Psychiat. 43*, 540-545 (1980).

Perucca, E., Garratt, A., Hebdige, S., and Richens, A. Water intoxication in epileptic patients receiving carbamazepine. *J. Neurol. Neurosurg. Psychiat. 41*, 713-718 (1978).

Parnas, J., Flachs, H., and Gram, L. Psychotropic effect of antiepileptic drugs. *Acta Neurol. Scand. 60*, 329-343 (1979).

Penry, J.K., and Daly, D.D. *Complex Partial Seizures and Their Treatment: Advances in Neurology, Vol. 11*. Raven Press, New York (1975).

Perez-Olea, J., Mordoh, I., and Quevedo, M. Efectos antiarritmucos de la carbamazepina. Estudio experimental y clinico. *Rev. Med. Chil. 107*, 203-209, (1979).

Peters, H.A. Carbamazepine in seizure management in acute intermittent porphyria. *Neurology 31*, 1579 (1981).

Pettilä, O., Neuvonen, P.J., Aho, K., and Lehtovaara, R. Interaction between doxycycline and some antiepileptic drugs. *Brit. Med. J. 2*, 470-472 (1974).

Pisciotta, A.V. Hematologic toxicity of carbamazepine, in *Complex Partial Seizures and Their Treatment: Advances in Neurology, Vol. 11*, J.K. Penry, and D.D. Daly, eds. Raven Press, New York, pp. 355-368 (1975).

Pisciotta, A.V. Carbamazepine: hematological toxicity, in *Antiepileptic Drugs*, D.M. Woodbury, J.K. Penry, and C. Pippenger (eds). Raven Press, New York, pp. 533-541 (1982).

Post, R.M. Lidocaine-kindled limbic seizures: behavioral implications, in *Kindling 2*, J.A. Wada (ed). Raven Press, New York, pp. 149-160 (1981).

Post, R.M., and Uhde, T.W. Biochemical and physiological mechanisms of action of carbamazepine in affective illness, in *Frontiers of Neuropsychiatric Research*. E. Usdin, M. Goldstein, A.J. Friedhoff, and A. Georgota (eds). MacMillan Press, London, pp. 175–192 (1983).

Post, R.M., Kotin, J., and Goodwin, F.K. Effects of sleep deprivation on mood central amine metabolism in depressed patients. *Arch. Gen. Psychat. 33*, 627-632 (1976).

Post, R.M., Pickar, D., Naber, D., Ballenger, J.C., Uhde, T.W., and Bunney, W.E., Jr.: Effect of carbamazepine on CSF opioid activity: relationship to antidepressant response. *Psychiatry Res. 5*, 59-66 (1981).

Post, R.M., Ballenger, J.C., Uhde, T.W., Smith, C., Rubinow, D.R., and Bunney, W.E., Jr. Effect of carbamazepine on cyclic nucleotides in CSF of patients with affective illness. *Biol. Psychiat. 17,* 1037-1045 (1982a).

Post, R.M., Uhde, T.W., Ballenger, J.C., and Bunney, W.E., Jr. Carbamazepine, temporal lobe epilepsy, and manic-depressive illness, in *Advances in Biological Psychiatry, Vol. 8: Temporal Lobe Epilepsy, Mania, and Schizophrenia and The Limbic System,* W.P. Koella and M.R. Trimble, eds. S. Karger AG, Basel, pp. 117-156 (1982b).

Post, R.M., Uhde, T.W., Ballenger, J.C., Chatterji, D.C., Green, R.F., and Bunney, W.E., Jr. Carbamazepine and its -10,11-epoxide metabolite in plasma and CSF: relationship to antidepressant response. *Arch. Gen. Psychiat. 40,* 673-676 (1983a).

Post, R.M., Uhde, T.W., Rubinow, D.R., Ballenger, J.C., and Gold, P.W. Biochemical effects of carbamazepine: relationship to its mechanisms of action in affective illness. *Prog. Neuropsychopharmacol. Biol. Psychiat. 7,* 263-271 (1983b).

Post, R.M., Ballenger, J.C., Uhde, T.W., and Bunney, W.E., Jr. Efficacy of carbamazepine in manic-depressive illness: implications for underlying mechanisms, in *Neurobiology of Mood Disorders,* R.M. Post and J.C. Ballenger, eds. Williams & Wilkins, Baltimore, pp. 777-816 (1984a).

Post, R.M., Putnam, F.W., Contel, N.R. and Goldman, B. Electroconvulsive seizures inhibit amygdala kindling: implications for mechanisms of action in affective illness. *Epilepsia 25,* 234-239 (1984b).

Privitera, M.R., Greden, J.F., Gardner, R.W., Ritchie, J.C., and Carroll, B.J. Interference by carbamazepine with the dexamethasone suppression test. *Biol. Psychiat. 17,* 611-620 (1982).

Pryse-Phillips, W.E.M., and Jeavons, P.M. Effects of carbamazepine (Tegretol) on the electroencephalograph and ward behaviour of patients with chronic epilepsy. *Epilepsia 11,* 263-273 (1970).

Puente, R.M. The use of carbamazepine in the treatment of behavioral disorders in children, in *Epileptic Seizures—Behavior—Pain,* W. Birkmayer, ed. Hans Huber Publishers, Bern/Stuttgart/Vienna, pp. 243-247 (1976).

Rahko, T., and Hakkinen, V. Carbamazepine in the treatment of objective myoclonus tinnitus. *J. Laryngol. Otol. 93,* 123-127 (1979)

Rajotte, P., Jilek, W., Jilek, L., Perales, A., Geard, N., Bordeleau, J.-M., and Tetreault, L. Proprietes antiepileptiques et psychotropes de la carbamazepine (Tegretol). *L'Union Med. du Canada 96,* 1200-1206 (1967).

Reynolds, E.H. Neurotoxicity of carbamazepine, in *Complex Partial Seizures and Their Treatment: Advances in Neurology, Vol. 11,* J.K. Penry and D.D. Daly, eds. Raven Press, New York (1975), pp. 345-353.

Reus, V.I., Targum, S.D., Weingartner, H., and Post, R.M. Effects of lithium carbonate on memory processes of bipolar affectively ill patients. *Psychopharmacology 63,* 39-42 (1979).

Robertson, M. Depression and epilepsy. *Proc. 15th Epilepsy International Symposium, Washington, D.C., Sept. 27, 1983.*

Robertson, M.M. and Trimble, M.R. Depressive illness in patients with epilepsy. *Epilepsia 24* (Suppl. 2), S109-S116 (1983).

Rodin, E.A., Rim, C.S., and Rennick, P.M. The effects of carbamazepine on patients with psychomotor epilepsy: results of a double-blind study. *Epilepsia 15,* 547-561 (1974).

Rootwelt, K., Ganes, T., and Johannessen, S.I. Effects of carbamazepine, phenytoin and phenobarbitone on serum levels of thyroid hormones and thyrotropin in humans. *Scand. J. Clin. Lab. Invest. 38,* 731-736 (1978).

Rosenberry, K.R., Defusco, C.J., Mansmann, H.C., and McGeady, S.J. Reduced theophylline half-life induced by carbamazepine therapy. *J. Pediatr. 102,* 472-474 (1983).

Roy-Byrne, P.P., Joffe, R.T., Uhde, T.W., and Post, R.M. Carbamazepine and thyroid function in affectively ill patients: clinical and theoretical implications. *Arch. Gen. Psychiat. 41,* 1150-1153 (1984).

Roy-Byrne, P., and Post, R.M. Carbamazepine in aggression, schizophrenia and other non-affective psychiatric syndromes. *International Drug Therapy Newsletter, 19,* 9-12. F. Ayd, ed. (1984).

Roy-Byrne, P., Uhde, T.W., and Post, R.M. Antidepressant effects of one night's sleep deprivation: clinical and theoretical implications, in *Neurobiology of Mood Disorders*, R.M. Post and J.C. Ballenger, eds. Williams & Wilkins, Baltimore, pp. 817-835 (1984a).

Roy-Byrne, P., Post, R.M., Uhde, T.W., Porcu, T., Davis, D. Life charting of the longitudinal course of recurrent affective illness. *Acta Psychiat. Scand., 71*, Suppl. #317, 5-34 (1985).

Roy-Byrne, P., Uhde, T.W., Post, R.M., and Joffe, R. Relationship of response to sleep deprivation and carbamazepine in depressed patients. *Acta Psychiatr. Scand. 69*, 379-382 (1984b).

Rubinow, D.R., Post, R.M., Gold, P.W., Ballenger, J.C., and Wolff, E.A. The relationship between cortisol and clinical phenomenology of affective illness, in *Neurobiology of Mood Disorders*, R.M. Post and J.C. Ballenger, eds. Williams and Wilkins, Baltimore, pp. 271-289 (1984).

Schou, M. Lithium in recurrent affective illness. *Sci. Proc. Am. Psychiatr. Assoc. 135th Annual Mtg.*, Toronto (1982), p. 39.

Shea, J.J., and Harell, M. Management of tinnitus aurium with lidocaine and carbamazepine. *Laryngoscope 88*, 1477 (1978).

Sheridan, W.P., King, R.W., and Gersiman, M. Fever as an adverse reaction to carbamazepine. *Aust. New Zeal. J. Med. 12*, 520-522 (1982).

Silberman, E.K., and Post, R.M. The 'march' of symptoms in a psychotic decompensation: case report and theoretical implications. *J. Nerv. Ment. Dis. 168*, 104-110 (1980).

Squillace, K.M., Post, R.M., Savard, R., and Erwin, M. Life charting of the longitudinal course of affective illness, in *Neurobiology of Mood Disorders*, R.M. Post and J.C. Ballenger, eds. Williams and Wilkins, Baltimore, pp. 38-59 (1984).

Steiner, C., Wit, A.L., Weiss, M.B., and Damato, A.N. The antiarrhythmic actions of carbamazepine (Tegretol). *J. Pharmacol. Exp. Ther. 173*, 323-335 (1970).

Stephan, W., Parks, R., and Tempest, B. Acute hypersensitivity pneumonitis associated with carbamazepine therapy. *Chest 74*, 463-464 (1978).

Stephens, J.H., and Shaffer, J.W. A controlled study of the effect of diphenylhydantoin on anxiety, irritability and anger in neurotic outpatients. *Psychopharmacologia (Berlin) 17*, 169-181 (1970).

Stephens, J.H., Shaffer, J.W., and Brown, C.C. A controlled comparison of the effects of diphenylhydantoin and placebo on mood and psychomotor functioning in normal volunteers. *J. Clin. Pharmacol. 14*, 543-551 (1974).

Stephens, W.P., Espir, M.L.E., Tattersall, R.B., Quinn, N.P., Gladwell, S.R.F., Galbraith, A.W., and Reynolds, E.H. Water intoxication due to carbamazepine. *Brit. Med. J., i*, 754-755 (1977).

Strandjord, R.E., Aandfrud, S., Myking, O.L., and Johannessen, S.I. Influence of carbamazepine of serum thyroxine and truodothyronine in patients with epilepsy. *Acta Neurol. Scand. 63*, 111-121 (1981).

Takezaki, H., and Hanaoka, M. The use of carbamazepine (Tegretol) in the control of manic-depressive psychosis and other manic, depressive states. *Clin. Psychiat. 13*, 173-183 (1971).

Thompson, P., Huppert, F., and Trimble, M. Anticonvulsant drugs, cognitive function and memory. *Acta Neurol. Scand. 62*, (suppl. 80) 75-81 (1980).

Trimble, M.R., and Richens, A. Psychotropic effects of anticonvulsant drugs, in *Advances in Human Psychopharmacology*, G.D. Burrows and J.S. Werry, eds. JAI Press, Greenwich, CT, 2, 181-202 (1981).

Uhde, T.W., and Post, R.M. Effect of carbamazepine on serum electrolytes: clinical and theoretical implications. *J. Clin. Psychopharmacol. 3*, 103-106 (1983).

Uhlenhuth, E.H., Stephens, J.H., Dim, B.H., and Covi. L. Diphenylhydantoin and phenobarbital in the relief of psychoneurotic symptoms. A controlled comparison. *Psychopharmacologia*

(Berlin) 27, 67-84 (1972).

Valsalan, V.C., and Cooper, G.L. Carbamazepine intoxication caused by interaction with isoniazid. *Brit. Med. J. 285*, 261-262 (1982).

Wada, J.A., and Osawa, T. Spontaneous recurrent seizure state induced by daily electric amygdaloid stimulation in Senegalese baboons (papio papio). *Neurology 26*, 273-286 (1976).

Wales, J.K. Treatment of diabetes insipidus with carbamazepine. *Lancet in*, 948-951 (1975).

Warren, J.W., Benmaman, J.D., Wannamaker, B.B., and Levy, R.H. Kinetics of a carbamazepine-ethosuximide interaction. *Clin. Pharmacol. Ther. 28*, 646-651 (1980).

Weingartner, H., Gold, P.W., Ballenger, J.C., Smallberg, S.A., Summers, R., Rubinow, D.R., Post, R.M., and Goodwin, F.K. Effects of vasopressin on human memory functions. *Science 211*, 601-603 (1981).

Wright, J.M., Stokes, E.F., and Sweeney, V.P. Carbamazepine intoxication due to isoniazid: a kinetic interaction. *Clin. Invest. Med.* (abstract) *4*, 7b (1981).

Wright, J.M., Stokes, E.F., and Sweeney, V.P. Isoniazid-induced carbamazepine toxicity and vice versa. *Med. Intelligence 307*, 1325-1327 (1982).

Yang, C.-P., and Nagaswami, S. Cardiac syncope secondary to glossopharyngeal neuralgia—effectively treated with carbamazepine. *J. Clin. Psychiat. 39*, 776-778 (1978).

Yassa, R. Carbamazepine: an alternative to lithium therapy? *Psychiatr. J. Univ. Ottawa 7*, 252-253 (1982).

Zawadzki, Z. Treatment of maladie de tics with carbamazepine. *Pediatr. Pol. 47*, 1105-1110 (1972).

Zucker, P., Daum, F., and Cohen, M.I. Fatal carbamazepine hepatitis. *J. Pediatr. 91*, 667-668 (1977).

III

ADJUNCTIVE MEASURES

11

The Use of New Antidepressants for Tricyclic-Resistant Patients

Robert Pohl and Samuel Gershon

INTRODUCTION

A number of new antidepressants have been introduced over the past decade, and the number of these drugs is sure to increase over the next decade. Unlike the first generation of tricyclic antidepressants (TCAs) and monoamine oxidase inhibitors introduced a quarter of a century ago, these drugs are usually novel structures, each different from the other. This "second generation" of antidepressants represents a significant addition to the clinician's armamentarium. Because these drugs have a varied pharmacology and are often much more selective in their effect on neurotransmitters, they will quite likely advance our knowledge of the pathophysiology of depression.

With the introduction of new antidepressants, clinicians will be exposed to various claims for efficacy. As always, it is important to see that efficacy studies are done by different investigators in a variety of settings, double-blind, and with random assignment to treatment condition. Data limited to outpatient studies may not be conclusive; these patients are more likely to respond to the nonspecific sedative or stimulating effects of a drug.

In the United States, new drugs that are not tested in placebo-controlled trials cannot be approved for use. Comparisons to standard drugs alone are potentially misleading because standard drugs are not always effective when compared to placebo. This can occur for a variety of reasons, including an insufficient number of patients or the nature of the study population. For example, a study population of TCA nonresponders may respond poorly to a TCA standard comparison drug. A study without a placebo group that shows that a new drug is comparable to a TCA leaves open two possibilities: the drugs were equally effective, or alternatively, equally ineffective.

A common characteristic of new antidepressants is that they appear to be no more effective than older drugs in group comparisons. Like TCAs, the new drugs all work two-thirds to three-quarters of the time. However, older drugs have problematic side effects. Of particular concern are the anticholinergic, cardiovascular, and sedative effects of TCAs; dietary restrictions have always precluded a primary role for the monoamine oxidase inhibitors. Therefore the impetus for developing new drugs is based on the need for drugs with fewer, or at least different, side effects. Because the main advantage of any new antidepressant is fewer side effects, clinicians need to pay special attention to the side effect profile of each new drug to determine its value over standard antidepressants. New drugs that are structurally similar to TCAs and have "me too" side effect profiles have no meaningful advantage over older drugs.

TRICYCLIC NONRESPONDERS

Tricyclic nonresponders fall into two categories. The first type is the patient who has not had an adequate dosage of a TCA for a long enough period of time. If the physician is knowledgeable and the patient compliant, troublesome side effects are almost always the reason for an inadequate trial. In this case, any subsequent antidepressant that is given an adequate trial is likely to work. A second-generation antidepressant is usually the logical choice, because side effects are the main advantage the new drugs have over the old. For any side effect associated with TCAs, a new antidepressant can be found that lacks that effect.

The second kind of nonresponder to consider is the patient who has not responded to an adequate trial of a TCA. These patients are known to sometimes respond to a second trial of another TCA. We would expect nontricyclic antidepressants to be at least as good in this regard as TCAs. Indeed, there is evidence that new antidepressants work for nonresponders. In a doubleblind randomized cross-over study (Abers-Wistedt, 1982), eight out of eleven nonresponders to desipramine responded to zimelidine (a new antidepressant recently withdrawn from the market). Conversely, of the five patients who did not respond to zimelidine, three responded to desipramine.

In another study (Stern et al., 1983), depressed inpatients with a history of never responding to a TCA were treated with bupropion or placebo. Bupropion produced a therapeutic response in about two-thirds of patients, and this response was significantly better than the minimal response produced by placebo. In treatment-resistant outpatients who typically had multiple trials of TCAs at adequate dosages and for adequate durations, about two-thirds of patients were again rated as much or very much improved. However, the same authors report preliminary unpublished evidence in a small number of patients that amitriptyline has antidepressant effects in "TCA nonresponders" comparable to bupropion; categorizing a patient as a TCA nonresponder may not predict future response to TCAs.

These findings suggest that many TCA nonresponders will respond to new antidepressants. Although we suspect that new antidepressants may be more effective for tricyclic nonresponders than a trial of a similar drug, this notion is difficult to demonstrate and remains to be proven.

Reasons for Nonresponse

Why should patients who failed to respond to an adequate trial of TCAs respond to second-generation drugs? The answer must be related to why the patient did not respond in the first place. Insufficient bioavailability is one possibility. Serum levels of tricyclic antidepressants in different patients taking identical dosages can easily vary ten-fold. Such dramatic individual differences in pharmacokinetics must explain the lack of response in at least some patients who have had otherwise adequate trials. Presumably, a structurally different antidepressant may have a better chance of working than another tricyclic.

TCA nonresponders may also respond to a new antidepressant because depression is a biologically heterogeneous disorder. In this model, more than one neurotransmitter has a role in producing depressive symptoms, and the relative importance of each neurotransmitter varies from one depressed patient to another. Patients may not respond to one antidepressant because the drug's predominant effect is on the wrong transmitter; using a drug that acts on a different neurotransmitter is then the next logical step. A patient who does not respond to a predominantly noradrenergic antidepressant should then be switched to a serotoninergic drug and vice versa. In this model, second-generation drugs have a great advantage because they often have a more selective effect on neurotransmitters, and in some cases affect neurotransmitters that are relatively unaffected by TCAs.

Biochemical Markers

If this model is correct, then biochemical markers that reflect neurotransmitter function should accurately predict response to treatment. One of these markers is 3-methoxy-4-hydroxyphenylethylene glycol (MHPG), a metabolite of norepinephrine. Maguire and Norman (1983) have reviewed ten studies that have used urinary MHPG to predict response to antidepressants. Many of these studies have small sample sizes, and the results may be difficult to generalize. Four studies found that low MHPG excretion was associated with a good response to desipramine, imipramine, or maprotiline. Three studies found that high or normal predrug MHPG excretion was associated with a good response to amitriptyline or nortriptyline, while four of the studies found no association between excreted MHPG and response to amitriptyline or nortriptyline. Although these results are mixed, the authors point out that the findings might be stronger if variables that affected MHPG, such as sex, activity, and diet, were taken into account. The use of new antidepressants with more selective effects on neurotransmitter systems may also strengthen the positive findings.

Subsequent studies have continued to show a mix of positive and negative findings. For example, two studies have again suggested that low urinary MHPG excretion is associated with a favorable response to maprotiline (Schatzberg et al., 1980; Gaertner et al., 1982), a drug that is selectively noradrenergic. However, in another study (Ridges et al., 1980), urinary MHPG and 5-hydroxyindoleacetic acid (5-HIAA), the metabolite of serotonin, had no relationship to a response to maprotiline or clomipramine.

Direct measurements of monoamine metabolites in the spinal fluid is likely to be a more powerful technique. Patients with a low cerebrospinal fluid level of 5-HIAA have responded significantly better to zimelidine, a selective serotonergic antidepressant, than those with high pre-treatment levels (Abers-Wistedt et al., 1980). In the same study, levels of 5-HIAA were not related to desipramine's therapeutic outcome. Similarly, in a double-blind study comparing the dopaminergic antidepressant nomifensine to the TCA clomipramine, the dopamine metabolite homovanillic acid (HVA) was measured from cisternal spinal fluid samples in 22 patients (Van Scheyen et al., 1977). The mean level of HVA was significantly lower in patients who responded to nomifensine, suggesting that there is a subgroup of depressed patients with diminished dopamine turnover who preferentially respond to the drug.

From the above, it can be seen that in general there is a tendency for the metabolites of norepinephrine, serotonin and dopamine to predict the response to treatment. When present, positive findings are surprisingly consistent with our knowledge of antidepressant pharmacology. On the other hand, not all studies show these findings, and it appears unlikely that depression can be divided into mutually exclusive subgroups. Although differences in response to treatment can be shown between groups, these differences are not large enough or reliable enough to predict antidepressant response in individuals.

STRATEGY

Patients who cannot complete an adequate trial of a TCA because of side effects can be immediately switched to an appropriate second-generation drug. The choice of drug simply depends on familiarity with each new antidepressant's side effect profile.

Managing the true TCA nonresponder is a more difficult, and less clear-cut, task. A reasonable first step is to ensure that the TCA trial is indeed adequate. This is the first time to question the patient about compliance, and to try manuevers that may improve the response rate, such as adding lithium (see Chapter 8), getting an antidepressant blood level (see Chapter 4) or adding thyroid (see Chapter 13). These manuevers are much less time consuming than a trial of second drug.

Once the patient's nonresponder status is firmly established, an alternative treatment must be considered. Severely ill patients may choose electroconvulsive therapy at this point because further drug trials usually take longer. Most patients, however, will be appropriate candidates for a second drug trial. Second-generation antidepressants are at least as good as any other drug treatment. Theoretically, a new antidepressant may be more likely to work than another TCA because of the biological heterogeneity of depressive illness. Although this assumption is unproven, it does suggest that it is best to choose an antidepressant that is different than the original drug in its structure and effects on neurotransmitter systems.

NEW ANTIDEPRESSANTS

The following drugs are well established as effective new antidepressants; some are available worldwide while others are not. This is, of course, only a partial list, and many more drugs are currently under investigation.

Amoxapine

Amoxapine is a tricyclic dibenzoxazepine, with a structure similar to imipramine. However, its structural similarity to the neuroleptic loxapine, of which it is the demethylated metabolite, makes amoxapine unique among tricyclic antidepressants. For this reason, and because it is new to both the U.S. and Europe, we will discuss amoxapine in this chapter.

Animal studies first suggested the antidepressant properties of amoxapine (Greenblatt et al., 1978) because of its ability to antagonize reserpine-induced hypothermia, promote yohimbine lethality and inhibit tetrabenzine-induced depression. Animal studies also demonstrated neuroleptic activity. Although amoxapine blocks the reuptake of both norepinephrine and serotonin, it is relatively specific for norepinephrine.

Studies comparing amoxapine to amitriptyline in depressed outpatients show that amoxapine is equally effective and has similar side effects but possibly a quicker onset of action (Hekimian et al., 1978; Donlon et al., 1981). In inpatients, amoxapine's efficacy and side effects are equivalent to amitriptyline, but with little difference in speed of action (James, 1982). Studies comparing amoxapine to imipramine have found that amoxapine is as effective, has similar or fewer side effects, and a more rapid onset of action (Bagadia et al., 1979; Holden et al., 1979; Takahashi et al., 1979). The above studies all lack placebo controls. There is only one study that demonstrates that amoxapine is superior to placebo as well as equal to a standard antidepressant (Rickels et al., 1980). The need for placebo controls is emphasized by the results of a study by Steinbook et al. (1979), who found that neither amoxapine nor imipramine were superior to placebo.

The recommended maximum and mean dose of amoxapine is twice that of standard antidepressants. Like typical tricyclic antidepressants, amoxapine can be given as a single daily dose (Ban et al., 1982).

The main advantage of amoxapine over other antidepressants is its apparent rapid onset of action. According to the manufacturer, 50 percent of all patients respond within one week, and 80 percent respond within two weeks. Clinicians should be skeptical, however, of claims for a rapid onset of action for any new antidepressant because of the number of variables involved in clinical studies. For example, it is unlikely that the dosage of any investigational drug is exactly equivalent to a comparison drug's dosage; it is possible that more aggressive dosing of the comparison drug would allow for a faster response.

The side effects of amoxapine are similar to those of other tricyclics, with one notable exception. As noted above, amoxapine has neuroleptic activity in addition to its antidepressant effect. Most of amoxapine's dopamine receptor blocking activity appears to be derived from its 7-hydroxy metabolite. Because this metabolite represents a small fraction of total drug at steady state, it can be argued that neuroleptic effects should be minimal (Donlon, 1981).

However, increased prolactin levels are an indirect measure of dopamine blockade, and amoxapine is associated with significant elevations of prolactin levels. This elevation has been compared to imipramine-treated controls, who had no elevation of serum prolactin (Cooper et al., 1981) and to loxapine-treated controls, who had qualitatively similar elevations (Robertson et al., 1982). More importantly, amoxapine has been associated with the same extrapyramidal side effects produced by neuroleptics, namely akathisia (Hullett and Levy, 1983; Ross et al., 1983); cog-wheel rigidity (Sunderland et al., 1983), and tardive dyskinesia (Lapierre and Anderson, 1983).

Because of amoxapine's neuroleptic effect, we advise a cautious approach to its use. The evidence to date raises the question of whether amoxapine is associated with a greater risk of long-term neurologic side effects compared to other antidepressants. Until this question is resolved, a reasonable strategy would be to not use amoxapine as a second-line drug, since other drugs are just as effective, but to use it for patients who have failed to respond to multiple drug trials.

Maprotiline

Maprotiline has been extensively used in Europe for years. However, it has only recently been introduced in to the U.S. and its tetracyclic structure is different from that of tricyclic antidepressants by virtue of an ethylene bridge across the central ring.

Maprotiline's most striking characteristic is its effect on neurotransmitter systems. Like tricyclic antidepressants, maprotiline inhibits norepinephrine uptake in peripheral and central neurons. However, unlike tricyclics, maprotiline's effect is highly selective, without any inhibition of serotonin uptake (Baumann and Maitre, 1979). The drug is well absorbed with a peak blood level from an oral dosage within 8 to 24 hours and a half-life that averages 43 hours (Alkalay et al., 1980).

Based on comparisons to standard drugs, maprotiline appears to be an effective antidepressant. Numerous controlled trials have shown it to be as effective as imipramine and amitriptyline, and to have similar side effects (Pinder et al., 1977). The onset of action has been reported to be faster than that of comparison tricyclic drugs in some studies (Silverstone, 1981) but the same in other studies (Sims, 1980). Our own belief is that it is very difficult to conclusively demonstrate a faster onset of action because of methodological problems, not the least of which is knowing whether the dosage of a comparison drug is truly equivalent. Once efficacy is established, examination of a drug's side effect profile is more important; a lack of side effects will allow for a more aggressive dosing regimen, and presumably a faster onset of action.

Although maprotiline's side effects are qualitatively similar to those of tricyclics, a few controlled trials suggest that side effects are less severe when compared to equal doses of imipramine (Singh et al., 1976) and amitriptyline (Botter, 1976). Like tricyclic antidepressants, maprotiline increases heart rate and delays cardiac conduction (Edwards and Goldie, 1983). However, symptoms of sinus tachycardia and postural hypotension may be less severe with maprotiline and comparable to the effects of doxepin (Hattab, 1976).

There are a number of reports of seizures with maprotiline (Holliday et al., 1982; Schwartz and Swaminathan, 1982; Hoffman and Wachsmuth, 1982). At present, it is not clear if maprotiline induces seizures more frequently than tricyclic antidepressants. However, drug rashes do appear to be more frequent with maprotiline (Settle, 1981). The dose range of maprotiline is the same as for standard tricyclics, that is, 100 mg to 300 mg daily. Bartholini (1976) retrospectively compared once daily dosage studies to divided dosage studies and found that once daily is equally effective and well tolerated.

Mianserin

Mianserin, a tetracyclic piperazino-azepine, has both a novel structure and pharmacology. First synthesized in 1966, mianserin was found to be a potent antihistamine and peripherally antiserotonergic. Although animal testing did not suggest an antidepressant effect, clinical observations of sedative and mood-lifting effects and quantitative EEG studies suggested mianserin would have antidepressant properties (Peet and Behagel, 1978).

Mianserin is clearly less potent than imipramine or amitriptyline in blocking serotonin and norepinephrine uptake, although to the extent that it does block amine uptake, it is selective for norepinephrine (Zis and Goodwin, 1979). In animals, it increases the turnover of norepinephrine but unlike tricyclic antidepressants does not also affect the turnover of serotonin. It also does not affect the turnover of dopamine (Leonard, 1977). Studies in man are consistent; mianserin reduces cerebrospinal MHPG but does not affect 5-HIAA or HVA (Mendlewicz et al., 1982). Mianserin's effect on the noradrenergic system may be the result of the drug's inhibition of presynaptic alpha adrenoceptors.

Mianserin has been compared to placebo, diazepam, amitriptyline, imipramine, clomipramine, doxepin, nortriptyline, maprotiline, nomifensine and trazodone (van Dorth, 1983). In these studies it is almost always superior to placebo and diazepam and equal in efficacy to other antidepressants. Unfortunately, many of the comparisons to active drugs do not include placebo groups. The importance of placebo-controlled trials is emphasized by Edwards and Goldie's (1983) study of 58 depressed outpatients. They found neither mianserin nor maprotiline were superior to placebo at 2 or 4 weeks and few patients completed the six-week trial because of a generally unsatisfactory response.

Mianserin is an effective antidepressant at doses that usually range between 30 mg and 60 mg/day. Its kinetics are similar to those of tertiary amine tricyclic antidepressants and the tetracyclic maprotiline; plasma levels show considerable interpatient variability, with a mean half-life of about 22 hours (Hrdina et al., 1983).

When compared to tricyclic antidepressants, mianserin causes fewer side effects. Rather than causing a dry mouth, mianserin actually increased salivary flow in one study (Wilson et al., 1980). In another study, amitriptyline diminished saliva production while mianserin was comparable to placebo (Kopera, 1983). Although mianserin has been shown to reduce resting pupillary size after treatment, this effect does not appear to be the result of adrenergic or cholinergic receptor activity because mianserm fails at the same time to affect pilocarpine-evoked miosis or tyramine and phenylephine-induced mydriasis (Shur et al., 1983).

Mianserin has no consistent effects on the ECG or heart rate (Peet et al., 1977) even when given to patients with cardiovascular disease (Kopera, 1983). It does not appear to affect cardiac conduction at the high dose of 60 mg/day (Burrows et al., 1979) and does not cause postural hypotension (Kopera, 1978). When compared to other drugs, mianserin does not produce the ECG findings associated with maprotiline (Edwards and Goldie, 1983) or amitriptyline (Burgess et al., 1980). In the latter study, mianserin did shorten the QS_2 interval and, like amitriptyline, shortened the left ventricular ejection time interval, but this effect was thought to be due to effects on the peripheral circulation rather than a direct action on the heart.

Unlike tricyclic antidepressants, mianserin does not interfere with the effects of anti-hypertensive drugs clonidine or methyldopa (Elliott et al., 1983) and there may be little interaction with guanethidine. Case reports suggest that mianserin also does not cause the carbohydrate hunger associated with tricyclic antidepressants when it is substituted for amitriptyline (Williams, 1980). However, like tricyclics, mianserin may precipitate mania in bipolar patients (Choppen et al., 1977).

Trazodone

Trazodone is a triazolopyridine derivative with a structure unlike other psychotropic drugs. Trazodone is a highly selective inhibitor of serotonin uptake, with relatively little effect on catecholamine uptake. For example, trazodone is a less potent inhibitor of serotonin uptake than clomipramine, but still four times more selective in its ability to inhibit uptake of serotonin compared to norepinephrine in an animal model (Riblet et al., 1979). Although the inhibition of serotonin uptake suggests a purely serotonergic effect, trazodone has also been discovered to have central serotonin antagonist activity and to occupy serotonergic binding sites in animals (Clements et al., 1980). In addition, trazodone, like mianserin, also blocks alpha-adrenoceptors (Clements et al., 1980).

The usual dosage of trazodone is twice that of standard antidepressants. After starting at 150 mg daily (lower in geriatric patients) the dose is titrated upward to as much as 600 mg daily. Trazodone is easily and fully absorbed after oral administration. The half-life is relatively short, about eight hours. Although there is no evidence that a single bedtime dose is as effective as divided doses, it is not uncommon for the major part of a daily dose to be administered in the evening to minimize sedative side effects.

Clinical experience with trazodone is extensive and includes more than 200 open and controlled trials involving more than 10,000 patients (Ayd, 1979). There is general agreement that trazodone is more effective than placebo and at least as effective as standard tricyclic antidepressants. A review of the literature (Saarma, 1974) and recent comparisons to imipramine (Fabre et al., 1979; Feighner, 1980; Kellams et al., 1979) indicates that trazodone may have a rapid onset of action with antidepressant effects within one week. These findings, however, are incidental to efficacy studies and are not present in other studies.

Trazodone has a definite sedative effect, but otherwise has a side effect profile quite different from tricyclic antidepressants. It slows the heart rate but does not appear cardiotoxic; there is no effect on cardiac conduction (Gomoll and Byrne, 1979). When given to geriatric patients, trazodone, like placebo, had no effect on heart rate and was not associated with any significant ECG effects (Hayes et al., 1983). In the same study, imipramine was associated with both an increased heart rate and isolated ECG complications.

Trazodone does have hypotensive effects, and has been associated with arrythmias in patients with pre-existing cardiac disease. In our own unpublished report of such a case, the patient developed frequent premature ventricular contractions (PVCs) with couplets. However, this may have been due to the discontinuation of desipramine before trazodone was started; tricyclic antidepressants may suppress PVCs, resulting in rebound arrythmias when the tricyclic is discontinued. Our patient continued to have frequent PVCs when trazodone was discontinued but showed dramatic improvement when desipramine was re-started.

Given our present knowledge, it appears that trazodone is an effective drug for patients who cannot tolerate the nonhypotensive cardiovascular effects of tricyclics. Sensible cautionary measures, such as follow-up ECGs, should be employed for patients with severe pre-existing cardiac disease when any antidepressant is given. Patients on tricyclic antidepressants with preexisting arrythmias need to be very carefully monitored when the tricyclic is discontinued.

In receptor binding experiments, trazodone lacks anticholinergic effects (Clements-Jewery et al., 1980). These findings are supported by clinical experience. The incidence of anticholinergic symptoms in trazodone patients is the same as for placebo patients and significantly less than the anticholinergic effects of imipramine in an analysis of the data from 15 multicenter studies involving 379 patients (Gershon and Newton, 1980).

In addition to sedation, trazodone is associated with dizziness, possibly related to hypotension, and with gastrointestinal upset in a small percentage of patients. These effects are usually mild. Trazodone has been tested in the elderly where it was found to be well tolerated and associated with fewer side effects than imipramine (Gerner et al., 1980). Trazodone has been reported to be effective for the treatment of anxiety and tremors (Brogden et al., 1981) and for withdrawal symptoms in alcoholics (Roccatagliata et al., 1980). Evidence for these latter indications is preliminary, however, and needs to be supported by larger, well-designed studies.

Nomifensine

Nomifensine is another second-generation antidepressant with a novel structure and a side effect profile that is substantially different from tricyclic antidepressants. A tetrahydroisoquinoline, nomifensine blocks the reuptake of both dopamine and norepinephrine but does not inhibit serotonin uptake at concentrations that would be expected during clinical use (Schacht et al., 1977). Amphetamines are also dopaminergic, and like amphetamines, nomifensine causes stereotypic movements in animal studies (Hoffman, 1977). However, unlike amphetamines, nomifensine does not promote the release of catecholamines.

Efficacy studies for nomifensine have been extensively reviewed by Brogden et al., (1979) and by Matz (1980). Nomifensine is as effective as imipramine, desipramine, amitriptyline, nortriptyline, clomipramine and doxepin at equal or similar doses in double-blind comparisons, and is clearly superior to placebo. The usual dose range for nomifensine is 50-200 mg daily. It is well absorbed and almost entirely excreted by the kidneys. Compared to other antidepressants, the half-life is relatively short, about two hours. The drug is effective when given as a single daily dose in the morning (Hanks et al., 1980).

As with most second-generation antidepressants, nomifensine's side effect profile is its main attraction. Nomifensine causes little or no sedation. Unlike tricyclic antidepressants, it does not affect alcohol or hexobarbital-induced sleeping time in animals (Hoffman, 1977). Similarly, when 75 mg of nomifensine is given with 754 ml of wine to volunteers, the subjective sedation and psychomotor performance are the same as for placebo with wine (Taeuber, 1977). A dosage of 75 mg of nomifensine also does not produce sedation and loss of concentration on subjective measures and does not affect psychomotor performance; on the other hand, 50 mg of amitriptyline significantly affects all of these measures (Chan et al., 1980).

Other studies also point to nomifensine's lack of sedative effects. During a simulated nighttime driving test in six normal volunteers, 50 mg of nomifensine had no effect on response time; 100 mg nomifensine actually improved response time (Hindmarch and Parrot, 1977). Nomifensine also had a central stimulating effect in a study that used Critical Flicker Fusion as a measure of sedation (Hindmarch and Parrott, 1977).

Nomifensine has minimal anticholinergic side effects. Seventy-five mg of nomifensine has no effect on salivary flow; 50 mg of amitriptyline reduces the flow (Chan et al., 1980). The anticholinergic side effects reported in drug comparison studies are relatively low for nomifensine compared to tricyclic antidepressants.

Cardiovascular effects of nomifensine appear to be minimal. In dogs, up to 10 mg/Kg of intravenously administered nomifensine has only a very slight effect on arterial blood pressure, blood flow or heart rate (Hoffman, 1977). High speed surface ECG recordings (Burgess et al., 1979) and his bundle electrocardiogram recordings (Burrows et al., 1978) fail to show significant cardiac effects in humans. Nomifensine, unlike tricyclic antidepressants, does not appear to prolong cardiac conduction time. The apparent lack of cardiotoxicity is supported by a low incidence of reported cardiac effects in clinical studies and a lack of serious cardiotoxicity in cases of nomifensine overdosage (Brogden et al., 1979).

Another interesting aspect of nomifensine is that it does not appear to lower the seizure threshold at usual doses. In photosensitive baboons, nomifensine at 10 mg/Kg does not lower the seizure threshold while maprotiline, clomipramine and imipramine all do. At 20 mg/Kg, all drugs produced seizures (Trimble et al., 1977).

Nomifensine also has no effect on animal seizures induced by nicotine, metrazole, or strychnine (Hoffman, 1977). Clinical data to support these findings are present, though sparse. In five depressed epileptic children, nomifensine had no adverse effects (Porath and Schreier, 1977). There are no reports of convulsions associated with nomifensine at either therapeutic doses or overdosage.

The most common side effects from nomifensine are sleep disturbances, restlessness, paranoid symptoms, nausea and tachycardia, and it provokes psychotic symptoms in schizophrenics (Brogden et al., 1979). The entire research program in the United States, involving more than 1,000 patients, failed to find medically significant changes with nomifensine treatment (Matz, 1980). There was a one percent incidence of drug-related fevers associated with nomifensine but all fevers have stopped when nomifensine was discontinued. There is also a report of two cases of hemolytic anemia associated with nomifensine (Eckstein et al., 1981). In general, however, side effects tend to be mild and either less frequent or less severe than the side effects associated with tricyclics.

Bupropion

Bupropion is another new antidepressant with a novel structure. Like nomifensine, bupropion is dopaminergic. When compared to imipramine and amitriptyline, it is 6 and 20 times more potent in inhibiting dopamine uptake. Unlike tricyclic antidepressants, bupropion is a relatively poor inhibitor of serotonin and norepinephrine uptake; for example, it is 60 times less potent as an inhibitor of norepinephrine uptake than amitriptyline (Soroko et al., 1977). Like other second-generation antidepressants, bupropion does not inhibit monoamine oxidase (MAO).

Although it affects dopamine uptake, bupropion does not affect prolactin or growth hormone levels (Laakmann et al., 1982). In animal models, it lacks anticholinergic activity, is not sympathominetic and is at least 10 times weaker than tricyclics as a cardiac depressant (Soroko and Maxwell, 1983). In man, the drug is rapidly and completely absorbed but with considerable first pass metabolism. The half-life shows a biphasic decline, with a first phase half-life of 1.5 hours, then 15 hours (Lai and Schroeder, 1983). The therapeutic dose ranges from 300-600 mg/day.

Bupropion's efficacy has been tested in a number of placebo-controlled trials in depressed inpatients (Fabre and McLendon, 1978; Zuns et al., 1983; Pitts et al., 1983; Fabre et al., 1983; Merideth and Feishner, 1983). The results of these trials are all quite similar. In addition to demonstrating efficacy, investigators note the absence of anticholinergic, cardiovascular and sedative side effects. In fact, many of the studies note that the incidence and severity of side effects with bupropion is indistinguishable from placebo. It has been suggested that bupropion's onset of action may be more rapid because its low side effect profile permits a more aggressive dosing regimen compared to tricyclics (Stern and Harto-Truax, 1980). There are also studies that demonstrate that bupropion is equal in efficacy to standard tricyclics (Mendels et al., 1983; Davidson et al., 1983).

The lack of cardiovascular effects in efficacy studies is supported by bupropion's lack of ECG effects in comparison to amitriptyline's prolongation of PR and QRS intervals (Wenser et al., 1983). Bupropion also did not affect blood pressure in patients who were withdrawn from tricyclics because of significant demonstrable orthostatic hypotension (Farid et al., 1983).

Unlike amitriptyline, bupropion is not associated with weight gain (Harto-Truax et al., 1983). In well over one thousand patients treated with the drug, the only adverse effect of medical significance in bupropion patients was major motor seizures. In outpatient, at lower doses, this occurs in one out of 1,000 patients; seizures may occur in about 1 out of 100 inpatients.

As with nomifensine, bupropion's dopaminergic effects raises the question of abuse potential. However, in volunteers with a history of amphetamine abuse, bupropion does not mimic amphetamine's effect on blood pressure, pulse, appetite or sleep (Griffith et al., 1983). Amphetamines and amitriptyline cause opposite and predictable effects on measures of auditory vigilance, tapping rates and subjective alertness but bupropion failed to affect any of these measures. Bupropion did abolish the sedative and impaired auditory vigilance effects of diazepam and alcohol, suggesting that it may act differently when combined with depressant drugs (Peck and Hamilton, 1983). In another study, subjects who were more alert, attentive, proficient, excited, interested and elated after dexamphetamine did not experience these same effects with either bupropion or nomifensine (Hamilton et al., 1982). It is possible that bupropion, like nomifensine, exacerbates schizophrenic symptoms.

CONCLUSION

Second-generation antidepressants are often indicated for patients who do not respond to a trial of a TCA. Although there is no evidence that a second trial of a new drug will be any more successful than another TCA, the new antidepressant option is attractive because most of these drugs are so different from TCAs and have more selective effects on neurotransmitter systems. One can therefore easily choose a drug with different effects on neurotransmitters than the original TCA. Maprotiline and mianserin are selectively noradrenergic; trazodone is serotoninergic and nomifensine and bupropion are dopaminergic. For patients who cannot tolerate an adequate trial of a TCA, a new antidepressant can avoid the problem of sedation (nomifensine or bupropion) or significant anticholinergic or cardiovascular effects (trazodone, mianserin, bupropion or nomifensine).

REFERENCES

Abers-Wistedt, A. Comparison between zimelidine and desipramine in endogenous depression. A cross-over study. *Acta Psychiat. Scand.* *66*(2), 129-138 (1982).

Abers-Wistedt, A., Jostell, K.G., Ross, S.B., and Westerlund, D. Effects of zimelidine and desipramine on serotonin and noradrenaline uptake mechanisms in relation to plasma concentrations and to therapeutic effects during treatment of depression. *Psychopharmacology (Berlin) 74*(4), 297-305 (1981).

Alkalay, D., Wagner, W.E., Jr., Carlsen, S., Khemani, L., Volk, J., Bartlett, M.F., and LeSher, A. Bioavailability and kinetics of maprotiline. *Clin. Pharmacol. Ther. 27,* 697-703 (1980).

Ayd, F.J. Trazodone: A unique new broad spectrum antidepressant. *Internat. Drug Ther. Newslett. 14,*33-40 (1979).

Bagadia, V.N., Shah, L.P., Pradhan, P.V., and Gada, M.T. A double-blind controlled study of amoxapine and imipramine in cases of depression. *Curr. Ther. Res. 26,* 417-429 (1979).

Ban, T.T., Fujimori, M., Petrie, W.M., Raghab, M., and Wilson, W.H. Systematic studies with amoxapine, a new antidepressant. *Internat. Pharmacopsychiat. 17*(1), 18-27 (1982).

Bartholini, E. Once daily dosage with maprotiline (Ludiomil). *J. Int. Med. Res. 36* (Suppl. 2), 101-108 (1976).

Baumann, P.A., and Maitre, L. Neurobiochemical aspects of maprotiline (Ludiomil) actions. *J. Int. Med. Res. 7,* 391-400 (1979).

Botter, P.A. A clinical double-blind comparison of maprotiline and amitriptyline in depression. *Curr. Med. Res. Opin. 3,* 634-641 (1976).

Brogden, R.N., Heel, R.C., Speight, T.M., and Avery, G.S. Nomifensine: A review of its pharmacological properties and therapeutic efficacy in depressive illness. *Drugs 18,* 1-24 (1979).

Brogden, R.N., Heel, R.C., Speight, T.M., and Avery, G.S. Trazodone: A review of its pharmacological properties and therapeutic use in depression and anxiety. *Drugs 21* (6), 401-429 (1981).

Burgess, C.D., Montgomery, S.A., Wadsworth, J., and Turner, P. Cardiovascular effects of amitriptyline, mianserin, zimelidine and nomifensine in depressed patients. *Postgrad. Med. J. 55,* 704-708 (1979).

Burgess, C.D., Montgomery, S.A., Montgomery, D.B., and Wadsworth, J. Cardiovascular effects of amitriptyline, mianserin and zimelidine in depressed patients. *Prog. Neuropsychopharmacol. 4* (4-5), 523-526 (1980).

Burrows, G.D., Vohra, J., Dumovic, P., Scoggins, B.A., and Davies, B. Cardiovascular effects of nomifensine, a new antidepressant. *Med. J. Aust. 1,* 341-343 (1978).

Burrows, G.D., Davies, B., Hamer, A., and Vohra, J. Effect of mianserin on cardiac conduction. *Med. J. Aust. 2,* 97-98 (1979).

Chan, M.Y., Ehsanullah, R., Wadsworth, J., and McEwen, J. A comparison of the pharmacodynamic profiles of nomifensine and amitriptyline in normal subjects. *Brit. J. Pharmacol. 9,* 247-253 (1980).

Clements-Jewery, S., Robson, P.A., and Chidley, L.J. Biochemical investigations into the mode of action of trazodone. *Neuropharmacology 19,* 1165-1173 (1980).

Cooper, D.S., Gelenberg, A.J., Wojcik, J.C., Saxe, V.C., Ridgway, E.D., and Maloof, F. The effect of amoxapine and imipramine on serum prolactin levels. *Arch. Intern. Med. 141* (8), 1023-1025 (1981).

Coppen, A., Ghose, K., Rao, V.A., and Peet, M. Mianserin: The prophylactic treatment of bipolar affective illness. *Internat. Pharmacopsychiat. 12,* 95-99 (1977).

Davidson, J., Miller, R., Van Wyck Fleet, J., Strickland, R., Manbers, P., Allen, S., and Parrott, R. A double-blind comparison of bupropion and amitriptyline in depressed inpatients. *J. Clin. Psychiat. 44* (5.2), 115-117 (1983).

Donlon, P.T. Amoxapine: a newly marketed tricyclic antidepressant. *Psychiat. Ann. 11* (11), 23-27 (1981).

Donlon, P.T., Biertuemphez, H., and Willenbring, M. Amoxapine and amitriptyline in the outpatient treatment of endogenous depression. *J. Clin. Psychiat. 42,* 11-15 (1981).

Eckstein, R., Riess, H., Sauer, H., and Mempel, W. Nomifensin-induced immune haemolytic anaemias (author's transl). *Klin. Wochenschr. 59* (11), 567-569 (1981).

Edwards, J.G., and Goldie, A. Mianserin, maprotiline and intracardiac conduction. *Brit. J. Clin. Pharmacol. 15* (Suppl. 2), 249S-254S (1980).

Edwards, J.G., and Goldie, A. Placebo-controlled trial of mianserin and maprotiline in primary depressive illness: a preliminary report. *Br. J. Clin. Pharmacol. 15* (Suppl. 2), 239s-248s (1983).

Elliott, H.L., McLean, K., Sumner, D.J., and Reid, J.L. Absence of an effect of mianserin on the actions of clonidine or methyldopa in hypertensive patients. *Eur. J. Clin. Pharmacol. 24* (1), 15-19 (1983).

Fabre, L.F., Brodie, H.K., Garver, D., and Zuns, W.W. A multicenter evaluation of bupropion versus placebo in hospitalized depressed patients. *J. Clin. Psychiat. 44* (5.2), 88-94 (1983).

Fabre, L.F., McLendon, D.M., and Gainey, A. Trazodone efficacy in depression: a double-blind comparison with imipramine and placebo in day-hospital type patients. *Curr. Ther. Res. 25*, 827-834 (1979).

Farid, F.F., Wenser, T.L., Tsai, S.Y., Sinsh, B.N., and Stern, W.C. Use of bupropion in patients who exhibit orthostatic hypotension on tricyclic antidepressants. *J. Clin. Psychiat. 44* (5.2), 170-173 (1983).

Feighner, J.P. Trazodone, a triazolopyridine derivative in primary depressive disorder. *J. Clin. Psychiat. 41*, 250-255 (1980).

Gaertner, H.J., Golfinopoulos, G., and Breyer-Pfaff, U. Response to maprotiline treatment in depressive patients relationship to urinary MHPG excretion and plasma drug level. *Pharmacopsychiatria 15* (5), 170-174 (1982).

Gerner, R., Estabrook, W., Steuer, J., and Jarvik, L. Treatment of geriatric depression with trazodone, imipramine, and placebo: A double-blind study. *J. Clin. Psychiat. 41*, 216-220 (1980).

Gershon, S., and Newton, R. Lack of anticholinergic side effects with a new antidepressant—trazodone, *J. Clin. Psychiat. 41*(3), 100-104 (1980).

Gomall, A.W., and Byrne, J.E. Trazodone and imipramine: Comparative effects on canine cardiac conduction. *Eur. J. Pharmacol. 57*, 335-342 (1979).

Greenblatt, E.N., Lippa, A.S., and Osterberg, A.C. The neuropharmacological action of amoxapine. *Arch. Int. Pharmacodyn. Ther. 233*, 107-135 (1978).

Griffith, J.D., Carranza, J., Griffith, C., and Miller, L.L. Bupropion: Clinical assay for amphetamine-like abuse potential. *J. Clin. Psychiat. 44*, (5.2), 206-8 91983).

Hamilton, J.J., Smith, P.R., and Peck, A.W. Effects of bupropion, nomifensive and dexamphetamine on performance, subjective feelings, autonomic variables and electroencephalogram in healthy volunteers. *Am. J. Psychiatry 139* (9), 1200-1201 (1982).

Hanks, G.W., Magnus, R.V., Myskova, I., and Mathur, G. Antidepressants in single daily doses: Studies with nomifensine in *Nomifensine*. P.D. Stonier and F.A. Fenner, eds. London: Academic Press, pp. 87-94 (1980).

Harto-Truax, N., Stern, W.C., Miller, L.L., Sato, T.L., and Cato, A.E. Effects of bupropion on body weight. *J. Clin. Psychiat. 44* (5.2), 183-186 (1983).

Hattab, J.R. The cardiovascular effects of ludiomil in comparison with those of some tricyclic antidepressants. Paper presented at Ludiomil Symposium (Malta) 1976.

Hayes, R.L., Gerner, R.H., Fairbanks, L., Moran, M., and Waltuck, L. ECG findings in geriatric depressives given trazodone, placebo or imipramine. *J. Clin. Psychiatry 44*(5), 180-3 (1983).

Hekimian, L.J., Friedhoff, A.J., and Deever, E. A comparison of the onset of action and therapeutic efficacy of amoxapine and amitriptyline. *J. Clin. Psychiat. 39*, 633-637 (1978).

Hindmarch, I., and Parrott, A.C. Repeated dose comparison of nomifensine, imipramine and placebo on subjective assessments of sleep and objective measures of psychomotor performance. *Br. J. Clin. Pharmacol. 4* (Suppl. 2), 167-173 (1977).

Hoffman, B.F., and Wachsmuth, R. Maprotiline and seizures. *J. Clin. Psychiat. 43* (3), 122 (1982).

Hoffman, I. A comparative review of the pharmacology of nomifensine. *Br. J. Clin. Pharmacol. 4* (Suppl. 2), 69-75 (1977).

Holden, J.M.C., Kerry, R.J., and Orme, J.E. Amoxapine in depressive illness. *Curr. Med. Res. Opin. 6,* 338-341 (1979).

Holliday, W., Brasfield, K.H., Jr., and Powers, B. Grand mal seizures induced by maprotiline. *Am. J. Psychiatry 139* (5), 673-674 (1982).

Hrdina, P.D., Lapierre, Y.D., McIntosh, B., and Oyewumi, L.K. Mianserin kinetics in depressed patients. *Clin. Pharmacol. Ther. 33* (6), 757-762 (1983).

Hullett, F.J., and Levy, A.B. Amoxapine-induced akathisia (letter). *Amer. J. Psychiat. 140* (6), 820 (1983).

James, B. A double-blind comparative clinical study of amoxapine and amitriptyline in depressed, hospitalized patients. *New Zealand Med. J. 709,* 391-393 (1982).

Kellams, J.J., Klapper, M.H., and Small, J.G. Trazodone, a new antidepressant: Efficacy and safety of endogenous depression. *J. Clin. Psychiat. 40,* 390-395 (1979).

Kopera, H. Anticholinergic and blood pressure effects of mianserin, amitriptyline and placebo. *Br. J. Clin. Pharmacol. 5* (Suppl. 1), 29-34 (1978).

Kopera, H. Lack of anticholinergic and cardiovascular effects of mianserin; studies in healthy subjects and heart patients. *Acta Psychiat. Scand. 302,* (Suppl.) 81-9 (1983).

Laakmann, G., Hoffmann, N., and Hofschuster, E. The lack of effect of bupropion HCL (Wellbatrin) on the secretion of growth hormone and prolactin in humans. *Life Sci. 30* (20), 1725-1732 (1982).

Lai, A.A., and Schroeder, D.H. Clinical pharmacokinetics of bupropion: A review. *J. Clin. Psychiat. 44* (5.2), 82-84 (1983).

Lapierre, Y.D., and Anderson, K. Dyskinesia associated with amoxapine antidepressant therapy: A case report. *Amer. J. Psychiat. 140* (4), 493-494 (1983).

Leonard, B.E., Some effects of mianserin (ORG GB 94) on amine matabolism in the rat brain. *Pharmackopsychiatr. Neuropsychopharmakol. 10,* 92-95 (1977).

Maquire, K.P., and Norman, T.R. Urinary MHPG and response to antidepressants, in *Antidepressants (Drugs in Psychiatry).* G.D. Burrows, T.R. Norman and B. Davies, eds. Elsevier Science Publishers, Amsterdam, pp. 35-41 (1983).

Matz, R.S. Clinical trials with nomifensine in the U.S.A., in *Nomifensine.* P.D. Stonier, and F.A. Fenner, eds. London: Academic Press, pp. 73-80 (1980).

Mendels, J., Amin, M.M., Chouinard, G., Cooper, A.J., Miles, J.E., Remick, R.A., Saxena, B. Secunda, S.K., and Sinsh, A.N. A comparative study of bupropion and amitriptyline in depressed outpatients. *J. Clin. Psychiat. 44* (5.2), 118-20 (1983).

Mendlewicz, J., Pinder, R.M., Stulemeijer, S.M., and Van Dorth, R. Monoamine metabolites in cerebrospinal fluid of depressed patients during treatment with mianserin or amitriptyline. *J. Affective Disord. 4* (3), 219-226 (1982).

Merideth, C.H., and Feishner, J.P. The use of bupropion in hospitalized depressed patients. *J. Clin. Psychiat. 44* (5.2), 85-87 (1983).

Peck, A.W., and Hamilton, M. Psychopharmacology of bupropion in normal volunteers. *J. Clin. Psychiat. 44* (5.2), 202-205 (1983).

Peet, M., and Behagel, H. Mianserin: A decade of scientific development. *Brit. J. Clin. Pharmacol. 5* (Suppl. 1), 5-9 (1978).

Peet, M., Tienari, P., and Jaskari, M.O. A comparison of the cardiac effects of mianserin and amitriptyline in man. *Pharmakopsychiatr. Neuropsychopharmakol. 10* 309-312 (1977).

Pinder, R.M., Brogden, R.N., Speight, T.M., and Avery, G.S. Maprotiline: A review of its pharmacological properties and therapeutic efficacy in mental depressive states. *Drugs 13*, 321-352 (1977).

Pitts, W.M., Fann, W.E., Halaris, A.E., Dressler, D.M., Sajadi, C., Snyder, S., and Ilaria, R.L. Bupropion in depression: a tri-center placebo-controlled study. *J. Clin. Psychiat. 44* (5.2), 95-100 (1983).

Porath, U., and Schreier, K. On the use of nomifensine in depressive mood in children and young people. Paper presented at Alival Symposium uber Ergebnisse der Experimentellen and Klinischen Prufung. Schattauer, Stuttgart, pp. 39-45 (1977).

Riblet, L.A., Gatewood, C.F., and Mayol, R.F. Comparative effects of trazodone and tricyclic antidepressants on uptake of selected neurotransmitters by isolated rat brain synaptosomes. *Psychopharmacology 63*, 99-101 (1979).

Rickels, K., Case, W.G., Werblowsky, J., Csanalosi, I., Schless, A., and Weise, C.C. Amoxapine and imipramine in the treatment of depressed outpatients: A controlled study. *Am. J. Psychiat. 138* (1), 20-24 (1981).

Ridges, A.P., Bishop, F.M., and Goldberg, I.J. Urinary amine metabolites in depression: A combined biochemical and general practice study: II. Biochemical aspects. *J. Internat. Med. Res. 8* (Suppl. 3), 37-44 (1980).

Robertson, A.G., Berry, R., and Meltzer, H.Y. Prolactin stimulating effects of amoxapine and loxapine in psychiatric patients. *Psychopharmacology (Berlin), 78* (3), 287-292 (1982).

Roccatagliata, G., Albano, C., Maffini, M., and Farelli, S. Alcohol withdrawal syndrome: treatment with trazadone. *Internat. Pharmacopsychiat. 15* (2), 105-110 (1980).

Ross, D.R., Walker, J.I., and Peterson, J. Akathisia induced by amoxapine. *Am. J. Psychait. 140 (1)*, 115-116 (1983).

Saarma, J. Trazodone—a review of the literature in *Modern Problems of Pharmacopsychiatry*, Vol. 9. T.A. Ban and B. Silverstrini, eds. Karger, Basel, pp. 95-109 (1974).

Schacht, U., Leven, M., and Backer, G. Studies on brain metabolism of biogenic amines. *Brit. J. Clin. Pharmacol. 4* (Suppl. 2) 77-87 (1977).

Schatzberg, A.F., Rosenbaum, A.H., Orsulak, P.J., Rohde, W.A., Maruta, T., Krueger, E.R., Cole, J.O., and Schildkraut, J.J. Toward a biochemical classification of depressive disorders. III: Pretreatment urinary MHPG levels as predictors of response to treatment with maprotiline. *Psychopharmacology (Berlin) 75* (1) 34-38 (1981).

Schwartz, L., Swaminathan, S. Maprotiline hydrochloride and convulsions: A case report. *Am. J. Psychiat. 139*(2), 244-245 (1982).

Settle, E.C., Jr. Maprotiline: Update 1981. *Psychiat. Ann 11* (11), 31-38 (1981).

Shur, E., Checkley, S., and Delgado, I. Failure of mianserin to affect autonomic function in the pupils of depressed patients. *Acta Psychiat. Scand. 67* (1), 50-55 (1983).

Silverstone, T. Relative speed of onset of the antidpressant effect of maprotiline. *Clin. Ther. 3* (5), 374-381 (1981).

Sims, A.C. Comparison of the efficacy of sustained-released amitriptyline with maprotiline in the treatment of depressive illness. *Curr. Med. Res. Opin. 6* (8), 534-539 (1980).

Singh, A.N., Saxena, B., Gent, M., and Nelson, H.L. Maprotiline (Ludiomil, CIBA 34, 276-BA) and imipramine in depressed outpatients: A double-blind clinical study. *Curr. Ther. Res. 19*, 451-462 (1976).

Soroko, F.E., and Maxwell, R.A. The pharmacologic basis for therapeutic interest in bupropion. *J. Clin. Psychiat. 44* (5.2), 67-73 (1983).

Soroko, F.E., and Maxwell, R.A., Ferris, R.M., and Schroeder, D.H. Bupropion hydrochloride (−1-) alpha-t-butylamino-3-chloropropiophenone HCl): A novel antidepressant agent. *J. Pharm. Pharmacol. 29,* 767-770 (1977).

Steinbook, R.M., Jacobson, A.F., Weiss, B.L., and Goldstein, B.J. Amoxapine, imipramine and placebo: A double-blind study with pretherapy urinary 3-methoxy-4-hydroxyphenylaglycol levels. *Curr. Ther. Res. 26,* 490-496 (1979).

Stern, W.C., and Harto-Truax, N. Two multicenter studies of the antidepressant effects of bupropion HCl versus placebo. *Psychopharmacol. Bull. 16,* 43-46 (1980).

Stern, W.C., Harto-Truax, N., and Bauer, N. Efficacy of bupropion in tricyclic-resistant or intolerant patients. *J. Clin. Psychiat., 44* (5.2), 148-152 (1983).

Sunderland, T., Orsulak, P., and Cohen, B. Amoxapine and neuroleptic side effects: A case report. *Amer. J. Psychiatry 140,* 1233-1235 (1983).

Taeuber, K. Dynamic interaction of nomifensine with alcohol. *Brit. J. Clin. Pharmacol. 4* (Suppl. 2), 147-151 (1977).

Takahashi, R., Sakuma, A., Hara, T., Kazamatsuri, H., Mori, A., Saito, Y., Murasaki, M., Oguchi, T., Sakurai, Y., Yuzuriha, T., Takemura, M., Kurokawa, H., and Kurita, H. Comparison of efficacy of amoxapine and imipramine in a multi-clinic double-blind study using the WHO schedule for a standard assessment of patients with depressive disorders. *J. Int. Med. Res. 7,* 7-18 (1979).

Trimble, M.R., Meldrum, B.S., and Anlezark, G. Effect of nomifensine on brain amines and epilepsy in photosensitive baboons. *Br. J. Clin. Pharmacol. 4* (Suppl. 2), 101-107 (1977).

van Dorth, R.M. Review of clinical studies with mianserin. *Acta Psychiat. Scand. 302,* (Suppl.) 72-80 (1983).

Van Scheyen, J.D., Van Praag, H.M., and Korf, J. Controlled study comparing nomifensine and clomipramine in unipolar depression using the probenecid technique. *Brit. J. Clin. Pharmacol. 4* (Suppl. 2), 179-184 (1977).

Wenser, T.L., Cohn, J.B., and Bustrack, J. Comparison of the effects of bupropion and amitriptyline on cardiac conduction in depressed patients. *J. Clin. Psychiat. 44* (5.2), 174-175 (1983).

Williams, W. Possible use of mianserin in cases of unacceptabel weight gain due to tricyclic antidepressant therapy (letter). *Med. J. Aust. 1* (3), 132-133 (1980).

Wilson, W.H., Petrie, W.H.,and Ban, J.A. Possible lack of anticholinergic effects with mianserin: a pilot study. *J. Clin. Psychiat. 41,* 63-65 (1980).

Zis, A.P., and Goodwin, F.K. Novel antidepressants and the biogenic amine hypothesis of depression. The case for iprindole and mianserin. *Arch. Gen. Psychiat. 36,* 1097-1107 (1979).

Zuns, W.W., Brodie, H.K., Fabre, L., McLendon, D., and Garver, D. Comparative efficacy and safety of bupropion and placebo in the treatment of depression. *Psychopharmacology (Berlin) 79* (4), 343-347 (1983).

12

Selective Monoamine Oxidase Inhibitors in Treatment-Resistant Depression

Dennis L. Murphy, Robert M. Cohen, Trey Sunderland, and Edward Mueller

INTRODUCTION

Over fifteen different monoamines found in brain are oxidatively deaminated by amine oxidase. It is only in the last few years that systematic investigations have been carried out to explore the possible therapeutic advantages of using drugs which selectively inhibit the oxidative metabolism of some monoamines, and not others, in psychiatric disorders. Conventional monoamine oxidase (MAO) inhibiting antidepressants currently available as prescription drugs in the United States (phenelzine, isocarboxazid, and tranylcypromine) have negligible substrate selectivity. While substrate-selective agents have thus far only been available for investigational use, the recent introduction of four new selective MAO inhibitors (amiflamine, cimoxatone, moclobemide, and CGP-11035A) into clinical investigational study phases, along with additional clinical studies with the "older" selective MAO inhibitors, clorgyline, deprenyl, and pargyline, indicate the broadening interest in the therapeutic potential of these agents.

THE SELECTIVE MAO INHIBITORS

The basis for the substrate-selective actions of the newer MAO inhibitors is the existence of two subtypes of MAO: MAO-A and MAO-B. While questions of additional subtypes of the enzyme or even a whole family of closely-related MAOs with a spectrum of affinities for different monoamines have been raised, the evidence currently available is reasonably compatible with two main enzyme forms which vary in immunogenicity, in electrophoretically identified fragments, in molecular weight, and in their substrate selectivity. The most clinically relevant distinction is their different sensitivity to certain inhibitors. The two enzyme forms are also differentially localized in certain cells and tissues. For example, MAO-B is found in primate platelets, rat astrocytes, pinealocytes, and brain serotonin-containing neurons, while MAO-A is the predominant form in peripheral sympathetic neurons and certain tumor cell lines grown in tissue culture, including N1E-115 neuroblastoma, C-6 glioma, and some hepatomas. Increasing evidence also points towards their differential requirements for lipids and, in cells which possess both enzyme forms, their different localization within the outer mitochondrial membrane. Several recent reviews and symposium monographs have been devoted to the MAO subtypes and selective MAO inhibitors (Singer et al., 1979; Beckmann and Riederer, 1983; Murphy et al., 1983; Youdim and Finberg, 1983). The first evidence for the existence of two monoamine oxidases actually came from studies of drugs which were later to be studied as potential antidepressants, clorgyline and Lilly 51461 (Johnston, 1968; Fuller, 1968). Clorgyline is probably the most highly selective inhibitor of MAO-A yet identified. Clorgyline, like its two congeners deprenyl and pargyline, contains an acetylenic group and inactivates the enzyme via formation of a covalent bond with the flavin adenine dinucleotide cofactor in the enzyme's active site. Deprenyl and to a lesser extent pargyline, are more selective MAO-B inhibitors and differ from clorgyline primarily in side-chain length, side-chain constituents, and the two chlorine atoms on clorgyline's ring. Other similar families of MAO-A and MAO-B inhibitors include the cyclopropylamines Lilly 51641 (an MAO-A inhibitor), Lilly 54781 (an MAO-B inhibitor), cimoxatone (MD 780515, an MAO-A inhibitor), and MD 780236 (an MAO-B inhibitor). An overall listing of many of the selective MAO-A and MAO-B inhibitors is presented in Table 1, together with identification of those compounds which have been studied clinically.

In regard to current thinking about the mode of action of antidepressants, presumptively the most important characteristics of the different selective MAO inhibitors are their effects on specific monoamine neurotransmitter or neuromodulator systems. As indicated in Table 1, MAO-A is relatively selective in functioning to inactivate serotonin, norepinephrine, and epinephrine, while MAO-B selectively deaminates phenylethylamine, dopamine (in primates but not in rodents), phenylethanolamine, tele-methylhistamine, and ortho-tyramine. Additional substrates such as para-tyramine, octopamine, and others show lesser selectivity for MAO-A or MAO-B . While inhibitors have been grouped as MAO-A or MAO-B selective in Table 1, it should be noted that the degree of selectivity (i.e., the ratio of MAO-A to MAO-B inhibition) varies among the different MAO inhibitors. Also, there are some data for within-class differences in that the MAO-A inhibitor amiflamine has been reported to be preferentially accumulated within serotonin nerve terminals and consequently to have greater effects on the serotonergic than noradrenergic neurotransmitter system in brain (Ask et al., 1983). Clorgyline, on the other hand, reduces the major norepinephrine metabolite

TABLE 1. Selective Inhibitors of the Monoamine Oxidases Studied in Man

Enzyme subtype	Selective inhibitors	Preferential subtrates in man
1. MAO-A	clorgyline Lilly 51641 amiflamine cimoxotone moclobemide CGP-11305 A	serotonin epinephrine norepinephrine
2. MAO-B	deprenyl pargyline MD 780236	phenylethylamine dopamine phenylethanolamine tele-methylhistamine ortho-tyramine
3. MAO-A and MAO-B (nonselective)	phenelzine tranylcypromine isocarboxazid	para-tyramine tryptamine (and others)

3-methoxy-4-hydroxyphenylglycol (MHPG) in brain to a greater extent than it does to the major serotonin metabolite (5-hydroxyindoleacetic acid), and hence its effects have been suggested to be most closely correlated with noradrenergic changes in brain (Murphy et al., 1984a).

An initial caveat, however, is needed concerning the selective inhibitors being regarded as necessarily like the conventional MAO inhibitors, and different only in having a narrower spectrum of action. We have presented some evidence elsewhere and reviewed the results from other studies suggesting that different classes of MAO inhibitors may have different clinical profiles in keeping with their different chemical and pharmacologic properties in vitro and in vivo (Murphy et al., 1983). This should not be surprising, as there is some evidence that two of the most well-studied conventional MAO inhibitors, tranylcypromine and phenelzine, may not be equivalent drugs (Himmelhoch et al., 1982; Quitkin et al., 1979), although this question has not yet been adequately investigated by direct comparisons using modern assessment and rating instruments in the same population of patients. One selective inhibitor, clorgyline, like the conventional drug tranylcypromine, has been found to compare favorably with the most well-studied tricyclic, imipramine, in more typical depressed patient populations, including severely depressed patients, whereas recent large-scale studies of phenelzine have provided the strongest evidence for its efficacy in outpatient populations with some atypical depressive features (Nies, 1983).

GENERAL ISSUES IN THE USE OF SELECTIVE AND NONSELECTIVE MAO INHIBITORS

Frequently, conventional MAO inhibitors have been turned to only after standard tricyclic antidepressants have been found ineffective or poorly tolerated, at least in severely depressed, "typical" patients (Pare, 1979). This second-line status has usually been attributed to three factors: (a) questions of the efficacy of MAO inhibitors relative to standard tricyclics in the majority of depressed patients, (b) questions regarding their potentially lethal toxicity due to hypertensive or CNS reactions related to dietary tyramine ingestion or certain drug interactions, (c) the inconvenience of dietary and drug restrictions required to minimize potential toxicity. The validity of these concerns and the benefit-risk ratios of conventional MAO inhibitor use are the subject of Chapter 6 of this book and several recent reviews (Kupfer and Detre, 1978; Quitkin et al., 1979; White and Simpson, 1981; Nies, 1983; Tollefson, 1983; Murphy et al., 1984b). Two areas of special interest for both the use of conventional MAO inhibitors and selective MAO inhibitors are their potential for benefit in "atypical" depressed patients, where conventional MAO inhibitors sometimes have been shown superior to standard tricyclics and advocated as the first line of treatment, and their use in combined treatment with tricyclics, lithium, and occasionally other agents, including monoamine precursors such as 5-hydroxytryptophan.

An important caveat needed in considering the question of the use of the selective MAO inhibitors in treatment-resistant patients is that treatment-resistance may be construed in several ways. New agents such as the selective MAO inhibitors may prove of therapeutic advantage not only if they work in patients who have failed to respond to standard treatments, but also if they can be used and are effective as antidepressants in patients who cannot tolerate adequate doses of conventional tricyclics and MAO inhibitors because of side effects or because of the coexistence of other medical disorders, or the required use of other drugs for other medical disorders which are incompatible with cotreatment with standard drugs. Some examples of situations such as these will be considered below.

SOME EXAMPLES OF PATIENT SUBGROUPS LIKELY TO BENEFIT FROM SELECTIVE MAO INHIBITOR TREATMENT

The selective MAO-A inhibitor, clorgyline, may be useful in severe, typical depressive syndromes. Unlike the conventional inhibitor phenelzine, for which there is contradictory evidence regarding its efficacy in severely depressed patients, but fairly strong evidence for its usefulness in "atypical," predominantly out-patient populations (Paykel et al., 1982), several studies have suggested that clorgyline may be effective across a fairly broad spectrum of patient populations. In the first random-assignment, double-blind study conducted with clorgyline, Herd (1969) reported that significantly more clorgyline-treated patients (14 of 16) than amitriptyline-treated individuals (7 of 15) were rated as "improved or recovered." Mean drug doses were not reported but ranged between 20-30 mg/day for clorgyline and 100–150 mg/day for amitriptyline. A second study compared clorgyline, 30 mg/day with imipramine, 100 mg/day in 92 depressed outpatients using a double-blind, random-assignment design (Wheatley, 1970). Both drugs were found to be equally effective and to yield a similar incidence of side effects.

In the only other double-blind study with clorgyline in the literature, which included a cross-over comparison with pargyline, Lipper et al. (1979) reported that clorgyline treatment yielded significant reductions in Hamilton, Beck, and other depression rating scale inventories while pargyline did not. In all the comparisons of the various rating scales in the cross-over design where significant differences in treatment response were found, the results uniformly favored clorgyline. In our extended study, which totaled 23 depressed patients treated with clorgyline (Murphy et al., 1981a), a significant association was demonstrated between initial severity of depression (as assessed by Hamilton scale ratings and several self-rating scales) and therapeutic benefit. This finding supported the observation made in our initial report (Lipper et al., 1979) that the most striking antidepressant responses to clorgyline, as indicated by a reduction of greater than 50% on the Hamilton rating scale, occurred in a subgroup of patients who had pretreatment Hamilton depression scale scores over 30 and who exhibited predominantly "endogenous"-type depressive symptoms, including weight loss, diurnal variation in mood, and psychomotor retardation.

Biochemical data from this clorgyline-pargyline comparative study strongly indicated that clorgyline, at the doses used (25-30 mg/day), markedly reduced MHPG concentrations in plasma and urine, with minimal effects on phenylethylamine or platelet MAO-B activity, and so could be considered as acting predominantly as a selective MAO-A inhibitor in these patients (Murphy et al., 1979; Murphy et al., 1981a). The pargyline doses used, however, were high enough (75-120 mg/day) to inhibit both MAO-B and MAO-A, and so could be considered to be acting nonselectively, as marked effects were observed on MHPG and phenylethylamine excretion, as well as on the dopamine metabolites, homovanillic acid and DOPAC, and on platelet MAO-B activity (Major, 1979; Murphy et al., 1979; 1981b). This is of some interest as a study conducted on the same inpatient research unit and with a comparable group of patients using the nonselective inhibitor phenelzine at an average dose of 60 mg/day revealed a very low response rate (4 of 22 patients recovered) despite evidence that platelet MAO-B was inhibited more than 80% (Murphy et al., 1975). Patients in all of our studies tend to have had prior outpatient and, in most cases, inpatient treatment, including trials with standard antidepressants, and hence can be considered as a group to be generally treatment-resistant.

Clorgyline has reported efficacy in a subgroup of rapid-cycling bipolar patients with treatment-resistant severe depressions. Potter and coworkers (1982) described five bipolar women with unusually treatment-resistant, severe, incapacitating symptoms of recurrent depressions. All had been given standard treatments including lithium, tricyclics, psychotherapy, thyroxine, propranolol, carbamazepine, and neuroleptics, and had been studied and treated for more than six months as inpatients before clorgyline administration in low dosage (2.5-10 mg/day) was begun. Each of the five patients experienced a longer duration of euthymic periods and a lesser severity of depressive symptoms upon the addition of clorgyline to their optimal conventional therapy (usually lithium). Some moderate lengthening of cycle duration had been observed with phenelzine and tranylcypromine, but depressive episodes were qualitatively more severe rather than less severe and included psychotic features with these conventional MAO inhibitors. Clorgyline in low doses was suggested to have anticycling as well as antidepressant effects in this small but extremely refractory patient group. In higher doses, however, clorgyline treatment may be associated with the precipitation of manic episodes in bipolar patients (Pickar et al., 1982), a common propensity of all MAO inhibiting drugs (Murphy, 1977). Because there have been other suggestions that bipolar patients may be less responsive to tricyclics and more responsive to MAO inhibitors, especially tranylcypromine (Kupfer and Detre, 1978; Himmelhoch et al., 1982), further study is needed to evaluate whether clorgyline possesses definite advantages in treatment-resistant bipolar depressed patients.

Clorgyline has possible special efficacy in depressed patients with mild to moderate hypertension. Conventional MAO inhibitors have moderate effects upon blood pressure, and one MAO inhibitor, pargyline, is marketed primarily for antihypertensive rather than antidepressant use. The development of orthostatic hypotension is a major side effect problem in some patients receiving MAO inhibitors or tricyclics.

Our studies with clorgyline and pargyline originally noted that several patients who completely recovered during clorgyline administration had mild to moderate hypertension prior to treatment (Lipper et al., 1979). Subsequent correlational analyses of data from a larger number of patients treated with clorgyline indicated that hypertensive patients became normotensive during clorgyline administration and tended to respond especially favorably to the drug (Roy et al., in press). Correlations between both pretreatment blood pressure and blood pressure reductions during clorgyline treatment versus depression rating reductions were fairly robust. Similar positive correlations were not observed with pargyline, although the small number of responders to pargyline and the smaller number of patients included in the pargyline trials lessen the meaningfulness of this information. Comparable studies of other MAO inhibitors are needed to evaluate whether this is a general finding with all MAO inhibitors or one specific to MAO-A inhibitors such as clorgyline. Our current interpretation of clorgyline's effects is that the drug leads to diminished central sympathetic outflow, associated with decreased plasma norepinephrine concentrations when measured both at rest and standing. As the blood pressure changes tend to develop only slowly during the course of chronic drug administration, and, in fact, parallel the course of clinical improvement and the delay required for adrenergic receptor numbers to change, we have hypothesized that these events may be interrelated (Cohen et al., 1980; Siever et al., 1982; Murphy et al., 1984a; Roy et al., in press).

Clinical antidepressant responses to other selective MAO-A inhibitors. Clinical trials are underway using cimoxatone, CGP-11305A and moclobemide (R011-

1163) but efficacy in a double-blind, random-assignment study has thus far only been verified for moclobemide (Larsen et al., 1983). No specific studies of treatment-resistant patients have yet been described.

Clinical antidepressant responses to MAO-B selective inhibitors. Early uncontrolled studies with the MAO-B inhibitor, deprenyl, reported beneficial effects in anergic, negativistic patients, several of whom had not responded to imipramine, electroconculsive therapy, and other treatments (Varga and Tringer, 1967). Deprenyl dosages in these early studies were in the range now known to be non-MAO-B selective. The first double-blind, random-assignment study of deprenyl in mild to moderately depressed outpatients using final doses of 20 mg/day showed lesser effects of deprenyl compared to placebo over the 4-week treatment period (Mendis et al., 1981). A second, more recent controlled study of a small group of predominantly unipolar inpatients given 15 mg of deprenyl per day for 40 days revealed significantly greater Hamilton depression scale reductions than in the placebo-treatment patients (Mendlewicz and Youdim, 1983). Prior treatment or possible treatment-resistant status was not discussed in these reports. One other open study with deprenyl (15-20 mg/day) in patient groups with endogenous depression suggested treatment efficacy (Mann and Gershon, 1980), but a more recent study by the same investigators indicated that primarily bipolar patients with endogenous-type symptoms and not endogenous unipolar patients responded (Mann et al., 1982). In fact, the highest response rate in this open study was in nonendogenous patients, who were described as having been nonresponsive to tricyclic antidepressants and to other experimental drugs under evaluation in the same clinic, arguing against a placebo effect in these patients. Mann et al. (1982) suggested that their nonendogenous depressed groups might represent a subpopulation of patients with phenylethy lamine or dopamine deficiency states who would benefit from MAO-B inhibition, in contrast to more typical unipolar patients with possible norepinephrine or serotonin abnormalities who might preferentially benefit from MAO-A inhibitors, in keeping with the hypothesis of a biochemical heterogeneity of affective disorders.

Our results with deprenyl in a small number of mixed depressive subjects, most with severe unipolar depression and histories of nonresponse to standard treatments, have thus far revealed no evidence for therapeutic efficacy in MAO-B selective doses of 10 mg/day. Small numbers of patients receiving 30 mg/day also showed negligible changes, but several patients receiving larger doses (60 mg/day) have shown partial antidepressant responses. This large deprenyl dose reduced MHPG excretion to nearly as great an extent as clogyline or tranylcypromine, and hence would appear to be acting also on MAO-A. These data, although preliminary, would seem to be compatible with our results from the clorgyline studies which indicate that some severe, treatment-resistant depressed patients may benefit from drugs which inhibit MAO-A. MAO-B inhibitors, in contrast, need to be studied further to evaluate whether possible beneficial effects might be found in nonendogenous patients.

Low doses of deprenyl appear to have lesser tyramine-potentiation effects than found with the usual doses of conventional MAO-inhibitors or clorgyline (Pickar et al., 1981; Mendis et al., 1981), and would have some advantage in this regard if antidepressant efficacy can be demonstrated in a patient subgroup. Like clorgyline, pargyline, and conventional MAO inhibitors, no direct anticholinergic effects occur, and so many troublesome side effects are avoided. Deprenyl may also possess fewer side effects of other types, including less orthostatic hypotension, and so may be of use in older patient populations, again if efficacy can be demonstrated. Deprenyl has been used safely in potentiating some effects of L-dopa therapy in Parkinson's disease (Lees et al., 1977), and Knoll (1982) has suggested that its use may theoretically be of greatest value in older patients not only in regard to depression and Parkinsonism but also other age-related behavioral changes. His hypothesis is predicated upon reports of MAO-B increasing with age and in certain types of age-related neuropathology, changes which may impair the modulation of dopamine and trace amine systems in the brain.

CONCLUSIONS

Only preliminary, essentially case-report type documentation exists supporting special benefits of selective MAO inhibitors in some subgroups of treatment-resistant patients. Much further study is needed to verify whether the suggestions that MAO-A inhibitors may be of special value for treatment-resistant severe endogenous patients, depressed patients with lithium-resistant recurrent depressions, or depressed patients with coexisting hypertension. Similarly, the delineation of other patient groups suggested to particularly benefit from MAO-B inhibitors, including nonendogenous and geriatric depressed patients, needs further exploration. The biochemical selectivity and postulated differential therapeutic spectra and side-effect profiles of currently available and newer selective MAO-inhibiting drugs may provide important tools to aid in the investigation of the undoubtedly heterogenous affective disorders.

REFERENCES

Ask, A-L., Fagervall, I., and Ross, S.B. Selective inhibition of monoamine oxidase in monoaminergic neurons in the rat brain. *Naunyn-Schmiedeberg's Arch. Pharmacol. 324,* 79-87 (1983).

Beckmann, H., and Riederer, P., eds. *Monoamine Oxidase and Its Selective Inhibitors: New Concepts in Therapy and Research.* Karger, Basel, 1983.

Cohen, R.M., Campbell, I.C., Cohen, M.R., Torda, T., Pickar, D., Siever, L.J., and Murphy, D.L. Presynaptic noradrenergic regulation during depression and antidepressant drug treatment. *Psychiat. Res. 3,* 93-105 (1980).

Fuller, R.W. Influence of substrate in the inhibition of rat liver and brain monoamine oxidase. *Arch. Intern. Pharmacodyn. Ther. 174,* 32-37 (1968).

Herd, J.A. A new antidepressant—M and B 9302. A pilot study and double-blind controlled trial. *Clin. Trials 6,* 219-225 (1969).

Himmelhoch, J.M., Fuchs, C.Z., and Symons, B.J. A double-blind study of tranylcypromine treatment of major anergic depression. *J. Nerv. Ment. Dis. 170,* 628-634 (1982).

Johnston, J.P. Some observations upon a new inhibitor of monoamine oxidase in brain tissue. *Biochem. Pharmacol. 17,* 1285-1297 (1968).

Knoll, J. Selective inhibition of B type monoamine oxidase in the brain: a drug strategy to improve the quality of life in senescence, in *Strategy in Drug Research,* J.A. Keverling Buisman, ed. Elsevier Scientific Publishing Company, Amsterdam, pp. 107-135 (1982).

Kupfer, D.J., and Detre, T.P. Tricyclic and monoamine-oxidase-inhibitor antidepressants: clinical use, in *Handbook of Psychopharmacology. Affective Disorders: Drug Actions in Animals and Man,* L.L. Iversen, S.D. Iversen, and S.H. Snyder, eds. Plenum Press, New York, pp. 199-232 (1978).

Larsen, J.K., Mikkelsen, P.L., and Holm, P. Moclobemide (RO 11-1163) in the treatment of major depressive disorder. A randomized clinical trial. *L'Encephale 9* (Suppl. 1), B6 (1983).

Lees, A., Kohout, L.J., Shaw, K.M., Stern, G.M., Elsworth, J.D., Sandler, M., and Youdim, M.B.H. Deprenyl in Parkinson's disease. *Lancet 2,* 791-795 (1977).

Lipper, S., Murphy, D.L., Slater, S., and Buchsbaum, M.S. Comparative behavioral effects of clorgyline and pargyline in man; a preliminary evaluation. *Psychopharmacology 62,* 123-128 (1979).

Major, L.F., Murphy, D.L., Lipper, S., and Gordon, E. Effects of clorgyline and pargyline on deaminated metabolites of norepinephrine, dopamine and serotonin in human cerebrospinal fluid. *J. Neurochem. 32,* 229-231 (1979).

Mann, J.J., Frances, A., Kaplan, R.D., Kocsis, J., Peselow, E.D., and Gershon, S. The relative efficacy of 1-deprenyl, a selective monoamine oxidase type B inhibitor, in endogenous and nonendogenous depression. *J. Clin. Psychopharmacol. 2,* 54-57 (1982).

Mann, J.J., and Gershon, S. L-Deprenyl, a selective monoamine oxidase type-B inhibitor in endogenous depression. *Life Sci. 26,* 877-882 (1980).

Mendis, N., Pare, C.M., Sandler, M., Glover, V., and Stern, G.M. Is the failure of L-deprenyl, a selective monoamine oxidase B inhibitor, to alleviate depression related to freedom from the cheese effect? *Psychopharmacology 73,* 87-90 (1981).

Mendlewicz, J., and Youdim, M.B.H. L-Deprenil, a selective monoamine oxidase type B inhibitor, in the treatment of depression: a double-blind evaluation. *Brit. J. Psychiat. 142,* 508-511 (1983).

Murphy, D.L. The behavioral toxicity of monoamine oxidase inhibiting antidepressants. *Adv. Pharmacol. Chermother. 14,* 71-105 (1977).

Murphy, D.L., Brand, E., Baker, M., van Kammen, D.P., and Gordon, E. Phenelzine effects in hospitalized unipolar and bipolar depressed patients: behavioral and biochemical relationships, in *Neuropsychopharmacology,* vol. 10, J.R. Boissier, H. Hippius, and P. Pichot, eds. Elsevier, New York, pp. 788-799 (1975).

Murphy, D.L., Cohen, R.M., Garrick, N.A., Siever, L.J., and Campbell, I.C. Utilization of substrate selective monoamine oxidase ihibitors to explore neurotransmitter hypotheses of the affective disorders, in *Neuriobiology of the Mood Disorders,* R.M. Post and J.C. Ballenger, eds. Williams and Wilkins Co., Baltimore, pp. 710-720 (1984a).

Murphy, D.L., Garrick, N.A., and Cohen, R.M. Monoamine oxidase inhibitors and monoamine oxidase: biochemical and physiological aspects relevant to human psychopharmacology, in *Drugs in Psychiatry. Vol. 1: Antidepressants,* G.D. Burrows, T.R. Norman, and E. Davies, eds. Elsevier/North Holland Biomedical Press, Amsterdam, pp. 209-227 (1983).

Murphy, D.L., Guttmacher, L.B., and Cohen, R.M. Recent developments regarding the use of monoamine oxidase inhibitors in psychopharmacology, in *Guidelines for the Use of Psychotropic Drugs,* H.C. Stancer, Z.M. Rakoff, and P.E. Garfinkel, eds. Spectrum Press, New York, pp. 77-93 (1984b).

Murphy, D.L., Lipper, S., Pickar, D., Jimerson, D., Cohen, R.M., Garrick, N.A., Alterman, I.S., and Campbell, I.C. Selective inhibition of monoamine oxidase type A: clinical antidepressant effects and metabolic changes in man, in *Monoamine Oxidase Inhibitors. The State of the Art,* M.B.H. Youdim and E.S. Paykel, eds. John Wiley and Sons, New York, pp. 189-205 (1981a).

Murphy, D.L., Lipper, S., Slater, S., and Shiling, D. Selectively of clorgyline and pargyline as inhibitors of monoamine oxidases A and B *in vivo* in man. *Psychopharmacology 62,* 129-132 (1979).

Murphy, D.L., Pickar, D., Jimerson, D., Cohen, R.M., Garrick, N.A., Karoum, F., and Wyatt, R.J. Biochemical indices of the effects of selective MAO inhibitors (clorgyline, pargyline and deprenyl) in man, in *Clinical Pharmacology in Psychiatry*, E. Usdin, S. Dahl, L.F. Gram, and O. Lingjaerde eds. Macmillan Press, London, pp. 307-316 (1981b).

Nies, A. Clinical applications of MAOI's, in *Drugs in Psychiatry*, vol. 1, G.D. Burrows, T.R. Norman, and B. Davies, eds. Elsevier, Amsterdam, pp. 229-247 (1983).

Pare, C.M.B. Monoamine oxidase inhibitors in resistant depression. *Internat. Pharmacopsychiatry 14*, 101-109 (1979).

Paykel, E.S., Rowan, P.R., Parker, R.R., and Bhat, A.V. Response to phenelzine and amitriptyline in subtypes of outpatient depression. *Arch. Gen. Psychiatry 39*, 1041-1049 (1982).

Pickar, D., Cohen, R.M., Jimerson, D.C., and Murphy, D.L. Tyramine infusions and selective monoamine oxidase inhibitor treatment. I. Changes in pressor sensitivity. *Psychopharmacology 74*, 4-7 (1981).

Pickar, D., Murphy, D.L., Cohen, R.M., Campbell, I.C., and Lipper, S. Selective and nonselective monoamine oxidase inhibitors: behavioral disturbances during their administration to depressed patients. *Arch. Gen. Psychiat. 39*, 535-540 (1982).

Potter, W.Z., Murphy, D.L., Wehr, T.A., Linnoila, M., and Goodwin, F.K. Clorgyline: A new treatment for refractory rapid cycling patients. *Arch. Gen. Psychiat. 39*, 505-510 (1982).

Quitkin, F., Rifkin, A., and Klein, D.F. Monoamine oxidase inhibitors. A review of antidepressant effectiveness. *Arch. Gen. Psychiat. 36*, 749-760 (1979).

Roy, B.F., Murphy, D.L., Lipper, S., Siever, L., Alterman, I.S., Jimerson, D., Lake, C.R., and Cohen, R.M. Cardiovascular effects of the selective monoamine oxidase inhibiting antidepressant clorgyline: correlations with clinical responses and changes in catecholamine metabolism. *J. Clin. Psychopharmacol.*, in press.

Siever, L.J., Uhde, T.W., and Murphy, D.L. Possible subsensitization of $alpha_2$-adrenergic receptors by chronic monoamine oxidase inhibitor treatment in psychiatric patients. *Psychiat. Res. 6*, 293-302 (1982).

Singer, T.P., Von Korff, R.W., and Murphy, D.L., eds. *Monoamine Oxidase: Structure, Function and Altered Functions*. Academic Press, New York (1979).

Tollefson, G.D. Monoamine oxidase inhibitors: a review. *J. Clin. Psychiat. 44*, 280-288 (1983).

Varga E., and Tringer, L. Clinical trial of a new type promptly acting psychoenergic agent (phenyl-isopropyl-methylpropinyl-HCl, "E-250"). *Acta. Med. Acad. Sci. Hung. 23*, 289-295 (1967).

Wheatly, D. Comparative trial of a new monoamine oxidase inhibitor in depression. *Brit. J. Psychiat. 117*, 547-548 (1970).

White, K., and Simpson, G. combined MAOI-tricyclic antidepressant treatment: A reevaluation. *J. Clin. Psychopharm. 1*, 264-282 (1981).

Youdim, M.B.H., and Finberg, J.P.M. Monoamine oxidase inhibitor antidepressants, in *Psychopharmacology 1*, D.G. Grahame-Smith, ed. Excerpta Medica, Amsterdam, pp. 38-70 (1983).

13

L-Triiodothyronine (T_3): Its Place in the Treatment of TCA-Resistant Depressed Patients

Arthur J. Prange, Jr.

In 1958 Kuhn published evidence that the substance G22355, later named imipramine (IMI), possessed antidepressant properties. In the decades that followed, most investigators, though not all, confirmed this finding (Kline and Davis, 1969), and IMI along with related tricyclic antidepressants (TCAs) became the mainstay of treatment for depression.

AN ADJUNCT FOR TCA TREATMENT

Despite their widespread use, the TCAs have three main drawbacks: they are slow to act; they are not always effective; even when effective, the remission they produce is sometimes less than complete. The second point in expanded form, i.e., the problem of drug-resistant depressed patients, is the subject of this volume, and one method of correcting drug resistance is the subject of the present essay. The remedy to be proposed is the use of the potent, fast-acting, quickly-removed thyroid hormone, L-triiodothyronine (T_3).

Some investigators and practitioners have used T_3 to correct all three disadvantages of TCAs. Its value is proven for shortening the latency of onset of TCA action, at least in women (Prange et al., 1969; Wilson et al., 1970), and for achieving acceptable outcome in TCA-resistant patients, men as well as women (see below). Anecdotal evidence suggests that T_3 improves the quality of remission, as induced and maintained by a TCA, though systematic investigation of this concept is lacking.

The early studies of T_3 as an adjunct to hasten the onset of TCA action, related animal investigations, and confirmatory reports have been extensively reviewed (Prange et al., 1976; 1984). A report by Earle (1970) illustrated the first use of T_3 as an adjunct to convert TCA non-responders to responders. Following Earle's work in the United States, four reports, two Japanese (Ogura et al, 1974; Tsutsui, et al., 1979) and two Hungarian (Banki, 1975; 1977) confirmed this phenomenon. These studies, like Earle's, were single blind, and interpretation was rendered difficult by variations in criteria for diagnosis and for outcome. Despite these variations, all authors reached the same conclusion, that a substantial majority of depressed patients who have previously been non-responsive to a TCA quickly become responsive if T_3 is added to their regimen. The usual dose of T_3 was 25 μg; the TCAs most often involved were IMI and amitriptyline (AMI).

A CONTROLLED STUDY

Goodwin and his colleagues (1982) reported a double-blind study of six men and six women (mean age 38 years) with major depressive illness who had not responded to IMI or AMI, 150-300 mg/day, for 26 to 112 days. Four patients showed the unipolar form of the illness, eight the bipolar form. All patients were proven to be euthyroid. All had shown only a minimal (or null) response to TCAs during the four weeks prior to the inception of the study, as judged by scores of routine behavioral ratings performed by nurses. A physician who was otherwise unconcerned with the study adjusted dosages of IMI or AMI upward to levels consistent with acceptable side effects (150-300 mg/day; mean ± SEM, 238 ± 14.3). After ratings continued to indicate no more than slight improvement, T_3 (25 μg/day, 10 patients; 50 μg, two patients) was given in the morning along with a TCA in coded capsules under double-blind conditions. The total number of capsules was held constant throughout the trial. Apart from the addition of T_3, all aspects of treatment, e.g. individual and group psychotherapy, were unchanged.

As a group, the 12 patients (who were studied during an 18-month period) began to show improvement within a week of starting T_3. By three weeks improvement was substantial, and their mean behavioral scores were compatible with clinical remission. Improvement was highly significant in nine patients but only slight in the other three. Even in these three, however, nursing notes suggested favorable changes. For example, one patient classified as a T_3 non-responder by systematic ratings was quoted as saying, "My girl friend says I'm the best she's ever seen me." Improvement was not related to subtype of depression, sex, type of TCA, dose of T_3, or degree to which T_3 suppressed plasma thyroxine (T_4). In the eight patients who were receiving IMI, T_3 had no effect on plasma levels of IMI or its derivative, desmethylimipramine (DMI), an observation consistent with the findings that T_3 did not affect TCA side effects and produced very few of its own.

CLINICAL CONSIDERATIONS

As described above, the report by Goodwin et al., like the ones that preceded it, is strongly positive, and no negative reports have appeared. Among the six published studies there is agreement that between two-thirds and three-fourths of patients promptly show a remarkable improvement that pertains about equally to all aspects of the depression syndrome. Resting on this evidence, the phenomenon of T_3 conversion of TCA failures can be characterized in broader clinical perspective. The first point to emphasize is that, across all studies, the phenomenon pertains equally to both sexes. Moreover, it appears to pertain about equally to the unipolar and bipolar forms of depression. Although bipolar patients, compared to unipolar patients, are more liable during most treatments to switch into mania or hypomania, T_3 does not increase this liability. Anecdotal evidence suggests that T_3 may also convert to responders patients who have failed to respond to a monoamine oxidase inhibitor (MAOI). However, neither the frequency nor the safety of the putative MAOI phenomenon has been established.

At what point in the treatment of a depressed patient should one employ T_3? The answer, of course, will depend on how the physician weighs the variables involved. If he regards the slow onset of action of TCAs as an undue hazard, through extended morbidity and risk of mortality through suicide, then he may use T_3 from the outset, at least in female patients (see below). If he regards slow onset of action as merely a nuisance to be tolerated, he will reserve T_3 to be used as a corrective measure in patients, men as well as women, who have not shown an adequate antidepressant response after, say, three weeks. In either case, he will ensure that his patient is euthyroid by usual criteria and that cardiovascular function is normal.

Cardiovascular function is assessed to confer full safety. Thyroid function is assessed for this reason and because a certain small number of depressed patients will be found to be hypothyroid. This should be corrected by usual means; such correction alone may relieve the depression. If hypothyroidism is not corrected then, as Avni (1967) has suggested on the basis of animal studies and human observations, TCA treatment is likely to be a useless exercise. Most authors who have studied the T_3-TCA interaction have proven that their patients were euthyroid and have excluded from studies those who were not.

The question remains, of course, whether in TCA non-responders one should add T_3 or try a different TCA. This problem has not been studied. Nevertheless, one gains the impression from the literature that the "rescue" rate is higher from adding T_3 than from switching drugs.

What T_3 accomplishes in TCA failures does appear to be something that cannot be accomplished merely by increasing TCA dosage. If T_3 merely increased TCA levels, it would be expected to increase TCA side effects, but it does not (Wheatley, 1972; Coppen et al., 1972). Moreover, both animal (Breese, et al., 1974) and human (Goodwin, et al., 1982; Garbutt, et al., 1979) studies have demonstrated that T_3 has no clear effect on TCA disposition or metabolism. Evidence bearing directly on the question has been provided by Banki (1975). Studying 96 TCA failures, he added T_3 to the treatment of 52, and 39 improved. He increased the TCA dose of 44, and only 10 improved. Later in a similar study, Banki (1977) found improvement rates of 23/33 for T_3, 4/16 for increased doses of TCA.

Side effects of T_3 in the dose range recommended, 25-50 μg per day, are difficult to detect. Nevertheless, when doses greater than 50 μg per day are used, toxicity may occur (Prange, 1971), presenting as activation of the sympathetic nervous system. In such a situation the advantage of quickly-removed T_3 (half-life about one day) over slowly removed T_4 (half-life about 7 days) becomes apparent.

The question is often asked as to how long T_3 should be given. The answer consists of only an approximation. If T_3 is given for less than three weeks, a certain small number of patients will relapse when it is stopped, while very few relapse if T_3 is continued for four weeks. A related question is the technique for stopping the hormone. If one prescribes 50 μg per day, which is usually unnecessary, one might reasonably reduce the dosage to 25 μg per day for a few days before discontinuing the hormone altogether. When 25 μg has been in use, there seems no need to taper dosage prior to discontinuation. These comments on stopping T_3, of course, avoid the issue as to whether T_3 would improve the quality of remission if it were continued along with a usual maintenance dose of a TCA.

What are the disadvantages of T_3 used in the fashion described above? Because side effects, including EKG abnormalities (Garbutt, 1979), are not increased and because T_3 is inexpensive, there appears to be only one, and it is minor. The use of

T_3, for its duration, invalidates usual blood tests of thyroid state. Most tests in common use measure T_4 or some aspect of T_4 kinetics. The use of T_3 partly suppresses T_4 secretion; thus even as the thyroid hormone T_3 is administered some laboratory tests, by tracking falling T_4 levels, will falsely suggest the development of hypothyroidism. In this situation, the measurement of some tissue response to thyroid hormones, such as secretion by the anterior pituitary gland of thyroid stimulating hormone (TSH), will provide an accurate index of thyroid state if one is needed.

SUPPORTING EVIDENCE

The use of T_3 to convert TCA non-responders to responders is closely related to the phenomenon of using T_3 to accelerate TCA response in previously untreated patients. From a descriptive point of view the two phenomena differ importantly in only one respect; the former, as described above, clearly pertains to both sexes; the latter is clearly established only in women. The validity of one phenomenon enhances the validity of the other, and in this connection it can be noted that all eight studies of the use of T_3 to "accelerate" (as opposed to "convert") have been double-blind. Six studies (Prange et al., 1969; 1971; 1976; Wilson et al., 1970; Wheatley, 1972; Coppen et al., 1972), involving 169 patients, have been positive; two studies involving 29 patients, have been negative. Feighner et al. (1972) gave larger doses of IMI (200 mg/day) and gave T_3 for a shorter time (10 days). For these and other reasons, they may have enhanced the risk of a false negative finding (Prange, 1972). Steiner et al. (1978) studied four patients in each of three treatment groups, increasing the risk of a false negative finding by reason of small group size.

After T_3 had been used in depressed patients for almost a decade, as an instance of therapeutic psychoendocrinology, a finding from diagnostic psychoendocrinology made it clear that the thyroid axis is in fact often disordered in depressed patients. A large minority of such patients, perhaps one-third, display a grossly subnormal, i.e., "blunted," TSH response after injection of a test dose of thyrotropin releasing hormone (TRH) (Loosen and Prange, 1982). Whether it is these patients who are most responsive to T_3 is uncertain, but Tsutsui et al. (1979) have adduced evidence that such may be the case. They identified 11 TCA non-responders who also showed blunted TSH responses to TRH. All were given T_3 as an adjunct to TCA, and 10 showed a remarkably favorable response. Other efforts to predict which TCA non-responders will respond to the addition of T_3 have been unsuccessful. The salient point, however, is that most do respond.

Finally, as indirect supporting evidence, at least as evidence that something is often amiss in the thyroid axis of depressed patients and that thyroid hormone treatment confers a benefit, attention should be given to patients who rapidly cycle from mania to depression. Patients with rapid-cycling bipolar illness, as contrasted to patients with non-rapid-cycling bipolar illness, demonstrate higher TSH levels, suggesting a degree of hypothyroidism (Cowdry et al., 1983). Such patients apparently can be treated successfully with hypermetabolic doses of T_4 (Stancer and Persad, 1982), and perhaps even with doses that have little measurable peripheral effect (Leibow, 1983).

THEORETICAL CONSIDERATIONS

A phenomenon, however consistently it may have been demonstrated on empirical grounds, is more readily accepted if a mechanism can be advanced as accounting for it. Conversely, if a phenomenon does win broad acceptance, then it can be used to investigate the mechanisms to which it may pertain. Thus TCAs were quickly accepted in the clinic not only by reason of empirical evidence of efficacy in most, though not all, trials (Kline and Davis, 1969) but also because they were shown to block the reuptake inactivation of certain released neurotransmitters, principally norepinephrine and serotonin, which were implicated in the pathophysiology of depression for reasons other than their reponsiveness to TCAs (Prange, 1964; Schildkraut, 1965; Bunney and Davis, 1965). Studies of TCA actions in animal brain were then employed to provide a fuller understanding of the pathophysiology of depression. This in turn has led to a reassessment of what TCAs do that is antidepressant. Because TCAs act slowly as antidepressants, but in animal preparations act quickly to block reuptake of transmitters, it has been suggested that reuptake blockade may not be fundamental to antidepressant action (Enna and Kendall, 1981). What is more concordant in time, effects in animal preparations compared to onset of antidepressant action, is the down regulation of β-adrenergic receptors in brain (Sulser et al., 1978). This observation has brought into question the fundamental postulate that brain transmitter systems are hypoactive in depressed patients. From one interpretation of the newer data, it is the *induction* of hypoactivity in these systems that is concordant with the onset of antidepressant action.

Interest in adrenergic receptors invites a consideration of thyroid hormones. Thyroid hormones penetrate the brain, are taken up in nerve ends, and appear to exert complex receptor effects in brain as elsewhere (Whybrow & Prange, 1981). Sulser (1984) has found that propranolol blocks the typical "down-regulating" effect of DMI in rat cortex; in this sense, the propranololized rat is TCA resistant. In such animals the typical TCA effect, down regulation of β receptors, is reinstated when animals are given T_3. Another view holds that it is increased α_1 noradrenergic receptor activity that accounts for TCA antidepressant effects.

Strombom et al. (1977), proponents of this view, found that T_3 enhances the behavioral activating effects of clonodine, an α_2 receptor agonist. Subsequently, receptor binding studies provided direct evidence that T_3 up-regulates central α-adrenergic receptors (Gross et al., 1981).

In laboratory work not yet published, we have taken the view that T_3 affects at least some of the actions of TCAs in brain and that this action or actions of T_3, in net effect, are antidepressant. We treated rats with DMI and observed the typical down-regulation of cortical β-adrenergic receptors. In other rats we added T_3 to the DMI regimen; T_3 *prevented* down-regulation. In a third group of rats, T_3 alone caused up-regulation. With this preliminary evidence one might suggest that down-regulation of β-adrenergic receptors, an "antiadrenergic" effect, is not the cause of TCAs being antidepressant but rather a partial compensation for some greater "proadrenergic" effect. Perhaps reuptake blockade *is* fundamental, as early believed; perhaps it simply needs to be in place for a few days before an antidepressant effect can be measured.

A question that is often asked has both clinical and theoretical implications: can T_4 be used in place of T_3 to enhance TCA clinical effects? There are no systematic data that bear on this point, though informal experience suggests that 100 μg T_4 can be used in place of 25μg T_3. Thyroxine has the advantage of not invalidating usual tests of thyroid state. Its longer half-life may confer a more even clinical effect; on the other hand, its longer half-life might be at least an inconvenience if toxicity is encountered. Thyroxine is readily converted to T_3; in fact, it is tissue conversion rather than thyroid gland secretion that produces most of the T_3 in the body (Ingbar and Woeber, 1981). Absent a rare deficiency in the deiodinase enzyme that performs this conversion, administered T_4 will be converted to T_3. On the other hand, the effects of T_4 and T_3 may not be identical, especially in brain (Dratman and Crutchfield, 1981), and it is possible that there may be tissue-specific deficiencies in conversion capacity (Visser et al., 1982). On balance, one must guess that thyroxine is probably as effective as T_3 as a TCA adjunct in depressed patients. It would be fascinating if it were not.

A final observation must be included in this brief account of theoretical points. In Chapter 8 of this volume, de Montigny and Cournoyer present the evidence, which seems compelling, that lithium carbonate, when given to TCA non-responders, often and quite promptly, converts them to responders. Lithium, of course, is an antithyroid substance, especially during the early days and weeks of its use. Thyroid hormones, one must think, are prothyroid. Then how can lithium and T_3 (or T_4) both remedy TCA non-responsiveness? The first possibility is that the two substances are effective in different patients, and this possibility needs direct clinical testing. However, if both substances, as seems the case, are effective in most patients, then their efficacy must overlap at least in part. Lithium, of course, has many effects. It may be that it is effective not because of its antithyroid property but in spite of it. Finally, and least appealing to the theoretician, is the possibility that what is important about the thyroid system in TCA non-responders is to change it. Perhaps a stimulus of either sign, pro-or antithyroid, will initiate a train of events within the thyroid axis that becomes manifest finally as an antidepressant effect.

CONCLUSIONS

The addition of T_3 to a usual TCA regime is a safe and effective remedy for most depressed patients who fail to respond to a TCA alone. The phenomenon may provide a useful means of exploring the pathophysiology of depression. Data pertain entirely to "first generation" antidepressants and mainly to IMI and AMI. Studies of interactions with "second generation" antidepressants would be valuable clinically; they would also be valuable theoretically as certain of these newer drugs are said to act on one or another transmitter systems with a high degree of specificity. A detailed study of how a thyroid hormone and lithium carbonate can have the same end results might provide new insights into the pathophysiology of depression.

REFERENCES

Avni, J., Edelstein, E.L., Khazan, N., and Sulman, F.G. Comparative study of imipramine, amitriptyline and their desmethyl analogues in the hypothyroid rat. *Psychopharmacologia 10*, 426-430 (1967).

Banki, C.M. Triiodothyronine in the treatment of depression. *Orv Hetil 116*, 2543-2547 (1975).

Banki, C.M. Cerebrospinal fluid amine metabolites after combined amitriptyline-triiodothyronine treatment of depressed women. *Eur. J. Clin. Pharmacol. 11*, 311-315 (1977).

Breese, G.R., Prange, A.J., Jr., and Lipton, M.A. Pharmacological studies of thyroid-imipramine interactions in animals, in *The Thyroid Axis, Drugs and Behavior*, A.J. Prange, Jr., ed., Raven Press, New York, pp. 29-48.

Bunney, W.E. and Davis, J.M. Norepinephrine in depressive reactions. *Arch. Gen. Psychiat. 13*, 483-494 (1965).

Coppen, A., Whybrow, P.C., Noguera, R., Maggs, R., and Prange, A.J., Jr., The comparative antidepressant value of l-tryptophan and imipramine with and without attempted potentiation by liothyronine. *Arch. Gen. Psychiat. 26*, 234-241 (1972).

Cowdry, R.W., Wehr, T.A., Zis, A.P. and Goodwin, F.K. Thyroid abnormalities associated with rapid-cycling bipolar illness. *Arch. Gen. Psychiat. 40*, 414-420 (1983).

Dratman, M.B. and Crutchfield, F.L. Interaction of adrenergic and thyronergic systems in the development of low T_3 syndrome, in *The Low T_3 Syndrome*, R.-D. Hesch, ed., Proceedings of the Serono Symposia, Vol. 40, Academic Press, New York, p. 115 (1981).

Earle, B.V. Thyroid hormone and tricyclic antidepressants in resistant depressions. *Amer. J. Psychiatry 126*, 1667-1669 (1970).

Enna, S.J. and Kendall, D.A. Interactions of antidepressants with brain neurotransmitter receptors. *J. Clin. Psychopharmacol. 1*, 12-165 (1981).

Feighner, J.P., King, L.J., Schuckit, M.A., Croughan, J., and Briscoe, W. Hormonal potentiation of imipramine and ECT in primary depression. *Amer. J. Psychiat. 128*, 1230-1238 (1972).

Garbutt, J.C., Malekpour, B., Brunswick, D., Jonnalagadda, M.R., Jolliff, L., Podolak, R., Wilson, I.C., and Prange, A.J., Jr. Effects of triiodothyronine on drug level and cardiac function in depressed patients treated with imipramine. *Amer. J. Psychiat. 136*, 980-982 (1979).

Goodwin, F.K., Prange, A.J., Jr., Post, R.M., Muscattola, G., and Lipton, M.A. L-triiodothyronine converts tricyclic antidepressant non-responders to responders. *Amer. J. Psychiat. 139*, 334-338 (1982).

Gross, G., Brodde, O.-E. and Schumann, H.-J. Regulation of alpha-1-receptors in the cerebral cortex of the rat by thyroid hormones. *Naunyn-Schmied. Arch. Pharmacol. 316*, 45-50 (1981).

Ingbar, S.H. and Woeber, K.A. The thyroid gland, in *Textbook of Endocrinology*, R.H. Williams, ed., W.B. Saunders Company, Philadelphia, pp. 117-247 (1981).

Klein, D.F. and Davis, J.M. *Diagnosis and Drug Treatment of Psychiatric Disorders*, The Williams & Wilkins Company, Baltimore (1969).

Kuhn, R. The treatment of depressive states with G-22355 (imipramine hydrochloride). *Amer. J. Psychiat. 115*, 459-464 (1958).

Leibow, D. *l*-Thyroxine for rapid-cycling bipolar illness. (Letter to editor) *Amer. J. Psychiatry 140*, 1255 (1983).

Loosen, P.T. and Prange, A.J., Jr. Serum thyrotropin response to thyrotropin-releasing hormone in psychiatric patients: A review. *Amer. J. Psychiat. 139*, 405-416 (1982).

Ogura, C., Okuma, T., Uchida, Y., Imai, S, Yogi, H., and Sunami, Y. Combined thyroid (triiodothyronine)-tricyclic antidepressant treatment in depressive states. *Folia Psychiatr. Neurol. Jpn. 28*, 179-186 (1974).

Prange, A.J., Jr. The pharmacology and biochemistry of depression. *Dis. Nerv. Syst. 25*, 217-221 (1964).

Prange, A.J. Therapeutic and theoretical implications of imipramine-hormone interactions in depressive disorders, in *Proc. V World Congr. Psychiatry*, Excerpta Medica, Amsterdam (1971).

Prange, A.J., Jr. Discussion of paper by Feighner, et al., *Amer. J. Psychiat. 128*, 55-58 (1972).

Prange, A.J., Jr., Wilson, I.C., Rabon, A.M. and Lipton, M.A. Enhancement of imipramine antidepressant activity by thyroid hormone. *Amer. J. Psychiat. 126*, 457-469 (1969).

Prange, A.J., Jr., Wilson, I.C., Breese, G.R., and Lipton, M.A. Hormonal alteration of imipramine response: A review, in *Hormones, Behavior and Psychopathology*, S.J. Sacher, ed., Raven Press, New York, pp. 15-19 (1976).

Prange, A.J., Jr., Loosen, P.T., Wilson, I.C., and Lipton, M.A. The therapeutic use of hormones of the thyroid axis in depression, in *Frontiers of Clinical Neuroscience*, R.M. Post and J.C. Ballenger, eds., Williams & Wilkins, Baltimore, pp. 311-322 (1984).

Schildkraut, J.J. The catecholamine hypothesis of affective disorders: A reviw of supporting evidence. *Amer. J. Psychiatry 122*, 509-522 (1965).

Stancer, H.C. and Persad, E. Treatment of intractable rapid-cycling manic-depressive disorder with levothyroxine. *Arch. Gen. Psychiat. 39*, 311-312 (1982).

Steiner, M., Radqan, M., Elizur, A., Blum, I., Atsmon, A., and Davidson, S. Failure of l-triiodothyronine (T_3) to potentiate tricyclic antidepressant response. *Curr. Ther. Res. 23*, 655-659 (1978).

Strombom, U., Svensson, T.H., Jackson, D.M. and Engstrom, G. Hyperthyroidism: Specifically increased response to central NA-(α)-receptor stimulation and generally increased monoamine turnover in brain. *J. Neurol. Transmission 41*, 73-92 (1977).

Sulser, F. Ventulani, J. and Mobley, P.I. Mode of action of antidepressant drugs. *Biochem. Pharmacol. 27*, 257-261 (1978).

Sulser, F. Antidepressant treatments and regulation of norepinephrine-receptor-coupled adenylate cyclase systems in brain, in *Frontiers in Biochemical and Pharmacological Research in Depresson*, E. Usdin, M. Asberg, L. Bertilsson and F. Sjoqvist, eds., Raven Press, New York, p. 249 (1984).

Tsutsui, S., Yamazaki, Y., Namba, T., Tsushima, M. Combined therapy of T_3 and antidepressants in depression. *J. Internat. Med. Res. 7*, 138-146 (1979).

Visser, T.J., Leonard, J.L., Kaplan, M.M. and Larsen, P.R. Kinetic evidence suggesting two mechanisms for iodothyronine t'-deiodination in rat cerebral cortex. *Proc. Natl. Acad. Sci. 79*, 5080-5084 (1982).

Wheatley, D. Potentiation of amitriptyline by thyroid hormone. *Arch. Gen. Psychiat. 26*, 229-233 (1972).

Whybrow, P.C. and Prange, A.J., Jr. Perspectives: A hypothesis of thyroid-catecholamine-receptor interaction. *Arch. Gen. Psychiat. 38*, 105-113 (1981).

Wilson, I.C., Prange, A.J., Jr., McClane, T.K., Rabon, A.M., and Lipton, M.A. Thyroid hormone enhancement of imipramine in non-retarded depressions. *New Eng. J. Med. 282*, 1063-1067 (1970).

14

Monoamine Precursors in Depression: Present State and Prospects

Herman M. van Praag

RATIONALE FOR THE MONOAMINE-PRECURSOR STRATEGY

Precursors of monoamines (MA) have been applied in depression ever since the introduction of the classical antidepressants in 1958. Yet the number of properly designed studies is surprisingly small. As far as the precursors of serotonin (5-hydroxytryptamine; 5-HT) are concerned, they are marginally sufficient for some cautious conclusions. The number of studies with catecholamine (CA) precursors is even smaller, barely enough for even tentative conclusions.

The therapeutic use of MA precursors in depression was prompted by two sets of observations/deliberations. First, the findings indicative of disturbed metabolism of MA—in particular 5-HT and noradrenaline (NA)—in depression (Review: van Praag, 1982; Baldessarini, 1983). Most findings suggested decreased MA metabolism. They have been interpreted in two ways, first as indicative of a primary decreased MA metabolism leading to diminution of MA-ergic function. The second hypothesis postulates a primary hyperactive MA-ergic system (possibly as a result of hypersensitive postsynaptic MA receptors) leading to compensatory diminution of MA metabolism (Figure 1). Assuming that the MA-ergic dysfunction is causally related to the depressive state, increased MA availability would make sense. According to the first theory this would increase the functional activity of MA systems; according to the latter theory it would down-regulate the hypersensitive postsynaptic MA receptors.

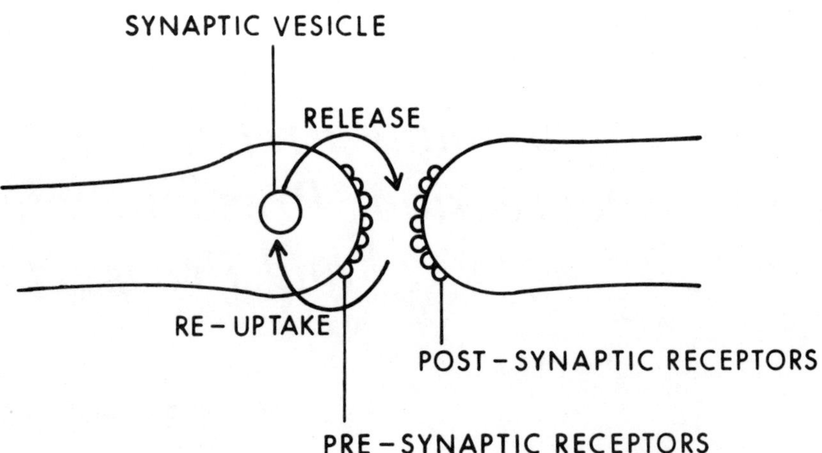

Figure 1. Schematic representation of a 5-HT-ergic neuron. A dynamic equilibrium is assumed to exist between transmitter availability in the synaptic cleft and sensitivity of the postsynaptic receptors. Increased transmitter availability in the synaptic cleft leads to down regulation of the postsynaptic receptor system, decreased transmitter availability to the reverse. Transmitter release is regulated via presynaptic receptors, whose activation by the transmitter decreases the transmitter output.

The second set of observations pertained to the phenomenon of antidepressant-resistant depression. Abundant evidence has accumulated that antidepressants are not equally effective in all types of depression. Most antidepressants are preferentially active in the syndrome of vital depression (van Praag et al., 1965; van Praag, 1978), a syndrome similar to the one described in anglosaxon literature under the heading of endogenous depression. The best fitting DSM III diagnosis is Major Depressive Episode, Melancholic Type. Only the group of the monoamine oxidase (MAO) inhibitors was found to be most active in so-called atypical depression, described mostly in the British literature. The syndrome is atypical in that it differs from the vital/endogenous syndrome, which is apparently considered as a more genuine depression type. This syndrome is roughly similar to the syndrome that has been otherwise named personal (van Praag, 1978), reactive, and neurotic. The closest DSM III diagnosis is Dysthymic Disorder.

Though most antidepressants acted preferentially in vital depression, some 30-40% of patients with this depression type turned out to be unresponsive. The explanation could not be found in pharmacokinetic factors. Another possibility was that the biochemical characteristics of the antidepressant and the biochemical characteristics of the depression did not "fit." In its simplest form: A depression in which 5-HT metabolism is predominantly disturbed would require a 5-HT potentiating compound and could not be expected to benefit substantially from a compound mainly increasing the availability of CA. The reverse would be likely for more "NA-related depressions." Since synthetic drugs with selectivity towards one particular MA only recently became available, MA precursors were resorted to in order to increase the concentration of MA selectivity.

In the following sections I discuss the following issues: (1) Do MA precursors have antidepressant potential? (2) Is their possible antidepressant effect related to signs of disturbed metabolism of a particular MA? (3) Have MA precursors improved prognosis of so-called treatment-resistant depression? (4) Are MA precursors really selective? (5) Is increased selectivity of antidepressants an appropriate goal, or would combined influence on 5-HT- and CA-driven systems provide the best conditions for therapeutic efficacy?

l-TRYPTOPHAN

Outcome

The results with tryptophan in depression are conflicting. In five studies tryptophan was tested against placebo. In two, a parallel placebo group was used (Mendels et al., 1975; Cooper and Datta, 1980); in the others, placebo substitution of tryptophan (Bunney et al., 1971; Murphy et al., 1974; Farkas et al., 1976). In no more than one of these studies tryptophan turned out to be superior to placebo (Murphy et al., 1974), and that only in bipolar, not in unipolar depressives. Tryptophan doses ranged from 3-16 mg/day and were generally high, i.e., ›6 mg/day.

Ten studies compared tryptophan with a tricyclic antidepressant in a double-blind design. In eight, the two compounds were found to be equivalent (Broadhurst, 1970; Coopen et al., 1972; Kline and Shah, 1973; Jensen et al., 1975; Herrington et al., 1976; Rao and Broadhurst, 1976; Chouinard et al., 1979b; Lindberg et al., 1979); in two studies, tryptophan was inferior (Worrall et al., 1979; Linnoila et al., 1980). Two studies report decreasing efficacy of tryptophan after two weeks of treatment (Herrington et al., 1976; Chouinard et al., 1979a).

In the largest and best designed tryptophan study to date, tryptophan (3 mg/day), amitriptyline (150 mg/day), the combination of the two compounds and placebo were compared in a double-blind design (Thomson et al., 1982). A total of 115 mild to moderately depressed out-patients were involved. The great majority were suffering from major depressive disorder according to DSM III criteria. All were treated by general practitioners. Tryptophan and amitriptyline were found to be equipotent and superior to placebo. The combination treatment was superior to either of the compounds alone.

One double-blind study compared tryptophan and the combination of lithium and tryptophan (Worrall et al., 1979). As mentioned, tryptophan showed no antidepressant effect; the combination treatment, however, did. Chouinard et al. 1979a) likewise reported potentiation of the antidepressant effect of lithium by tryptophan, in particular in bipolar patients.

In four open studies, tryptophan was compared to electroconvulsive treatment (ECT). In two of them, tryptophan had no antidepressant effect in contrast to ECT (Carroll et al., 1970; Herrington et al., 1974). One study considered both treatments as equipotent (Coppen et al., 1967). Mac Sweeney's (1975) considered tryptophan superior to ECT. Tryptophan appeared to have no practical value for potentiating the antidepressant efficacy of ECT (d'Elia et al., 1977; Kirkegaard et al., 1978).

The four controlled studies in which tryptophan or placebo were combined with a MAO inhibitor all found tryptophan to be superior in potentiating the antidepressant response (Coppen et al., 1963; Pare, 1963; Glassman and Platman, 1969; Ayuso Gutierrez and Lopez-Ibor Alino, 1971). The combination studies with tricyclics, on the other hand, are inconclusive. In three, no potentiation was found (Lopez-Ibor Alino et al., 1973; Chouinard et al., 1979a; Shaw et al., 1975); in two, tryptophan seemed to be better than placebo (Walinder et al., 1976; Walinder et al., 1981). The selective 5-HT reuptake inhibitor zimelidine was found not to be potentiated by tryptophan (Walinder et al., 1981; Walinder et al., 1983).

Conclusions

The difference in outcome of the placebo- and the antidepressant-controlled tryptophan studies is striking. It is not unlikely that the generally small sample size was a contributing factor. In 6 out of 8 studies, less than 20 patients were involved. Since (1) approximately 25% of potentially antidepressant-responsive patients are apt to respond to placebo as well and (2) the percentage of antidepressant-responders in the group of vital depression is not greater than approximately 60-65%, in small samples a possible difference in therapeutic potential between two substances would easily be blurred.

Adding tryptophan to a MAO inhibitor seems to potentiate their therapeutic efficacy. It should be noted, however, that this combination entails the risk of psychotic-LSD-like side reactions (van Praag, 1962). The results of combination treatment with tricyclic antidepressants tend to be inconclusive. Why MAO inhibitors and tricyclics differ in this respect is unclear.

Possible Explanations for the Conflicting Therapeutic Results

Assuming that the observed indications of a central 5-HT deficit in certain forms of depression have causal significance, the tryptophan results are rather unexpected. Tryptophan, after all, leads to increased 5-HT synthesis in 5-HT-ergic neurons, the only locus of tryptophan hydroxylase, i.e., the first and rate-limiting enzyme in the synthesis of 5-HT. This is clear in animals and likely in humans since, in the latter, tryptophan administration leads to substantial increase in probenecid-induced 5-HIAA accumulation in CSF. 5-HIAA is the main degradation product of 5-HT. Accumulation of 5-HIAA in CSF after probenecid is an indicator of 5-HT metabolism in the CNS (Review: van Praag, 1977a).

A possible explanation of the equivocal results may lie in the fact that very few studies have measured 5-HT related variables before treatment and correlated them with treatment outcome. The group of Møller et al. (Review: Møller et al., 1983) did and found evidence that depressed patients with low plasma ratio of tryptophan/competing amino acids (CAA) are more responsive to tryptophan treatment than those who show a tryptophan/CAA ratio in the upper normal range. They also found indications that some depressives show elevated plasma levels of CAA which might be attributed to disturbed plasma clearance of these compounds. Decreased tryptophan/CAA ratio would lead to decreased transport of tryptophan from the bloodstream into the CNS (Wurtman, 1982) (Figure 2). Decreased availability of CNS tryptophan will reduce the synthesis rate of 5-HT. It is not known if and how low tryptophan/CAA plasma ratio relates to other signs of disordered 5-HT metabolism as have been found in depression.

It is conceivable that the so-called 5-HT deficient subgroup of vital (endogenous) depression is preferentially responsive to tryptophan and that failure to make this differentiation has blurred the potential therapeutic value of this compound.

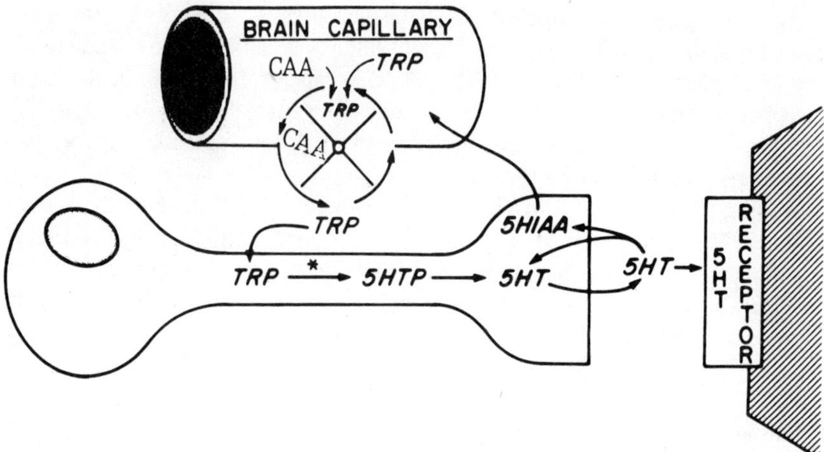

Figure 2. The so-called neutral amino acids compete for the same transport mechanism from plasma to CNS. These competing amino acids (CAA) are: tryptophan, tyrosine, valine, leucine, isoleucine, and phenylalanine. Since the carrier is satiable, the ratio tryptophan/CCA and tyrosine/CCA determines the influx of tryptophan and tyrosine in the CNS. The CNS availability of those amino acids is an important regulator of 5-HT and catecholamine synthesis respectively (adapted from Fernstrom, 1982).

A second possible explanation is inadequacy of the tryptophan dosage. Around 98% of tryptophan is metabolized in the liver (Hagen and Cohen, 1966). This metabolism, down the so-called kynurenine pathway, is initiated by the enzyme tryptophan pyrrolase, which is induced by its substrate tryptophan (Knox and Auerbach, 1955) (Figure 3). As a result, the amount of tryptophan available for 5-HT synthesis is very small indeed. The effect of the kynurenine-shunt gets even more pronounced if large quantities of tryptophan are administered. Under such circumstances the plasma level of kynurenine is raised substantially and kynurenine competes with tryptophan for transport into the brain (Green and Curzon, 1970). Plasma cortisol, often elevated in depression, causes induction of tryptophan pyrrolase in the liver (Green and Curzon, 1968; Green et al., 1976; Green and Aronson, 1983). This will further detract from the efficiency of a tryptophan dose to raise brain 5-HT. Consistent with this interpretation, Singleton and Marsden (1979) found that the rise in brain tryptophan in mice seen after 3 days on a high tryptophan diet had largely disappeared by the 18th day on such a diet.

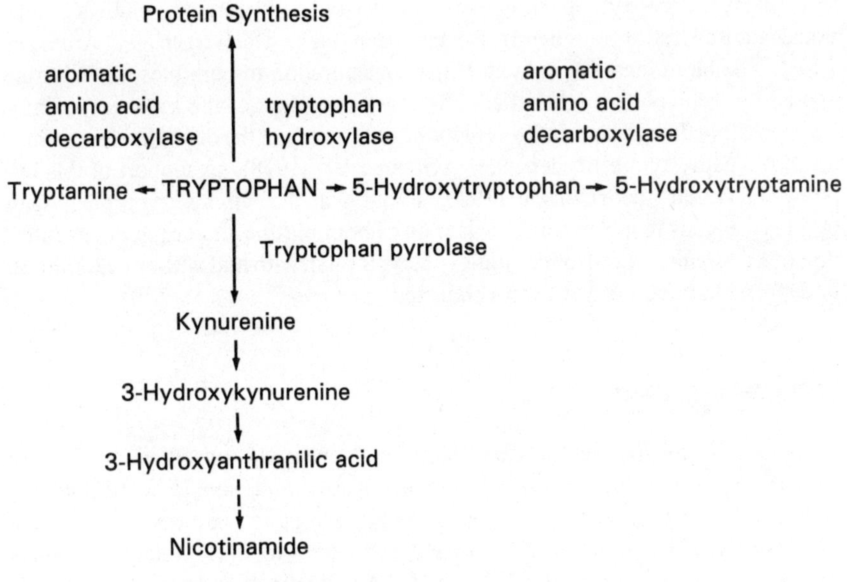

Figure 3. Schematic representation of tryptophan metabolism.

Conceivably, high doses of tryptophan can work against the aim of its administration, i.e., raising brain 5-HT. Another counterproductive mechanism could possibly be at work. The amino acids competing with tryptophan for the same carrier mechanism into the brain are tyrosine, leucine, isoleucine, valine, and phenylalanine. Raising plasma tryptophan and kynurenine can be assumed to diminish tyrosine transport into the brain (Wurtman, 1982) (Figure 3). Diminished availability of tyrosine will reduce CA synthesis. According to the CA hypothesis of depression, this constitutes a depressogenic factor.

Tryptophan dose, therefore, seems to be a critical issue. Too little, as well as too much, will fail to increase brain 5-HT sufficiently. Moreover, too much could initiate depressogenic mechanisms.

In order to circumvent the kynurenine pathway, the combined administration of tryptophan and a pyrrolase inhibitor—such as allopurinol or nicotinamide—has been suggested. Both compounds have been used in conjunction with tryptophan (Shopsin, 1978; McSweeney, 1975; Chouinard et al. 1979b), but since a tryptophan/placebo group was lacking, the usefulness of these compounds were not really clarified.

To decrease the tryptophan-depleting effect of the kynurenine pathway additional administration of vitamin B6 has been suggested (Green and Aronson, 1983). The large increase in kynurenine concentration in both plasma and urine caused by tryptophan might reflect a relative saturation of the kynurenine pathway, possibly due to vitamin B6 depletion, since many of the degradative enzymes down the pathway are B6-dependent (Green et al., 1978). In support of this hypothesis, Green and Aronson (1983) found that combining tryptophan with pyridoxine leads to a substantial reduction of both plasma and urinary concentration of kynurenine. Controlled studies of tryptophan with and without vitamin B6 in depression have not yet been conducted.

Conclusion

The status of tryptophan in depression treatment is still unsettled. In order to solve the issue, in future research the following conditions should be fulfilled: (1) large enough sample size, (2) careful patient classification in terms of syndrome and severity, (3) correlation of treatment outcome with 5-HT related variables measured before treatment (e.g., CSF 5-HIAA and ratio of tryptophan/CAA), (4) monitoring of plasma ratio tryptophan/CAA and kynurenine during treatment.

Finally it would seem to make sense to study whether combining tryptophan with a pyrrolase inhibitor, viamin B6, or tyrosine will increase its efficacy.

Prophylactic Value of Tryptophan

There is some scattered data that suggests tryptophan to be of prophylactic value in depression (Chouinard et al. 1979; Beitman and Dunner 1982). No systematic study has been undertaken.

l-5-HYDROXYTRYPTOPHAN (5-HTP)

Therapeutic Applications

In 1963, Kline and Sacks reported antidepressant effects produced by a single intravenous injection of small amounts of *dl*-5-HTP in patients under treatment with a MAO inhibitor. However, they were subsequently unable to confirm this observation (Kline et al., 1964).

In the late sixties we started systematic studies of *l*-5-HTP in depression. Before using the precursor therapeutically, we made the following preliminary observations (Review: van Praag, 1977a). (1) Oral 5-HTP increased the probenecid-induced accumulation of 5-hydroxyindoleacetic (5-HIAA) in CSF. The accumlation of 5-HIAA in CSF after probenecid is a crude indication of 5-HT metabolism in the brain. (2) Depressed patients with diminished CSF 5-HIAA accumulation after probenecid are able to transform 5-HTP to 5-HT. This was concluded from the observation that an oral 5-HTP load increased CSF 5-HIAA accumulation after probenecid to the same degree in patients with normal and those with subnormal 5-HIAA response to probenecid. (3) In rat brain 5-HTP is transformed into 5-HT at least in part in 5-HT ergic neurons (Korf et al., 1974). (4) Combination of 5-HTP with a peripheral decarboxylase inhibitor greatly enhances its efficiency (Westenberg et al., 1982).

In several double-blind studies, controlled with placebo (van Praag et al., 1972; van Praag, 1979) and/or tricyclic antidepressant (van Praag, 1979), we demonstrated 5-HTP in combination with a peripheral decarboxylase inhibitor superior to a placebo and equipotent to a tricyclic antidepressant. The combination of 5-HTP and a tricyclic was superior to either compound alone (Figure 4). Those who had a subnormal CSF 5-HIAA response to probenecid before treatment responded preferentially to 5-HTP (Figure 5). Several uncontrolled and controlled studies (Review: van Praag, 1981) confirmed our therapeutic findings. The study relating pretreatment CSF 5-HIAA to treatment outcome has not yet been replicated.

Three studies (one open, two placebo-controlled) have so far yielded negative results. The open study (Takahashi et al., 1976) focused on brief therapy (7 days) with small doses of 5-HTP. The study of Brodie et al., (1973) was placebo-controlled but concerned only 7 patients, who likewise were treated (too) briefly (1-15 days). Mendlewicz and Youdim (1980) compared the antidepressant effects of three medications: a MAO inhibitor combined with 5-HTP, 5-HTP alone, and a placebo. The combined therapy was superior to that with the placebo. The effect of 5-HTP alone did not significantly differ from that obtained with the combination. Nevertheless, the difference between 5-HTP and the placebo was not significant. The possible explanation is that (a) the groups studied were small, and (b) the number of responders in the placebo group was unusually large.

Few antidepressants have so far been tested in combination with 5-HTP. The therapeutic effect of the tricyclic antidepressant clomipramine is potentiated by *l*-5-HTP in combination with carbidopa (van Praag et al., 1974; van Praag, 1979) and by 5-HTP alone (Nardini et al., 1983). Some striking results have been obtained with this combination in therapy-resistant vital depressions (van Praag et al., 1974). No other tricyclic antidepressant has so far been tested in combination with 5-HTP.

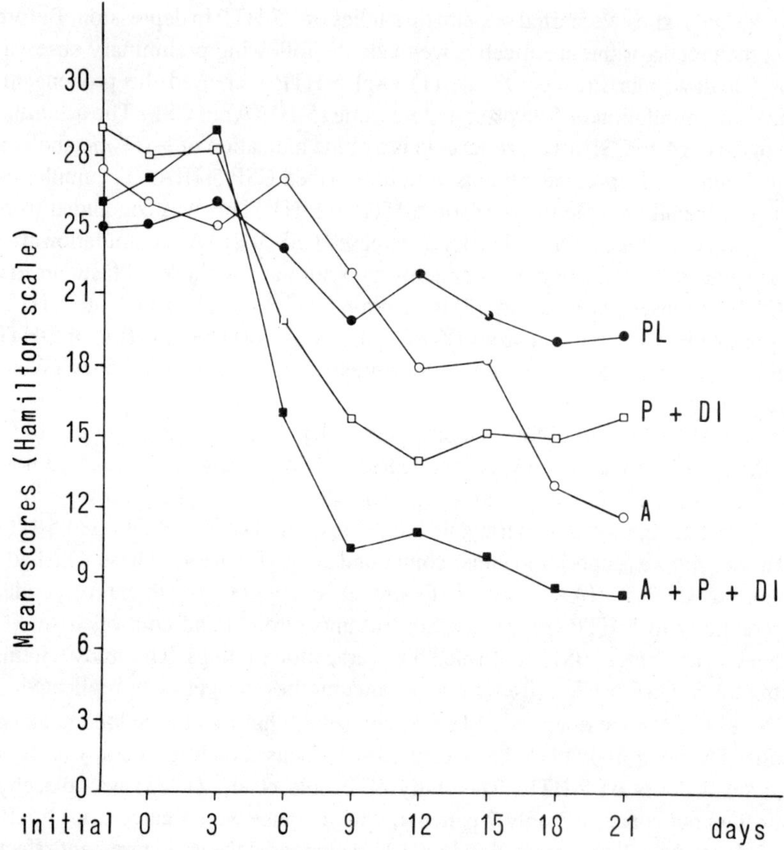

Figure 4. Hamilton scores in 4 groups of 10 patients suffering from vital depression with uni- and bipolar course, before and during a 3-week treatment period with 5-HT potentiating compounds. The groups consisted of 10 patients each, treated, respectively with clomipramine (225 mg per day, A), *l*-5-HTP (P, 200 mg per day, in combination with 150 mg MK 486, a peripheral decarboxylase inhibitor: DI), combination of clomipramine with 5-HTP (A+P+DI) and placebo (PL). The design was double-blind.

Two compounds of the group of MAO inhibitors have been tested in this context: nialamide and clorgyline. The effect of the former is potentiated by 5-HTP (Lopez-Ibor Alino et al., 1976). Mendlewicz and Youdim (1980) found that clorgyline in combination with 5-HTP is more effective than 5-HTP alone and than placebo. A group of patients given clorgyline alone was not included in the design. Strictly speaking, therefore, the conclusion that 5-HTP potentiates the MAO inhibitor is not warranted.

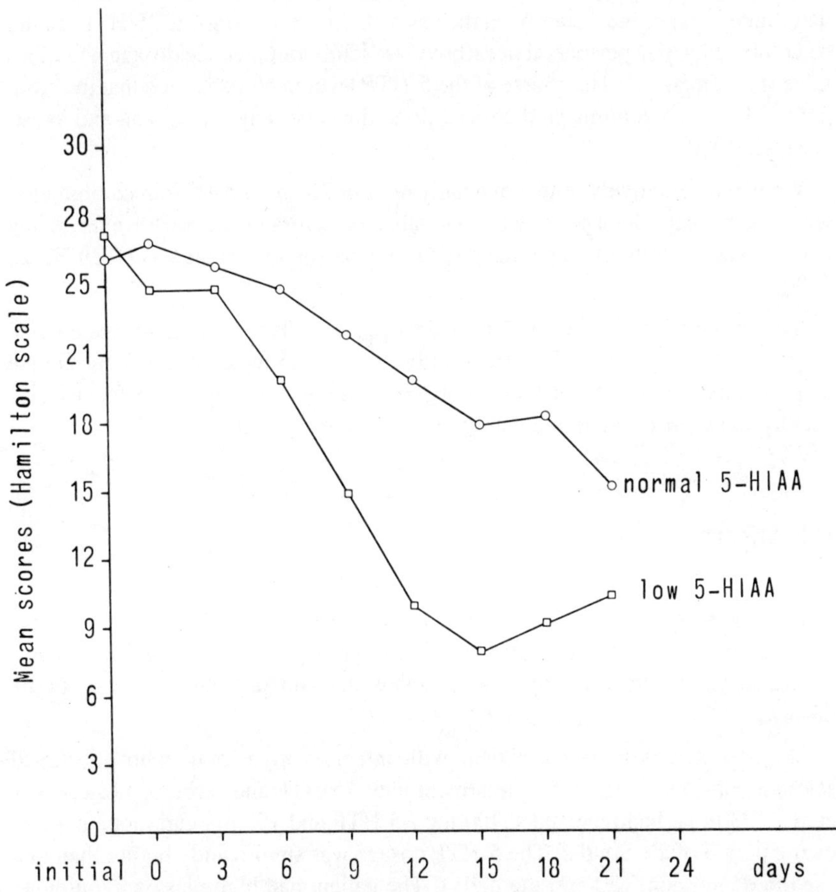

Figure 5. Hamilton scores of 30 patients suffering from vital depression with uni- and bipolar course before and during a 3-week treatment period with 5-HT potentiating compounds, i.e., clomipramine alone, *l*-5-HTP (together with a peripheral decarboxylase inhibitor) alone, and those drugs in combination. The lower curve depicts treatment results in patients with subnormal pretreatment 5-HIAA response to probenecid (n±13), the upper curve depicts results for patients with normal pretreatment 5-HIAA responses (n±17).

Dosage

Different dosages were used in the various 5-HTP studies and, consequently, it is not yet possible to give firm guidelines on dosage. Only the following points were established with certainty: (1) A given dosage scheme leads to widely different blood 5-HTP levels in different subjects. Since nothing is known as yet about a minimum (and possibly a maximum) therapeutic dose, this makes it necessary to determine dosages individually on the basis of clinical findings. (2) 5-HTP should be combined with a peripheral decarboxylase inhibitor to reduce dosage and minimize side effects. (3) The course of the 5-HTP level in blood is such that the compound should be administered at least three times per day (van Praag and Westenberg, 1983).

We would tentatively hold that a daily dose of 200 mg *l*-5-HTP in combination with 150 mg carbidopa per day is acceptable as a gross average. However, many patients can do with less, and many require more (up to 500 mg/day) (van Hiele, 1980).

It is advisable to increase the 5-HTP dosage gradually in order to reduce the risk of gastrointestinal side effects. We usually start with 25 mg daily and in the course of 10-14 days increase to an average of 200 mg daily. A therapeutic effect (if any) usually does not occur immediately but only after 5-20 days.

Side Effects

The only side effects of practical importance are gastrointestinal: nausea, vomiting, and diarrhea (Review: Sourkes, 1983). These effects are dose-dependent. Tolerance can be improved by coating tablets and using a gradual build-up of the dosage.

The literature describes a patient with intention myoclonus who developed scleroderma-like illness during treatment with *l*-5-HTP and carbidopa (Sternberg et al., 1980); he had received 1,400 mg *l*-5-HTP and 150 mg carbidopa per day over a period of 20 months. The 5-HTP dosage was significantly higher than that used in depressions (50-500 mg daily). The patient had high plasma kynurenine levels, which remained high when the 5-HTP/carbidopa combination was discontinued. However, the levels rose further upon drug rechallenge, suggesting that the drug unmasked an abnormality of one of the enzymes that catabolize kynurenine. Scleroderma-like syndromes have been associated with disorders of both the kynurenine and the 5-HT pathways of tryptophan metabolism.

Conclusions

The number of controlled studies comparing 5-HTP with a placebo or with a standard antidepressant is still small. A final evaluation is, therefore, not yet possible. The results obtained so far, however, indicate the likelihood that 5-HTP has antidepressant properties and that the combination of 5-HTP with clomipramine or with the MAO inhibitors nialamide and clorgyline is superior in effect than either of these substances separately. Whether this potentiating effect also applies to other tricyclic compounds and MAO inhibitors remains to be established. In any case, this combined medication merits consideration in depressions of the vital (endogenous) group that show an insufficient response to traditional antidepressants.

Two other observations likewise indicate an influence of 5-HTP on mood: 5-HTP was found to have a euphoric effect on normal test subjects (Trimble et al., 1975; Puhringe et al., 1976). When used as a therapeutic in myoclonus patients (van Woert et al., 1977; Thal et al., 1980), 5-HTP was found to cause (hypo)manic disinhibition as a side effect.

The principal side effects of 5-HTP are gastrointestinal. They can be largely avoided by giving 5-HTP (a) in coated tablets, (b) in combination with a peripheral decarboxylase inhibitor, or (c) in accordance with a gradually increasing dosage scheme, respectively.

Considering group averages, 5-HTP can be described as roughly equal in therapeutic efficacy to traditional antidepressants. Should the observation that the low 5-HIAA subgroup of vital depressions preferentially responds to 5-HTP (van Praag 1978, 1979) be confirmed, then the net yield of 5-HTP therapy could probably be increased by determining the (post-probenecid) 5-HIAA accumulation in CSF in advance. It is not yet known whether peripheral 5-HT related variables do or do not correlate with probenecid-induced 5-HIAA accumulation in CSF.

Prophylactic Use of 5-HTP

So far only one prophylactic study has been conducted in which 5-HTP and placebo were compared in a double-blind cross-over design (van Praag and de Haan, 1980). Three observations prompted this study. First the demonstration that low post-probenecid CSF 5-HIAA is state-independent in a majority of patients (van Praag, 1977b). Moreover, we demonstrated that the low 5-HIAA subgroup of vital (endogenous) depression had an increased relapse risk (van Praag and de Haan, 1979). Finally, low CSF 5-HIAA was shown to correlate with increased depressive morbidity in the family (Sedvall et al., 1980). Those data suggested low CSF 5-HIAA to be a depression-predisposing factor. If that were so, increasing 5-HT availability in the CNS could be expected to have a prophylactic effect.

The study of van Praag and de Haan (1980) confirmed this prediction. 5-HIAA (in combination with a peripheral decarboxylase inhibitor) turned out to be superior to placebo (Table 1) and equipotent to lithium in unipolar vital depression. In bipolar depression, 5-HTP seemed inferior to lithium, probably because it did not prevent (hypo)manic episodes, and in fact might have even provoked them (van Praag and de Haan, 1981).

TABLE 1. Patients with Unipolar and Bipolar Vital Depression and High Relapse Rate Given 1 Year of 5-HTP Medication (with a Peripheral Decarboxylase Inhibitor) and 1 Year of Placebo Medication (van Praag and De Haan, 1980)

	Number of test subjects[a]	Number of patients who developed relapses		Number of relapses	
		Placebo period	5-HTP period	Placebo period	5-HTP period
Group A[b]	10	9	3	14	3
Group B[c]	10	8	3	10	4

[a]The number of patients who relapsed and the total number of relapses were significantly larger during the placebo than during the 5-HTP periods.
[b]One year of 5-HTP medication followed by 1 year of placebo medication.
[c]One year of placebo medication followed by 1 year of 5-HTP medication.

So far this study has not been replicated. If confirmed, 5-HTP prophylaxis would be the first form of aimed chemoprophylaxis in psychiatry. "Aimed" is to say: aimed at a suspected pathogenetic factor in certain types of vital depression.

COMPARISON OF 5-HTP AND TRYPTOPHAN IN DEPRESSION

Therapeutic Comparison

The data on tryptophan in depression seem to be more ambiguous than those on 5-HTP. We, therefore, felt a comparative study to be indicated. This is the first comparative study of the two 5-HT precursors (van Praag, 1984).

Forty-five patients were involved whose characteristics are summarized in Table 2. They were treated for 4 weeks with either tryptophan (5 g per day), 5-HTP (200 mg/day) in combination with the peripheral decarboxylase inhibitor carbidopa (150 mg/day) or placebo.

TABLE 2. Comparability of the Patients Participating in the Comparative Tryptophan/5-HTP/Placebo Study (van Praag, 1984)

	Tryptophan	5-HTP	Placebo
Severity (Hamilton)	26 ° 6	25 ° 5	23 ° 5
Precipitated/nonprecipitated	10/15	12/15	9/15
First episode/unipolar/bipolar	3/9/3	2/8/5	4/8/3
Male/female	4/11	6/9	4/11
Age	21-64	19-62	24-63

Tryptophan was found to be slightly better than placebo but not significantly so. 5-HTP on the other hand was superior to both placebo and tryptophan (Figure 6).

Biochemical Comparison

We were interested in the possible cause of the therapeutic discrepancy between the two 5-HT precursors. One possible explanation is that they influence catecholamine (CA) metabolism differently. Indeed, in animals 5-HTP has been demonstrated to increase the metabolism not only of 5-HT but also of dopamine (DA) and noradrenaline (NA) (Awazi and Goldberg, 1978; Everett, 1979). The possible reason is that 5-HTP is transformed in 5-HT not only in 5-HT-ergic neurons but in CA-ergic neurons as well. This "ectopical" 5-HT could act as a false transmitter, with increase of CA production as a compensatory consequence. Tryptophan failed to exert this effect supposedly because tryptophan hydroxylase, in contrast to 5-HTP decarboxylase (= DOPA decarboxylase) is only present in 5-HT-ergic neurons. We found evidence that the same difference seems to occur in humans (van Praag, 1983). Both after single and chronic administration, oral 5-HTP increased 5-HIAA and the CA metabolites homovanillic acid (HVA) and 3-methoxy-4-hydroxyphenylglycol (MHPG) in CSF (Figure 7). Tryptophan increased CSF 5-HIAA but failed to have an influence on CA metabolites both after single and longer term administration (Figure 8).

A second set of data support the notion that it could be the stimulating effect on both 5-HT *and* CA that gives 5-HTP a therapeutic edge over tryptophan. In the 15 years we have been studying 5-HTP in depression, we observed that in some 20% of patients who respond initially, the therapeutic effect wears off after the first month of treatment (although seldom to the point of complete relapse). This effect could not be explained by pharmacokinetic factors. The 5-HTP plasma levels remained stable over time.

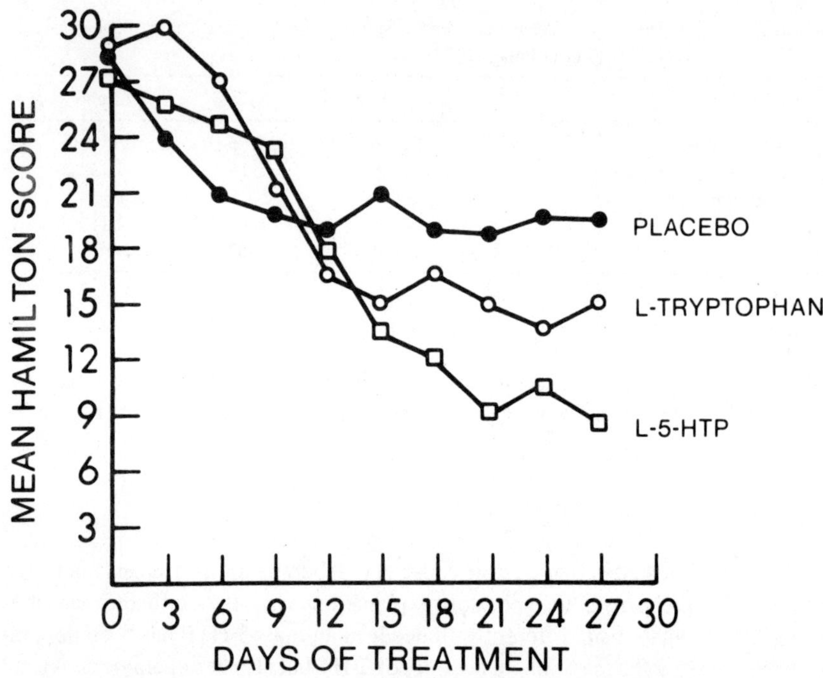

Figure 6. Comparative, controlled study of *l*-5-HTP (200 mg/day) in combination with carbidopa (150 mg/day), *l*-tryptophan (5 g/day) and placebo in patients suffering from the syndrome of vital (endogenous) depression. 5-HTP is significantly superior to tryptophan and placebo. Tryptophan treatment is not significantly different from placebo treatment.

Next we studied whether the influence of 5-HTP on central MA metabolism changes over time (van Praag, 1983; 1984). In two independent studies we demonstrated that while in the first month of 5-HTP treatment, CSF concentration of both 5-HT, DA and NA metabolites are increased, the situation in the second month of treatment is different. CSF 5-HIAA remains elevated; however, the concentrations of the CA metabolites return to pretreatment values. In particular this was the case in the patients who (partially) relapsed in the second month of 5-HTP treatment (Figure 9).

On the basis of these observations, we hypothesized that (1) the antidepressant effect of 5-HTP is based on its combined effect on 5-HT and CA metabolism; (2) the diminution of 5-HTP's effects on CA after the first month is responsible for the partial relapse one might observe after the first month of 5-HTP treatment; (3) the

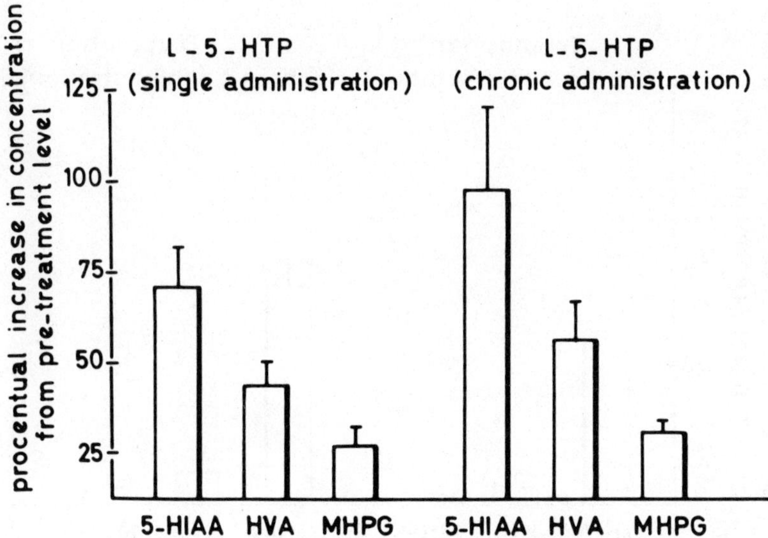

Figure 7. Percent increase in the concentrations of 5-HIAA, HVA, and MHPG in lumber CSF after administration to test subjects of a single dose of *l*-5-HTP (200 mg orally) and after administration of the same dose for a week. In the acute experiment, the patients were pretreated with carbidopa 150 mg/day, for 3 days. In the chronic experiment, *l*-5-HTP was combined with carbidopa in the same dose. In all cases the increase in concentration in relation to the medication-free period was significant. The lumbar CSF was withdrawn after probenecid loading (5 g/5 hour), 8 hr after starting the load.

inferior therapeutic effects of tryptophan in comparison to 5-HTP is related to the inability of the former to increase CA metabolism.

L-TYROSINE

Up to the present time no more than four controlled studies with tyrosine in depression have been published. Negligence of tyrosine was due to the erroneous notion that tyrosine-hydroxylase was completely saturated. In recent years, it was demonstrated that, under certain conditions, an extra supply of tyrosine definitely can increase the catecholamine (CA) synthesis (Wurtman et al., 1974; Scally et al., 1977).

Gelenberg et al. (1982) conducted a double-blind, placebo-controlled study in 14 patients with major depressive disorder. Tyrosine was given for 4 weeks, in a

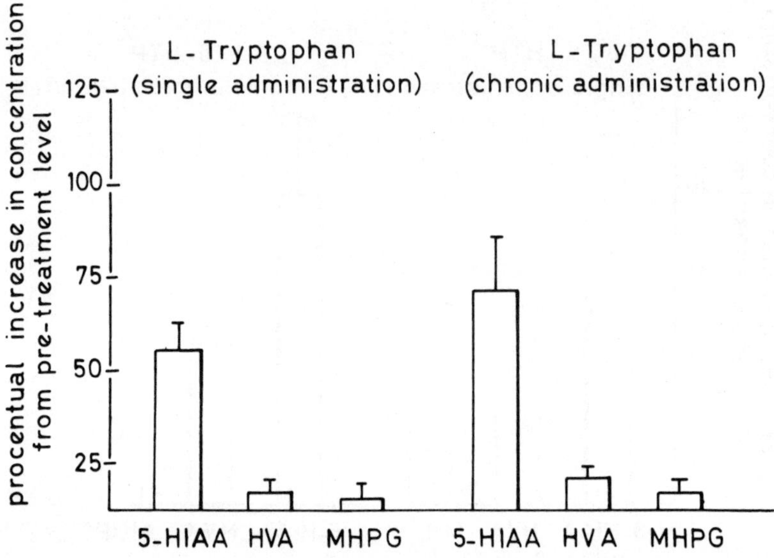

Figure 8. Percent increase in the concentrations of 5-HIAA, HVA, and MHPG in lumbar CSF after administration to test subjects of a single dose of *l*-tryptophan (5 g orally) and after administration of the same dose for a week. In all cases the increase in 5-HIAA concentration in relation to the medication-free period was significant. Changes in post-probenecid HVA and baseline MHPG were insignificant. The lumbar CSF was withdrawn after probenecid loading (5 g/5 hr), 8 hr after starting the load.

dose of 100mg/kg/day. Five placebo nonresponders were likewise treated with tyrosine in an open trial. Although the numbers were too small for more definitive conclusions, the results were considered to be encouraging (Table 3). Urinary MHPG excretion increased an average of 24%. The increase of fasting plasma tyrosine averaged 27%. A trend toward positive correlation between improvement and rise in plasma tyrosine was noted.

Van Praag (1983) reported 2 studies in which 5-HTP was combined with tyrosine. The rationale for the studies has been described in the preceding paragraph. Briefly, it was observed that the effect of 5-HTP on CA metabolism tended to decline over time in some patients and that this "habituation" was possibly related to diminishing antidepressant efficacy of 5-HTP. Accordingly, (re)-augmentation of CA metabolism could be expected to be beneficial.

So far, two small pilot experiments have been carried out. In one, four patients

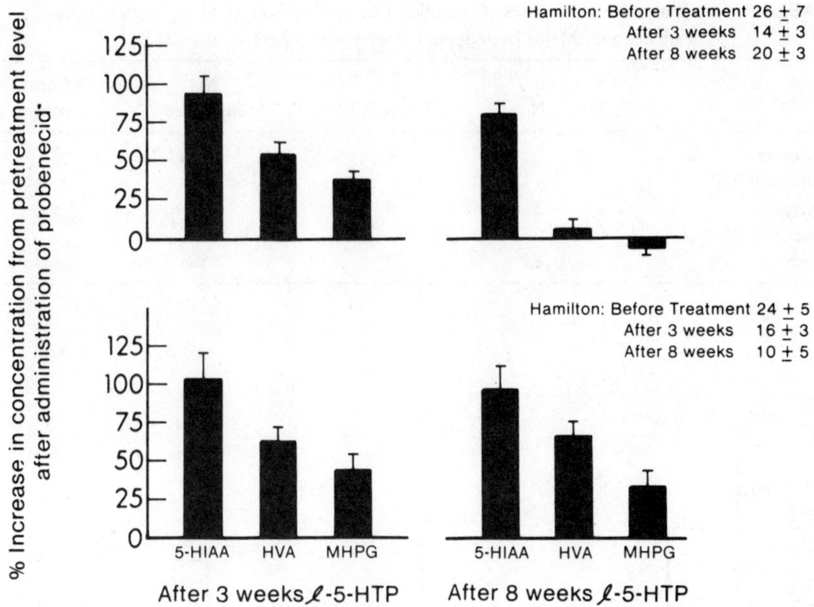

Figure 9. Concentrations of 5-HIAA, HVA, and MHPG in CSF after probenecid loading in 5 patients who continue to improve on 5-HTP treatment and in 5 patients who showed a (partial) relapse after the first month of 5-HTP treatment. In the first group MA metabolite concentrations are increased both in the first and second month of 5-HTP treatment. In the latter group, the concentration of all three metabolites is increased in the first month. In the second month, however, the CA metabolites had returned to pretreatment levels, whereas the 5-HIAA concentration remained elevated.

who had relapsed in the second month of 5-HTP treatment were treated, in addition, with either placebo or tyrosine in a cross-over design. In all four patients, adding tyrosine coincided with a remission. This was not the case with placebo (Figure 10). The second experiment was a two-group experiment in which the treatment consisted of either 5-HTP and tyrosine or 5-HTP and placebo. The first combination was superior to the latter.

Although the size of the studies is too small for definite conclusions, both findings point in the same direction, i.e., potentiation of the antidepressant effect of 5-HTP by tyrosine.

Finally, van Praag and Lemus (1985) provided evidence that the addition of l-tyrosine raises l-tryptophan to the level of an effective antidepressant.

TABLE 3. Double-Blind, 4-Week, Controlled Placebo/Tyrosine (100 mg/kg/day) Study in 14 Patients with Major Depressive Disorder (Gelenberg et al., 1982)

	N	Improved	Not Improved	Percent Improved
Tyrosine (double-blind)	6	4	2	67
Tyrosine (open)	5	3	2	60
Placebo	8	3	5	38

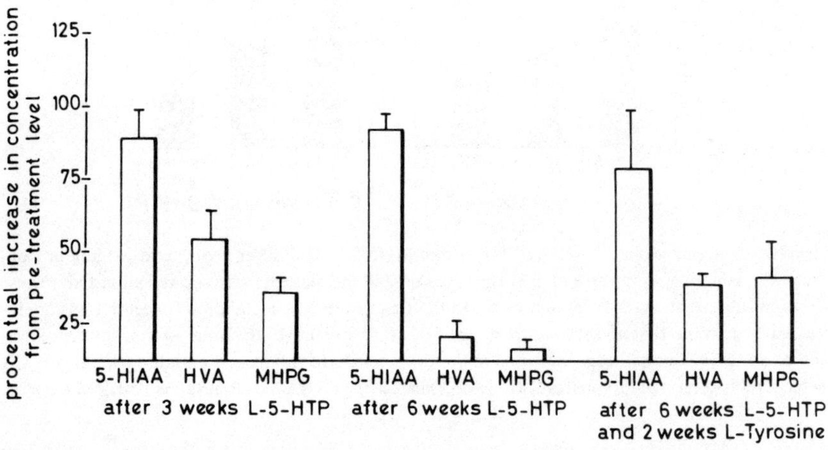

Figure 10. Four patients with vital depression ((two) unipolars and (two) bipolars) were treated with *l*-5-HTP (200 mg/day) and carbidopa (150 mg/day). After an initial therapeutic response, the efficacy diminished in the second month of treatment. The partial relapse coincided with normalization of post-probenecid CSF, HVA, and MHPG. CSF 5-HIAA remained elevated. Adding tyrosine to the therapeutic regime led to (1) clinical remission and (2) increase of post-probenecid CSF, HVA, and MHPG.

L-DOPA

If peripherally administered, this CA precursor is predominantly transformed into dopamine (DA) in the CNS. The number of DOPA studies in depressives is very small (Goodwin et al., 1970; van Praag, 1974; van Praag and Korf, 1975).

Their conclusions are quite similar. DOPA in depressives is better than placebo. It increases motor activity and drive, in particular when those functions are diminished as in retarded depression, but seems to have little effect on mood.

We studied DOPA in depressed patients of which five were selected for subnormal response of CSF homovanillic acid (HVA) to probenecid, while in the other five this response was normal. This selection criterion was chosen because we had demonstrated that motor retardation in depression strongly correlates with low post-probenecid CSF HVA. Post-probenecid CSF HVA is an indicator of DA metabolism in the CNS.

Again, it was found that motor retardation was most pronounced in the low HVA group. The therapeutic (activating) effect of DOPA was evident only in the low HVA group. Under the influence of DOPA post-probenecid CSF HVA rose to (high) normal values (Table 4).

TABLE 4. DA Metabolism Before Treatment and Treatment Response to L-Dopa in Depression (van Praag and Korf, 1975)

Patients	N	HVA accumulation (ng/ml)[a]	Motor retardation[a]	
			Before treatment	After treatment
DA-deficient	5	74 (65-90)	6.8 (4-8)	2.7 (0-3)
Non-DA-deficient	5	121 (107-143)	2.1 (0-3)	2.4 (0-3)

[a]Group mean and range.

The *conclusion* seems justified that DOPA can have therapeutic value in (retarded) depression and that its potential has been underestimated and underanalyzed.

SUMMARY AND CONCLUSIONS

5-HT precursors seem to have therapeutic potential in depression, presumably in particular if the vital (endogenous) symptomatology is prominent. The data are most unequivocal for 5-HTP, more controversial for tryptophan.

In the only controlled comparative study of both 5-HT precursors, 5-HTP was superior to placebo, tryptophan was not. Two possible reasons for the discrepancy have been discussed: (1) By decreasing the plasma tyrosine/CAA ratio tryptophan decreases tyrosine entrance in the CNS and with that CA synthesis. By increasing plasma kynurenine tryptophan decreases its own entrance in the CNS and, by that, 5-HT synthesis. Those effects could detract from tryptophan's therapeutic efficacy. (2) 5-HTP increases not only 5-HT metabolism but CA metabolism as well. Tryptophan lacks the latter effect, which is likely to contribute to its lesser antidepressant potential.

If these considerations are valid, study of the combination of tryptophan and tyrosine would make sense, while monitoring plasma levels of competing amino acids and kynurenine, i.e., substances competing for the same carrier system into the CNS. The first tryptophan/tyrosine combination study yielded positive results.

The therapeutic effect of 5-HTP sometimes wears off in the second month of treatment. This effect is possibly related to normalization of the initially increased CA turnover. Combination of 5-HTP and a CA precursor such as tyrosine, therefore, seems to be a sensible measure. Preliminary data seem to confirm this theoretical notion.

Another way to increase the yield of 5-HT precursor treatment seems to be a differentiation of patients in those with and those without signs of disturbed central 5-HT metabolism, under the assumption that the former category will be preferentially responsive. Very few studies of that kind have been conducted, using post-probenecid CSF 5-HIAA accumulation and plasma ratio tryptophan/CAA as 5-HT indicators. The results are promising in that these 5-HT related variables indeed seem to predict treatment outcome. These studies should be repeated and extended.

The number of 5-HT precursor studies in depression is still small. In other words, the subject has been insufficiently studied. The available data do not justify this negligence.

The data on CA precursors in depression are even more scanty. Yet the data on DOPA are unanimous. DOPA improves motor activity and drive and normalizes post-probenecid CSF HVA in retarded endogenous depression. The effect on mood, per se, seems to be slight. The possible practical value of this drive-increasing substance as a supplement to antidepressant medication has been underestimated.

Tyrosine is represented with no more than four small controlled studies. The preliminary data are interesting. In one study, tyrosine turned out to be better than placebo; in the three others, it potentiated the antidepressant effect of 5-HTP and tryptophan. Likewise, there is every reason to study this CA precursor in more depth for its therapeutic potential in depressive disorders.

With the probable exception of 5-HTP, the practical value of MA precursors in depression treatment is still uncertain. The question whether they have something special to offer vis-à-vis the traditional antidepressants is likewise unanswerable. My guess is that they have. Chemical subtyping of depression and tailoring antidepressant treatment accordingly, is a logical lead for future research and could result in "de-resistization" of so-called treatment-resistant depression. MA precursors, alone or in combination, seem to be appropriate ingredients to compose such "tailor-made" treatments.

REFERENCES

Awazi, N., and Goldberg, H.C. On the interaction of 5-hydroxytryptophan and 5-hydroxytryptamine with dopamine metabolism in rat striatum. *Naunyn-Schmeidebergs Arch. Pharmac. 303,* 63-72 (1978).

Ayuso Guttierrez, J.L., and Lopez-Ibor Alino, J.J. Tryptophan and an MAOI (Nialamide) in the treatment of depression. A double-blind study. *Internat. Pharmacopsychiat. 6,* 92-97 (1971).

Baldessarini, R.J. *Biomedical Aspects of Depression.* American Press, New York, (1983).

Beitman, B.D., and Dunner, D.L. L-Tryptophan in the maintenance treatment of bipolar II main-depressive illness. *Amer. J. Psychiat. 139,* 1498-1499 (1982).

Broadhurst, A.D. L-Tryptophan versus ECT. *Lancet i,* 1392-1393 (1970).

Brodie, H.K.H., Sack, R., and Siever, L. Clinical studies of *l*-5-hydroxytryptophan in depression, in *Serotonin and Behavior,* J. Barchas and E. Usdin, eds. Academic Press, New York, pp. 549-559 (1973).

Bunney, W.E., Brodie, H.K., Murphy, D.L., and Goodwin, F.K. Studies of alpha-methyl-para-tyrosine, L-dopa, and L-tryptophan in depression and mania. *Amer. J. Psychiat. 127,* 872-881 (1971).

Carroll, B.J., Mowbray, R.M., and Davies, B. Sequential comparison of L-tryptophan with ECT in severe depression. *Lancet i,* 967-969 (1970).

Chouinard, G., Jones, B.D., Young, S.N., and Annable, L. Potentiation of lithium by tryptophan in a patient with bipolar illness. *Amer. J. Psychiat. 136,* 719-720 (1979a).

Chouinard, G., Young, S.N., Annable, L., and Sourkes, T.L. Tryptophan-nicotinamide, imipramine and their combination in depression. *Acta Psychiat. Scand. 59,* 395-414 (1979b).

Cooper, A.J., and Datta, S.R. A placebo controlled evaluation of L-tryptophan in depression in the elderly. *Can. J. Psychiat. 25,* 386-390 (1980).

Coppen, A., Shaw, D.M., and Farrell, J.P. Potentiation of the antidepressive effect of a monoamine-oxidase inhibitor by tryptophan. *Lancet i,* 79-80 (1963).

Coppen, A., Shaw, D.M., Herzberg, B., and Maggs, R. Tryptophan in the treatment of depression. *Lancet ii,* 1178-1180 (1967).

Coppen, A., Whybrow, P.C., Noguera, R., Maggs, R., and Prange, A.J. The comparative antidepressant value of L-tryptophan and imipramine with and without attempted potentiation by liothyronine. *Arch. Gen. Psychiat. 26,* 234-241 (1972).

D'Elia, G. Lehmann, J., and Raotma, H. Evaluation of the combination of tryptophan and ECT in the treatment of depression. 1. Clinical analysis. *Acta Psychiat. Scand. 56,* 303-318 (1977).

Everett, G.M. Effects of 5-hydroxytryptophan on brain levels of monoamines and the dopamine metabolic DOPAC, in *Catecholamines: Basic and Clinical Frontiers,* E. Usdin, I.J. Kopin, and J. Barchas, eds. Pergamon Press, New York (1979).

Farkas, T., Dunner, D.L., and Fieve, R.R. L-tryptophan in depression. *Biol. Psychiat. 11,* 295-302 (1976).

Fernstrom, J.D. Acute effects of tryptophan and single meals on serotonin synthesis in the rat brain, in *Serotonin in Biological Psychiatry,* B.T. Ho, J.C. Schoolar, and E. Usdin, eds. Raven Press, New York (1982).

Gelenberg, A.J., Wojcik, J.D., Gibson, C.J., and Wurtman, R.J. Tyrosine for the treatment of depression, in *Research Strategies for Assessing the Behavioral Effects of Foods and Nutrients,* H.R. Lieberman, and R.J. Wurtman, eds. Proceedings of a conference held at the Massachusetts Institute of Technology, Cambridge, Massachusetts (1982).

Glassman, A.H., and Platman, S.R. Potentiation of a monoamine oxidase inhibitor by tryptophan. *J. Psychiat. Res. 7,* 83-88 (1969)

Goodwin, F.K., Brodie, H.K.H., Murphy, D.L., and Bunney, W.E. L-DOPA, catecholamines and behavior: a clinical and biochemical study in depressed patients. *Biol. Psychiat. 2,* 341-366 (1970).

Green, A.R., and Aronson, J.K. The pharmacokinetics of oral *l*-tryptophan; effects of dose and of concomitant pyridozine, allopurinol or nicotinamide administration. *Adv. Biol. Psychiat. 10,* 67-81 (1983).

Green, A.R., Bloomfield, M.R., Woods, H.F., and Seed, M. Metabolism of an oral tryptophan load by women and evidence against the induction of tryptophan pyrrolase by oral contraceptives. *Brit. J. Clin. Pharmacol. 5,* 233-241 (1978).

Green, A.R., and Curzon, G. Decrease of 5-hydroxytryptamine in the brain provoked by hydrocortisone and its prevention by allopurinol. *Nature Lond. 220,* 1095-1097 (1968).

Green, A.R., and Curzon, G. The effect of tryptophan metabolites on brain 5-hydroxytryptamine metabolism. *Biochem. Pharmacol. 19,* 2061-2028 (1970).

Green, A.R., Joseph, M.H. and Woods, H.F. Tryptophan metabolism in the isolated perfused liver of the rat: effects of tryptophan concentration hydrocortisone and allopurinol on tryptophan pyrrolase activity and kynurenine formation. *Brit. J. Pharmacol. 57,* 103-114 (1976).

Hagen, P.B. and Cohen, L.H. Biosynthesis of indolealkylamines: physiological release and transport of 5-hydroxytrptamine, in *Handbook of Experimental Pharmacology,* Erspamer, F. ed. Springer, Berlin, pp. 182-201 (1966).

Herrington, R.N., Bruce, A., Johnstone, E.C., and Lader, M.H. Comparative trial of L-tryptophan and ECT in severe depressive illness. *Lancet ii,* 731-734 (1974).

Herrington, R.N., Bruce, A., Johnstone, E.C., and Lader, M.H. Comparative trial of L-tryptophan and amitriptyline in depressive illnesses. *Psychol. Med. 6,* 673-678 (1976).

Jensen, K., Freunsgaard, K., Ahlfors, U.G., Pihkanen, T.A., Tuomikoski, S., Ose, E., Dencker, S.J., Lindberg, D., and Nagy, A. Tryptophan/imipramine in depression. *Lancet i,* 920 (1975).

Kirkegaard, C., Møller, S.E., and Bjørum, N. Addition of L-tryptophan to electroconvulsive treatment in endogenous depression. A double-blind study. *Acta Psychiat. Scand. 58,* 457-462 (1978).

Kline, N.S., and Sacks, W. Relief of depression within one day using an MAO inhibitor and intravenous 5-HTP. *Amer. J. Psychiat. 120,* 274-275 (1963).

Kline, N.S., Sacks, W., and Simpson, G.M. Further studies on one day treatment of depression with 5-HTP. *Amer. J. Psychiat. 121,* 379-381 (1964).

Kline, N.S., and Shah, B.K. Comparable therapeutic efficacy of tryptophan and imipramine: average therapeutic ratings versus "true" equivalence. An important difference. *Cur. Ther. Res. 15,* 484-487 (1973).

Knox, V.E., and Auerbach, V.H. The hormonal control of tryptophan peroxidase in the rat. *J. Biol.*

Chem. 214, 307-313 (1955).

Korf, J., Venema, K., and Rosbema, F. Decarboxylation of endogenous *l*-5-hydroxytryptophan after destruction of the cerebral raphe system. *J. Neurochem. 23,* 249-252 (1974).

Lindberg, D., Ahlfors, U.G., Dencker, S.J., Fruensgaard, K., Hansten, S., Jensen, K., Ose, E., and Pihkanes, T.A. Symptom reduction in depression after treatment with L-tryptophan or imipramine. *Acta Psychiat. Scand. 60,* 287-294 (1979).

Linnoila, M., Seppala, T., Mattila, M.J., Vihko, R., Pakarinen, A., and Skinner, J.T. Clomipramine and dexepin in depressive neurosis. *Arch. Gen. Psychiat. 37,* 1295-1299 (1980).

Lopez-Ibor Alino, J.J., Ayuso Gutierrez, J.L. and Iglesisa, M.L.M.M. 5-hydroxytrptophan (5-HTP) and a MAO I (nialamide) in the treatment of depression. A double-blind controlled study. *Internat. Parmacopsychiat. 11* 8-15 (1976).

Lopez-Ibor Alino, J.J., Ayuso Gutierrez, J.L. and Montejo, M.L. Tryptophan and amitriptyline in the treatment of depression. A double-blind study. *Internat. Pharmacopsychiat. 8,* 145-151 (1973).

MacSweeney, D.A. Treatment of unipolar depression. *Lancet ii,* 510-511 (1975).

Mendels, J., Stinnett, J.L., Burns, D., and Frazer, A. Amine precursors and depression. *Arch. Gen. Psychiat. 32,* 22-30 (1975).

Mendlewicz, J., and Youdim, M.B.H. Antidepressant potentiation of 5-hydroxytrptophan by *l*-deprenil in affective illness. *J. Affect. Disord. 2,* 137-146 (1980).

Møller, S.E., Kirk, L., Brandup, E., Hollnagel, M., Kaldan, B., and Ødum, K. Tryptophan availability in endogenous depression—relation to efficacy of *l*-tryptophan treatment. *Adv. Biol. Psychiat. 10,* 30-46 (1983).

Murphy, D.L., Baker, M., Goodwin, F.K., Miller, H., Kotin, J. and Bunney, W.E. *l*-tryptophan in affective disorders: indoleamine changes and differential clinical effects. *Psychopharmacologia 34,* 11-20 (1974).

Nardini, M., De Stafano, R., Iannuccelli, M., Borghesi, R., and Battistini, N. Treatment of depression with *l*-5-hydroxytrptophan combined with chlorimipramine, a double-blind study. *Internat. J. Clin. Pharm. Res. iii,* 239-250 (1983).

Pare, C.M.B. Potentiation of monoamine-oxidase inhibitors by tryptophan. *Lancet ii,* 527-528 (1963).

Puhringe, W., Wirx-Justice, A., Graw, P., Lacoste, V., and Gastpar, M. Intravanous *l*-5-hydroxytryptophan in normal subjects: an interdisciplinary precursor loading study. I. Implication of reproducable mood elevation. *Pharmakopsychiatrie 9,* 260-268 (1976).

Rao, B., and Broadhurst, A.D. Tryptophan and depression. *Brit. Med. J. i,* 460 (1976).

Scally, M.C., Ulus, I., and Wurtman, R.J. Brain tyrosine level controls striatal dopamine synthesis in haloperidol-treated rats. *J.Neurol. Trans. 41,* 1-6 (1977).

Sedvall, G., Fyro, B., Gullberg, B., Nyback, H., Wiesel, F.A., and Wode-Helgodt, B. Relationships in healthy volunteers between concentration of monoamines metabolite in cerebrospinal fluid and family history of psychiatric morbidity. *Brit. J. Psychiat. 136,* 366-374 (1980).

Shaw, D.M., MacSweeney, D.A., Hewland, R., and Johnson, A.L. Tricyclic antidepressants and tryptophan in unipolar depression. *Psychol. Med. 5,* 276-278 (1975).

Shopsin, B. Enhancement of the antidepressant reponse to *l*-tryptophan by a liver pyrrolase inhibitor: a rational treatment approach. *Neuropsychobiology 4,* 188-192 (1978).

Singleton, L., and Marsden, C.A. Increased responsiveness to 5-methoxy, N.N-dimethyl tryptamine in mice on a high tryptophan diet. *Neuropharmacology 18,* 569-572 (1979).

Sourkes, T.L. Toxicology of serotonin precursors. *Adv. Biol. Psychiat. 10,* 160-175 (1983).

Sternberg, E., van Woert, M.H., Young, S.N., Magnussen, J., Baker, H., Gauthier, S., and Osterland, C.K. Development of a sclerodermalike illness during therapy with *l*-5-hydroxytryptophan and carbidopa. *New Engl. J. Med. 303,* 782-787 (1980).

Takahashi, S., Takahashi, R., Masamura, I., and Miike, A. Measurement of 5-hydroxyindole compounds during 5-HTP treatment in depressed patients. Folia Psychiat. *Neurol. Jap. 30,* 463-473 (1976).

Thal, L.J., Sharpless, N.S., Wolfson, L., and Katzman, R. Treatment of myoclonus with *l*-5-hydroxytryptophan and carbidopa. Clinical, electrophysiological and biochemical observation. *Ann. Neurol. 7,* 570-576 (1980).

Thomson, J. and Rankin, H., Ashcroft, G.W., Yates, C.M., McQueen, J.K., and Cummings, S.W. The treatment of depression in general practice: a comparison of *l*-tryptophan, amitriptyline, and a combination of *l*-tryptophan and amitriptyline with placebo. *Psychol. Med. 12,* 741-751 (1982).

Trimble, M., Chadwick, D., Reynolds, E., and Marsden, C.D. *l*-5-hydroxy-tryptophan and mood. *Lancet i,* 583 (1975).

van Hiele, L.J. *l*-5-hydroxytryptophan in depression. The first substitution therapy in psychiatry? *Neuropsychobiology 6,* 230-241 (1980).

van Praag, H.M. Monoamine oxidase inhibition as a therapeutic principle in the treatment of depression. Thesis, Utrecht (1962).

van Praag, H.M. Towards a biochemical typology of depressions. *Pharmakopsychiatr. 7,* 281-292 (1974).

van Praag, H.M. *Depression and schizophrenia. A Contribution on Their Chemical Pathologies.* Spectrum Publications, New York (1977a).

van Praag, H.M. Significance of biochemical parameters in the diagnosis, treatment and prevention of depressive disorders. *Biol. Psychiat. 12,* 101-131 (1977b).

van Praag, H.M. *Psychotropic Drugs. A Guide for the Practitioner.* Brunner/Mazel, New York (1978).

van Praag, H.M. Central serotonin: its relation to depression vulnerability and depression prophylaxis, in *Biological Psychiatry Today,* Y. Obiols, C. Ballus, E. Gonzalez Monclus, and Y. Pujols, eds. Elsevier North-Holland Biomedical Press, Amsterdam (1979).

van Praag, H.M. Management of depression with serotonin precursors. *Biol. Psychiat. 16,* 291-310 (1981).

van Praag, H.M. Neurotransmitters and CNS disease: depression. *Lancet ii,* 1259-1264 (1982).

van Praag, H.M. In search of the action mechanism of antidepressants. 5-HTP/tyrosine mixtures in depression. *Neuropharmacology* 22, 433-440 (1983).

van Praag, H.M. Studies in the mechanism of action of serotonin precursors in depression. *Psychopharm. Bull. 20,* 599-602 (1984).

van Praag, H.M., and de Haan, S. Central serotonin metabolism and frequency of depression. *Psychiat. Res. 1,* 219-224 (1979).

van Praag, H.M., and de Haan, S. Depression vulnerability and 5-hydroxytryptophan prophylaxis. *Psychiat. Res. 3,* 75-83 (1980).

van Praag, H.M., and de Haan, S. Chemprophylaxis of depression. An attempt to compare lithium with 5-hydroxytryptophan. *Acta Psychiat. Scand. 290* (suppl.), 191-205 (1981).

van Praag, H.M., and Korf, J. Central monamine deficiency in depression: causative or secondary phenomenon. *Pharmakopsychiatr, 8,* 321-326 (1975).

van Praag, H.M., Korf, J., Dols, L.C.W., and Schut, T. A pilot study of the predictive value of the probenecid test in the application of 5-hydroxytryptophan as an antidepressant. *Psychopharmacologia 25,* 14-21 (1972).

van Praag, H.M., and Lemus, C. Uses of nutrients in treating psychiatric disease, in *Nutrition and the Brain,* R.J. Wurtman, and J.J. Wurtman, eds., New York, Raven Press (1985).

van Praag, H.M., Uleman, A.M., and Spitz, J.C. The vital syndrome interview. A structured standard interview for the recognition and registration of the vital depressive symptom complex. *Psychiat. Neurol. Neurochir. 68*, 329-346 (1965).

van Praag, H.M., van den Burg, W., Bos, E.R.H., and Dols, L.C.W. 5-hydroxytryptophan in combination with clomipramine in 'therapy-resistent' depression. *Psychopharmacologia 38*, 267-269 (1974).

van Praag, H.M., and Westenberg, H.G.M. Treatment of depression with *l*-hydroxytryptophan, in *The Treatment of Depression with Monoamine Precursors*, H.M. van Praag, and J. Mendlewicz, eds., Basel, Karger (1983).

van Woert, M.H., Rosenbaum, D., Howieson, J., and Bowers, M.B. Long-term therapy of myoclonus and other neurological disorders with *l*-5-hydroxytryptophan and carbidopa. *New Engl. J. Med. 296*, 70-75 (1977).

Walinder, J. Combination of tryptophan with MAO inhibitors, tricyclic antidepressants and selective 5-HT reuptake inhibitors. *Adv. Biol. Psychiat. 10*, 82-93 (1983).

Walinder, J., Skott, A., Carlsson, A., Nagy, A., and Roos, B.E. Potentiation of the antidepressant action of clomipramine by tryptophan. *Arch. Gen. Psychiat. 33*, 1384-1389 (1976).

Walinder, J., Carlsson, A., and Persson, R. 5-HT reuptake inhibitors plus tryptophan in endogenous depression. *Acta Psychiat. Scand. 63*, 179-190 (1981).

Westenberg, H.G.M., Gerritsen, T.W., Meijer, B.A., and van Praag, H.M. Kinetics of *l*-5-hydroxytryptophan in healthy subjects. *Psychiat. Res. 7*, 373-385 (1982).

Worrall, E.P., Moody, J.P., Peet, M., Dick, P., Smith, A., Chambers, C., Adams, M., and Naylor, G.J. Controlled studies of the acute antidepressant effects of lithium. *Brit. J. Psychiat. 135*, 255-262 (1979).

Wurtman, R.J. Nutrients that modify brain function. *Sci. Amer. 246*, 42-51 (1982).

Wurtman, R.J. Larin, F., Mostafapour, S., and Fernstrom, J.F. Brain catechol synthesis: Controlled by brain tyrosine concentration. *Science 185*, 183-194, (1974).

15

Sleep Deprivation in Resistant Depression

Willem A. Nolen

Sleep deprivation (SD) has been reported to produce an elevation of mood in depressed patients. Schulte (1969) was the first to report beneficial effects in a patient who stayed awake for a whole night on his own initiative. Pflug and Tölle (1971) were the first to study systematically the effect of SD as a treatment for depression. In most studies SD has been combined with antidepressants, but it has also been given as a single treatment, i.e., used on its own. Van den Burg and van den Hoofdakker (1975) deprived ten endogenous depressed patients for two nights, interrupted by one "recovery" night during which the patients were allowed to sleep. In general they observed a positive effect after each SD, with two patients showing a substantial improvement. As a rule, however, the recovery night was followed by a relapse. Amin (1978) obtained a response to SD in twelve of 20 patients, but seven of them worsened after the next night. Gerner et al. (1979) studied 25 patients with a major depression with a single SD. They observed a positive effect, defined as a mood elevation from baseline, in 16 of them, but after a recovery night only five of them remained well and the difference was no longer significant. Similar results were reported in another report of this group, obtained with some of the same patients (Duncan et al. 1980). Knowles et al. (1981) treated six patients with two SDs during a study period of eleven days. SD produced a beneficial but transient effect in four of them. In two less well documented studies similar findings were obtained (Larsen et al. 1976; Kvist and Kirkegaard, 1980).

Combining these studies we may conclude that between 50% and 70% of the patients show a positive effect immediately after SD, but an unspecified percentage (below 20%) of patients show a more or less durable effect when SD is given as a single treatment, i.e., not combined with antidepressants.

Before treatment with SD most patients in these studies had already received antidepressants. The washout period before SD varied from 1.5 days to four weeks. In most studies further information about these antidepressant treatments is lacking as regards "adequate dose," duration of treatment, and the specific antidepressants given in advance. Consequently it is not clear whether these patients were suffering from resistant depressions. Therefore, we decided to investigate the effectiveness of SD in such patients.

METHODS

Description of the Follow-Up Study

The actual study forms a part of a larger follow-up study of resistant depressives. Because this publication is a chapter in a book on the treatment of resistant depression, some information on this follow-up study is presented below; more details will be published elsewhere. For the study, patients who suffer from a "major depressive episode" according to DSM-III, and who already have been treated unsuccessfully with at least one antidepressant during the current depressive episode, were selected. These antidepressants (reuptake inhibitors) must have been given in an adequate dose (i.e., 150 mg imipramine or a comparable dose of another antidepressant) for at least four weeks. All patients had to have an entry score on the Hamilton Rating Scale for Depression (HRSD-17 items) of at least 18 points. Thus the study deals with the subgroup of 10-30 percent of depressed patients who do not respond to antidepressant(s), in which we have compared the effects of two antidepressants of the so called "second generation," SD, the serotonin precursor 5-HTP, and the MAO inhibitor tranylcypromine. The protocol of this follow-up study is presented schematically in Table 1.

Depressed patients, selected as described above, were given oxaprotiline (a selective noradrenalin reuptake inhibitor) or fluvoxamine (a selective serotonin reuptake inhibitor). These drugs were given in a double-blind cross-over design for four weeks with a maximum dose of 300 mg/day. When no response was

TABLE 1. Protocol of Follow-Up Study in Therapy-Resistant Depressed Patients.[a]

Period	Length	Treatment
Pretreatment period	2 weeks	Totally medication-free
First treatment period,	4 weeks	Oxaprotiline or fluvoxamine, double-blind
Washout period	1 week	No antidepressant treatment
Second treatment period	4 weeks	Crossover of first treatment
Washout period	1 week	No antidepressant treatment
Third treatment period	2 weeks	Sleep deprivation, 4 treatments
Fourth treatment period	4 weeks	5-HTP (+ carbidopa) or tranylcypromine
Washout period	1 week	No antidepressant treatment
Fifth treatment period	4 weeks	Crossover of fourth treatment
Further follow-up	Not specified	ECT Continuation of one of treatments mentioned above Combination of two of the treatments mentioned above Other treatment, for instance with neuroleptics

[a]Entry criteria: Major depression (DSM-III); HRSD (17 items) score ≥ 18; patients between 20 and 65 years old; no or insufficient response to an adequate treatment with antidepressants

obtained with the first drug, the opposite drug was given after a washout period of one week. The patients who did not respond to the above drugs, were then subjected to SD, given as a single treatment and applied four times during two weeks.

Finally, those patients who showed no or only a temporary response to SD were subsequently given 5-HTP (together with carbidopa) or tranylcypromine. 5-HTP was given with a maximum dose of 200 mg/day, tranylcypromine with a maximum dose of 100 mg/day.

Prior informed consent was obtained from all patients. Degree of depression was scored weekly on the HRSD obtained by one well-trained nonblind observer. Response to any treatment during the whole follow-up study was defined as a decrease of at least 50% in the total HRSD score on the last treatment day of each treatment, compared to the entry score of the total study, i.e., the day before the first treatment (oxaprotiline or fluvoxamine). Thus, patients were admitted to each following step in the study, when they had not recovered by at least 50% through the former treatment. Before the first treatment the patients were kept medication-free for 14 days, during which period several laboratory investigations were performed.

The Current Study

When both oxaprotiline and fluvoxamine, given as outlined above, remained unsuccessful SD was applied after a new washout period of one week, following the second drug. During two weeks a maximum of four SDs was given. Psychoactive drugs were not allowed, with the exception of benzodiazepines (lorazepam) in the case of anxiety or agitation, once or twice a day, but not as a sleeping medication. The weekly HRSD scores were obtained on the days immediately following the second and fourth SD. For evaluating the effect of SD these scores were compared not only with the entry score before the first drug was given, but also with the scores two days before treatment with SD was started, i.e., the scores at the end of the washout period following the second drug. As SD produces the best results on the day after the treatment, the HRSD scores on these days reflect the acute effect and might lead to false-positive results with regard to the long-term effect. The patients were therefore also scored on a global rating scale indicating the overall profit for the patient at the end of two weeks treatment with SD. This scale ranged from ++ (= longlasting response), via + (= substantial response with relapse) and ± (= moderate or small response with relapse), to − (= no response or deterioration).

Patients

Twenty-four patients were treated with SD, out of a total of 43 patients treated according to the protocol described (see Table 2). During the first two treatment periods five patients responded to oxaprotiline and four to fluvoxamine. Two patients withdrew themselves from the study after being treated unsuccessfully, and another patient committed suicide after a temporary response to oxaprotiline. Three patients were treated with ECT when a further deterioration occurred during the first or second treatment period. One patient initially responded (to oxaprotiline) and was kept on this drug, but nevertheless relapsed after several months. At that time the study had stopped. Thus, we were left with 27 patients who had not responded to oxaprotiline and fluvoxamine. Three refused SD, two of them because they had been treated with SD unsuccessfully earlier in their lives, and the third refused to stay awake.

The remaining group of 24 patients who were given SD consisted of 9 men and 15 women. Their ages varied from 32 to 65 years (mean age 56 years). Seventeen patients suffered from a recurrent major depression, while four of them had also suffered from hypomanic episodes (cyclothymic disorder or bipolar II). One patient had a depressive episode in the course of a bipolar disorder. The remaining six

TABLE 2. Treatment Results During First and Second Treatment Periods

	Response	Temporary or no response: Drop-out or ECT	Temporary or no response: Continuation
First treatment period: 43 patients			
Oxaprotiline (n = 19):			
response	2		
temporary response			
suicide after relapse		1	
drop-out after relapse		1	
continuation to next treatment			2
no response			
continuation to next treatment			13
Fluvoxamine (n = 24):			
response	1		
earlier termination of treatment			
continuation to ECT		1	
no response			
continuation to next treatment			22
Second treatment: 37 patients			
Fluvoxamine (n = 15):			
response	3		
earlier termination of treatment			
continuation to ECT		1	
no response			
continuation to next treatment			11
Oxaprotiline (n = 22):			
response	3		
temporary response			
continuation to next treatment			4
continuation to new protocol		1	
no response			
drop-out		1	
continuation to ECT		1	
continuation to next treatment			12

patients were suffering from their first depression. The HRSD-scores at the end of the washout period following the second drug show that 7 of the 24 patients had a score below 18 points, which is one of the entry criteria of the total follow-up study. In six of them these scores were above the 50% mark of the original HRSD-scores on the days before the first drug, so they were considered as nonresponders to both drugs and were then selected for SD. One patient with a HRSD-score of nine points had in fact responded (more than 50% reduction on oxaprotiline), but continued to complain of further severe mood fluctuations and was therefore selected for further treatment according to the protocol. (The results obtained in the first two treatment periods will be published in more detail elsewhere.)

RESULTS

The results obtained with SD are presented in Table 3. Only 14 of the 24 patients performed all four scheduled SDs. Five patients refused further SDs after the first week and in one patient a further treatment with SD was stopped, because a severe deterioration followed the first SD. Three other patients completed only three SDs. The tenth patient was not given the last two SDs, having responded after the first two. This patient showed a switch into a short hypomanic episode followed by a complete recovery and was then put prophylactically on lithium with success.

The acute effects obtained with SD are best shown by the HRSD scores obtained on the days immediately following the second and fourth SD (see also Figure 1).

During the first week a mean improvement of 5.1 points was obtained (SEM 1.2) on the HRSD, compared to an initial score before SD of 23.3 points (SD 8.0) which represents a mean improvement of about 21%. Seventeen patients continued with SD during the second week, after a mean improvement during the first week of 6.5 points (SEM 1.1), 16 of them showing at least some improvement. During the second week, only three patients showed a further improvement. The mean deterioration in all 17 patients was 2.6 points (SEM 1.1). This contributed to a mean overall improvement over both weeks of 3.9 points (SEM 1.1).

The global ratings after two weeks give the clearest picture of the long-term effect of SD. Only one of the 24 patients showed a lasting recovery. Only short-term effects were obtained in 14 patients. In these patients the response was substantial (nine patients) or moderate/small (six patients). Nine patients showed no response or even a deterioration.

Further Follow-Up

The further follow-up of the 23 patients who did not respond lastingly to SD is also shown in Table 3, and *together with* the remaining three patients who refused SD in more detail in Table 4.

TABLE 3. Effects of Sleep Deprivation During Third Treatment Period (24 Patients)

Patient	Age	Diagnosis[a]	Initial HRSD	First week number SDs	First week HRSD	Second week number SDs	Second week HRSD	Global rating scale[b]	Further follow-up[c]
1	58	R, P	35	2	26			−	T ++
3	65	R, P	30	2	21	2	25	−	−
8	48	R, P	42	2	42			−	T ±
15	58	Rc	9	2	4	2	4	+	T ++
17	63	Rc	11	2	6			++	−
18	59	NR, P	13	2	10	2	10	+	T ++
19	60	NR, P	29	2	18	2	19	±	T ++
20	59	NR	32	2	26	2	32	−	−
21	64	R	30	2	23	1	30	±	T ++
22	61	NR	16	1	13	2	20	−	−
24	63	R	15	1	24			−	T ++
25	54	R	30	2	25	2	31	−	−
27	59	Bip	23	2	21	2	17	±	−
28	56	R	19	2	19	2	15	±	−
29	32	NR	19	2	18	2	21	−	T +
30	34	R,P	30	1	14			+	T ++
31	63	Rc	24	2	10	2	10	+	T ++
32	55	NR	24	2	24	2	21	±	T ++
34	57	R	16	1	16			−	T ++
35	63	R,P	24	2	23			+	T +
36	60	R	23	2	12	2	19	+	−
37	58	R	16	2	15	2	15	±	T ++
38	45	R	25	2	10	1	22	+	T +
40	42	Rc	25	2	17	2	17	+	T +

[a]R = Recurrent major depression;
NR = non-recurrent major depression;
Rc = recurrent major depressive episode [with cyclothymic disorder;]
Bip = major depressive episode in bipolar disorder;
P = psychotic;
[b]++ = Longlasting response;
\+ = substantial response followed by relapse;
= = moderate or small response followed by relapse;
− = no response or deterioration;
[c]T++ = Response to tranylcypromine during fourth or fifth treatment period;
T+ = response to tranylcypromine during further follow-up;
T= = temporary response to tranylcypromine followed by suicide;
− = no or only partial response (to tranylcypromine, 5-HTP, and other treatments).

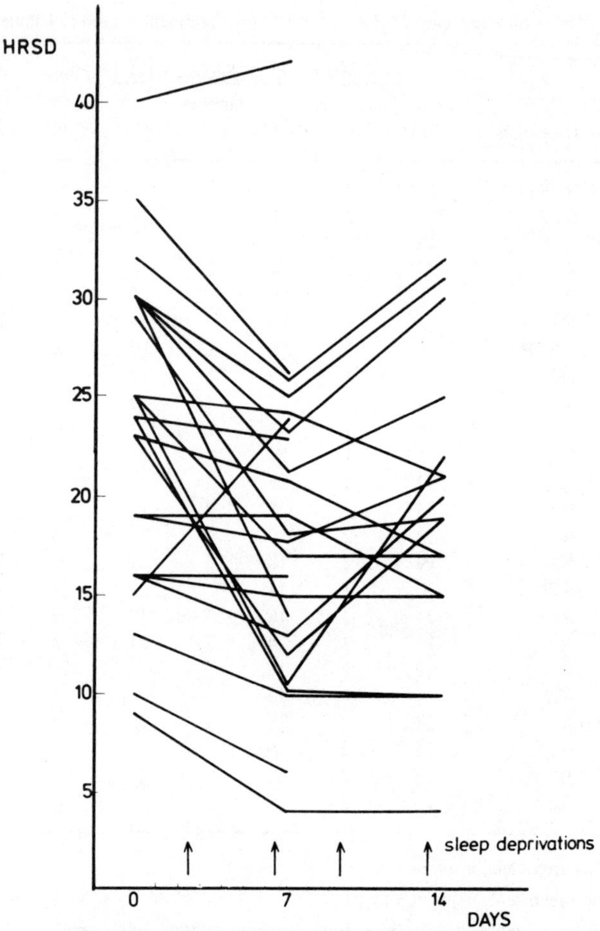

Figure 1. Effects of sleep deprivation as scored on HRSD before and after one and two weeks. The nights with SD are indicated with ↑.

Fifteen of these 26 patients responded to tranylcypromine; one had a temporary response but later committed suicide when he was confronted with the fact that he could not return to his job. Seventeen of the 26 patients were also treated with 5-HTP, none of them showing a response. Thus, at the end of the fourth and fifth treatment-periods we were left with ten patients who had not responded to any treatment. In five of them we continued with tranylcypromine, which ultimately

TABLE 4. Treatment Results During Fourth and Fifth Treatment Periods

Fourth treatment period: 26 patients	Response	Temporary or no response: Drop-out	Temporary or no response: Continuation
Fourth treatment period: 26 patients			
Tranylcypromine (n = 14):			
response	7		
temporary response			
suicide		1	
no response			
continuation to next treatment			6
5-HTP + carbidopa (n = 12):			
no response			
continuation to next treatment			12
Fifth treatment period: 18 patients			
5-HTP + carbidopa (n = 6):			
treatment refused			1
no response			
continuation to next treatment			5
Tranylcypromine (n = 12):			
response	8		
no response			
continuation to next treatment			4
Further follow-up: 10 patients			
ECT (n = 1) temporary response			1
Tranylcypromine (n = 5) response	2		
partial response			3
Oxaprotiline (n = 2) partial response			2
Sulpiride (n = 2) partial response			2

led to a positive response in two more patients, and a partial remission (less than 50%) in the other three. One patient was subjected to ECT which led to temporary remissions on two subsequently given series of ECT. Of the remaining four patients, two continued with oxaprotiline (with partial remission) and the other two were switched to another treatment (sulpiride), which also led in both cases to some positive effect. (Details of this part of the follow-up study will also be published elsewhere.)

Table 5 shows how temporary responders to SD subsequently responded to

TABLE 5. Response to SD, Compared to Response to Subsequent Treatment with Tranylcypromine

	Effect of tranylcypromine			
	Response	Temporary response	Response during further follow-up	No response
Improvement on HRSD (n = 15)	10	1	1	3
No improvement on HRSD (n = 8)	3		1	4

tranylcypromine. Twelve of the 15 patients who showed an acute response to SD on the HRSD improved with tranylcypromine during the further follow-up. Of the eight patients who showed no acute response to SD, only four improved with tranylcypromine (differences not significant, Fisher's Exact Test, two-sided: $p = 0.18$).

DISCUSSION

The long-term results with sleep deprivation in our study were rather poor. Only one patient showed a complete recovery after two SDs. Having a low HRSD score of ten points before SD, this patient was perhaps already coming out of her depression. This poor long-term effect of SD, given as a single treatment, indicates that SD on its own is of little therapeutic value in resistant depression. In 14 patients (65%) an acute (but no long-lasting) effect was observed. In eight of them the response immediately after SD was substantial. Comparable findings have been reported by others, who studied SD given as a single treatment (van den Burg and van den Hoofdakker, 1975; Amin, 1978; Gerner et al., 1979). The good short-term effect obtained with SD is remarkable in view of the fact that our patients have proved to be resistant to several antidepressants, both from the first and the second generation.

Another remarkable fact is that a temporary response to SD may be related to a subsequent response to the MAO inhibitor tranylcypromine. Our results, as presented in Table 5, show that most temporary responders to SD improved on treatment with tranylcypromine (and not on 5-HTP). Thus our study supports the hypothesis that a positive temporary response to SD is likely to be followed by a positive response to subsequent treatment with antidepressants. Wirz-Justice et al., (1979) found that 24 out of 34 (temporary) responders to SD also responded to subsequent treatment with several antidepressants, while twelve out of 18 nonresponders to SD also failed to improve with drugs. This finding has more or less been confirmed in the already mentioned study by Amin (1978) who observed response to SD in twelve of 22 patients, ten of them also responding to antidepressants. Of the ten nonresponders to SD six also failed on drugs. The impression left by these studies is that patients who show a temporary response to SD are likely to respond to antidepressants. In a recent study Fähndrich (1983) subjected 60 patients with a depression to one SD. Then he divided them into two groups of 30 patients who were treated, probably in an open way, with clomipramine or maprotiline. Twenty patients, 15 of whom had also responded to SD, responded to clomipramine. Twenty-one patients responded to maprotiline, only five of whom had responded to SD. Fähndrich suggests that (temporary) response after one SD predicts a positive response to a serotonin reuptake inhibitor like clomipramine, while nonresponders to SD respond better to noradrenergic antidepressants like maprotiline. However, clomipramine is not a real serotonergic drug as it is metabolized into desmethyl-clomipramine which is also a noradrenalin reuptake inhibitor. This assumption is not substantiated by the studies of Wirz-Justice et al. and Amin. Both groups were using several different antidepressants and do not mention differences in response to these drugs in relation to response to SD. Our study cannot give any answer on this question, as all our patients were treated unsuccessfully with both a noradrenalin and a serotonin reuptake inhibitor before SD, whereas many of them subsequently showed a temporary response to SD.

In most studies SD has been combined with antidepressants and this combination produces better results than SD given as a single treatment. Pflug (1976) reports good effects with the combination in 124 patients, although he does not present much specific data. Van Scheyen (1977), with as far as we know the only study that gives some detailed information on the earlier treatment given to his patients, studied 29 patients who had already been treated unsuccessfully with antidepressants (clomipramine or amitriptyline 150 mg/day for three weeks), in ten of them in combination with ECT. When these patients did not respond, he subjected them to SD (mean number 4.9) once weekly, and also continued with the antidepressants. He saw temporary responses in many of his patients after the first SD, but after more SDs this improvement lasted for a longer period, and ultimately 20 patients recovered. When we compare this positive result to the poor long-term result of our study with single SD, we would like to hypothesize that SD and antidepressants can be mutually beneficial. This hypothesis is supported by the study of Loosen et al. (1976), who compared the effect of clomipramine 150 mg/day alone to clomipramine in combination with one SD given on the day before starting clomipramine. They observed a quicker response to the combined treatment than to clomipramine alone. Elsenga and van den Hoofdakker (1980; 1983) studied three groups treated with clomipramine alone, SD combined with placebo, and SD combined with clomipramine. Four SDs were given during two weeks. The combination of clomipramine and SD led to a quicker response than clomipramine alone, while both led to a better result than SD combined with placebo.

Subsequent refusals by patients who undergo SD have hardly been reported. Only Kretschmar and Peters (1973) and Elsenga and van den Hoofdakker (to be published) mention difficulties in motivating patients. Lit (1979), for instance, describes how easily he can obtain the cooperation of patients, because SD "has a good press among them." In our group of patients, who had all agreed to the total follow-up study, three patients nevertheless refused SD completely, while eight other patients only accepted to undergo two or three treatments. In one patient further treatment had to be stopped because severe deterioration followed the first SD. Also, side effects have been reported only rarely. In some studies a few cases are mentioned of worsening of symptoms, or a hypomanic or even psychotic reaction with a duration of at the most a few days (van den Burg and van den Hoofdakker, 1980; Fähndrich, 1981; van Scheyen, 1977).

Finally, one might wonder why ECT was not given earlier and/or more frequently during this study. This reflects the situation in the Netherlands, where ECT is hardly used for political/psychological reasons, after many debates in newspapers and on radio and television. In a recent governmental report (Gezondheidsraad, 1983) it is stated that in 1979, 46 patients in the Netherlands were treated with ECT on a total population of 14 million inhabitants.

CONCLUSION

Although SD as a single treatment seems of little value for depressed patients who have not responded to antidepressants, we are still using SD in special situations: in patients who have shown only a partial response to an antidepressant (reuptake inhibitor or MAO inhibitor) *and* no response to several other antidepressants. In these patients we combine SD with the antidepressant that has produced the partial effect, in the hope that both treatments can be mutually beneficial. Our preliminary and subjective impression is that these combinations are most useful in patients who show a substantial response after the SD, whatever the duration of this response. It can help patients and their relatives to realize themselves that the depression is changeable, which can produce hope for the patient's future.

ACKNOWLEDGMENTS

I wish to thank the nursing staff of the department of biological psychiatry for their patience during all SD nights, professor Rudi van den Hoofdakker for several comments after the first version of this publication, Hans Kamp for his help in selecting the references, and Nicoline van der Salm who did all typing.

REFERENCES

Amin, M. Response to sleep deprivation and therapeutic results with antidepressants. *Lancet*, p. 165 (1978).

Duncan, W.C., Gillin, J.C., Post, R.M., Gerner, R.H., and Wehr, T.A. Relationship between EEG sleep patterns and clinical improvement in depressed patients treated with sleep deprivation. *Biol. Psychiat. 15*, 879-889 (1980).

Elsenga, S., and van den Hoofdakker, R.H. Sleep deprivation and clomipramine in endogenous depression, in: *Sleep 1978*, Fourth European Congress on Sleep Research. Karger, Basel, pp. 625-628 (1980).

Elsenga S., and van den Hoofdakker, R.H. Clinical effects of sleep deprivation and clomipramine in endogenous depression. *J. Psychiat. Res. 17*, 361-374 (1983).

Fähndrich, E. Effects of sleep deprivation on depressed patients of different nosological groups. *J. Psychiat. Res. 5*, 277-285 (1981).

Fähndrich, E. Effect of sleep deprivation as a predictor of treatment response to antidepressant medication. *Acta Psychiat. Scand. 68*, 341-344 (1983).

Gerner, R.H., Post, R.M., Gillin J.C., and Bunney, W.E. Biological and behavioral effects of one night's sleep deprivation in depressed patients and normals. *J. Psychiat. Res. 15*, 21-40 (1979).

Gezondheidsraad, Governmental report. *Advies Inzake Electroconvulsie-Therapie, the Hague* pp. 121 (1983).

Knowles, J.B., Southmayd, M.A., Delva, N., Prowse, A., MacLean, A.W., Cairns, J., Letemendia, F.J., and Waldron, J. Sleep deprivation: outcome of controlled single case studies of depressed patients. *Can. J. Psychiat. 26*, 330-333 (1981).

Kretschmar, J.H., and Peters, U.H. Schlafentzug zur Behandlung der endogenen Depression, in: *The Nature of Sleep*. U.J. Jovanovic, ed. Fisher, Stuttgart (1973).

Kvist, J., and Kirkegaard, C. Effect of repeated sleep deprivation on clinical symptoms and the TRH test in endogenous depression. *Acta Psychiat. Scand. 62*, 494-502 (1980).

Larsen, J.K., Lindberg, M.L. and Skorgaard, B. Sleep deprivation on treatment for endogenous depression. *Acta Psychiat. Scand. 54*, 167-173 (1976).

Lit, A.C. Depressies en doorwaakte nachten. *Tijdschrift voor Psychiatrie 21*, 137-144 (1979).

Loosen, P.T., Merkel U., and Amelung, U. Kombinierte Schlafentzugs-/Chlorimipramin-Behandlung endogener Depressionen. *Arzneim-Forsch. 26*, 1177-1178 (1976).

Pflug, B., and Tölle, R. Therapie endogener Depressionen durch Schlafentzug. *Nervenarzt 42*, 117-124 (1971).

Scheyen, J.D. van Slaapdeprivatie bij de behandeling van unipolaire (endogene) vitale depressies. *Ned. T. Geneesk. 121*, 564-568 (1977).

Schulte, W. Klinische Erfahrungen über das Herausgeraten aus der melancholischen Phase, in: *Das depressive Syndrom*. H. Hippius and H. Selbach, eds. Urban Schwarzenberg, München, pp. 415-420. (1969).

Van den Burg, W., and van den Hoofdakker, R.H. Total sleep deprivation in endogenous depression. *Arch. Gen. Psychiat., 32*, 1121-1125 (1975).

Wirz-Justice, A., Pühringer, W., and Hole, G. Response to sleep deprivation as a predictor of therapeutic results with antidepressant drugs. *Amer. J. Psychiat. 136*, 1222-1223 (1979).

REFERENCES

16

Bright Light Used to Treat Sleep and Mood Disorders

Alfred J. Lewy and Robert L. Sack

This chapter discusses how to use bright artificial light in the treatment of patients with major depression who are unresponsive to other treatments. Preliminary data suggest that some of these patients may be helped by bright light exposure, an intervention that avoids toxicity and side effects associated with pharmacotherapy; bright light can also be easily administered in combination with medication.

The goals of this chapter are: (1) to outline the theoretical basis for bright light therapy, (2) to describe how it is used, and (3) to review the types of disorders that might most likely benefit from a trial of bright light exposure. One such disorder, winter depression, has already been shown to be extremely responsive to bright light therapy (Lewy et al., 1982, 1984, 1985b; Rosenthal et al., 1984, 1985a, 1985b). Although some of these patients also benefit from medication, many do not and others are not able to tolerate the side effects of antidepressant medications.

Biological rhythms are thought to be important components of sleep and mood disorders (see Table 1). Patterns of recurrence, particularly of the seasonal type,

TABLE 1. Biological Rhythm Abnormalities in Affective Disorders

1. Patterns of recurrence, especially seasonal
2. Diurnal variation of mood (depression worse in the morning)
3. Sleep disturbances
4. Phase advanced or phase delayed circadian rhythms

suggest that biological responses to recurring changes in the environment might be involved in the timing of some affective episodes (Halberg, 1968; Kripke et al., 1978). Diurnal variation of mood (depression worse in the morning than in the evening) is quite striking in many patients with melancholia. Perhaps most significantly, mood disorders are frequently accompanied by sleep disturbances. In the last few years, details of actual circadian rhythm abnormalities have been documented (reviewed by Wehr and Goodwin, 1981). Most recently, the discovery that bright light might be able to manipulate biological rhythms (Lewy et al., 1982, 1984, 1985b; Wever et al., 1983), based on the finding that bright light can suppress nighttime melatonin production in humans (Lewy et al., 1980), has opened the door to future treatment possibilities (Lewy et al., 1982, 1984, 1985b; Kripke et al., 1983; Rosenthal et al., 1984, 1985a, 1985b).

REGULATION OF SEASONAL AND CIRCADIAN RHYTHMS BY LIGHT

Before we examine human biological rhythms further, some background from the animal literature is in order (Aschoff, 1981). In animals, there appear to be two types of biological rhythms that are regulated by light: seasonal rhythms and circadian (24-hour) rhythms (see Table 2).

Seasonal rhythms are ubiquitous in animals. Examples are reproduction (estrus), hibernation, and migration, among many others. The most important time cue (zeitgeber) for regulating seasonal or annual rhythms is day length (photoperiod). Studies have shown that animals measure day length as the interval between dawn and dusk. Seasonal rhythms in many animals are regulated by the

TABLE 2. Effects of Light

1. Suppression of nighttime melatonin production
2. Entrainment of circadian rhythms
3. Regulation of seasonal rhythms

duration of nighttime melatonin production. Melatonin is produced only at night during the dark; consequently, the duration of melatonin production is greater in the winter than in the summer.

Animal studies have shown that light (i.e., the 24-hour light-dark cycle) also synchronizes (entrains) circadian rhythms. Circadian rhythms are endogenously generated and are self-sustaining. In the absence of the light-dark zeitgeber, they become "free running." Free-running periods are usually slightly greater than or slightly less than 24 hours. It is important that the intrinsic (free-running) periods of animals differ slightly from 24 hours or else steady-state entrainment to a 24-hour zeitgeber would be extremely difficult.

When human subjects are studied under conditions of temporal isolation, such as in caves or in underground laboratories, their circadian rhythms free run at their intrinsic periods. The intrinsic periods of most humans studied under temporal isolation are almost always greater than 24 hours, although a few people have been reported to have intrinsic periods slightly less than 24 hours. The average intrinsic period for humans is 25 ± 0.5 hours (Wever, 1979) and varies between individuals. The intrinsic period of an individual can change from time to time and can be affected by environmental factors.

Phase and Period

Two aspects of entrainment, period and phase, are related. The period of a circadian rhythm is about 24 hours. The phase of a circadian rhythm is determined by comparing arbitrary points between rhythms; for example, if the maximum of rhythm A occurs earlier than the maximum of rhythm B, then rhythm A has an advanced phase with respect to rhythm B (or, conversely, rhythm B is phase-delayed with respect to rhythm A). Real time or the light-dark cycle can also be used as a reference base for determining whether a rhythm is phase advanced or phase delayed. For example, a rectal temperature minimum that occurs at 0100 is phase advanced, because in most individuals the minimum occurs around 0400.

The Phase Response Curve (PRC)

Although relatively little is known about how animals are entrained by the light-dark cycle in nature, much is known about how light affects these rhythms in the laboratory. The light-dark and dark-light transitions appear to be most important for entrainment. Entrainment to external time cues and maintenance of stable phase relationships between the various circadian rhythms are explained by what is called a phase-response curve (PRC). The PRC is a plotted graph (see Figure 1): the abscissa is (circadian) time; the ordinate shows the direction (below the abscissa for delay shifts, above the abscissa for advance shifts) and the magnitude of the phase shift that is caused by a pulse of light at a particular time.

To determine a PRC, an animal is placed in constant darkness. It immediately begins to free run (as measured by some device such as an activity wheel). The animal is then exposed to a short (15-minute) pulse of light every few weeks and is then observed for a shift in the phase of its activity-rest cycle. The period of its activity-rest cycle continues to be around 24 hours, but a phase shift occurs after each light pulse (a few days of "transients" may pass before the full effect of the light pulse takes hold). The animal then continues to free run at its usual intrinsic (free-running) period. The direction [advance (shift to an earlier phase) or delay (shift to a later phase)] and the magnitude of the phase shift depend on when the light pulse occurs in relation to the animal's subjective activity-rest cycle. Because the animal is in continuous dark, with the exception of these brief, infrequent light pulses, there is no actual day or night, but we can denote a subjective day and night: for diurnal animals, subjective day is the activity portion of their free running activity-rest cycle and subjective night is the rest portion; for nocturnal

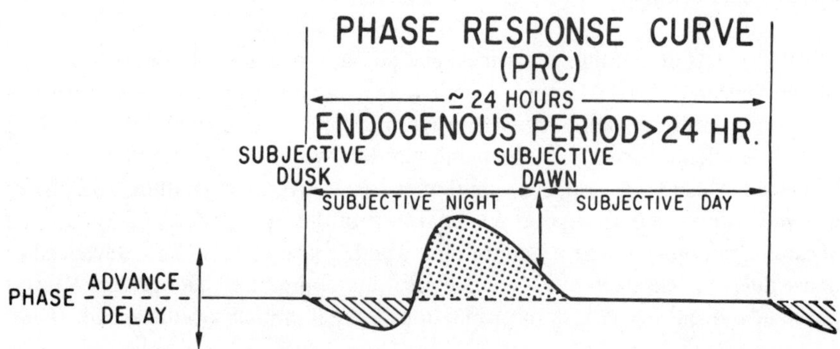

Figure 1. Our hypothesized phase response curve for humans. Bright light exposure during the day should have little effect. Bright light exposure during the first part of the night should delay (shift to a later time) circadian rhythms; bright light exposure during the last part of the night should advance (shift to an earlier time) circadian rhythms. The further away from dusk and dawn, the greater should be the magnitude of the shift. Because humans generally have intrinsic endogenous circadian rhythms with periods greater than 24 hours, the area under the advance portion of the PRC illuminated by daylight should be greater than the area under the delay portion. This curve is based on PRCs obtained in a variety of species of animals and on the experimental evidence we have obtained in humans. From Lewy et al., 1983.

animals, subjective day is the rest portion and subjective night is the activity portion.

The precise shapes of these curves vary greatly, but certain features appear to be universal for both diurnal and nocturnal animals (Pittendrigh and Daan, 1976; Hoban and Sulzman, 1985). If the light pulse occurs during subjective day, there is a minimal phase-shifting effect. The most pronounced effects result only if the light pulse occurs during subjective night. Generally, the closer the light pulse is to the middle of subjective night, the greater is the magnitude of the phase shift. The direction (delay or advance) of the phase shift depends on whether the light pulse occurs in the first or second half of subjective night, respectively. If the pulse of light occurs in the first half of subjective night (i.e, near subjective dusk), the animal will delay its phase position. For some animals, if the light pulse occurs one hour after subjective dusk, the animal will delay one hour; if the light pulse occurs two hours after subjective dusk, the animal will delay two hours, etc. If the pulse of light occurs during the second half of subjective night (i.e, near subjective dawn), the animal will advance its phase position. For some animals, a light pulse that occurs one hour before subjective dawn might advance the animal by one hour; if the light pulse occurs two hours before subjective dawn, the animal will advance two hours etc. In the middle of subjective night, there is an inflection point: the time for producing the greatest phase delay might be separated by only a few minutes from the time for producing the greatest phase advance.

Entrainment to the Natural Photoperiod

From the experimental origins of PRCs, we can speculate about how the light-dark cycle entrains circadian rhythms in nature. It can be hypothesized that morning light advances rhythms and evening light delays them (Lewy et al., 1983), and therefore, every day our clocks are gently nudged in each direction. The net effect of these phase shifts should depend on the animal's PRC and on its intrinsic period. For humans, whose intrinsic periods are generally around 25 hours, we must make a net advance of approximately one hour per day. Otherwise, we would gradually drift later and later each successive cycle. Furthermore, evening light might cause an additional delay each day. Suppose we delay 0.5 hours each day as a result of evening light, then we must use morning light to advance 1.5 hours each day. The net effect of morning and evening light will then be a one-hour advance, which is what is necessary to keep us stably phased and entrained to the 24-hour day-night cycle, assuming our intrinsic periods are 25 hours.

As will be discussed in the next section, bright light (above the intensity of ordinary room light) appears to be necessary for the regulation of human biological rhythms. Given the general features of PRCs, dawn and dusk should be the important times for light exposure for the day-to-day entrainment of both circadian and seasonal rhythms, because these are the times when sufficiently bright light illuminates the higher-amplitude portions of the PRC. Morning light advances our circadian rhythms; evening light delays them. In addition, the interval between dawn and dusk, the photoperiod, is crucial for cueing seasonal rhythms to the time of the year.

THE HUMAN RESPONSE TO LIGHT

Until recently it was widely held that humans lacked the above mentioned responses to light. Chronobiologists thought that light was of limited, if any, importance in the regulation of biological rhythms in humans (reviewed by Czeisler et al., 1981). Similarly, pineal physiologists were also of the opinion that light did not effect humans in ways in which light seemed to affect all other species (reviewed by Lewy et al., 1980).

Bright Light Suppresses Human Melatonin Production

In 1980 (Lewy et al.), we showed that previous studies of retinally mediated nonvisual effects of light used insufficiently intense light for demonstrating these effects in humans. Humans appear to require light four or five times brighter than ordinary room light for suppression of melatonin production (Figure 2). Once a threshold has been reached, the brighter the light, the greater the suppression. Humans require light of about 2500 lux for suppression of nighttime melatonin production to near daytime levels, whereas some animals need only 10 lux. Ordinary room light is rarely above 500 lux (one lux is about 10 foot-candles.) Outdoor sunlight is 10,000 to 100,000 lux, depending on the cloud cover (see Table 3).

Our findings concerning suppression of human melatonin production by bright light had at least two implications. One implication was that humans had biological rhythms that were regulated by sunlight (ordinary room light is probably not bright enough to perturb the rhythms that are cued by sunlight). The second implication was that these rhythms could be experimentally (and perhaps therapeutically) manipulated, using exposure to sufficiently bright artificial light. The next section will discuss the initial studies in healthy control subjects, and later sections will review findings in patients with chronobiologic sleep and mood disorders.

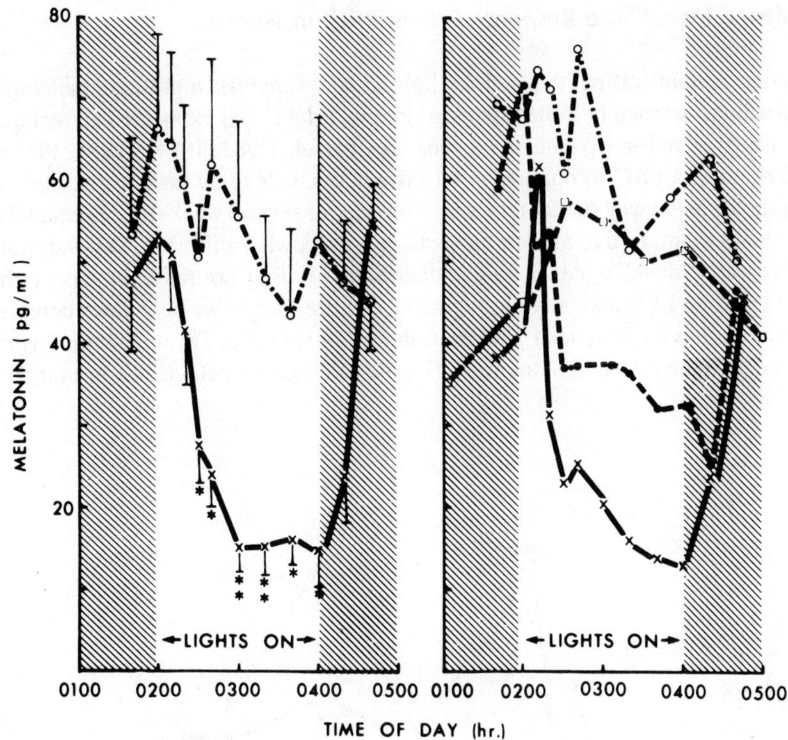

Figure 2. Suppression of nighttime melatonin production. (Left) Six normal volunteers were awakened between 2 and 4 A.M. and exposed to different intensities of light. 500 lux (o) had little effect, whereas 2500 lux (x) caused significant suppression (* = p <.05, ** = p <.01). (Right) Two volunteers were also exposed to 1500 lux (●), which suppressed melatonin production to an intermediate extent. There was no suppression of melatonin production when these subjects slept in the dark (□). Reproduced by permission (Lewy et al., 1980).

TABLE 3. Intensities of Light, by Source

Source	Lux
Outdoor sunlight, sunny day	100,000
Outdoor sunlight, cloudy day	10,000
Bright artificial light	2000-2500
Ordinary room light	200-500

Evidence for a Phase Response Curve (PRC) in Humans

After demonstrating that bright light could suppress nighttime melatonin production, we then became interested in how bright light exposure can manipulate (shift) circadian rhythms in humans (Lewy et al., 1983, 1984, 1985b, 1985c). Determining a PRC in humans is an extremely challenging task, particularly if done in the usual way (under temporal isolation for several weeks). Consequently, we chose to study our human subjects in a somewhat different way—shifting "dawn" and "dusk" under entrained conditions. In four normal volunteers (who slept between 2300 and 0600 throughout the entire study), we held dawn constant for a week, having advanced dusk from about 2100 to 1600. The melatonin rhythm shifted earlier by the end of the week (Figure 3). Then we held dusk constant for a

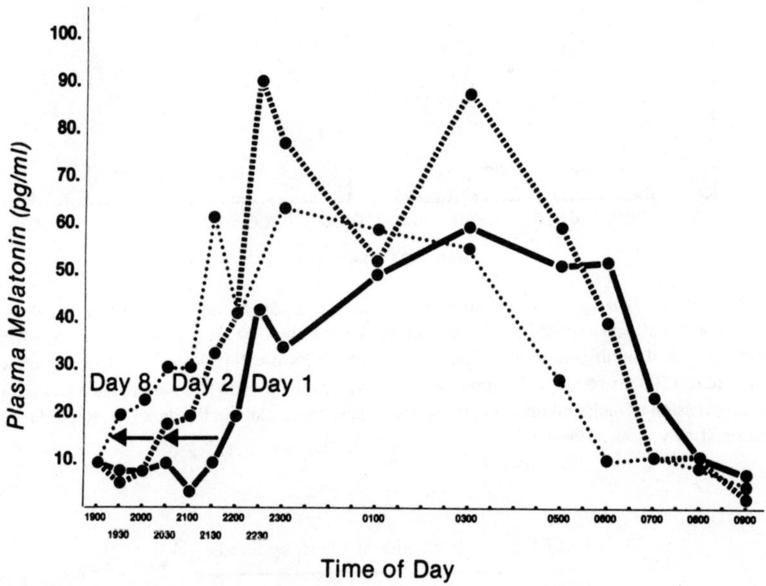

Figure 3. Patterns of melatonin production under different photoperiods. Four normal volunteers slept between 2300 and 0600 throughout the entire study. Only the means are plotted; the SEMs can be found in another publication (Lewy et al., 1985b). On day 1, "dusk" was between 1930 and 2100 and "dawn" was between 0600 and 1730. Dusk was shifted to 1600 on day 2 and held constant for the remainder of the study. The first day of advanced dusk (day 2), the melatonin onset shifted. 1.5 hours earlier (15 pg/ml was used as the level to determine the nighttime melatonin onset). By the seventh day of advanced dusk (day 8), the melatonin onset shifted earlier by another hour and the melatonin offset also appeared to shift earlier by about one hour. Reproduced by permission (Lewy et al., 1985c).

week and delayed dawn from about 0600 to 0900. The melatonin rhythm subsequently was delayed (Figure 4). These data are consistent with the existence of a PRC in humans, with delay responses to light in the evening and advance responses to light in the morning. These data suggest that to delay circadian rhythms, subjects should be exposed to bright light in the evening; to advance circadian rhythms, subjects should be exposed to bright light in the morning (see Table 4).

The Dim Light Melatonin Onset (DLMO) as a Marker for Circadian Phase Position

We also found that the evening melatonin onset occurred much earlier the first night of advanced dusk, too soon to be a shift of the clock; thus, we think that bright light in the evening can also suppress the onset of melatonin production if the photoperiod is sufficiently long. Consequently, we are now recommending the

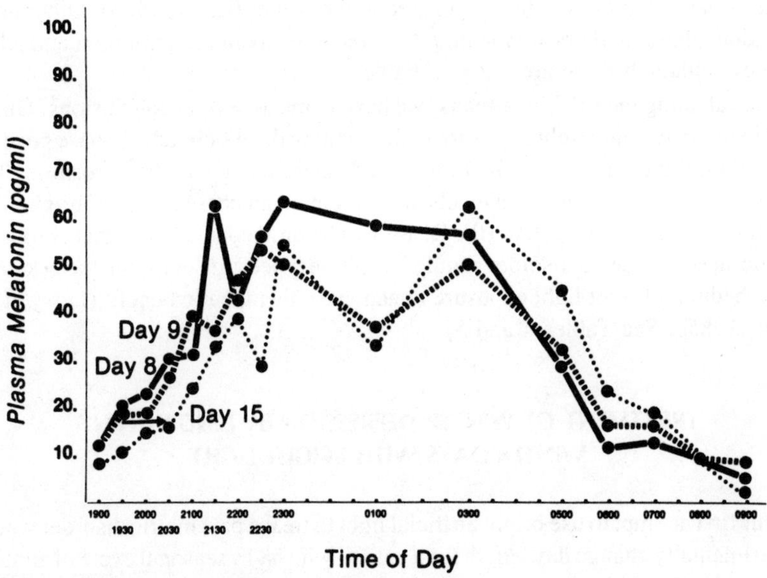

Figure 4. Patterns of melatonin production under different photoperiods. On day 9, dawn was shifted to 0900 and was held constant for the remainder of the study. No immediate change was noted the first day of the shift (day 9). However, by the end of the week (day 15), both the onset and the offset delayed by about one hour. Reproduced by permission (Lewy et al., 1985c).

TABLE 4. Morning and Evening Bright Light Have Opposite Effects on Shifting Circadian Phase Position

Direction of phase shift	Schedule bright light exposure	Avoid light
To advance phase	in the morning	in the evening
To delay phase	in the evening	in the morning

use of the dim light melatonin onset (DLMO) for marking circadian phase position (Lewy et al., 1984, 1985b, 1985c). After 5 P.M., subjects are asked to remain in a room shielded from sunlight and bright artificial light exposure. Then blood is sampled every 30 minutes between 6 P.M. and 11 P.M.

The time of rise of the melatonin levels is a useful marker for circadian phase position. However, too few patients and normals have been studied to determine the normal range of circadian phase positions. Time of the year may also be a crucial variable and we have hypothesized that circadian phase position may be more advanced in the summer compared to the winter (Lewy, 1983). Other good circadian phase markers are the nighttime rectal temperature minimum and REM latency, although these are not as reliable.

In evaluating the PRC in humans, we have come to several conclusions. One is that in humans bright light exposure in the evening delays circadian phase position and bright light exposure in the morning advances circadian phase position. The second is that to use melatonin levels to mark circadian phase position, bright light should be avoided after 5 P.M. (the DLMO). The third conclusion is that chronobiologic sleep and mood disorder should be "phase typed" to determine the best time for scheduling bright light exposure to achieve a therapeutic benefit (Lewy et al, 1984, 1985b; See Tables 4 and 5).

TREATMENT OF WINTER DEPRESSION BY LENGTHENING WINTER DAYS WITH BRIGHT LIGHT

Our first attempt to use bright artificial light to treat a psychiatric disorder was to experimentally change day length for a patient who had a seasonal cycle of annually recurring major depressive episodes (Lewy et al., 1982). This patient had recurrent depressions for at least 13 years that generally began when the days grew shorter and remitted when the days lengthened. We experimentally increased the

TABLE 5. Phase Typing of Chronobiologic Sleep and Mood Disorders

Phase type	Sleep	DLMO	Temp. minimum	REM latency
Advanced	early morning awakening	early	early	short
Delayed	morning hypersomnia	late	late	normal or long

length of his winter days by exposing him to bright light between 6 and 9 A.M. and between 4 and 7 P.M. Within 4 days, his depression began to remit, two months before the expected time.

Since the publication of our first case report on winter depression and its treatment using bright light exposure, several other studies have been completed. In the following winter (1981), nine subjects were crossed over to dim (yellow) light (Rosenthal et al., 1984). Because dim light did not suppress human melatonin production, it was thought that light of this intensity would not be chronobiologically active and therefore could be used as a placebo control. Patients had a robust antidepressant response to lengthening their winter days with 2500 lux light; the dim light had no statistically significant effect. Generally, light exposure appears to be required for the antidepressant effect for the duration of winter until the days naturally lengthen in the spring.

In the winter of 1982, the NIMH group investigated the role of sleep deprivation in winter depression, (Rosenthal et al., 1985), because, in the 1981 study, patients were asked to arise slightly earlier than their normal time. They concluded that sleep deprivation did not account for the antidepressant effect of bright light. In the winter of 1983, the NIMH group investigated the role of melatonin in this disorder. A group of eight winter depressive patients who were treated with bright light exposure were fed melatonin in the morning and evening (Rosenthal et al., 1985b). Some, but not all, of the symptoms of winter depression returned with replacement of melatonin, whereas administration of a placebo had no effect. This is an interesting finding, but it is certainly not conclusive at this time.

The NIMH group had also begun to use bright light exposure in the evening without concomitant morning exposure. They are currently reporting that five hours of bright light in the evening is sufficient for the antidepressant response. (Rosenthal et al., 1985a). Futhermore, they claim that morning light does not appear to be critical for the antidepressant response in patients with seasonal affective disorder.

TREATMENT OF PHASE DELAYED WINTER DEPRESSIVE PATIENTS WITH MORNING BRIGHT LIGHT

On the other hand, we have found that winter depressive patients have a much better response to morning light (6-8 or 9 A.M.) than to evening light (7 or 8-10 P.M.) (Lewy et al., 1984, 1985b) (Figure 5). (When treating chronobiologic disorders, bright light exposure at these times permits patients to obtain a full night's sleep.) The response to morning light is even greater than the response to light exposure during both times. Evening light alone is ineffective. This is consistent with our observation that most of these patients appear to be phase delayed. Unlike the typical endogenous (melancholic) depressive, who appears to be phase-advanced as evidenced by a history of early morning awakening, winter depressive patients generally complain that they have difficulty arising in the morning and are therefore probably phase-delayed. Figures 6 and 7 are overnight temperature and activity curves for a winter depressive patient who was phase-delayed as evidenced by the sleep-wake cycle. After scheduling his sleep for one week between 11 P.M. and 6 A.M.., the nighttime temperature minimum was at 5 A.M., which

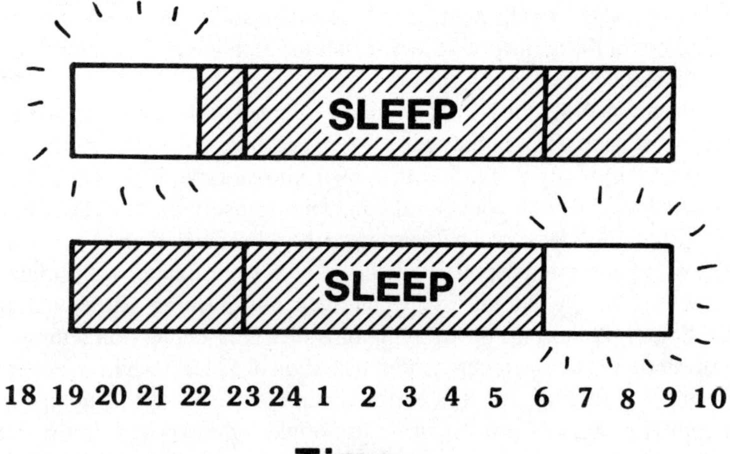

Figure 5. Subjects and patients can be shifted according to our hypothesized PRC. Whenever possible, sleep is held constant between 2300 and 0600. (Top) To delay circadian rhythms, subjects are exposed to bright light in the evening between 1900 and 2200 and are kept away from bright light between 0600 and 0900. (Bottom) To advance circadian rhythms, subjects are kept away from bright light after 1700 and are exposed to bright light in the morning between 0600 and 0900.

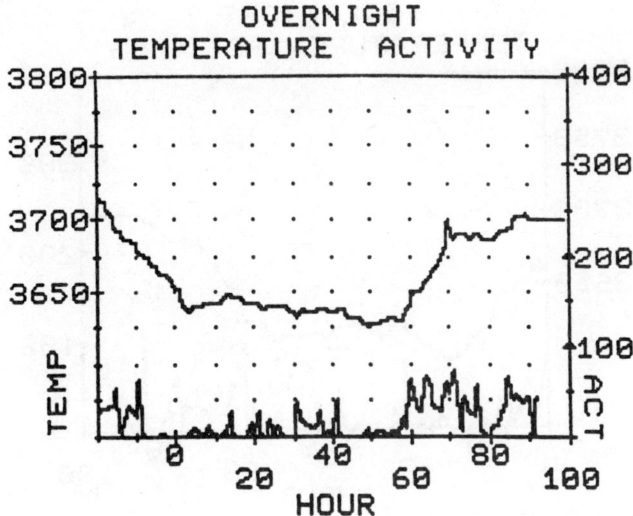

Figure 6. Overnight rectal temperature and wrist locomotor activity curves in a patient with winter depression. Time is shown on the abscissa (0 = midnight, 100 = 10 A.M.). Temperature in centrigrade and activity counts are shown on the ordinates. Pretreatment, this patient had a slightly phase delayed temperature with the nighttime minima occurring at about 5 A.M., which is consistent with how we phase typed this patient by clinical history. Sleep offset had been at 6 A.M., as scheduled by the investigators. From Lewy et al., 1985b.

was slightly phase-delayed (and certainly not phase-advanced; see Figure 6). After one week of morning bright light exposure, the temperature minimum shifted earlier to 12:30 A.M. (Figure 7) and the patient's depression remitted.

Thirty minutes of morning bright light exposure (6-6:30 A.M.) may be sufficient to induce a remission in some winter depressive patients. Indeed, some winter depressive patients may actually respond better to this schedule of bright light exposure than to two hours of morning bright light (6-8 A.M.); these patients may become overly phase advanced by too much morning bright light exposure and may complain that their morning hypersomnia has now become early morning awakening. Although the response to light is usually complete within a week, some patients will take up to a week longer to achieve their maximum response, especially if they had to get up early (advance their sleep-wake cycle) to accommodate the morning bright light exposure. It may also be possible to treat patients with winter depression by delaying their sleep so that they are waking up into bright morning sunlight (Lewy et al., 1985b).

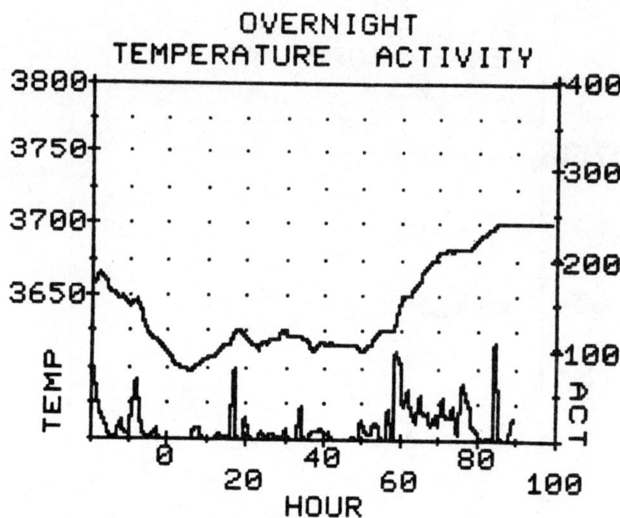

Figure 7. Overnight rectal temperature and wrist locomotor activity curves in the same winter depressive patient after one week of bright light exposure between 6 and 9 A.M. (avoiding bright light after 5 P.M.). The temperature minimum shifted earlier to 12:30 A.M. and the patient's depression remitted. From Lewy et al., 1985b.

TREATMENT OF PHASE ADVANCED ENDOGENOUS DEPRESSIVES WITH EVENING BRIGHT LIGHT

We have also studied a relatively small number of patients with endogenous depression who have early morning awakening. After 2-3 days of bright light exposure in the evening, the early morning awakening was ameliorated. Evaluation of the other symptoms of depression after light treatment is in progress. It should be pointed out that Kripke and colleagues (Kripke, 1981; Kripke et al., 1983) have been treating these presumably phase advanced patients with bright light exposure in the morning. However, according to our hypothesized PRC, morning light would advance circadian rhythms; therefore, we have hypothesized that evening light exposure should be best for these patients (Lewy et al., 1983; Lewy, 1984). Figure 8 is an example of an endogenously depressed patient with phase advanced circadian rhythms. In this case we have plotted the dim light melatonin onsets DLMOs). On admission (AD), the DLMO was occurring at 7:50 P.M. One week of morning bright light (avoiding bright light in the evening) advanced the DLMO to 7:10 P.M. During one week of dim light morning and evening, the DLMO

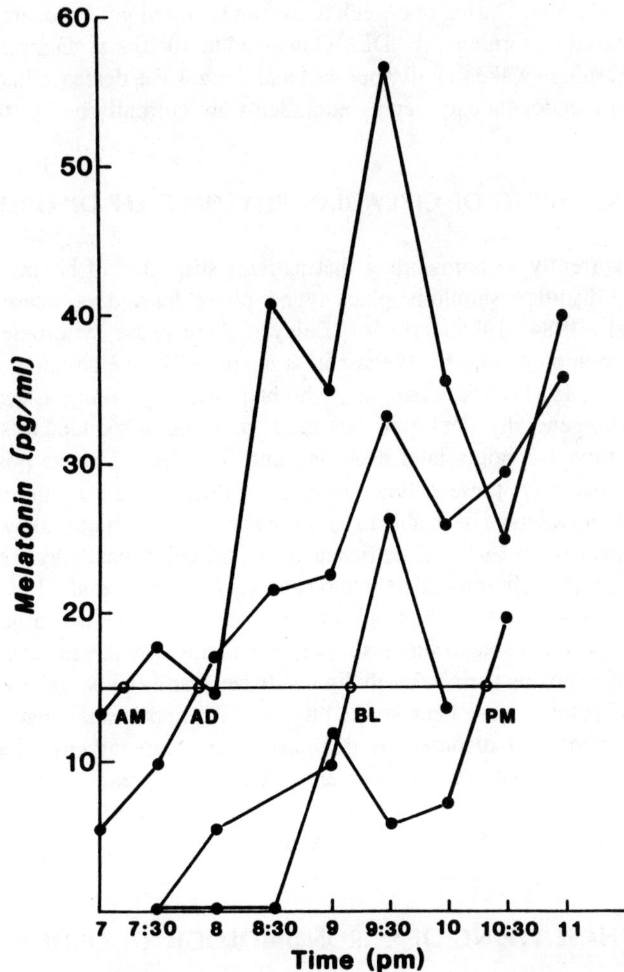

Figure 8. Dim light melatonin onsets (DLMOs) in a patient with endogenous depression. This study was done during February and March. The 15 pg/ml threshold was selected as the basis for defining the nighttime rise in melatonin production (levels are quite low throughout the day until the evening). On admission (AD), the DLMO occurred at about 7:50 P.M., which is somewhat phase advanced (and is consistent with how we had phase typed this patient by clinical history). After a week of bright light exposure (AM) between 6 and 9 A.M. (avoiding bright light in the evening), the DLMO shifted slightly earlier (to about 7:10 P.M.). After a week of dim light morning and evening, the DLMO delayed to 9:10 P.M. (BL) After a week of bright light exposure between 7 and 10 P.M. (avoiding bright light in the morning), the DLMO delayed to 10:20 P.M., during which time the patient responded (PM). From Lewy et al., 1985b.

delayed to 9:10 P.M. During one week of evening bright light exposure (avoiding bright light in the morning), the DLMO delayed to 10:20 P.M. During this week the early morning awakening disappeared and there was a decrease in depression ratings. More endogenously depressed patients are currently being studied.

PHASE TYPING OF CIRCADIAN RHYTHM SLEEP DISORDERS

We are currently recommending that patients suspected of having chronobiologic sleep disorders should be phase typed: phase delayed vs. phase advanced (Lewy et al., 1984, 1985b, 1985c). Delayed sleep phase syndrome was first treated chronobiologically by Weitzman et al. in 1981 (Weitzman et al., 1981; Czeisler et al., 1981). These patients, who had difficulty falling asleep before 3 A.M. and who generally slept quite late in the morning, responded to scheduling their sleep time 1-3 hours later each day until the desired phase position was reached. Apparently, these patients have great difficulty advancing their sleep time. However, we have been able to advance these patients quite easily by scheduling their sleep times ½-1 hour earlier each day, provided that they are exposed to one hour of bright light immediately upon awakening (Lewy et al., 1984, 1985b). After a few days, these patients fall asleep earlier and wake up earlier.

We have also been able to successfully treat patients with advanced sleep phase syndrome by exposing them to bright light between 8 and 10 P.M., although only a few of these patients have been studied to date. We hypothesize that depression differs from pure sleep disorders, in that in sleep disorders, all circadian rhythms may be phase-displaced to the same extent, whereas in depression, the sleep-wake cycle may not be as phase-displaced as the other endogenous rhythms, thus creating a phase-angle disturbance in depression (Lewy et al., 1985b).

PHASE TYPING OF CHRONOBIOLOGIC DISORDERS

On the basis of our theoretical understanding of the phaseresponse curve and of our preliminary treatment results, we recommend that patients with sleep or mood disorders suspected of having a chronobiologic component should be phase typed into either the phase advanced or phase delayed type (Lewy et al., 1984, 1985b, 1985c; see Table 5). Phase-typing can often be done based on the sleep-wake cycle. A patient who goes to bed late and arises late is probably phase delayed; similarly, a patient who goes to sleep early and arises early is probably phase-advanced. Such disturbances in phase position are not necessarily pathological unless a change is desired, either for social reasons or because the patient seeks symptomatic relief. For example, some patients complain that they have become increasingly phase-shifted over several years; for others, a change in their work or school schedule dictates that they must get up earlier.

What is the most likely phase type for a patient who has trouble falling asleep and who has early morning awakening, or vice versa? Sleep offset is probably more important than sleep onset (Lewy, 1983), when using sleep time for phase typing. Measurement of some physiological circadian phase marker may also be informative. We recommend the DLMO (Lewy et al., 1984). However, REM latency and temperature (Lewy et al., 1984, 1985b), may also be useful.

Taking a light-exposure history is important. Determining the intensity of light exposure around dawn and dusk is critical. Outdoor light is generally sufficiently intense except for the hour or so of twilight. Cloudiness, fog, or other obstructions to sunlight may influence the duration of twilight, but generally, even very cloudy days are sufficiently bright. Indoor light is usually subthreshold under most circumstances. Windows act like point sources for the inverse square law. That is, light intensity decreases as a function of the square of the distance from the light source. Consequently, being a few inches from a window may be suprathreshold. Direct sunlight through a window may be adequately intense at a distance of several feet.

The exact threshold for entrainment has not yet been determined. Furthermore, some people may be more sensitive to light than others. In fact, patients with a history of bipolar affective disorder may be supersensitive to light in that light exposure between 2 and 4 A.M. suppresses their melatonin levels to twice the extent as in normal control subjects (Lewy et al., 1981, 1985a). We are all probably more sensitive to light in the morning compared to other times of the day. For this reason and because we must use dawn more than dusk for entrainment (if our intrinsic periods are greater than 24 hours), light exposure is probably more critical at dawn than at dusk.

TREATMENT OF JET LAG USING SCHEDULED BRIGHT LIGHT EXPOSURE

The hypothesized PRC can also be used to guide the optimal schedule for bright light exposure at one's destination after traveling through several time zones (Daan and Lewy, 1984). Following transmeridian flight, much of the higher-amplitude portion of the PRC will be illuminated without interfering with sleep.

The hypothesized PRC can be used in the treatment of jet lag in the following way. After traveling through three time zones to the west, for example, bright light exposure in the late afternoon is optimal. After traveling through three time zones to the east, morning bright light is best. However, after traveling through nine time zones to the east, morning bright light would now be illuminating the delay portion of the hypothesized PRC and would retard adaptation to the new time zone; consequently, bright light exposure beginning a few hours after dawn would be best. (See Figure 9).

SUMMARY

We have just begun to evaluate the potential use of bright light exposure as a therapeutic modality. The wavelengths for maximal suppression of melatonin production in humans appear to be around 509 nM—similar to the action spectrum for rhodopsin (Brainard et al., 1985). This is near the middle of the visible spectrum and most white light sources have a substantial representation here. We use fluorescent lamps with plexiglas diffusers. This is probably one of the safest ways to administer bright light. The intensity of the light source is measured at various distances and a distance is selected that produces a response of 2000-2500 lux on a light meter with a photopic sensor. (One lux is about 10 foot-candles). Patients do not have to look at the light all the time, but are encouraged to look in that direction for a few seconds every few minutes. The eyes must be open. Patients should be evaluated for prior eye disease, and, of course, are never instructed to look directly at the sun when outdoor light exposure is scheduled.

Scheduling bright light exposure is based on phase typing the individual (Lewy et al., 1984, 1985b, 1985c) and on the hypothesized phase-response curve (Lewy et al., 1983). If a person is phase-delayed, bright light exposure in the morning should be most effective. If a person is phase-advanced, bright light exposure in the evening is most effective. Bright light should be avoided at that time of the day when it might hinder the phase shift. (This principle was illustrated in the above discussion of jet lag.) For example, patients who are exposed to bright light in the morning should avoid bright light in the evening. Patients who are exposed to bright light in the evening should avoid bright light in the morning. Avoiding bright light can be accomplished in dimly lit rooms or by wearing welder's goggles (Lewy et al., 1985b). These goggles exclude light from every direction and lenses can be interchanged depending on the intensity of the ambient light.

Patients generally respond within 3-4 days, and the response is mostly completed by the end of a week. Once the timing of sleep has normalized, it is held constant. This is particularly important in depressed patients, in whom we have hypothesized that the phase angle between the sleep-wake cycle and the other circadian rhythms may be pathogenic (Lewy et al., 1985b). The number of minutes of exposure necessary per day is not known at the present time. This may vary among

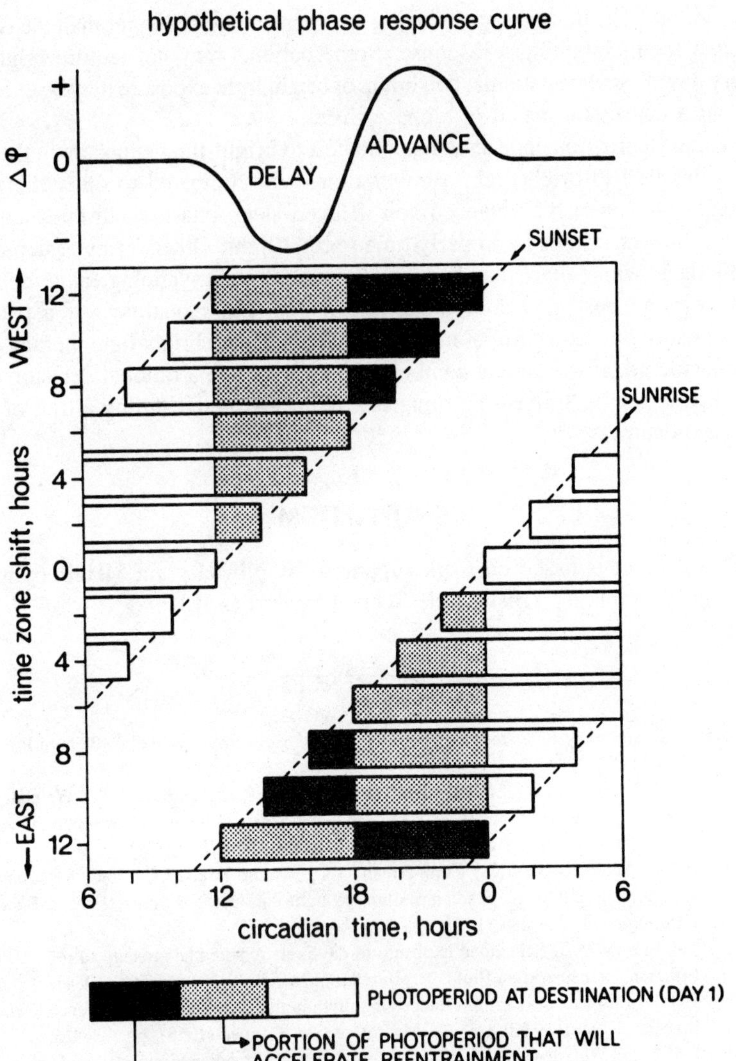

Figure 9. Use of the PRC for reducing jet lag. Assuming a photoperiod length of 12 hours, Figure 9 has been constructed for recommending the best times to obtain and to avoid bright light exposure the first few days after arriving at the new destination. The bars indicate the photoperiod at the destination. The gray areas indicate the times to obtain light exposure; the black areas indicate the times to avoid bright light exposure. From Daan and Lewy, 1984.

individuals. The duration for inducing a response may be longer than the duration needed for maintaining a response. Some patients may not require bright light every day. For some patients, two hours of bright light exposure may be excessive, in that it causes too much of a phase shift.

Winter depression appears to respond best to bright-light exposure in the morning compared to bright light at other times and compared to other therapeutic modalities. Similarly, advanced and delayed sleep phase syndromes appear to have robust responses to properly timed bright light. Other forms of depression, particularly where there may be many biological and psychological components, may respond best to a combination of therapeutic modalities. If a patient is suspected of having a chronobiologic component, then bright light therapy should be considered. If the patient can be phase typed, then a rational decision can be made as to the best time—morning or evening—for scheduling a trial of bright light exposure.

ACKNOWLEDGMENTS

This chapter is based on work supported by NIMH grant MH40161 and the Chicago Community Trust Searle Scholar Award (AJL).

REFERENCES

Aschoff, J. *Handbook of Behavioral Neurobiology, Biological Rhythms*, vol 4. Plenum Press, New York (1981).

Brainard, G.C., Lewy, A.J., Menaker, M., Fredrickson, R.H., Miller, L.S., Weleber, R.G., Cassone, V., and Hudson, D. Effect of wavelength on the suppression of nocturnal melatonin in normal volunteers. *Ann. N.Y. Acad. Sci.*, *453*, 376-378 (1985).

Czeisler, C.A., Richardson, G.S., Zimmerman, J.C., Moore-Ede, M.C., and Weitzman, E.D. Entrainment of human circadian rhythms by light-dark cycles: A reassessment. *Photochem. Photobiol. 34*, 239-247 (1981).

Daan, S., and Lewy, A.J. Scheduled exposure to daylight: A potential strategy to reduce "jet lag" following transmeridian flight. *Psychopharmacol. Bull. 20*, 566-568 (1984).

Halberg, F. Physiologic considerations underlying rhythmometry, with special reference to emotional illness. *Symposium Bel-Aire III*, Masson et Cie, Geneve (1968), pp. 73-126.

Hoban, T.M., and Sulzman, S.M. Light effects on the circadian timing system of a diurnal primate—the squirrel monkey, *Amer. J. Physiol* R274-R280 (1985),

Kripke, D.F. Photoperiodic mechanisms for depression and its treatment, in *Biological Psychiatry 1981*, C. Perris, G. Struwe, and B. Jansson, eds. Elsevier, Amsterdam (1981), pp. 1249-1252.

Kripke, D.F., Mullaney, D.J., Wolf, S., and Adkinson, M. Circadian rhythm disorders in manic-depressives. Biol. Psychiatry 13, 335-350 (1978).

Kripke, D.F., Risch, S.C., and Janowsky, D. Bright white light alleviates depression. *Psych. Res. 10*, 105-112 (1983).

Lewy, A.J. Biochemistry and regulation of mammalian melatonin production, in *The Pineal Gland*, R. M. Relkin, ed. Elsevier North-Holland, New York (1983), pp. 77-128.

Lewy, A.J. Human melatonin secretion (II): a marker for adrenergic function, in *Neurobiology of Mood Disorders*, R.M. Post, and J.C. Ballenger, eds. Williams & Wilkins, Baltimore (1984), pp. 215-226.

Lewy, A.J., Kern, H.E., Rosenthal, N.E., and Wehr, T.A. Bright artificial light treatment of a manic-depressive patient with a seasonal mood cycle.*Am. J. Psychiatry 139*, 1496-1498 (1982).

Lewy, A.J., Nurnberger, J.I., Wehr, T.A., Pack, D., Becker, L.E., Powell, R.L., Simmons-Alling, S., Goodwin, F.K., and Gershon, E.S. Supersensitivity to light may be a trait marker for manic-depressive illness. *Amer. J. Psychiatry 142*, 725-727 (1985a).

Lewy, A.J., Sack, R.L., Fredrickson, R.H., Reaves, M., Denney, D.D., and Zielske, D.R. The use of bright light in the treatment of chronobiologic sleep and mood disorders: The phase-response curve. *Psychopharmacol. Bull. 19*, 523-525 (1983).

Lewy, A.J., Sack, R.L., and Singer, C.M. Assessment and treatment of chronobiologic disorders using plasma melatonin levels and brigth light exposure: The clock-gate model and the phase response curve. *Psychopharmacol. Bull. 20*, 561-565 (1984).

Lewy, A.J., Sack, R.L., and Singer, C.M. Treating phase typed chronobiologic sleep and mood disorders using appropriately timed bright artificial light. *Psychopharmacol. Bull.*, 21, 368-372 (1985b).

Lewy, A.J., Sack, R.L., Singer, C.M. Immediate and delayed effects of bright light on human melatonin production: Shifting "dawn" and "dusk" shifts the dim light melatonin onset (DLMO). *Ann. N.Y. Acad. Sci.*, *474*, 253-259 (1985c).

Lewy, A.J., Wehr, T.A., Goodwin, F.K., Newsome, D.A., and Markey, S.P. Light suppresses melatonin secretion in humans. *Science 210*, 1267-1269 (1980).

Lewy, A.J., Wehr, T.A., Goodwin, F.K., Newsome, D.A., and Rosenthal, N.E. Manic-depressive patients may be supersensitive to light. *Lancet 1*, 383-384 (1981).

Pittendrigh, C.S., and Daan, S. A functional analysis of circadian pacemakers in nocturnal rodents. V. Pacemaker structure: a clock for all seasons. *J. Comp. Physiol. 106*, 333-355 (1976).

Rosenthal, N.E., Sack, D.A., Gillin, J.C., Lewy, A.J., Goodwin, F.K., Davenport, Y., Mueller, P.S., Newsome, D.A., and Wehr, T.A. Seasonal affective disorder. *Arch. Gen. Psychiatry 41*, 72-80 (1984).

Rosenthal, N.E., Sack, D.A., Carpenter, C.J., Parry, B.L., Mendelson, W.B., and Wehr, T.A. Antidepressant effects of light in seasonal affective disorder. *Am. J. Psychiatry 142*, 163-170 (1985a).

Rosenthal, N.E., Sack, D.A., James, S.P., Parry, B.L., Mendelson, W.B., Tamarkin, L., and Wehr, T.A. Seasonal affective disorder and phototherapy. *Ann. N.Y. Acad. Sci. 474*, 260-269 (1985b).

Wehr, T.A., and Goodwin, F.K. Biological rhythms and psychiatry, in *American Handbook of Psychiatry*, vol. 7, 2nd ed., S. Arieti, and H.K.H. Brodie, eds. Basic Books, New York (1981), pp. 46-74.

Weitzman, E.D., Czeisler, C.A., Coleman, R.M., Spielman, A.J., Zimmerman, J.C., Dement, W., Richardson, G., and Pollak, C.P. Delayed sleep phase syndrome: a chronobiological disorder associated with sleep-onset insomnia. *Arch. Gen. Psychiatry 38*, 737-746 (1981).

Wever, R.A. *The Circadian System of Man*. Springer-Verlag, New York (1979).

Wever, R.A., Polaske, J., and Wildgruber, C.M. Bright light affects human circadian rhythms. *Pflugers Arch. 396*, 85-87 (1983).

17

Psychostimulant (Amphetamine or Methylphenidate) Therapy for Chronic and Treatment-Resistant Depression

Frank J. Ayd, Jr., and Joseph Zohar

In an editorial entitled "The Use of Dextroamphetamine in Medically Ill Depressed Patients" (Pitts, 1982), Ferris N. Pitts Jr., M.D., editor-in-chief of the *Journal of Clinical Psychiatry*, lamented that "what *is* in the medical literature on the usefulness of amphetamines in the treatment of depression has had little impact on the medical community." This, he noted, accounts for the fact that in the United States some board-certified, competent and responsible psychiatrists have had hospital privileges suspended or have had their medical licenses suspended because they had prescribed a psychostimulant, either dextroamphetamine or methylphenidate, for chronic depressives who had not responded to "psychotherapy plus adequate doses of various tricyclics, neuroleptics, and monoamine oxidase inhibitors." After treatment with prudent and proper doses of a psychostimulant, these patients had become less depressed and more functional without developing tolerance for or abusing the psychostimulant to which they had responded. Hence, Dr. Pitts concluded: "Amphetamines are effective in the treatment of depression, and it can be good medical practice to utilize them carefully and rationally as adjunctive agents in the treatment of patients shown to be inadequately responsive to other treatments for depression." Dr. Pitts also could have made the same conclusion regarding methylphenidate.

For more than three decades, psychostimulants have appeared to be an attractive possibility for the treatment of depression (Myerson, 1936; Landman et al., 1958; Hare et al, 1962; Kiloh et al., 1974; Katon and Raskind, 1980; Kaufmann and Murray, 1982). On the surface it has seemed very plausible to give a stimulant to a person who is depressed, apathetic and withdrawn, and even more to a patient who has not been responding to standard antidepressant treatments, i.e., in a case of treatment-resistant depression. In addition, for many years now conscientious clinicians have prescribed psychostimulants for chronic depressives who are medically ill and intolerant of tricyclic antidepressants, or whose medical condition makes treatment with a tricyclic contraindicated. Unfortunately, many patients who are candidates for psychostimulant therapy for chronic depression have been and will continue to be denied such treatment for two reasons, namely, that many doctors are unaware of the potential benefits and safety of proper psychostimulant therapy for specific subgroups of depressed patients, and many others are afraid of possible abuse of and/or addiction to a psychostimulant and of being censured for prescribing such a drug, particularly since it has been classified as a controlled substance. The objectives of this chapter are to present clinical data that should overcome these obstacles to appropriate psychostimulant therapy by describing the candidates for it, the effective daily dosages, and the duration and safety of judiciously prescribed psychostimulant therapy.

CANDIDATES

Although it may seem that any depressed patient may be a candidate for psychostimulant therapy, this simply is not true. Over thirty years' clinical experience throughout the world has provided data documenting that there are subgroups of depressed patients who are candidates for and who may benefit from psychostimulant therapy. These are discussed below.

Mild to Moderately Chronic Dysphorics

These are the individuals whose illness began in childhood, adolescence, or in their early twenties. Characteristically, the majority of these patients never or rarely consult a psychiatrist. Instead, they are treated by family physicians, internists, and gynecologists, often those with whom they are socially acquainted and friendly. The number of these patients is unknown, but they are considered to constitute only a small percentage of the numerous victims of affective disorders who are or become chronically depressed, an estimated 10% to 20% of all affective disorder patients.

Typically, these individuals suffer early-onset dysthymia without subsequently superimposed acute major depressions. The latter distinguishes these individuals from other chronic depressives whose premorbid dysthymic pattern also began in early life with superimposed major depressive episodes followed by a return to the premorbid dysthymic baseline; these have become known as "double depression" (Keller and Shapiro, 1982). The latter also are known as chronic depressive personality, the Research Diagnostic Criteria (RDC) for which are listed in Table 1.

The chronically dysphoric patients who are candidates for psychostimulant therapy have many of the traits of those with a chronic depressive personality, except they do not have a history of superimposed acute major depressions. When these patients consult a physician, they do not complain of the characteristic vegetative, emotional, and psychological manifestations of an endogenous depression. On the contrary, they seek relief from many years of mild anhedonia, self-pity, overreactivity, pessimism, feelings of inadequacy, lack of energy, and easy fatiguability, and preoccupation with negative events. Although these low-grade chronic depressives may seem to have a characterologic depression, they do not. Their personalities conform to Schneider's (1958) depressive typology: (1) quiet, passive and nonassertive; (2) gloomy, pessimistic, and incapable of fun; (3) self-critical, self-reproaching, and self-derogatory; (4) skeptical, hypercritical, and complaining; (5) conscientious and self-disciplining; (6) brooding and given to worry; and (7) preoccupied with inadequacy, failure, and negative events to the point of morbid enjoyment of failures. Hence, they have been labeled as having *a subaffective dysthymic disorder* by Akiskal (1983; Chapter 1 this volume.)

As doctors get to know these low-grade depressives in the office, they realize that they are self-centered, demanding, and attention-seeking. Rarely do they seem to be a candidate for treatment with a tricyclic antidepressant. In fact, if such an antidepressant had been prescribed for them, they usually intensely disliked its sedative and anticholinergic effects, promptly discontinued it, and vowed they would never take an antidepressant again. Quite often these patients insist they cannot tolerate any antidepressant and that they need something to pep them up, not to make them slower than usual. Furthermore, the majority of these patients do not seem to believe they need a psychiatrist and imply that they would be offended by and would refuse a referral to a psychiatrist.

For the reasons just enumerated, these chronic dysphorics have cajoled a few

TABLE 1. Research Diagnostic Criteria for Chronic Depressive Personality

This category is for individuals who characteristically are bothered by depressive mood not attributable to any other psychiatric condition described in these criteria. Patients with this condition may also have other episodic conditions superimposed on them, including Major Depressive Disorder or an episode of a psychotic illness. A through D are required.

A. Since early adulthood has been bothered by depressive mood (e.g., sad, blue, hopeless, low, "don't care anymore") to a noticeably greater degree than most people, for at least several days of almost every month of almost every year. The depressive mood or the symptoms in B dominate the clinical picture. (Includes a person in his twenties who has been this way for at least 5 years.)

B. Since early adulthood at least 3 of the following traits have been present to a noticeably greater degree than in most people and were not limited to discrete affective episodes of illness:
 1. Easily disappointed, self-pity, or feelings of being short-changed
 2. Over-reactive to stressful situations
 3. Pessimistic
 4. Feelings of inadequacy
 5. Bothered by low energy or fatigue
 6. Preoccupation with negative aspects or events or situations
 7. Demanding or complaining behavior
 8. Dramatic attention-seeking behavior

C. The chronic condition (other than a superimposed episode of another condition) has resulted in 1 of the following:
 1. Impairment in functioning socially, with family, at home, at school, or at work
 2. Taking medication
 3. Seeking or being referred for help from someone
 4. A suicidal gesture or attempt
 5. Someone has complained about some manifestation of the condition

D. Depressive mood can not be attributed to any other psychiatric condition noted in this manual,* such as Cyclothymic Personality or Briquet's Disorder, or to premenstrual tension

*From: Spitzer R.K., Endicott J., Robins E. (1975): *Research Diagnostic Criteria*, 2nd edition, Biometrics Research, New York State Psychiatric Institute.

doctors to cautiously prescribe small doses of an amphetamine, for example, 5 mg twice or three times a day, or of methylphenidate, 10 or 20 mg two or three times daily, for them. Such psychostimulant doses often have produced dramatic and prompt symptomatic relief. Thereafter, attempts to reduce the dose of the psychostimulant have been followed by symptom resurgence that can be promptly abolished by reinstitution of the previously effective dose. For many years therafter these patients continue to take the same daily psychostimulant dose without developing signs and symptoms of tolerance and without abusing it. For this subgroup of chronic depressives, who may have a lifetime disorder, psychostimulant therapy seems to be a form of replacement therapy analogous to insulin for the diabetic. For them, many years of psychostimulant therapy is necessary and safe and should be considered as respectable as insulin therapy for diabetes. As a rule, after many years of consistent daily doses of a psychostimulant, many of these patients can gradually discontinue it without any withdrawal reactions and without any resurgence of their dysphoric symptoms.

Chronic Unipolar Depressives with or without Psychosis Refractory to Tryicyclic Antidepressants

In 1971 Wharton and his associates (1971) reported the successful treatment of seven patients with recurrent refractory psychotic depressive illness by administering an antidepressant (imipramine) long enough to achieve individual steady-state blood levels and then attempting to alter the blood level by the superimposition of methylphenidate. Their working hypothesis was that increased blood levels of the antidepressant would be induced by methyphenidate enzymatic inhibition of the metabolism of imipramine and desipramine. This in turn, they reasoned, would result in higher concentrations of the antidepressant and its primary metabolite at the site of action in the nervous system with a concomitant clinical improvement. They chose methylphenidate instead of dextroamphetamine because the latter has negligible effects on imipramine metabolism. The result of their preliminary trial indicated that methylphenidate treatment 10 mg twice daily for 10-21 days (average 14 days) may substantially inhibit the metabolism of imipramine and desmethylimipramine in some patients and, in some way, markedly increase their blood levels and subsequently enhance the therapeutic effectiveness of the parent drug. In three of their patients the plasma level of imipramine and desipramine combined was 30% to 400% higher after methylphenidate was added; one patient's combined level rose from 350 to 650 ng/ml.

Although Wharton and his collaborators assumed that methylphenidate's action was an increase in tricyclic levels, Drimmer and his associates (1983) have disputed this. They pointed out that Glassman et al. (1977) showed "in the same laboratory that the combined level of imipramine and desipramine in the blood correlated with therapeutic effect and that the combined levels of 225 ng/ml or greater were associated with maximal response" (Drimmer et al., 1983). The levels of two of Wharton et al.'s patients were well above the therapeutic threshold even before the addition of methylphenidate, and the level of the third patient was near the threshold. Hence, Drimmer et al. concluded that "it is unlikely that the increase in plasma levels observed with the addition of methylphenidate was responsible for the therapeutic effect" (Drimmer et al., 1983). Furthermore, they pointed out, "the observed increase in combined antidepressant levels was due primarily to an increase in the imipramine level; the desipramine levels were less affected in the two patients for whom data were given" (Drimmer et al., 1983).

Drimmer et al. (1983) successfully treated with combined desipramine-methylphenidate therapy a chronically depressed bipolar II man who had been refractory to various tricyclics, including amoxapine and lithium. After 4 weeks treatment with desipramine in doses up to 200 mg daily which produced a plasma level of 90 ng/ml, which is reported to be in the therapeutic range (Friedel et al., 1979), this man was still very depressed. Methylphenidate 10 mg twice daily was added to his desipramine. Marked improvement in mood and agitation was noted in 3 days. Discontinuation or tapering of methylphenidate resulted in the recurrence of depressive symptoms on two occasions. Remission was achieved within 4 days when methylphenidate was restarted. Measurements of plasma desipramine levels after methylphenidate disclosed a decrease rather than an increase. It was because of the latter that Drimmer and his associates concluded that methylphenidate's mechanism of action "does not involve an increase in plasma levels," as assumed by Wharton et al. (1971). Instead, Drimmer and his collaborators speculated that the effect of methylphenidate on response to tricyclic antidepressants is due to its action on the dopaminergic system (Drimmer et al., 1983).

In the twelve years since the Wharton et al. (1971) report, clinicians have treated an indeterminate number of treatment-resistant patients (chiefly nonpsychotic unipolars) with combined tricyclic-methylphenidate therapy. More recently a smaller number of such patients have been treated with a second generation antidepressant such as maprotiline plus methylphenidate, with varying degrees of success. In the majority of patients the dose of methylphenidate has been 10 to 20 mg twice or three times daily. We are unaware of any published or unpublished reports of serious adverse effects provoked by such combined therapy. Nor could we find any reports of such patients developing a tolerance to methylphenidate or abusing it.

Medically Ill Depressed Geriatric Patients

In 1975 Kaplitz (1975) reported the outcome of a double-blind randomized six-week trial which showed that methylphenidate (10 mg twice daily), as compared to placebo, "was singularly effective in 44 withdrawn, apathetic geriatric patients," all over age 60 (range 61 to 95) and victims of various age-related medical disorders. Their improvement was documented by the results of tests for mental status, ward behavior (nurses' rating), target-symptom response, and physicians' and nurses' global evaluations. For this reason, and because there were no side effects, Kaplitz concluded that "this form of antidepressant therapy should be considered in the treatment of previously unresponsive or oversedated patients."

In 1980 Katon and Raskind (1980), after deciding that the usefulness and safety of psychostimulants may be age-related, treated with methylphenidate some depressed medically ill elderly patients. They were encouraged to do this because several published reports indicated that psychostimulants may have a place in the geriatric population. They cited a placebo-controlled but nonblind study (Jacobson, 1958) which showed that menthylphenidate was significantly superior to placebo in the treatment of 54 elderly depressed patients. They also pointed out that two studies had demonstrated methylphenidate to be effective in treating secondary depression in patients in whom the affective signs and symptoms were superimposed on an underlying dementia (chronic organic brain syndrome). One of these was the Kaplitz study reviewed above. The other (Holliday and Joffe, 1965) indicated that depressed demented patients responded better to methylphenidate than they did to the tricyclic antidepressant protriptyline.

As noted above, faced with the dilemma of instituting an effective treatment for elderly depressed patients who were intolerant of tricyclic antidepressants, Katon and Raskind (1980) elected to treat with methylphenidate three patients who were either unable to tolerate tricyclic antidepressants or had a medical illness that contraindicated tricyclic therapy. These patients were 82, 75, and 85 years old. The 82-year-old man had been depressed for 1 year. Attempts to treat him with 50 mg amitriptyline daily produced acute urinary retention. Later, desipramine was prescribed for him. After the dose has been gradually increased to 75 mg/day over 2 weeks, he again developed urinary retention without improvement in his depression. After a 10-day drug-free period, treatment with methylphenidate, 10 mg twice daily, was started. Two days later his mood was brighter and his ability to concentrate on everyday tasks was improved. Steady improvement followed and he returned to part-time work. There were no side effects and no indications of psychostimulant habituation or abuse. Methylphenidate was discontinued after 4 months' treatment. At 1-year follow-up no signs or symptoms of depression could be detected.

The 75-year-old woman studied by Katon and Raskind (1980) had adult onset diabetes mellitus and bilateral amputations below the knee for peripheral vascular disease. Over a 3-month period she had become quite depressed. A 4-week course of imipramine 100 mg daily in divided doses produced no benefit but did produce side effects such as an unpleasant tremor, constipation, nocturnal sweats, and increased dysphoria. Imipramine was stopped and amitriptyline, 75 mg/day in divided doses, was prescribed. During the next week she became increasingly lethargic and fell twice due to severe postural hypotension. Amitriptyline was discontinued and 1 week later treatment with methylphenidate, 10 mg twice daily, was started. Within 3 days this woman began to improve and over the next month fully remitted from her depression. Methylphenidate was continued for another 2 months. There were no side effects. At 6-months follow-up she was symptom-free.

The 85-year-old woman studied by Katon and Raskind (1980) had been hospitalized for treatment of a dislocated right hip. She became depressed, anorexic, progressively lost weight, and refused to participate in physical rehabilitation. Electrocardiogram revealed first degree atrioventricular block and a right bundle branch intraventricular block. For this reason tricyclic antidepressants were considered contraindicated. Treatment with methylphenidate, 10 mg twice a day, was started. Within three days she was eating well, participating in physical activity, and sitting up most of the day. She was alert, her mood was much improved, and she showed renewed interest in her rehabilitation and discharge from the hospital. Her improvement in mood and activity level persisted and she was discharged 10 days later to continue her convalescence in an intermediate care facility.

In their discussion of these cases, Katon and Raskind (1980) stressed the rapid improvement 10 mg methylphenidate twice daily produced, in each case beginning within three days. Furthermore these clinicians commented: "Of perhaps greater importance was the absence of significant adverse effects from methylphenidate in these three patients. The same patients who either could not tolerate tricyclic antidepressants or for whom tricyclics were felt to be contraindicated easily tolerated a course of low-dose methylphenidate. We did not observe the adverse effects that have been attributed to the psychostimulants, such as appetite suppression, hypertension, palpitations, cardiac arrhythmias, nervousness, headaches, dyskinesias, precipitation of paranoid ideation or overt psychosis, insomnia, rapid tolerance to euphoriant effects, and abuse of these agents. This absence of adverse effects may have been fortuitous or secondary to the low dose of medication, but it is consistent with the low incidence of adverse effects secondary to methylphenidate in previous geriatric studies (Kaplitz, 1975; Jacobson, 1958; Holliday and Joffe, 1965; Gilbert et al., 1973; Crook et al., 1977; Bare and Lin, 1977 (Katon and Raskind, 1980: p. 965). Based on their data and those of earlier investigators, Katon and Raskind concluded that "methylphenidate is a reasonable candidate for closer scrutiny as an antidepressant drug for the elderly depressed patient."

In 1982 Kaufmann and Murray (1982) described a positive therapeutic response to d-amphetamine in three medically ill depressed patients in a general hospital. Their ages were 15, 57 and 82. The 15-year-old boy had been hospitalized for surgical treatment of an osteosarcoma. His depressive symptoms included sad mood, terminal insomnia, anorexia and a 20-pound weight loss. Post operatively his depression worsened and his pain responded only partially to repeated doses of morphine. Within a day of starting d-amphetamine 2.5 mg/d, he began to improve.

He tolerated well a second operation (below knee amputation) both physically and psychologically without any reappearance of depression. d-amphetamine was continued for one month with further improvement and a significant weight gain.

The 57-year-old woman patient studied by Kaufmann and Murray (1982) was admitted after a serious amitriptyline overdose following her realization that she could not read or write, and a 2-year deterioration in cognitive function. (She knew her family history of Huntington's chorea.) To avoid the anticholinergic effects of tricyclic antidepressants on an already compromised brain (a fact established by various tests), d-amphetamine 10 mg/d was administered. Within 48 hours she began to improve and a week later she was transferred less depressed to a neurology unit for further assessment of her cognitive impairments.

The 82-year-old woman described by Kaufmann and Murray (1982) had been admitted for arthritis, abdominal pain, constipation, weight loss, and depression. She did not respond either to psychotherapy or consecutive trials of imipramine and maprotiline, each of which caused intolerable drowsiness, dizziness, and hypotension. Within 2 hours of her first dose of 10 mg d-amphetamine she began to improve. Four days later she was discharged fully recovered. The d-amphetamine was continued and at a 6-month follow-up she had no side effects and no recurrence of depression.

At the end of their report Kaufmann and Murray commented, "The response to d-amphetamine in these three cases illustrates three points: (1) quick remission of depression after a small dose of medication, (2) lack of toxic side effects, and (3) the lack of recurrence of depression in the cases in which follow-up was possible" (Kaufmann and Murray, 1982: p. 464). They referred to Hackett's (1978) description of the usefulness of d-amphetamine in diagnosing and effectively treating medically ill, apathetic, weakened patients, in whom depression might easily be masked by concomitant illness and stated: "The rapid improvement in the physical and psychological symptomatology speeds recovery, in some cases dramatically. This rapid response to treatment, usually within 24-48 hours, is of additional benefit in this population, whose concurrent medical illness makes it undesirable, if not hazardous, to wait 10 to 14 days for the onset of tricyclic antidepressant action" (Kaufmann and Murray, 1982).

The successful treatment with methylphenidate of four depressed postcardiac surgery patients has been reported by Kaufmann and his colleagues (1984). These patients, ages 52, 67, 60 and 70, besides having a secondary depression, i.e., a clinical depression meeting DSM-III criteria for major affective disorders preceded by or concurrent with a medical illness, had developed cardiac complications after cardiac surgery that contraindicated the use of tricyclic antidepressants. Methylphenidate, 10 mg twice daily, produced in each a rapid remission of depressive symptomatology with no adverse effects.

The 52-year-old woman (Kaufmann et al., 1984) had a history of a minor depressive episode 12 years earlier that remitted spontaneously. Following mitral and tricuspid valve replacement she developed a third-degree A-V block which required the implantation of a temporary pacemaker, and moderate congestive heart failure only partially responsive to diuretics. Her depression was manifested by crying spells, anorexia, impaired concentration, middle insomnia, anergia, loss of interest in her recovery, intense feelings of sadness and emptiness, and a feeling that life was not worth living. She was started on methylphenidate 10 mg b.i.d. Within 24 hours, her appetite improved, her mood was brighter, and she started to express more interest in her recovery. Two days later, she showed progressive remission in her remaining psychological and vegetative signs of depression. Methylphenidate was continued for 8 days without side effects and then discontinued. She remained hospitalized for 2 months, with no recurrence of depression.

The 67-year-old woman studied by Kaufmann et al. (1984) had been hospitalized for triple coronary artery bypass. She had had a major depression followed by a suicide attempt 15 years prior to admission that required ECT and hospitalization. She had shown signs of mild depression preoperatively. Postoperatively she had a complete heart block requiring a temporary pacemaker and her depression worsened. Twenty-four hours after starting on methylphenidate, 10 mg twice a day, she started ambulating and developed renewed interest in her rehabilitation. By the seventh postoperative day, her appetite had improved significantly and she was no longer dysphoric. Methylphenidate was continued for a week at which time she was discharged. No depressive relapse had occurred at 6-month follow up.

The 60-year-old man described by Kaufmann et al. (1984) was hospitalized for aortic and mitral valve replacement and coronary bypass grafting of the circumflex artery. Preoperatively he had been manifesting some depressive symptoms for about a year following development of congestive heart failure. Postoperatively his depression worsened. Because he also had a left bundle branch block and had required cardioversion for rapid atrial fibrillation and also had required further surgery for an infected sternotomy with mediastinitis, tricyclics were considered contraindicated. Within 48 hours of starting methylphenidate, 10 mg twice daily, there was a dramatic remission of his depressive symptomatology. He became involved with his rehabilitation and exhibited a sense of well-being, with complete disappearance of vegetative and psychological symptoms of depression. Methylphenidate was continued for 2 weeks with no side effects and discontinued prior to discharge. At 6-month follow-up he was still free of depression.

The 70-year-old woman described by Kaufmann et al. (1984) had been hospitalized for mitral valve replacement. She had had a depression at age 40 from which she recovered after 2 years' psychotherapy. Depressive symptoms began again about 1 year preoperatively. Postoperatively she had an embolic stroke in the right middle cerebral artery region followed by a left hemiparesis and conjugate deviation of the eyes to the right. Her depression worsened considerably and because of hypotension and a right bundle branch block with left hemiblock, tricyclics were contraindicated. Within 24 hours of starting methyphenidate, 10 mg twice daily, there was a dramatic improvement followed by a disappearance of all signs of depression. Methylphenidate was continued for 9 days with no side effects. It was discontinued prior to discharge and at 6-month follow-up she was free of any signs of depression.

As Kaufmann and his associates stressed, these four cases document three main aspects of methylphenidate therapy in medically ill depressed patients: (1) the quick remission of depression after a small dose of the medication, (2) the lack of toxic side effects, and (3) no recurrence of depression in the cases followed for 6 months. To these we would add that the short duration of methylphenidate therapy needed for inducing remission from depression precluded any risk of tolerance or habituation to methylphenidate.

COMMENT

Experienced clinicians know how difficult it is to deal with the geriatric patient who cares little, if at all, about his surroundings, himself, or his future. Such a patient may or may not have organic pathology; generally, however, his mood alteration, that is, his depression, is accompanied either by psychomotor retardation or agitation. Such troubled, despondent persons obsessed with guilt, self-condemnation, hopelessness, and thoughts of suicide cannot cooperate with a medical and nursing regimen designed to better their condition.

Experienced clinicians also have learned that d-amphetamine or methylphenidate in modest doses can be an effective and safe therapy for such depressed individuals between 60 and 90 with all types of medical problems. Initiating treatment with a low twice daily dose can be followed, if necessary, by an increase to three times a day dosage, all before 1 or 2 P.M. Such patients should not be given the psychostimulant after 4 P.M. to avoid interfering with sleep onset. In such patients this therapy often produces an increase of alertness, dissipates early morning depression and fatigue, and helps to break the communication barrier to psychotherapy or counselling for them. Often such improvement is rapidly induced and usually it persists as long as the patient continues the effective daily dose of the psychostimulant. Rarely does tolerance develop with continued treatment and the risk of abuse or addiction of an effective psychostimulant is minimal. Should a person relapse, reinstitution of the previously effective dose is usually effective again. Clearly, advanced age is not a contraindication to psychostimulant therapy for depressed elderly individuals. Nor do hypertension, cardiovascular disease, diabetes, or other aging disabilities preclude treatment with a psychostimulant, particularly methylphenidate. The latter induces alertness, improves psychomotor performance and elevates mood usually without production of sympathomimetic side effects that amphetamines may cause.

Finally, there are data substantiating that d-amphetamine and methylphenidate can be a safe and effective pharmacotherapy for selected subgroups of depressed patients refractory to other therapies. Many patients should not be considered absolutely treatment-resistant until they have had a trial of psychostimulant therapy for their seemingly refractory depression.

REFERENCES

Akiskal, H.S. Overview of chronic depressions, in *Affective Disorders Reassessed: 1983*. F.J. Ayd Jr, I.J. Taylor and B.T. Taylor, eds. Ayd Medical Communications, Baltimore, pp. 124-137 (1983).

Bare, W.E., and Lin, D. A stimulant for the aged. II. Long-term observations with a methylphenidate-vitamin-hormone combination. *J. Am. Geriatr. Soc. 10*, 539-544 (1977).

Crook, T., Feris, S., Sathananthan, G., et al. The effect of methylphenidate on test performance in the cognitively impaired aged. *Psychoparmacology 52*, 215-255 (1977).

Drimmer, E.J., Gitlin, J.J., and Gwirstman, H.E. Desipramine and methylphenidate combination treatment for depression: Case report. *Amer. J. Psychiatry 140*, 241-242 (1983).

Friedel, R., Veith, R., Bloom V., et al. Desipramine plasma levels and clinical response in depressed patients. *Commun. Psychopharmacol. 3*, 81-87 (1979).

Gilbert, J.G., Donnelly, K.J., Zimmer, L.E., et al. Effect of magnesium pemoline and methylphenidate on memory improvement and mood in normal aging subjects. *Int. J. Aging Hum. Dev. 4*, 35-51 (1973).

Glassman, A., Perel, J., Shostak, M., et al. Clinical implication of imipramine plasma levels for depressive illness. *Arch. Gen. Psychiat. 34*, 197-204 (1977).

Hackett, T.P. The use of stimulant drugs in general hospital psychiatry. *Audio-Digest Tape*, Vol. 7, number 12. Audio-Digest Foundation, Glendale, Ca. (1978).

Hare, E.H., Dominian, J. and Sharpe, L. Phenelzine and dexamphetamine in depressive illness. *Brit. Med. J. 1*, 9-12 (1962).

Holliday, A.R., and Joffe, J.R. A controlled evaluation of protriptyline compared to methylphenidate hydrochloride. *J. New Drugs 5*, 257 (1965).

Jacobson, A. The use of Ritalin in psychotherapy of depression. *Psychiatric Quarterly 32*, 475-483 (1958).

Kaplitz, S.E. Withdrawn, apathetic geriatric patients responsive to methylphenidate. *J. Am. Geriatr. Soc. 23*, 271-276 (1975).

Katon, W. and Raskind, M. Treatment of depression in the medically ill elderly with methylphenidate. *Amer. J. Psychiat. 137*, 963-965 (1980).

Kaufmann, M.W., and Murray, G.B. The use of d-amphetamine in medically ill depressed patients. *J. Clin. Psychiat. 43*, 463-464 (1982).

Kaufmann, M.W., Cassem, N., Murray, G., and Macdonald, D. The use of methylphenidate in depressed patients after cardiac surgery. *J. Clin. Psychiat. 45,* 82-84 (1984).

Keller, M.B., and Shapiro, R.W. "Double depressions": Superimposition of acute depressive episodes on chronic depressive disorders. *Amer. J. Psychiat. 139,* 438-442 (1982).

Kiloh, L.G., Neilson, M., and Andrews, G. Response of depressed patients to methylamphetamine. *Brit. J. Psychiat. 125,* 496-499 (1974).

Landman, M.E., Preising, R., and Perlman, M. A practical mood stimulant. *J. Med. Soc. New Jersey, 55,* (1958).

Myerson, A. Effect of benzedrine sulfate on mood and fatigue in normal and in neurotic persons. *Archs. Neurol. Psychiat. Chicago, 36,* 816-822 (1936).

Pitts, F.N. Jr. The use of dextroamphetamine in medically ill depressed patients. *J. Clin. Psychiat. 43,* 438 (1982).

Schneider, K. *Psychopathic Personalities,* translated by M.W. Hamilton, Cassell, London (1958).

Wharton, R.N., Perel, J.M., Dayton, P.G., and Malitz, S. A potential clinical use for methylphenidate with tricyclic antidepressants. *Amer. J. Psychiat. 127,* 1619-1625 (1971).

18

The Role of Estrogen in Treating Resistant Depression

Gerald Oppenheim, Joseph Zohar, Baruch Shapiro, and Robert H. Belmaker

INTRODUCTION

There is a longstanding general agreement that the common menopausal syndrome with vasomotor symptoms and mild "depression" is relieved by the administration of estrogen (Ripley et al., 1940). Hermann and Beach (1978) have summarized studies of the therapeutic effects of estrogen on menopausal symptoms. The psychological symptoms that occur at the time of the menopause, their relationship to catecholamines, and the role of estrogen in this relationship are the subject of a recent review (Coulam, 1981).

However, a possible true antidepressant effect of estrogen in the equivalent of major depression (DSM-III) has received very little systematic evaluation. An early, negative study of estrogen therapy in depressed menopausal women (Ripley et al., 1940) apparently discouraged further investigation. More recently, Klaiber et al. (1979) performed a twelve week, double-blind, placebo-controlled study of very high doses of estrogen (average 21.5 mg/day of conjugated estrogen) in a group of 40 pre- and postmenopausal women with severe and resistant depression diagnosed by Research Diagnostic Criteria (Spitzer et al., 1977). A significant antidepressant effect was seen in the estrogen treated group (average Hamilton Depression Scale reduction of 10 points), with the group improving "from a severely to moderately depressed condition." The significance of these results was amplified by the study's inclusion criterion of at least two years' unsuccessful treatment with conventional therapies including electroconvulsive therapy (ECT) and antidepressant drugs.

In a more recent but open study, the effects of four weeks' treatment with 0.06 mg/day of ethinyl estradiol was investigated in 10 premenopausal and 10 postmenopausal women with endogenous depression (Holsboer et al., 1983). A decrease in Hamilton Depression Score of at least 12 points was achieved in seven postmenopausal and four premenopausal patients.

In a report of the comparative antidepressant effects of the combined prescription of estrogen and 150 mg imipramine versus placebo and imipramine (Prange, 1972), differential effects were seen with 0.05 mg and 0.025 mg ethinyl estradiol. With the higher dose combination, less improvement was seen after 1 week; with the lower dose combination a greater improvement was seen after 1 week, but at 3 weeks both treatments were equally effective.

In a clinical study of a postmenopausal patient whose depressive illness was totally unresponsive to various antidepressant drugs over a six-month period (Oppenheim, 1984), the addition of conjugated estrogen (up to 4.375 mg) to her most recent but ineffective antidepressant drug (dibenzepin) induced the condition of rapid mood-cycling, which has become recognized as a direct complication of various agents with antidepressant activity (Oppenheim, 1982).

POSSIBLE NEUROPHARMACOLOGICAL MECHANISMS

Enhanced Availability of Central Norepinephrine

The frequently cited catecholamine hypothesis of affective disorders is based partly on the finding that clinically effective antidepressants of the tricyclic and monoamine oxidase inhibitor (MAOI) classes have a rapid action in enhancing brain norepinephrine (NE) availability (Schildkraut, 1965).

An increase in brain NE content following ethinyl estradiol administration to mice pretreated with monoamine oxidase inhibitors may represent the induction of increased NE synthesis (Grenngrass and Tonge, 1974). An estrogen-induced increase in bioavailability of NE is suggested by reports of estrogen inhibition of monoamine oxidase in both animal (Kobayashi et al., 1966) and man (Klaiber et al., 1972). More recently, estrogen has been demonstrated to induce the release of endogenous catecholamines within the hypothalamus (Paul et al., 1979). Thus, estrogen may act in depression through its effect on central NE levels.

Effects on Neurotransmitter Receptor Mechanisms

Adrenergic and Serotonergic Systems

In recent years abundant research has demonstrated that long-term antidepressant treatments induce consistent changes in adrenergic and serotonergic receptor sensitivities which suggest that "modulation of receptor sensitivity may be a mechanism of action common to tricyclic antidepressants, 'atypical' antidepressants, monoamine oxidase inhibitors, and electroconvulsive therapy" (Charney, 1981).

Estrogen has been found to have a direct effect on serotonin and α-adrenergic receptor binding in rabbit platelets (Roberts et al., 1979; Elliott et al., 1980); platelets have numerous properties in common with central monoaminergic neurons (Campbell, 1981). Further suggestive evidence is seen in the recent finding of an estrogen-dependent decrease in serotonin-2 receptor binding in rat cerebral cortex during long-term imipramine administration (Kendall et al., 1981). This decreased receptor binding was abolished by ovariectomy and reestablished by administration of estrogen. In this regard, Peroutka and Snyder (1980) demonstrated an antidepressant drug-induced decrease in neurotransmitter receptor binding, most marked for serotonin-2 receptor sites.

Dopaminergic System

Standard antidepressant treatments have been shown to have effects on the dopaminergic system, which suggest a treatment-induced desensitization of presynaptic dopamine (DA) autoreceptors (Chiodo and Antelman, 1980). The resultant dopaminergic hyperactivity has been postulated as a mechanism of the treatment's antidepressant effect (Post et al., 1978); these authors report DA agonists such as pirebedil to have clinically significant antidepressant effects and to be capable of inducing rapid mood-cycling. The role of DA agonists in affective illness has recently been reviewed. (Post et al., 1981).

Within the brain, estrogen has been shown to alter the sensitivity of presynaptic DA autoreceptors in the substantia nigra (Chiodo and Caggiula, 1980). It has also been shown to increase the number of postsynaptic dopaminergic binding sites in the striatum (Hruska and Silbergeld, 1980). In addition, estrogen may effect the γ-aminobutyricacid-mediated feedback regulation of nigrostriatal DA (Gordon et al., 1977). Further evaluation is needed of various factors in estrogen's effect on the dopaminergic system, e.g., whether the above effects represent a direct action or an indirect action via other neurotransmitter or hormonal systems, and the differential effects of acute versus chronic estrogen administration and its timing (Chiodo et al., 1981).

How estrogen may alter receptor binding characteristics is at present unknown, but theories include a direct allosteric effect on receptor affinity (Elliott et al., 1980) and an indirect effect via stimulation of RNA and, therefore, protein synthesis (Buller and O'Malley, 1976).

Thus, a role for estrogen in the treatment of depression may be linked to its induction of changes at the neurotransmitter or receptor levels, or to the enhancement of such changes as a result of its use in combination with antidepressant drugs. Such a facilitatory role in drug-resistant patients has already been proposed for thyroid hormone (Whybrow and Prange, 1981; Goodwin et al., 1982) and for lithium carbonate (Montigny et al., 1981; Nelson and Byck, 1982).

CAN ESTROGEN POTENTIATE FAILED ANTIDEPRESSANT DRUG TREATMENT?

In the light of the above findings we have performed a double-blind, placebo-controlled, crossover study comparing the effects of imipramine plus estrogen versus imipramine plus placebo in a group of depressed women who have failed to respond to an adequate trial of antidepressant drug treatment. The hypothesis we tested is that estrogen may potentiate the antidepressant effect of a drug which has failed to improve the patient's depression.

Methods

Patient Selection

Eleven female patients suffering from major depression (DSM-III) unresponsive to an adequate trial of antidepressant treatment were the subjects of the study. Patients were premenopausal (3) or postmenopausal (8) women between the ages of 26 and 74, and were admitted to the study only after an illness duration of at least six months despite treatment including two antidepressant drugs given for six weeks each at dosages equivalent to 250 mg per day imipramine.

Routine pretrial gynecological and medical evaluation was performed and any patient with breast or endometrial carcinoma, a past history of thromboembolic illness, or active or severe liver disease was excluded. Informed consent was obtained from each patient and her family.

Medication Procedure

All patients received imipramine 200 mg per day throughout the study. Night sedation was allowed if needed (nitrazepam 10 mg), but other medication was avoided.

Conjugated estrogen (Premarin) was added to the imipramine beginning at 1.25 mg (1 capsule) per day for 2 days, 2.5 mg per day on days 3 and 4, and reaching the full dose of 3.75 mg per day on day 5. This gradual dose increase was aimed at minimizing any side effects including breast tenderness. This full dose was then continued for 16 days, followed by a similar gradual decrease over five days to zero. The exact same procedure was carried out with identical placebo capsules. Patients were randomly assigned to begin with the active agent or placebo. In premenopausal women the estrogen or placebo was begun with the onset of menses. On the day of estrogen or placebo cessation (day 26) norethisterone acetate (Primolut-Nor) 10 mg/day was begun for a five-day period in order to induce menses.

Depression Rating

The Hamilton Depression Rating Scale (Hamilton, 1960) was administered once weekly to all patients throughout the crossover study. Each score takes into account the patient's self-rating and staff ratings for the previous week. The scorer was blind to estrogen or placebo administration.

Possible Risks

A recent review of the safety of estrogen replacement therapy shows an apparent protective effect of estrogen in lowering the mortality from all causes in postmenopausal women (Bush et al., 1983). We consider our low-dose, time-limited protocol of negligible risk.

RESULTS

As seen in Table 1, no overall improvement in depression score was seen with estrogen or placebo. In one patient (No. 11), a striking improvement was seen after one week of estrogen, and after two weeks she was no longer depressed—a remission which has continued for six more weeks including the four weeks of placebo.

TABLE 1. Effects on Depression Score of Addition of Estrogen or Placebo to Failed Antidepressant Drug.

		Hamilton Depression Rating Scale scores					
		Estrogen			Placebo		
Subject No.	Age	Pre	Post	Change	Pre	Post	Change
1	59	33	32	+1	32	36	−4
2	62	22	22	0	33	22	+11
3	33	28	Florid mania on day 9 and trial discontinued.				
4	55	31	28	+3	30	31	−1
5	26	33	30	+3	30	19	+11
6	38	36	48	−12	39	36	+3
7	74	30	31	−1	31	32	−1
8	60	30	30	0	29	30	−1
9	57	31	27	+4	27	29	−2
10	59	23	29	−6	23	23	0
11	62	28	4	+24	4	12	−8
		Total change:		+16	Total change:		+8
		Mean change:		+1.6	Mean change:		+0.8

It should be emphasized that this patient's depression had been resistant to prolonged, high doses of different antidepressants. This rapid response to the addition of estrogen resembles the above-mentioned reports of the potentiation of antidepressant drug by thyroid hormone and lithium carbonate.

Another striking response was the florid mania which began nine days after the addition of estrogen in a 33-year old woman (No. 3) previously resistant to treatment. Bunney et al. (1977) suggest that an increased receptor sensitivity during the depressive phase might predispose to a switch towards mania if a large or rapid increase in the level of available NE should occur; the evidence suggesting estrogen's potential to induce such an increase in NE has been summarized earlier in this chapter.

In patient No. 2, an 11-point improvement in depression score followed placebo administration. This chronically depressed woman had for weeks waited anxiously to receive the "hormone treatment." In the dosage used here, side effects were not a significant problem. Two patients suffered temporary breast tenderness, which needed no change in treatment. Two others had uterine bleeding (beginning on days 4 and 6 of estrogen) which ceased after temporary dosage lowering. The toxic side effects previously reported from a combination of 150 mg imipramine and 0.05 mg ethinyl estradiol (Prange, 1972; Khurana, 1972) were not seen with the antidepressant-conjugated estrogen combination used in our study.

DISCUSSION

This study represents the first investigation in resistant depression of an antidepressant-estrogen combination rather than estrogen alone. In the group of patients studied here, no significant improvement was seen following the addition of conjugated estrogen to the patient's antidepressant drug treatment.

The evidence reported here both from neuropharmacological and from clinical reports, suggests that in some patients and under as yet undefined conditions, estrogen may demonstrate antidepressant or antidepressant-potentiating activity. It is possible that such a potentiating effect of estrogen may be more effectively elicited using a higher dosage, a longer administration period, or another form of estrogen administration. Estrogen may also be more likely to potentiate a different antidepressant whose predominant influence is on an alternative transmitter system. The possibility that estrogen may have a preferential effect in unipolar or bipolar patients also remains to be excluded.

REFERENCES

Buller, R.E., and O'Malley, B.W. The biology and mechanism of steroid hormone receptor interaction with the eukaryotic nucleus. *Biochem. Pharmacol. 25*, 1-12 (1976).

Bunney, W.E. Jr., Post, R.M., and Andersen, A.E. A neuronal receptor sensitivity mechanism in affective illness (a review of evidence). *Commun. Psychopharmacol. 1*, 393-405 (1977).

Bush, T.L., Cowan, L.D., Barrett-Connor, E., Criqui, M.H., Karon, J.M., Wallace, R.B., Tyroler, H.A., and Rifkind, B.M. Estrogen use and all-cause mortality. *J.A.M.A. 249*, 903-906 (1983).

Campbell, I.C. Blood platelets and psychiatry. *Brit. J. Psychiat. 138*, 78-80 (1981).

Charney, D.S., Menkes, D.B., and Heninger, G.R. Receptor sensitivity and the mechanism of action of antidepressant treatment. *Arch. Gen. Psychiat. 38*, 1160-1180 (1981).

Chiodo, L.A., and Antelman, S.M. Tricyclic antidepressants induce subsensitivity of presynaptic dopamine autoreceptors. *European J. Pharmacol. 64*, 203-204 (1980).

Chiodo, L.A., and Caggiula, A.R. Alterations in the basal firing rate and autoreceptor sensitivity of dopamine neurones in the substantia nigra following-acute and extended exposure to estrogen. *European J. Pharmacol. 67*, 165-166 (1980).

Chiodo, L.A., Caggiula, A.R., and Saller, C.F., Estrogen potentiates the stereotypy induced by dopamine agonists in the rat. *Life Sci. 28*, 827-835 (1981).

Coulam, C.B. Age, estrogens, and the psyche. *Clin. Obstets. Gynecol. 24*, 219-229 (1981).

Elliott, J.M., Peters, J.R., and Grahame-Smith, D.G. Estrogen and progesterone change the binding characteristics of alpha-adrenergic and serotonin receptors on rabbit platelets. *European J.*

Pharmacol. 66, 21-30 (1980).

Goodwin, F.K., Prange, A.J., Post, R.M., Muscettola, G., and Lipton, M.A. Potentiation of antidepressant effects by L-triiodothyronine in tricyclic nonresponders. *Amer. J. Psychiat. 139*, 34-38 (1982).

Gordon, J.H., Nance, D.M., Wallis, C.H., and Gorski, R.A. Effect of estrogen on dopamine turnover, glutamic acid decarboxylase activity and lordosis behavior in septal lesioned female rats. *Brain Res. Bull. 2*, 341-346 (1977).

Grenngrass, P.M., and Tonge, S.R. The accumulation of noradrenaline and 5-hydroxytryptamine in three regions of mouse brain after tetrabenazine and iproniazid: Effects of ethinyloestradiol and progesterone. *Psychopharmacologia 39*, 187-191 (1974).

Hamilton, M.A rating scale for depression. *J. Neurol. Neurosurg. Psychiat. 23* 56-62 (1960).

Hermann, W.M., and Beach, R.C. The psychotropic properties of estrogens. *Pharmakopsychiat. 11*, 164-176 (1978).

Holsboer, F., Benkert, O., and Demisch, L. Changes in MAO activity during estrogen treatment of females with endogenous depression. *Mod. Probl. Pharmacopsychiat. 19*, 321-326 (1983).

Hruska, R.E., and Silbergeld, E.K. Estrogen treatment enhances dopamine receptor sensitivity in the rat striatum. *European J. Pharmacol. 61*, 397-400 (1980).

Kendall, D.A., Stancel, G.M., and Enna, S.J. Imipramine: Effect of ovarian steroids on modifications in serotonin receptor binding. *Science 211*, 1183-1185 (1981).

Khurana, R.C. Estrogen-imipramine interaction. *J.A.M.A. 222*, 702-703 (1972).

Klaiber, E.L., Broverman, D.M., Vogel, W., and Kobayashi, T. Effects of estrogen therapy on plasma MAO activity and EEG driving responses of depressed women. *Amer. J. Psychiat. 128*, 1492-1498 (1972).

Klaiber, E.L., Broverman, D.M., Vogel, W., and Kobayashi, T. Estrogen therapy for severe persistent depressions in women. *Arch. Gen. Psychiat. 36*, 550-554 (1979).

Kobayashi, T., Kobayashi, T., and Kato, J. Cholinergic and adrenergic mechanisms in the female rat hypothalamus with special reference to feedback of ovarian steroid hormones, in *Steroid Dynamics*, G. Pincus, T. Nakao, and J. Tait, eds., Academic Press, New York, pp. 303-309 (1966).

Montigny, de C., Grunberg, F., Mayer, A., and Deschenes, J.P. Lithium induces rapid relief of depression in tricyclic antidepressant drug non-responders. *Brit. J. Psychiat. 138*, 252-256 (1981).

Nelson, J.C., and Byck, R. Rapid response to lithium in phenelzine non-responders. *Brit. J. Psychiat. 141*, 85-86 (1982).

Oppenheim, G. Drug-induced rapid cycling: Possible outcomes and management. *Amer. J. Psychiat. 139*, 939-941 (1982).

Oppenheim, G. Rapid mood cycling with estrogen: Implications for therapy. *J. Clin. Psychiat. 45*, 34-35 (1984).

Paul, S.M., Axelrod, J., Saavedra, J.M., and Skolnick, P. Estrogen-induced efflux of endogenous catecholamines from the hypothalamus in vitro. *Brain Res. 178*, 499-505 (1979).

Peroutka, S.J., and Snyder, S.H. Long-term antidepressant treatment decreases spiroperidol-labeled serotonin receptor binding. *Science 210*, 88-90 (1980).

Post, R.M., Gerner, R.H., Carman, T.S., Gillin, C., Jimerson, D.C., Goodwin, F.K., and Bunney, W.E., Jr. Effects of a dopamine agonist pirebil in depressed patients. *Arch. Gen. Psychiat. 35*, 609-615 (1978).

Post, R.M., Cutler, N.R., Jimerson, D.C., and Bunney, W.E., Jr. Dopamine agonists in affective illness: Implications for underlying receptor mechanisms, in *Apomorphine and Other Dopaminomimetics, Vol. 2. Clinical Pharmacology*, G.U. Corsini and G.L. Gessa, eds.,

Raven Press, New York, pp. 77-91 (1981).

Prange, A.J. Estrogen may well affect response to antidepressant. *J.A.M.A. 219*, 143-144 (1972).

Ripley, H.S., Shorr, E., and Papanicolaou, G.N. The effect of treatment of depression in the menopause with estrogenic hormone. *Amer. J. Psychiat. 96*, 905-915 (1940).

Roberts, J.M., Goldfien, R.D., Tsuchiya, A.M., Goldfien, A., and Insel, P.A. Estrogen treatment decreases alpha adrenergic binding sites on rabbit platelets. *Endocrinology 104*, 722-728 (1979).

Schildkraut, J.J. The catecholamine hypothesis of affective disorders: A review of supporting evidence. *Amer. J. Psychiat. 122*, 509-522 (1965).

Spitzer, R.L., Endicott, J., and Robins, E. Research Diagnostic Criteria (RDC) for a Selected Group of Functional Disorders. Biometrics Research, New York State Psychiatric Institute (1977).

Whybrow, P.C., and Prange, A.J. A hypothesis of thyroid-catecholamine-receptor interaction. *Arch. Gen. Psychiat. 38*, 106-113 (1981).

19

Addition of Reserpine to Tricyclic Antidepressants in Resistant Depression

Joseph Zohar, Daniel Moscovich, and Roberto Mester

Three groups examined the use of reserpine addition to an ongoing tricyclic antidepressant (TCA) treatment in TCA nonresponder depressed patients (Poldinger, 1963; Haskovec and Rysanek, 1967; Hopkinson and Kenny, 1975. Poldinger was the first to report (Poldinger, 1959) on positive therapeutic potentiation of ongoing imipramine treatment after addition of reserpine. He gave 7-10 mg reserpine i.m. for 1 or 2 days on the third and fourth day of imipramine treatment. Seven of 11 patients who had not yet responded to 4 days of imipramine treatment showed immediate favorable response to reserpine addition. He next treated 7 depressive patients who had been taking desipramine for 3 days (Poldinger, 1963). Four patients from this group responded to one or two injections of reserpine 2.5-7.5 mg or to a single i.v. or i.m. injection of tetrabenazine 50-100 mg. Two out of the four who did not respond had received only 2.5 mg reserpine i.m. Summing up these two clinical observations, 11 out of 18 depressed patients had a favorable response to reserpine or tetrabenazine added after 4 days of imipramine or desipramine treatment. The response started with an excited state following the injection which rapidly passed into a marked improvement in clinical state. The adverse effects included excitation, increased pulse, mydriasis, perspiration, tremor, insomnia, vertigo, and headache. All the adverse effects were short-lived and lasted for several hours. Poldinger concluded the two studies by saying that "patients resistant to imipramine or desipramine could be made responsive to the drug by some injections of reserpine or tetrabenazine." However, it now seems that four days of tricyclic treatment is too short a period to determine whether a patient is resistant to this treatment or not. Therefore the relevance of Poldinger's studies to resistant depression is questionable. It might be that those patients would have been tricyclic responders if they would have been given the treatment for another two or three weeks and that the addition of reserpine had just speeded up the process.

Haskovec and Rysanek (1967) studied reserpine addition to imipramine-resistant depressive patients under more rigorous conditions. All their 15 depressed patients were diagnosed as having "endogenous depression" independently by two psychiatrists. The average duration of treatment with imipramine before reserpine was 92 days with a range of 21-308 days. The daily dose of imipramine was gradually increased to 300 mg. All the patients received reserpine 7.5-10 mg i.m. injection for two successive days. The clinical condition of the patients before and after the reserpine administration was evaluated by two psychiatrists independently, according to Overall's Rating Scale. A six-month follow-up was also carried out. Their findings fully support Poldinger's clinical experience. Out of the 15 endogenous depressed patients studied, 14 responded to the combination of imipramine and reserpine. The response was described as dramatic in some but in 8 patients it was only temporary; it lasted 2–17 days and then the patients relapsed into their original state of depression. In 6 patients the improvement lasted throughout the follow-up period of six months. As far as side effects are concerned, blood pressure, pulse, and temperature were very slightly decreased; by contrast psychiatric patients treated with reserpine alone in much lower doses demonstrate a more marked decrease in blood pressure and pulse rate in the very early stages of treatment (Bonati et al., 1956; Masini et al., 1956; Kirkpatrick and Sanders, 1955). All patients exhibited a conspicuous vasodilation and increase of intestinal peristalsis. These symptoms are regularly observed during the administration of reserpine alone, but they were accentuated and prolonged when imipramine had been previously administered. Profuse diarrhea was observed in one patient. Haskovec and Rysanek (1967) concluded that "the administration of reserpine in adequate doses during imipramine therapy was associated with a conspicuous stimulatory effect." They described this effect as rapid, dramatic, and resembling the "switch process" (Bunney, 1972) from depression to mania. Usually it started on the second day of reserpine administration. Moreover, according to their pilot study, doses of 5-7.5 mg of reserpine injected i.m. for 1 day to three endogenously depressed patients who had been treated with an ongoing tricyclic treatment was completely without antidepressive effect.

Hopkinson and Kenny (1975) conducted the only double-blind study concerning the therapeutic effects of adding reserpine to tricyclic nonresponding depressive patients. They had two randomly allocated groups composed only of females. One group consisted of eight depressed patients who received injections of 5 mg reserpine on 2 successive days simultaneous with continued administration of current tricyclic medication. The second group consisted of six depressed patients who received saline injection on 2 successive days with concurrent medication. Only patients with endogenous depression were allowed to participate in the study. Failure to respond to any of the tricyclic antidepressants for a minimum of 3 weeks, 150 mg daily, was considered to be the minimum acceptable duration and dosage. The day before and the day after reserpine administration, each patient was independently assessed by a clinical psychologist using the Hamilton Depression Rating Scale. The rater was blind to the patient's medication status. The experimental population included patients on imipramine, trimipramine, and amitryptiline. No drugs were added or changed during the four days of the experiment. Changes in Hamilton depression ratings for pre- and post-trial periods were analyzed by means of a two-way analysis of variance. The reserpine group produced a significantly ($p < 0.01$) greater drop in depression rating than did the control group. No alarming side effects were noted. Three patients complained of nasal stuffiness; one patient experienced facial flushing, followed by a transient morbiliform rash which lasted 2 days. One patient complained of mild excitation which lasted a few hours and was followed by a good recovery. Mania did not occur. It is of special interest to note that one patient from the reserpine group who responded favorably was a tricyclic nonresponder and electroshock nonresponder (8 shocks). In a 3-month follow-up none of the reserpine patients had relapsed, except for one patient who showed a mild recurrence of her depressive symptoms after 5 days. The patient was given two further injections of reserpine and responded well. None of the eight patients who received reserpine required electroshock therapy. Of the six patients who received placebo all but one needed ECT before discharge.

We added 1 mg reserpine i.m. on 2 consecutive days to the ongoing tricyclic treatment of four tricyclic nonresponder major depressive patients. Three of these patients had an immediate dramatic favorable response after a brief period of agitation with manic features. The fourth patient did not respond to the treatment.

Case 1. This was the third psychiatric hospitalization of a 43-year-old married woman, mother of four, who was admitted because of restlessness, insomnia, social withdrawal, and inability to function for the past two months. Two years before and also fifteen years before, she was hospitalized with the same clinical presentation. In each hospitalization, antidepressant drugs were ineffective and the depression cleared up only after electroconvulsive treatment. Her mother also suffered from depressive bouts, and was also treated with ECT. After the patient did not respond to one month of imipramine 300 mg/day, 1 mg reserpine i.m. was added to the ongoing imipramine treatment for 2 consecutive days. On the third day the patient developed euphoric affect and hyperactivity which was followed by a very mild depression. After several weeks, the patient was discharged in full remission without further changes in her medication. This time, as opposed to previous hospitalizations, she did not require electroconvulsive treatment. The patient was in a stable remission at one-month follow-up, while still on medication.

Case 2. This was the first psychiatric hospitalization of a 22-year-old married woman who had given birth three months previously. On admission she appeared to be depressed and claimed that she was a witch and demanded to be killed. This condition began shortly after the birth with loss of appetite, insomnia, tension, and inability to take care of her child. Her father and her elder sister had histories of affective disorder, manic type. Following combined tricyclic and neuroleptic treatment her depressive delusions decreased, yet she remained severely depressed. After another month in which only amitryptiline 300 mg/day was administered, she continued to be depressed. She was then given reserpine 1 mg i.m. for 2 consecutive days while still on amitryptiline 300 mg/day. Immediately following the second injection she developed rapid speech, became hyperactive, hypersexual, and euphoric. This situation lasted for 3 days and receded spontaneously to what seemed to be her premorbid personality. Shortly afterwards she was discharged and tricyclic treatment was discontinued. At 3-month follow-up she continued to be well without medication.

Case 3. Mr. D. was a 22-year-old single man who was admitted to his third psychiatric hospitalization because of manic episodes. His first and second hospitalizations were for the same reason. He had also undergone several depressive episodes which had subsided with ambulatory treatment. His mother had had four psychiatric hospitalizations and was diagnosed as schizophrenic. During his hospitalization, and following treatment with chlorpromazine 1000 mg/day and lithium 1500 mg/day for two months, Mr. D. developed severe depression with manifestations of guilt feelings, despair, reduced psychomotor activity, and suicidal ideations. Since two months of imipramine treatment (up to 300 mg/day) proved fruitless, reserpine 1 mg/day i.m. for 2 consecutive days was administered.

The next day his depression vanished. This situation continued, with some fluctuation, for the next 4 months. During this period the patient was discharged from the hospital, returned to his premorbid activity, and all medication except for lithium maintenance was discontinued.

The above clinical observations are in accordance with those of Poldinger (1959, 1963), Haskovec and Rysanek (1967), and Hopkinson and Kenny (1975). However, in our study we gave reserpine 1 mg i.m./day for 2 consecutive days, while in the studies mentioned, the dose administered ranged between 2.5 and 10 mg reserpine i.m. for 2 consecutive days.

Reserpine induces enhancement of monoamine concentration in the synaptic cleft for brief periods (Cooper et al., 1978). Tricyclics derive their antidepressive effect by blocking of the monoamine reuptake in the synaptic cleft. The amine theory of depression (Schildkraut, 1965) postulates that depression is associated with a reduction of monoamines in critical synapses within the CNS. It would therefore seem logical that addition of reserpine for short periods in a patient already taking tricyclics would add to the clinical potency of the tricyclic. Clinical observations demonstrate that adding reserpine to an ongoing tricyclic treatment causes enhancement of monoaminergic activity. It was reported that this combination causes autonomic side effects (heightened pulse, mydriasis, perspiration, tremor; Poldinger, 1963), as well as conspicuous vasodilation and increase of intestinal peristalsis (Haskovec and Rysanek, 1967), which resembles crises of patients with argentaffinoma. Moreover, in animal experiments (Osborne, 1962; Scheckel and Boff, 1964; Sulser et al., 1964; Garattini et al., 1962) this combination causes the animals to become aroused and excited instead of the typical sedative and depressive effects of reserpine when it is administrated alone. Some authors relate this reserpine reversal phenomenon to the action of catecholamines (Scheckel and Boff, 1964; Spector, 1963; Sulser et al., 1965); some suggest serotonin (Green and Erickson, 1962) and others suggest that both amines are involved (Graeff et al., 1965).

Simultaneous measurement of epinephrine, norepinephrine, and serotonin metabolite excretion during a course of combined imipramine and reserpine administration might give us a clue in this regard. In 10 patients who were on this combination (Haskovec and Rysanek, 1967), 24-hour urine specimens were collected and assessed for 3-methoxy-4-hydroxymandelic acid (5-HIAA). In this study, an association between increased 5-HIAA excretion rate during the first day of reserpine administration and later favorable response to the combined treatment was found. No such relationship was found for VMA. These findings suggest a possible link between 5-HT activity and the relief of depression in this combined treatment. However, lack of a control group and the limited validity of urine measurement of monoamines as the only indicator for CNS activity (Kopin et al., 1983) limited the importance of these findings. Yet there might be a parallel to these findings from the clinical observations and biochemical studies on lithium addition to an ongoing tricyclic treatment in tricyclic-resistant patients (de Montigny and Cournoyer, Chapter 8 of this volume). Both lithium and reserpine seem to cause an immediate and dramatic switch process of the depression 24-48 hours after their administration to some tricyclic-resistant depressive patients. Since both lithium (Blier and de Montigny, 1983; Treiser et al., 1981) and reserpine (Garattini et al., 1959) result in an enhanced release of 5-HT in the synaptic cleft, it would be tempting to propose that 5-HT neurotransmission is involved in this process. However, it is still difficult to explain how a transient augmentation of 5-HT transmission induces a long-lasting desirable therapeutic effect.

CONCLUSION

We have reviewed four studies, three of them open and one double-blind. Out of the 45 depressive patients who were treated with the combined treatment of tricyclic antidepressant plus reserpine, 38 had a favorable response. Bearing in mind the limited number of patients, the lack of control group in three of the studies and the absence of recent studies, these results are promising. Since it takes only a couple of days and since no alarming adverse effects were noted, it might be justifiable to try reserpine in TCA nonresponders. More carefully designed studies of this combined treatment will undoubtedly have clinical as well as theoretical importance.

REFERENCES

Blier, P., and deMontigny, C. Enhancement of serotonergic neuro-transmission by short-term lithium treatment: electrophysiological studies in the rat. *Neurosci. Abst. 9*, 126.5 (1983)

Bonati, F., Cucurachie, L., and Urbani, M. Le modificazioni della pressionc arteriosa della frequenza cardiaca e del quadro electro cardiografico in psicopatici sottoposti ad intensa terapia reserpinica, in *Symposium nazionale sulla reserpina e clorpromazina in neuropsichiatria*. Vita e pensiero, Milano, pp. 150-153 (1956).

Bunney, W.E. Jr., Goodwin, F.K., and Murphy, D.L. The "switch process" in manic-depressive illness. *Arch. Gen. Psychiat. 27*, 312-317 (1972).

Cooper, J.R., Bloom, F.E., and Roth, R.H. *The Biochemical Basis of Neuropharmacology*, 3rd edition, Oxford University Press, New York, pp. 213-214 (1978).

Garattini, S., Mortavi, A., Valsecchi, A. and Valzelli, J. Reserpine derivatives with specific hypotensive or sedative activity. *Nature 183*, 1273-1274 (1959).

Garattini, S., Ginchetti, A., Jori, A., Pieri, L., and Valzelli, L. Effects of imipramine, amitryptiline and their manomethyl derivatives on reserpine activity. *J. Pharm. Pharmacol. 14,* 509-514 (1962).

Graeff, F., Garcia, L.J., and Silva, R. Role played by catechol- and indolamines in the central action of reserpine after monoamine oxidase inhibition. *Int. J. Neuropharmacol. 4,* 17-26 (1965).

Green, H., and Erickson, R. Further studies with tranylcypromine (monoamine oxidase inhibitor) and its interaction with reserpine in rat brain. *Arch. Int. Pharmacodyn. 135,* 407-425 (1962).

Haskovec, L., and Rysanek, K. The action of reserpine in imipramine-resistant depressive patients. *Psychopharmacologia 11,* 18-30 (1967).

Hopkinson, G., and Kenny, F. Treatment with reserpine of patients resistant to tricyclic antidepressants. *Psychiatria Clin. 8,* 109-114 (1975).

Kirkpatrick, W., and Sanders, F. Clinical evaluation of reserpine in state hospital. *Ann. N.Y. Acad. Sci. 61.* 123-143 (1955).

Kopin, I.J., Gordon, E.K., Jimerson, D.C., and Polinsky, R.J. Relation between plasma and cerebrospinal fluid levels of 3-methoxy-4-hydroxyphenyl-glycol. *Science 219,* 73-76 (1983).

Masini, A., Pescetto, G., and Tosca, L. Effetti somatici ed impiego psichiatrico della reserpine, in *Symposium naqionale sulla reserpina e clorpromazina in neuropsichiatria.* Vita e pensiero, Milano, pp. 137-144 (1956).

Osborne, M. Interaction of imipramine with sympathomimetic amines and reserpine. *Arch. Internat. Pharmacodyn. 138,* 493-505 (1962).

Poldinger, W. Diskussionsbemerkung an der der 129. Verslag der Schweiz Ges. fur psychiatrie. Schweiz. *Arch. Neurol. Psychiat. 84,* 327 (1959).

Poldinger, W. Combined administration of desipramine and reserpine or tetrabenazine in depressive patients. *Psychopharmacologia 4,* 308-310 (1963).

Scheckel, C., and Boff, E. Behavioral effects of interacting imipramine and other drugs with d-amphetamine, cocaine and tetrabenazine. *Psychopharmacologia (Berl.) 5,* 198-208 (1964).

Schildkraut, J. The catecholamine hypothesis of affective disorders: a review of supporting evidence. *Am. J. Psychiat. 122,* 509-522 (1965).

Spector, S. MAO in control of brain serotonin and NE content. *Ann. N.Y. Acad. Sci. 107,* 856-864 (1963).

Sulser, F., Bickel, M., and Brodie, B. The action of desmethyl-imipramine in counteracting sedation and cholinergic effect of reserpine-like drugs. *J. Pharmacol. Exp. Ther. 144,* 321-329 (1964).

Treiser, S.L., Cascio, C.S., O'Donohue, T.L., Thoa, N.B., Jacobowitz, D.M., and Kellar, K.J. Lithium increases serotonin release and decreases serotonin receptors in hippocampus. *Science 213,* 1529-1531 (1981).

20

Beta-2 Adrenergic Agonists for Depression as a Potential Treatment

Joseph Zohar, Bernard Lerer, and Robert H. Belmaker

The catecholamine hypothesis of depression suggested that depression is associated with a reduction in functional noradrenaline levels at some central synapses (Schildkraut, 1965). This theory implied that a direct agonist at noradrenaline receptors may be effective in depression. However, available agonists either did not cross the blood-brain barrier or caused cardiac arrhythmias after more than brief use.

Simon and his group (Lecrubier et al., 1977; Simon et al., 1978; Lecrubier et al., 1980) first reported antidepressant efficacy for salbutamol, a β-2 adrenergic receptor agonist used routinely in the treatment of asthma. (Heart noradrenaline receptors are predominantly β-1, and so cardiac side effects of salbutamol are negligible.) Salbutamol has been widely used for its peripheral effects and its penetration into brain has not been well-studied. However there are case-reports of addiction (Edwards and Holgate, 1979; Gaultier et al., 1976), and of induction or exacerbation of psychosis (Gluckman, 1974; Feline and Quentin, 1975), as with other antidepressants. Moreover, recently, Hallberg et al. (1980) found effects of systematically administered salbutamol in rats on brain monoamine metabolism. The function of β-2 receptors in human brain is not known. However, several studies of adrenergic receptor function in untreated depressed patients (Pandey et al., 1979; Extein et al., 1979) have reported interesting changes in the leukocyte β-receptor, which is β-2 in nature (Gelfand et al., 1979).

The pharmacokinetics of salbutamol have been studied in animals and in man. Several human studies have shown absorption after an oral dose of 4 to 8 mg to be between 60% and 80% (Martin et al., 1971; Evans et al., 1973). It is thus unclear why Simon et al. (1978) have been impressed with the drug's "poor bioavailability" and have given the drug only by infusion to depressed patients. Salbutamol for maintenance treatment in asthma is used orally with doses up to 4 mg four times daily. Martin et al. (1971) gave labeled salbutamol 25 mg/kg orally to rats and studied distribution into several tissues including brain. While very little salbutamol seemed to penetrate into brain tissue in this study, it should be noted that data on only 12 rat brains are reported and hepatic clearance in the rat and conjugation of salbutamol seemed to proceed differently from that in humans.

The present clinical literature on salbutamol is almost entirely due to the efforts of Simon and his group (Lecrubier et al., 1977; Simon et al., 1978; Lecrubier et al., 1980). In one uncontrolled study (Simon et al., 1978) 49 depressed patients were treated with 3 mg of salbutamol per day in two daily infusions of 250 ml isotonic glucose. The infusion was given at a rate of 20-40 drops per minute, and the dose was increased over several days to a total of 6 mg per day salbutamol in the two i.v. infusions. Patients were treated for a total of 6-10 days. There were 8 bipolar depressives and 14 endogenous unipolars, of whom only 2 failed to respond. Simon et al. report that effects were clear by the third day and sometimes by the first day. The clinical impression was of even improvement in the whole depressive syndrome, including "mood, psychomotor retardation, suicidal ideas, and anxiety." Among 18 patients with severe reactive depressions in Simon's uncontrolled study, 15 were reported to have a clear therapeutic effect. Among 9 less severe depressive reactions, Simon et al. reported some disinhibiting effects, relaxation, and some mild euphoria. All patients who responded were reported to do so quickly, within three days. However, no follow-up data is given for any of the patients. Since salbutamol was only given intravenously, it would be especially important to know how many of these patients were treated afterwards with oral tricyclics and how many were able to be discharged after salbutamol treatment alone. It would also be important to know whether any manic episode were precipitated among the bipolar patients. One patient in a previous study was said to have a transient hypomania after the sixth day of salbutamol treatment (Lecrubier et al., 1977).

In a controlled study of salbutamol versus chlorimipramine, Lecrubier et al. (1980) gave salbutamol again in two daily infusions, each over 2-3 hours. Dosage was progressively increased to 6 mg daily. Chlorimipramine dosage was 150 mg daily, also given in two daily infusions. Treatment in this study was extended for 15 days and 10 patients were studied in each drug group. Salbutamol was significantly superior to chlorimipramine by day 5 of treatment, and this difference was still present by day 15. Eight of the ten salbutamol-treated patients responded very well, including three bipolars, a delusional depressive and four endogenous depressives.

However, this study does not meet the usually accepted criteria of placebo control in depression research. The chlorimipramine group showed no improvement from day 5 to day 15, and without a placebo group this fact is difficult to interpret. However, since salbutamol was significantly superior to chlorimipramine, this procedural objection is perhaps technical and the study should be accepted as valid. The salbutamol clinical literature is therefore limited more by its paucity than its quality. A single study could yield results due to chance; also, all best efforts notwithstanding, the double-blind between salbutamol and chlorimipramine must be difficult to maintain, given a typical coarse tremor with salbutamol and absence of cholinergic effects. It is unfortunate that no follow-up data is available from the controlled study of Lecrubier et al. (1980), as it would be crucial to know whether salbutamol-treated patients relapsed or were dischargeable after salbutamol alone. Also, a 21-30 day comparison of salbutamol with chlorimipramine is crucial, as chlorimipramine side effects could conceivably appear to worsen depression early in treatment, thus causing an apparent superiority for salbutamol.

Our own unit's experience with salbutamol is entirely open in design and thus adds little proof of efficacy to Simon's work. However, we have added experience with salbutamol given orally rather than intravenously, with salbutamol for 21 days of treatment (Lerer et al., 1981), with salbutamol in combination with lithium (Zohar et al., 1982), and in addition we have follow-up on response to other treatments in relation to salbutamol treatment.

It should be emphasized that permission to study salbutamol as an antidepressant is available to us only for resistant depressive patients, so that our two series (totaling 17 separate patients as three patients were studied both with and without lithium) represent a highly select group of tricyclic nonresponder depressives. All patients were drug-free for at least 14 days before starting salbutamol, except for the lithium plus salbutamol patients who have been receiving lithium for at least 17 days before starting salbutamol. Salbutamol was started at 2 mg four times daily for three days, and dosage then raised to 4 mg four times daily. Treatment was continued for 21 days in the salbutamol-only protocol, and for 9 to 17 days in the salbutamol plus lithium protocol. In order to test the peripheral β-adrenergic adenylate cyclase, patients were given 0.25 mg salbutamol i.v. in a 10-minute push before onset of oral treatment, and then again after about one week and three weeks of oral treatment in the salbutamol-only study, and after about two weeks of treatment in the salbutamol plus lithium study.

The marked biochemical findings reported (Lerer et al., 1981, Zohar et al., 1982) suggest that absorption of salbutamol into the blood was satisfactory, as was patient compliance in our setting. Side effects were minimal and the tremor reported by Simon et al. (1978) was mild if present at all in our patients. An elevation of basal heart rate by 5-10 beats per minute was noted on almost every patient in the salbutamol-only study, but seemed to be blocked by concurrent treatment with lithium, as in other studies (Belmaker et al., 1979).

Nine of our patients had unipolar depression, seven had bipolar disease, and one was schizoaffective. Ten were female and there were seven males; their age varied from 29 to 72 years, with an average of 55 years. All but three were tricyclic nonresponders, four also did not respond to an adequate trail of ECT, and two were also MAO inhibitor nonresponders. Twelve patients had a trial of neuroleptics and ten did not respond to lithium treatment. Only three of 17 patients failed to show some improvement in Hamilton Depression Scores (Hamilton, 1967) with salbutamol treatment. The three patients who participated in both salbutamol and salbutamol-plus-lithium protocols improved to about the same degree during each salbutamol treatment, despite their relapse after the salbutamol alone that justified their trial with salbutamol plus lithium. However, the response was neither rapid nor dramatic. The course of the antidepressant response over 7-21 days seemed comparable to that of other antidepressant treatments. Several salbutamol responders were restarted on salbutamol after a 4-day placebo period after the first 21 days of salbutamol therapy. All of these patients relapsed within 2-3 weeks despite continued salbutamol treatment. Two of these patients later had clear responses to other drug combinations or to ECT, whereas at least one seemed resistant to all available treatment. No hypomanic responses to salbutamol were seen, despite the fact that three patients had manic responses to other treatments during the follow-up period. Despite the overall evidence of improvement with salbutamol in almost all patients, only one patient could be discharged directly after salbutamol treatment, and this was a patient with excellent social support and little past hospitalization despite his chronic depression. That the group was capable of responding to some biological treatment is evidenced by four patients who responded well and were discharged after ECT, and two patients who responded very well to lithium plus phenelzine. None of these patients were dischargeable at the end of the salbutamol trial.

One patient, a 56-year-old woman schoolteacher with a long history of alternating mania and depression, developed a severe delusional psychosis during treatment with lithium plus salbutamol. She had not had such symptoms in the past. The psychosis did not respond to withdrawal of salbutamol, but improved after 10 days of treatment with chlorpromazine. Interestingly, she was then maintained on chlorpromazine 100 mg daily without depressive relapse.

The frequent and significant decline in Hamilton scores without achievement of full remission could suggest an amphetamine-like action for salbutamol. In our studies, however (Belmaker et al., 1981), the acute infusions of 0.25 mg salbutamol in these patients were not accompanied by mood or psychomotor changes. Recently the effect of another β-2 agonist, pirbuterol, on resistant depressive patients, was studied by another group (Nurnberger et al., submitted). In this trial they added pirbuterol up to 60 mg per day, to an ongoing lithium treatment of five resistant depressive women. Their clinical impression was that "most patients experienced transient improvement on pirbuterol but that this improvement was not sustained despite continuation of medication at the same dose." Salbutamol, as well as pirbuterol, is a drug which may have poor penetration across the blood-brain barrier (Martin et al., 1971; Nurnberger et al., submitted). The question of psychoactive effects of β-2 receptor agonists that can cross the blood-brain barrier better is an exciting one. Recently, such a compound named clenbuterol became available for human studies. Simon et al. (1983) reported that clenbuterol was as effective as chlorimipramine in unselected depressive patients. Therefore, it seems that β-2 receptor agonists that cross the blood-brain barrier warrant further research in depression in general, and in resistant depression in particular.

REFERENCES

Belmaker, R.H., Lerer, B., Ebstein, R.P., Lettik, H., and Kugelmass, S. A possible cardiovascular effect of lithium. *Amer. J. Psychiat. 136*, 577-579 (1979).

Belmaker, R.H., Lerer, B., and Ebstein, R.P. Noradrenaline, dopamine and mood, in *Advances in the Biosciences*. Vol. 31, Recent Advances in Neuropsychopharmacology, B. Angrist, G.D. Burrows, M. Leder, O. Lingjaerde, G. Sedvall and D. Wheatley, eds. Pergamon Press, Oxford, pp. 17-29 (1981).

Edwards, G.J., and Holgate, S.T. Dependency upon salbutamol inhalers. *Brit. J. Psychiat. 134*, 624-626 (1979).

Evans, M.E., Walker, S.R., Brittain, K.T. and Paterson, J.W. The metabolism of salbutamol in man. *Xenobiotica 3*, 113-120 (1973).

Extein, I., Tallman, J., Smith, C.C., and Goodwin, F.K. Changes in lymphocyte Beta-adrenergic receptors in depression and mania. *Psychiat. Res. 1*, 191-197 (1979).

Feline, A., and Quentin, A.M. Ventolin psychosis. *Nouvelle Presse Medicale 4*, 2808-2809 (1975).

Gaultier, M., Gervais, P., Lagier, G., and Danan, L. Pharmacodependence psychique au salbutamol en aerosal chez asthmatique. *Therapie 31*, 465-470 (1976).

Gelfand, E.W., Dosch, H.M., Hastings, D., and Shore, A. Lithium: A modulator of cyclic AMP-dependent events in lymphocytes. *Science 203*, 365-367 (1979).

Gluckman, L. Ventolin psychosis. *New Zealand Med. J. 80,* 411 (1974).

Hallberg, H., Almgren, O., and Svensson, T.H. Increased brain serotonergic and noradrenergic activity after repeated systemic administration of the β-receptor agonist salbutamol, a putative antidepressant drug, in Abstracts of the 12th CINP Congress, Goteborg, Sweden (supplement to *Progress in Neuropsychopharmacology)* (1980).

Hamilton, M. Development of a rating scale for primary depressive illness. *Brit. J. Social Clin. Psychol. 6,* 278-296 (1967).

Lecrubier, Y., Jouvent, R., Puech, A.J., Simon, P., and Widlocher, D. Effect antidepressant d'un stimulant β-adrenergique. *Nouvelle Press Medicale 6,* 2786 (1977).

Lecrubier, Y., Puech, A.J., Jouvent, R., Simon, P., and Widlocher, D. A β-adrenergic stimulant salbutamol vs. clorimipramine in depression: A control study. *Brit. J. Psychiat. 136,* 354-358 (1980).

Lerer, B., Ebstein, R.P., and Belmaker, R.H. Subsensitivity of human β-adrenergic adenylate cyclase after salbutamol treatment of depression. *Psychopharmacol. 75,* 169-172 (1981).

Martin, L.E., Hobson, J.C. Page, J.A., and Harrison, C. Metabolic studies of salbutamol-^{3}H: A new bronchodilator in rat, rabbit, dog and man. *Eur. J. Pharmacol. 14,* 183-199 (1971).

Nurnberger, J.I., Kessler, L., Simmons-Alling, S., Nadi, N.S., Berrettini, W.H. and Gershon, E.S. A clinical trial of the β-2 agonist Pirbuterol as an antidepressant. Submitted.

Pandey, G.N., Dysken, M.W., Garver, D.L., and Davis, J.M. β-adrenergic receptor function in effective illness. *Amer. J. Psychiat. 136,* 675-677 (1979).

Schildkraut, J.J. The catecholamine hypothesis of affective disorders: A review of supporting evidence. *Amer. J. Psychiat. 122,* 509-522 (1965).

Simon, P., Lecrubier, Y., Jouvent, R., Puech, A.J., Allilaire, J.F., and Widlocher, D. Experimental and clinical evidence of the antidepressant effect of a β-adrenergic stimulant. *Psychol. Med. 8,* 335-338 (1978).

Simon, P., Puech, A.J., Lecrubier, Y., and Widlocher, D. Abstract of VII World Congress of Psychiatry, Vienna (1983).

Zohar, J., Lerer, B., Ebstein, R.P., and Belmaker, R.H. Lithium does not prevent agonist-induced subsensitivity of human adenylate cyclase. *Biol. Psychiat. 17,* 343-350 (1982).

21

Opioids as a Possible Treatment for Resistant Depression

Hinderk H.M. Emrich

INTRODUCTION

Since the time of Hippocrates the therapeutic potential of opium, not only for pain relief, but also as a psychotropic agent (sedation, tranquilization, anti-panic, and euphorogenic effects) has been recognized (Verebey and Gold, 1984). As early as 1901, at which time modern psychiatry was in its infancy, Emil Kraepelin recommended the "opium cure" in slowly increasing and later decreasing doses, in particular for patients with agitated depression. Though no standardized evaluations of this therapy have been undertaken, the original clinical reports suggest a genuine antidepressant effect of tinctura opii, morphine and other opiates (Weygandt, 1935). To circumvent the problem of opiate dependence, the opiate dosage was reduced stepwise prior to discharge of the patient. It was not reported that the patients became opiate-addicted as a consequence of this therapy.

Subsequent to the discovery of modern thymoleptic drugs, interest in possible opiate treatment of depressed patients decidedly waned. Fink et al. (1970), alone, investigated the action of the, at that time, novel mixed agonist/antagonist cyclazocine in depressed patients. In an open study, Fink applied 1.0-3.0 mg cyclazocine to 10 severely depressed patients and observed an about 50% reduction of the items "depressed mood" and "apathy." This particular substance was used, since a lower dependence liability of the partial agonistic compound was anticipated. However, it emerged that cyclazocine exerts psychotomimetic effects in normal probands (Jasinski et al., 1967). As a result, these investigations were discontinued.

A real resurgence in interest as to a possible connection between opioids and depression was prompted by the discovery of the endorphins (for a summary see Emrich, 1981; Bloom, 1983). It has been proposed that these endogenous opiate-like peptides may be deficient in depression and that, therefore, a rational therapy might be the substitution for this by opioids (Herz and Emrich, 1983). Kline and co-workers (1977) were the first to report beneficial effects of i.v. beta-endorphin in depressed patients (open study, 2 patients, 1.5-6.0 mg). Angst et al. (1979) observed a switch to hypomania/mania after beta-endorphin infusions (10 mg, i.v.) in 3 out of 6 depressed patients. Furthermore, Gorelick et al. (1981), in 10 depressed patients, found an unequivocal antidepressive action of i.v. beta-endorphin infusions (double-blind design, 1.5-11.5 mg). Also, the use of the synthetic enkephalin analogue FK 33-824 in 10 patients with endogenous depression produced a remarkable improvement in 3 of them and a tranquilizing effect in 4 patients (Nedopil and Rüther, 1979). Additionally, Gold et al. (1982) reported data suggesting potential antidepressant and antianxiety/antipanic effects of opiates. The possible impact of opioids in the theory and treatment of depresssive disorders has recently been discussed (Gold et al., 1982; Herz and Emrich, 1983). Furthermore, it has recently been documented that patients suffering from senile dementia accompanied by depression show remarkable effects upon application of deodorated tincture of opium (Abse et al., 1982). Codeine, on the other hand, turned out to be ineffective in depression (Varga et al., 1982).

THE USE OF THE PARTIAL AGONIST BUPRENORPHINE IN RESISTANT DEPRESSION

The finding that the opiate mixed agonist/antagonist buprenorphine (Lewis, 1980) had mood-improving effects in postoperative patients (Harcus et al., 1980) and the most important fact that this strong analgesic substance is devoid of psychotomimetic effects and has a very low abuse potential (Jasinski et al., 1978; Mello et al., 1981) suggested the performance of a clinical trial in resistant depression. Furthermore, it had been shown by Mello and Mendelson (1980) that buprenorphine exerts extremely positive subjective effects in opiate addicts. The aim of the investigation was to develop a new opioid substance with a strong anti-depressant potency and a high degree of drug safety.

Methods

The study was performed by use of a double-blind A_1/B/A_2 design ($A_{1,2}$ = placebo; B = buprenorphine). Thirteen patients who met the research diagnostic criteria (Spitzer et al., 1978) for major depressive disorders gave their informed consent to participate in the study. The duration of the three therapeutic phases varied; A_1 was from 1-7 days; B was from 5-8 days; A_2 was from 0-4 days. The patients were free of conventional thymoleptic drugs. Before the beginning of the trial, a washout period of 4 days was performed. During the buprenorphine treatment phase, two sublingual tablets (0.2 mg per day) were given at 8:30 and 16:30 h. Psychopathological evaluation was performed by a trained psychiatrist every two days in the afternoon by use of the IMPS (Lorr et al., 1962) and the Hamilton Scale for Depression (Hamilton, 1960). Additionally, the global impression of depression and, as a screening of side effects, the symptoms "nausea," "vomiting," "dizziness," and "euphoria" were evaluated by use of the VBS (Verlaufs-Beurteilungs-Skala; Emrich et al., 1977).

The mean results of the Hamilton scores before (A_1), during (B_1; B_2; B_3) and after (A_2) buprenorphine treatment are depicted in Figure 1. The data B_1–B_3 represent the average values of the Hamilton score at the beginning of the blind buprenorphine treatment (B_1), in the middle of buprenorphine treatment phase (B_2), and at the end of buprenorphine treatment (B_3). A_2 represents the average data of the Hamilton scores at the end of the second placebo treatment period. As can be seen in Figure 1, there is a reduction in the Hamilton scores during the phases B_1-B_3 in comparison with the placebo phase A_1 and, to a lesser degree, also in comparison with the second placebo phase A_2. These differences are significant ($p < 0.02$, Wilcoxon test).

An evaluation of the data of individual patients (data not shown) reveals that about 50% of the patients responded very strongly to buprenorphine, whereas the other 50% were, apparently, nonresponders. Since practically all of the patients included in the study were nonresponders to conventional thymoleptic therapy, this is a significant result. Most of the patients experienced some degree of slight nausea, dizziness, and sedation (vomiting in one case) in the course of the study, but these side effects, with the exception of the one case of vomiting, never became a problem during therapy.

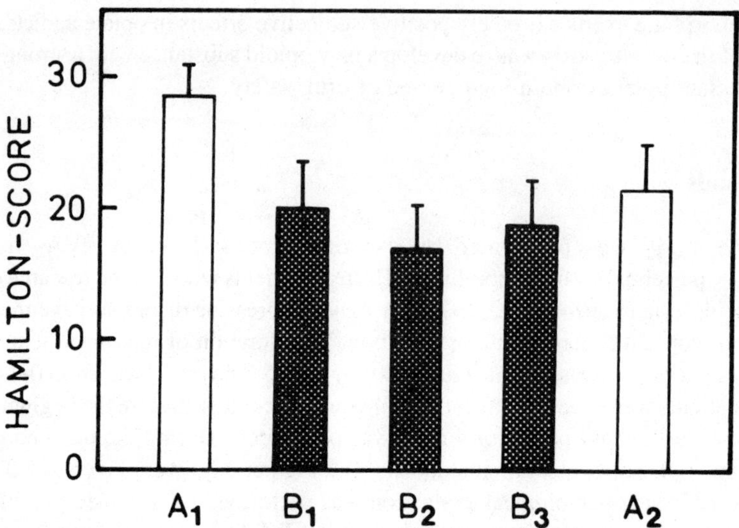

Figure 1. Averaged Hamilton scores of 13 depressed patients before (A_1), during (B_1-B_3), and after (A_2) buprenorphine treatment. Bars = Sem; for details see text.

DISCUSSION

There are several investigations documenting a blunted prolactin response in depressed patients following infusion of methadone/morphine (Extein et al., 1980; Judd et al., 1982; 1983). These findings may be regarded as representative for a hint as to a possible defective operation of endorphinergic systems in endogenous depression, possibly at the receptor level. On the other hand, it has been shown that electroconvulsion exerts activating effects on endorphinergic systems in animals as well as in man: Holaday's group (Belenky and Holaday, 1979; Holaday and Belenky, 1980) obtained compelling evidence for an activation of central endorphinergic systems by ECT. In line with these results are the findings of Emrich et al. (1979), in which an increase in plasma levels of beta-endorphin immunoreactivity was observed 10 minutes following electroconvulsion in depressed patients, a result that has recently been reproduced by Alexopoulos et al. (1983). Therefore, a possible endorphinergic component of the mode of action of electroconvulsion may be hypothesized.

Bearing these facts in mind, it appears plausible to consider the administration of an opioid in patients who fail to respond satisfactorily to conventional thymoleptic treatment. In the investigation documented above, about 50% of thymoleptic nonresponders showed a rapid and pronounced response to buprenorphine. Subsequent to termination of the present double-blind study of buprenorphine in resistant depression, a number of patients have been treated under open conditions. The percentage of positive results was again about 50%. It has also been observed that the combination of buprenorphine with tricyclic antidepressants presents no problems and that, after appearance of a positive opioid response, treatment with a tricyclic compound may be continued after withdrawal of buprenorphine. Although the dependence liability of buprenorphine is relatively low (Jasinski et al., 1978), buprenorphine-dependence has been observed in cases of chronic pain (Richert et al., 1983); therefore, the buprenorphine treatment of resistant depression cannot be performed in outpatients. However, it should be mentioned that the development of buprenorphine dependence in depressed patients has not, as yet, been described. Presently, this type of therapy may be regarded as an alternative to electroconvulsion in patients who prove resistant to conventional thymoleptic therapy.

REFERENCES

Abse, D.W., Rheuban, W.J., and Akhtar, S. The poppy: therapeutic potential in cases of dementia with depression. *Ann. N.Y. Acad. Sci. 398*, 79-82 (1982).

Alexopoulos, G.S., Inturrisi, C.E., Lipman, R., Frances, R., Haycox, J., Dougherty Jr. J. H. and Rossier, J. Plasma immunoreactive beta endorphin levels in depression. *Arch. Gen. Psychiat. 40*, 181-183 (1983).

Angst, J., Autenrieth, V., Brem, F., Koukkou, M., Meyer, H., Stassen, H.H., and Storck, U. Preliminary results of treatment with beta endorphin in depression, in *Endorphins in Mental Health Research,* E. Usdin, W.E. Bunney Jr., and N.S. Kline, eds., Macmillan, London, pp. 518-528 (1979).

Belenky, G.L., and Holaday, J.W. The opiate antagonist naloxone modifies the effects of electroconvulsive shock (ECS) on respiration, blood pressure and heart rate. *Brain Res. 177*, 414-417 (1979).

Bloom, F.E. The endorphins: a growing family of pharmacologically pertinent peptides. Ann. Rev. Pharmacol. *Toxicol. 23*, 151-170 (1983).

Emrich, H.M., ed. *The Role of Endorphins in Neuropsychiatry (Modern Problems in Pharmacopsychiatry, Vol. 17).* Karger, Basel (1981).

Emrich, H.M., Cording, C., Pirée, S., Kölling, A., von Zerssen, D., and Herz, A. Indication of an antipsychotic action of the opiate antagonist naloxone, *Pharmakopsychiat. 10*, 265-270 (1977).

Emrich, H.M., Höllt, V., Kissling, W., Fischler, M., Laspe, H., Heinemann, H., von Zerssen, D., and Herz, A. β-Endorphin-like immunoreactivity in cerebrospinal fluid and plasma of patients with schizophrenia and other neuropsychiatric disorders. *Pharmakopsychiat. 12*, 269-276 (1979).

Extein, I., Pottash, A.L.C., Gold, M.S., Sweeney, D.R., Martin, D.M. and Goodwin, F.K. Deficient prolactin response to morphine in depressed patients. *Amer. J. Psychiat. 137*, 845-846 (1980).

Fink, M., van Simeon, J., Itil, T.M., and Freedman, A.M. Clinical antidepressant acitvity of cyclazocine—a narcotic antagonist. *Clin. Pharmacol. Therapeut. 11*, 41-48 (1970).

Gold, M.S., Pottash, A.C., Sweeney, D. Martin, D., and Extein I. Antimanic, antidepressant, and antipanic effects of opiates: Clinical, neuroanatomical, and biochemical evidence. *Ann. N.Y. Acad. Sci. 398*, 140-150 (1982).

Gorelick, D.A., Catlin, D.H., and Gerner, R.H. Beta endorphin studies in psychiatric patients. *Mod. Probl. Pharmacopsychiat. 17*, 236-245 (1981).

Hamilton, M. A rating scale for depression. *J. Neurol. Neurosurg. Psychiat. 23*, 56-62 (1960).

Harcus, A.H., Ward, A.E., and Smith, D.W. Buprenorphine in post-operative pain: results in 7500 patients. *Anaesthesia 35*, 382-386 (1980).

Herz, A., and Emrich, H.M. Opioid systems and the regulation of mood: Possible significance in depression? in *The Origins of Depression: Current Concepts and Approaches*, J. Angst, ed., Springer, Berlin, pp. 221-234 (1983).

Holaday, J.W., and Belenky, G.L. Opiate-like effects of electroconvulsive shock in rats: a differential effect of naloxone on nociceptive measures. *Life Sci. 27*, 1929-1938 (1980).

Jasinski, D.R., Martin, W.R., and Haertzen, C.A. The human pharmacology and abuse potential of N-allyl-noroxymorphone (naloxone). *J. Pharm. Exp. Therapeut. 157*, 420-426 (1967).

Jasinski, D.R., Pevnick, J.S., and Griffith, J.D. Human pharmacology and abuse potential of the analgesic buprenorphine. *Arch. Gen. Psychiat. 35*, 501-506 (1978).

Judd, L.L., Risch, S.C., Parker, D.C., Janowsky, D.S., Segal, D.S., and Huey, L.Y. Blunted prolactin response. *Arch. Gen. Psychiat. 39*, 1413-1416 (1982).

Judd, L.L., Risch, S.C., Janowsky, D.S., Segal, D.S. and Huey, L.Y. Methadone and metoclopramide may differentially affect prolactin secretion in depressed patients. *Psychopharmacol. Bull. 19*, 482-485 (1983).

Kline, N.S., Li, C.H., Lehmann, H.E., Lajtha, A., Laski, E., and Cooper, T. β-Endorphin-induced changes in schizophrenic and depressed patients. *Arch. Gen. Psychiat. 34*, 1111-1113 (1977).

Kraepelin, E. *Einführung in die Psychiatrische Klinik,* Joh. Ambrosius Barth-Verlag, Leipzig, p.11. (1901).

Lewis, J.W. Buprenorphine—a new strong analgesic, in *Problems in Pain,* C. Peck and M. Wallace, eds. Pergamon Press, Oxford, pp. 87-89 (1980).

Lorr, M., Klett, C.J., McNair, D.M., and Lasky, J.J. *Inpatient Multidimensional Psychiatric Scale*. Consulting Psychologists Press, Palo Alto, California (1962).

Mello, N.K., and Mendelson, J.H. Buprenorphine suppresses heroin use by heroin addicts. *Science 207*, 657-659 (1980).

Mello, N.K., Bree, M.P., and Mendelson, J.H. Buprenorphine self-administration by rhesus monkey. Pharmacol. *Biochem. Behav. 15*, 215-225 (1981).

Nedopil, N., and Rüther, E. Effects of the synthetic analogue of methionine enkephalin FK 33-824 on psychotic symptoms. *Pharmacopsychiat. 12*, 277-280 (1979).

Richert, S., Strauss, A., von Arnim, Th,. Vogel, P., and Zech, A., Medikamentenabhängigkeit von Buprenorphin. *Münch. med. Wschr. 125*, 1195-1198 (1983).

Spitzer, R.L., Endicott, J. and Robins, E. *Research Diagnostic Criteria (RDC) for a Selected Group of Functional Disorders*. 3rd ed., New York Biometrics Research, New York State Psychiatric Institute, New York (1978).

Varga, E., Sugerman, A.A. and Apter, J. The effect of codeine on involutional and senile depression. *Ann. N.Y. Acad. Sci. 398*, 103-105 (1982).

Verebey, K. and Gold, M.S. Endorphins and mental disease, in *Handbook of Neurochemistry. Pathological Neurochemistry, Vol. 10,* A. Lajtha (ed.) Plenum Publishers (1985).

Weygandt, W. *Lehrbuch der Nerven-und Geisteskrankheiten,* Marhold Verlagsbuchhandlung, Halle, p. 507 (1935).

22

Treatment of Therapy-Resistant Depression with Drip Infusions of Chlorimipramine

P. Kielholz

THERAPY-RESISTANT DEPRESSIONS

Studies carried out in various countries have repeatedly shown that, when patients suffering from endogenous or psychogenic depression are given oral treatment with antidepressants in combination with psychotherapy, 60-70% of them show an encouraging response within two weeks (Klein et al., 1980). A further 10-15% respond to antidepressive medication when switched to another antidepressant with a suitable activity profile. Approximately 15%, however, fail to improve under oral medication combined with psychotherapy and must therefore be regarded as therapy-resistant cases.

The term "therapy-resistant" is thus applicable to those patients with endogenous or psychogenic depression who have still showed no response after oral treatment with two correctly dosed antidepressants, each possessing an appropriate activity profile and each administered one after the other for two weeks.*

In order to narrow down the indications for electroconvulsive therapy, we embarked some 15 years ago on a study of the question as to what other possibilities there might be of overcoming this problem of therapy-resistance. At that time we began by giving these patients intravenous treatment with chlorimipramine, which, in the light of pharmacokinetic considerations, we later administered in combination with maprotiline. What prompted us to resort to intravenous therapy were the following points:

1. When antidepressants are given by mouth, 20%-60% of the active substance becomes at least partially inactivated owing to the "first-pass" effect in the liver and because of binding to proteins (Riegelman, 1972).

2. Numerous biochemical studies had already been undertaken in an attempt to confirm the so-called transmitter hypothesis that endogenous depressions, and apparently also certain forms of psychogenic depression, are due to a deficiency of, or an imbalance between, biogenic amines (chiefly serotonin and noradrenaline) or, as has recently been postulated, to the fact that the post-synaptic receptors display reduced sensitivity to such amines. Hence the concept of administering treatment with two antidepressants, one exerting a serotonergic and the other a noradrenergic effect.

3. When, as shown in studies performed by Gram et al. (1982), an antidepressant is given in combination with a neuroleptic, the plasma levels of the antidepressant rise. Also, in animal experiments, Ortman et al. (1982) have recently demonstrated that such combined medication is associated with a significant increase in the turnover of serotonin. In view of these findings, additional administration of a neuroleptic drug might also prove of therapeutic value, particularly in forms of depression attributable mainly to a serotonin deficit.

THE CONCEPT OF COMBINED INFUSION THERAPY

Assuming that confirmation is forthcoming for the hypothesis that biogenic amines play a major role in the pathogenesis of depression, it should be possible to induce therapy-resistant depressions to lift by raising the concentrations of transmitter substances in the synapses. Such an increase in their concentrations can be achieved by administering antidepressants. For this purpose, we use two

*_Editor's note_: see also Chapters 2 and 5 for a detailed discussion of this subject.

antidepressants with differing pharmacological properties, namely chlorimipramine and maprotiline. Chlorimipramine inhibits the reuptake of serotonin, and maprotiline the reuptake of noradrenaline, from the synaptic cleft into the presynaptic depots. Due to this blockade, the transmitter substances are able to build up to higher levels in the synapses. The infusion treatment with chlorimipramine and maprotiline is given together with a neuroleptic drug in order to relax the patient, and is also supplemented by psychotherapy and physiotherapy.

ADVANTAGES

Combined infusion treatment offers a number of advantages:

1. More rapid onset of effect achieved by circumventing the problem, firstly of delayed gastro-intestinal absorption of the antidepressive substance and, secondly, of its degradation in the liver.
2. Lower dosage made possible because the active substance reaches the brain directly.
3. Increased plasma levels of the antidepressants, attained by giving them in combination with a neuroleptic.
4. Fewer side effects thanks to the use of lower dosages.
5. Increased concentrations of serotonin and noradrenaline in the synapses, resulting from the use of chlorimipramine (serotonergic) in combination with maprotiline (adrenergic).

CONDUCT OF TREATMENT

Where a patient is suffering from an endogenous or psychogenic depression which has proved therapy-resistant (within the meaning of the term as already defined), the diagnosis is first thoroughly checked again and a five-day course of intramuscular relaxation therapy then instituted with a neuroleptic drug. For this purpose, we employ neuroleptics which also have a mild antidepressive effect, e.g., 20-40 mg clotiapine t.i.d. or 15-30 mg chlorprothixene t.i.d. Immediately after this course of injections we commence daily intravenous drip infusion treatment. Each infusion contains 0.5-2 ampules (12.5-50 mg) of chlorimipramine and of maprotiline in 250 ml physiological saline or 5% glucose solution; in most cases we employ 250 ml of a mixture of these two solutions in a ration of 1:2, administered at a rate of 60 drops per minute over a period of about 90 minutes, given for 10-20 days.

Once a start has been made on the infusion treatment, we switch the patient to oral doses of the neuroleptic. These oral doses—reduced after a few days to one evening dose of 0.5-1 tablet of clotiapine, for example—are continued until the treatment has been completed. The neuroleptic not only reinforces the effect of the two antidepressnts but also helps to combat sleep disturbances.

After the depression shows clear signs of lifting, we transfer the patient to oral medication with the antidepressants, administered as a rule in daily doses equivalent to double the dosage that had been given by infusion, e.g., 50 mg chlorimipramine in the morning and 75 mg maprotiline in the evening.

Where anxiety states accompanied by cardiac signs and symptoms (tachycardia, precordial pain, pseudo-angina, extrasystoles) are a prominent feature of the clinical picture, we prescribe a beta-blocker in addition, provided of course that such treatment is not contraindicated. In some cases, a dose of only 1 tablet of 40 mg oxprenolol t.i.d. proves sufficient to interrupt, often almost at once, the vicious circle operating between the patient's anxiety and his cardiac symptomatology. Treatment with a beta-blocker also serves to ensure that the enhanced risk of suicide in severe anxiety states is already diminished before the antidepressive medication has begun to exert its full effect.

In comparison to oral medication, intravenous infusions prove significantly superior in terms of the speed with which they induce brightening of the mood in therapy-resistant cases of depression (Figure 1). By the time the patients are discharged from the hospital, however, their scores on the Beck and Hamilton Scales are roughly the same (Kielholz et al., 1979).

RESULTS OF TREATMENT

In all, we have now employed combined infusion therapy in 250 patients (102 men and 148 women), as listed in Table 1. Of these 250 patients, 145 were diagnosed as suffering from endogenous depression and 105 from psychogenic depression (Table 2). The four patients with endogenous depression who failed to respond to the treatment were severely anxious and agitated women suffering from involutional depression with strong overtones of hypochondriasis.

Already after the first few infusions many of the patients felt relaxed. Side effects such as slight dryness of the mouth, tiredness, tremor of autonomic nervous origin, and sleep disturbances occurred only in isolated instances. Five patients who got up immediately after completion of an infusion complained of palpitation and dizziness. For this reason, we subsequently instructed all patients to remain lying down for one hour after the infusion, whereupon such cardiovascular side effects were no longer observed.

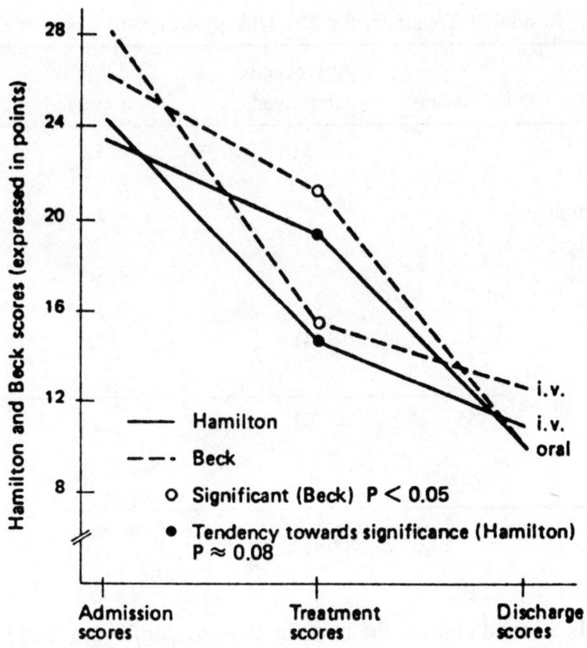

Figure 1. Comparison of results obtained with oral (N = 17) and intravenous (N = 15) treatment foı depression.

TABLE 1. Nosological Classification of 250 Therapy-Resistant Cases of Depression

	Men	Women
Endogenous depressions (unipolar, bipolar, involutional depression)	58	87
Psychogenic depressions (exhaustion depression)	44	61
Total 250	102	148

REPETITION OF THE TREATMENT

If a patient fails to respond to the treatment or shows only an inadequate response, we repeat the course of infusions after having first rechecked the diagno-

TABLE 2. Results of Treatment for 250 Therapy-Resistant Cases of Depression

	Remission	Appreciably improved	Slightly improved	No effect
Endogenous depressions (unipolar, bipolar involutional depression)	98	31	12	4
Psychogenic depressions	57	31	12	5
Total 250	155	62	24	9
	62%	25%	13%	

sis. During the second course, the infusion therapy can be intensified by supplementary treatment either with *L*-5-hydroxytryptophan (100-300 mg daily) or with *L*-tryptophan, which is administered intravenously. In therapy-resistant cases of endogenous depression, sleep deprival during the infusion treatment may sometimes lead to a slight brightening of the underlying depressive mood, a brightening which can occasionally be stabilized or even further improved by the infusions.

After the patients have been discharged from hospital, even in cases where the depression has completely lifted, treatment with chlorimipramine and maprotiline is continued by the oral route until they have become completely rehabilitated both in their private and social milieu and at their place of work.

SUMMARY

In 250 depressive patients who had proved resistant to therapy, intravenous infusion treatment with chlorimipramine and maprotiline was carried out after an initial five-day course of intramuscular medication had been given with a neuroleptic drug in order to relax them. The patients received one daily infusion for 10-20 days, after which the two antidepressants were administered orally. From the start of the infusion therapy until their treatment had been completed, neuroleptics were also prescribed orally in an evening dose.

After four weeks, 68% of the endogenous depressions and 54% of the psychogenic depressions had completely lifted. In cases where a patient fails to respond, a second course of infusion therapy can be instituted in combination with *L*-5-hydroxytryptophan or sleep deprivation in the hope that it may still be possible to obtain the desired response.

REFERENCES

Gram, L.F., Pedersen, O.L., Kristensen, C.B., Bjerre, M., and Kragh-Sorensen, P. Drug level monitoring in psychopharmacology: usefulness and clinical problems, with special reference to tricyclic antidepressants. *Ther. Drug Monit. 4*, 17-25 (1982).

Kielholz, P., Terzani, S. and Gastpar, M. Treatment for therapy resistant depressions. *Internat. Pharmacopsychiat. 14*, 94-100 (1979).

Klein, D.F., Gittelman, R., Quitkin, F., and Rifkin, A., in *Drug Treatment of Psychiatric Disorders*, 2nd ed., Williams and Wilkins, Baltimore/London, pp. 276-283, (1980).

Ortman, R., Bischoff, S., Radeke, E., Buech, O. and Delini-Stula, A. Correlation between different measures of antiserotonin activity of drugs. Study with neuroleptics and serotonin receptor blockers. *Arch. Pharmacol. 321*, 265-270 (1982).

Riegelman, S. Physiological and pharmacokinetic complexities in bioavailability testing. *Pharmacology 8*, 118-141 (1972).

23

Psychosurgery for Resistant Depression

Paul Bridges

INTRODUCTION

The topic of psychosurgery still tends to evoke hostility that is not always reasonable. In the past the lesions were large, the side effects could be severe, and this treatment was perhaps overused. All that has changed; the indications for psychosurgery are now clearer and more limited, and the operations highly refined (Bridges and Bartlett, 1977). Indeed, although psychosurgery is the treatment of last resort for affective disorders, when all other treatments have failed, the results can be quite dramatic, even with longstanding illnesses. Therefore, patients with refractory depression no longer need remain incapacitated and desperate, because psychosurgery may help.

This treatment should not be considered in isolation. There is a quite widely held view that psychosurgery, being an unusual treatment, is more appropriate for atypical illnesses. This is wrong, and it is people with intractable affective disorders, where the diagnosis is clear from the presence of typical symptoms, who can most confidently be expected to do well with psychosurgery. Thus, psychosurgery is an extension of therapy progressing from antidepressant medication, to electroconvulsive therapy (ECT), and, when both come to fail in their effectiveness, or the improvement is of short duration, psychosurgery follows. Equally, it is a treatment that is much less likely to be effective for a depressive illness that has never responded either to ECT or antidepressant medication. It is an important clinical observation that whereas most recurrent affective disorders continue to respond to either antidepressants or ECT to a varying extent, there are a small number of cases where there has been a response in the early phases of the illness but subsequent attacks become resistant to these forms of therapy. In such cases psychosurgery can produce total recovery and, even when the response is partial, then sometimes medication and ECT, ineffective preoperatively, come to produce improvement again.

Psychosurgery is a particularly controversial subject largely because it involves an irreversible cerebral lesion, and so it is the ultimate physical treatment in psychiatry. There is a widespread belief that physical treatments in general are undesirable in psychiatry and tend to be used in the absence of more time and willingness to care for mentally ill patients by psychodynamic methods. This erroneous view is popularly held and is also the opinion of a number of psychiatrists who remember Freudian theory but sometimes forget the intervening psychopharmacological revolution of the 1950s. During a comparatively few years, new drugs were discovered by chance which had totally novel psychotropic activities.

For the first time antipsychotic and antidepressant medication became available. The study of these drugs in animals clarified their actions and this gave important clues to the metabolic abnormalities involved in both schizophrenia and the affective disorders. Both of these so-called "functional" psychoses seem to be associated with neurotransmission abnormalities and hence they may be briefly defined as inherited neurotransmission disorders which have prominent psychological symptoms. Nonetheless they may not be essentially different from other neurotransmission disorders. This tends to be confirmed by observations that treating one of these diseases can produce another as a side-effect. Thus, treating schizophrenia with a neuroleptic can produce Parkinsonism. Treating depression with a monoamine oxidase inhibitor may result in hypertension or hypotension, while treating hypertension with methyldopa can cause endogenous depression. On this basis therefore, as it used to be appropriate to treat Parkinsonism by means of neurosurgery, then, equally, neurosurgery is appropriate for intractable endogenous depression.

This view helps to dispose of some major fallacies. One concerns the definition of psychosurgery, which is given by Stone (1975) as "any procedure . . . for the purpose of altering behaviour or treating a psychiatric illness"; by the World Health Organization (1976) as, "the selective surgical removal or destruction . . . of nerve pathways . . . with a view to influencing behaviour"; and by

O'Callaghan and Carroll (1982) as "brain surgery conducted explicitly to amend specific aspects of human behaviour. . . ." A review of the literature (Valenstein, 1980) will show that psychosurgery is most commonly carried out for psychiatric illness, where the aim is to control psychological symptoms while retaining normal emotional responsiveness, when behavior is not directly affected at all. Second, there is frequent criticism that psychosurgery involves lesions in "normal" brain tissue. Of course, affective disorders undoubtedly involve functional but not structural abnormalities. Finally, it is important to realize that psychosurgery, like ECT, was initially devised as a treatment for schizophrenia but subsequently was found to be more appropriate for affective disorders. Schizophrenia is not now an indication for psychosurgery but some schizoaffective conditions are.

HISTORICAL DEVELOPMENT

There are some early suggestions that melancholia was treated by perforating the skull, although this probably involved the ancient idea that with mental illnesses there are undesirable substances that need to be released from the brain. In the nineteenth century Burckhardt, a daring Swiss physician-superintendant, carried out the six earliest brain operations on psychiatric patients but, he reported, the results were not good. In more modern times, it was John Fulton, a neurophysiologist, who unwittingly initiated psychosurgery in 1935 when describing the results of experiments in which the frontal lobes of two chimpanzees were removed. The surgery caused considerable emotional blunting in the animals and Mòniz, professor of neurology at Lisbon, who was in the audience, decided that a similar technique might help very disturbed schizophrenic patients. With his colleague, Lima, professor of neurosurgery, he began operating in that year and their method involved the removal of three cores of frontal lobe tissue on each side. In 1936 Freeman and Watts, respectively professors of neurology and neurosurgery in Washington, in the United States, devised their own operation, (Freeman and Watts, 1950) called prefrontal lobotomy (or leucotomy in Britain) and it was this operation that was very widely used, mainly for schizophrenia but also for depression, for the next fifteen years or so (Tooth and Newton, 1961). Nonetheless, from the early days Moniz observed that the technique was more effective in cases of depression, but schizophrenia was the greater clinical problem at the time. Prefrontal leucotomy, which was a wide-ranging operation that involved a 3% chance of effects on the personality so severe that discharge was impossible for this reason alone, became obsolete in the 1950s when chlorpromazine (Largactil) was introduced. It then became clear that the neuroleptics were a much more effective and safer treatment for schizophrenia.

Thereafter, psychosurgical operations became increasingly modified and were used primarily for cases of intractable depression, tension, anxiety, and obsessional disorders. John Fulton, although a neurophysiologist, obviously became interested in psychosurgery and published a prescient book in 1951 in which he reported studies of the actual cerebral lesion produced by surgery, assessed postmortem, in relation to the psychiatric effects of the lesion (Fulton, 1951). The operative death rate for prefrontal leucotomy was about 4% but some patients subsequently died from other causes. Prefrontal leucotomy involved a "free-hand" technique which therefore lacked precision and was associated with considerable variation from one case to another. Propitiously, this limitation in the surgical method enabled Fulton to study the relationship between the size and site of the lesion and its psychological effects which led him to conclude that prefrontal leucotomy involved a lesion that was too extensive and too imprecisely placed. He suggested that the psychosurgical lesion should be confined to the ventromedial quadrants of the frontal lobes bilaterally, the area that gave the best psychiatric results with the fewest side effects. This remains the target for most psychosurgery carried on at present, although it is not the only target site for contemporary operations.

STEREOTACTIC SUBCAUDATE TRACTOTOMY

Fulton's work suggested that an accurately placed lesion of controlled size was needed in the ventromedial quadrants of each frontal lobe producing minimal trauma on entry. Knight, the initiator of modern psychosurgery, met these partly contradictory requirements most ingeniously and remarkably effectively by the use of radioactivity to produce the lesions. Measured beta-radiation is introduced in small ceramic rods containing radioactive yttrium (^{90}Y). Each rod is 7 mm x 1 mm and is introduced on a thin probe so there is little damage on entry. The rods are sited by stereotaxis with an accuracy of 1-2 mm and they can be built up into any pattern, thus the size and site of the lesion is under complete control. Yttrium 90 has a half-life of about four days and decays to zirconium 90, which is stable. The rods thus become inert and remain in situ indefinitely (Figure 1).

The operative technique for stereotactic subcaudate tractotomy has been described by Knight (1964), and the clinical results by Ström-Olsen and Carlisle (1971) and by Göktepe et al. (1975). Depending on the diagnosis, 50% or more of the patients operated on recover completely, either with no further treatment needed or still taking some medication. This is a remarkable result considering the severe and intractable cases which come to have this operation. Significant effects on the personality are very unlikely to occur and of 1,100 patients now operated on there has been only one death attributable to the operation, which happened some three months later (Knight, 1973), and no major side effects have been

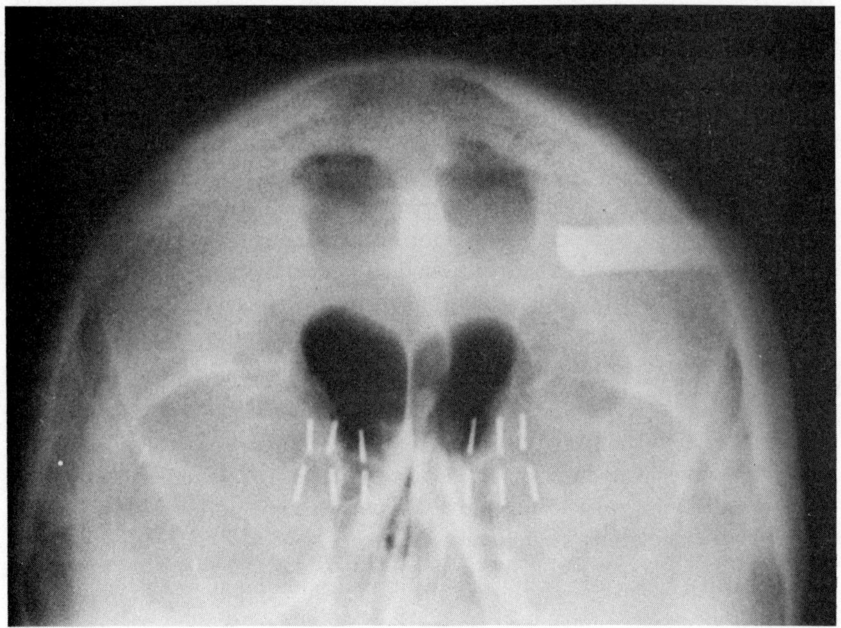

Figure 1. X-ray of yttrium rods. Stereotactic subcaudate tractotomy.

encountered up to now. There is an incidence of epilepsy postoperatively of 1-2% and patients who have been assessed as suitable are, of course, warned of this and other potential side effects such as hemorrhage and infection, when they are offered the operation.

While a few patients show almost immediate improvement, for the majority the recovery is gradual and may take up to six months or more. Sometimes the delay can be overcome by giving antidepressants, and occasionally ECT may be needed. The slow improvement has important implications for rehabilitation which, accordingly, has to be slowly progressive in the demands on the patient.

Stereotactic subcaudate tractotomy is carried out at the Geoffrey Knight Unit at the Brook General Hospital in London where over 90% of the psychosurgical operations in Britain are performed at present (Bridges and Bartlett, 1973). Patients are admitted about one week before, for routine investigations. At the operation an anesthetic is always used and the head does not require shaving. The technique takes about one and a half hours with most of the time for taking X-rays and developing plates with which the stereotactic calculations are made. The operation causes little distress to the patient, who is in bed for only forty-eight hours afterwards and is then up and about normally. Early, temporary side effects include some degree of headache, but this is not invariable. Occasionally there are lethargy and confusion.

The indications for stereotactic tractotomy (Bartlett et al., 1981) with a large pair of subcaudate lesions are:

Depression: Of endogenous type, either chronic or persistently recurrent, with a limited or absent response to routine therapies. The prognosis for bipolar illnesses is not yet clear from the few operations so far carried out for such cases, but while the results are not so striking as with unipolar depression, there is usually worthwhile amelioration and no special postoperative problems have so far been encountered.

Anxiety and tension: Chronic or recurrent episodes of anxiety or tension, or intractable phobic anxiety states.
A behavioral assessment may need to be arranged before offering a psychosurgical opinion, and postoperative behavior therapy is often required as part of the rehabilitation programme.

Obsessional neurosis: In cases with associated prominent symptoms of depression.

Schizoaffective illnesses: Definite affective symptoms, such as intractable depression, anxiety or tension, may be relieved in some patients, and the schizophrenic component ameliorated as a result.

There is no upper age limit, but with the elderly the physical risks of surgery are naturally higher.

Knight (1973) summarized his early findings by reporting that over a twelve-year period the results were consistent in showing that "more than 50% of cases of resistant depression can be set free of medical care and another 25% at least can be improved." The outcome at 2-4 years postoperatively for two detailed studies (Ström-Olsen and Carlisle, 1971; Göktepe et al., 1975) is given in Table 1.

With regard to side effects, in 23 out of 284 cases (8%) the relatives reported personality changes, but none were severe. In any case the significance of these figures has been reconsidered recently because the staff of the unit have not observed obvious personality changes. It is possible that some relatives who have grown accustomed to a chronically depressed and dependent individual describe aspects of improved function in terms of undesirable side effects. Complaints that the patient has become excessively talkative and argumentative may really refer to the emergence of greater independence and assertion (Honig et al., in preparation). Cognitive impairment has not been shown to occur with the modern stere-

TABLE 1. Outcome 2-4 Years after Stereotactic Tractotomy

Outcome	Depression N (%)	Anxiety N (%)	Obsessional N (%)	Other N (%)	Totals N (%)
I	58 } (62)	21 } (49)	14 } (50)	1 } (13)	94 } (53)
II	37	13	5	2	57
III	34 (22)	16 (23)	9 (24)	9 (39)	68 (24)
IV	24 (16)	20 (29)	9 (24)	11 (48)	64 (23)
V	-	-	1 (3)	-	1 (0.4)
Total	153	70	38	23	284

Key:
I=recovered, no symptoms and no treatment required
II=well; mild residual symptoms, little or no interference with daily life
III=improved but significant symptoms remain, which interfere with the patient's life
IV=unchanged
V=worse

otactic techniques (Bridges, 1972; Mitchell-Heggs, et al., 1976). Indeed some have reported significant postoperative increases in the intelligence quotient, no doubt due to improved performance on recovery from the depressive illness. A number of professional patients have undergone stereotactic tractotomies and have been able to return to their demanding work when relieved of depression.

When a case is being considered for possible referral for psychosurgery, the following aspects (Bridges and Bartlett, 1977) need to be taken into account:

Without operation	With operation
Fatal suicide possible (perhaps 15% in the case of uncontrolled depressive illnesses)	One or more seizures (about 1%-2%)
Continuing distress of the patient	General surgical risks
Functional impairment of the personality resulting from chronic illness	Uncommon and mild effects on the personality
Small risks from medication and ECT	

CINGULOTOMY

While the subcaudate area is the commonest target for operations for affective disorders in Great Britain, the most frequently performed operation elsewhere in the world for this indication is that of anterior cingulotomy. This involves a lesion placed into the cingulate gyrus, although with earlier techniques there was bilateral removal of the anterior half of the gyrus, when the operation is then termed cingulectomy (Whitty et al., 1952). However, as cingulectomy involves the removal of quite a large amount of cerebral tissue, this is likely to impair the blood supply to surrounding tissue secondarily, thus in effect increasing the size of the lesion beyond that part of the brain removed. Hence, the more refined cingulotomy operation should now be the technique of choice.

Another aspect of cingulotomy is that, in the USA in particular, it is almost as frequently used for complaints of pain as for psychiatric illnesses (Donnelly, 1978). Donnelly has reported that 1,039 psychosurgical operations were carried out in the USA by 195 neurosurgeons in 1971-73 although the number specifically of cingulotomy operations is not given. With regard to cingulotomy, Ballantine, et al. (1977) reported that of 68 patients operated on between 1962 and 1969, by 1970, 78% were said to have been "significantly improved," that is, they were assessed as being "well," "markedly improved," or "moderately improved." Unfortunately, this six-point outcome classification does not readily relate to that used for the studies with stereotactic tractotomy. Taking the total series of 345 operations involving 238 patients, no operative deaths or serious complications occured, although these figures indicate that a number of repeat operations were necessary. Postoperative seizures occurred in 1.2%, and Ballantine et al. note that in a series of 154 of the patients there were as many as seven suicides postoperatively. (Figure 2)

Bailey et al. (1977) have reported the most recent information from an ongoing series of cingulate operations (Bailey et al., 1971; 1973). Of 200 patients, 80% were included in the upper three categories of a five-point scale which omitted a category, "worse." The diagnoses included affective disorders, both unipolar and bipolar, and "chronic anxiety-depressive states, with or without phobic features." It was considered that patients accepted for this treatment should preferably have "a sound personality structure with reasonable potential for adjustment to life stress, and at least average, and preferably well above average, intelligence." Also it was desirable for patients to show "a reasonable level of super-ego development." Postoperatively, 86% of 94 cases specially studied showed an improvement in intellectual function. There was death by suicide postoperatively among 2% of the total series of 200 patients. It is unclear why such stringent personality characteristics and high intelligence are so necessary. These qualities are not considered particularly relevant for stereotactic tractotomy.

DIAGNOSES APPROPRIATE FOR PSYCHOSURGERY

The basic problem is that there is no reliable objective indication of the presence of any psychiatric diagnosis. Therefore diagnoses in psychiatry are necessarily

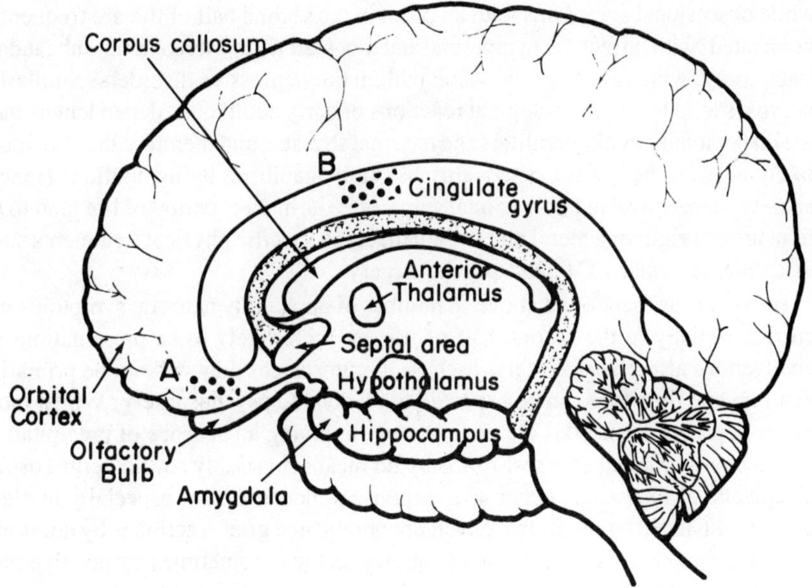

Figure 2. Sites of the two main current operations. (A) Subcaudate tractotomy and (B) Anterior cingulotomy.

made on the grounds of the presence or absence of specific symptoms and signs, and by clinical experience of the progress of an illness, taking into account the past and family histories.

Studies using factor analysis of symptoms when the patient was accepted for psychosurgery, in association with the outcome after stereotactic tractotomy, point to the importance for a good outcome of a positive family history, previous control of attacks with ECT, and the presence of specific symptoms such as diurnal variation of mood. Hence, it seems likely that, using the DSM-III criteria (American Psychiatric Association, 1981) these observations point to the presence of an inherited major depressive disorder and exclude neurotic conditions such as hysteria, obsessional neurosis, anxiety states and neurotic depression. Nonetheless, as the DSM-III makes clear, other symptoms can be associated with major depressive episodes, especially including phobic anxiety, chronic anxiety, tension and obsessional symptoms.

Our clinical experience (Bartlett, et al., 1981) is that the onset of an obsessional neurosis in adolescence or early adulthood is usually unassociated with major depression and does better with limbic leucotomy (Mitchell-Heggs, et al., 1976), while obsessional symptoms with an onset in the second half of life are frequently associated with affective symptoms and do well with stereotactic subcaudate tractotomy, which is of special value with major depressive disorders. Similarly, neuroses tend to be psychological reactions of early adulthood, dependent as they are on personality vulnerabilities and external stresses, and therefore they are more likely to occur before the personality has fully stabilized by maturation. Hence, anxiety, depressive and obsessional symptoms during this period of life tend to be of neurotic origin in general and not amenable to specific physical treatments such as antidepressants, ECT, and psychosurgery.

However, as mentioned above, a number of apparently neurotic symptoms occurring initially in the second half of life are more likely to be presentations of endogenous affective disorders. In these circumstances they will not be primarily neurotic and therefore can be expected to respond to psychosurgery. Whilst most major depressive episodes are endogenous, implying an absence of precipitation due to environmental stresses, this is by no means invariably so. Sometimes such an episode of illness can occur as a response to bereavement, especially in older people, and its differentiation from an uncomplicated grief reaction is by duration, severity, the presence of specific symptoms and also sometimes by positive past and family histories.

The absence of any reliable objective method of diagnosis in psychiatry at present has been mentioned, but currently much interest is centered on the dexamethasone suppression test (Carroll et al., 1981), which seems to at least increase the confidence with which a diagnosis of endogenous depression can be made. Other possible biological markers include the tyramine load test (Bonham-Carter et al., 1978) and TSH stimulation (Loosen and Prange, 1982).

Clinically, the most important diagnostic factors include the presence of a family history of a similar illness and the detection of the specific symptoms of endogenous depression, which includes early morning waking, diurnal variation of mood, loss of interest and energy, feelings or delusions of worthlessness, guilt and pessimism. Another characteristic symptom found in the more severe affective illnesses but not often reported in the literature is an unpleasant sensation of epigastric "churning" or "butterflies in the stomach."

Taking these points into account, selection for psychosurgery can be, at its most basic, fairly simple and straight forward. Thus:

A positive family history of affective disorders.	This suggests the presence of an inherited metabolic abnormality likely to respond to physical treatments such as psychosurgery

Previous response to antidepressants and/or ECT, with recovery and normal social function between episodes of illness	This observation suggests that personality function is essentially normal between episodes of illness. It also shows that the illness has responded satisfactorily to physical treatments in the past and so can be expected to respond to psychosurgery
Failure in recent months or years in the efficacy or antidepressants and ECT, despite earlier effectiveness	Thus psychosurgery is the next treatment to be considered
Evidence of serious incapacity, frequent or lengthy hospital admissions, suicidal behavior	These are aspects which suggest that decisive treatment is needed soon before the personality becomes unduly impaired by persistent lack of confidence and institutionalization. Sometimes, treatment is urgently indicated because of dangerous suicidal behavior
The patients describe early morning waking when they feel at their worst, with mood improving somewhat during the day, appetite and weight loss, and unreasonable guilt	This confirms that the appropriate illness is present because of the symptoms described which are specific

This simple information, by itself, suggests the need for psychosurgery and that a good outcome is likely, although the complete management of the case will require a more detailed history, together with appropriate investigations.

POSTOPERATIVE REHABILITATION

Because the risk of side effects with contemporary psychosurgical operations is not great, this treatment must not be left as a last desperate resort when the patient's personality function has been significantly impaired by chronic and/or severe uncontrolled illness. Psychosurgery is the final treatment in sequence, as has been shown, but when other forms of suitable therapy have failed, no lengthy wait is necessary before psychosurgery is at least considered, provided of course the patient is interested in the possibility of being accepted for this form of treatment. Patients can be told that affective disorders are spontaneously relapsing and remitting illnesses and, in time, most attacks will remit untreated. The patient should then become involved in a decision as to how long he wishes to wait for such an event. If there is desperation and the indications are correct then surgery can be considered before the patient has been housebound for too long, or institutionalized in hospital, with the result that impoverishment of the personality has become irreversible. With stereotactic tractotomy, circumstances are recognized in which, when the outcome is assessed one or more years postoperatively, then it may be found that the surgery was successful but rehabilitation failed. This means that the patient recovered from depression but never regained sufficient social confidence to live independently or to accept placement away from hospital.

A frequent observation which has very important implications for rehabilitation is failure in the marriage (Honig et al., to be published). In a rough survey of twenty consecutive cases considered for psychosurgery, marital problems were noted among half. This is because spouses find chronic psychiatric illness extremely difficult to tolerate. The inevitable self-absorption of the patient and his preoccupation with his persistent symptoms impairs marital relationships and the spouse becomes decreasingly tolerant of chronic complaining and helpless dependence. Sometimes, the decisive improvement after operation causes problems for the spouse's adaptation. A husband or wife may have become adjusted to the partner's being passive, dependent and helpless. Indeed, sometimes the marriage depends on these circumstances and the appeal of the patient to the spouse to some extent is the patient's sickness role. But with postoperative recovery, the relative may have difficulty in accepting a more independent, communicative, and assertive spouse. It has been noted above that this may cause relatives to regard the personality changes associated with recovery as undesirable side effects of the operation which they call, for example, excessive outspokenness and aggressiveness.

Clearly, if the illness is allowed to continue so that the marriage breaks up, this will make rehabilitation that much more difficult or even impossible. After a long admission to hospital it takes some time and careful encouragement for patients to slowly resume a life at home when they have a supportive spouse, but if the marriage has failed patients may find it quite impossible to return home to live alone even though they have largely recovered from their depression.

The aim of rehabilitation is to counter the ingrained pessimism and helplessness produced by chronic and intractable affective disorders and to encourage patients to realize the new potentials resulting from surgery. Nearly all patients having psychosurgery suffer from overdependence on others and usually serious loss of self-confidence. Considerable skill, effort and patience is needed to reverse these traits, but failure to do so will mean that the patient does not gain the maximum benefits from the operation. Sometimes clinicians have said that the patient, after psychosurgery, has had the ultimate therapy for their condition and nothing more can be done, the treatment will in time either succeed or not. Psychosurgery essentially requires renewed therapeutic endeavor afterwards.

INFORMED CONSENT

In the past, informed agreement to undergo psychosurgery by schizophrenic patients must have been only infrequently obtainable. Schizophrenia is much more usually associated with loss of insight than are the affective disorders. The majority of patients with severe depression, anxiety, and tension are likely to be able to agree or otherwise to an offer of psychosurgery if their illness is considered appropriate. Indeed, it is the experience of clinicians involved with psychosurgery that many patients become so desperate with the failure of their illness to respond to routine treatments that they seek other possibilities of therapy themselves and may suggest to their psychiatrist or general practitioner the possibility of psychosurgery, perhaps encountered in a magazine.

It is the policy of the Geoffrey Knight Unit not to accept patients who are compulsorily admitted on a legal order. While there are circumstances where such a Section would be desirable, such as with persistent and determined suicidal behavior, compulsory admission would invite suspicions of compulsory psychosurgery, which is of course totally out of the question and unthinkable. In practice, quite severely disturbed and perhaps very suicidal patients settle reasonably well when they have been offered the chance of such a potent form of therapy when all else has failed, and so they can nearly always be managed with careful nursing rather than by compulsory detention. Our rule is that when a patient refuses psychosurgery this is always accepted even if the refusal is due to illness. Thus, some patients say that they realize that help is being offered but they feel so unworthy, so guilty and the future looks so black, that they decline any help and insist that they deserve to die or they feel they must go on with their distressing symptoms as deserved punishment which will lead to death. This refusal is clearly due to delusional ideas, but we consider that it must be accepted nonetheless.

There are also stuporous patients who are unable to communicate but are clearly very ill. Usually, these patients refuse food and have often lost a good deal of weight, hence surgery can be considered, in the more extreme cases, as being essential treatment not only saving the patient's life but also restoring him to health when he has no control whatsoever over his own condition. In these circumstances most would agree that, ethically, surgery should by carried out because of grave illness in the absence of agreement but also in the absence of refusal. With such cases, a balanced judgment is obviously needed and the agreement of close relatives is clearly necessary. Ethical problems in relation to psychosurgery have been considered by Gostin (1980, 1982).

REFERENCES

American Psychiatric Association. DSM-III: *Diagnostic and Statistical Manual of Mental Disorders. 3rd ed.* APA. Washington, DC. (1981).

Bailey, H.R., Dowling, J.L., and Davies, E. Studies in depression. III. The control of affective illness by cingulotractotomy: a review of 150 cases. *Med. J. Australia, ii,* 366-371 (1973).

Bailey, H.R., Dowling, J.L., and Davies, E. Studies in depression IV. cingulotractotomy and related procedures for severe depressive illness. In *Neurosurgical Treatment in Psychiatry, Pain and Epilepsy.* W.H. Sweet, S. Obrador, and J.G. Martin-Rodriguez (eds.) University Park Press, Baltimore, Maryland, pp. 229-251 (1977).

Bailey, H.R., Dowling, J.L., Swanton, C.H., and Davies, E. Studies in depression, I. Cingulotractotomy in the treatment of severe illness. *Med. J. Australia, i,* 8 (1971).

Ballantine, H.T., Levy, B.S., Dagi, T.F. and Giriunas, I.B. Cingulotomy for psychiatric illness: Report of 13 years experience. In *Neurosurgical Treatment in Psychiatry, Pain, and Epilepsy.* W.H. Sweet, S. Obrador, and J.G. Martin-Rodriguez (eds.) University Park Press, Baltimore, Maryland, pp. 333-351 (1977).

Bartlett, J.R., Bridges, P.K. and Kelly, D. Contemporary indications for psychosurgery. *Brit. J. Psychiat. 38,* 507-511 (1981)

Bonham-Carter, S., Sandler, M., Goodwin, B.L. Sepping, P., and Bridges, P.K. Decreased urinary output of tyramine and its metabolites in depression. *Brit. J. Psychiat., 132,* 125-132 (1978).

Bridges, P.K. Psychosurgery today: psychiatric aspects. *Proceedings of Royal Society of Medicine, 65,* 1104 (1972).

Bridges, P.K., and Bartlett, J.R. The work of a psychosurgical unit. *Postgrad. Med. J. 49,* 855 (1973).

Bridges, P.K., and Bartlett, J.R. Psychosurgery: yesterday and today. *Brit. J. Psychiat, 131,* 249-260 (1977).

Carroll, B.J., Feinberg, M., Greden, J.F., Tarika, J., Albala, A.A., Haskett, R.F., McI. James, N., Kronfol, Z., Lohr, N., Steiner, M., de Vigne, J-P., and Young, E. A specific laboratory test for the diagnosis of melancholia. *Arch. Gen. Psychiat. 38,* 15-22 (1981).

Donnelly, J. The incidence of psychosurgery in the United States, 1917-1973. *Amer. J. Psychiat., 135,* 1476-1480 (1978).

Freeman, W., and Watts, J.W. *Psychosurgery, 2nd ed.* Charles C. Thomas, Springfield, Illinois (1950).

Fulton, J.F. *Frontal Lobotomy and Affective Behaviour: A Neurophysiological Analysis.* W.W. Norton, New York (1951).

Göktepe, E.O., Young, L.B., and Bridges, P.K. A further review of the results of stereotactic subcaudate tractotomy. *Brit. J. Psychiat. 126,* 270-280 (1975).

Gostin, L.O. Ethical considerations of psychosurgery: the unhappy legacy of the pre-frontal lobotomy. *J. Med. Ethics 6,* 149-154 (1980).

Gostin, L.O. Psychosurgery: A hazardous and unestablished treatment? A case for the importation of American legal safeguards to Great Britain. *J. Social Welfare Law, March,* 83-95 (1982).

Knight, G. The orbital cortex as an objective in the surgical treatment of mental illness. *Brit. J. Surg., 51,* 114-124 (1964).

Knight, G. Further observations from an experience of 660 cases of stereotactic tractotomy. *Postgrad. Med. J. 49,* 845-854 (1973).

Loosen, P.T., and Prange, A.J., Jr. Serum thyrotropin response to thyrotropin-releasing hormone in psychiatric patients: a review. *Amer. J. Psychiat. 139,* 405-416 (1982).

Mitchell-Heggs, N., Kelly, D., and Richardson, A. Stereotactic limbic leucotomy—a follow-up at 16 months. *Brit. J. Psychiat. 128,* 226-240 (1976).

O'Callaghan, M.A.J., and Carroll, D. *Psychosurgery. A Scientific Analysis.* MTP Press Ltd., Lancaster, England (1982).

Stone, A.A. Psychosurgery in Massachusetts: A task force report. *Mass. J. Ment. Health 5,* 26-46 (1975).

Ström-Olsen, R., and Carlisle, S. Bifrontal stereotactic tractotomy. *Brit. J. Psychiat. 118,* 141-154 (1971).

Tooth, G.C., and Newton, M.P. *Leucotomy in England and Wales 1942-54. Reports on Public Health and Medical Subjects No. 104.* Ministry of Health, London, HMSO (1961).

Valenstein, E.S. (ed.) *The Psychosurgery Debate.* W.H. Freeman and Co., San Francisco (1980).

Whitty, C.W.M., Duffield, J.E., Tow, P.M., and Cairns, H. Anterior cingulectomy in the treatment of mental disease. *Lancet, i,* 475-481 (1952).

World Health Organization. *Health Aspects of Human Rights.* Geneva. WHO (1976).

Index